God's Autopsy and the Living Truth of Soul

God's Autopsy and the Living Truth of Soul

A History of Western Consciousness

Hal Childs

WIPF & STOCK · Eugene, Oregon

GOD'S AUTOPSY AND THE LIVING TRUTH OF SOUL
A History of Western Consciousness

Copyright © 2022 Hal Childs. All rights reserved. Except for brief quotations in critical publications or reviews, no part of this book may be reproduced in any manner without prior written permission from the publisher. Write: Permissions, Wipf and Stock Publishers, 199 W. 8th Ave., Suite 3, Eugene, OR 97401.

Wipf & Stock
An Imprint of Wipf and Stock Publishers
199 W. 8th Ave., Suite 3
Eugene, OR 97401

www.wipfandstock.com

PAPERBACK ISBN: 978-1-6667-3730-1
HARDCOVER ISBN: 978-1-6667-9658-2
EBOOK ISBN: 978-1-6667-9659-9

08/18/22

Scripture quotations from the New Revised Standard Version Bible, copyright © 1989 National Council of the Churches of Christ in the United States of America. Used by permission. All rights reserved worldwide.

Wolfgang Giegerich, excerpts from *The Soul Always Thinks*. Copyright © 2010 by Wolfgang Giegerich. Excerpts from *Soul-Violence*. Copyright © 2008 by Wolfgang Giegerich. Reprinted with permission of Routledge c/o Copyright Clearance Center.

Charles B. Guignon, excerpts from *Heidegger and the Problem of Knowledge*. Copyright © 1983 by Charles B. Guignon. Reprinted with the permission of Hackett Publishing Company, Inc.

J. N. D. Kelly, excerpts from *Early Christian Doctrines*. Copyright © 1960, 1965, 1968, 1977, by John Norman Davidson Kelly. Reprinted with the permission of Continuum Publishing, an imprint of Bloomsbury Publishing Plc.

Jack Miles, excerpts from *God: A Biography*. Copyright © 1995 by Jack Miles. Used by permission of Georges Borchardt, Inc. and Alfred A. Knopf, an imprint of the Knopf Doubleday Publishing Group, a division of Penguin Random House LLC. All rights reserved.

Friedrich Nietzsche, excerpt from *The Gay Science*, translated by Walter Kaufman. Copyright © 1974 by Walter Kaufman. Used by permission of Penguin, an imprint and division of Penguin Random House LLC. All rights reserved.

Albert Schweitzer, excerpts from *The Quest of the Historical Jesus: A Critical Study of Its Progress from Reimarus to Wrede*. Copyright © 1968 by James M. Robinson, renewed 1996. Reprinted with the permission of Scribner, a division of Simon & Schuster, Inc. All rights reserved.

Stephen Hawking, excerpts from "Does God Play Dice?" (1999). Reprinted with the permission of The Estate of Stephen Hawking.

Dedicated to the Guild for Psychological Studies,

providing a home for soul-work for over seventy years.

Books are food for God

—Author's Dream

Contents

Acknowledgments | ix

Introduction: Fundamental Concepts | 1

Chapter 1 Is There a Modern Soul? | 16
Chapter 2 Bible as Soul's Dream of Itself | 56
Chapter 3 Abram: Archaic Soul Leaves Home | 87
Chapter 4 Yahweh's Violent Rupture: Soul's Revolution | 123
Chapter 5 Yahweh Defeats Himself to Save Himself | 154
Chapter 6 Job: A Crack in the Armor | 195
Chapter 7 Yahweh Kills Himself, Christ Sublates the Flesh | 246
Chapter 8 Reason: The Sublation of Christ (Death of God) | 289
Chapter 9 Soul's Thought of Itself Today Is *Consciousness* | 323

Afterword: White Supremacy Is Christian Supremacy | 377

Recommendations for Further Reading | 385
Bibliography | 387
Author Index | 391
Name Index | 393
Ancient Document Index | 395

Acknowledgments

THE ACT OF WRITING is indeed a solitary event, and I have enjoyed many lonely hours in the writer's cell. But, the seeming solitude is also peopled by a host of others, without whom nothing would have been written. There are many people to acknowledge and thank. But, I also want to express my gratitude to the realm of living ideas and to the history of consciousness itself that impinges its necessity on me, addressing its question and wanting my answer. There is an entire history of thought, with misty origins and unfinished futures, within which thought occurs. I am immensely grateful to participate in the stream of thought where books are food for the voracious appetite of consciousness. This is one small nibble contributed to that enormous banquet.

I want to thank the late John Petroni, mentor and colleague, who first introduced me to Wolfgang Giegerich's *The Soul's Logical Life*, now over two decades ago. After that, there was no going back. My collegial group in the Guild for Psychological Studies, Harry Henderson, Jennifer Morgan Mansfield, Faith Mason, and Patricia Calcagno Stenger, read each chapter in early drafts. I am deeply grateful for their support and ongoing encouragement. The seeming solitary process of soul-work also requires its village. Harry Henderson also provided needed guidance in areas of science I explore in this work but for which I have no formal training. He also has a knack for succinct expression in psychological thinking, which has brought welcome clarity to my own thought.

Throughout, the Guild for Psychological Studies provided a quality of support hard to articulate. This organization, devoted to facilitating deep soul-work, has always been there, a home nurturing and challenging personal development and the honing of thought. The Guild also provided financial support at critical stages of the work. For all of this I am thankful.

Over a seven-year period I guided a group of psychological-spiritual seekers in Washington DC through monthly essays exploring the work of C. G. Jung and novel

Acknowledgments

psychological interpretations of scripture. Their enthusiastic interest in my work supported my exploratory thinking and writing, nudging it toward this book. I am especially grateful to Susan Thompson for her leadership in making that work possible, and all the participants who worked on their own journeys with great integrity: Collie Agle, Betsy Agle, Matthew Black, Barbara Black, Pete Eveleth, Ed Kneedler, Lynn Kneedler, Steve McLaughlin, Gregory Niblett, Karen Falk, Penelope Farley, Betty Foster, Josie Jordan, Hester Ohbi, Nancy Van Scoyoc, and Marilu Sherer.

I am thankful for the editing expertise (and magic) of Jacqueline Tasch who made much of my writing less convoluted. Because of her, the book is more readable and clear, and she helped me keep the reader in view. My agent Arnie Kotler provided a steady and encouraging hand in guiding the manuscript toward the appropriate publisher, and I am grateful for his support and expertise in helping the book find a home.

Hugh Leonard was an enthusiastic reader who brought an early chapter to a study group, providing important feedback in the process. He gave me important insights in how to frame the search for a publisher, for which I am grateful. A very big thank you to Tim Sanderson, a long-time conversation partner in all things soul, personal and professional. His steady presence in my life is a gift as we wrestle with big ideas and banter about basketball and the weather.

I am indebted to colleagues in the International Society for Psychology as the Discipline of Interiority (ISPDI.org) for their support of my work and the opportunity to present papers at conferences where the furnace of public presentation tempers thought. Michael Caplan read an early version and provided helpful suggestions. Peter White volunteered a close reading of several chapters with critical and helpful insights. Greg Mogenson provided insightful comments and advice. I am also grateful for the supportive encouragement received from Gabriel Eckert and Jane Smith-Eivemark. I owe a huge debt of gratitude to Wolfgang Giegerich who's incisive body of work is the inspiration at the heart of this whole project. It was his thinking that enabled an implicit inchoate understanding within me to become explicit, and it is not too much to say, saved me from logical homelessness. Thought that had been groping, found its home.

This book is my own working out an explicit statement of soul, and it is also a gesture of gratitude.

Introduction

Fundamental Concepts

We are living in the *kairos* for a "metamorphosis of the gods," that is, of the fundamental principles and symbols. This concern of our time, which is certainly not of our choosing, expresses the changes that are going on in the inner and unconscious man.[1]

The gods are the first immediacy of consciousness's becoming conscious of itself—first immediacy because although in the gods consciousness has become conscious of itself, it does not in any way know that what it is conscious of is its own inner logical functioning.[2]

Consciousness is now on the way to comprehending itself
as mindedness, as logical form and logical life.[3]

FOR APPROXIMATELY ONE THOUSAND five hundred years, the reality of God *was* the central category of meaning and truth, the central organizing principle, for the Christian West. For the last two to three hundred years, God has *not* been that cornerstone. Of course, many continue to zealously affirm God's existence and relevance, and others equally zealously deny that God *ever* existed. Religious traditionalists will say that God is an eternal truth and that humans in their frailty have drifted away from God, while rational atheists will say that God, and gods, have always been merely superstitious beliefs existing only in the primitive and unenlightened mind of humankind.

---

1. Giegerich, "Jung's Idea of a Metamorphosis," 533 (cited and trans. modified by Giegerich); see Jung, *Civilization*, ¶ 585.
2. Giegerich, "Jung's Idea of a Metamorphosis," 539.
3. Giegerich, "Jung's Idea of a Metamorphosis," 542.

God's Autopsy and the Living Truth of Soul

The "death of God," a notion brought to explicit awareness by Friedrich Nietzsche in 1882, does indeed mark and identify our modern Western centuries. Of course, to say that "God is dead" is still to think in terms of God, and the question of what happened to the God that died remains unanswered. In order to answer this question, I will conduct an autopsy of God. I aim to cut open the "body" of God and move beyond either dismissal or rehabilitation. What has happened to God? Is God alive, or is God dead? Or, is something else afoot for which the words *God*, *alive*, and *dead* are no longer relevant or helpful?

The process of an autopsy examines a corpse in order to determine the cause of death. For my purposes, the corpse of the God of Western civilization is the corpus of Judeo-Christian Western consciousness, beginning with the Bible, the Old Testament and the New Testament, and most especially the particular qualities of the two gods, Yahweh and Christ, in their original context. The idea or image of death in symbolic contexts, in mythology, religion, dreams, and intuitive divinatory systems, always means change and transformation, and not biological death.[4] Such symbolic contexts are about *consciousness* as it manifests in the ideas and values shaping society. Death in the realm of consciousness points to the death of one form or state of consciousness and the birth and emergence of another status of consciousness.

For consciousness, that is, the world of meaning, death is simultaneously an end and a beginning. My autopsy of God is not simply to determine the cause of death but also to understand the process of death as an emergent birth of a new form of consciousness. My contention is that God, and gods and goddesses, were indeed real in the past but are no longer real in the present because their truth and reality have undergone a historical change of the form or shape of consciousness. I will suggest a new option for understanding what happened to God—and what is happening today to modern culture—as the latter undergoes a cataclysmic reorientation. Although this will provide an answer to the question, "Whence and wither God," my larger goal is an interpretation of the history of Western consciousness. I am interested in why the particular God of the Judeo-Christian tradition emerged in the first place approximately three thousand years ago, and how this God has undergone several transformations, so that, in a manner of speaking, this God appears to have disappeared itself.

As I reinterpret our history, I will examine not only consciousness but the notion of *soul*. Within this work, *consciousness* and *soul* are synonymous, and thus together form a new determinative category that has digested and transformed the category of God. These words have new meaning in this book, and the book is an extended demonstration of this new meaning. Here I will briefly touch on each concept.

---

4. For example, the Death card (No. 13) in the Tarot means change, transformation, and transition.

Fundamental Concepts

What Is Consciousness?

I make a crucial distinction between personal consciousness and general consciousness, or what is also the distinction between foreground consciousness and background consciousness. In an important sense, when we are born we do not have a personal self-aware consciousness. Rather we are born into an already existing consciousness that is made up of all the implicit beliefs, ideas, values, assumptions, and practices of our family, community, society, culture, and historical time. We gradually absorb this preexisting consciousness like a sponge—an instinctive process needing no instructions. We are social beings first, shaped and formed by the social environment, before we develop an individual sense of self. For example, at every level of the general consciousness, from family to our historical epoch, we are informed how to be a boy or a girl, a woman or a man, but there is almost nothing to tell us about other kinds of gender identities. Although this is changing, in general it is still mostly true that if you do not fit into the cultural consensus of the binary norm of gender identity (one is either male or female), you have a problem becoming true to yourself. Today, the fact that gender identity is becoming much more fluid and less clear-cut is only one example of a profound and widespread transformation of the underlying background of consciousness I will be tracing throughout this book. Gender identity is but one example of a specific type of shared social consciousness (that is mostly unconscious, or implicit), but I am aiming for something larger and more inclusive.

General consciousness, or the background consciousness, is like a form or shape of consciousness within which we live, not unlike the way we live in a house without really being aware of the house; later, I will speak of the general consciousness in terms of the water that fish (we) swim in. This shape of consciousness gives us our fundamental and taken-for-granted orientation to reality. It makes our personal consciousness possible in the first place. Just as we can make an architectural history of human dwellings and observe how they have changed over thousands of years, I argue that we can study how general consciousness has changed dramatically and significantly over several thousand years. The distinction between general and personal consciousness also means that my historical overview of consciousness is not about human beings but about consciousness itself, consciousness as a phenomenon in its own right.

Our general tendency is to think that human consciousness today is more enlightened than it was fifty thousand years ago, ten thousand years ago, two thousand years ago, or even five hundred years ago. We certainly see that human society and culture have changed over these thousands of years, but has consciousness changed? Of course, when we think of the evolution of consciousness, the idea of evolution is implicitly associated with change for the better, that consciousness improves. But what are the criteria by which we would say that consciousness has improved over thousands of years? Those criteria are based on our values today, which we assume are universal in some way and thus serve as a kind of benchmark against which we can judge whether or not consciousness has evolved. But, such an assumption on our part would be naive. My view is that the background form of consciousness has changed, but the judgment as to whether it has changed for the better is reserved for later after we understand what exactly has changed and how it has changed.

Cultures and societies are informed and shaped by implicit values that most take for granted. Although they appear to be universal within a culture or society, we should not assume they are universal. For example, in the ancient past, human and animal sacrifice made to gods and goddesses was normal and expected. Today we find such sacrifices in the name of a god abhorrent. We take for granted that religious practices do not require the sacrifice of human persons or animals, and that the God of the Judeo-Christian tradition (as we will come to see) was a god who gave up and rejected his own desire for human and animal sacrifice. Does this mean that our consciousness today is better or that it is simply different? We might also remember that modern society has "sacrificed" millions of human beings in wars of national pride as well as for other ideological values and principles, and we continue to "sacrifice" hundreds of millions of cattle, pigs, and chickens for food and profit.

To us (Western society) it is obvious that we are separate individuals because our modern collective cultural consciousness has created this reality; the shape of modern general consciousness is, in a manner of speaking, broken up into personal and individualized identities (we think first in terms of "I" and only secondarily in terms of "we"). However, while my focus is on our general deeply shared consciousness, our collective background consciousness, I do not want ideas like "group consciousness" and "collective mind" to bleed toward mystical, esoteric "new age" ideas that suggest some kind of "spiritual" reality beyond our ordinary existence. I have nothing of the sort in mind, and I will not suggest any ideas that cannot withstand the scrutiny of modern critical consciousness. I hope to step back from our ingrained and automatic assumptions and view our cultural history from a new perspective that recognizes culture and history themselves as collective phenomena that have nothing mystical or spiritual about them but are simply the existential condition of our human species. My focus is our "world" of consciousness, which is primarily the world of culture, of language, of knowledge and meanings.

We really are not creatures that *have* consciousness; we *are* fundamentally creatures of the shared overarching general consciousness that is embodied as language, as culture, as history. Of course, we live within a real physical environment, a real natural world, real physical bodies, but we access this real material world through language and cultural meanings. Our *human* world is rooted in a primary shared consciousness, the world of *meaning*, which is, paradoxically, unconscious in the sense that we are not aware of it, but it is the ground of what we take as the real. This primary shared *unconscious consciousness* embraces all the implicit assumptions, values, and ideas that shape a culture. I hope to make this invisible shape of consciousness a little more visible.

The other word I use that is synonymous with our unconscious consciousness, the logical form of consciousness, is *soul*.

The Living Truth of Soul

The word *soul* is problematic because of its history. The notion that each of us has a nonphysical soul is an antique mythological personification that has no place in our rational, critical, and secular modern consciousness. An old-fashioned way of thinking, it has been completely expunged from biology and science in general as well as psychology. Informed by our Western rational culture in general, we no longer speak of soul, but of mind.

But the idea of soul offers two advantages: (1) it allows us to remain in touch with our true history, in which mythology and religion did indeed play major roles not all that long ago, and (2) it helps us remember that the noetic quality of culture and history, the mindedness of general consciousness itself, is not first of all under our control. Since antiquity, soul has been conceived as an impersonal autonomous function that is independent of human agency. In whatever way soul is conceived, the human person does not create it; it would be more like a gift from the gods. The traditional mythological and religious idea of soul is connected to my idea of modern soul, in that soul remains impersonal and not subject to the individual's manipulation.

The modern secular antagonism against the idea of soul has to be accepted, and so to reintroduce the idea of soul, it must have nothing occult, romantic, religious, or nostalgic about it. The sense of soul I propose is not related to the divine, nor is it the archaic principle of life that departs the body at death. Soul is related instead to the notion of *general consciousness*, the *shape of consciousness*, or our *background consciousness*, which is our given and shared larger context. In my usage, soul is synonymous with the *dynamic process* of the general consciousness that we see at work as culture and history, and which also impinges on us personally.

The cultural soul, our here and now, is self-generating in the way that culture is a self-generating cauldron of ideas. Soul in this sense primarily points to the dimension of cultural ideas that are taken for granted, that live and churn below the obvious surface of things, the big ideas that can shape an entire society, such as the "Yahweh" of ancient Judaism, the "Christ" of late antiquity and medieval Europe, and the "Reason and Science" of modernity. These are the big living ideas that shape entire historical epochs. This dimension of soul, the general consciousness, is also known as the *syntax* of consciousness in contrast to the *contents* of consciousness. Just as the syntax of language implicitly orients those who speak it, the syntax of (cultural) consciousness orients an entire historical and cultural era, and it establishes what a culture takes for granted as the true and the real—this is soul. Soul is living thoughts, the living ideas that implicitly shape a culture's self-understanding.

For the work of this book, the idea of soul is that dimension of public mind that informs us and of which we are generally unaware. It is completely existential, it is the living here and now. Soul is our *human* source of life but only in the sense that it is the world of meanings which makes us human and exists separate from but in relation to the biological life of the body. If we were not constituted by soul-life (a world of cultural meanings), we would be the equivalent of animals and would not know that we existed. Today, in our contemporary world we have become aware that we exist as soul and that soul is now conscious of itself. Consciousness has become conscious of itself, and we can now view history and cultural phenomena as soul speaking about itself; the world and history of *meaning* can now be examined with a kind of self-reflexive analysis. In an important sense, one of the achievements of the historical development of soul is that consciousness can now step outside of itself and observe itself. History and culture are also forms of "soul's autobiography," a subject I will take up in more detail in chapter 1.

God Died *and* Did Not Die

Soul and *consciousness* are ordinary words that we first automatically associate with individual persons. In my usage, they become new categories pointing to the syntax of consciousness (our shared background consciousness) that shapes cultural and historical epochs. We readily understand that the worlds of culture, of language, have a degree of autonomy about them, have a life of their own, that is not ours to control or direct. Certainly, language is a living thing that exhibits historical development, which is always out ahead of standard usage. We play catch up by creating dictionaries and altering the rules of grammar. We certainly participate in culture, and we influence culture, but we do not ultimately control it.

In modern times, we came to think of human beings as the authors of history and culture, a new idea in contrast to the earlier prevailing theological idea that God was in charge of history. I will suggest that the complex of culture-history is authoring itself, telling its own story, weaving its own complex web of reality. It merely uses us to write the historical record. For my reading of the history of general consciousness, the gods, goddesses, and God were absolutely real during antiquity as personifications of soul, expressing the syntax of consciousness of that time. General consciousness, public mind, is the invisible ground of our being, and it undergoes transformations which can be read in the historical record. And, let me be clear that the concept of soul is not a way to smuggle the old idea of God into the discussion. God was indeed a real metaphysical being or ontological entity, he existed, but he is no more. Soul is the process of consciousness itself; soul does not exist in some mysterious way behind, above, below, or even within culture and history. *Soul is the process of thought unfolding itself (as culture-history).*

From the particular psychological perspective of soul and consciousness I adopt, it is not that some entity named God has died in an ordinary sense of death. Rather, the reality and cultural meaning that lived under the name "God" was irrevocably transformed into a new form of consciousness, which became the European Enlightenment (the Age of Reason). That new consciousness, our modern secular and mostly rational consciousness, appears to be a simple negation of the former God-centered consciousness that dominated Western civilization for a thousand years. However, my contention is that the God-consciousness of antiquity and the Middle Ages transformed itself from within and became the consciousness of the Enlightenment and modernity. Although one gave birth to the other, they are radically incompatible. Something monumental happened to what was formerly known as "God," and the form of our shared consciousness (our world) was changed forever. Today it certainly seems like soul is undergoing another monumental revolution that is changing and challenging our global civilization.

The Origin of the Book

My personal autobiography plays a significant role in the ideas explored in this book, but it includes far more than the temporal frame of my personal life. Although I was born in 1946, the ideas that have formed the course of my life are far older. I will explore an important event of early childhood at the beginning of chapter 1, but here I want to describe the specific entry point where my autobiography and the autobiography of soul (Western history) intersect. I have suffered from a curious interest and preoccupation with the problem of the quest for the historical Jesus. Although I personally rejected the Christianity of my father, who happened to be a liberal Protestant clergyman, I found myself immersed in a novel, experiential, psychologically focused, study of the (non-Christian) historical Jesus. During more than three decades of such immersive study, I began to sense that something was not quite right about the quest for the *historical* person of Jesus.[5]

---

5. From 1973 through the early 2000s. My first exposure to an experiential immersion in the Synoptic Gospels combined with a rigorous historical-critical method was with Walter Wink at Union Theological Seminary. I have since worked with the Guild for Psychological Studies offering weeks-long intensive seminars that promote both emotional and critical engagement with the historical figure of Jesus, such that each participant must think for themselves, and become conscious of unconscious preconceptions. At these seminars, the imaginal movement of soul on a personal level is also supported through expressive arts and other nonverbal methods. Because of the focus on the historical figure of Jesus there has been a misunderstanding that the Guild was a Christian group (Kirsch, *Jungians*, 76), but that was never the case. The Guild was always orientated through Jung's depth psychology, but primarily focused as a personalistic psychology and not the psychology with soul I emphasize in this book. The tenor of the seminar work has changed dramatically over the years, partly in response to the ideas I explore here. For an overview of the Guild's traditional theoretical orientation and methodology, as well as a lively memoir of lived seminar experience in which one person is challenged by the non-Christian historical Jesus, see Norris, *Reflections of a Passerby*.

God's Autopsy and the Living Truth of Soul

I was originally convinced, as most are, that a real historical person, Jesus of Nazareth, was at the heart of the gospel message. On the other hand, the more I studied the gospels, the less historical and the more literary and mythological they seemed to me. At the same time, the study of Jung's depth psychology revealed deep archetypal patterns in the psyche that have a greater sense of reality in some respects than mere historical facts. I began to sense that deep strata of the psyche invisibly shape our reality before so-called historical facts influence us. As Victor Hugo stated, "Nothing is as powerful as an idea whose time has come," which suggests that primal or fundamental *ideas* are the driving forces of history and influence our response to events.

I began to conclude that the process of history and cultural development results from an ongoing ferment of competing and conflicting ideas, which emerge gradually and imperceptibly. Before we are conscious of it, before it is articulated, this implicit level of thought shapes people and the culture of its time. We often see this only in historical hindsight because in the thick of the historical moment, things are too complex and multifaceted, too many ideas are competing all at once, to distinguish which cultural trend will emerge and become dominant.

The question that emerged for me was this: Could one man, a historical Jesus, even with a few followers, really account for the emergence of the Christ myth and the spread of Christianity? I began to doubt it. In the first centuries of the Christian era, a plurality of christianities emerged, many unique and differing expressions of a widespread archetypal pattern; the Christianity we know today, even in its many different forms, is but one example. In the light of Jung's insights about the objective psyche, Christianity seemed to me to be the emergence of a new cultural truth growing out of an already existing truth. At first, it was a Jewish development, an extension and evolution of Yahweh. Within the new perspective of an objective psyche, I saw not a historical man standing at the origin of Christianity, but the transformation and evolution of a god: A new living idea, incarnation, eventually expressed that change.

It is important to recognize that interest in the historical person of Jesus has been a decidedly modern phenomenon. Prior to the eighteenth century, the dominant cultural reality was the incarnate Christ, who was also known as the Second Person of the Trinity of Christian truth (dogma); within the Christian world the divine Christ was a "historical" fact, that is, a theological "historical" fact. The Christ, as the incarnation of God, was the living reality at the heart of Christianity and Western culture. The dichotomy represented by the ideas of a Christ of faith and a Jesus of history did not exist. The modern distinction between a historical man and a divine Christ is rooted in the great difference between our modern form of consciousness and the form of consciousness of antiquity. The contemporary interest in the historical person of Jesus emerged only during the Enlightenment in Western Europe, representing a radical disjuncture with the prevailing cultural consciousness of Medieval Christian civilization. Chapter 7 will address this difference in more detail when I examine the emergence of Christianity and its function as a prelude to Enlightenment consciousness.

One of the critical turning points for me was when I began to see that "history" is not a simple factual account of the past but a *written* construction based on other written constructions, always grasped indirectly and incompletely. What we think of as history is a function of literacy. No writing, no history. What we know as history is a written interpretation of shared memories. I remember clearly the moment when this "intellectual" insight into history's interpretive foundation produced a decidedly physical vertigo. My unconscious and naive notion of history as solid fact simply dissolved under me, and I was suspended over an abyss: I felt a certain degree of fear and disorientation before I experienced any sense of freedom.[6]

I began to recognize the quest for the historical Jesus, not as a technical historical problem that could be solved with better historical methodologies, but rather as a problem of consciousness. This led to a different kind of historical problem. I saw that consciousness itself is not historically uniform—it is not the same across historical periods. I had become quite suspicious of modern historical consciousness and its attempt to discern a historical Jesus in the New Testament documents, written some two thousand years ago within another kind of consciousness, one truly alien from our own. This recognition applied well beyond the story of Jesus and the question of whether or not he existed in history.[7]

The Bible has been devotedly poured over, word by word, ever since it emerged in the West as the source of ultimate truth. For most of our Western history, the Bible has been a vital and living culture-shaping document: As direct divine revelation, the Bible *was* the word of God. When the Bible *was* the source of God's revealed truth, the text was sacrosanct and had a final authority. And the rise of rational thinking during the Enlightenment did not diminish this fascination, which has dissected and analyzed the Bible from every conceivable scientific perspective. During the last few hundred years, however, the Bible has become one literary work among many, and it is viewed as the product of human hands at very specific social and historical times and places. Today, the sciences of archaeology, anthropology, sociology, historical criticism, literary criticism, textual transmission, and philology, especially in relation to ancient Hebrew and Greek, inspect and analyze the text. They have given us a deeper understanding of how difficult it is not only to translate the Bible, but to really understand it.

Other perspectives, such as philosophical hermeneutics as well as feminist and postcolonial criticism, for example, have brought awareness of cultural and systemic bias, prejudice and preconceptions that influence interpretation, not only of the Bible,

---

6. See "Critical Historiography," in Childs, *Myth*, 59–95. Among those who influenced my view of history are Munz, *Shapes of Time*; Stevenson, *History as Myth*; Stock, *Listening for the Text*; Veyne, *Writing History*; White, *The Content of the Form*.

7. These issues are explored in depth in my book *The Myth of the Historical Jesus and the Evolution of Consciousness*. There I point out the unwitting positivism permeating the idea of history guiding the contemporary scholarly search for the historical Jesus, and offer another approach integrating recent historiography, hermeneutics, and Jung's analytical psychology.

but of literature and culture in general. The Bible may be familiar to many but familiarity does not mean understanding. The modern study of the Bible should impress upon us how utterly alien from our own was the biblical world, the world of the ancient Near East. As the Bible shaped an entirely new European civilization for a thousand years of Christianity, we lost touch with the Bible's original context. And even more so today, all the modern hermeneutic approaches to the Bible rest in the core logic of Enlightenment humanism. And yet, our modern form of consciousness is radically different from the consciousness of antiquity when the Bible was written.

The Death of God Is the Living Truth of Soul

To illuminate the history of meaning—that is, soul—and how it has changed itself over three millennia of written history, I focus solely on the history of consciousness of the Judeo-Christian West, and from the broadest of historical perspectives. The continuous thread of background consciousness that we inherit has its seeds in the ancient mythological and religious traditions of our ancestors. This is why I will spend most of my time examining the god of the Judeo-Christian tradition.

The writing of history involves an ongoing tension between the trees and the forest, with some histories more focused on the trees—the activities of human persons—and others on the forest. The trees and forest metaphor is another way to think about the difference between contents of consciousness (trees) and the syntax or form of consciousness (forest). My analysis of the history of consciousness is involved almost exclusively with the primary religious texts that have carried and conveyed the meaning of existence for us. My focus is on the forest far more than the trees, tracking broad overarching themes in the history of the form of consciousness.

My project assumes that the God of the Bible is finished. That God was a historical personification of the truth of soul in its time, and served as a stepping stone in soul's ongoing historical self-transformations. The historical movement of soul has left that god behind because that form of consciousness has accomplished its work. Soul, as the always changing *form* of consciousness, is still at work today but in an entirely new form—hidden, I will suggest, in the exponential explosion of digital technology and media. To combine my history of the form of consciousness with an analysis of the Bible is to do an autopsy on the idea of God from a new perspective. How did soul create itself as an emergent new consciousness in the form of Yahweh over twenty-five hundred years ago, and how did that syntax or shape of consciousness develop itself over the centuries?

The Design of the Book

This book serves two purposes: it introduces psychology with soul, or psychology as the discipline of interiority, and it offers a novel interpretation of the Bible in its historical function to develop Western consciousness. These two purposes interweave throughout the book and build on each other. We get a glimpse of where our particular form of Western consciousness originated and where it might be going today.

Chapter 1 develops what I mean by *modern soul* in contrast with traditional understandings of soul. I include a brief introduction to how consciousness developed historically over about three thousand years, using the Bible's *I Am* and the Western philosophical and psychological traditions. In chapter 2, I describe how I reinterpret the Bible (and history itself) as soul's historical dream of itself, differentiating ego or pragmatic consciousness from soul or psychological consciousness. Chapters 1 and 2 reorient our everyday practical consciousness to the deeper soul-oriented consciousness I will use to interpret the Bible beginning in chapter 3.

Chapter 3 begins a sequence of discussions based on the Old Testament and its god Yahweh, beginning with the patriarch Abraham, interpreted as the personified form of soul leaving the archaic, preliterate form of itself and embarking on the long and arduous journey into the status of consciousness known as literacy. I find major turning points on that road in Yahweh's peculiar interest in human sexuality and in the sacrifice of Isaac. In chapter 4, I look to the relationship of Yahweh and Moses, where the god is a violent force, separating himself from his original nature-based Canaanite bull-storm-god manifestation. Yahweh represents the movement of soul toward transcendence, imageless spirit, and written word. Yahweh was the Western god of writing and literacy, a tremendous liberation of the form of consciousness from its original preliterate fusion with nature. Within the Yahweh form of soul we watch soul discriminate itself from itself. Chapter 5 highlights Yahweh's decision to separate from the world of nature-fused gods and goddesses and his subsequent intolerance of that polytheistic cosmos. Yahweh demands singular absolute obedience from the people, but Israel cannot put aside the other gods and goddesses. Their relentless disobedience leads to extremes of punishment that almost destroy the people and Yahweh himself. In this drama, soul is struggling to preserve itself in the face of near annihilation. Soul does save itself by refocusing on the torah as the external form of the mind of God, and *study* replaces *war* as Yahweh's new passion. The *thoughts* of God and *thought* itself gain greater value; illiteracy is sinful, and literacy is sacred.

Chapter 6 takes up the story of Job, in which Yahweh suffers a disturbing insight, as the god's absolute value and power begin to transfer to the morally superior Job. The syntax of consciousness personified as a "god" (universals) is cracking open and shifting some of its value to the particulars (the human). And so, in chapter 7, I explore the idea of incarnation, as soul continues to shift from a divine Yahweh to a human subject. Each historical transformation is soul's self-negation in service to a new status of consciousness, and here soul appears as a new shape of meaning, Christ, or God made Man. The Christ form of soul represents a revolutionary change in, and further discrimination of, the form of consciousness.

With chapter 8, I leave the Bible as a text behind, but continue to follow the "Yahweh/Christ" impulse through soul's postbiblical developments. Key iconic thinkers reflect the development of soul during the Enlightenment. Among others, Martin Luther, Francis Bacon, and René Descartes represent soul's difficult and painful move into the development of human potential and eventually the "death of God" (Friedrich Nietzsche). Radically different from the consciousness of antiquity and the medieval era, modernity splits soul into the ontologically separate categories of subject and object, or mind and matter. The human subject achieves a new and extraordinary freedom, while at the same time it becomes isolated and alienated from the once predominant larger narrative of Meaning (Christianity).

Chapter 9 brings us into contemporary times, with the development of depth-psychology, the notion of the unconscious, and the scientific discoveries of uncertainty, probability, and the role of the observer in experimental outcomes. Philosophy has its own, so to speak, "death of God" moment in Martin Heidegger's realization that there can be no final, universal foundation on which to base truth or human existence. The certainty promised by modern science is undermined, and everything is seen to be in flux. These developments of soul, of our form of consciousness, reveal we are no longer split apart as subject vs. object, but rather that we exist as a subject-and-object continuum. We are waking up to the idea that we are no longer "children of God" but rather psychological adults constituted as consciousness. Soul is conscious of itself as consciousness. Consciousness has come home to itself.

Chapter 10 offers a brief, and admittedly speculative, analysis of the social problems of genocide, misogyny, and racism in the light of the analysis of the preceding chapters recording how the Western form of consciousness developed. Strangely enough, the hidden imperative at the heart of Western consciousness—driving genocide, misogyny, and racism—might be found in Yahweh's and Christ's intolerance of the nature gods and goddesses.

The work of God's autopsy requires a new set of categories that put the phenomenon of "God" in a new light. The new categories enable us to see God's disappearance as a natural historical transformation of the ground of cultural consciousness itself—that is soul, the logical form of consciousness. Over these chapters, I show how soul's operations on itself throughout history lead to changes in what is taken as the real and the true during particular cultural eras: from the far distant preliterate, nature-based, myth-ritual cultures, through antiquity and the rise of religious literate culture, into modernity and science, and now our contemporary digital and media-saturated time.

On Referring to God and Yahweh

Throughout the book I make use of the varied terms Yahweh, the Yahweh god, and God or god. The simple *God* reminds us that from the Bible's perspective, there is one unified and unifying God. In popular usage, the word *God*, capitalized, refers to the

God at the beginning of Genesis, the God of the New Testament, and whatever God might mean today—a single God. Our modern mindset no longer thinks in terms of multiple gods. Our Western consciousness has been long imbued with monotheism and its purported yet implicit moral superiority, which contributes to the general pervasive sense of our own superiority; it is a deeply ingrained thought habit.

To use the name *Yahweh* is to place us in the historical world of the biblical traditions, where cultural and historical contexts shaped the idea of any god. The old gods are indeed as strange to us as is the name Yahweh, although certainly not as strange as Moloch or Chemosh, El, Baal, and Asherah, to name only a few of the hundreds of ancient Near Eastern gods who have disappeared. To say "the Yahweh god," though awkward, reminds us that this god was simply one among many and, in relation to the great ancient civilizations (Assyria, Egypt, Babylonia, Persia, Greek, Rome) surrounding the Hebrew tribes and then Israel, a minor god at that. Our ingrained assumptions about God, whether positive or negative, are difficult to navigate.

God and gods are psychologically historical, culturally contingent, and complex; it takes effort not to unconsciously settle into the thought habit of "One God." In a manner of speaking—and not unlike *literacy*, monotheism has basically colonized global consciousness, and we are all infected by it. However, this God is no more; our tradition's monotheistic consciousness is breaking up, undermining itself, and a new form of consciousness is emerging.

In antiquity, gods and goddesses were fluid, sharing and changing their identities, even contradictory identities and qualities, with other gods and goddesses, adapting to local circumstances. The prevailing and common world of polytheism was widely tolerant and inclusive, gods and goddesses slipping in and out of various cultures and societies, adapting and reshaping themselves, as well as shaping their culture. Every locale had its deities, and as they were always associated with, and embodied in, natural phenomena, they were literally thousands. The deities were the heart and soul of society and culture. This was the world in which the Bible emerged.

The Tanakh and the Old Testament

Tanakh is the conventional Jewish, but postbiblical, term used to refer to the Hebrew Bible. Both the Tanakh and the Old Testament are collections of the same books, all thirty-six of them, beginning with Genesis, but the interesting and significant difference between the two volumes is the order of their books. The word Tanakh is an acronym derived from the initial letters of the Hebrew words that describe three separate groupings: *torah*, "teaching"; *nebi'im*, "prophets"; and *ketubim*, "writings," and this is their order in the Tanakh.[8] The Old Testament changes the order of the second two groupings so that it begins with the *torah*, the first five books.[9] Next are

---

8. Miles, *God*, 18.
9. In both the Tanakh and the Old Testament it is the first nine books that are the same. The four

the "writings" (such as Job, Psalms, Proverbs, etc.) and then the "prophets" which lead right into the New Testament, because for the Christian point of view the yearning expressed in the prophetic writings was fulfilled by the Christ. It is the Christian view of reality that interprets the Christ principle as a continuous thread running throughout the entire Tanakh and leading inexorably to the Christ revelation, which is the New Testament. Therefore, the Tanakh represents the Jewish story of God before the Christian influence rearranged the order of the books. The Old Testament then represents Christianity gathering up the Jewish story of God and incorporating it into its new form of consciousness.

This is important for my story because the unfolding of the Hebrew-Jewish God comes before that of the Christian God, and my psychological interpretation depends on the historical development of consciousness. It is still possible to reach back through the ages and get a glimpse of how consciousness emerged and developed, and the Bible is the key document for this new psychological interpretation.

While I follow the order of the Tanakh as representing an internal development in its own right, all of the biblical quotations in this work are from the New Revised Standard Version (NRSV) unless noted otherwise.

The Labor of Conscious Reading

Our culture and society is literate, defined and dominated by the consciousness that reading and writing have shaped. We learned to read and write as children and so were absorbed into this style of consciousness unconsciously. We read without thinking about the process of reading, and we love writing that flows along seamlessly. When we encounter misspelling, odd grammar, and anomalous syntax we become irritated and annoyed, thinking this is bad writing, but we usually do not become conscious of the writing or reading in themselves. Literacy has consumed and digested our consciousness and uses it as its own form of being in the world without our being the least bit aware of it. Obviously we cannot step outside of our literate world in order to gain another perspective on it, and we cannot choose to become illiterate, and unlearn reading and writing. Therefore, to become conscious of the form of our consciousness, which is essentially invisible to us, we are dependent on reading and writing offering a way to reflect on itself. Hopefully the writing and reading of this book will give us a glimpse of the nature and quality of the collective literate consciousness that we take for granted, and which has shaped our fundamental sense of self over about two thousand years.

These ideas will pose challenges for readers. I ask you to note your personal consciousness and reactions, and at the same time bracket them, as you allow soul to tell its own story and to stay with me as this story evolves. I believe you will find a

---

books after the Torah, called the "Former Prophets," describe the "history" of the Hebrew people becoming the nation of Israel.

reward, first perhaps an interesting and novel insight into the deeper meaning of biblical narratives and historical ideas that are the ground of today's consciousness. More importantly, I hope you will come to share a deeper understanding of how this history of the form of consciousness, i.e., soul, helps to explain what has been happening to us as a species, which is the tale of the following chapters.

Chapter 1

Is There a Modern Soul?
Consciousness as the Shape of Meaning

As humans we live *primarily* in a linguistic cosmos, not in the body. We see what is and happens not directly, not as things-in-themselves, but only in terms of the words and concepts that we have of them.[1]

Soul or consciousness is the All, and everything real, just as much as everything imaginable, has its place in soul and consciousness.[2]

"I MIGHT AS WELL be praying to a brick wall." The thought simply appeared, as the young boy, perhaps six or maybe a bit older, said his bedtime prayers. His dutiful mother, young wife of her clergyman husband, had taught him to do what she surely believed to be right and good. The boy learned simple childhood prayers and continued to say them, more or less by rote, when the spontaneous idea of the brick wall interrupted his innocent prayer ritual.

Now, as the man writing this book, the event takes on new significance. All I remember is the one thought, "I might as well be praying to a brick wall." No emotion, surprise, or shock. I simply knew this was true and stopped my prayers. No crisis of faith, no further reflection on the thought itself (not something a six-year-old would do). The thought simply appeared, changed my behavior, and was gone. Not until early adulthood, during a prolonged psychological analysis, did the memory of this event resurface.

Seen from my perspective today, over sixty years later, this simple childhood event depicts a profound ambivalence and conflict within soul in relation to religion

---

1. Giegerich, *What Is Soul?*, 74.
2. Giegerich, *What Is Soul?*, 75.

and modern rational thought. It is not my personal ambivalence. The thought that I might as well be praying to a brick wall represents a conflict between religion and reason inherent in modern consciousness that is still unresolved. Even after the achievements of the Enlightenment and science over the last four hundred years, and the absence of God in modern secular society, the problem of the conflict between religion and reason has not been fully worked through. On a historical cultural level, which is the dimension of soul that concerns me, the outer practice (praying) has not caught up with the inner truth (brick wall). We as a culture are still embroiled in ongoing confusion about the relationship between Religion and Reason.

My childhood prayer event raises the question of soul. The problem of Religion versus Reason is not merely my personal problem; it is soul's problem. Here I wish to explore the notion of a modern soul in contrast to traditional mythological and religious notions of soul. This is the question the entire book addresses. One reason for the significant confusion about Religion and Reason is that these very concepts are today inadequate as primary categories. Soul itself has outgrown them. Our concepts for thinking about essential matters have not caught up with what has already happened culturally and historically. I hope to show that the concepts *soul* and *consciousness* can function as new categories that constitute an emergent and revolutionary understanding of psychology and offer a new way to interpret historical cultural change. A psychology oriented with soul is needed to help us understand the profound cultural shifts we are undergoing today. A psychology with soul pushes off from the prevailing ideas of Religion and Reason, while at the same time it incorporates them into a new framework. The categories of Religion and Reason are negated, preserved, and transformed, as I hope to show, in a psychology with soul.

To begin with, soul is not an entity but a living *process*. In the scene of my interrupted prayer, soul is not an actor in the background making things happen. Soul did not interpose a brick wall between me and God. God *was* nothing more than a brick wall in my thought. The nature of soul is that it does not make things happen, it *is* what happens. But the interior meaning, the deeper meaning of what is happening is not obvious. Soul itself is a kind of intent buried in the happening. We are in the position of needing to learn how to understand it, which is the discipline of learning to allow soul to speak about itself. In this case, "my" childhood thoughts are the happening of soul, and what I personally think or feel about what happened is not at the heart of what soul is trying to say. The modern notion of *soul* entails a radical shift in perspective from the common personalistic and anthropocentric view of ourselves, society, and culture, to a wider and deeper kind of background, an impersonal field of consciousness, of which we are all a part. We are immersed in it (or *soaked* in it, as a friend likes to say) as our shared reality, but it is not of our *personal* making or doing. Like culture, soul exists, and we are born into it. Soul is the dynamic field of *meanings* already here when we arrive.

Instead of asking, why did I as a young boy have that thought, I want to ask, why did soul think that thought *as if* it were my thought? The idea that God was nothing more than a brick wall was a complex thought, a problematic thought, quite beyond the intellectual means of a young boy. And yet, in hindsight, the thought gave voice to a problem that soul needed to work on, which then became my life work, a kind of vocation or calling. I did not choose it. Rather, it chose me and maintained a hold on me as the only thing worth thinking about. At the time, there certainly was no such sense of a calling. The thought happened, disappeared, and was forgotten. However, it was the seed of the problem that would inform my life's deepest concerns: it was a true, or living, thought that would have to think itself all the way through, and my life would be the medium for that soul-thought's work.

The personalistic interpretation of this event uses the categories of conventional psychology, or ego-psychology, or more broadly, psychology within the logic of humanism or anthropology, and views it as only my personal conflict and problem. Conventional psychology is human-centered, in contrast to a soul-centered psychology. As my father was a clergyman, a Freudian personalistic interpretation would see the symptom of an Oedipal conflict; or, more simply, the naive rejection of a family mythology along the lines of realizing that Santa Claus is not real. While either of these interpretations has some truth, conventional psychology sees the mind, or psyche, as encapsulated and self-contained within the individual, and even identifies the mind with the brain and keeps it all inside the skull. This is the modern scientific and humanistic view of the person as a discrete and disconnected individual, about which I will have more to say later. The conventional personalistic perspective actually prevents awareness of another form of consciousness, a soul-oriented consciousness, in which soul is both impersonal and autonomous and not subject to control by human agents. The concept of *soul* points to a broader, general, and unconscious, or implicit, *form* of consciousness, which is first of all social and cultural. Of course, we are individual bodies and persons, we have our own thoughts and feelings, and experience ourselves as separate from each other. However, the notion of soul proposes another dimension to our being that is impersonal, shared, and social, that has its own life. From soul's perspective, "my" idea that God was nothing more than a brick wall was much more than my own thought. The idea of the brick wall was soul's thought, produced spontaneously. It was soul's thought about itself of which I was both a recipient and a co-creator. Not unlike a dream, which is not created consciously by my personal ego, and which if not taken literally but symbolically, can reveal meaning, a modern view of soul invites us to change our perspective. Soul is first of all not my personal experience. The "brick wall" is a cultural and historical living idea that appears to me of its own accord. I am the location where this soul thought happens. Thus, I become responsible for the thought, but I am not its origin or creator.

From the point of view of soul, the image of the brick wall introduced a complex set of ideas to the mind of a child who was incapable of understanding them, but understanding is not necessary (at first) when the impact of the event is the mark of soul. With the image that "God" was a "brick wall," I intuitively understood that there was no God at all. It did not mean that God was still there as a silent, mute, and deaf presence. It meant that instead of a presence (personified as God), there was only empty nothingness—there was no one, no thing, there! The idea of God, the word "God," was revealed as hollow, an empty husk. What expressed itself with the experience of the brick wall was the meaning of Friedrich Nietzsche's well-known phrase, "God is dead," stated only about sixty years before my brick wall thought. When I realized I was praying to nothing, I experienced the truth of our modern age. Our modern truth is that metaphysically and theologically there really are no longer any transcendent deities or presences beyond ourselves: we are alone in the sense of no longer contained in a mythological or religious cosmic meaning or story that societally and culturally would be taken for granted. The heavens have long been emptied of their presences, and the gods and goddesses only populate textbooks and story books; we hear of them secondhand. The idea that our modern age is secular and godless is not new.

What is new is to see the historical role of soul in creating our modern general consciousness—soul *is* the happening that we call history and culture. It is common to blame humankind for killing off the gods (as Nietzsche metaphorically claimed in his parable)[3] and to blame the rise of science as a human activity for separating us from the sacred. But from the point of view of a soul-oriented psychology, this was soul's own doing as a historical process. The death of God and the rise of science are soul's own happening, soul's own production. As a child, to stop praying, was simply getting in tune with the prevailing truth, which I, of course, had no inkling of at the time. Later in childhood and life, this truth contributed to deep anxiety and loneliness, the terrible personal underside of the pervasive cultural loss of meaning. Such anxiety and loneliness were first experienced as only my personal suffering, without any understanding of a deeper cultural truth. At the time, however, the innate meaning of the brick wall simply registered as true, and that was that. As we will come to see, truth and soul are identical, and they share an objective quality in the sense that they are a public, cultural reality that is not merely an individual's personal and subjective belief (*objective* in this sense does not mean eternal or permanent). We have been born into the (objective) truth of our age, which is a fundamentally different truth from former ages. Here *objective* simply means a truth that exists independently of our personal beliefs or preferences.

---

3. "Whither is God?" he cried. "I will tell you. *We have killed him*—you and I. All of us are his murderers." We will read the full parable in chapter 8.

Exploring the Experience

Several aspects of modern soul are introduced by the brick wall experience. These are, in no particular order:

- soul does manifest as a (psychological) event
- soul is spontaneous
- soul thinks, so to speak, for itself
- soul is related to truth (the public taken-for-granted assumptions of any culture)
- soul is the only concern of psychology
- soul's thoughts are different from, independent of, our personal human thoughts
- soul is the living cultural present, while the historical record preserves dead soul
- soul, as public truth implicitly accepted by everyone, is not reducible to human subjectivity
- soul creates itself, destroys itself, recreates itself, continually
- soul will disrupt and disturb convention, which soul had a hand in creating
- soul does not care whether we are ready for its truth or not
- soul as truth is far out in front of where we actually are, individually and as a people
- soul makes a claim on us, both collectively and personally, experienced as a necessity

These varied aspects of soul will unfold as we proceed.

One might think it cruel that soul would rob a child of his innocent belief in God, but then we would be casting soul within human terms and human values. Soul is, first of all, not human and not a human attribute. Soul, in its autonomy, is like the weather: indifferent to our personal comfort. A conventional understanding of soul is that it is *one's* immortal soul, that dimension of one's being that connects the individual to the divine, and thus to that which is traditionally understood as absolute, eternal, infinite, and unchanging. The conventional and popular idea of the transcendent is of some(actual)thing entirely separate from the here and now. The soul in this traditional context is linked to ideas of God, the Absolute, and the Eternal, religious or spiritual notions of a transcendent essence. But, even in this traditional sense, the soul is not human either, but divine (however, today the word "divine" is a harmless and mostly comforting romantic adjective employed by the alienated ego, and has nothing to do with the terrible truth of a deity). Yet, if our modern era is marked by the truth that "God is dead," does this mean that "soul" is dead, too? Is soul absent and lost to us in the same way the gods are? Yes, the traditional idea of soul has died, but what I hope to show is that the original idea of soul has changed and become a *modern soul,* and modern in such a way that does not offend modern consciousness for whom the gods have indeed faded away.

It is crucial to see that in the modern psychological understanding of soul, neither the gods, or God, have died in any literal sense. Nietzsche's story was a metaphorical expression of what had already become a historical and culture-wide truth. The sense of a "modern soul" points to an emergent, historical process that develops culture and pushes culture into new possibilities. Soul is the historical process; it is at the heart of cultural paradigms and itself undergoes change. As soul changes, what a culture takes as truth changes, which changes the culture's institutions and organization. The psychological understanding of soul as modern is that history and culture are how soul creates and develops itself and that human persons are the cultural-historical medium with which soul does its work.

A soul-view shifts from the conventional focus on the discrete individual person to the larger and broader world of culture and history, the living dynamic here and now, as the true locus of soul. If soul is to be *modern*, we can no longer conceive of soul as a transcendent some-thing that operates on us from outside culture. Soul *is* a living truth that animates culture; soul is the structural form of a culture's consciousness; soul is an embedded, or interior, intent. It is familiar as what we might call the *Zeitgeist*, the spirit of an age. Like language, soul is a quality of shared we-ness, with a life of its own, the dimension of what we can call public mind that makes us what we *are* without thinking about it. Soul in this modern sense is the shape of implicit shared meaning that gives our age, our historical epoch, its definition, and thus our basic and implicit self-understanding at this cultural time.

If the images and ideas of myth and religion are transformed and no longer relevant for modern consciousness, why continue to use the word *soul* at all? If we are redefining *soul*, why not redefine the idea of God and maintain the historical continuity with this powerful idea? Certainly, contemporary theologians have been rethinking the notion of God more abstractly, as process, as patterning, incorporating ideas from science. But, from my point of view, the reason not to rehabilitate the idea of God is that it is not up to us. That would be an ego choice rather than seeing what soul itself has done with its own self-definition.

Soul has already modernized itself and redefined itself in the word *psychology*. The ancient word *soul* (*psyche*) is preserved in the contemporary word *psyche-logy*. Of course, the conventional meaning of psychology refers to the scientific study of the individual person's psyche. But our modern word has ancient Greek roots: *psyche* means soul and *-logy* derives from *logos*, which is related to word, speech, and to give an account. Another meaning of psychology altogether opens up with the notion of "soul's logos," or "soul's speech about itself." In antiquity, the Greek idea of *logos* did not mean human thought but was first of all *the Logos*, a cosmic principle of divine Reason. It was the gift of higher thought that came to humankind from the gods, an ordering principle and the ability to think and reflect that separated humankind from the animals. In mythological cultures, language and speech were of a nonhuman origin, either gifted by a god or in some indigenous cultures, by an animal.[4] Language and speech were not at all human inventions. Psychology, understood as "soul's logos," inherits this phenomenology while at the same time understanding that the time of gods and divine gifts is over. What this means for me is that for the purposes of this book, psychology shifts from being focused on the human person to an activity and dimension of soul itself that is distinct from, yet also related to, humankind.

Soul is historically associated with the phenomenology of mythology and religion, and within that context, it was independent and transcendent in relation to humankind, and yet it was also intimately related to the human person. My view of modern soul will retain its autonomy, but within a very different framework. Even though soul is not a human attribute, the human person cannot escape soul. Thinking biologically, the idea of life is similar. Life as such, biological life, does not belong to any individual creature, plant, animal, or human, as an attribute, such as being big or small. When we are alive, Life is something we *are*. Soul is also a kind of life, but of a different order, a *logical* life, that is, the life of mind, of language, of consciousness and culture. Culture and language are shared social realities that function with a life of their own independent of human persons, and yet human persons are the place where culture and language happen. Soul is the public mind that we are born into, and within which we gradually become individuals. The idea of modern soul preserves its autonomous function without taking on any conventional theological or metaphysical entities or purposes. This refers to the idea that modern soul is an emergent cultural life that happens now; it is the present, and does not know ahead of time where it is going. Soul is a self-creating process that works itself out in the fertile ferment of culture. Soul is a *telos*, or soul is in itself telic, without a formal teleology, as the future cannot be known ahead of time. Soul is intentionality itself without specific content. Speech functions in a similar way. When we speak extemporaneously, speech happens of its own accord, creating itself as it happens.

---

4. The story of the Ten Commandments in Exodus most likely reflects an older origin-of-written language myth, as it is the god who *writes* the words on a mountain top, which then come down to the human world. The mythology of some indigenous peoples includes animals who have speech before human beings do. The California Native American tribe Winnemem Wintu believe they received language and speech from the salmon so that they could speak for the salmon. "Language" in this sense is something magical and preexists human beings. Even today, linguists consider that the search for the origin of language may be the hardest scientific problem (https://en.wikipedia.org/wiki/Origin_of_language). Here I also want to emphasize the difference between orality, spoken language, and written language, the written word. It is obviously easier to determine when writing emerged because we have artifacts, while the origin of spoken language remains lost in the mists of preliterate and prehistorical cultures. As we will see, *writing* is peculiar and critical to the form of consciousness introduced by the Old Testament god Yahweh.

Soul and Language

Heidegger has stated, "Language is the house of Being. In its home man dwells."[5] It is not a stretch to say that "language is the house of soul." But, language is itself an artifact that disappears within, or behind, the *meaning* that it conveys. When I say "house" I am not conscious of the phonetic quality of the sound of the word. When I write "house" I am not conscious of the five letters as black marks that are visible against the white background. I am preoccupied with the meaning the word *house* conveys, and the meaning of the larger context within which I use that word. Fundamentally, we are creatures of *meaning*, which is also to say, creatures of *consciousness*, which is *soul*. In this sense, meaning is our home, where we dwell.

Language and soul are almost indistinguishable in that both are socially and culturally shared meanings that we live within, or better, that we live *as*. We *are* these cultural meanings that give us our way of relating to the world. Our use of language is very personal, but language is also a reality that extends beyond us that we do not control. We do not choose our language; we are born into it. Language has a life of its own, and we are playing catch-up to its evolving meanings. We also do not experience language as a divine presence, as an entity or a thing. Language is a nonexistent reality, a matrix of meanings, that makes us human and lifts us out of nature. With language, we have already left behind animal existence, that level of unconscious embeddedness in the environment. (I explore this historical movement of soul in chapter 4.) Language is the medium in which Mind (or soul, or consciousness) expresses itself and creates itself. When we speak of *world*, we really mean the human world of public mind, language, and culture, which constitute soul and consciousness at large: the *world of meaning* that we *are* first of all.

Psychology with soul is concerned with the everyday phenomena that make up our cultural world of tacitly shared meanings, the human world of Mind and Culture. A psychology with soul undertakes the work of bringing the implicit and unconscious dimension of soul into an explicit and conscious articulation or interpretation. This is the process of soul making in which we attempt to see through the surface of everyday phenomena and interpret their soulful meaning. This is why a psychology with soul is not focused, first of all, on the inner world of the individual but rather on the shared world of soul, which is the collective structure and syntax of consciousness itself. Such everyday cultural phenomena are, for example, television, money and global markets, the World Wide Web, the nuclear bomb, smart phones, software, globalization, media saturation, and advertising. From the psychological perspective, their meaning does not first of all have to do with human persons, but with soul itself. Human-centered psychology, conventional psychology as a science, has its objects of interest and investigation outside of itself: the feelings, thoughts, fantasies, behaviors, of the individual.

---

5. Heidegger, "Letter on Humanism," 193.

The radical shift of consciousness that has already occurred in our contemporary world, and that I am concerned with here, is that *psychology has come to the realization that it is its own object.* Jung realized that the psyche is both subject and object, that is, that psyche is its own subject and object at the same time. Psychology in this sense is the psyche investigating itself. Our ordinary orientation assumes that we, as a subject, look out at objects as separate from us. But we have never before been aware of the nature of our looking, of what structures and conditions our looking. What does give our consciousness its basic orientation? We certainly are aware that personal attitudes affect how we see things. The classic example is how optimists and pessimists see a partially filled glass of water as either half full or half empty. When we are in love, we see things very differently than when we are depressed. This is the personal level, the individualistic approach of conventional psychology, but it shows how we are predisposed by certain general states of mind to see and relate to the world in specific ways.

My interest is in how soul looks at things. The level of soul's looking is consciousness-at-large, the general consciousness of culture at large. Psychology with soul is a psychology that views soul as itself the structure of our looking, the structure and nature of the consciousness with which we look. Psychology with soul is a psychology of consciousness as such, consciousness that has become conscious of itself. Today consciousness has discovered itself as a phenomenon in its own right. This is a kind of new "enlightenment" that has already occurred historically. If we were fish, it would be like becoming conscious of the water that has been our taken-for-granted context all along. But with the image of fish and water, we must take another step and imagine that the water is becoming conscious of itself as the total context, and the only possible context, of all fishiness.

Consciousness now knows that it is the context of *all* knowledge, and as such it is a cultural phenomenon more than a property of the individual. In this sense, it is more accurate to think of ourselves as radio receivers in relation to the collective prevailing form of consciousness. We are born into a given quality and style of consciousness that is represented by the family, the community, the culture at large, and we absorb all the unspoken nuances of all these different levels of culture unconsciously. As we grow, we learn to use the cultural givens within the limits of our creative capacities, which stretch soul in new directions. Yet, it is really soul that uses us to stretch itself into new directions, its inner telic impulse always pushing, trying new ideas, new things.

We are accustomed to thinking of consciousness as that space in which we are aware of the physical objects of our environment, as well as immaterial objects like thoughts, ideas, feelings, images, sensations, and so on. Consciousness, historically, has naturally been preoccupied with those objects, and not at all aware of itself as the space within which those objects appear. But, now, consciousness is capable of turning its attention to that "space" that is its own awareness of itself. Consciousness is turning its attention to consciousness as such. This is the provenance of psychology with soul.

Is There a Modern Soul?

This thought presented itself to me in the following dream, in which this new form of consciousness is making a statement about itself:

> A middle-aged female research scientist, wearing a white lab coat, working in a laboratory of perhaps the 1950s, is looking through a microscope. The tables, cabinets, and floor are a dark wood, and so the room has a warm quality. The dream scene shifts to an outdoor rural setting with some farm or ranch buildings nearby, where basketball player Klay Thompson is looking up through a pair of binoculars. The two of them become aware that they are seeing each other seeing each other, which brings a warm knowing smile to the woman's face.[6]

I think the dream is fairly self-explanatory, but a few comments will flesh it out. The microscope and the binoculars suggest the seeing involved here is seeing beyond the surface, beyond the contents seen by the unaided eye, beyond ego seeing. This seeing is also the seeing, seeing itself. The two people, looking through their instruments not only see each other, they also see each other seeing each other. While as individual persons, the two dream figures represent separate moments of personal consciousness, in the mutual seeing, which is seeing itself, they become a unified dialectical ouroboric consciousness. They symbolize the logical form of *consciousness of consciousness*. This dream in particular seems to be soul's thought about itself, soul's own logos. The two dream figures are not people in any ordinary sense, but symbolic of how consciousness as such can reflect itself within itself, or to itself: consciousness as self-relation.

As the dreamer, I had a startled response when I realized that the female research scientist looking through the microscope was seeing the human world, which we do not ordinarily think of as microscopic. The microscope and the binoculars, as scientific instruments, are symbolic of consciousness having achieved a radical new perspective on reality and itself. It brings to mind the image of the earth from outer space, which at that distance becomes, in a sense, microscopic. Then, too, when we look up or out, through binoculars or a telescope, we become aware of the vast scale of the universe in which the earth is indeed a microscopic dot. The perspective available through the scientific instruments reflects what has happened to consciousness. The instruments have enhanced consciousness in such a way that we now know that what we have always seen with the unaided eye is an extremely limited slice of "reality," or an extremely limited slice of consciousness itself. Our ability to see our planet from "outer space" also symbolizes this shift in consciousness, the ability of consciousness to see itself from a new perspective, and thus shift into a new logical status that now includes within a larger order of consciousness its former manifestations. Both religion and science are now sublated moments within soul's new consciousness of itself. This means that psychology with soul includes a religious sensibility or sensitivity without being a religion, as well as employing the critical phenomenology of science without reducing reality

---

6. Author's dream: April 8, 2018.

to materialism. Soul is no longer external to us but has become, through its own self-transformations, a quality of consciousness that we can cultivate.

Interpretation (Psychology) as Choice

Returning to the image of the brick wall that intruded into my boyhood prayers, viewing it as a soul event is a conscious choice. I make no claim of something ontological beyond the interpretation itself. One could choose to stay completely on the human level and interpret it in terms of my personal development within my particular family. To approach it psychologically as a soul event, however, is to choose to interpret it as the irruption of the already true background form of modern consciousness into my awareness. For psychology with soul, the "brick wall" is the symbol of the absence of the gods and the emptiness of the heavens, a truth the soul is speaking about itself. The "brick wall" is not merely a personal matter but a truth of consciousness at large that is making itself known. The very idea of *soul* is itself a choice of a particular interpretive perspective. With choice we either make soul or ignore soul. It is important to see that it is choice that makes a soul truth explicit, and this is what soul-making is, making soul conscious. The choice of a soul-oriented interpretation is not arbitrary but is consistent with soul's historical unfolding, as I hope to demonstrate.

In the ancient past—and the Bible is a fine and ready example here—dreams were known as revelations of divine truth. Dreams, as the speech of God, or a god/goddess, had a substantial presence and guided events and foretold the future. The dream made a claim on the dreamer. To make a claim is a core characteristic of soul. It claims us, either collectively or individually. We can see how the idea of "the Christ" claimed the cultures of late antiquity throughout the Mediterranean and medieval Europe, how the idea of "evolution" claimed nineteenth-century Europe, and how "television and smart phones," not as gadgets but as soul-ideas, have claimed contemporary culture. The individual is claimed when a creative project or idea takes over their life and must be pursued; or a dream jars us into action; or even a pathological symptom like an addiction or anxiety dominates our existence. These are the surface manifestation of a claim of soul that seeks our attention, an implicit idea that wants to be addressed, understood, and realized consciously. As for dreams, our modern scientific view does not acknowledge any claim. Dreams are thought to be neurological processes that have no existential meaning other than as biological functions of the brain. This is the biological point of view, and within its own framework, it is its own truth. The scientific framework of biology has done away with all inherent meanings in life processes. No animism, no spirits, no gods, no soul, no personally meaningful significance, just chemically based physiological processes. The framework of biology is materialism: blind matter doing its thing according to physical laws. Any sense of broader meaning is excluded. But what about those dreams from which we awake shaking, terrified, weeping, or elated? Within that emotional intensity, the claim such a dream makes on us, a dream-meaning, is pressing to be unearthed.

In contrast to the scientific framework, the psychological point of view is another framework that gives priority to thoughts and meanings working on themselves; consciousness at large is the life of mind, interpreting and reinterpreting its own truths. We can choose which framework we want to work with, but neither framework should claim an absolute or final truth for itself. As we will see later, although soul once had the status of an Absolute, as God, as Being, as Reason, modern soul, knowing itself as consciousness of consciousness, has dissolved all absolutes. A traditional, metaphysical Absolute is not time-bound or contingent, but, today soul sees itself as essentially historical, as a process, as time itself. The choice to work as a psychologist with soul is the choice to adopt a specific attitude and approach, to take on a methodological discipline that does not lead to a universal truth, nor any basis for dogmatism. Psychology posits an autonomous soul as its foundation, and modern soul is aware that consciousness is conscious of itself as the context of all knowing. Consciousness of consciousness is the circular structure of soul, and within psychology, truth is also aware of itself as constituted by language, interpretation, thought, and meaning. Soul, as the structure of consciousness that informs culture, creates itself using the dynamic tools of language, thought, invention, social organization, human persons. Soul, as the historical-cultural implicit shape of consciousness, is truth itself, and as truth it also creates and re-creates itself throughout history.

Truth

Within a psychology oriented to soul's logos, the notions of soul and truth are synonymous. Truth is the syntax of the consciousness of its particular historical time and place. Truth is that deep ground of being that a culture takes for granted, does not question. Truth is the water that the fish swim in. In antiquity, truth was identified with the gods and goddesses or a God; as such it was external to human persons and objective, also in the sense that the gods, goddesses, and God were public facts, cultural taken-for-granted realities. They were, in their time, as real and as ordinary as our roads and highways, along with the extensive "priesthood" of civil engineers that builds and maintains them, on which we are fully dependent, taking for granted they will always be there. The nature of truth changes the world we inhabit as soul transforms itself historically.

The worldview that emerged out of the world of antiquity and Medieval Europe, that of the Enlightenment and the Age of Reason, defined truth in scientific terms. Science makes truth in terms of empirical, verifiable facts that are public and objective; this truth is also external to human persons. Scientific facts are supposed to be independent of personal belief and opinion. The truth of science is grounded in a view of the universe that is at bottom materialistic; the fundamental basis of reality is matter and energy, and truth is grounded in the functioning of natural laws. Science is the basic world of truth we have simply and unconsciously inherited as modern persons. The assumptions of science are our unconscious background of consciousness, the water we swim in. The materialism of science is still the implicit prevailing ground of our public mind today. But, the dogmatic logic of science as the only way to view reality is being undermined by new soul developments, which began about one hundred years ago and are obviously ongoing.

Today, psychology with soul represents yet another transformation of truth, because truth itself (soul) sees itself in a new light. The psychological view of truth is a dialectic of objective-subjective within the circle of consciousness of consciousness. This is how soul (truth) now sees itself. Soul now knows itself to be a unified difference within itself. Previously soul/truth knew itself as a difference that was separated from itself, as either gods/God vs. humankind, or as humankind vs. nature. Now, consciousness recognizes that it reflects itself to itself *as* the medium of culture, language, thought, and uses human persons in the process. But, even to use the word *medium* creates too much distance between what we mean by soul and consciousness, language and thought. Rather, culture, language, and thought constitute soul's reality and our reality as beings of consciousness, creatures of meaning. We do not create consciousness, but we participate in consciousness. One of the manifestations of this new consciousness in contemporary society is the growing fluidity and dissolution of identities and boundaries (new family structures, same-sex marriage, new gender identities, nation-states challenged by the world wide web, global economy, and the climate crisis). The political attempt to harden old identities and boundaries (the rise of nationalism) is a regressive reaction born of deep anxiety. The attempt to bring back prior notions of truth that have already transformed themselves is like shutting the proverbial barn door after the horse has escaped. While truth is indeed fluid as never before, and the truth of our culture is not of our personal making, just as we are personally responsible for soul-making, we are also responsible for truth-making. On the historical-cultural level, truth comes to us unbidden, as a given; so also on the personal level, our truth, our soul-task, comes to us unbidden, and it is our responsibility to take up its claim on us and bring it into reality. While this view of soul and truth is transpersonal and impersonal, broadly historical and out of reach of human control, the telos of soul, soul's fundamentally telic nature, is also at work in individuals. Our individual work at establishing our truth, of responding to our deepest truth, no matter how modest, is necessary for the creation of meaning and a life worth living. We have to come to terms with the fact that in the face of soul, we, as human beings, do not have much influence on the macro level, but on the micro level of our personal lives, we do have the power to bring our meaning and truth to birth.

Is There a Modern Soul?

Sublation: Soul's Self-Negation and Self-Preservation

Sublation, an idea that comes from Hegel, is used by Giegerich to describe the way soul works on itself as a historical process of change and development. To sublate means to negate and preserve, that is, to negate one form of an idea and preserve its essence in a new more comprehensive framework. The notion of sublation views culture and history at large as a whole unto itself, with a life of its own. In the context of psychology with soul, sublation describes the process of history as the place where consciousness develops itself through a series of transformations (sublations) that I seek to demonstrate throughout this book. Viewing the history of Western consciousness as a series of sublations enables us to see an essential continuity of consciousness running through the polytheistic nature gods and goddesses, the loss of those gods under the monotheistic God, and the death of the monotheistic God with the emergence of Reason and science, and now the world-rattling changes occurring through technology, media, and software. This broad historical view and these profound cultural transitions, have one thread in common: the self-sublations of the logical form of consciousness, or the self-sublations of the shape of (cultural) meanings.

Some analogies may help us understand sublation. The individual letters of the alphabet have discrete limited meanings when they stand alone. As soon as the letters are brought into a word, however, their individual meaning and distinctness is completely absorbed, sublated, into the meaning of the word. When we say, or read *the*, the discrete individuality of the separate letters, *t*, *h*, and *e*, is negated, and at the same time, some essence of the individual letters is preserved in the more comprehensive meaning of the word as a whole. What we call an alphabet is made up of abstract markings on a page or computer screen. When we look at the marks of an unknown language, such as (for me) Chinese or Arabic, we see only abstract markings that have no meaning. It is the *meaning*, that is, soul, that appropriates, that is sublates, the markings into its world of meanings. When we recognize the letters and words of our own language, the marks on the page disappear into the meanings they convey. If we repeat a word out loud over and over again until all we hear is a meaningless sound, then we experience the separation of meaning (soul) from the abstract and arbitrary sound that is the spoken word. It is the *meaning* that sublates the sounds and marks of language, which themselves make the *meaning* explicit and shareable. Words themselves are negated and sublated in sentences, and so on in ever-expanding literary contexts. In the linguistic universe (our everyday world), the process of sublating meanings into larger contexts just happens as a function of language. It is an automatic, invisible process that simply happens by itself. In our experience of language, the individual letters simply disappear, and in this sense, they have dissolved into meaning created by soul. Not unlike, to use a physical analogy, how a sugar cube dissolves in coffee. While its outer form disappears, the essence of the sugar, its sweetness, is still present.

Giegerich uses this sugar cube analogy when he speaks of what has happened to God and religion: "Religion had been the objective representation, in imaginal or conceptual form, of the inner logic of human existence."[7] Religion and God, once upon a time, really were the true and concrete expression of soul's logical form of consciousness. God and religion, once the very ground and taken-for-granted foundation of culture, society, and mind at large, have disappeared. Their visible form has dissolved into a new status of consciousness: "Consciousness has recognized *itself*, its own structure, in its formerly projected or extrajected contents. It has comprehended them as the mind's self-portrait."[8] Here "projected" does not mean human projection in the conventional sense, as that simply reduces the gods, or God, to a human function. Soul, in its primordial manifestation as gods and a God, projected itself in the form of gods and a God, and now recognizes that those outer historical forms of itself have dissolved into the form of consciousness itself. The project of this book is to trace the historical sublations of soul and show how the gods and God have indeed disappeared (at the logical level), and have become psychology, understood as the soul's logical life. The word *logical* in this psychological context is not related to the conscious procedures and rules of rational logic but is rooted in the idea of *logos* as speech, word, related to mind. The *logical form of consciousness* is the background quality of a group consciousness, or shared cultural mind, that gives a *people* its identity. It is a field of consciousness that belongs to everyone and that everyone accepts as a fundamental and unquestioned truth. As an adjective, logical is akin to archetypal, as an invisible, or unconscious, background that informs and characterizes a group consciousness. The ideas of *soul*, *logical form of consciousness*, and *public mind* are synonymous. I am tracing the historical development of the logical form of consciousness, i.e., soul.

Soul's Progressive Metamorphosis from God to Psychology

The following brief overview will illustrate a psychological reading of soul's historical self-transformations. This will serve as an introduction to the chapters that follow in reading the Bible and our Western history psychologically. In general, the Bible is read either theologically as telling us something about a god, or historically and humanistically, as a historical document telling us something about human persons. These are the two basic choices: it is either a document of divine revelation or a document of human ideas. I offer a third approach: viewing the biblical text as a soul document and interpreting it psychologically as soul's speech about itself, and in this light, as an account of an evolution of consciousness. The psychological interpretation is actually the product of the cultural achievements of both the theological and humanistic interpretations, which have developed over approximately three thousand years. Psychology with soul is aware of both the theological and humanistic points of view, and

7. Giegerich, "End of Meaning," 222.
8. Giegerich, "End of Meaning," 222.

it also contains them both within its own point of view as sublated aspects. Because of psychology's critical awareness of the unspoken assumptions that guide theological and humanistic interpretation, psychology's interpretation can bracket the tacit logic of theological and humanistic points of view and prevent them from intruding into its interpretation.

I am reading not only the Bible, but the whole history of Western civilization, and the same interpretive principles apply throughout. Psychology asks of the historical texts, what is soul, as the background structure of consciousness, saying about itself? This is the singular question that guides my interpretation of God's autopsy, which at the same time, is soul's autobiography, the living truth of soul.

The verb "to be" appears at three key moments in the Bible and Western history in its first-person form: "I Am." The first "I Am" takes the form of the Lord in Exodus, and the second is the "I Am" of Christ in the Gospel of John. The third emergence of the "I Am" occurs with René Descartes and represents the Enlightenment and the modern era. A fourth manifestation appears, first, as an intuition in the psychological work of Carl Jung. However, Jung's intuition is incomplete until it finds a more fully thought-out realization in the psychological work of Wolfgang Giegerich. I will focus on these manifestations of the "I Am" beginning with the Jewish and Christian traditions and then its continuation in modern thought.

First, however, as a preface to the "I Am," I examine the initial appearance of *light* at the beginning of the creation myth in Genesis.

In the Beginning: Light Is Not Natural

In the creation myth of Genesis, *light* is created before the sun is created. It is not until the fourth day that the natural sources of light (sun, moon, stars) are put in the dome of the sky. What kind of *light* is this first light if it is not natural light? The myth begins by setting the initial condition:

> In the beginning when God created the heavens and the earth, the earth was
> a formless void and darkness covered the face of the deep, while a wind from
> God swept over the face of the waters. (Gen 1:1–2)

Viewed psychologically, this is a statement by soul about soul, and it gives us a glimpse as to how soul imagines itself at the very beginning, that is, how soul thinks its own beginning with the opening line of this ancient text. Viewed in terms of soul speaking about itself, the story at the beginning of Genesis has nothing to do with the creation of the physical universe, nor is it about some absolute beginning of soul itself. It is about how consciousness sees itself at the beginning of the Jewish myth, which, for all intents and purposes, is the origin myth of Western civilization, and, in turn, the basis of Western consciousness.

Two general forces, two tendencies, are present at this beginning. One is disorder (formless void, darkness, waters), and the other is order (God and a wind or spirit of God). While they present themselves as distinct and opposed to each other, within the context of soul, they are a dialectical unity. In other words, although disorder and order contradict each other in our everyday experience, within soul their difference is a unity; they are the same; they presuppose each other. Order and disorder must define themselves in the context of each other. Neither exists in isolation, but rather they in-form each other. Consciousness can know order only with its contradiction of disorder, and it can know disorder only with its contradiction of order. As a dialectical unity, they are the same and different at the same time. Order and disorder comprise a dynamic unity and difference, each giving rise to the other. They are not separate truths that logically (in the traditional sense of rational logic) negate each other. As a dialectic, they are an identity; they are each other.

As concepts, order and disorder are constituted by consciousness (i.e., soul), which itself is a self-contained unity and totality. The dialectical identity is another way of saying that soul negates itself and re-creates itself, depending on the circumstances in which it finds itself. Within our creation myth, chaos and order represent soul's conflict with itself. This is a creation story after all, and in this version, the process of creation and creativity is rooted in the dynamic tension of the twin forces of disorder/chaos and order/form. But, chaos and order are empty abstractions that can be applied anywhere, and in themselves tell us nothing about what soul is up to in the particular historical context of the ancient Near East. The psychological view is that soul is always contingent and temporal, soul is always a living *specific* cultural context. Soul is the interiority, the purpose and meaning, of a culture; it is what animates and drives a culture; it does not transcend and then intrude into culture. In this sense soul is the (secret) life of culture. Through hindsight and examining the written records of history, we can interpret soul's unfolding. So, what is the specific chaos this God of order is up against?

My view is that the darkness and formless chaos at this "beginning" is a symbolic representation of the already existing and well-established polytheistic cosmos that was the natural form of consciousness throughout the ancient Near East. The image of God creating order in the context of a formless void echoes the cosmic battle in the Babylonian creation myth between the hero god Marduk and Tiamat, the terrible dragon goddess of the ocean and chaos. Going further, I suggest that the "chaos" at the beginning of the Bible represents the nature-based polytheistic cosmos at large, the status of consciousness when soul and nature were fused with each other. The "chaos" is the prevailing polytheism that predates God and is the context in which the new monotheistic God will create his world.

The God of the Judeo-Christian tradition did not emerge in a vacuum, nor all at once. The god of the early Hebrew people, before Israel became a nation, was but one minor tribal god among many other gods and goddesses. The God that we recognize today as the ground of monotheism emerged only after a protracted life-and-death struggle taking about one thousand years. That God more than once narrowly escaped being reabsorbed into the wider polytheistic cosmos that characterized all other peoples and nation-states of the ancient Near East.

The Jewish God was a developmental amalgamation and synthesis of multiple gods and goddesses and their qualities, resulting in an uncomfortable and difficult deity full of tension and conflict. Polytheism was an ever-present danger to this new god. From the point of view of emergent monotheism, the polytheistic universe would be seen in such terms as "the earth was a formless void and darkness covered the face of the deep." But more than this simple distinction, we need to understand the relation of each theism to nature. Polytheism was the condition of soul in nature, or nature *as* the presence and aliveness of soul. In polytheism, nature itself was numinous and personified, animated as hundreds, even thousands, of local gods and goddesses. Soul was embedded in and identified with nature. Monotheism was a movement in another direction. The Hebrew God, who becomes the God of Israel and then the Jewish God, was *a God of spirit, word, and text*. The general movement of soul and consciousness in the form of monotheism was away from nature, extracting itself out of the natural world into new forms of culture and consciousness that transcend nature. The God of the Tanakh was not a nature deity and was at war with the prevailing nature gods and goddesses.

It will become clear later that the Bible is a record of a historical development told from the point of view of the winner. The Bible is essentially a polemic by the Judeo-Christian monotheistic God against the "evils" of polytheism. My tracing of this development as soul's autobiography is not a judgment on either polytheism or monotheism. I see a soul development directed internally by soul's own auto-telic nature, a movement that is not directed by humankind: we are where soul happens, but we are not its genesis. My analysis, this autopsy of God, is a phenomenological examination, not a critical judgment as to whether it was right or wrong, good or bad. From the point of view of soul, it simply happened. Of course, this was a cultural development in which human persons participated, but humankind did not cause or generate this development. We help it along, but mostly we are carried along.

Another distinction to keep in mind is between soul and experience, or what I will also refer to as negativity and positivity. In the narrative world of the Bible and in our own human experience, the forces of disorder and order are presented and experienced separately, usually in succession, one after the other. Our everyday world of experience and things is the world of positivity, that which is visible, empirical, and manifest. The world of soul is negative in that we must think it and reflect it in ideas and concepts. The idea of negativity simply means that soul does not exist as an empirical or material thing; it does not exist as a positivity. Soul is negative in the way that consciousness and ideas are negative because they have no mass, weight, size, or physical dimension; we cannot measure an idea, a concept, or meaning. But ideas and concepts, the world of consciousness, in the context of soul are not mere intellectual abstractions, but living ideas or existing concepts that are realities in their own right. They are social and cultural truths, vital animating principles that give life to a culture or civilization. Here the concepts of negative and positive are not value judgments, they are not separate categories or realms of being, nor are they the dichotomy of spirit and matter. They are a way to differentiate and think soul in its dialectical relation with itself. The negativity of soul's thoughts become real as positive cultural productions.

The idea "God" is instructive. In the Bible, which represents the world of antiquity, the ideas of God and gods and goddesses are clearly vital living ideas that are the shared background and public truth for whole peoples. And yet, God is a negativity as God does not exist as a material manifest being or entity: God was spirit. Even though God appears in the biblical narratives in the form of natural phenomena (fire, storm, light, smoke) or even sometimes in the form of a person, this is understood to be a temporary appearance and not reflective of the essential reality of God, which remains a negativity as a powerful, real, and *living idea* that is the ground of the whole people or tribe. In a very real sense, the *Mind* of the tribe in antiquity is *God* as a corporate, societal truth. The logical form of consciousness that soul took in antiquity was God, or gods and goddesses. In the Bible, this fundamental and unquestioned background form of consciousness, the logic or syntax of consciousness, is known by the one word, *God*. But God is not a discrete private personal content of an individual's belief or an individual's mind. The notion of God was the one general thought that was the ground, even the general shape, of what we can call the public mind. Because we are so conditioned to think of God as an entity, or with some kind of personhood, it is hard to step back and see that in the ancient past, gods, goddesses, and God symbolized the overall frame or structure, syntax, of the general consciousness that created the public mind. This contained and conditioned all the thoughts that individuals would have. The thought that *was* God, was not an intellectual abstraction, but a true, real living presence, as a prevailing, general (group-mind) form of consciousness.

The dialectical unity of soul at the beginning of our biblical story manifests as a conflict between the single God of spirit, on one side, and polytheistic nature, symbolized as a formless dark void, on the other. They are about to interact. The first action is one of separation:

> Then God said, "Let there be light"; and there was light. And God saw that the light was good; and God separated the light from the darkness. God called the light Day, and the darkness he called Night. And there was evening and there was morning, the first day. (Gen 1:3–5)

While God is presented as the creator of all things, the text clearly tells us that God did not create the formless void and the dark waters. The formless dark waters are uncreated; they exist along with God from the beginning. In this sense, the uncreated darkness is older than the created light. And while the text itself does not tell us, the newly emergent Hebrew-Jewish God is a newcomer, far younger than the long-established polytheistic deities. Although in the Jewish telling of the story of God, God appears full blown all at once, in the historical cultural context, this God is a young and inexperienced God, an emotionally reactive and impulsive figure, who learns what he is about through his relationship with people.

The formless dark waters paired with God are not only the general polytheistic cosmos, but also represent a goddess partner with whom God is entangled and in conflict. In the polytheistic world, most gods and goddesses existed as male and female pairs. But the God presented in the Tanakh, the official Jewish text, is a singular God, without any divine parents, friends, companions, or consorts. This singular God is not a simple God; he is a complex mixture of multiple god and goddess types trying to achieve a unified identity over at least a thousand-year period.[9] The evolution of God described in the Bible is the work of soul, a complex soul in conflict with itself. It was a conflict between polytheism and monotheism that represented a deeper struggle internal to consciousness as the syntax of consciousness evolved into a new form. God is in conflict with himself, which I read as soul in tension and conflict with itself. The internal tension and conflict generates the energy, is itself the engine, driving the creative process that leads to the development of a new form of consciousness.

In the Beginning: Separation

The first impulse in our creation story is for separation: light and darkness are separated into Day and Night. Something is pushed apart. A self-enclosed embrace is broken open in order to create a space or clearing that is called light. Light can exist only in the context of darkness, and so here is another pair of dialectical opposites, a unity with an internal difference of tension and conflict. Soul is telling the story of its own beginning within the context of this particular cultural setting, the beginning of its beginning. The space or clearing that is created by the prying apart of darkness and light is an early image of consciousness and language. Language is where the separation that creates a clearing happens. Soul imagines itself in this state of formless void and darkness, a state of being prior to language, culture, and consciousness.

Deeply immersed in language and culture as consciousness, we cannot know what existence without language and culture would be like. We can think of it only as an abstract state of pure nature and animal existence in which there is no difference between life and environment: all is undifferentiated oneness, which is a state of unconsciousness. But even then, we have to use language in order to think about life without language, and so we are inextricably contained within language. Language, as the medium of *meaning*, is our existential cocoon, our human world, and there is no

---

9. For the full treatment of the development of God's character, see Miles, *God: A Biography*; in this instance, esp. 64, 66, and 85–95.

exit from this world. We live as languaged-meaning. It is impossible to *know* what life without language or consciousness is.

Still, the nature of consciousness, of soul, is to make up a story about where it came from, a story about what it was, and what gave rise to it, before it became what it is. We do know that consciousness is constituted by difference and separation. To be conscious of nature, we have to be separate from nature. Our creation myth shows a process whereby soul imagines itself creating itself through a separation that occurs with the emergence of language. We cannot ignore the fact that this God creates with language, with speech, by the action of speech: "Let there be light." Language, the spoken word, creates light and engenders the separation of light and darkness. But, and this is critically important, the stories of the origin of this particular god are in writing. The *written word* in this particular text is the presence of the god. This god is a god of literacy and emerges out of generally preliterate cultures.

The most we can say is that somehow language and consciousness created itself, and continues to create itself through a kind of historical developmental process—languages are not static. We have to say "somehow" because we can never get on the other side of language in order to know language's origin. The same holds true for soul. Out of what, or how, did soul emerge as the meaning-context of language, culture, and consciousness for *Homo sapiens*? Even today, of course, soul will make up stories about its origin, but we can never truly know the origin of soul. We do not need to know the origin of soul in order to trace the tendencies of soul in the great cultural and historical narratives we have, the Bible being one of these with which soul defined and developed itself in the past. It is important for us to note that for ancient Mind, the source of language, culture, and all of creation, is a god, or gods and goddesses. For ancient mythological and religious Mind (i.e., soul) the idea *God* was the ultimate origin of all things. The living, pervasive idea of Godness, of divinity, was original in the fundamental meaning of original—it was the primary foundation. The idea of God(s) was the absolute bottom line, there was no getting behind God(s), and all things were explained through God(s). This was the logical form of consciousness that constituted soul in antiquity.

The Bible is one of the great narratives with which soul describes its self-development, thus *soul's autobiography*, in the form of a God story. In reading the Bible as soul's autobiography I am interested in how the Bible depicts soul's development, soul's development from within itself, as a series of self-transformations. My view is a soul view, not a God view, and thus I cannot stop at God as the final explanation. The psychological perspective interprets God as a symbol, a personification, of the process of soul as language, culture, and consciousness undergoing historical transformations. Within psychology God is not the final bottom line, but rather language, culture, and consciousness are the ways soul manifests itself as our world, as the *world* within which we live, or even better, the world *as* which we live. It is the perspective of modern soul that views language, culture, and consciousness (soul) as the fundamental nature of our being, our truth and reality. This does not mean that we live within some mental bubble with no contact with a physical reality. The physical world is real and we have real contact with it. The problem for us is to realize how consciousness is the context and nature of our contact with reality. And we have to grasp how language, culture, and consciousness are not private personal subjective realities, but socially shared public truths, that for the most part remain invisible, unconscious, and taken-for-granted. *Soul* is our world, it is the unconscious taken-for-granted basis of our existence as beings of language, culture, and consciousness. Psychology (with soul) is the work of attempting to make the implicit (unconscious) basis of our existence explicit (conscious).

In the Beginning: Light as a Symbol

The first *light* is not a natural light, it is not sunlight constituted by photons, not a positivity. I view it as a symbol of the emergence of language and consciousness, and as soul's own doing, soul's own happening to itself. The first light is a negativity, that is, it is the ancient image of a living idea that required separation for it to come into existence. The first light appears as the separation of the original eternal embrace (a state of fusion and oneness, or nature in its primordial state) of a god and goddess by an eruption of spoken language that creates Day and Night (day and night are personified in antiquity as god and goddess). The separation creates a space of nascent consciousness which acts as the thought, the reflection, that gives the names, *Day* and *Night*. Soul makes a move here from being unconsciously embedded in nature, to separating itself just enough to look at itself as nature from outside with language, through the process of naming. Soul imagines its own early emergence in terms of the speech of God, as God was the fundamental category with which to think about essential and ultimate things.

Today our public thinking takes place within scientific categories, like big bang and evolution; our modern tendency is to look for material causes. The idea of modern soul informing psychology and consciousness creates another set of fundamental categories: soul, psychology, and consciousness. Consciousness as a general evolutionary phenomenon is not simply an attribute of humankind, something derivative or secondary that is only human. Consciousness is itself a new category that has emerged as a result of soul's own evolution. For modern consciousness, God is no longer the final category. Of course, modern thought is still primarily dominated by scientific and humanistic categories, and *materialism* is the fundamental idea or category that has replaced God. But for psychology (with soul) consciousness is a category that overcomes, actually encompasses, both the categories of God and materialism, by the historical process of sublation. Modern psychological *consciousness* exists as both sublated religion and sublated science, because it retains important aspects of each while negating their original dogmatic logic:

> [Psychology] is sublated religion inasmuch as it negates the immediate religious interpretation *with which* the contents of the inner experience *come*, but it also preserves the religious contents and atmosphere, however only as a "moment" of the new Notion of the realty of the soul. It is likewise sublated science because it negates the naive positivistic reductivism of the scientific approach to the psychological, but it also preserves the critical rationality of the sciences as a "moment" of its own stance by *not regressing* behind the intellectual achievement of the project called Enlightenment.[10]

Psychology, as sublated religion, retains a religious sensibility without buying into the surface form of religious intuitions. The gods, or God, and spirits are taken as real; not real in their presentation, but real as in their symbolic status requiring interpretation in terms of an evolving consciousness. As sublated science, psychology retains the stance of a critical phenomenology, without buying into the foundational materialism that science claims as its dogma. As we will see, psychology is the result of earlier historical sublations within religion and science.

Sublation points to an organic and natural dynamic process of soul's own self-unfolding. The reading of the Bible as soul's autobiography will illustrate the process of sublation, and the overview here of the development of the "I Am" shows how sublation works as a historical cultural process. Sublation is an internal process in which soul operates on itself. We have already noted that our modern period is characterized by the absence of gods and God. The human-centered point of view tells us that humankind, through the development of science, chose to "kill off" mythology and God. But the psychological point of view shows us a process of sublation in the historical radical shift in which mythological/religious consciousness transformed itself into the forms of Reason and science. The end of religion as a culture-wide public truth is not the act of humankind, but rather the evolution of consciousness itself. From soul's point of view, it is an inside job. In this sense, the *essence* of religion has shed its former skin, left it behind, and has become a new kind or mode of being in the world that carries us along with it.

The first light is not a natural light, it is not seen by the natural eye. The first *light* of Genesis 1:3 is the symbolic representation of a mode of thought, the first glimpse of soul's *telos*, in which a certain tendency or direction is at work. The gods, or God, have always been known to have direction and purpose. They are depicted as knowing what they want and having a will that makes a claim on humankind. The assertion of first light by this god indicates a development that characterizes the intent of sublation. Within the tension of the dialectic dynamic inclusive of the God (spirit) vs. polytheism (nature), consciousness (i.e., soul) wants to make the implicit contradiction explicit, through a negation and then a reemergence in a more encompassing consciousness that preserves their unity and difference in a new form. Thus, in our story, the first light is the result of the negation of darkness (nature) by the light (spirit), which is

---

10. Giegerich, *Soul's Logical Life*, 67.

then reordered in a new totality, a higher encompassing status of consciousness, one that includes them both in Day and Night, morning and evening, here called "the first day." Spirit (Day) and nature (Night) are differentiated, and at the same time united in the concept of "first day." However, while God calls the light "good," he does not call the darkness good. He separates the light from the darkness, and while we cannot say he ignores the darkness (it gets the name Night), clearly the light has the upper hand. Later we will see that the struggle of God to unify himself in the context of polytheism is not so simple, but a terrific life-and-death struggle. Now we are ready to move to the overview of the development of the "I Am," which will give us a picture of soul's self-sublation over the course of approximately two thousand five hundred years.

The First *I AM* Is Not Human

The first light, which appears at the very beginning of our biblical story, is the first implicit glimmer of the phenomenology of the "I Am." The first explicit statement of the "I Am" appears in a dialogue between God and Moses at the beginning of Exodus. For the psychological approach, the literary figures of God and Moses personify a dialogue soul has with itself, or, a dialogue public mind has with itself ("public mind" is "public meaning," which is what soul is). The narrative context of this dialogue is also soul's self-portrait, and it portrays the tensions soul is struggling with in relation with itself, the interiority of a conflict the culture has with itself.

Biblical scholars and liberal thinkers, ignoring the fundamentalist literal appropriation of the Bible, see the Bible as a whole, but especially the books of Genesis and Exodus, not as records of historical events in our modern sense of history. Certainly, the Bible reflects historical circumstances of its time, and the Bible itself is a text written within specific historical contexts. But above all, the Bible is a cultural document, a document of soul's unfolding itself, of far-reaching significance. I read the Bible psychologically oriented to the logical form of consciousness, or the character of truth, that the Bible preserves as soul's historical autobiography. What form did truth, as publicly shared and assumed, take in the past, and how has it evolved? I am interested in what constituted God and where the God of the Tanakh came from.

At the beginning of Exodus, the Hebrew people are in Egypt, and their population is exploding at a rate that alarms the Egyptian political hierarchy. Their fear is that Hebrews will eventually outnumber Egyptians and threaten the stability of the nation. With this story line, we see the problem soul is struggling with, the conflict between the expansion of a new idea (the Hebrew people and emergent monotheism) and the need to maintain the stability of the status quo (Egyptian polytheism). The boundaries of the Egyptian state act like a pressure cooker, as the increasing population of the foreign ethnic group intensifies. The king of Egypt tries to gain control of the rapidly multiplying Hebrews through the ancient birth control method of killing male babies.

First, he enlists the midwives to do the dirty work, but when that fails he orders male Hebrew babies thrown into the Nile.

Here the story of Moses begins, as he is one of the threatened male Hebrew babies. His mother, after nursing and protecting him for three months, realizes she can no longer keep him safe. As she places Moses in a basket hidden among the reeds on the river's edge, she releases Moses to Fate. Soul's irony in this story is that Moses is found by Pharaoh's daughter and is raised in Pharaoh's court. The very thing the king of Egypt tried to eliminate, the source of his anxiety over national instability and chaos, is now under his very nose, hidden in his own house—it is Moses who will one day lead the rebellion disrupting Egyptian society. Soul is working against one form of itself, toward another form.

Unable to limit the growing population of the Hebrew people, the Egyptians attempt to control them through enslaved forced labor. As an adult, Moses witnesses the harsh and oppressive conditions of the Hebrew people. Although himself raised as an Egyptian in the king's court, he knows himself to be Hebrew and that these are his people. One day, he sees a brutal Egyptian overlord beating a Hebrew. Incensed, he impulsively kills the Egyptian and buries him in the sand, believing the act was not witnessed. However, obviously, the Hebrew man he rescued told everyone all about it. Moses learned he was a marked man and that Pharaoh was out to kill him. He fled to another country as a fugitive murderer. There he married, had a child, and worked as a shepherd keeping flocks for a number of years. Let's keep in mind this initial portrait of Moses: sensitive to oppressive cruelty as well as impulsive and violent. As we will see, Moses' character is a mirror image of the God, Yahweh, who claims Moses to liberate his people. The new god Yahweh makes his claim in the context of a very unusual scene:

> Moses was keeping the flock of his father-in-law Jethro, the priest of Midian; he led his flock beyond the wilderness, and came to Horeb, the mountain of God. There the angel of the LORD appeared to him in a flame of fire out of a bush; he looked, and the bush was blazing, yet it was not consumed. (Exod 3:1–2)

The symbolism in this passage points to a nonordinary state of consciousness outside of daily life. Putting Moses beyond the wilderness and far away from human habitation sets him in the realm of soul, another status of consciousness altogether. He is on a holy mountain and has apparently wandered into a local nature deity's sacred grove. The Lord, that is, Yahweh, appears as both an angel and an inexhaustible fire in a bush, as if the bush were the wick of a candle. An image that defies the laws of physics puts us in the realm of soul, the world of soul's thoughts in contrast to human thoughts. In terms of the text, we are in the presence of an impressive God; in psychological terms, we are in the presence of soul's logic in contrast to everyday logic.

Moses is overwhelmed and fears for his safety as this powerful numinous presence erupts in front of him. This God has designs on Moses:

> The cry of the Israelites has now come to me; I have also seen how the Egyptians oppress them. So come, I will send you to Pharaoh to bring my people, the Israelites, out of Egypt. But Moses said to God, "Who am I that I should go to Pharaoh, and bring the Israelites out of Egypt?" (Exod 3:9–11)

Moses is not a weak or timid man, and yet his immediate reaction to this assignment is "Who am I?" Whatever confidence the phrase "I am" might hold is here reversed in the plaintive or fearful, "Who am I?" As we are not reading this in human terms, we must see that Moses' "Who am I?" is not about the state of his personal self-esteem, nor is it simply the classic resistance every prophet experiences when the claim from God comes. Within the context of soul, the human figure in this story is also one of the moments in soul's internal dialectic. In this dialogue, one side of the dialectic, symbolized by the human person, does not have an "I am" of its own. What we take for granted as our modern sense of subjective identity is actually an achievement of soul over hundreds, thousands, of years. Here we get a glimpse of the beginning development of subjective consciousness, but historically, it first appears as a deity, not as human. In the face of Moses' reticence, God tries to reassure him that he, God, will be with him for this undertaking. However, Moses needs convincing, especially in the pervasive polytheistic world in which he lives. It is not at all clear which god is approaching him; he needs to know this god's name:

> But Moses said to God, "If I come to the Israelites and say to them, 'The God of your ancestors has sent me to you,' and they ask me, 'What is his name?' what shall I say to them?" God said to Moses, "I AM WHO I AM." He said further, "Thus, shall you say to the Israelites, 'I AM has sent me to you.'" (Exod 3:13–15)

Here the other moment of soul's dialectic shows itself with God's disclosure of his essence, his name. At this stage of soul's development, the God *is* the "I Am," and the human person is not. Humankind in general is dependent on the God for this status of consciousness. Moses symbolizes humankind in general during the period of antiquity, and at that stage of the development of consciousness, the gods and goddesses, not people, embodied the power and value associated with the "I Am." In general, today we easily associate "I am" with our personal identity and subjectivity and leave it at that. But, the *I Am* is much more than simply a personal designation, carrying as it does the power *to be* in the first place. *I Am* is the form of soul's agency, and an independent self. Let's take a closer look at the name this God gives himself.

I Am as an Action Verb

The Hebrew word that is translated "I AM WHO I AM" is related to the verb *hayah*, meaning "to be." The sacred name of the Jewish God is abbreviated as YHWH, and pronounced Yahweh. In the Bible, translation tradition substitutes "the LORD," spelled with capital letters, for YHWH. Thus, when we encounter the words "the LORD" in the

God's Autopsy and the Living Truth of Soul

biblical text we are reading an action verb. The sense of "being" in ancient Hebrew is not at all like our associations with a Greek or metaphysical sense of Being, with its philosophical connotations of the absolute and eternal. The Hebrew God "I AM WHO I AM" is an intensely personalized active force in the present. Because God is the speaker of his own name, it is written in the first person, but YHWH is the third-person form of the verb, and so it could be translated, "He causes to be." The emphasis is on action, so it means "I am what I do," or even more simply, "I will act."[11] The force and direction of Yahweh here in the context of the Exodus story is liberation, to disrupt the prevailing consciousness represented by the oppressiveness of Egypt and to create a new consciousness, symbolized by the emancipated Hebrews. The force of *I Am* is both disruptive and liberating; it is not a passive or static identity. Yahweh personifies the dynamic truth of I Am as initiative, intent, purpose, movement, and power. The I Am is the compelling force that makes a claim, theologically referred to as "God's will." Moses is the object of the I Am's claim: he is the one to liberate the Hebrew people from the oppressive Egyptians. The I Am is the initiative, the imperative, that makes its claim. Making a claim is one of the core characteristics of soul, and in this text, it is experienced as, and voiced by, a god, the familiar God of our Judeo-Christian tradition.

Today we recognize such an imperative as a personal calling or an inner creative necessity, but what I want to emphasize here is that during antiquity, over two thousand years ago, the motivating power of I Am belonged to the gods, and it came to the human person as a force or claim from outside. The I Am was first experienced as a god separate from the human person. The god was the source of the power *to be*, the power to create and liberate. The god was the agency to act and to make things happen. The power of I Am did not belong to the human person yet. The logical essence of I Am is creation and liberation, and it makes creation and liberation happen in reality. The syntax, or form, of the I Am at this stage is the god, not the human being.

Let me be clear that I am not suggesting that empirical human persons in antiquity did not ever act on their own, that they had no personal agency. Of course, daily life went on without a god determining every action. I am thinking here of the general *concept* of the human in relation to the God, or gods, and for really important matters, the gods were indeed looked to first. Ultimate value, true value, resided with the gods, not human beings. Today we think of the subject-object relationship as one in which humans as independent subjects are separate from and observers of the objects of the world. In antiquity, the subject-object relationship should be understood as humankind being the object unconsciously fused with the greater Subject of the god. That is, at this stage, the subject-object separation we take for granted has not occurred. Rather, humankind is an object at the mercy of the gods, who are the first subject from the point of view of soul's evolution. At this stage in the development of consciousness, soul's agency and intent is a numinous power experienced by humankind as external

---

11. Miles, *God*, 98–99.

and compelling, as a god or goddess. It has not yet become what we experience today as a personal sense of subjectivity and agency, our personal status as an *I am*.

The *I Am* of Christ

Psychologically and phenomenologically, the historical event of Christianity truly was an extraordinary moment in soul's development.[12] Christianity was the result of a metamorphosis of the soul, the internal transformation of Yahweh within the historical cultural context of Judaism. From an external historical point of view, it appears that a new religion, Christianity, co-opted Judaism and claimed to supersede it. But, from soul's point of view, it was God who changed himself from within as an act of sublation. Religious figures personify the self-sublation of consciousness, or public mind. Yahweh, from within, negates and transforms his form of the *I Am*, which within Christianity becomes the *I am* of Jesus Christ. The very structure or shape of public *meaning* undergoes a transformation.

One simple and essential fact: Yahweh is not a human person. Yahweh can become quite intimate with his human creatures, but the distinction between the God on one side and the human person on the other is absolute and uncrossable. This unbridgeable gap undergoes a remarkable change in Christianity. Soul as Yahweh, dissolves itself and takes on a completely new form in the figure of Jesus Christ. Soul re-creates itself as the powerful and living *idea* of a historical person who is at the same time God. For now, I am not concerned with whether or not Jesus Christ was an actual historical person. From the perspective of soul's logos, my concern is with the living *idea* of *Jesus Christ*, which inspired well over a thousand years of christological and theological reflection and created an entire civilization. From soul's perspective, we have a new truth: Jesus Christ is the mythological image of a "historical" incarnation of the Jewish god. The myth of the incarnation was, in its time, a truth of soul's manifestation; its powerful claim became a reality in the form of a new culture and society. As an emerging and grippingly real soul-truth, a new reality of cultural-Mind, the idea of the incarnation presented a terrific problem for the mind of antiquity: The very premise of the incarnation, the union of a man and a God, was a fundamental impossibility. In effect, soul created a new reality for itself, a new form of public consciousness which it did not know how to think.

The category difference between gods and humankind was taken-for-granted in antiquity: the gods were absolute and the gods were not human. Thus, the incarnation

---

12. The modern distinction between a Christ of faith and a Jesus of history is a thoroughly modern separation, which never existed for about the first fifteen hundred years of Christian culture, during antiquity and medieval Europe. This modern distinction introduces a significant complication in our attempt, as modern consciousness, to think about the Christ of early Christianity, which was an entirely different consciousness. I will address this problem in chapter 7. For this summary overview of the development of the I am, I will stay focused on the mythological, or theological, Jesus Christ of the incarnation as the new form that soul took at that time.

presented a profound challenge to the traditional mytho-logical arrangement, releasing an energy that drove Christology through the many struggles and conflicts that emerged between orthodoxy and heresy. At the time, it was not merely an intellectual academic problem for theological or philosophical specialists. It was the struggle for Ultimate Truth. As the objective collective mind of antiquity, soul had to think it all the way through. The great minds of the ancient world poured enormous energy into coming to terms with the new truth of the incarnation.

One of those minds was the author of the Gospel of John in the Christian New Testament. Here we find the connection between the Christ and the God of the Tanakh most clearly asserted. Even more than a connection, the opening lines of the book of John claim for the Christ *an identity* as the preexistent *logos* (the Word), the same status as the creator god of Genesis:

> In the beginning was the Word [logos], and the Word was with God, and the Word was God. He was in the beginning with God. All things came into being through him, and without him not one thing came into being. What has come into being in him was life, and the life was the light of all people. The light shines in the darkness, and the darkness did not overcome it. (John 1:1–5)

With these words soul speaks about itself and shows us the new light within which soul sees itself. In those first four sentences of John, soul gathers up everything that came before, all the way back to the beginning of Genesis, encompassing all that soul has been into this new image of itself as the creating Word that is simultaneously God, life, and light. But this "life" and "light" is not contained in biology or physics, in contrast with the terms and assumptions of the Genesis creation story, where God's original words and speech created the physical world and biological life.

The Word that appears now as the Christ is an entirely new order of *life* and *light*; soul is re-creating itself as a new form of consciousness, a new truth and reality, a new *Logos*, that has never existed before. The Christ, as soul's new idea of itself, takes up and trans-forms the *I am* as its own identity:

> I am the bread of life. (John 6:35)

> I am the light of the world. (John 8:12)

> I am the way, and the truth, and the life. (John 14:6)

> I am the true vine. (John 15:1)

Lest there be any doubt about the extent of the reach of the new Logos, the Christ explicitly claims the very name of God as his own when he says, "Very truly, I tell you, before Abraham was, I am" (John 8:58). Soul was sublating its prior form as Yahweh into a fusion of formerly incommensurate categories, God and man, as a unified God-man. This God-man was also a new dialectic structure, both a unity and difference within itself, for soul now existed as both fully God and fully man, something truly unheard of before. The God-man was a powerful and gripping *idea* that was the result of soul (cultural-consciousness) transforming itself. The foundational consciousness, the general truth of the age, was undergoing a profound change from within. The internal logical structure of *I Am* was incorporating a new categorical dimension into itself, becoming a wholly new reality.

The essence of the I am in the form of Yahweh is the imperative of creation and liberation; the I am is soul's intent to create and make free. The new image of the Christ negates the form of Yahweh and, at the same time, preserves the essence of the I am in the new idea of the incarnation. Soul, in its manifestation as Yahweh, sublates itself into the form of the Christ. The *I am* as God becomes the *I am* of a God-man. Within the Christian framework, Christ brought salvation (that is, liberation and a new creation) to the whole world and all of history. The Christian myth was the transformation of the logical status of creation at large because a new *creation* is a new consciousness. The agency of I Am as what makes real and free moves to a new level in the image of an incarnation of a god into a human person, coming down from the heavens as it were and walking on the earth. *Heaven* and *earth*, each representing a once completely separate status of consciousness, are now united: "And the Word became flesh and lived among us" (John 1:14).

Even though the form of the I am in this particular myth has now taken on that of a human person, the power of the I am still belongs only to the Christ—it is not really accessible to everyone else yet, except through a kind of "inner" Christ.[13] The I am is fully contained in the personified image of the Christ as a new form of deity. And while the Christ represents a new truth universally accessible to everyone, the I am remains in the self-contained and discrete form of the Christ. It is not yet a general function of human consciousness, a step that will come with the Enlightenment. Here I want to remember that the Christ, as a manifestation of soul's logical form, is not an actual empirical human person. The *idea* of the Christ symbolized the syntax of an emergent consciousness that took hundreds of years to develop itself and become a new general foundation of consciousness. In the process, it created a new civilization, Christian Europe. The Christ, as the form of consciousness that soul had taken, becomes the unconscious ground of everyone's consciousness, whether they are a professing Christian or not.

The changes within the nature of the subject-object relationship help us see how soul, as the syntax of consciousness, is transforming itself through these historical periods. For the historical period of Yahweh-consciousness, humankind is an object in thrall to a Greater Subject, God as I Am. With the Christ, the structure of the subject/object relation undergoes a partial shift. Although the I am has taken on human form as the Christ, it remains distinct from actual human persons. The human person is

---

13. "But if Christ is in you, though the body is dead because of sin, the Spirit is life because of righteousness" (Rom 8:10). Even though "Christ" may be within, there remains a categorical difference between this Christ and the "flesh," that is, the person himself, who remains identified with "sin."

still an object in relation to a greater subject. The ultimate value of the human person is located in the Christ, even if the Christ is "within" the person as an inner truth. The idea that human persons have their own innate ultimate value simply as ordinary human persons, an ideal of humanism, is a modern development. For Christian-consciousness, ultimate value lies with the Christ. The structure of consciousness that the Christ represents is a move in the direction of soul becoming the *I am* subject and agent of human persons.

Within Christianity, it will take about another two thousand years for the I am form of consciousness Christ represents to become *psychological*, to become modern soul. During antiquity, as both Yahweh and Christ, soul is manifesting as a subject, but manifesting as a god. It is certainly unconscious of itself as consciousness. At this stage, soul is completely contained within mythological images and theological ideas, and these ideas are realities in their own right. In their time and place, God and Christ were real; they were not figments, constructs, or projections of human imagination. They were the way soul made itself known, and the process of change that leads from God to Christ is soul's own doing.

The conventional interpretation of the incarnation is that God is embodied, enfleshed, humanized. God comes down to earth; God walks among us. Such a human-centered interpretation misses what had happened to *Word*, *life*, and *light*. All three are no longer the Word, life, and light of Genesis, of material creation, but have become the Word, life, and light of a different order altogether. Yahweh was intent on establishing himself with a house (temple) and an empirical political and social kingdom on earth. Christ's kingdom, however, was of *heaven*, and the kingdom of heaven, or the kingdom of God, was "not from this world" (John 18:36); it was a spiritual world, a spiritual truth. Thus, it represented an entirely different order of consciousness, although at the time it was certainly not understood in terms of *consciousness*, but as the soul-truth and reality of a very new kind of *Christ*, that is, messiah.

The movement from the I am of Yahweh to the I am of Christ as incarnate Word, entails a revolution of consciousness. This was not simply the exchange of one object (God) for another object (another God). It was the radical transformation of one form of consciousness into another—soul's own sublation of itself: negating the Yahweh form of I am and preserving the essence of I am in the new form of the Christ. Soul, in this new Christian form, then had to spend hundreds of years thinking this through, reformatting the basic categories of God and Man. Although this thinking was focused on the nature of Jesus Christ and his relationship with God, indirectly the trend was to raise the status of humankind in general to an ontological, or fundamental, equivalence with God, which diminished the ontological significance of God. The logical status of the human, the *concept* of the human, was getting an upgrade, so to speak, while the *concept* of God was gradually downgraded. This shift in the valence of significance began to fully realize itself during the historical period known as the Enlightenment.

Is There a Modern Soul?
"I think therefore I am."

The next move of soul in its evolution as consciousness takes about one thousand years, and makes its symbolic appearance in the famous statement of René Descartes, "I think therefore I am" (*cogito ergo sum*). That new status of the *I am* was soul's achievement as the Western European Enlightenment. The period, also known as the Age of Reason, is generally dated during the seventeenth and eighteenth centuries. Descartes rejected the inherited legacy of thought received from the Greek and Roman traditions and set out to think for himself, to show that the *mind* could be the locus of truth independent of perception and tradition. Notice what has shifted here. With Descartes, truth does not come from a divine source or hallowed traditions thoroughly oriented to the divine, but from the human mind itself. With this move, Christ as the Word, as "the light of the world," underwent another sublation in the form of Descartes's *I am* and, so to speak, dissolved into a new light, the light of Reason. This Reason is not the divine Logos, but human reason. The light of Reason has now become available to everyone. Through the power of Reason, people could think for themselves, independent of received tradition and belief. Enlightenment's reason is not personified as a deity but is a function of human consciousness in general. In leaving behind its manifestation as a deity, soul moves to another level of abstraction, or maybe better, soul differentiates itself from its personified divine form into a human function. This is when God died as the logical form of consciousness, long before Nietzsche made his famous statement.

Reason, as the new form of soul, also functioned as a creator and liberator. The heady ambition inspired by Reason, which still prevails widely, was to liberate humankind from all its ills, even death. Under the critical and questioning force of Reason, the world of the gods and spirits diminished, and the realm of matter, the world of physics, became the really real. Science and critical thought came to dominate the cultural landscape. In this phase of the soul's evolution, there are no gods, and there is no such thing as an unconscious dimension to humankind. The notion of soul in its traditional sense, along with God, fades to nothing. For the modern world, the essence of being is rational consciousness, and humankind is excited to realize its own agency and to create its own fate. The idealized "messianic" vision of rational consciousness was that now science would determine truth and reality, freeing us from church dogma, superstition, and religious mythology. Through science and reason, human beings were now masters of their own fate, the authors of their own history. Reason created a new type of human being, liberated into its own agency independent of tradition and God. The prevailing logic at the heart of the definition of the human was transformed. The logical status of humankind had been as *child of God*. Now, its logical status is as *adult* (no more parent God).

Formerly it was Yahweh, and then Christ, who critiqued the human condition from the distance of transcendence. Now this function of criticism, the phenomenon of a critical perspective, is manifest in the methods of science and rational critical thought. In a kind of turnabout, soul, now in the form of human critical thought, turns on itself and critiques its previous form as God into nonexistence. The psychological perspective views these profound changes as soul's own activity, changing its form, changing the structure of consciousness. Reason enables a critical distance on the form of consciousness that enwrapped us in a mythological and religious cosmos. As the agency of *I am*, soul has become the function of human thought as Reason. Humankind now experiences itself as a free subject which can carry out this kind of thinking. The American and French revolutions of the eighteenth century are social examples of soul's logical status, the new form of consciousness, working itself out in changing fundamental social structures and assumptions: from a divinely informed monarchy to democracy run by free citizens.

In the Cartesian subject-object framework, the function of subject is now the human person, and the object is everything else—but the "everything else" is devoid of soul. Soul has left nature behind, has left Yahweh behind, and now leaves Christ behind and becomes Reason, and rational thought is now the activity, even the duty, of human persons. As the source of meaning and purpose, soul is now constituted as Reason, a function of human subjectivity (not divine Logos). Soul resides in the human subject alone. When looked at closely in the light of soul's development, this is an achievement of the differentiation (liberation) of consciousness out of unconscious fusion with nature, the gods-goddesses, religious beliefs, and traditions. Soul continues its march of freedom, not for humankind, but for itself. From our human point of view, we believe we benefit from this new freedom accorded by Reason, but from soul's point of view, this is a by-product and not the aim of soul's efforts.

The Word, life, and light that were spiritualized by soul's Christian form are now spiritualized even more deeply into themselves. They move to another level of abstraction as the freedom and independence of thought itself, with its own agency taking up a new location in human persons. We certainly think we are the thinkers, but it is more accurate, at least from the point of view of psychology with soul, to see that soul thinks its thoughts as us. Reason emerged as a result of soul's turning in on itself, when the Word, the life, and the light of Christ went through a sublation and became human functions. This led to another round of soul becoming independent and critical of itself, and psychological consciousness began to emerge.

Is There a Modern Soul?

Psychological Consciousness—Soul Is Now Conscious of Itself as Consciousness

> The emergence of subjectivity and the concept of "the I" is the sign that the soul had shed its previous logical form of substance and otherness and taken on the form of subject.[14]

In this broad historical overview through Yahweh, Christ, and Descartes, the *I am* made its appearance explicitly through the serendipity of our texts (and, of course, their translation into English), and the actual words "I am" showed themselves. Now, however, the *I am* as such disappears and does not show itself as obviously. There is no iconic post-Enlightenment text that stands out as a symbolic declaration of *I am* in some new form . . . except—if we look at the general field of psychology as it developed during the twentieth century, we can speak of the *ego*. We can thank the English translators of Freud for introducing the Latin word *ego* to modern society as the now popular form of the I am. Freud himself simply spoke of "*das Ich*," or "the I," to refer to the personal consciousness of the individual whose job, he felt, was to mediate between social reality and the unconscious. The Latin word *ego*, however, harks back to Descartes's *cogito ergo sum* and carries a certain metaphysical weight and significance that Freud was not thinking of at all; Freud was simply designating the everyday person. When Freud was translated, however, Latin still carried a weightier scientific status than ordinary English, and the promoters of Freud certainly wanted to emphasize his scientific standing. Today the word *ego* has become quite ordinary and simply stands for the prosaic sense of "I am" that we all assume ourselves to be.

The great historical trajectory of the sublations of the *I am* from the I Am of God all the way to our modern moment, results in the human person occupying the implicit status that once belonged only to God. This does not mean that the individual person is a God in any inflated or literal sense—that would be identifying the empirical person with God. But, the essential phenomenology of the *I am* of the God, an independent subject with the powers of creation and liberation, is now assumed to belong to the individual as their inherent right. The right of God to be free and creative is now embedded implicitly in the "natural rights of man." The individual is now considered to be free and creative, the author of their own destiny, enjoying innate dignity, equality, and the right to pursue happiness. What has changed is the broad syntax of consciousness that defines what it means to be human. This represents the development of the soul into the form of humanism, and Freud was thoroughly immersed in the traditions of science and humanism. But, for Freud—and Jung—the ego as "I am" no longer stands alone as the Cartesian ego had up until this point. Depth psychology asserts that the ego exists in an intimate relation with something called "the unconscious," which leads to a fundamental new understanding of the nature of consciousness.

---

14. Giegerich, *What Is Soul?*, 273.

God's Autopsy and the Living Truth of Soul

Psychological consciousness began to emerge as Reason gradually realized there was more to reality than Reason could account for. At the same time, the light of Reason was turned on itself: Mind began to investigate mind, and psychology came to the forefront of modern society. This occurred first when psychology emerged as a conventional science out of the field of medicine. The year 1900, when Freud's *The Interpretation of Dreams* was published,[15] is a convenient symbolic historic date that marks the next shift toward a radical new form of consciousness. This broad cultural (soul) shift reflected itself in all fields, but it was especially noticeable in art and physics, along with the massive upheavals of the two world wars. Three broad significant insights emerge from Freud's theories, in spite of the reductive scientific and biological nature of his basic orientation, which profoundly undermine Reason's monolithic and rational hold on consciousness:

1. Dreams have meanings that are not dependent on divine revelation.
2. The idea of the "unconscious" itself becomes culturally significant, a *living* concept that permeates modern thought in general.
3. The very idea of the unconscious challenges the one-dimensional nature of rational consciousness and introduces the presence of an autonomous function of mind that is independent of rational consciousness (or, ego).

Reason itself comes to realize that it is not as free nor in control as it once thought. We begin to realize that mind is not simply personal consciousness, not only conscious thought, but a complex duality, composed of both conscious and unconscious dimensions. With Carl Jung, the fundamental principles of a more complex structure of consciousness, implicit in Freud's thought, become explicit, and the broad significance of consciousness for history becomes apparent.

With Jung, the idea that soul is now conscious of itself emerges as a truly radical new status of consciousness, a status of consciousness that is both the product of, and encompasses, its previous historical forms, the ancient mythological/religious and the modern scientific/humanistic. Consciousness (soul) begins to see itself for what it is: culture, language, interpretation, and fundamentally historical (that is, neither eternal nor absolute, no longer transcendent, and fully contingent). It realizes that it is the medium, the context, of all knowledge. Consciousness, as the shape of *meaning*, is the matrix within which we live; it is our reality. Mind recognizes itself as Mind expressing itself as culture and history: culture and history are the autobiography of Mind (soul)—again, my emphasis is on public mind in contrast to private (personal) mind. Jung began to glimpse the larger historical and cultural—and, we could say with qualification, "ontological"—significance of consciousness during a trip to Africa. Jung had the insight that consciousness was fundamental and foundational for everything we know, including our knowledge that the world exists.

---

15. Actual publication date was November 4, 1899.

Is There a Modern Soul?

Jung's story of his 1925 trip to Africa, when he was fifty years old, appears in his autobiography, *Memories, Dreams, Reflections*.[16] It is worth repeating here significant portions of his report of the dawning of the cosmic meaning of consciousness:

> From Nairobi we used a small Ford to visit the Athi Plains, a great game preserve. From a low hill in this broad savanna a magnificent prospect opened out to us. To the very brink of the horizon we saw gigantic herds of animals: gazelle, antelope, gnu, zebra, warthog, and so on. Grazing, heads nodding, the herds moved forward like slow rivers. There was scarcely any sound save the melancholy cry of a bird of prey. This was the stillness of the eternal beginning, the world as it had always been, in the state of non-being; for until then no one had been present to know that it was this world. (255)

Here Jung senses nature in its primordial state, completely unconscious of itself. In Jung's modern worldview, there is no God who automatically bestows an *a priori* knowing and meaning on creation. Jung was a child of the Age of Reason, and his consciousness could not assume he was a "child of God," as would have been true in antiquity. Nature now is no longer a divine creation, but a material phenomenon blindly following the laws of biology and physics. Jung, imagining the original world of nature without the presence of humankind, begins to sense the significance of human knowing:

> I walked away from my companions until I had put them out of sight, and savored the feeling of being entirely alone. There I was now, the first human being to recognize that this was the world, but who did not know that in this moment he had first really created it. (255)

Jung thinks that recognizing the world as the world is also "creating" the world. Jung seems to imagine himself as an early man, maybe even prehistoric, who recognizes the world as world, but the ability to know that he knows the world is not yet possible until today. But, what does Jung mean by "create"? We cannot take Jung's words literally here. Something important about consciousness was emerging:

> There the cosmic meaning of consciousness became overwhelmingly clear to me. "What nature leaves imperfect, the art perfects," say the alchemists. Man, I, in an invisible act of creation put the stamp of perfection on the world by giving it objective existence. This act we usually ascribe to the Creator alone...
>
> My old Pueblo friend came to my mind. He thought that the *raison d'être* of his pueblo had been to help their father, the sun, to cross the sky each day. I had envied him for the fullness of meaning in that belief, and had been looking about without hope for a myth of our own. Now I knew what it was, and knew even more: that man is indispensable for the completion of creation; that, in fact, he himself is the second creator of the world, who alone has given to the

---

16. See pp. 255–56.

world its objective existence—without which, unheard, unseen, silently eating, giving birth, dying, heads nodding through hundreds of millions of years, it would have gone on in the profoundest night of non-being down to its unknown end. Human consciousness created objective existence and meaning, and man found his indispensable place in the great process of being. (255–56)

Jung was acutely and painfully aware that his European civilization had lost its mythic or divine ground of meaning and that the Christian religion was no longer his culture's myth, that he and Western civilization were no longer contained within what was once a meaningful and purposeful world and cosmos. He was also acutely aware that the dominant rational consciousness of modern civilization was at its core lifeless and meaningless. And so, he "had been looking about without hope for a myth of our own." Jung's concern for a myth of meaning was not merely personal and private; he had the fate of Western civilization in view. He knew that something was amiss on a large scale. A pervasive malaise clung to modernity, and he wanted an alternative to a strictly rational worldview, which he believed had gone off the rails. The answer he was groping for became clear to him when he realized the "cosmic meaning of consciousness." Something about human consciousness itself became profoundly meaningful to him. But, what does Jung mean by "he himself is the second creator of the world, who alone has given to the world its objective existence"? Again, Jung could not mean that consciousness creates the physical universe. Rather, what he must be getting at is that consciousness has become objective to itself as distinct from the world. Only a consciousness that recognizes itself as distinct from the world can, in Jung's "second creator" sense, view the world "objectively," that is, as an object that is a function of consciousness.

Until Jung, the Cartesian ego was fascinated and preoccupied with all the objects (the world of nature) that it observed in a new light (the light of science and Newtonian mechanics) as if for the first time. Although the Cartesian ego was looking out there, it was not yet aware of itself as the looker. Jung has the insight that it is consciousness itself that is aware of the world, and so he becomes aware of not just the world, but of his consciousness itself as what is aware of the world. This does not challenge the reality of a material world existing "out there" as it were, independently of us, or whether any kind of world exists independently of us. Yes, the material world, and the cultural world of mind, exist independently of our individual minds, our individual consciousness. But, now, *consciousness in general as it knows the world, both the natural world and the cultural world of mind, is aware of itself.* This is the key shift for understanding modern soul and psychology with soul. Knowledge, or mind as such, what we are also calling soul, has become conscious of itself, which historically, is a completely new status of consciousness in general. The *I am* has become consciousness-as-subjectivity in relation to itself as also object. Rather than saying that consciousness has created the object (world), it is more accurate to say that consciousness has *created* itself (become conscious of itself) as self-reflexive: The structure of consciousness is now recognized as circular, in contrast to its previous linear structure. Or we could say that Cartesian consciousness has been primarily a horizontal consciousness in relation to a world out there, but now consciousness adds a vertical dimension as its consciousness of itself, and it is now aware of its own infinite depth. Now consciousness is not only human consciousness, but psycho-logical, that is, constituted as soul's logos, soul's speech about itself. In other words, *meaning*, as shared cultural meanings, exists independently of individual human persons, and it is self-generating. The cauldron of ideas that is culture is the place where soul's auto-telic process takes place. Now, soul, consciousness, meaning, is aware of this condition, this status of itself, as not our creation, but the place where we live.

Scientific humanistic consciousness, the Cartesian or Enlightenment syntax of consciousness, has a linear structure. It goes out to the object, and it retrieves information about the object, out and back, in a kind of straight or horizontal movement. This scientific consciousness is completely focused on the object and is not aware of itself. In this phase, soul, as the logic of reason and science, achieved a new access to the material world it could not have had before, but in this form, it is not aware of itself as itself a particular style of consciousness. In this sense, soul, in its scientific and humanistic form, apprehends the world naively, taking its materialistic and empirical view of the world for granted. In this way, the logic of humanism is blind to any other possibilities of consciousness, and this is also why humanism is fundamentally atheistic in a strict sense. Humanism can entertain the gods only as the projections of *human* longings, desires, fears, and hopes. The possibility that the gods, and God, were their own truth *sui generis*, real phenomena for their stage of soul's development, is closed to humanism, that is, the logic or syntax of humanism as a form of consciousness in itself. (Individual humanists can believe whatever they want, but that is a function of private mind in contrast to the internal logic of public mind humanism.) However, as the linear form of consciousness probed more deeply into matter, it was at the same time probing more deeply into itself, and its linear direction turned back on itself, first in recognizing an unconscious dimension of the human mind, and now in recognizing itself as circular, as self-aware, as consciousness-of-consciousness, as itself both subject and object.

The unified duality of consciousness that now characterizes this late modern development of soul also shows up in how Jung viewed the structure of the human psyche, which he saw as both ego and self. Ego refers to the center of personal consciousness, and the idea of the self is seen as a larger transpersonal organizing center, a source of meaning and purpose that is distinct from the ego. The ego is a kind of everyday pragmatic consciousness oriented to the coping tasks of social adaptation. The self then is a kind of mountaintop perspective that intuits a larger, more meaningful goal for the individual. The self is the seed that guides the individual toward becoming their true or authentic self, not just going along but contributing creatively to society in some individual and specific way. The ego and the self are different styles or modes of consciousness, and together they constitute the horizontal and vertical dimensions of consciousness as a whole. Consciousness in its fullest sense, in this schema, is the combination of both ego and self, as they mirror and reflect each other in a combination of both subjective and objective consciousness. Here is just one statement by Jung on this relationship:

> I have defined the self as the totality of the conscious and unconscious psyche, and the ego as the central reference-point of consciousness. It is an essential part of the self, and can be used *pars pro toto* when the significance of consciousness is borne in mind. But when we want to lay emphasis on the psychic totality it is better to use the term "self." There is no question of a contradictory definition, but merely of a difference of standpoint.[17]

In spite of Jung's insistence on a dimension of consciousness beyond the nineteenth century's paradigm of personalistic and rational consciousness, in spite of his words about an "objective psyche" and the "collective unconscious," Jung's view of the psyche and the self was primarily confined to the human individual. The individual was the sole carrier of consciousness, and it was the "great man" who moved culture and history forward. Jung did not fully achieve the insight that consciousness at large, that the unconscious structure, or syntax, of consciousness is an autonomous cultural phenomenon (public mind) largely independent of individuals. As individuals, we are constituted by and participate in public mind, but we do not ultimately control or direct it. This vision of soul as the syntax of consciousness, or the background and hidden grammar of our current historical consciousness, escaped Jung.

It is Wolfgang Giegerich who brings the background syntax of consciousness (public mind) to the forefront of psychology and makes it psychology's primary interest. While Jung understood that the psyche was investigating itself, Giegerich puts this new awareness of the logical structure of consciousness (its circular, ouroboric nature) at the center of psychology's self-understanding. A psychology with soul is not primarily focused on what goes on inside individual persons. It is first of all interested in the syntax of consciousness in general, which is what actually makes personal experience possible in the first place. We see again that the *I am* is fundamentally not personal. We do see, however, that our *personal* and modern sense of I am as a free agent is an achievement of soul that has taken place over a few thousand years. Today soul appears to be moving on from this achievement, pushing on to new forms of consciousness (what we on the surface see as, among other things, technology, media, virtual reality, and artificial intelligence) that challenge our conventional understanding of what it means to be human.

---

17. Jung, *Mysterium*, ¶ 133.

Is There a Modern Soul?

In my brief historical overview, the *I am* first personified itself as a deity, Yahweh. That personification furthered itself into a new form as the *I am* of a God/Man, the Christ as the incarnation, a new kind of deity. These were not nature deities, but deities of word, of spirit, of logos. They were deities of the book insofar as they personified the consciousness that emerged with literacy and writing. Next, the personified image of the *I am* disappeared into Reason itself and became the reasoning capacity of humankind. Today—and I do not say "finally" because who knows where this is going—the *I am* has dissolved into the form, or syntax, of consciousness itself, as consciousness of consciousness. The *I am* is now a dialectical unity and difference, interiorized into itself as both a personal (ego) and a non-personal (soul) form of consciousness. It is, first, the general logical structure of consciousness at large (manifesting through contemporary technological and media-saturated culture) and, second, the ground of our personal experience of ourselves.

Is there a modern soul? From the psychological perspective I adopt here, yes there is, and it is soul that has made itself modern. It is soul that has made itself psychological. From God to psychology traces an evolution of soul at the level of a logical form of cultural consciousness, the evolution of a kind of cultural shared mind. As human persons, we are taken along for the ride. Of course, our participation is not that passive; we and soul shape each other. But, we do not have the control over history that we typically assume, and in large measure, continue to think we have. But as long as we are the place where consciousness happens we are essential to the process of soul-making, essential for making soul real. If soul is really using us for its purposes and we are not using soul for our purposes, do we have any real effect on the direction of soul? Does our consciousness of this new historical status of soul, in relation to soul, make any difference? Certainly, a new perspective on the arc of historical consciousness can be liberating to individuals, especially when the traditional received meaning has died. Even though humankind is decentered in this view of soul, the new meaning brought to soul by soul provides a meaningful home in contrast to modernity's existential and ontological homelessness.

Chapter 2

Bible as Soul's Dream of Itself
Consciousness as Methodological Choice

> The psychological sense of soul is only a methodological one, a way of looking at things brought to bear on given phenomena or material. It is not in any way an ontological one. Like music, it needs to be made. It *is* only in the process or performance of truly psychological interpretation (interpretation of *meanings*, not of letters).[1]

> For psychology this means that it can today only be the discipline that it is if it is nothing but a particular methodological *procedere*, an approach to (potentially all kinds of) possible experience, a *mode* or *style* of perceiving, reflecting, interpreting, and reacting, a form of consciousness.[2]

> The soul now has *itself* attained the form of psychology. It has lost its abstract form as a doctrine *about*, and turned into method, a method, moreover, which animates the real process in contrast to a merely subjective method applied from outside to the real process.[3]

BURIED IN THE MASS of Carl Jung's vast writings is a brief statement that provides an awe-inspiring and liberating insight: a new way to read myths, fairy tales, and dreams—and, of course, the Bible, which is the source text for this book. Historically speaking, we have had two options for reading the Bible: the theological or religious perspective, which reads the Bible as divine revelation, and the humanistic or scientific perspective, which turns the Bible into a product of the human mind. Jung's alternative emerges from an important insight into the nature of soul:

1. Giegerich, *What Is Soul?*, 83.
2. Giegerich, *What Is Soul?*, 288.
3. Giegerich, *What Is Soul?*, 290.

> In myths and fairytales, as in dreams, *the soul speaks about itself*, and the archetypes reveal themselves in their natural interplay, as "formation, transformation / the eternal Mind's eternal recreation."[4]

The essence of the statement—*soul speaks about itself*—points us in the direction of *modern* soul. From the perspective of *psychology with soul*, myths, fairy tales, and dreams are not about people's ideas nor about divine revelation, but about soul. Soul is a reality unto itself, and it speaks about itself, which implies a function with a certain independence from human speech. This autonomy is complicated because obviously, soul can speak only with the aid of human persons and human language. People are the place where myths, fairy tales, and dreams arise, where they find their voice, but Jung's insight gives us a new way to understand the creative matrix out of which they arise and what they are saying. Jung's concept of soul reaches toward a psychological soul, in contrast to a mythological, metaphysical, or human soul. Soul, in its manifestation as the creative ferment of culture, language, thought, and history, creates itself. Anyone who sits in silence long enough will experience and observe the inexhaustible fountain of the mind's self-production, an unending stream of thoughts, fantasies, fears, desires, plans, hopes, regrets, and more, that simply flow forth. The perpetual and prodigal production of the individual mind is magnified on the cultural level as soul, as consciousness at large, as public mind.

Of course, we participate in soul's self-generation, but we are not the creators of soul, no more than we are the creators of our own thoughts or dreams. Psychological consciousness differentiates between ego as personal and soul as impersonal, holding them together as a unified totality. This differentiated unity is the *psychological difference*, that difference between the psychic and the psychological, the surface and the depth, or content and form (syntax).[5] The "psychological difference" is the awareness that there is more to consciousness than our personal, ego, consciousness. This is how soul is brought into the picture of what we *are* as both personal and cultural beings. It points to the difference between the face value, the surface or immediate presentation, and that which emerges through thoughtful reflection and interpretation. It is also the difference between the message and the medium,[6] in which the message emerges from the medium and the medium has no life without its message—they must exist as a differentiated unity. Of course, the message that emerges from any medium—in our case, the Bible—is dependent on the point of view of the interpreter. The psychological difference is a step beyond the theological difference, which would make a religious interpretation in terms of a god's speech, and a step beyond the subject-object difference, which would make an interpretation in terms of science or humanism, as only human speech. Instead of looking outside the myth, fairy tale, or dream for

---

4. Giegerich, *What Is Soul?*, 44 (cited and translation modified by Giegerich; emphasis added); see Jung, *Archetypes*, ¶ 400.

5. Giegerich, *What Is Soul?*, 101–2.

6. Giegerich, *Soul's Logical Life*, 109.

its meaning, psychology stays with the words and images themselves, and through a process of negating the immediate surface presentation, asks what is consciousness saying about itself from within the psychological difference that is the constitution of the consciousness asking the question. Consciousness is the source of its own answer, but that answer is aware of the difference between ego and soul, and thus soul's speech about itself does not come from the ego but from its own depth, the inexhaustible depth of soul's own self-production.

Looked at psychologically, the Bible is, or has been, the myth or dream of Western civilization, our collective dream, even though it has hardly any public presence anymore and has almost completely disappeared as far as modern society is concerned. Jung's insight provides a dazzling new way to read the myths and dreams that compose the Bible. During antiquity, the theological/mythological cosmos was reality and truth. The gods and goddesses, and all the other magical, wonderful, and dreadful creatures, were real as the truth of shared cultural-mind; they were the soul's manifestation in that time. That whole taken-for-granted reality changed with the emergence of science and Reason, when the basic logic of consciousness was transformed and the ground of the real shifted to empirical facts and measurable quantities: materialism and physics. In the light of science, the realm of the goddesses and gods, and animated nature, have faded away. Scientific rationalism, or materialism, is still the prevailing logic of our modern era, the logic of humanism, which tells us that myths, fairy tales, dreams, and the Bible are the product of the subjective human mind and relegated to the status of superstition with no authoritative status. It is common to see the word *myth* used as a synonym for false, untrue, and mistaken. The innate logic of modernity asserts that all narratives that are not historical, not grounded in objective empirical evidence, are fictions, constructs of the *human* mind. In general, during the modern era, the divine realm, God, is no longer considered to be the source of the revelation of sacred scripture, myth, or dreams. The distinction between the theological/mythological form of consciousness and the scientific/humanistic form of consciousness is a historical one and not a judgment or criticism about whether one or the other is better or more valuable. Each does have its own form of truth, but my larger question is whether or not soul still inhabits those forms of truth, or has soul (the syntax of consciousness) moved on to another form?

The psychological idea—that an autonomous soul speaks about itself—represents a radical historical shift in the very ground of consciousness with which we look at the world and ourselves. During the Middle Ages, theology was the queen of the sciences. It was the overarching standard that encompassed all fields of knowledge and study (our word *science* simply means "knowledge"), and this was the form of soul during antiquity and the medieval period. The religious form of soul then transformed itself into the materialistic scientific outlook and humanism, the view that humankind is the author of all culture. Psychology with soul is a new option for consciousness, and it is the historical result of the sublation of the religious and scientific outlooks.

This new psychological consciousness encompasses the former religious and scientific forms within itself, seeing them as earlier forms of consciousness. This raises our contemporary consciousness to a new level that is conscious of itself as consciousness, manifesting in profound cultural and technological changes we are struggling to understand. In a very real sense, this new self-aware consciousness has already happened; it is logically already true, and it is we, humankind, who are grappling with trying to make what has already happened conscious.

First Impression and Soul Depth (Immediacy and Reflection)

Jung's insight that myths, fairy tales, and dreams are soul speaking about itself leads to another insight about the two traditional approaches. The religious and the humanist perspectives are fundamentally "first impression" approaches to the Bible. While their fundamental assumptions are very different, each takes the content of the Bible at face value. For the mythological/religious form of consciousness, the gods and goddesses, and any magical creatures and animals, are the reality that the stories are about. In the ancient past, soul personified its truth in these mythological beings. As we saw briefly in the previous chapter, truth was external to human beings and resided with, or as, the gods and goddesses. In antiquity, gods and goddesses symbolized the general form or syntax of general consciousness itself; they were the taken-for-granted ground of everyone's consciousness. For the modern mind, which is a scientific and human-centered form of consciousness, holy scripture and magical tales are the product of the *human* mind, the *human* imagination. The old stories are read as expressions of *human* feeling and emotion, *human* hopes and fears. Belief in gods is taken as an early naive stage in the development of *human*kind. Even when modern consciousness appreciates the old stories, they are viewed as metaphors about the human condition, human faith, human belief—they are stories created by human persons, not truths revealed by a god. Religious and humanist forms of consciousness cannot escape the inner logic of their own syntax as completely deity-centered or human-centered; this is what defines them. Psychology's soul-centered option is radically significant.

Our Historical Difference

The psychological understanding of soul gives us an entirely different and heretofore unavailable option for how to interpret the Bible. The psychological perspective allows soul to speak about itself, lets us see soul's logos at work. Of course, the word *soul* itself has fairly unshakable religious and metaphysical associations from its origins. However, the idea of sublation, which points to historical change in the foundation of consciousness, reminds us that the need to negate traditional associations is an ongoing activity. While soul on the cultural level may have already negated itself, I need to continue to negate the religious and humanist associations that stubbornly cling to the word. At the same time, I want to recognize that the essence and phenomenology of traditional soul continue in its new form as psychology, as soul's recursive speech about itself.

Jung's statement about soul includes a quotation from Goethe: "Formation, transformation / the eternal Mind's eternal recreation," links "soul" with "eternal Mind." I want to avoid stumbling over any metaphysical mystifications, such as taking the idea *eternal* literally and chronologically, or thinking of *Mind* in any personalistic sense. This greater Mind is more akin to my notion of soul as that fertile, always changing, yet invisible, web of being, the realm of shared meanings as our historical-cultural Mind. While both soul and eternal Mind are personifications, I am learning to think of them in nonpersonal ways. The idea of cultural-Mind (soul) points to the basis of our fundamental and yet unconscious way of being in the world, determined by our cultural-historical time and place; it is our unconscious orientation to the world at large. In the context of our modern consciousness, "modern soul" is about consciousness in its broadest and most public sense (in contrast to our private personal consciousness).

Another way to think of the two traditional approaches to myth, fairy tales, and dreams is in terms of authority. In the ancient world of myth and religion, the basis of reality and truth was the numinous and powerful personified authorities (gods) that existed external to humankind. That authority was the self-evident, the taken-for-granted, syntax of ancient consciousness. The truth and reality of divinity was not a mistaken belief on the part of humankind, not a content of the personal mind; it was humankind's form of the world-consciousness in that historical time. I would say it was the governing shape of public mind. What I am referring to as the syntax, or the logic, of consciousness, is not a content that one can choose to believe or not believe, choose to agree with or not. The syntax or logic refers to the essence or form of mind itself, which *psychology with soul* recognizes has gone through historical transformations. In the context of the modern era's science and humanism, this authority is now lodged within humankind itself. Humankind sees itself as the final authority, and this human-centric authority characterizes the general consciousness of our age. In the brief overview I presented in chapter 1, the "I Am" sublated itself, emerging first as God, then into the new form as Christ, on to the next form as Reason, and now as an ego-soul circular form of psychological consciousness.

I want to recognize the world-changing difference between the two traditional forms of consciousness, or modes of interpretation, and the psychological form of consciousness. The traditional forms of consciousness are completely contained in their own essential logic, or syntax, either as gods or as science, and remain unaware of themselves (as forms of consciousness). From a psychological perspective, they are naive apperceptions of the world. Psychological consciousness, an entirely new status of consciousness, has become *self*-conscious. Within psychology, soul now speaks about itself; consciousness is now aware of itself as consciousness. A new and more inclusive order of consciousness, this perspective on psychology means that *psychology with soul* is sublated religion and metaphysics and sublated science and humanism; consciousness in general is aware of itself as the larger container, so to speak, of its former syntaxes (religion and science). Religion and science are no longer the ruling paradigms of consciousness but rather contents within a new more inclusive paradigm. From this point of view, myths, fairy tales, and dreams are not the only instances of soul speaking about itself; *all* products of culture, all forms of knowledge, are shared soul (cultural-mind) speaking about itself. Psychology gives us the option not to take the surface presentation at face value and to look for a deeper significance that is neither God-centered nor human-centered, but a new logic, an unfolding of soul's logical life.

One iconic and popular image of the move of consciousness outside of itself is the view of the planet Earth from outer space. The feat of traveling away from planet Earth and turning our cameras back on ourselves, seeing ourselves as a whole from a distance, reflects the historical shift of the very constitution of soul itself. Our cultural-mind now understands itself in a way completely different than ever before, in a way that was never possible before. This is our historical difference, and we exist as this difference. During the 1960s, an enormous cultural urgency pushed the race into space, and public mind poured all of its resources into that achievement. What we tend to think of as a technological achievement was animated by the shift of consciousness already underway within soul itself. To see the planet Earth from outer space mirrors the movement of soul outside of itself, soul becoming conscious of itself as consciousness as we see ourselves from space. The view of the planet, really the view of ourselves, from outer space is symbolic of the changing logic of modern soul. The factual move into outer space is not simply an action humankind achieved, but a radical shift in our interpretive ground, the lens with which we see and understand our world and ourselves. Our historical difference is also the psychological difference, and it is a rupture with all prior forms of consciousness. It is as if we have been pushed out of a womb, born out of a former logic of consciousness that once contained us, and there is no going back. It is our responsibility to learn what the new form of consciousness is teaching us.

Semantics and Syntax, Content and Form

A sentence is composed of both the individual words and their meanings, as well as the grammatical structure of the sentence itself. When we analyze a sentence in terms of its semantics and syntax, we are thinking a difference that is itself a unity as far as the meaning of the sentence goes. The syntax is an invisible form that conveys the meaning of the sentence, while the semantic content is indeed visible as the individual words. This grammatical arrangement is helpful in thinking about soul. We could even say that the invisible syntax of a sentence is a kind of animating quality that breathes life into the words as it brings them together into a meaningful whole. Words by themselves have their own definitions, but they do not have a living meaning or purpose until they are arranged by syntax. Syntax works as an energizing force that brings the isolated "dead" words together into a living presence, which then sparks to life in a receptive mind.[7] It is interesting to note that as children learn to speak, they are taught words but never syntax. The syntax of any language is its invisible meaning structure (and every language has its own syntactical idiosyncrasies), which is simply absorbed unconsciously. The grammatical structure of a language, its syntax, is an invisible, unconscious orientation of our consciousness that everyone shares and that is conveyed and absorbed by default; we just learn it without knowing that we have done so. Thus the syntax of consciousness shapes who we *are*, our deepest sense of being, which remains implicit and unthought, as a member of a particular language culture.

The difference between semantics and syntax, content and form, shows us the nature of the relationship between soul and the real. Soul is never, so to speak, *not* incarnate as some cultural product, whether that product is Christianity, the Bible, television, the nuclear bomb, or any phenomenon that helps to define a culture. The idea of modern soul views soul as the animating "spirit," or thought, at the heart of cultural production. Soul in this sense is happening all the time, but usually we can discern the meaning, or the living truth, or the soul of the matter, only in hindsight. Syntax and form are not "things" outside of us but rather refer to the mode of perception that invisibly shapes our perception of reality, along the lines of those "rose-colored glasses" that inform our view.

The analogy of a lens is another helpful way to think about soul. When I look through the windshield while driving, I am not aware of the windshield but of all the many objects beyond it. When we wear glasses or contact lenses, we are not aware of the lens itself but of the objects we are looking at. The objects, the contents of our consciousness or the semantic level, take all of our attention, and so the windshield or the glasses remain invisible and unconscious. One of the opportunities available through psychotherapy is to examine how our personal "windshield" (consciousness) may be distorted, obscured, or colored. We are also aware of how our interactions with other people affect and color our consciousness, changing how we "see" things. The family we grew up in has lent a certain character and quality to how we see ourselves, others, and the world: Do we see the world as a place of opportunity or a place of threat and danger? Do we see ourselves as capable or incapable? These simple examples should bring home the difference between the form or syntax of consciousness and the content or semantics of consciousness. We are, however, more familiar with how our personal moods, assumptions, biases, addictions, and neurotic tendencies influence our personal consciousness than we are with the idea of a broad historical-cultural syntax of consciousness which is where the idea of modern soul is focused. A psychology with soul is concerned with the syntax of consciousness, public mind, and its development during different historical-cultural periods.

7. Giegerich, *What Is Soul?*, 56.

My psychological reading of the Bible as myth, fairy tale, and dream addresses the changes the syntax of consciousness has undergone historically. I will view the characters in the Bible, both divine and human, as the soul's unified self-presentation. While the Bible contains many different stories and characters in many historical periods and social circumstances, as well as multiple images of God, I will view the whole as a unity that symbolizes the unfolding of the general cultural consciousness (soul). Viewed as a soul document, the Bible as a whole is a unity in relation with itself; viewed in this way it gives us access to soul's development, insights into what I call "God's autopsy," and an overview of the living truth of soul. My approach to myth and dream in terms of "soul speaks about itself" reinforces the choice to put the syntax of theological and historical perspectives aside and to read the figure of God—as well as human characters like Moses, Abraham, and all the others—as *symbolic personifications* of soul working on itself, as soul's speech about itself as a process of developing consciousness. As I read the Bible, I will bracket the assumptions of both theological and historical consciousness and attempt to discern soul at work.

While it imposes a certain set of restrictions, reading the Bible psychologically as soul's autobiography also liberates a new vision of the psychological history of the Judeo-Christian tradition. To read the Bible psychologically means to explicitly exclude theological (traditional) and historical (humanistic) points of view. Psychology aims to allow a phenomenon to reveal itself as soul speaking about itself, and it views the phenomenon as self-sufficient in this regard, a self-sufficiency that does not need, and does not allow, other points of view, other fields of inquiry, to intrude on and thus distort soul's speaking. To exclude theological and historical readings does not mean I am unaware of the varied theological approaches, from the most conservative to the most liberal, nor of what historical and other scientific studies have taught us about the Bible and its world of origin. I am wary not so much of the content of theology, as of the logical form of consciousness that it represents. In fact, the psychological reading I bring to the Bible is already informed by the theological readings and the frame of mind that is historical consciousness, which came earlier. As noted in the brief overview of the history of the development of the "I Am," modern psychological consciousness is the product of those prior forms of consciousness.

Psychology (with soul), or modern psychological consciousness, is the still early result of the broad historical and cultural influence of both Jewish and Christian ideas as well as the scientific worldview. Psychology does not take religious ideas or images at face value, as divine revelation, as a god speaking, but it does take them seriously as symbolic statements soul is making about itself in the light of the history and evolution of consciousness. In a similar manner, psychology brackets the historical and scientific reading of the Bible because historical and scientific consciousness is informed by its own logic, which precludes any notion of "soul speaking about itself." Historical scientific consciousness takes the Bible at face value as a statement of history, as a collection of texts, physical artifacts written by human authors and produced by and for specific social circumstances. Historical consciousness seeks the origin of the texts in the realms of sociology, politics, economics, anthropology, tribal identity formation, history of religions, and history of ideas; these points of view are governed by a general human-centric, or humanistic, form of consciousness. The biblical text is no longer understood or accepted as a self-evident truth, as being of divine origin; instead it is taken as human belief and a human construct. And, of course, soul has no place in the scientific-humanistic syntax of consciousness. The restriction that a psychological reading of the Bible chooses to enforce is not merely to exclude the content of fields that are alien to psychology as soul's logos; what I really want to exclude is the logical form of consciousness that perpetuates the stance of externality, the logic of science and humanism. Psychology works with the logic of interiority, which is not the subjective interiority of the human person but interiority as soul's truth or syntax, the meaning and purpose of consciousness; this emerges from the phenomenon under investigation, in our case, the Bible. To help us understand how the restriction works and how it releases the Bible to speak on its own terms, I want to introduce the literary reading of the Bible undertaken by Jack Miles in his book, *God: A Biography*. This remains an extraordinary work of interpretation and speculation about God as a literary character, which is, in my view, underappreciated.

God: A Biography—a Methodological Model

Miles undertook a strictly literary reading of the Bible, approaching the Bible as if it were the evidence for a biography of God. He reads the *Tanakh* (in contrast to the *Old Testament*) from beginning to end, allowing only the text itself to expose the character of God one page at a time. In effect, he approaches this character as if he had never heard of him, and the only evidence is the biblical report. For his reading, the Bible contains all the evidence for God's character, and nothing more is needed or wanted. He starts at the beginning of God's life, God's first appearance in the book of Genesis—in this sense, with his infancy—and reads the Bible as if it were the chronological unfolding of God's development. We know only what the text in front of us tells us and not what is coming next. All prior knowledge about God, theological presuppositions and traditional claims are excluded from this reading. This is the effect of the discipline of this purely literary reading. We should take note of the fact that such a literary reading is possible only because we are the heirs of a modern consciousness in which the theological presupposition is no longer the only and all-encompassing framework with which to think about the Bible. Miles has the freedom to choose how to focus his reading and what to exclude. This freedom to choose how to read the Bible is so common, so obvious and taken for granted, that it is difficult to truly appreciate. We are not that far removed from the time when the theological dogmatic framework was the unconscious dominant background of the functioning consciousness that permeated all our institutions. Today, the theological perspective is simply one point of view among others within the framework of modern secular culture. Bracketing out theological concerns is one exclusion. Our psychological reading requires another exclusion if it is to produce its own results.

The discipline of the literary reading brackets historical consciousness in a special way. The Bible is approached as a literary whole in its own right. Our modern knowledge, by way of critical historical consciousness, tells us that the Bible is a varied collection of many books, many authors, many literary genres, brought together and repeatedly edited over hundreds of years. Miles's literary discipline is aware of the historical circumstances, but he keeps this awareness off to the side as he reads the Bible as a literary whole. Although Miles called his book a biography based on the Bible as evidence, one could also say it views the Bible as a novel with God as the central character. While the historical investigation of the biblical narratives gives us invaluable information about their formation and context, it also breaks up the biblically unified story of God into unconnected chunks. Of course, it was precisely historical and scientific consciousness that created the critical distance and independence from the unquestioned and dominant theological view that had been the prior form of consciousness, and which had given birth to the Bible in the first place. Miles's decision to treat God as a *literary* character and to keep his interpretation sealed within this confined literary space is an impressive achievement and a kind of consciously chosen naiveté. His narrow and restricted focus allows the text of the Tanakh to teach us who God is without the intrusion of theological assumptions or historical-humanistic reduction. God, as literary character, is allowed to be God and to tell us about himself through this text. Miles's literary approach parallels my choice to restrict and exclude the theological and historical frameworks from our psychological reading. Just as Miles's method allows God to speak about himself, I will attempt to let soul (developing consciousness) speak about itself as if the text (Bible) were a dream.

God has no extratextual authority in Miles's literary reading, and the unfolding of his character is confined to what the biblical, and only the biblical, texts tell us. Although Miles, as a former Jesuit trained in religious studies and Near Eastern languages, is very well aware of both the theological and the historical-critical readings of the Bible, he does not allow the logic of either approach to intrude. That is, the text is not read in terms of humankind's thoughts and feelings about God, nor is it read as a historical document about the Hebrew/Jewish people. Although the main character in Miles's biography, the protagonist, is God, the traditional theological God is kept entirely out of the way of the literary God. Miles does not focus on the human characters in the Bible except insofar as they play an essential role in the development of God's self-understanding. So, just as Jung tells us that myth is soul speaking about itself, the Tanakh, in Miles's literary reading, is God speaking about himself. What we learn about God as a purely literary character, taken at face value, contradicts and undermines all of our popular and conventional assumptions about God. Miles's books about God and Christ are a salutary read against the pious and popular pablum that substitutes for a careful reading of the actual text. This god is neither omniscient nor omnipotent. He is an imperfect deity who actually learns and develops by way of his interactions with the image of himself that he created. Here I do want to read the Bible, in a sense, at face value, insofar as I want to take what it actually says seriously. According to God's own words, humankind is the extension of God's own self, or mind:

> Then God said, "Let us make humankind in our image, according to our likeness; . . ." So God created humankind in his image, in the image of God he created them; male and female he created them. (Gen 1:26–27)

God made a reflection of himself, and not only was the human creature tied to and dependent on this God, but God himself was inextricably tied to and dependent on his likeness. It turns out that God had no idea that creating an image of himself would cause so much trouble for him. God and humankind form a kind of circle, and each is inexorably bound to the other; neither has any existence without the other. The self-enclosed circle of God and humankind mirrors soul's self-reflecting and recursive structure—soul is also symbolized as the ouroboros, the mythical serpent devouring its own tail. Soul is continually turning back on itself and pushing off from itself, just as God and humankind turn each other back on themselves and also push off from each other and, as narrative entities, are transformed in the process. For my psychological reading of the Bible, God and humankind are the symbolic presentation of the living truth of soul, or soul's speech about itself.

By reading the Bible psychologically, I am examining the archetypal DNA of the Western psyche. The Bible represents the skeleton, nervous system, and marrow of Western consciousness. We have grown so far away from the Christian atmosphere that once was Western civilization's prevailing form of consciousness that we have little sense today of how important the Bible once was. This psychological examination is not unlike a dissection of a dimension of Western mind that has fallen so out of favor in general that it has become invisible and unconscious. Those still proclaiming a Christian God are shouting to no avail against the prevailing winds. The claim that God is still alive is a humancentric project that has little to do with where soul is today. My psychological concern is with what soul might be saying about itself, or has already said about itself, through the Bible. For my approach, the Bible is not the Bible but a soul-document. For psychology, the Bible has no inherent authority. Precisely because the Bible was historically the once preeminent syntax of the Western mind, however, it is crucial to interpret again its historical significance. So today, as a result of the development of Western mind, the Bible is only one text among many, and yet, I believe that the Bible is perhaps the most significant text for understanding the creation and achievement of modern consciousness. From soul's point of view, if God is dead, then the Bible is also dead, and God's autopsy includes this autopsy of the Bible. The truth of the Bible was once God's truth, but that truth is now dead. I want to know today what truth has been concealed in the biblical record, which until the emergence of psychology with soul has been invisible because inconceivable. If we can't conceive it, we cannot see it. The psychological notion of soul enables a new kind of seeing into our tradition that was simply not possible heretofore. The psychological autopsy will reveal a new truth and at the same time create that new truth through the process of articulation, making it explicit.

The Bible itself is clear that the monotheistic God emerged in the historical and cultural context of the polytheistic ancient Near East, and it did so with great difficulty, slowly and violently. The plurality of the gods and goddesses that was the norm in that larger cultural environment became, within the God of Western psychological history, an inner complex plurality of ambivalence and self-contradiction. The conflicts that exist between gods and goddesses in a polytheistic cosmos became the conflicted personality of God himself.[8] And because in the biblical narrative humankind is God's self-image, the strife and conflict that also exists between God and humankind mirrors not only God's own conflict with himself, but also the conflicts that constitute soul's dynamic evolution.

Bible as Dream

Reading the Bible as if it were a dream parallels the literary method of Miles. Here I want to address how I will approach humankind as an essential character in our reading of the Bible. Of course, the character of God interacts with human beings, but within the literary method, they are literary characters and not historical persons. In a literary or psychological reading, we are not concerned with whether or not they were historical persons, and even if they were, we are not focused on their reality as historical persons. In literature and dream, they function as symbols. As literary characters, their primary function within the Bible as a self-contained text is not as actual historical actors once upon a time but as God's self-image. Within the Bible as a self-contained whole, the seemingly separate characters of God and humankind function as a unified totality. In an important sense, it is not God who is the main character but the *relationship* of God and humankind—that is certainly where the action is. I want to grasp the biblical fact that humankind is God's self-image, and then I must always think in terms of God *and* humankind mirroring each other; the action of one will always have an effect on the other. The fact that they are inextricably joined at the hip, for better or for worse, is the clue to seeing their dynamic as the unified soul, a self-interpreting process, working on itself.

Dreams are more often than not real emotional experiences, and yet, we are asleep when they occur. Thus, we should know that the reality of dream is not the same as the reality of ordinary waking life. In antiquity and in the Bible, dreams were the direct communication of a god; in the Bible, the ability to interpret dreams was also from

---

8. Miles, *God*, 85–95.

God (both Joseph and Daniel credit God, and not themselves, as the source of their interpretations).⁹ Today we have choices about how to understand dreams, ranging across a spectrum from the scientific perspective of random neurological activity, to symbolic images from the unconscious, personal or collective, with potential meaning, and even to literal indications of another "spirit" world, or, as I am suggesting, "soul speaking about itself." We need not debate different approaches to dreams as I have already selected the soul approach. The psychological reality of dream, however, will help in understanding the psychological approach to the Bible.

Psychology views dreams as soul speaking about itself using metaphor, image, emotion, and thought. Although we dream about actual people and about ourselves, the dream is its own reality, and the figures inhabiting the dream are not the actual people we encounter in daily life, but rather psychological images and ideas. In other words, there are no human beings in dreams, just as there are no real objects in dreams. One could say that all the people and things in a dream are the *thoughts* and *ideas* of consciousness thinking out loud about itself. Dreams, from the point of view of psychology, are one way that consciousness processes its own self-relation, its own development and possibilities, its own awareness of itself. To choose to read the Bible as a dream is to read it as a soul-document and only a soul-document; it is to read it in the terms of the syntax of consciousness processing itself at specific times in history. My view of soul is historical and developmental. That is, soul operates on a historical scale and continually complexifies and expands itself, what I call sublation. I want to understand history from the perspective of soul, or psychologically, and also to view soul in a historical light. The psychological point of view takes the Bible as soul's autobiography, as demonstrating stages in soul's history; the Bible is soul's account of itself.

Psychology with soul views all the characters in the Bible as if they personify aspects of soul. On a personal level, the people in our dreams personify our thoughts and attitudes, our own multiple qualities and points of view, and most often those attitudes and feelings we are not aware of; yet, we still know ourselves as one person (even if conflicted). Psychologically, we are a unity and a multiplicity at the same time. This can be very painful when we suffer violent conflict, torn between competing values and desires or duties. Still, we are a unity as ourselves, and we struggle to contain our conflicts and learn what they have to teach us. This often requires the growth of a larger more expansive consciousness to encompass our conflicts. Consciousness will at times simply outgrow the conflicts that occupy us at particular times. The point here is to see that we are both the same and different; we are a unity of both unity and difference in our essential makeup. This is the nature of soul, and it is how I choose to view the Bible. The Bible as a soul-document is a single whole, constituted as a unified multiplicity (soul) that is undergoing metamorphosis over time. There are many ways to view the variety and conflicts of history and culture. A psychology with soul is one such choice, and with this choice, I will undertake an overview of Western history

9. Gen 41:16 and Dan 2:27–28; 4:18.

and culture as the place where the dynamic interior self-relation of the one soul works itself out. This perspective steps back far enough to see the unity of the whole forest, while not forgetting the individual trees.

It is easy to get caught up in the pressing reality of dreams, to get taken in by their immediate and concrete presentation. Dreams can be surprisingly real and convincing, and in the moment of the dream, we know it is a fact and true. But, just as we have learned that physical reality is not what it seems to our senses, that matter is composed of atoms, subatomic particles, and force fields, so the first immediate experience of a dream is not what it seems. The psychological perspective enables us to work with and then through the immediate surface presentation of a dream and release the deeper thoughts buried within the images and emotions of the dream. Psychology as the discipline of interiority works with and through the surface to hear what the dream may be saying about itself as soul-speech. My psychological approach to the Bible is similar. I do not want to take the characters in the Bible at face value, as they first present themselves, as a story about gods and people. I am curious about the animating principle, or soul truth, that the biblical characters are expressing. I will read them as soul, as the syntax of consciousness, giving an account of itself, its inner conflicts, and purposes.

Language and Soul

Language and soul have an interlocking relationship that is almost an identity. I want to explore language here in order to amplify our understanding of modern soul. I am especially focused on written language and the difference between preliterate, oral cultures and literate, writing cultures. Certainly language is what has created our uniquely human capacities and being, but the emergence of literacy and written language marked the occasion when history and culture took off and outpaced the slow and gradual development that had marked biological evolution and preliterate cultures.[10] Soul refers to our world of shared meanings, and language is the medium with which our shared-meaning world is communicated. Language is the medium of meaning (which is what Heidegger meant when he stated, "Language is the house of Being.")[11]

Soul's otherness and transpersonal quality is like the nature of language. While we all use language individually, it has a shared meaning in which we all participate; no single person or group controls the development of language. In a sense, *Homo sapiens* speaks one language because all the different languages of the world can, more or less, be translated into each other. Language has a life of its own. Dictionaries can catalogue the words that are part (and only part) of language, but they can neither control nor direct language. We can document or catalogue language, but we cannot steer it. Language creates itself, and we are in the position of catching up to language's

10. Harari, *Sapiens*, 41.
11. Heidegger, "Letter on Humanism," 193.

perpetual movement and development. It is the phenomenon of *meaning* (i.e., soul) that uses language to express itself and develop itself.

What is language? Where does language come from? Language is the medium in which culture, society, history, story, meaning, and memory exist, but it is impossible for language to know its own origin. Language cannot remember its own beginning, any more than we can individually remember our first use of language. Language emerged somehow, but it is clearly a collective, socially shared phenomenon. The meaning (soul) embodied in language is what combines brain, mind, body, and society into a field phenomenon because language in general expresses a kind of group shared mindedness. Language is first of all a body of socially shared meanings. No expression of language is so completely idiosyncratic that it cannot be understood by others, and if it is incomprehensible, then it is not language anymore, but a purely private and isolated phenomenon.

Language is first of all a social field of shared meanings that binds a group, tribe, or society together and invisibly defines it. This dimension of language is autonomous and transcends any individual's creative activity, even evades the group's attempt to control it. This is my definition of modern soul, the social field of shared meanings, the deep consciousness that defines the social group in the living here and now. The dimension of shared meanings I am pointing to are deeply unconscious and invisible. Soul speaks about itself in these shared meanings, but it is not easy to discern what soul is saying. The world of languaged meanings is our world, that is, the world, as beings-of-language, that we inhabit, or even better, that we *are*. We do not really live "in" language, we *are* language. And because we *are* language, we do not live immediately in nature but mediated to nature by way of language. The human world is the language-world, and I mean language in its broadest cultural productions sense.

Language is not natural to the extent that it separates us from the animal's unconscious embeddedness in nature. We know that we come from an evolutionary lineage of animals that existed without language, and yet language emerged at some point and separated us from that existence embedded in nature. Language forms the world of culture separate from the world of nature. Language is also a closed circle, a closed self-referential phenomenon. We cannot understand language from outside of language. We can understand words only by using other words. Language can understand itself only by way of itself, through itself. Language can never get outside of itself, can never find a vantage point that is not language, which is why language can never find or know its own origin, its own beginnings. To know a beginning as a fact, one would have to know what came before that beginning, and in the field of language, that is impossible. Which is why, as language-beings, our beginnings are stories, creation stories, whether mythological, theological, or scientific, stories told and created long after the actual beginning, whenever that might have been. Stories are interpretations, soul's speech about itself, woven with words.

Our actual *world* as human beings *is* the world of meaning, mediated by language. We relate to the natural world, the world of matter, through and with language. This is not to suggest that there is no real material world, that the only reality is mind. Rather, our relationship with reality is mediated by language, and our being is fundamentally linguistic. We are irrevocably cut off from the immediacy (unconscious containment) of nature by language. It is as impossible for us to be unconsciously immersed in nature as it would be to forget or expunge our native tongue. Our relationship with the natural world is no longer immediate and direct as it is for animals, plants, and minerals but is mediated, reflected, as meaningful, as soul.

The modern philosophical speculation that we might exist only as a mind, that no material world is "out there," is purely a product of the form of consciousness known as modern humanism, the logic of which is the idea of the isolated subjectivity of the individual. The idea that we are only "mind" is an extreme expression of the realization that we are indeed fundamentally linguistic beings. This philosophical position signals an unconscious intuition that we are indeed "trapped" inside language, with no way out. And while this is true, that we are indeed inescapably languaged beings, only the logic of modern consciousness can formulate the thought that we could be only mind. During antiquity, no such thought would have been possible because the form of soul (the logical form of consciousness) had not yet taken on the form of the privatized, subjectively isolated, encapsulated mind of the solitary individual. In antiquity, reality and truth (soul) was constituted as social, public, shared mythologies in which we and the world were the creations of preexisting and world-constituting gods and goddesses. The empirical human person existed primarily as a *We*, a corporate entity, constituted first by the truth of the god, myth, and tribe, all three inextricably wrapped together as a collective truth. In antiquity, the individual as we today understand subjective individuality, which we take unthinkingly for granted, did not exist. The modern "I am" did not exist. The "I Am," as seen in the previous chapter, was identified with the god Yahweh, who vouchsafed the people's existence and world.

Just as only modern consciousness can seriously ask the question about whether or not God exists, such a thought would have been impossible in antiquity. Only modern consciousness can conceive of existence in terms of a mind cut off from matter (the natural world), or we might say cut free from matter. Still, such skepticism does follow the trajectory of language, which has cut itself free, in a sense, from matter. Language is *contra naturam*. And, as we will see in future chapters, Yahweh, the god of the Tanakh, was against nature. I will show in chapter 4 that Yahweh personified the logical form of consciousness that was the historical emergence of literacy, the written word. As such, Yahweh represented a revolutionary rupture from within the prevailing polytheistic nature-based and mostly preliterate cultures.

Language as a whole, as a living process, does not exist anywhere as a thing. It is a web of meanings that is culturally shared. In itself it is a whole, a unity, but it is constituted by multiple and conflicting meanings. Language is truly only alive, or real, when a mind, or minds, express themselves with language. Words in a book or dictionary are not language, or if they are, they are dead words, dead language. Words and language come alive when a mind engages with them, and their meaning comes alive with the spark of the living mind. Language is an activity and lives as shared meanings in the context of people and culture. Language in itself, as a whole, is a single unity, but it is also constituted by many different, conflicting, and developing ideas.

Language is, at the same time, both a unity and a difference in relation to itself. Language also develops historically and is not under the control of human users. Language has a life of its own, and we are the ones who have to catch up to its new developing edges. What is it that moves language and directs language? It is nothing external to language. Language creates itself from within itself; it is itself alive, animated. Language, as culture, both creates and destroys meanings. New ideas emerge, and old ideas fall out of favor and die. I could say that language and soul are identical, but it would be more accurate to say that language is the visible manifestation of soul, and that soul is the world of *meaning*. And language is the medium by which meaning (i.e., soul) creates itself as our world. Language, as the form of thought, like soul, does not exist; soul is not substantial, not divine, not spiritual, not eternal or immortal. Soul is the dynamic, turbulent, creative, roiling edge of now. In order to know soul, we cannot stop at the surface of things, at the level of thing-ness; soul is a process, a meaning, a living idea. Language, like soul, is autotelic, that is, it is akin to a living organism in that it is self-directing, although like soul, it does not know ahead of time where it is going.

Externality vs. Interiority

Psychology, or soul, does not have an external relationship with itself or any other object, in contrast to the position of externality that characterizes the methods of the sciences. According to the inner logic of humanism, which is also the logic of science and materialism, the human person is the conscious subject observing an external object; things exist in space outside of us. Consciousness, or the subject as observer, is external to its object, what it is studying or investigating, whether a rock or a poem. Within the logic of humanism, subject and object are separate and divided, discrete. The "objective observer" is the ideal position of science, and the status of reality exists independent of the observer. The scientific standard of objective observer seeks to separate the bias, prejudice, superstition, needs, and desires of the observer, the subject, from what is being observed and studied. The subjective state of the observer should not interfere with or contaminate what is observed. In the state of externality, consciousness is working with, looking at, objects in front of it as *contents* of consciousness. The logical (as in the syntax of consciousness) separation between subject and object was an enormous historical achievement on the part of soul. The deep divide between subject and object, however, between person and world, has now become a serious problem for consciousness. It is at the heart of the infamous Western dualism or Cartesian dualism, which is considered an illegitimate split in the nature of reality and a fatal flaw in our view (consciousness) of reality. I also want to make the distinction between the *method* of science and the *logic* of science. The basic method is to bring a certain critical awareness to observations of reality and to be ready to question assumptions. However, soul has already left behind the logic of science, the syntax of consciousness that informs science, which established the ontological split between subject and object at the very heart of reality. As we will see in chapter 9, the scientific logic of externality has dissolved.

The prevailing critique of Cartesian dualism needs to be modified in the psychological perspective, which sees the separation of subject and object as a historical achievement of soul itself. It was soul's own doing through its self-transformations. We cannot undo the separation through some romantic return to nature or new vision of wholeness. This would be only an intellectual and superficial band-aid that seeks to sooth a guilty modern ego, which has unfortunately taken this huge historical transformation of consciousness personally, that is, as a human fault. Intellectual efforts to paper over the so-called ontological gap do not touch the soul depth, the logical form of consciousness, where this change has occurred. A new unified consciousness must be more complex and on a higher level than the Cartesian dualism of subject and object, or mind and nature (spirit and matter). It must encompass and overcome the dualism in a new consciousness that accepts the dualism as the current status of consciousness and then interiorizes the dualism into itself as a new form of consciousness.

Dualistic consciousness places subject and object vis-à-vis each other on a horizontal plane. The critique of dualism is still thinking from the position of externality, of consciousness here (subject) and world (objects) there. Only a shift at the logical level of consciousness, in terms of consciousness itself, can move beyond the dualism by encompassing the dualism in a new consciousness. This new consciousness, informed by a psychology with soul, places subject and object on a dialectical continuum that is fundamentally circular and whose movement is from implicit to explicit, or unconsciousness to consciousness. This point of view will be developed further in later chapters. Psychology is now aware of the historically different logical forms of consciousness and how they inform our experience of what we call reality. What we do know now—and this is the revolution of consciousness—is that consciousness (the world of meaning) *is* our reality.

The revolutionary change that contemporary consciousness has undergone is that consciousness at large, public mind, has come to the realization that it is conscious of itself: the status of consciousness of consciousness. This means that the subject (consciousness) realizes it is its *own* object and that consciousness is observing itself. During the era we call modernity, consciousness was completely fascinated with the objective world, the world of nature, and was also completely unconscious of itself. The subject, the observer, thought that he or she was completely separate from and

God's Autopsy and the Living Truth of Soul

independent of what was observed. But then the observer began to observe the mind. At first the mind was taken as a separate object just like the rest of nature, but Jung had the insight that the mind as observer is the subject taking itself as its own object. Thus consciousness (mind, soul) wakes up to its circular nature and realizes that all knowledge is implicated in this structure of consciousness. At the same time as Jung, the philosopher Martin Heidegger called this state of affairs the hermeneutic circle. Working independently, Heidegger developed an extended critique of Cartesian dualism in his work *Being and Time*. His phenomenological analysis of Being showed that the hermeneutic circle was an essential structure of human existence. He said, "Any interpretation which is to contribute understanding must already have understood what is to be interpreted."[12] The work of interpretation is what makes explicit, or conscious, what is already understood, that is, "known" implicitly.

Today it is possible to see that subject and object are a unity within a circular consciousness from which there is no escape. The subject (consciousness) now realizes that it is an object to itself because it has become self-aware as an observing consciousness. In all situations, consciousness is aware of its inextricable epistemological entanglement with every object; every object is constituted by consciousness. This leads to the realization that we can never get outside of consciousness, just as we can never get outside of language. This is not our personal consciousness, however, but the logical form of consciousness that we exist as. We experience it personally, but it is our shared human reality. Consciousness is aware of itself as its own background. Our sense of reality is affected too because now truth itself is constituted by this self-reflecting structure. Truth is no longer simply objectively "out there," the stance of externality, but rather a complex entanglement of subjective-objective, as we are aware that we participate in creating truth and making truth real, which is psychology's stance of interiority. The circular structure (syntax) of consciousness is our reality.

Soul's Creation Myth

In the previous chapter, I touched on that early moment in the Genesis creation myth when God created light before the natural sources of light were created. I suggested that the first light, not being natural light, had something to do with the "I Am" that emerges later and that the "I Am" of Yahweh, because it is personified as a god, is a continuation of soul's development in the form of subject. Historically, soul emerges first as a personified subject in all the personalities of the many gods and goddesses of the polytheistic cosmos. In our Judeo-Christian tradition, we first see the "I Am" as God, then as Christ, and next as the function of human reason. As Reason then developed itself, soul as subject finds its concrete realization in the form of the human ego. As the human ego becomes conscious of itself, soul realizes that it is both subject and

---

12. Heidegger, *Being and Time*, 194. Heidegger's contribution to the circular logic of consciousness and the overcoming of Cartesian dualism will be examined in chapter 9.

object in relation to itself. Modern soul comes to know itself as a *unity* of its unity and difference, in contrast to the disunity of Cartesian consciousness. Now the relation between subject-object is no longer a separated duality but rather a differentiated unity. I am reading the Bible from the perspective of this new status of consciousness. The creation myth that has stood at the beginning of Judeo-Christian Western civilization is not really about the creation of the physical universe. It is soul's own self-creation of its world—soul is dreaming its own origin dream. With this creation myth, soul tells the story of the creation of a new world, really a new cosmos, in the context of the prevailing cosmos of nature-polytheism. A new soul-form, Yahweh, emerges as the result of its own making.

It is true that the surface content of the beginning of Genesis is about a god's creation of the material world, the known universe. As I shift my perspective and take this creation story as a dream, as soul speaking about itself, I can ask what the act of creation is saying about itself in the terms of a development of consciousness. A world is indeed created, but it is not a material world, but a new world of consciousness, a new meaning-world. The world that soul was creating was the world of monotheism, pushing off from the world of polytheism. Before the Bible, soul's world was the natural world of polytheism, which was, speaking generally, a world of sophisticated and complex, highly organized, myth-ritual cultures. That world was in no way less intelligent, less truthful, less beautiful, less good, less profound, less meaningful than the biblical world that followed, or our modern world today. It was certainly a profoundly different world, with values and practices that we today would find abhorrent (for example, human and animal sacrifice to the gods was the norm, as were temple-based sacred sexual rites), but it was not less of a cultured world. Our horror at human sacrifice or our moral judgment of sacred so-called prostitution is simply the result of our modern form of consciousness, long conditioned by monotheism, and our inability to appreciate how soul-infused the world of nature was with nature deities. The moral judgments of Judaism and Christianity against the ritual practices of mythological-polytheistic cultures were the result of soul pushing off from its former manifestation. For this movement of soul to be as successful as it was, soul mobilized the powerful energies of hate and war against the other gods and goddesses, their people, their practices, and their land. As we will see, anything that smacked of polytheism was an abomination to the god of the Bible. Psychology, however, does not make moral judgments but observes the phenomenology of soul as it goes through its historical process of re-creating itself and thus creating new cultural worlds.

In the creation story of Genesis, the speech of God creates the new world. God speaks, not *the* world into existence, but rather *his* new world, his world of monotheism, a world of word and spirit, which will establish itself in contrast to and against the prevailing world of soul's already achieved manifestation as the polytheistic nature world. In this story, the word is soul's creative medium:

God's Autopsy and the Living Truth of Soul

> Then God said, "Let there be light"; and there was light. And God saw that the light was good; and God separated the light from the darkness. God called the light Day, and the darkness he called Night. And there was evening and there was morning, the first day.
>
> And God said, "Let there be a dome in the midst of the waters, and let it separate the waters from the waters." So God made the dome and separated the waters that were under the dome from the waters that were above the dome. And it was so. God called the dome Sky. And there was evening and there was morning, the second day.
>
> And God said, "Let the waters under the sky be gathered together into one place, and let the dry land appear." And it was so. God called the dry land Earth, and the waters that were gathered together he called Seas. And God saw that it was good. (Gen 1:3–10)

Speech, the spoken word, is the creative act that brings this new world into being. Language, in and of itself, has a mysterious, magical power to light up, to create, a world. Listening to the Bible as our myth, fairy tale, and dream, we hear soul speaking about itself in this creation story. For soul, this is a self-creating, self-generating story, creating a new soul-world, that will, over some thousand-plus years, gradually become monotheism, a fully new logical form of consciousness, a new syntax of consciousness, that ultimately succeeds in destroying polytheism. To "destroy polytheism" means soul sublates one form of itself in order to become a new form. In other words, what happened to polytheism historically and culturally is the reflection of the transformation within soul at the level of syntax, at the level of the form of consciousness. In the process of one God taking over from all the many gods, soul is extracting itself from nature, moving further away from nature, changing itself into a form that will have more to do with spirit in the form of word, sacred scripture, study, and thought. Psychologically, it is a move from image located in material nature as the basis of consciousness to written concepts not tied to specific locations as the basis of consciousness. It is the emergence of literacy, the *written* word, as the basis of culture. This deep change in the form of consciousness is reflected in how central the study of the Torah became for Judaism and how profoundly sacred the book, the New Testament, became for Christianity. While idols (physical symbols of gods and goddesses) are destroyed and prohibited, the Torah and the New Testament, the revealed *word* of God, become the actual presence of God. Soul moves from being present as nature gods, to being the presence of God as a book. The entire Tanakh, read as a soul-document, is the story of this self-transformation and sublation of soul.

When God creates humankind, he gives them dominion over the natural world, and this charge is to this day still taken literally as the divine authorization for humankind to have supreme authority over nature and therefore to use nature however it wants. But, if we go beneath the surface reading, and remember the polytheistic context of this story, a different interpretation sees this new god Yahweh claiming *his* dominion over all the other nature deities. In antiquity, there is no separation between nature and the gods and goddesses: the gods and goddesses *are* nature. Polytheism is the living natural world. On the sixth day of creation, God claims his dominion (supreme and final authority) through his self-image, or surrogate, humankind, over all of nature:

> Then God said, "Let us make humankind in our image, according to our likeness; and let them have dominion over the fish of the sea, and over the birds of the air, and over the cattle, and over all the wild animals of the earth, and over every creeping thing that creeps upon the earth."
>
> So God created humankind in his image, in the image of God he created them; male and female he created them. God blessed them, and God said to them, "Be fruitful and multiply, and fill the earth and subdue it; and have dominion over the fish of the sea and over the birds of the air and over every living thing that moves upon the earth." God said, "See, I have given you every plant yielding seed that is upon the face of all the earth, and every tree with seed in its fruit; you shall have them for food. And to every beast of the earth, and to every bird of the air, and to everything that creeps on the earth, everything that has the breath of life, I have given every green plant for food." And it was so. (Gen 1:26–30)

The gods and goddesses of nature, of animal husbandry, of agriculture, of nature's productive yield, of fertility and abundance, as well as drought, famine, and flood, of land, seas, and weather, are usurped. The functions of the other gods and goddesses are now taken over by one God, who creates and takes charge of everything. Even though this god grants dominion to his human creatures, they are his self-image, and together they represent a singular soul movement. Soul is creating a new world of new meanings, new significances, new relationships and duties, as soul, in the form of this new style of God, one singular God, who will have a distinct and unique direction and function in his new world. This is indeed a new creation, but it is the creation of a new world of meanings, a new culture, in the midst of an already existing world, the polytheistic cosmos.

Another example of the different direction of this new god is a linear sense of time in contrast to a circular sense of time. In the nature-based polytheistic cosmos, time follows the repetitive round of nature's seasons, and there is little sense of linear history. The new god, the Lord Yahweh of Judaism, has historical aims and goals for himself and his people that break out of the circular round of nature. This new god transcends the natural order, and he must continually take extreme measures to maintain his new status. Soul's story of its own self-transformation into new forms is a violent one. The new god will claim complete authority over his new world, and he will demand complete and absolute obedience from his human subjects. Because humankind is his self-image, I read this demand for obedience as God's requirement of complete mastery over himself. His demand for absolute obedience will have a great cost, one that almost costs this new god his very existence, a turn of events we will meet in future chapters. But, even God does not have complete control over his creation or even over himself. As we will see next in soul's self-creation myth, one of God's own creatures, indeed his very self-image, turns against him.

God and Serpent: Soul's Conflict with Itself

The new god establishes himself as the creator and controller of his world. He also claims supreme authority over everything, usurping the powers of the other gods and goddesses and taking them as his own. He creates a self-image in the form of human beings, and they also have dominion over the created order. Next, we meet an element in the created order that is potentially disturbing of that order and about which God is naturally ambivalent:

> Then the LORD God formed man from the dust of the ground, and breathed into his nostrils the breath of life; and the man became a living being. And the LORD God planted a garden in Eden, in the east; and there he put the man whom he had formed. Out of the ground the LORD God made to grow every tree that is pleasant to the sight and good for food, the tree of life also in the midst of the garden, and the tree of the knowledge of good and evil. (Gen 2:7–9)

This text represents another creation myth that is independent of and different from the first one, which immediately precedes it. The author(s) of Genesis have no problem putting two different versions of creation side by side. But, we ask, human beings have already been created, so how can there be a second creation of the same beings? This is the kind of question that our modern critical and rational consciousness asks, the kind of consciousness that discovered, during the eighteenth and nineteenth centuries in Europe, that the Bible, which had been the unquestioned word of God and the truth of God, could be questioned. The literary contradictions could be examined, and then seen as a human-created literary collection of varied traditions and authors, woven together into a more or less coherent narrative. The contradictions and inconsistencies in the Bible have contributed to our seeing the Bible in a new light. But, the psychological perspective, while it includes the rational position, remembers that the Bible is our dream, and as such I do not expect it to be historically true nor logically consistent. Within the Bible as dream, a second creation story presents another point of view resting next to the first without contradicting it, but rather enhancing it. Dreams do this all the time with their dislocations of time and space, their abrupt non sequiturs and amalgamations of persons known and unknown. Dreams are a process of thinking that uses poetic and dramatic symbolism, rather than rational exposition.

In the biblical dream story, soul is talking about itself as it struggles to establish its new and different, even contrary, world in the context of the already prevailing well-established world of nature polytheism. The problem that would continually bedevil the god of the Tanakh was how to keep the original world of polytheism and its deeply ingrained truths of the nature gods and goddesses from intruding into, contaminating and corrupting, the newly emerging monotheistic world. The biblical story of the new god emerges within a context in which soul already exists as a widespread multiplicity of gods and goddesses, every river, spring and lake, every grove of trees and high hillside, every group, people, and city, had their own local gods and goddesses and cultic practices. The new god personifies soul's new impulse toward monotheism; he wants to be absolutely singular and consistent. No matter how deeply he longs to be the Only One to his self-image (humankind), we see that he is himself deeply riven by his own inconsistencies and self-contradictions, which are the very other gods and goddesses that soul is trying to integrate into one deity. I contend, in an unusual interpretation, that the knowledge of evil in the garden is the ever-present surrounding threat of polytheism. The presence of the tree of the knowledge of good and evil in the garden, taken as a truth soul expresses about itself, I interpret as the inescapable fact that nature-polytheism is the logical form of consciousness of the cultural mind in antiquity. Polytheism, from the point of view of monotheism, is evil. Even though the impulse toward a theistic singularity has emerged, it has hardly established its own secure ground, existing as nothing more than one minor god among a vast profusion of other gods and goddesses. This will become clear in chapters 4 and 5.

God's own breath, as the "breath of life," animates the dust of the ground to become a living being. The "breath of life" that comes from a god is an ancient image of soul as the animating principle of biological life. This is one of the traditional ideas of soul as a divine principle that links the human person to the divine and continues within the human person as one's immortal soul. This ancient notion of soul, its divine origin and its realness, is linked to the psychological idea of "modern soul," but soul, through its evolutionary process of sublation, has left behind both its biological and divine forms and is now a psychological function, the awareness of the form of consciousness as such. Here we see the intimate link between God and his human creature, in that the breath of each is one and the same, both God and humankind have the same breath, the same soul-function. In this version of the creation story, humankind is not the self-image of the god. Here the same breath ties them together in a similar way, however. If either one stops breathing, will the other one also stop breathing? Of course, I am not thinking of God as a biological being that breaths the air, but the soul-image of breath and breathing is what unites God and his human creature. What is the "breath of life" if we do not take it literally as a gas composed of nitrogen and oxygen? Here, in the context of the creation story, the breath of life is associated with biological life. But, in the Bible as a whole, *life* is clearly understood in terms of living according to the word of God, God's statutes, ordinances, and laws, or the torah. The existence of God and humankind is rooted in a mutually dependent agreement (covenant) to live according to God's commandments, and if either one fails to follow this agreement, both will cease to exist. If one stops breathing, the other will too. This mutual dependence between God and humankind, also reflects my view of soul as an ouroboric self-reflexive totality. I noted earlier that both soul and the hermeneutic circle have a similar phenomenology in their movement from implicit to explicit, from unconsciousness to consciousness. In the arrangement established between God and humankind in the Tanakh, God is the implicit dimension that is dependent on humankind to become explicit, to become real in the world. Through the "dust of the ground," God's breath becomes visible, explicit, and real.

The garden itself is both aesthetically beautiful and nourishing. As a "garden," we assume it is a protected place in which God provides what is needed for an abundant and secure life. This idyllic scene is even anchored by the tree of life, a universal image of the source and power of the Life force. However, just as we are settling into this paradise, this "new world," there is an abrupt change, a disturbance, as we hear of the "tree of the knowledge of good and evil." A foreboding ripples through paradise. Evil? Simply the appearance of the knowledge of evil in the midst of this scene of beauty and safety is disruptive. Why does God introduce the inherent tension and conflict of knowledge of good and evil? Does God know what he is doing? Isn't God in control? We could wax philosophical about the nature of reality and the necessity for moral discrimination, and search for other rationalizations, theological or human, to resolve this internal contradiction in God's character. Such questions are not silly because they point out unsupported theological and conventional presuppositions about God that slip into our thinking—that is their only purpose—to undermine taken-for-granted assumptions about the nature of God. Within the psychological approach, there is no God we have to worry about because God is not the problem. Such questions about God are irrelevant when we take the Bible as a soul-document and attempt to psychologically discern the movement of soul, manifesting as cultural-consciousness. This tree, however, does have a fence around it:

> The LORD God took the man and put him in the garden of Eden to till it and keep it. And the LORD God commanded the man, "You may freely eat of every tree of the garden; but of the tree of the knowledge of good and evil you shall not eat, for in the day that you eat of it you shall die." (Gen 2:15–17)

Now a new quality of God's character appears. After his generous gift of creation, providing abundance, fertility, and dominion to humankind, he commands and prohibits, he erects a barrier around one part of creation that is also good for eating and nourishment. This is not merely one of those plants that happens to be poisonous. This one is also good to eat, and here it is in plain sight, but God explicitly states, "Look, but don't touch." Wouldn't it have been easier just not to put it in the garden in the first place? That is the question our adult commonsense mind asks. But, as noted, we are in the realm of myth, dream, and soul, not commonsense; we are, in an uncommonsense, an upside-down, world.

I want to be aware that the first impulse is to approach this story from the standpoint of externality, anthropomorphically (commonsense again). We see an authority figure giving instruction to another adult, who could then consider whether or not to obey. However, this is why we should not think in terms of people but rather the dynamics of soul working on itself, when interpreting such a story. Generally speaking, when a god gives instruction, it personifies deeply held unconscious beliefs that are simply taken for granted as truth. When as young children, we learn the "rules" of the family, we simply absorb them as truth, especially when they are absorbed nonverbally, unavailable for reflection or questioning. The movement of this story is a movement within soul itself, which means that soul has set up a prohibition in relation to itself. God wants to keep his self-image, and thus himself, unconscious of matters that would become complex and troubling. It is God who does not want to know, that is, to become truly conscious of his own good and evil. Or, in other words, soul does not want its already implicit self-contradiction to become explicit. Fortunately for consciousness, God is not a unilateral totalitarian entity in spite of his hopes, and as the Bible story unfolds (looking ahead now), God is gradually initiated into knowledge of his innate self-contradictory nature. This will come fully into view when we read the book of Job. My view is that the serpent is God's own internal, dialectical contradiction: The serpent is another point of view that God is supposedly aware of (it is right there in the garden) and yet, he is trying to suppress it. The text itself reveals the development that will make the contradiction explicit:

> Now the serpent was more crafty than any other wild animal that the LORD God had made. He said to the woman, "Did God say, 'You shall not eat from any tree in the garden'?" The woman said to the serpent, "We may eat of the fruit of the trees in the garden; but God said, 'You shall not eat of the fruit of the tree that is in the middle of the garden, nor shall you touch it, or you shall die.'" But the serpent said to the woman, "You will not die; for God knows that when you eat of it your eyes will be opened, and you will be like God, knowing good and evil." (Gen 3:1–5)

The conventional translation of the Bible uses the singular form "God," or the "Lord God," for the divine entity but really several different gods are at work in the book of Genesis. In the serpent's phrase, "you will be like God, knowing good and evil," the word for God should be "gods," plural and lower case "g." And earlier in Genesis, in the first creation myth, God spoke in the plural, "Let us make humankind in our image, according to our likeness." In the ancient Near East, gods and goddesses were many and fluid, competing, cooperating, and overlapping, and the experience of the Hebrew people was no exception. Our consciousness and civilization, however, have been so thoroughly conditioned to monotheism and the singularity that the word *God* refers to, that God's original polytheistic context has long been lost to us. We can think historically and imagine the polytheistic worldview, but we have to accept that we cannot know what a polytheistic consciousness would have been like from the inside. Still, our modern historical vantage point enables us to see that the Bible is the story of a particular kind of monotheism gradually consolidating itself over about two thousand years, within and over against a general cultural context of polytheism. The God of the Hebrews, Israelites, and Jews (these different names for the same people represent stages in God's historical development) is always in conflict with the other gods and goddesses. For psychology, the conflict between God and gods/goddesses personifies soul's conflict with itself, soul pushing off from itself into a new form of consciousness.

The serpent states openly that God knows good and evil, and this knowledge was kept from humankind in order that they do not become like God. What could "good and evil" refer to if we are to understand this pair of terms as not merely an abstraction, a generalization about the opposition that is necessary for consciousness in the first place? The story can be taken on a human level in terms of a personalistic psychology, which is about an awakening, a coming of age, an emergence of consciousness out of an earlier state of unconsciousness. Such an ego-oriented interpretation views God as representing the tendency to maintain a state of unconscious innocence in paradise, a childlike state in subservience to the higher authority. It is well known that to leave childhood and grow up, we have to disobey our parents, break some family rules, on the way to finding our own moral ground. The serpent, in this case, could be the personification either of God's own self-doubt or ambivalence about this state of affairs, or of the human capacity for disobedience as the first step toward claiming authority. Either way, the serpent represents a conflict at the heart of creation and God's own intentions. Here is one of our first clues that God does not know what he is doing ahead of time. He created order, but did he realize that order triggers disorder? It is helpful to realize that the word *know* in the biblical context does not mean intellectual or theoretical knowledge, but experiential knowing, knowing through experience; *to know* in Hebrew also means to have sexual relations and thus refers to intimate knowledge. It is really God who does not want to *know* the extent of his own good and evil. If his self-image knows both good and evil, then God will have to know it, too. The story says that the gods already know good and evil, but do they know that they know? Until knowledge is reflected, it is not really known, it has not become consciousness. In like manner, we can know something intellectually long before it is integrated as an aspect of our consciousness ("Why do I keep doing the same stupid thing over and over again?!").

As I speak about "God," I want to remember that I am interpreting soul's speech about itself. It is soul that wants to know itself, and at the same time does not want to know itself. That is, soul wants to become real as a new form of consciousness (the monotheistic god) and also does not want to leave behind its current form of consciousness (nature polytheism). In this historical cultural process of change, soul is in conflict with itself. For soul, the ambivalent relationship with "knowing" is at the heart of why God created a self-image in the first place. Soul needs to become known in order to be real. Ideas that are not acted on languish as unrealized possibilities. The ancient god Yahweh was a new idea, a new cultural idea ready to shape a new form of public mind. That idea (God) needed an active partner of his own creation so that this *idea* (God) could become a concrete living reality, and not simply remain an unrealized possibility. Just so, soul, as those cultural ideas that shape consciousness, becomes real through concrete cultural products; soul is the idea that animates culture's creative projects. Monotheism was one of those soul-ideas that indeed shaped an entire civilization.

Another interpretive option for this story may seem farfetched but is worth considering, given the ancient context of consciousness within which the Bible emerged. This is an ancient creation story that already existed in some form within the world of nature polytheism. My view is that soul's new monotheistic impulse repurposed the story as its own myth of origin, and it is not too hard to link "good" with monotheism and "evil" with polytheism (as noted above). Throughout the Tanakh, as we will see, the word *evil*, along with words like *abomination*, are almost exclusively used in relation to polytheism, its symbols and practices, its gods and goddesses. God does not want his new creation, the world of monotheism, to be contaminated with evil polytheism. Of course, the *gods know* "good and evil" because they *are* already many. The monotheistic impulse, however, wants to create monotheistic people out of the already existing polytheistic people because only through people can soul's monotheistic impulse become concretely real. So, God has to put a hedge around his people to protect them from the dangers and evils of polytheism and from being polytheists, which of course they already are, all the way through their being. Polytheism was not an intellectual choice (the way we think religion is a choice today), but rather it was the ontological ground, the very being, of the people of antiquity in general. Almost all of the laws associated with ancient Judaism have to do with separating and protecting the emerging monotheistic impulse from the already existing polytheistic surround. The polytheistic surround is not just "out there" as society: It constitutes the very heart, mind, and body, the very soul, of every group and every person. Everyone is already long soaked in nature-bound polytheism, and so for monotheism to make any headway, it has to take extreme measures. So, whether God knows what is going on or not, there is certainly a profound conflict between God and the serpent, as well as with his self-image, which show us that God is in serious conflict with himself. Perhaps this story was a kind of mythological cautionary tale about how to avoid death, that is, the deathly ways of the other gods and goddesses, and remain true to the monotheistic way of Life that was to be this new God's way.

What does it mean when God becomes a figure tormented by his own incompatible and violent inconsistencies? What is happening to soul, to consciousness itself, when this happens? To *know* good and evil in the biblical sense does not mean some kind of moral superiority above good and evil, but rather to *know* both as one's own tendencies, one's own conflicted truths. As God's self-image, Adam and Eve, representative of humankind, also suffer the terrible conflict of soul's cosmic struggle to move in another direction. In this particular cultural context of the biblical world, soul itself is constituted by the tension between the urge to monotheism and the still very alive and vital natural world of polytheism. Soul is trying to establish a new order of consciousness; the resistance to this new order, while it is very deep, is nothing more than the eternal rhythm of the seasons, the movement of game and the hunt, the coming or not coming of the rain, the fertility of the fields, and the perpetual sacrifices needed to keep everything in its natural flow. Soul, in this original state, is embedded as nature and as the nature gods/goddesses, and yet soul is now, as Yahweh, trying to extract itself, to move itself to a new state as a new form of consciousness.

One detail of this story that has always been a problem for Christianity is the relationship between nakedness and shame, and thus by association, sexuality and procreation. Long before Christianity turned the disobedient act of Adam and Eve into the theological doctrine of *original sin* (which has its own soul significance), this new monotheistic god showed an outsized preoccupation with sexuality and procreation. We can check our modern and Christian-trained morality at the door as we reach back to these early stories of soul speaking about itself long before Christianity emerged. What would make nakedness, sexuality, and procreation (fertility) of concern to soul's monotheistic impulse as it develops in a polytheistic environment? What is the place of sexuality and fertility psychologically (that is, phenomenologically) in that particular soul environment of nature-polytheism? Before monotheism, fertility and sexuality are themselves both primordial soul forces and essential, vital natural powers, which have little to do with the individual person at first. Fertility and sexuality are at the very heart of nature's self-procreating cycle. They express a universal life force, and humankind, whole cultures, serve these natural forces as gods and goddesses. In polytheistic cultures, nature and soul are united, fused together, bonded in ritual, practice, and necessity. Nakedness, sexuality, and fertility have to do with the gods and goddesses of land, rain, and sun, agriculture, the power of storms and magnificent bulls impregnating cows, the irrepressible power of life, the inescapable necessity and pleasure of mating, all fused with the inevitability and numen of soul. Sexuality and fertility, however, are fundamentally nature-bound processes. Yahweh, the new god, will seek to sublate the natural processes of sexuality and fertility into a more spiritual process of conception, giving birth to concepts, words, ideas, thought, and the creation of the written word. This is a transformation from bodies giving birth to other bodies, to mind giving birth to mindedness and the freedom of thought.

The monotheistic impulse is the struggle of soul to extract itself from its fusion with nature. Our modern humanistic consciousness tends to separate the gods and goddesses, even God, from human persons, and turn them into beliefs and constructs that humans "have," or "had," as if they were possessions one could pick up and put down. The gods and goddesses of antiquity were not *contents* of consciousness, but the very *syntax* of consciousness. Consider unlearning your native language. Our language is inextricably intertwined with who we are, how we understand ourselves, invisibly shaping our deep cultural identity. The ancient connection with the gods and goddesses, and with God, was an identity: We cannot separate the gods and goddesses from people, as they constitute together a cultural identity embedded in the natural processes of life. Today it is a different story. The gods and goddesses, even God to a great extent, are only names in history books; their visceral and concrete reality has disappeared because the cultures and societies that made their truth real, that were the context of their identity, have disappeared.

The new god of our Genesis creation myth is clearly not pleased that the cat is out of the bag, that the knowledge of good and evil has escaped its fenced-in area. If anything has died, in terms of the threat that death follows knowing, it is God's own innocent hope that simply declaring the "knowledge of good and evil" off limits would take care of matters and protect God from his own internal polytheistic contradictions, his own plurality. God is still *gods*. The reaction of God to the serpent's and Adam and Eve's "disobedience" is extreme. The terrible curse he lays on them echoes to this day down through two thousand years of Judeo-Christian Western culture. God in this instance is hardly thoughtful or reasonable. He does not discuss this matter nor show any restraint. In the words of Miles, it is "an explosion of fury," a ruthless "vindictive reaction," of "brutal impatience":[13]

> YHWH, God, said to the snake:
> Because you have done this,
>   damned be you from all the animals and from all the living-
>   things of the field;
>   upon your belly shall you walk and dust shall you eat, all the days
>   of your life.
>   I put enmity between you and the woman, between your seed
>   and her seed:
>   they will bruise you on the head, you will bruise them in the
>   heel.
> To the woman he said:
>   I will multiply, multiply your pain (from) your pregnancy,
>   with pains shall you bear children.
>   Toward your husband will be your lust yet he will rule over you.
> To Adam he said:
>   Because you have hearkened to the voice of your wife
>   and have eaten from the tree about which I commanded you,
>   saying:
>   You are not to eat from it!
>   Damned be the soil on your account,

13. Miles, *God*, 32–38.

God's Autopsy and the Living Truth of Soul

with painstaking-labor shall you eat from it, all the days of your
life.
Thorn and sting-shrub let it spring up for you,
when you (seek to) eat the plants of the field!
By the sweat of your brow shall you eat bread,
until you return to the soil,
for from it you were taken.
For you are dust, and to dust shall you return.[14]

The curse is the first glimpse, right at the beginning of the biblical version of soul's autobiography, of just how intolerant this god is, and will be, of disobedience. Soul, in the form of God here in the Tanakh, will have a policy of zero tolerance. Capital punishment will be the consequence when the people break the commandment which demands they stay true to the new monotheistic god and his claim that they too must become monotheistic in their essence. The curse reveals just how unsettled and volatile God is in his new identity, and how dire is the threat of incomplete mirroring by his self-image. Viewing this story through psychology with soul, God's emotional volatility and the struggle with the disobedience of his self-image (in God's eyes, disobedience is humankind's trademark) all reflect the struggle of soul to move to a new form of consciousness.

Right after the curse, and before God throws them out of the garden, God displays a stunning moment of tenderness: "The Lord God made garments of skins for the man and for his wife, and clothed them" (Gen 3:21). Here God appears intimate and literally touching as he brings them garments. This parental touch, while caring, is also controlling in that God is in charge of what will be worn. The garments are symbolic of God's ideas, his laws and commandments, about how to live as a monotheist. God will teach his creatures thoroughly how to be *his* people. He wants his people to be singular (not poly) throughout their being in order to fulfill his own longing to be singular throughout. This is only the beginning of the journey, however, and God is a mass, even a mess, of conflicting desires and needs. He is the personification of a new soul-desire in conflict with itself, but its central defining vision is looking forward toward a new consciousness that has aspirations that point away from the original natural world where soul first found itself. Soul is preparing to leave its first home.

---

14. Fox, *Five Books*, Gen 3:14–19.

Chapter 3

Abram: Archaic Soul Leaves Home
Consciousness Creates Itself

> In a kind of self-bootstrapping, the soul first made itself through killing, it *killed itself into being,* and this is why I consider sacrificial killings as the primordial soul-making. With great effort the soul liberated itself, *within* its immersion in the merely-biological, *from* this immersion—from an immersion, however, that continues to prevail even after it has been overcome.[1]

> The terrific quality is due to the fact that the event of consciousness is in fact something outrageous, because it bursts, invades frighteningly, into ordinary natural life.[2]

THE STORY OF ABRAM/ABRAHAM and his immediate descendants occupies 80 percent of the book of Genesis, chapters 12–50. On its face, it is a complicated narrative, beginning with Yahweh's command that Abram pick up his family and move from his ancestral home to a new land that god will designate. There follows Yahweh's repeated but long-unfulfilled promise to give Abram and Sarai a son. And finally, we will confront the puzzling account of Yahweh/El's directive that Abraham must sacrifice that son, Isaac.

Even if these stories were historical, and they are not, and even if Abraham had been an actual person, and he was not,[3] my focus is as always concerned with com-

---

1. Giegerich, "Killings," 205.
2. Giegerich, "Killings," 227.
3. Traditional biblical scholarship had long accepted the so-called historical narratives in Genesis at face value. More recent appraisals over the last decades have led to the realization that there is no real history nor historical persons in these texts. These ancient stories are now considered constructs of collective memory, idealized tales about the origins of the identity of a people that derive from a particular relationship with a particular god (Levenson, *Inheriting Abraham*, 1–17). Regarding the

pletely different categories (consciousness and soul vs. history and human persons) informed by the question: What is soul doing to itself? In this regard, Abram/Abraham's story reads as an early stage of soul's creating itself, focusing on the process of soul being at home and leaving home. My approach to this movement of soul is first to examine the nature of symbol as an example of soul's presencing. Clues for how soul develops itself come from Jung's description of the nature of a symbol.

A symbol is a living process with its own inner logic; it is soul's presence. Just like myths, fairy tales, and dreams, a symbol is soul's speech about itself. For Jung, a symbol is a psychic reality that both lives and dies:

> So long as a symbol is a living thing, it is an expression for something that cannot be characterized in any other or better way. The symbol is alive only so long as it is pregnant with meaning. But once its meaning has been born out of it, once that expression is found which formulates the thing sought, expected, or divined even better than the hitherto accepted symbol, then the symbol is *dead*, i.e., it possesses only an historical significance.
>
> A symbol really lives only when it is the best and highest expression for something divined but not yet known to the observer. It then compels his unconscious participation and has a life-giving and life-enhancing effect.
>
> The living symbol formulates an essential unconscious factor, and the more widespread this factor is, the more general is the effect of the symbol, for it touches a corresponding chord in every psyche.[4]

The essence of a symbol is not fixed. It is historical; it lives in time and is not eternal. Symbols are born, live, and die. When a symbol is born and alive, soul is at home in the symbol, giving the symbol its emotional charge, its claim on us, its compelling full-of-meaning presence—a symbol is life-giving and life-enhancing. The symbol, *pregnant* with meaning, is the potential of a newly emergent consciousness. Soul's movement appears as symbol, intent to realize something. Most often symbols, especially religious symbols, are thought of as timeless and constant, representative of eternal truths. However, Jung's view sees them as transitional, mediating and midwifing a movement from one status of consciousness to another. Once the new consciousness realizes itself, once it is born, the symbol "dies" because soul has left that home. The meaning of the symbol then takes on a new form. The manifestation of the symbol becomes like a shed snakeskin or dried husk—empty of its former life.

---

role of collective memory in constructing ancient Israel's self-understanding, see Smith, *Memoirs of God*. For my psychological perspective, what seem to be historical narratives in the Bible are really origin myths, constructed by soul, dream-tales, as it were, depicting the developmental history of the *form* of consciousness.

4. Jung, *Psychological Types*, ¶ 816, 819, 820.

The symbol dies, loses its compelling charge, when soul leaves that particular home and moves on—and by soul, I mean its quality as consciousness. A symbol represents a certain quality and status, or stage, of consciousness. Here a personal example may help us feel our way into this soul process. The moment of sunrise once held symbolic power for me. I made an effort to rise before dawn and go to a favorite lookout to watch the sun rise. I simply had to seek out and experience the quality of that moment when the sun peeked over the horizon. At some point, I dreamt that I went to see the sunrise and found that the sun was already high in the sky; I had missed the sunrise. The dream suggested that the meaning of the sunrise had moved on to a new position (higher in the sky), and the actual moment of sunrise was no longer as magical. The strong pull to witness the actual sunrise faded. The quality of consciousness that the sunrise represented had become a quality and function of my everyday consciousness. The meaning of the sunrise had become the syntax of my consciousness, and the sunrise as a living symbol had served its purpose. Soul had left its home as the magical moment of sunrise and was now in a sublated form as a quality of ordinary daytime consciousness.

When soul leaves home in this sense, it is a logical event, that is, an event of soul's logos, an event of consciousness. A personal symbol might last an entire lifetime, but more often, it is alive during a period of development. Once the symbol has served the purpose of that development, if it was an actual object, we might notice it gathering dust, and then we move it from its place of honor on a personal altar to a drawer or storage box. If it was a person who fascinated us for a while and who has come to be seen as an ordinary person, the symbol's meaning has moved on, and what had been a living symbol is now a historical marker no longer alive, no longer charged. The living symbol is the outer manifestation of a potential of consciousness, and as such, it has a fascinating power and a magical aura that draws us to it because it is our own potential, or, not to speak so personalistically, it is soul's own potential, that wants to become real as the form of consciousness, a quality of day-to-day life. We are indeed where soul (i.e., consciousness) happens, but we, our personal awareness, is not what consciousness has in mind. Soul is an autonomous intent that moves through humankind like waves move through water. It looks like the water is moving, but it is actually the energy-impulse that moves. *Homo sapiens* is the medium, so to speak, in which soul (the historical evolution of *meaning*) moves.

Now let's turn to the civilization-shaping cultural historical symbol I am most concerned with at the early stage of soul's development. That symbol is God, the god of the Judeo-Christian Western tradition. The historical overview of the changing form of the *I Am* has shown us one way in which the cultural symbol of God has lived and died, birthing new forms of itself, over a few thousand years. The life and death of this central symbol has transformed the syntax of our cultural consciousness. Now I will look for each historical stage of consciousness, and its preparation for the next stage, in the biblical story of God and his people, and then, after God as symbol has died, in readings of selected cultural expressions of modernity. The living symbol is a manifestation of soul's internal telos, and that urge wants to move from implicit to explicit, from pregnancy to birth, from unconscious to conscious. The symbol is in effect a future possibility that moves soul forward. But, from the point of view of the current status of consciousness, the future "not yet" possibility of consciousness is an impossibility. The current state of consciousness cannot envision its next step because the logic of a particular form of consciousness is, by definition, trapped in its own logic. This is why the next stage appears first as a compelling symbol. The living symbol provides the energy that will move what appears to be impossible to become possible, for without the attracting power of the symbol, the present state of consciousness would not even try to move forward. The symbol's fascinating lure embodies soul's own future and provides the motive power to move out of the *status quo*, move away from what has already been achieved, and reach toward a new status of consciousness, something that seems impossible, and both promising and frightening. This is true for both individuals and cultures or societies.

On a personal level, a seemingly unreachable goal to which we are nevertheless ineluctably drawn is such a symbol, prodding us forward. On a cultural level, an entire society will pour enormous resources into a project without fully understanding why it is simply necessary to do so, such as building the cathedrals in medieval Europe and the pyramids in ancient Egypt, or in our modern world, putting a man on the moon, or building a world wide web of software connected through computers and smart phones. This is the work of soul. The process of the symbol's living and dying, its being at home and leaving home, is not something that human persons do or make happen. This is soul's process that happens to us and around us, and not everyone enjoys it. Throughout all major historical and cultural periods of change and upheaval, many are brought along and many are left behind. Soul's changes bring the new and entail suffering. The symbol's transformation, on the personal or cultural level, is soul pushing off from itself in order to become a new form of consciousness.

The Command to Leave Home

The relationship of Abraham and Yahweh once constituted a living cultural symbol that was moving in a new direction. The two are a unity that reflects the process of consciousness generating itself at a time in the ancient past. This is the story of an archaic form of consciousness *leaving home* and self-generating a new form of consciousness. The approximate time frame for this "event" is three thousand years ago, at least as far as the story represents itself within a historical sense of time that is still quite mythical. The writing down and development of the story occurred much later.

In reading the Bible as a dream, as soul's speech about itself, the focus is on how the biblical narrative personifies the transformations of the background form of consciousness (the logical form of consciousness), the movement from polytheism to monotheism, from natural sensual *image* (the gods and goddesses of nature symbolized in metal, stone, and wood) to abstract spiritualized *idea* (writing) (monolatry prohibits images of the deity and focuses on sacred texts/the written word). This shift in how consciousness will constitute itself is tectonic in scale. It was an enormous rift in a natural world that had existed for tens of thousands of years.

At the time—and the matter of "the time" is complex—one minor god, Yahweh, among many (El, Baal, Asherah, Astarte, to name a few) took hold of an anonymous, most likely Canaanite tribal group (loosely organized under the name Hebrew) in the ancient Near East and demanded that they leave their common ancestral home. The biblical narrative tells the story of "leaving home" in terms of geographical relocation, but for the psychological perspective, "leaving home" represents a change in the logical form of consciousness, a change in the syntactical status of consciousness. The *land* is the home of the god or goddess, and to leave the land is to leave behind that god and the consciousness that god represents.

With regard to the "time" of these events, there are three time frames to keep in mind, both ancient and modern: (1) the purported historical time of Abraham; (2) the time when the story of Abraham was written and revised; and (3) today. The purported time of Abram, what is known as the *patriarchal* or the *premonarchic* tribal period, is conventionally dated at approximately 1300–1000 BCE. The writing of these stories, however, took place over several hundred years; the dates are debated, perhaps the eighth through fifth centuries BCE. Thus, the writing of these stories (and they are stories, not records of events) took place hundreds of years after the so-called events. The scholarly consensus today is that "what seems at the beginning to look like history ends up looking like a mixture of historical facts with cultural echoes and memories from different periods."[5] What we think of as history—of any kind, ancient and modern, biography and autobiography—is written in hindsight, created from the distance of the present looking back on the past. Historical writings are in fact distant reflections that bring organization, meaning, and purpose into the narrative from the point of view of the time when the writing takes place. Historiography and biography create a narrative structure in hindsight for events, which at the time they were happening did not have a narrative form.

Life happens spontaneously, and the writing of history produces history by organizing it into a meaningful narrative. Speaking broadly, this is how soul functions: Soul is culture reflecting on itself historically, that is, after the fact, creating meaning through a narrative form. The reflection, or interpretation, that I am engaged in is a thoroughly contemporary re-reading of an ancient story, the Bible, including the implications of this reading for a new interpretation of modernity. At the various times of its writing, the Bible itself was a contemporary rereading and reinterpretation of older stories, shaping themselves in the light of a new idea. In the Bible's case, the new idea was emergent monotheism. For the psychological reading, the idea of *consciousness*—specifically, the significance of the evolution of the syntax of consciousness, the

---

5. Smith, *Memoirs of God*, 6.

logical form of consciousness—is at the heart of these stories. Rather than a history of social and political events, I am interested in the history of an idea, the idea of monotheism read psychologically as the history of soul's self-transformations. I want to be clear, though, that the idea of monotheism was not simply an intellectual idea promulgated by some people who might have wanted power over other people (as the view from externality is sometimes put forward). The *idea* of monotheism created itself as the truth and reality of Yahweh, a living presence, which, in this interpretation, was *the living idea* as soul's presencing.

Although I have stated that a psychological reading is not concerned with actual historical events or people, a psychological reading is thoroughly imbued with a historical consciousness because soul imagines and interprets itself historically. Modern consciousness itself is essentially historical in its own self-understanding, and modern soul, as I have outlined it, imagines itself historically in terms of radically different and changing forms of consciousness. Recognizing that contemporary consciousness is radically different from the consciousness of ancient man enables us to enter into the mind of Abraham, that is, "Abraham" as an exemplar of public mind (i.e., soul) at that stage of its development. Abraham personifies a form of ancient Mind, the syntax of that consciousness, undergoing a transformation—Abraham represents the status of archaic soul and the process of archaic soul leaving home.

Soul Pushes Off from Itself

The story of Abraham begins abruptly. At the beginning, Abraham is not yet Abraham, but simply Abram. Later, the god changes Abram's name, which also reflects the deeper change in soul I am tracing. I will explore the name change later in its narrative context. Abram's story begins with a command from a nonhuman source:

> Now the LORD said to Abram, "Go from your country and your kindred and
> your father's house to the land that I will show you." (Gen 12:1)

The idea to leave home does not come from Abram; it is not his personal idea, but the Lord's idea. In the mythological worldview, the motive power for any important decision is always a god or goddess. In antiquity, land and territory are not merely measured acreage. Land is the basis of life, crops, animals, communities, and it is the provenance of a god and/or goddess. In terms of the logical form of consciousness of antiquity, land and deity are fused as one. The land *is* a god or a goddess.[6] When Abram is told to leave his country, his kindred, and his father's house, it means leaving the gods of his ancestors, his family gods. Here I want to strongly emphasize

---

6. This connection is particularly important in shedding psychological light on the invasion and conquering of the so-called promised land, the land Yahweh promised to the Hebrew people after their liberation from Egypt. For my psychological perspective, Yahweh's eradication of indigenous gods and goddesses, and the occupation and possession of a land for himself, symbolizes a transition of the logical form of consciousness, soul's self-negation for a new status.

that the fusion and unity of land and god/goddess constituted the general consciousness, and so, the command to leave home is an ancient god's command to himself, to leave his home, his original context, which would be the general cultural world of the many gods and goddesses. The Lord addressing Abram represents an emergent monotheistic consciousness pushing off from its current form as polytheistic consciousness. For some reason, soul is pushing off against itself, against being embedded in a polytheistic natural world, toward something new, which is put in terms of the promise to Abram of "the land I will show you." The "new land" will be a new god. Yahweh himself, originally a nature god, a Storm and Bull god, does not want to share the land any longer with other gods and goddesses. He wants his own place, his own land, in order to fulfill his singular purpose, which will be radically different from the prevailing processes of nature. Yahweh is undergoing an internal transformation that is separating him from himself. Historically, this will take centuries, but this is the aim.

Abram appears to obey this god's command easily and without question. The story at this point gives no hint of any struggle within Abram. According to the biblical story, this sort of movement had already happened in Abram's life. His father, Terah, "took his son Abram and his grandson Lot son of Haran, and his daughter-in-law Sarai, his son Abram's wife, and they went out together from Ur of the Chaldeans to go into the land of Canaan; but when they came to Haran, they settled there" (Gen 11:31). Although soul's move is not a geographical move, a map of that time tells us something about soul's context and soul's state of mind (as it were).

Ur was the capital city of a southern Mesopotamian empire, where today we find Iraq and its eastern border with Iran (Persia). Ur was a thriving, cultured, wealthy city, a major trading center on the southern end of the Euphrates River. Full of large lavish buildings and its own ziggurat (pyramidal temple) dedicated to the city's deity, Nanna, a moon god. The large temple complex was both a city administrative center and a shrine to the moon god. This was clearly a civilized, cultured, and polytheistic context for the origin of this particular Hebrew clan. The ancestral land and the ancestral gods are identical. The geography is interesting because it puts some of the actual details in perspective. From Ur to Canaan (modern-day Palestine and Israel), where Abram's father, Terah, was originally headed, is about six hundred miles west. From Ur to Haran, where Terah ended up, is about six hundred miles north, along the Euphrates River, and from Haran, Canaan is about four hundred miles south. We cannot know why Terah went north instead of directly to his goal, but it would certainly have been easier to travel along a river when immediately west of Ur is the Arabian desert.[7]

There is not a word of what motivated Terah to take such a journey. How long would such a journey take, moving a clan with all its possessions? After his father

---

7. Although this speculation about distances and directions is admittedly from the point of view of externality, as if such a journey actually happened, and has little relevance for the soul story I am following, it nevertheless reminds us that soul always thinks its own thoughts in the context of the real, our actual world. This is not a myth that takes place in an imagined world of gods or heroes, but occurs right here on earth.

dies, Abram hears the command of the Yahweh god to make his move and perhaps complete the interrupted journey to Canaan, which is Yahweh's goal. The modern historical explanation of these stories speaks in terms of migration and population movements from Mesopotamia into Canaan during the second millennium BCE. But the story we are reading is soul's story, soul personified as Yahweh-Abram, remembering that Abram is the "likeness," the "self-image" of Yahweh. And, the question about motivation remains, especially if it is not about what motivates a human person to take such a journey. What did this god at that time really want?

I do not want to get confused by the historical fact that this particular Canaanite-Hebrew tribe was somewhat nomadic, lived in tents, and took part in real migrations. The story of their geographical movement, looked at psychologically, is not just another horizontal move of the tent, not a geographical relocation, but a real rupture, a radical leave-taking from a particular tribal/cultural frame of mind. Soul is undergoing a dislocation, a vertical and logical transformation of consciousness. It was not simply an individual's mind that changed, but a cultural-Mind that was changing itself. This was a soul change, or a change on the logical or archetypal level of identity. Abram's leaving home symbolizes a soul move on a deeper logical, or psychological, level. Soul is actually taking leave of itself, pushing off from itself, for a new idea that is dimly thought and not yet known. As the matrix of living ideas that constitute societal identities, that generate themselves within the creative, fertile, and conflicting mix of existing concepts, soul is experiencing the birth of a new concept ("leave home"), a rupture with prevailing concepts. I am not concerned here with any actual migratory move on the part of someone named Abram, whether such a move occurred or not, but with the biblical narrative of that move. The narrative (Bible) is where soul's move is recorded. Again, not a horizontal or geographical move, but a historical vertical psychological move.

Home as Original, Fundamental (Unconscious) Self-Containment

The idea of home is complex and paradoxical. Home is that place of which we say "There is no place like home" and "Home is where the heart is." The *homeland* is our origin and identity. Home in general is usually associated with safety and security. But, home is also that place, especially that state of mind, we must leave if we are to grow up and become adults in our own right. Birds are pushed out of the nest, and the mare kicks the foal away from her teat. We must leave our original home if we are to make our way in the world and create our own home. The womb itself is an apt image of our original biological home that must be left if life is to continue. Leaving the womb through birth is a profound change in that we leave a blind, dark, and watery world for a sighted, light-filled, airy world. This involves a radical transformation of the form of life, which obviously is not under our direction. Literal birth happens to us, against our will so to speak; we do not choose to be born, but we also do not *not* choose; we do not choose at all one way or the other, we are simply born. Birth itself chooses to birth. The autonomy of the biological birth process mirrors the character of soul. When soul gives birth to itself in terms of leaving one cultural-Mind form behind in order to create a new cultural-Mind form, we are taken along for the ride. We do not choose the historical time when we are born; it happens to us whether we like it or not. God's command to Abram to leave home for a new unknown home is this very process in action on the cultural, or soul, level. The god's command to Abram is the representation, or personification, of soul's action, soul pushing off from itself, leaving the father-land, the *Abram* identity, for the land that will become *Abraham's* land; leaving the father-gods for the new single, One Abraham-God. To recall Jung's formulation, with Abram/Abraham, we witness the death of one symbol (polytheism) and the birth of a new symbol (monotheism): Soul leaves home.

Again, in general, we think of home in terms of comfort, security, and a sense of belonging. And, feeling "at home" in relation to ourselves often indicates the sense of living congruently with our deepest truth or authentic self. The idea of home has dual dimensions. On the personal level, in our personal lives, we must literally leave one home in order to seek and create our own home. We leave our parents' home, where we have been unconsciously contained, where everything was done for us, in order to make a home for ourselves, where we become responsible for our well-being.

Leaving home and coming home are two movements that depict an evolutionary direction. The definition of home, the meaning of home, is psychologically ambiguous and unstable. Sometimes circumstances force us to leave home if the inner natural movement of life is not strong enough. The pull to stay in the nest, to stay attached to the teat, is strong. This is why on the soul level, the level of society and culture, the shift from one soul-form of culture to another is often violent and cruel. It explains why the God of the Tanakh gives no thought to comfort, to family ties, to biological needs, to the call of other gods and goddesses; it is why disobedience to the demands of this God is a capital offence, punished by death. This too is symbolic to the extent that there is no (human) life without soul. With Abram, the way of life associated with soul (not biology) is undergoing a major revolution.

The first home is a fundamental unconsciousness that cannot be known or recognized until it is left. Only after leaving home are we able to look back and reflect on where we were. The original home becomes a construction of memory and reflection after it has been left behind. While we are fully contained within that original home—whether it is the womb, the parent's home, the tribe, the myth, the logical form of consciousness of an entire culture or civilization—we are unconscious of it. We exist fully embedded in it with no differentiation. Our being, our sense of self, is fully identified with "home"; we *are* that home, and it is our basic identity. On the level of individual psychology, such an unconscious state and lack of differentiation is an *ego-syntonic* condition. In Jung's thought, the phrase *participation mystique* (borrowed from the philosopher Lévy-Bruhl) describes a condition of blurred boundaries and shared identity between persons, or between persons and objects, or ideas. Lévy-Bruhl first applied this idea to so-called "primitive" mentality, or ancient peoples, but we know today that no one is exempt from the condition of *participation mystique* in its more general sense. For psychology, psychology as "soul's logos," the word *soul* describes our unconscious identification with the fundamental ideas, assumptions, and presuppositions of our form of consciousness, whether of the family, society, nation, race, ethnicity, or religion, but most especially of the culture at large. The idea of soul is a comprehensive term that refers to the form of consciousness that defines our historical time, the larger syntax of consciousness that encompasses all the other smaller and local forms. None of us are exempt from being shaped in our most fundamental sense of self by soul, and none of us are exempt from the historical changes that soul undergoes—none of us are exempt from history.

Today we tell our origin story in terms of scientific cosmology and biological evolution. For us, our original home was nature, but for us nature is a scientific object, not a soul-infused abode of the gods and goddesses. Our view is that biological life evolved from simple organic forms to highly complex forms. On the level of culture, we also see an evolution from smaller social forms of extended family tribes to highly complex civilizations. The development of the individual also proceeds from fairly simple forms of personal consciousness to increasingly complex forms of consciousness, or from the innocent and simple consciousness of childhood to the conflicted, confused, and complex consciousness of adulthood. Adult consciousness, by definition, is burdened by a more comprehensive awareness and experience of the problems of life, while childhood consciousness should not be so burdened. We proceed along stages or levels of unconsciousness, one stage of unconsciousness giving way to another stage of unconsciousness that is a little deeper or broader so as to include the earlier, but still, in its own fundamental assumptions and structure, a state of unconsciousness from which we can never escape. We will always be unconscious of our own status of consciousness because consciousness can only reflect on itself, see itself, in hindsight, historically. This contemporary realization of historical stages of consciousness is itself a new status of consciousness because consciousness can now at least know this much about itself. From the point of view of modern soul, soul is always leaving home, arriving at a new home, and leaving again.

Psychologically, polytheism was the original *logical home* of the Hebrew people. They were at home in that form of soul. Polytheism represented the eternal round of nature, birth and death, planting and harvest. Nature was Fate, personified by the gods and goddesses, and accepted as such. Polytheism, in this psychological history of consciousness, was an early form of the syntax of consciousness. The syntax of consciousness is what gives us our sense of the real; it is the ground of reality that we simply take for granted. Abram gives us a glimpse of life embedded in psychological nature, a life dominated by nature gods and goddesses and regular cultic ritual practices. Nature was psychological when it was inherently meaningful as soul-infused in contrast to our view of nature as inert raw materials for industrial production. The conflict at the heart of Abram's story is that Abram and his god reveal soul beginning to restrain and focus the prodigal forces of nature, particularly the natural forces of sexuality and reproduction, in its move toward monotheism and away from nature. The cost of monotheism was high, however, requiring both genocide and poly-deicide. Not only people were killed and displaced, but all the other gods and goddesses were killed too, as we will see in future chapters. Yahweh became a warrior god who shed blood freely for his own purposes. Violence was a vital force in the development of monotheism. Empirical history is riddled with violence, but I am writing a history of consciousness, the history of mind's foundation, its logical form. Violence and killing in the biblical dream portray the enormous and fierce energy required to change consciousness. The violence is real, but it is the violence of soul acting on itself. This is not an indictment of Yahweh or monotheism, nor a critique of violence. Moral judgments have their place, but they are the point of view of externality and belong in a different work. Like astronomers observing exploding stars, I am observing the phenomenology of soul, and I stand in wonder at its dynamism, its inevitability, and its living truth. From the point of view of personal human feeling, soul is as distant and cold and impersonal as those exploding stars and evolving galaxies.

Soul's First Logical Home Is Nature

The entire Bible presupposes and pushes off from the prevailing polytheistic myth-ritual cultures of the ancient Near East. For these cultures, nature was alive with soul. Bulls, groves of trees, rivers, springs, and hillsides were the living presence of gods and goddesses. For us today, the experience of nature as intelligently alive is less than a vague memory. However, there are still echoes of this old reality, such as when a contemporary northern California Native American tribe remembers that it was Salmon who gave them the power of speech. The Winnemem Wintu Tribe, celebrating the autumn return of the salmon at a spot where mountain rivers enter the Pacific Ocean, knows that their tribal existence is identified with the salmon:

> "The salmon are intricately tied to our culture," he said. "We are to them as they are to us. In our creation story, we were brought out of a sacred spring on Mount Shasta by the creator, but we could not speak. The Salmon gave us their power of speech as long as we promised we would always speak for them."[8]

Within that indigenous context, "the salmon" are "Salmon," a people in their own right, who give the power of speech to the human creatures. The Salmon people symbolize

---

8. "Returning salmon welcomed in Native American ceremony in Glen Cove," *Vallejo Times Herald*, September 17, 2016. Gary Mulcahy, of the Winnemem Wintu Tribe, explained that the size of salmon populations today in the McCloud River are only one percent of what they were in the 1800s when his ancestors tended to the river.

a soul-infused nature, an animated, intelligent, and purposeful nature. Though this soul-nature has died for us, its memory lives in the Bible. Abram represents a mythological ritualistic people, clearly premonotheistic, and essentially preliterate, for whom trees and stones are local theophanies:

> So, Abram went, as the LORD had told him . . . When they had come to the land of Canaan, Abram passed through the land to the place of Shechem, to the oak of Moreh. At that time, the Canaanites were in the land. Then the LORD appeared to Abram, and said, "To your offspring I will give this land." So, he built there an altar to the LORD, who had appeared to him. (Gen 12:4, 5b–7)

Shechem was a thriving Canaanite city during the Stone Age, the second millennium BCE, the empirical time in which Abram's mythical emigration is situated. These stories, written hundreds of years after the so-called events are said to have happened, represent the retrojection of the monotheistic impulse into the past, a mythological and legendary past. The literary memory is the monotheistic impulse creating its own origin. Although Abram represents the original Canaanite identity of the Hebrew people, the monotheistic impulse presents itself as coming in from the outside. The oak of Moreh, which means "oracle giver," or Diviners' Oak, was a known sacred tree, referred to several times in the Bible.[9] The tree marks a well-known nature sanctuary, featuring the numinous presence most likely of a goddess, a place of ritual and sacrifice. The altar that Abram builds would be stones set up as pillars, with some kind of platform for sacrifice; in fact, the more accurate translation of the Hebrew word for *altar* is "slaughter-site."[10] Stones mark the living presence of a divine appearance, and are themselves sentient, as in the following:

> Joshua wrote these words in the book of the law of God; and he took a large stone, and set it up there under the oak in the sanctuary of the LORD. Joshua said to all the people, "See, this stone shall be a witness against us; for it has heard all the words of the LORD that he spoke to us; therefore it shall be a witness against you, if you deal falsely with your God." (Josh 24:26–27)

The stone is an "intelligent" presence, soul-infused, that hears, remembers, and witnesses what the people say and binds them to their commitment. The people know that the stone is their witness because the ancient logical form of consciousness linked

---

9. "So they gave to Jacob all the foreign gods that they had, and the rings that were in their ears; and Jacob hid them under the oak that was near Shechem" (Gen 35:4). "As you know, they are beyond the Jordan, some distance to the west, in the land of the Canaanites who live in the Arabah, opposite Gilgal, beside the oak of Moreh" (Deut 11:30). "So Joshua made a covenant with the people that day, and made statutes and ordinances for them at Shechem. Joshua wrote these words in the book of the law of God; and he took a large stone, and set it up there under the oak in the sanctuary of the Lord" (Josh 24:25–26). "Gaal spoke again and said, 'Look, people are coming down from Tabbur-erez, and one company is coming from the direction of Elon-meonenim'" (Judg 9:37) (The location is Shechem, and Elon-meonenim means Diviners' Oak.)

10. Fox, *Five Books*, Gen 12:7.

the aliveness of the stone and the people in a shared intelligible world. Sacred groves and hillsides, stones, trees, pillars, and carved symbols were common and ever present. Soul is what unconsciously orients us to the world in a certain way, and it also *is* our world (remembering the analogy of the water fish swim in). In antiquity, nature was alive and knowing, in the way that people knew they were known by the gods/goddesses. For the world of archaic soul, the reality and truth of soul were experienced as an external other, as nature and the nature gods and goddesses. The many god and goddess presences were the normative cultural truths that guided all aspects of life throughout all the major civilizations of the ancient Near East. Nature as a living presence was the first home of soul, as it appeared to human awareness as if "out there." And the living presence of nature made a compelling claim on human persons and groups. The Salmon extract a promise for the sake of speech, and the stones, as witnesses, extract commitment and accountability. But, in our story, the Yahweh-Abram pair represent an anomaly as monotheism begins its gradual emergence to supplant and replace the widespread and vibrant nature-based poly-deistic truths. The Yahweh-Abram pair is the new idea that guides the small tribal group, which itself is the literary personification of the emergent new form of soul. A new cultural mindset, a new logical form of consciousness, a new form of soul, is making itself known, by way of the literary creation known as the book of Genesis.

Consciousness Changes Its Form

The gods and goddesses of polytheism were the already existing concepts and living ideas that constituted the broader cultural context, the soul-context, as which Abram already existed. The name *Abram* personified the identity and cultural context of polytheism, of that status of soul fused with nature, the natural world, the forces and cycles of natural life. The living idea of monotheism is not yet real, but it makes its initial appearance here in God's imperative, "Go from your country." With this command, the monotheistic impulse is on the move toward becoming an existing concept named Yahweh, as Hebrew and Israelite cultural identity begins to shape itself. This is not an ordinary move in the realm of empirical positivity, like a sight-seeing trip during which nothing fundamental changes. Abram's move depicts a change in the background form of consciousness, which, until that move happens, remains taken for granted and unconscious. Abram's move represents a differentiation between the existing background (logical) form of consciousness and a new logical form that is beginning to emerge. And, it is not just Abram who is leaving, but the Yahweh-Abram identity that is taking leave of itself, its archaic form of nature-rooted consciousness, and becoming something new and at that time unheard of.

In the ancient world, gods and goddesses were identified with nature and natural forces; each place, land, and town or city had its god or goddess. The name of the god or goddess was not a label attached to a physical place; that would be our modern rational explanation. The god or goddess *was* the land's living presence: Land and god/goddess were a natural unity, known intuitively and lived spontaneously, and certainly not thought about consciously. Certain natural features and natural events, imbued with god and goddess power, would be marked as such with stones, carvings, and altars, and because the gods and goddesses made claims and demands as soul's presence, these functioned as places of worship, sacrifice, and ritual. Deity was anchored to place. The god who comes and says, "Get up and move to an unknown land," is initiating something different and contrary to what exists. Abram is told to go, and he goes. In this we also recognize an idealized type and not a real person who would naturally have resistance to such an idea.

The fact that a god makes the decision to leave home is typical of the logical form of consciousness of antiquity, of the ancient mind. Soul, in its self-representation in ancient myth, presents itself as a god in relation to human persons and societies, and the implicit and taken-for-granted authority of soul's intent or desire is located in the figure of the god. For the human person in ancient society, the authoritative nature of the edicts and commands of the god were self-evident. That's why no true questions about the god's motives or aims are ever raised. Only modern consciousness can raise the questions, "Who gave you all the power?" and "Why are you always right?" The status of consciousness for which the Bible is evidence could not even entertain such questions. With regard to the ancient world's gods, might was right. Although, for me, as a modern person, to use the phrase "might is right" implies a moral judgment, which belongs to the modern mind and not the ancient mind. The gods were not dictators sitting over and above human subjects. They were the form of mind itself, and their power, *as nature*, was self-evident. Today, we do not make moral judgments about the impersonal power of nature because we know, with scientific certitude, that the laws of nature are impersonal. The gods had the same taken-for-granted neutral (amoral) status in antiquity that nature has for us. The gods were simply accepted as the way things were, divine Fate.

The even more fundamental question, "Does God exist?" was an impossibility for biblical consciousness, ancient consciousness. It is interesting to note that in the Bible, some people negotiate with God in an attempt to temper God's hot-headed destructive impulse. Abraham talks God down from killing everyone in Sodom and Gomorrah (but that does not last long, and the cities are destroyed anyway). Moses talks God out of destroying all the people he brought out of Egypt because of their stiff-necked and brazen rebellion in the golden calf incident (but, mightily incensed himself, Moses goes on a murderous rampage and with his warriors kills three thousand Hebrews).[11] These amount to ethical interventions and do not question the fundamental authority of God and certainly not the existence of God. The fact that there

---

11. Abraham negotiates with God: Gen 18:22–33; God destroys Sodom and Gomorrah: Gen 19:24–25. Moses negotiates with God: Exod 32:7–14; Moses has three thousand killed: Exod 32:19–29. I will examine the golden calf incident in detail in chapter 4.

is a conversation with God, even though an argument, simply assumes the reality of God. The incontrovertible authority and reality of the god remains in place.

In general, humankind has always experienced soul as external to itself, when in fact, from the psychological perspective, soul is consciousness, but in its ancient form as a god, is a consciousness in the status of not-yet-aware-of-itself and not yet embodied as a human subject. Soul is also fundamentally process and movement, so we see in our story of Abram an early form of consciousness on the move. In ancient cultures, consciousness is not recognized as consciousness as such, showing itself instead in the form of personifications as gods, goddesses, spirits, animals, natural phenomena (storms, earthquakes, volcanoes, floods, drought, etc.), and also in the form of special individuals who are heroes, priests, warriors, kings, prophets, and so on. Therefore, if God created Abram as his self-image, then, telling Abram to leave home, to leave "your country and your kindred and your father's house," is in fact soul taking leave of itself, taking leave of one form of itself for another form that is beginning to reshape itself. Abram is told to leave his "country," his "kindred," and his "father's house." He is told to cut himself off from his roots, his family tradition, his ancestry, the land that gives him life, and the gods and goddesses that he serves in that land. Everything he is told to leave is what identifies him as him; his identity is not in himself as it is for us moderns, but in the land, in the ancestors, in his father's house and the household gods. He is told to leave his *natural* context, those blood ties that define him. This new god, commanding Abram to leave home, acts against the natural ways and the natural gods/goddesses. This god wants to break out of the closed self-contained natural world, to leave the womb of Mother Nature. Abram is an archetypal personification of both a particular god and a particular people. His is the name the biblical narrative gives to a transformation soul is undertaking. Abram is told to cut himself off from his ancestors, and yet, at the same time, the biblical narrative makes a point of establishing his genealogical roots.

Prior to Abram leaving home, the narrative presents an ancient genealogy linking Abram to Shem, the son of Noah, which connects to an earlier list of generations that link Noah back to Adam and Eve.[12] These genealogies, neither biological nor historical (in our modern sense), represent a genealogy of soul's intent, a genealogy of meaning created by soul's monotheistic impulse. The logic of soul's monotheistic impulse reframes itself, by way of the genealogy, as beginning at the beginning of its own myth. As the personification of his particular cultural logic, Abram was a nature- and image-based polytheist. Throughout the biblical narrative, monotheism reframes all of Hebrew cultural history in its own terms. Monotheism was not the original form that soul took; rather, monotheism was creating itself, the myth or narrative of itself, as a contradiction internal to polytheism. Yahweh had to differentiate himself from all the other deities. At first he was tolerant, as polytheism in general is tolerant. But

---

12. Noah to Abram, Gen 11:10–26; Adam to Noah, Gen 5:1–32.

later, in an attempt to conquer and destroy the other deities, he will institute a reign of fierce zero tolerance.

Tradition and ancestors, especially in ancient indigenous societies, were where soul resided because the gods and goddesses gave birth to and created the ancestors and the traditions. The living looked back to the ancestors for knowledge of soul and to learn what soul wanted. Tradition in ancient societies embodied soul-truth. When God tells Abram to leave his father's house, this is soul cutting itself off from itself, soul leaving home. That was a revolutionary move on soul's part. The ancient mythological story shows us soul negating one status of itself for another status. A particular cultural consciousness, the natural world of polytheism, was undergoing a metamorphosis. What is the source of the energy for this deep transformation of the background logic of consciousness? From the story's point of view, the god is the motive power of this move, but what is changing for this god, who is one nature deity among many others? As we will see, this god, in relation to Abram in particular, is preoccupied with sexuality and procreation, and he wants to control and focus it in a particular way. Perhaps the new god's focus on sexuality will have something to do with the energy that drives the engine of Abram's transformation to Abraham, the name change signaling a new status of consciousness.

Soul Promises Itself Greatness (to Become a Great Word)

Soul, in the form of God, has movement, intent, direction, and motive power. But, what does this intent want? God's explanation is a vague, open-ended promise that hardly seems galvanizing:

> I will make of you a great nation, and I will bless you, and make your name great, so that you will be a blessing. I will bless those who bless you, and the one who curses you I will curse; and in you all the families of the earth shall be blessed. (Gen 12:2–3)

This grand promise reveals something of the new god's aims. What motivates soul to create such profound upheavals for itself, to disrupt itself and leave home? The promise states that Abram's name will become great and that his greatness will influence all the families of the earth; all will be blessed. The *name* is the *word* that will be made great and change the world into its image. In other words, our world will become a world of the *word* through soul's movement from preliterate culture (soul's preliterate form of consciousness) to literate culture, which indeed came to dominate and shape the cultural world all over the globe, certainly in part, through the Judeo-Christian influence. Abram portends a huge revolution in consciousness, as soul's oral and prehistoric form of consciousness transforms itself into a literate and historical form of consciousness.

Soul's Telos

What does Yahweh-Abram want? If the promise is to make Abram great, a great nation, a great name, and a great blessing, and Abram is this god's self-image, then it follows that the Yahweh god wants to be great, and under then-current conditions he was not. He was a minor local deity among many, but apparently one with great ambition. The "I" that speaks ("I will make of you a great nation") and promises to make Abram great, by extension, will make himself great. Why does this Yahweh god want to be great, and why does he want his own land? The question about Yahweh is at the same time the question about soul: What does soul want?

What does soul want in its guise as Yahweh-Abram? As dream image, this combined character represents aspects of soul in relation with itself, a development of consciousness in a mythological guise. The story itself makes no mention of *consciousness* because consciousness is a modern idea emerging in public discourse only during the seventeenth century.[13] The question, "What does soul want?" also means, "What does consciousness want?" Or even, in what direction was the logic or syntax of *meaning* itself moving? Put this way, the question intentionally personifies the notions of both soul and consciousness, even though these ideas are abstractions. Psychological thinking chooses to see Yahweh-Abram as a personification of soul, which is a deliberate methodological choice to adopt a certain style of thinking. This is not an ontological assertion about soul because soul is not a spiritual, theological, or mythological entity, not a thing or substance, but a process, and more specifically a process of thought. To think psychologically about soul is to think about the forms of thinking that soul has taken. Soul itself is thought. That is, today, for our modern time, soul is a form of thought, and, I must remind myself, not conscious, personally directed thought, but thought directing itself (soul-directed thought). The psychological approach chooses to view soul and consciousness as a *telos*, an intent, but this does not mean it is a plan known ahead of time, nor is this telos an ultimate end. It is a drive and process to develop itself, and it cannot know in the moment where it will end up. This is a style of thinking that psychology adopts as its own self-definition. Psychology does not posit a traditional teleology with a final goal in mind, which would be an ontological or theological assertion in the terms of traditional truths. Teleology in the traditional formal sense was the province of metaphysics and theology, but not for psychology with soul. Psychology has in mind a process of emergence, a development of unexpected and unknown consequences, and yet, soul, from our vantage point today, does seem to have a trend. The call of Abram is expressive of this trend of soul, soul is on

---

13. While the word "conscience" entered usage during the thirteenth century, the use of "consciousness" as personal awareness entered general usage during the seventeenth century, and then continued to refer to the personal consciousness of the individual. Originally, the word "conscience," as "con" (with) and "scire" (to know), meant "knowing with" or shared knowing, among individuals or a people. Only later during modernity did both conscience and consciousness become the exclusive property of only the individual. *Oxford English Dictionary*, 845–47.

the move and has a direction in mind, with no guarantee that soul will get what it wants. In general, soul seems to want to fulfill its telos, its creative impulse, wherever it leads. Of course, the stories themselves, written in hindsight, show God always in control and an end result that is a foregone conclusion. It can also be said that my story of soul's historical development, also told in hindsight, is a foregone conclusion, but this is a truism of any historiography. Still, as regards the future, we, and soul, remain blind as to what soul will do next. What soul has done does not predict what it will do. The amazing thing is that the biblical story and its traditions have had such tremendous power and influence for the development of Western civilization, as well as world history at large.

In nature we can see a telos without teleology. The twin instinctual desires of sexual reproduction and eating have an internal telos that transforms energy from one form to another. This is the desire, or telos, of biological life, and it is basically blind. The desire that characterizes nature is embedded and enclosed in its own cycle, on the one hand circular and repetitive, on the other hand with a direction that we call evolution, a developmental telos of the progressive complexification of life forms. If evolution has a goal in mind, we do not know what it is, but we do see evolution's results so far. From the point of view of consciousness, however, biological processes are not aware of themselves; they have no recognizable or visible consciousness that reflects on itself, no culture, no language, no history. Nature and biology are completely self-contained in a self-enclosed whole we can refer to simply as nature, or silent nature.

Consciousness, by definition—that is, as culture, language, history (memory)—must have some distance from nature in order for nature to be reflected in consciousness. Consciousness is a form of distance, even a break, from a former state of unconsciousness, from that state of nature that is blind to its own processes. Each developmental state of consciousness (cultural and personal) is always relative in relation to the former state of consciousness, as each state of consciousness is more or less unaware of itself. When we get a new perspective, we see the former perspective with more clarity in hindsight than we can see the new perspective itself. This process of continuously unfolding consciousness reflects soul's infinity; that is, this process is inexhaustible. Each status of consciousness will lead to a new sublation, as soul pushes off from itself and creates a new form of consciousness, over and over. The manifestation of consciousness at large, the manifestation of soul, is culture and history. In a figurative way of speaking, culture builds itself on top of nature; culture is not embedded in nature the way animal life is completely and unconsciously at home in its environment. Culture is a step out of nature. Culture leaves the home of nature and builds a new kind of home, necessarily linked with nature, but also distinct from nature. Abram, in leaving home, personifies soul's journey as it steps out of one form of itself, the stage of being embedded in nature in the form of polytheism. Soul shapes itself into a new form, which will be the new Yahweh god, a god who will refuse any concrete images of himself; he will insist on being an imageless god who is not bound to natural phenomena.

Originally Yahweh Was a Bull God

The Bible, with its emphasis on Yahweh as a transcendent imageless spirit god, tries to erase the true origins of Yahweh as a bull. But, it was Yahweh's full immersion in nature as a bull that was the source of his later preoccupation with sexuality and procreation. Yahweh will channel the procreative drive of sexuality as the energy that helps drive Yahweh out of nature. As we will see, he will take control of Abram's penis and use it to create ostensibly an heir for Abram, but really a future for Yahweh. But, first we want to see how thoroughly Yahweh was one Canaanite polytheistic bull among many.

The bull has always been an animal that inspires awe at its embodiment of raw power, its generative power, its power to work and to wreak havoc. Throughout the ancient world, the bull was a sacred animal identified with the power of life itself, often the object of ritual slaughter (sacrifice). From at least 7000 BCE through the first millennium BCE, the bull was a god, identified with deities like El and Baal and Yahweh throughout Mesopotamia and the Levant (broadly, the eastern Mediterranean from Egypt to Turkey).[14] The bull was a moon god, its pointed curved horns like the crescent moon, and thus a god of death and rebirth, as well as royal power (the central god of Ur, Abram's ancestral origin, was the moon god Nanna). Nanna, a Sumerian name, became identified with the Akkadian or Semitic moon god, Sin. Sin was a "lord of wisdom," "father of the gods," and "chief of the gods," as well as "creator of all things." He rode on a winged bull. Sin's father, Enlil, was the "Bull of Heaven."[15] Yahweh and the moon are connected through the timing of the Passover celebration, its date determined by the first full moon after the vernal equinox. The identities of the gods and goddesses in the ancient world were manifold and fluid. They are all interrelated, some more prominent to specific locals. Throughout the broad area of the Levant, the bull was ubiquitous and centrally important. The bull was the potency of life and a leader, in that this power takes the lead, leads the way. The bull is the irrepressible impulse of Life itself; it is a god. This was soul-infused Nature, Nature as the Divine presence of generative and destructive power.

The biblical depiction of Yahweh is clear: He is against all the other gods, he is apart and separate from other gods. There are no pictorial, carved, or cast images of Yahweh, and Yahweh is not an animal deity, not a nature deity. Biblical Yahweh is not a Bull god! The larger historical record is invaluable, in this case, as is reading between the lines of the Bible itself. The cultural context clearly shows Yahweh sharing identities

---

14. Black, *World History Atlas*, 37, http://semiramis-speaks.com/the-origins-and-evolution-of-the-bull-cult-in-the-ancient-mediterranean/.

15. *Wikipedia*, s.v. "Sin (mythology)," last updated April 30, 2022, https://en.wikipedia.org/wiki/Sin_(mythology).

with other Canaanite gods, such as El and Baal, and the Bible, in spite of itself, clearly reveals Yahweh as a nature deity. Yahweh takes over the functions of the nature and fertility gods, which we will see especially in relation to Abram and his wife, Sarai. The close connection between the Canaanite gods and goddesses and the biblical record became clear when numerous cuneiform clay tablets, written in a language unknown at the time of their discovery, were accidentally discovered on the coast of the Mediterranean in what is now Syria (near Turkey) in 1923. These tablets represented the royal archives of the ancient kingdom of Ugarit, and the language belonged, with Hebrew and Aramaic, to the northwest Semitic languages. "The evidence suggests that Israelite theology was not as radically discontinuous with Canaanite religions as was once thought. Yahweh was imbued with characteristics associated with El and Baal."[16] Psalm 29 is a text now considered to have been originally a Canaanite chant to Baal, a storm god closely related to Yahweh. Here are some representative verses in which I include Baal along with Yahweh (and forgo the words Lord and God):

> The voice of Baal/Yahweh is over the waters;
> > Baal of glory thunders,
> > Baal/Yahweh, over mighty waters.
> The voice of Baal/Yahweh is powerful;
> > the voice of Baal/Yahweh is full of majesty.
>
> The voice of Baal/Yahweh breaks the cedars;
> > the Baal breaks the cedars of Lebanon.
>
> The voice of Baal/Yahweh flashes forth flames of fire.
> > The voice of Baal/Yahweh shakes the wilderness;
>
> The voice of Baal/Yahweh causes the oaks to whirl,
> > and strips the forest bare;
> > and in his temple all say "Glory!"
>
> Baal/Yahweh sits enthroned over the flood;
> > Baal sits enthroned as king forever.
> May Baal/Yahweh give strength to his people!
> May Baal/Yahweh bless his people with peace!

Storm, thunder, and lightning, torrential rain and powerful winds, volcanic eruption and earthquake, here the "voices" of Baal/Yahweh, *are* the presence of Baal/Yahweh. The storm god is a fertility god, rain impregnates the earth, bringing forth crops; water is essential to life, and as such, the storm god is the life of the people.

Psalm 18 is another text that combines storm imagery with Yahweh as a powerful warrior (representative verses):

16. Metzger, "Ugaritic," 785.

> The LORD [Yahweh] is my rock, my
> > fortress, and my deliverer,
> > my God [El], my rock in whom I
> > take refuge.
>
> ...
>
> Then the earth reeled and rocked;
> > the foundations also of the
> > > mountains trembled
> > and quaked, because he was
> > > angry.
> Smoke went up from his nostrils,
> > and devouring fire from his
> > > mouth;
> > glowing coals flamed forth from
> > > him.
> He bowed the heavens, and came
> > down;
> > thick darkness was under his
> > > feet.
> He rode on a cherub, and flew;
> > he came swiftly upon the wings
> > > of the wind.
> He made darkness his covering
> > around him,
> > his canopy thick clouds dark
> > > with water.
> Out of the brightness before him
> > there broke through his clouds
> > hailstones and coals of fire.
> The LORD [Yahweh] also thundered in the
> > heavens,
> > and the Most High uttered his
> > > voice.
> And he sent out his arrows, and
> > scattered them;
> > he flashed forth lightnings, and
> > > routed them.

Our modern mind reads this poem as a metaphor. The wind, lightning, rock, and earthquake are merely adjectives to describe God. But, for the ancient mind, nature in all its wild power *is* the presence of the god, the *real presence* of the "Bull of Heaven," the Canaanite high god El, as well as Baal—in the form of Yahweh, in this case—called upon to protect the psalmist from his enemies. Yahweh, though never explicitly shown in the image of a bull in the Bible,[17] is himself originally and essentially a Storm-Bull god.

Another explicit connection that is hidden by the English translation at Genesis 49:24 (also Ps 132:2) is the title "bull of Jacob," ordinarily translated as "the Mighty One of Jacob." This derives from the bull imagery of El, as does the image of Yahweh having horns "like the horns of the wild ox," in Numbers 24:8.[18] While the general biblical polemic against Baal is obvious, the cumulative historical and cultural evidence is clear that "on the whole Baal was an accepted Israelite god, that criticism of his cult began in the ninth or eighth century, and that despite prophetic and Deuteronomistic criticism, this god remained popular through the end of the southern kingdom [587 BCE]. There is no evidence that prior to the ninth century Baal was considered a major threat to the cult of Yahweh."[19] The word *ba'al* undergoes a complex development in both the Bible and other sources. It can refer in general to various Canaanite storm gods who would have their own ritual practices and specific sanctuaries in numerous locations. Both the varied manifestations of El and Baal are conflated in the biblical traditions and become absorbed into the singular divine character of Yahweh, so we know that the Bull gods El and Baal were interchangeable with Yahweh.[20] Yahweh was, unequivocally, originally, a Bull god and a Storm god!

Abram, as one of God's created beings, was also, and most importantly, a self-image of God: "Let us make humankind in our image, according to our likeness" (Gen 1:26). It follows that Abram, as associated closely with Yahweh god, is also a bull, and thus a generative father. He is promised literally to be the father of countless descendants, the father of a great nation, so he will be a Great Bull in his own right. The name *Abram* means "exalted or high father, or ancestor,"[21] and this too links him indirectly with El and Baal as bull. Abram becomes the generative father of the nation of Israel through the blessing of the Bull god Yahweh. Abram is not divine in any sense, but the qualities of bull and father intermingle and overlap in the symbiotic relationship between Abram and Yahweh. As I stated earlier, Abram and Yahweh are a unity symbolizing soul's development.

---

17. Except for the case I will explore in chapter 4 when, in Exodus, the people forge a golden calf and declare of the bull calf, "These are your gods, O Israel" (Exod 32:4). The "calf" designation in that text, as we will see, is belittling and points to Yahweh's contempt for his bull form.

18. Smith, *Early History of God*, 51. The Hebrew word is *abir*, which is, without exception, translated in English Bibles as "mighty," but Smith states is "bull," as derived from "the bovine imagery of El." This is another example of how thoroughly normative monotheistic consciousness has erased its original derivation in the world of nature-polytheism.

19. Smith, *Early History of God*, 47.

20. Smith, *Early History of God*, 41, 47–48.

21. *New Interpreter's Bible*, 1:456, 459.

The Bull God Negates Itself—from Natural to Supernatural

Over the course of Abram's life, Yahweh promises him uncountable descendants, not once, but many times, and yet his wife Sarai remains barren and the children never come. Seven distinct promises of progeny are made, six of them coming over a period of twenty-five years before any child is finally born. At one point, Yahweh promised Abram all the land he can see with his eyes, north, south, east, and west, as well as innumerable offspring: "I will make your offspring like the dust of the earth; so that if one can count the dust of the earth, your offspring also can be counted" (Gen 13:16). This promise induced Abram to move his tent and settle by the oaks of Mamre, near Hebron, where he built an altar (slaughter-site) to Yahweh. The oak at Mamre was another great and ancient tree, known widely as a sacred site of ritual sacrifice.[22] Trees in the ancient Near East were associated with goddesses, and Yahweh, contrary to the biblical image of monotheism, is one among many deities. This is another indication, more or less hidden in the biblical record, of the thoroughly nature-based polytheistic cosmos Abram and Yahweh both called home.

Abram's and Sarai's childlessness, a serious problem, becomes a crisis. Abram complains angrily to Yahweh: "O Lord God, what will you give me, for I continue childless . . . You have given me no offspring, and so a slave born in my house is to be my heir." Abram no longer believes the promise because they still have no children. Yahweh however tells Abram, "Look toward heaven and count the stars, if you are able to count them . . . So shall your descendants be" (Gen 15:2–5). Well, another grandiose promise, but now "Sarai, Abram's wife, bore him no children" (16:1). Sarai, however, does not think this is her personal fertility problem, and points to Yahweh as the source: "You see that Yahweh has prevented me from bearing children; go in to my slave-girl; it may be that I shall obtain children by her" (16:2). Sarai voices the logic of the consciousness of antiquity. Yahweh himself, the Bull god, is causing her barrenness. Sarai's inability to conceive is not a human problem, or a biological problem; it is a conflict within soul that Yahweh represents. Why would Yahweh make extravagant promises of fertility and descendants, and at the same time prevent conception? Is Yahweh intentionally blocking (damming up) sexual procreative power for a reason? This is soul's internal self-contradiction. Here we see the power of the bull restrained, perhaps directed for another purpose beyond natural reproduction. A shift is brewing, from biological reproduction to logical reproduction. Soul's interest seems to be turning toward the creativity of mind, of the living concept and the conception of ideas. Yahweh is at the heart of this transformation of consciousness.

Years go by and now Abram is ninety-nine and Sarai is ninety, and still no children. At this age, naturally, it is not just a problem, but a biological impossibility, for Sarai is far too old to bear children (if we take the text at face value as the narrative asks us to). But, "the Lord" appears to Abram, again, and this time Yahweh has a new name:

---

22. *Wikipedia*, s.v. "Mamre," last updated May 2, 2022, https://en.wikipedia.org/wiki/Mamre.

"I am God Almighty [El Shaddai]; walk before me, and be blameless. And I will make my covenant between me and you, and will make you exceedingly numerous." Then Abram fell on his face; and God said to him, "As for me, this is my covenant with you: You shall be the ancestor of a multitude of nations. No longer shall your name be Abram, but your name shall be Abraham; for I have made you the ancestor of a multitude of nations. I will make you exceedingly fruitful; and I will make nations of you, and kings shall come from you." (Gen 17:1–6)

El is the name of the Canaanite high god and is used interchangeably with Yahweh. The Hebrew word *Shaddai* is obscure and traditionally translated as "almighty," but also as "of the mountains." In Genesis, the term *Shaddai* is most often associated with promises of human fertility, and so it also belongs with bull imagery.[23] The covenant El Shaddai refers to here is going to get a special definition because the Bull god, with his bull image Abraham, will restrain and redirect the phallic power they both share. Sexuality and procreation will no longer simply be natural and cyclical but will come to serve a specific direction, the future. In this way, they are brought into history, brought out of the eternal cycle of nature to serve the idea of a history with future goals. The "future goal," the idea of a historical goal, is itself the new identity that Yahweh wants as the *one and only* god of Israel. Here we see history breaking out of biology,[24] the endless timeless round of nature is ruptured for a future historical goal. This represents a fundamental revolution in the nature of the basic ground of consciousness, the syntax of consciousness.

The name change from Abram to Abraham is on the surface minor. The latter is simply a dialect variation that basically means the same thing as Abram: "the [divine] ancestor is exalted."[25] The ancestor in antiquity is not only a human ancestor but ultimately the god. Abram/Abraham is here closely associated with the high god El, who is also a bull by name, and, thus, a shared identity. But now the identity of "the ancestor is exalted," Abraham as the Bull god, is raised to a new status. The logical status of the ancestor is undergoing a change. El, Yahweh, and Abram, with their overlapping identities and names, take on a new dimension with this text. The fundamental orientation of the ancestor is changed. In the Hebrew language, the word Abraham is similar to "ancestor of a multitude," which we can see in the following English translation:

> No longer shall your name be called Avram,
> Rather shall your name be Avraham,
> For I will make you *Av Hamon Goyyim* / Father of a Throng of Nations![26]

23. Fox, *Five Books*, Gen 17.1n.
24. Harari, *Sapiens*, 41.
25. Gen 17:5n NRSV.
26. Fox, *Five Books*, Gen 17:5.

The transformation of Abram's name, as situated in this text, is actually a profound shift in soul's relation to time itself. Not only is Abram's identity changed, but Yahweh's identity changes as well. An orientation focused on the past and the present while immersed in the traditions of the ancestors and nature's endlessly repeating seasons, shifts to a new future orientation, a historical future stretching out in a linear progression, going somewhere. Abraham, as "ancestor of a multitude," as the source of the promised uncountable descendants that are still to come, represents the birth of a new cultural consciousness (soul) that uncoils the closed circle of nature into a linear forward-looking goal. The orientation that the new name Abraham suggests breaks out of the annual fertility cycle, the round of natural life, and now has a direction and a purpose that creates a new sense of time, time as a history oriented to a still unknown but promised future, one that will be great in land and progeny. The Bull god is first of all Nature's prodigal fertility, but now Yahweh is beginning to show himself as a fertile cultural mind, a mind giving birth to goals and ideas for a future that pushes off from the natural cycle. I interpret Yahweh's self-imposed limitation on Abram and Sarai's ability to have children as the inhibition of natural procreative power in order to channel it in a new direction, one mirrored in the new names, Abraham and Sarah, who participate in the Bull god becoming a word god, a god of texts, eventually of Torah. The natural process of fertility, giving birth to biological children, is undergoing sublation in the direction of soul (in the form of Yahweh's fertile *mind*) giving birth to new ideas, a consciousness that emerges as the form of writing and a new abstract (cut free from nature) form of literacy. Yahweh is also on the way to becoming a supernatural deity, that is, one who acts on nature from outside in contrast to a deity whose being is identified with natural phenomena.

Cut, Blood, and Archaic Soul

At the time of the covenant promise, when Abraham is ninety-nine years old, there is another unexpected development. Yahweh will now take control of the bull's phallic power through the rite of circumcision:

> God [El] said to Abraham, "As for you, you shall keep my covenant, you and your offspring after you throughout their generations. This is my covenant, which you shall keep, between me and you and your offspring after you: Every male among you shall be circumcised. You shall circumcise the flesh of your foreskins, and it shall be a sign of the covenant between me and you . . . Both the slave born in your house and the one bought with your money must be circumcised. So shall my covenant be in your flesh an everlasting covenant." (Gen 17:9–13)

The Hebrew word that is universally translated as *covenant* in the Bible is *berit*, which means "to cut." Generally speaking, a covenant is an agreement, promise, commitment, or bond between people; it can be thought of as a contract or guarantee, and thus binding. For us today, binding agreements are *written* legal contracts that are managed by courts of law. We live within an implicit social contract that empowers the laws governing agreements and contracts among people. Modern covenants are grounded in humanistic values and, for us, the unspoken power of the written word. For us, the binding power of a contract is in the writing. The paper with the writing on it is what resolves and mediates differences of understanding and binds us to what is written. But, the ancient idea of covenant as a "cut" brings up the image of blood. What does blood have to do with an agreement and commitment? How does blood play a role in a bond between people? The ancient cult of "blood brothers" offers a clue as to the power of blood. Natural brothers are related through blood by birth, but "blood brothers" are two men who take part in a ritual of cutting themselves on the hand, arm, or finger and binding their wounds together. In sharing their blood and an oath they are bound together as "brothers." But to appreciate the depth of this blood bond, we need to recognize the difference between our modern consciousness and archaic consciousness, or the modern soul and archaic soul.

The natural tendency of our modern humanistic consciousness is to see the "blood brother" compact in personal terms, emotional terms, a personal commitment and agreement between two separate individuals who, though sharing in a common compact, remain separate individuals, a kind of ego-to-ego promise. But, for the archaic soul, the blood brother ritual was not personal at all. The bond was not metaphorical but metaphysical in the sense that its reality was grounded in a truth beyond the personal. It connected the two men in a logical, even cosmic unity that literally made them, *psychologically*, one person, and they were committed to revenging each other's honor as if it was their own.[27] When one was killed in battle, their life force would merge with the one who was still alive. One form of the blood brother ritual involved cutting a strip of sod so that it could be lifted and held aloft with their spears, while remaining attached to the earth at the ends. Then the two men would pass under the earth, allow their blood to trickle into the earth, and make their common oath invoking the gods. The earth was the world or cosmos, and the blood was the "life force," both objective realities that were god-infused, or psychologically, soul-infused. The identities of the men, and archaic humankind in general, were constituted by these extra-human realities that were substantial and public. Their blood brotherhood brought them together as one within an already existing substantial unity of earth-cosmos and blood-life force, that was not personal at all. Through the blood ritual they became a substantial unity, and let's remember they were not (modern) separate individuals to start. Humankind's sense of self-hood was constituted very differently within the conditions of archaic soul: "Man had his true substance, his very self, his ultimate being not in himself, but in something larger, in the *encompassing cultic reality*

---

27. Giegerich, "Blood Brotherhood," 267–315.

in which he had his place."[28] The archaic blood brotherhood is but one example of the substantial binding power of blood rituals, and it was the "encompassing cultic reality," those constant rituals of blood-letting sacrifices, that defined the essence of the archaic soul.

Blood occupied a unique position in archaic culture as a concrete presence of soul, as soul and blood were substantially identical. Blood was not a symbol of the soul in our modern sense; archaic man did not think mistakenly, but for obvious reasons, that blood was not just the literal source of life, but a kind of spiritual life force. For archaic humankind, blood *is* soul and soul *is* blood. The god or goddess who embodied the inner imperative of blood sacrifice was the very affirmation of life. As the knife cut into the living animal, soul was reaching for something beyond the merely animal, beyond biological life. In chapter 15 of Genesis, there is an echo of a very ancient covenant ritual sacrifice whose original meaning has been lost, but it comes just two chapters prior to the requirement of circumcision. It has been worked into one of the covenant promises Yahweh makes to Abraham:

> Now he said to him:
> I am Yhwh
> who brought you out of Ur of the Chaldeans
> to give you this land, to inherit it.
> But he said:
> My Lord, Yhwh,
> by what shall I know that I will inherit it?
> He said to him:
> Fetch me a calf of three, a she-goat of three, a ram of three, a
>   turtle-dove, and a fledgling.
> He fetched him all these.
> He halved them down the middle, putting each one's half toward
>   its neighbor,
> but the birds he did not halve.
> Vultures descended upon the carcasses,
> but Avram drove them back.
> Now it was, when the sun was coming in,
> that deep slumber fell upon Avram—
> and here, fright and great darkness falling upon him!
> . . .
> Now it was, when the sun had come in,
> that there was night-blackness,
> and here, a smoking oven, a fiery torch
> that crossed between those pieces.

---

28. Giegerich, "Blood Brotherhood," 295.

God's Autopsy and the Living Truth of Soul

> On that day
> Yhwh cut a covenant with Avram,
> saying: I give this land to your seed,
> from the River of Egypt to the Great River, the river Euphrates[29]

During the "night-blackness," Yahweh passes between the cut animal pieces in the form of the "smoking oven" and the "fiery torch." Abraham prepares the animals and the ritual setting, and Yahweh acts to seal the agreement by passing in between the cut parts of the animals. Yahweh initiates the blood-letting cut when he says, "Fetch me" a calf, a she-goat, a ram, and birds. Soul, not humankind, wants the killing, cutting, and blood-letting, which is why we must seek the meaning of ritual killings beyond anything biological or practical. The cut of sacrifice involves blood-letting, a lot of blood, and of course the death of the animals. Sacrificial killing for the gods had little to do with pragmatic biological needs like getting food (which is not to say that the animals ritually killed were not also eaten). If it was a *soul event*, sacrificial killing was meaningful in itself; as a blood ritual, it was a fulfillment of soul in itself, without the need of our thoroughly modern rational explanations. In other words, sacrifice did not have a biological evolutionary purpose; it was a soul event, soul itself straining against the mute enclosure of mere biological life, soul's telos wanting something. Within sacrificial killing was the press of meaning, the intent of meaning (i.e., soul), to develop itself. The sacrificial promise-agreement ritual between Abraham and Yahweh created and affirmed a substantial binding between human person and the god. In Leviticus 17:11, 14 (Fox) we hear explicitly that blood *is* life:

> For the life of the flesh—it is in the blood;
> I (myself) have given it to you upon the slaughter-site, to effect-
>   ransom for your lives,
> for the blood—it effects-ransom for life!
> . . .
> For the life of all flesh—its blood is its life!
> So I say to the Children of Israel:
> The blood of all flesh you are not to eat,
> for the life of all flesh—it is its blood,
> everyone eating it shall be cut off!

Blood is life. The god is life, and the god is the source of Life and Death. Not only animal sacrifice but human sacrifice and child sacrifice were common in the ancient world. Sacrifice, the bloody cut of the knife, cutting into life, releasing the life into the earth, was the norm, was a decisive element in the relationship between humankind and the gods. This truth of the archaic soul is truly alien to our modern minds. The very thought of killing animals for a god, let alone other human beings, is repugnant to us today. Blood sacrifice remains incomprehensible as a disgusting superstitious

---

29. Fox, *Five Books*, Gen 15:7–12, 17–18.

relic from a former ignorant age. To consider that sacrifice had an inherent value and meaning in itself, that it embodied a living truth in its own right, we must exercise an effort of imagination to feel and think the bond of the "blood brother" compact. Archaic soul, the logic and syntax of the consciousness of ancient culture, existed as a blood-bond between the gods and humankind—as if the god and humankind were "blood brothers." The bloodletting was the mingling of the life of the god and humankind so that the life-giving powers of the god, the bull, the Yahweh, would continue to infuse both parties of the "cut." For us this is a metaphor, but for archaic soul, it was a substantial reality. Yahweh needed the sacrificial blood just as much as Abraham did; the dynamic of Life flowed in both directions. The blood was soul's logical lifeline that united the gods and humankind. Nature-god-life-humankind existed as a logical unity, and blood sacrifice was soul's claim, affirming its life-giving power. The cut kept both god and humankind alive insofar as they both existed within, or *as*, the medium of soul's meaning. And ritual sacrifice was at the heart of meaning, creating itself out of biological life.

Circumcision, a ritual of initiation into adulthood that occurred sometime during adolescence, was practiced by other tribal or social groups. The Jewish tradition of bringing the rite of circumcision to the eighth day after birth (Gen 17:12) was an innovation. But, Abraham was ninety-nine, and all the other men of his household were adults as well. Circumcision generally occurred in indigenous societies with the awakening of sexuality and the power of manhood, as well as bringing young males and their untamed power into the circle of the rules of manhood in a particular society. In other words, the penis is not totally free to do whatever it wants and is circumscribed by social rites and traditions. In the case of Abraham, Yahweh now takes charge of Abraham's penis. At the same time, reading the story through the psychological lens, Yahweh takes action and changes the character of his own bull nature. As we know today, ejaculated semen contains hundreds of millions of sperm, another fitting analogy for the countless descendants that Abraham is promised. All of this potency will now be channeled according to Yahweh's purposes and aims, which at this point we understand to be his ambition to have a great nation, a great name, wide lands and kings that are his and his alone. Yahweh has circumscribed, restrained, and redirected Abraham and Sarah's fertility to show that fertility is under a new authority and a new goal; Yahweh even transcends the normal biological limits of fertility. No one would expect any of the other fertility gods or goddesses to enable a couple of ninety-nine and ninety to conceive and have a child. Yahweh wants to show that he is more powerful than all the other gods and that he controls nature, from outside of nature, for his own purposes. Yahweh is on the way to becoming a supernatural (abstract) deity no longer constrained by natural limits. However, Abraham himself, in the story, does not know this about Yahweh yet. He is only human after all (as far as the story is concerned) and he does not believe Yahweh's promise anymore!

> God said to Abraham "As for Sarah your wife, you shall not call her Sarai, but Sarah shall be her name. I will bless her, and moreover I will give you a son by her. I will bless her, and she shall give rise to nations; kings of peoples shall come from her." Then Abraham fell on his face and laughed, and said to himself, "Can a child be born to a man who is a hundred years old? Can Sarah, who is ninety years old, bear a child?" And Abraham said to God, "O that Ishmael might live in your sight!" God said, "No, but your wife Sarah shall bear you a son, and you shall name him Isaac." (Gen 17:15–19a)

Finally, the child, the promised heir, does come, but only after Yahweh has delayed fertility for decades, delayed it, in fact, until it is too late to have children naturally, and only after the rite of circumcision, which in this case is the turning of the penis, the bull, toward a historical, abstract (unnatural) future. Yahweh, originally a nature god, one among many other gods and goddesses, as he emerges in his new form, is a god *contra naturam*; he is becoming a new direction, a new desire. He and Abraham together express soul's impulse for an unfolding history, sublating natural procreation into the creation of history, that is, time with an unnatural purpose. Soul is pushing itself off from its embeddedness in nature for a new kind of consciousness that will rise above nature.

Yahweh the bull negates himself in his nature form, as bull, and with this negation pushes off from nature toward a consciousness that will shape itself through the written word, text, scripture, and literacy. Looking ahead, we can see this as a move from the sacrifice of literal bulls to the sacrifice needed for study of the holy word, the Torah that will become Yahweh's new abode. In this particular historical-cultural context, Yahweh personifies that logical form of consciousness that is defined by the *written* word. Yahweh is the historical emergence of cultural literacy that will lead to the development of the Western style of consciousness.

Human Sacrifice and Abraham as Historical Watershed

If we read the story of Abraham from the conventional human perspective, we see God (for no clear or compelling reason) directing Abraham to leave the home of his father under the promise that he will be the father of innumerable descendants destined to become the nation of Israel and that God (again for reasons unknown) will give him large territories of land. We see Abraham struggle with God over infertility, over who will control the male organ of reproduction, and over repeated unkept promises of countless future descendants. We witness the circumcision covenant involving ritual sacrifice and finally the miraculous birth of the promised son and heir, Isaac. Throughout all this, although Abraham was at times angry with God and argued with God, he has in the main been true with God, and God true with him, and they have together sealed themselves within a covenant by way of a ritual blood sacrifice. It would be hard to argue that Abraham needs to prove anything more about his loyalty to Yahweh. Although my perspective is psychological, and thus impersonal, as I examine Abraham and God in terms of soul's struggle with itself, a story about the evolution of the syntax of consciousness, let us stay on the human level for a moment longer in order to feel the impact of what comes next.

After everything these two have been through together, quite suddenly and with no preparation, the narrative takes an unexpected and shocking turn. Quite out of the blue, God wants to "test" Abraham and commands him to sacrifice his son Isaac as a burnt offering to God! If the story we have been reading has any internal coherence, we can only be astonished at this development. What?! What an extraordinary contradiction! First, why does Abraham need to be tested at this stage, and second, God—clearly the one who wants the innumerable descendants and the land for himself, who chose Abraham through whom all this would happen, and who, after many frustrated promises, finally contrary to nature brings about the birth of Isaac—will now have Isaac killed? On the surface, from a human perspective, this is crazy. Why would God negate his own promise to himself?

God is contradicting himself, again. This seems to be the norm for God, self-contradiction. Promise innumerable descendants and prevent descendants. Bring about a miraculous birth, then kill that very child. And at the beginning of Genesis, we remember, God contradicted himself with the serpent in the garden. The *human* reader cannot make heads or tails of this turn of events. But, the soul perspective reveals the meaning in the upside-down world. The command for Abraham to sacrifice his son Isaac is a negation of common sense, which takes us below the surface perception for the sake of a deeper purpose. What is this divine self-contradiction about, especially since, as we find out, this is all set up ahead of time (for the reader) as a "test" of Abraham, and Isaac is not sacrificed after all?

Our point of view as we read this story makes all the difference. Within traditional Jewish or Christian frameworks, the story is about theological principles regarding human faith and trust in God. Abraham is held up as a model of absolute trust in God, no matter what the personal consequences, right up to sacrificing his own beloved son. But, traditional Jewish and Christian frameworks are themselves isolated and abstracted out of the context of the larger polytheistic cosmos of the ancient Near East. What is the larger cultural context of this story? This story makes no sense whatsoever if human sacrifice is not already an existing norm. One detail of the text that affirms human child sacrifice was culturally normative is neither Abraham nor Isaac make any protest, and, as we have seen, Abraham had no compunction about either being angry with Yahweh or arguing against his aims (Sodom and Gomorrah).

What we have here is an older story of human sacrifice, reframed in service to a biblical narrative that is a protest *against* human sacrifice. However, framing the divine request for the son's sacrifice as a "test" would make no sense if human sacrifice was not a generally accepted norm: The firstborn of both animals and humans was routinely given back to the god who provided them. There is no "test" if Abraham does not know that God's request is the cultic ritual norm, even expected. Human and animal sacrifice to the god and for the god was a long-standing practice, probably for thousands of years, practiced by the myth-ritual nature-embedded polytheistic cultures of the ancient Near East, and throughout the world. This particular story would make no sense if that had not been the case. Just imagine today someone suggesting that a divinity's command to ritually slaughter one's firstborn son or daughter was a required test of faith. That person would be officially diagnosed as criminally insane, and rightly so. Our general public form of consciousness does not support such acts and thoughts. However, the *logical form* of consciousness of the archaic soul was rooted in such acts, and this means that the *meaning and the purpose* of archaic consciousness was established by such acts of ritual slaughter. Before we discuss this any further, here is the story in its entirety. I have added italics in order to point out two different textual traditions I will discuss below, that are identifiable by the different names of the god (El or Yahweh) brought together in this story:

> After these things God [El] tested Abraham. He said to him, "Abraham!" And he said, "Here I am." He said, "Take your son, your only son Isaac, whom you love, and go to the land of Moriah, and offer him there as a burnt offering on one of the mountains that I shall show you." So Abraham rose early in the morning, saddled his donkey, and took two of his young men with him, and his son Isaac; he cut the wood for the burnt offering, and set out and went to the place in the distance that God [El] had shown him. On the third day Abraham looked up and saw the place far away. Then Abraham said to his young men, "Stay here with the donkey; the boy and I will go over there; we will worship, and then we will come back to you." Abraham took the wood of the burnt offering and laid it on his son Isaac, and he himself carried the fire and the knife. So the two of them walked on together. Isaac said to his father Abraham, "Father!" And he said, "Here I am, my son." He said, "The fire and the wood are here, but where is the lamb for a burnt offering?" Abraham said, "God [El] himself will provide the lamb for a burnt offering, my son." So the two of them walked on together.
>
> When they came to the place that God [El] had shown him, Abraham built an altar there and laid the wood in order. He bound his son Isaac, and laid him on the altar, on top of the wood. Then Abraham reached out his hand and took the knife to kill his son. *But the angel of the Lord [Yahweh] called to him from heaven, and said, "Abraham, Abraham!" And he said, "Here I am." He said, "Do not lay your hand on the boy or do anything to him; for now I know that you fear God [El], since you have not withheld your son, your only son, from me." And Abraham looked up and saw a ram, caught in a thicket by its horns. Abraham went and took the ram and offered it up as a burnt offering instead of his son. So Abraham called the place "The Lord [Yahweh] will provide"; as it is said to this day, "On the mount of the Lord [Yahweh] it shall be provided."*

Abram: Archaic Soul Leaves Home

> *The angel of the LORD [Yahweh] called to Abraham a second time from heaven, and said,* "By myself I have sworn, *says the LORD:* Because you have done this, and have not withheld your son, your only son, I will indeed bless you, and I will make your offspring as numerous as the stars of heaven and as the sand that is on the seashore. And your offspring shall possess the gate of their enemies, and by your offspring shall all the nations of the earth gain blessing for themselves, because you have obeyed my voice." So Abraham returned to his young men, and they arose and went together to Beer-sheba; and Abraham lived at Beer-sheba. (Gen 22:1–19)

Historical biblical criticism, as it reconstructs the various sources for biblical stories like this one, sees two separate sources woven together in the fact that two different names for the deity are used. The Hebrew word translated as "*God*" is El, or *elohim*, and the Hebrew word translated as *the LORD* is *Yahweh*. The source that uses El is called "E" (for Elohist), and the source that uses Yahweh is called "J" (for Yahwist).[30] In this biblical story, we see two versions of a story of child sacrifice, one in which Abraham *does* ritually kill Isaac and one in which he does not.[31] Read the story and omit the italicized text, which is from the Yahwist source, and you read a story of ritual sacrificial slaughter, commanded by El (and not interrupted by Yahweh): "Then Abraham reached out his hand and took the knife to kill his son. 'By myself I have sworn: Because you have done this, and have not withheld your son, your only son, I will indeed bless you, and I will make your offspring as numerous as the stars of heaven and as the sand that is on the seashore, etc.'" However, read the story and include the Yahwist source—recognizing that the "angel" of the Lord is indeed the Lord—and the sacrifice of the child is halted and a ram is substituted. The use of different names for God points to different historical strata of tradition, different authors, and different cultural contexts, and it suggests that the story of the son's ritual sacrifice is a tradition older than the biblical version.

In addition to the two sources using different names for God, another interesting narrative detail raises the question about whether this story preserves an earlier version of a completed human sacrifice. Early in the story, when Abraham and Isaac are walking toward the mountain where the sacrifice is to take place, the phrase "So the two of them walked on together," referring to Abraham and Isaac, is used twice. The emphasis on the two of them together unifies them, binds them together as sacrificer and sacrificed. At the end of the story, after a sacrifice has taken place, after God blesses Abraham, we read, "So Abraham returned to his young men, and they arose and went together to Beer-sheba." Where is Isaac? Why is Isaac not at Abraham's side ("together") when he returns from the mountain of sacrifice? Isaac's absence here,

---

30. These scholarly designations often derive from German words, and this one is no exception. The German form of Yahweh is *Jahwe*. (It is not unusual to see the Old Testament god referred to as Jehovah.)

31. Levenson, *Inheriting Abraham*, 86.

in the light of the earlier emphasis on their "togetherness," is very loud. Of course, in such ancient texts, an omission like this proves nothing. However, the absence of Isaac at this crucial point reinforces the impression that in one version of the story he was indeed sacrificed. This, of course, leads to a pragmatic problem when we wonder, if Isaac was indeed sacrificed, who was the father of Jacob? Because, as the biblical version of the narrative will continue, Isaac is very much alive, he goes on to marry Rebekah, and they have two sons, Jacob and Esau, who are pivotal in the further history of Israel. This pragmatic conundrum remains unresolved because it is the Jahwist that contains the Isaac story and there are no surviving documents that might tell us what the Elohist source thinks about the parentage of Jacob.[32] But, even more than any textual variations the Bible may contain between the lines, we are not reading empirical history in this narrative, but soul's autobiography, a history of meaning developing itself. In reading this text as a dream, soul's speech about itself, we can let go of rational consistency. But, for my psychological point of view, the historical-critical detective work on ancient biblical texts is illuminating because it reveals internal contradictions that point to the evolution of consciousness. The textual traditions are also psychological traditions that soul takes up and massages and reworks as it goes through the process of negating earlier versions of itself for the sake of the next stage of consciousness.

What is important for my purposes is that we do in fact have two stories about human sacrifice embedded within this one story: one that includes human sacrifice and one that excludes human sacrifice. We can ignore the particulars of the narrative characters, especially the idea that they were actual human personalities, because that is not our focus. The focus is on what soul is saying about itself with this story. This is soul's watershed, that point at which a fundamental division occurs, the division between the archaic soul and what has become modern soul.[33] The archaic soul is so thoroughly foreign and alien to our consciousness because we are far on this side of soul's continental divide. It is nearly impossible for us to think and imagine that human and animal sacrifice was a meaningful soul-event, that the event of sacrifice *was* the soul's own doing, and that the sacrificial-event *was* the presence of a god, the presence and actualization of highest meaning. The dividing point symbolized by the Abrahamic story of the binding of Isaac, in which human sacrifice is forestalled by the god himself, is a foundational and revolutionary change in which soul breaks with itself. Soul breaks out of its containment within nature, its complete identification as nature. In this case, soul manifesting as the Bull god El/Yahweh is undergoing a self-negation and moving toward a new cultural status of consciousness as a nature-transcending god. The two stories, one of human sacrifice and one of no human sacrifice, conflated here into one story, represent the dividing point in history where prehistory streams into the distant past and (our) history streams into the future, further and further

---

32. Levenson, *Inheriting Abraham*, 86.
33. Giegerich, "Sacrifice of Isaac," 171–87.

away from that archaic situation. The change is so profound that we are irretrievably separated and alienated from what we, in our position, can only call, the archaic soul. Archaic soul was prehistorical, even, in a sense, pre-soul, in that soul had to liberate itself from nature. But, we must not think of "soul" as some *thing*, something spiritual or ontological, that already existed and had to be freed. No, soul—and here is where Giegerich is extremely helpful—had to create itself out of, so to speak, nothing, and thousands of years of ritual sacrificial killings awakened something we now call soul:

> Soul is *logical* (noetic) life (logical movement), and is, as such, self-generating. In man and through him, the soul as "conscious-being" gradually generated and edified itself by means of innumerably many incisive acts [ritual killings]. In a kind of self-bootstrapping, the soul first made itself through killing, it *killed itself into being*, and this is why I consider sacrificial killings as the primordial soul-making. With great effort the soul liberated itself, *within* its immersion in the merely-biological, *from* this immersion—from an immersion, however, that continues to prevail even after it had been overcome.[34]

That last phrase points to the contradiction that exists in our Abraham and Isaac story. Human sacrifice, in principle, is stopped, but it also continues along with animal sacrifice. These stories are not historical, empirical, but logical, psychological. A change on the soul level does not lead to an immediate change in social practices, which take a long time to catch up to soul's new status. In fact, throughout history, there is often much resistance to soul-change, a logical change of consciousness, and so archaic consciousness and practices continued for a long time alongside the development of a future-oriented historical consciousness and the new cultural development of writing and literacy. We will see this reflected in Yahweh's fierce contests with polytheistic practices that the Hebrew and Israelite people were in no hurry to abandon.

The particular story of Abraham and Isaac, along with the larger Abrahamic narrative and the biblical narrative in general, symbolizes the creation of time itself out of non-time. Time as historical (that is, as linguistic, cultural, mnemonic, linear, and text-based) is created by the intervention of Yahweh against himself. With this action, Yahweh stepping in and negating his own desire for sacrifice, indeterminate time becomes determinate. Again, thinking psychologically and remembering this narrative actually condenses a soul-process that took countless centuries, Yahweh intrudes into his own desire for sacrifice, abruptly and decisively, even urgently, with the words, "Abraham, Abraham!" and then, "Do not lay your hand on the boy or do anything to him." This intrusion is itself incisive, a cut into a sacred cultic practice so normal and routine that no one raised the slightest doubt or question about carrying it out. Something within the El/Yahweh god awakened itself, as a result of countless ritual killings. Something awakened, soul's glimmer of itself, creating a new space of reflection, thus creating soul itself through the act of killing. The blind and endlessly

---

34. Giegerich, "Killings," 205.

God's Autopsy and the Living Truth of Soul

repeated ritual killings awakened a new kind of seeing within that very blindness. A dim consciousness dawned within the archaic act where a god was already present. Something of that meaning, the god's presence in the sacrificial killing, awakened to itself. A new kind of *meaning* emerged.

To awaken in the morning is to kill the status of sleeping when we are asleep to ourselves. To awaken is to find ourselves in a conscious space separate from the sleeping state. When asleep we do not know we are asleep. When awake we know we are awake. The sacrificial killings of the myth-ritual stage of culture that preceded the "religious" stage of culture, which we see developing in the Tanakh over about a thousand years, was a function of soul, by soul, and for soul alone. The nature of *meaning* (i.e., the logic of consciousness) was awakening to a new level of itself:

> In the institution of sacrificial slaughter, the creation of man *as* man took place and the creation of the world *as* the world of man, that is to say, the "world" as one that speaks to us and appears to us in the form of persons and figures. Sacrifices are the event in which the self-generation of what we call soul, consciousness, meaning happened.[35]

From the perspective of a psychology with soul, sacrificial killings serve no practical purpose, no biological or evolutionary purpose. Viewed psychologically, they were soul-events: events of meaning, acts that were meaningful in themselves. The act of ritual killing was the appearance and the presence of the god. Meaning was not *attached* to them (that would be our modern attempt to find a rational explanation, and an external explanation at that). Ritual killing was in fact, the very essence of the logical form of consciousness, and the fulfillment of the syntax of consciousness, of that prehistoric time. As abhorrent as this may seem to our consciousness today, we have to reach back across the ages and imagine a form of consciousness that found its highest fulfillment, its sacred apotheosis,[36] in the ritual act of killing another living being—the act of ritual slaughter was the theophany of the god. Only when we can imagine such a truth for archaic soul will we be able to appreciate the enormous scale of soul's project, which began with Yahweh's call to himself to leave the home of his ancestors and will continue with his attempt to create a new land and a new people, a new identity, for himself. Soul's push to leave home, to cut itself out of its containment within nature, to become a consciousness differentiated from nature, is the goal of Yahweh throughout the Bible.

---

35. Giegerich, "Sacrifice of Isaac," 183–84.
36. Giegerich, "Sacrifice of Isaac," 173, 178.

Chapter 4

Yahweh's Violent Rupture: Soul's Revolution

Consciousness Liberates Itself

The purpose of emancipation and an increase of consciousness directly *aims* for change. It catapults consciousness to higher stages and statuses of itself.[1]

The purpose of emancipation *from* the soul is itself a soul purpose![2]

WESTERN CULTURE SEES IN the book of Exodus the story of Moses bringing his people out of Egypt against the opposition of the pharaoh and leading them to a promised land. The dramatic images are powerful: the angel of death passes by the Hebrew houses, the pursuing Egyptian armies are swallowed in the Red Sea, Moses goes to the fiery mountaintop and brings from his encounter with Yahweh new commandments for his people, then returns to find them dancing around a golden calf.

These mesmerizing stories have captured the Western imagination for over a thousand years. Their emotional power, like a dream we cannot forget, still resonates and lends them well to the psychological reading. The stories are full of decisive acts, and among them, in my interpretation, Yahweh castrates himself and divorces his wife Asherah. Yahweh does not act alone as he has a necessary accomplice on earth in the figure of Moses; they are partners in the violent actions, fulfilling soul's impulse to liberate itself. There is a ferocious revolution in consciousness as soul wrenches itself free of its preliterate polytheistic status for a future in which writing and the human will become dominant. This chapter explores the often brutal and blood-soaked unfolding

---

1. Giegerich, *What Is Soul?*, 321.
2. Giegerich, *What Is Soul?*, 322.

of these profound changes in soul, and in the soul document known as Exodus, Moses and Yahweh are the personifications of the struggle.

Yahweh Divorces Asherah

The news that Yahweh (God) had a wife may indeed be startling, even shocking, given the long-standing conventional image of our Western god as a singular and celibate deity. The evidence is clear that Yahweh did indeed have a consort, but this has only come to light relatively recently. Today biblical scholars and archeologists agree that Yahweh, along with all the other ancient male Near Eastern deities, had a wife, or consort.[3] Evidence both within and outside of the Bible supports this divine marriage. The Bible, but most especially the Tanakh, is both a polemic against the goddess and a lengthy divorce decree. From the point of view of the history of soul's logical transformations, the "goddess" in this ancient context, in a broad symbolic sense, represents the status of archaic soul and its immersion in an unreflective and unconscious natural world, standing in contrast to the emergent Yahweh.[4] In order to make this case, I will undertake a close examination of several biblical texts throughout this chapter.

I claim that Yahweh divorces Asherah, and so a word on the emotional dynamics of divorce among human persons may be helpful. Whether or not we have personally gone through a divorce, most people recognize that a measure of hate is necessary to break the intimate entanglement of marriage. Marriage is a powerful emotional bond because it is constructed not only by cultural-religious values and expectations both social and internal, but also by deep personal desires and needs that are often quite unconscious. The bond of marriage is primarily psychological, a deep logical or archetypal bond, which makes it a mutually impersonal unconscious identity. The connection of marriage is deep, persistent, and stubborn in maintaining itself. The Bible speaks to the depth of the marriage union when it states, "Therefore a man leaves his father and his mother and clings to his wife, and *they become one flesh*."[5] The idea of becoming "one flesh" is ancient and, in spite of our modern enlightened individuality, still infuses our experience of marriage. The biblical assertion is a religious injunction, a divine claim: Even if we no longer believe in God, it lives on in the unspoken hinterland of our cultural traditions and the deeper recesses of the psyche. To break the marriage bond requires a great deal of energy, which often takes—needs to take—the form of hate. The tragedy is when the hate is acted out in bitter animosity, or crimes of passion. For my purposes, I want to keep the tenacity of the marriage bond in mind

---

3. Dever, *Did God Have a Wife?*; Metzger, "Asherah," 62; Smith, *Memoirs of God*, 111–12.

4. The "goddess" in my usage here symbolizes a stage of soul's logical development that must be differentiated from how humankind behaves and acts out with regard to gender, ethnic, and racial differences. See the afterword for a reflection on the hidden connection between soul's logic and the human actions of genocide, misogyny, and racism.

5. Fox, *Five Books*, Gen 2:24, emphasis added.

as we shift from the personal to the impersonal perspective of soul. Now we consider Yahweh, who himself is destined to commit just such crimes of passion over and over again for centuries.

Yahweh came to hate his consort Asherah and was compelled not only to divorce her but to completely erase her existence. With violent mythological imagery, soul negates itself, working to break out of its closed self-containment within the world of nature. My exploration is not about gods, goddesses, and people but about a radical movement of the logical form of consciousness whose seed was planted long ago. I am thinking not theologically or humanistically, but psychologically and phenomenologically, viewing Yahweh and Asherah not as divine entities, nor even as cultural models, but as symbolic personifications of a soul phenomenon, as ancient forms of the *syntax of consciousness*. In this autopsy, undertaken as a psychological analysis, they personify the shape of *meaning* itself. Yahweh's move to divorce Asherah—and he will divorce her violently—is soul's move to liberate itself.

The legacy of monotheism is deeply ingrained in our modern consciousness. Even though we are historically distant from the great and dramatic revolution in consciousness the new Yahweh represented, monotheism is so taken for granted that it's hard for us to realize how profoundly consciousness has changed. While our psychological distance from archaic soul is vast, that antique text, the Bible, gives us clues about what happened. And, I must add and acknowledge, today we in Western civilization are on the side of the winner of that ancient war against the gods and goddesses. The general cultural consciousness we take for granted today is the direct result of Yahweh's victory. We cannot return to a polytheistic-nature consciousness any more than we can leave our culture, unlearn our language, and return to a prelinguistic mode of existence. We can be aware, however, of an ancient form of consciousness profoundly different from our own, acknowledging that something revolutionary changed as a result of Yahweh's divorce from Asherah. Again, my interpretation is that Yahweh represents the shift from preliterate consciousness to literate consciousness, so that writing became the manifestation of a new dominant mode of consciousness. I touched on these ideas in relation to Abraham's story and the notion of soul leaving home. Here I look at the same theme through the lens of the relationship between ancient, prebiblical Yahweh and a goddess, and between Yahweh and his own bull essence.

Biblical Chronology and Historical Chronology

The Bible has its own internal chronology, separate from the historical chronology when its books were composed. The stories of Abraham and Moses and the Exodus were written hundreds of years after the purported events themselves, and they tell the stories from a point of view that did not exist in that ancient past. Dating these ancient times is a speculative undertaking that keeps changing as scholars recalibrate eras according to new discoveries. Dating with a broad brush, however, puts the cultural practices and truths that Abraham and his family represent around 1800–1300 BCE (and earlier), while the Exodus events are linked to a time around 1300 BCE.[6] The stories were composed, however, after the Babylonians conquered the southern kingdom of Judah and destroyed the Jerusalem temple, in 587 BCE. The Persian empire displaced the Babylonian from 539–333 BCE, which is when most of the Tanakh was put together, taking the form familiar to us today.

The Tanakh itself took shape in a process occurring over hundreds of years of writing, rewriting, and reframing, as the monotheistic point of view developed. Monotheism does not really consolidate itself until after Israel as an independent kingdom and its cultic center, the Jerusalem temple, are destroyed. During the Babylonian exile, educated Jewish aristocrats composed and compiled much of the Tanakh's literary text as the way to preserve their religious identity in relation to Yahweh. While my primary focus is soul and not history, soul is not itself ahistorical or atemporal. In the psychological approach, soul is an interpretation of history—or better, history interpreting itself—as soul responds to historical circumstances. Yahweh himself will change in response to historical circumstances, that is, Yahweh as the personification of soul's movement, something I will look at more closely in the next chapter.

The idea that Yahweh was the one and only God for the Israelites gained strength and definition during the sixth and fifth centuries BCE, and then was retrojected into the biblical narrative almost one thousand years into a past before the monotheistic idea was born. As we have seen, and will continue to see, monotheism created, and will continue to create, its own origin myth, by way of history as written narrative, reinterpreting itself. This broad historical overview gives us a context for soul's history, helping to keep in view the larger historical-cultural frame in which biblical history wrote its own story. Yahweh's story gives us a history of the psychological form of consciousness, which became our Western consciousness. The *story* of Yahweh, and the evolution of Yahweh, has become the form of our consciousness, a kind of archetypal DNA of soul's development, working on itself through the culture and history of Western civilization. Biological DNA is the invisible genetic framework of our physiological constitution, and soul is the invisible syntax, or framework, constituting our consciousness, both public mind and our individual mind. The Bible's story of Yahweh, our God, has been the living heart of Western civilization for two thousand years and remains deeply embedded in our collective psyche, or better really, not a *thing* embedded, but the *form* of our consciousness itself. While God is no longer the living form of our contemporary cultural consciousness, nor of our historical time,

---

6. The linkage to a general date range is speculative and does not mean there is any evidence for an actual large population of slaves escaping from Egypt, either Egyptian historical or archaeological evidence. The exodus story, from a modern perspective, is fiction. But fiction is a poor category because it is generally dismissive, and loses sight of what is at stake psychologically—the transformation of the very real Yahweh and the logical form of consciousness he represents. Whether or not there is material historical truth in this story is beside the point, because the focus here is on the real and profound psychological (historical) truth, transforming itself during antiquity.

the lingering residue of God and the popular and conventional misunderstanding of God continue as an invisible and pervasive influence. That's why, at this time, an autopsy is appropriate for understanding in a new way the influence of the dead "God."

Yahweh Liberates Himself

The early Hebrew people, the people collectively identified with Abraham and his family, were Canaanites and polytheists, worshipping many gods and goddesses. The biblical story brings the early Hebrew people into a thoroughly polytheistic Egypt, where literally fourteen hundred to two thousand or more gods and goddesses were known.[7] Along with this vast array of local and national deities, the king of Egypt, the pharaoh, was also a deity. The traditional story of Exodus, read naturalistically as if it is about people, tells us of the liberation of the Hebrews, who had been oppressed and enslaved under the cruel hand of the Egyptians, by a Yahweh who had become a great warrior. A closer look at the whole story, however, beginning in Genesis, from our soul-development point of view, reveals that the problem of Egypt was Yahweh himself. The exodus from Egypt, read psychologically, was about Yahweh extracting himself from the polytheistic cosmos; Egypt was the perfect symbol of that cosmos, in which Yahweh was originally at home.[8] In this story Yahweh takes another step in freeing himself from the all-pervading world of nature polytheism that Egypt symbolized. He intended to have his own land where he alone could reign supreme. For psychology, the Exodus story of the liberation of the Hebrews is only secondarily about the people insofar as they are the self-image of Yahweh; Yahweh needs the people in order to become real himself. The Hebrew people, the characters in this narrative, symbolize the empirical (historical) embodiment of Yahweh's intent. Yahweh and the people are a symbiotic pair in which each cannot exist without the other. Yahweh, in trying to become a deity who transcends nature, who is superior to the other nature gods and goddesses, is fighting for his own life, his own liberation. Ancient Yahweh represented a soul impulse that wanted to break free from its existence in and as natural phenomena. Today, soul's seeming tendency to continue its self-liberation project is still at

---

7. *Wikipedia*, s.v. "Ancient Egyptian deities," last updated April 20, 2022, https://en.wikipedia.org/wiki/Ancient_Egyptian_deities.

8. During the fourteenth century BCE, Akhenaten, who ruled Egypt for about twenty years, tried to introduce the worship of one god, Aten, a solar deity, and to eradicate the prevailing polytheism. That was a short-lived failure. After his death, natural polytheism returned, and Akhenaten's memory was eradicated by succeeding rulers, only to be rediscovered by nineteenth-century archaeologists. Perhaps Akhenaten's attempt was inspired by soul's general inclination toward monotheism, but in that cultural context it failed and was swallowed up by polytheism. Akhenaten's attempt also appears to have been an external imposition of an idea, while the new idea of Yahweh appears to have developed from within itself, an internal development within the gods and goddesses that permeated the consciousness of a people. But, it is also important to remember that monotheism did not become the form of consciousness of a civilization until the spread of Christianity.

work.[9] Yahweh, in his original form as a Bull-Storm god, was undergoing a powerful metamorphosis, and the divorce from Asherah actually required self-castration, that is, he had to cut himself off from himself. Yahweh was compelled to renounce his natural bull form and become an imageless spirit (no graven images, no idols). The dramatic story of how this cut is carried out begins with the book of Exodus.

Yahweh Sets the Stage Against Himself

Read from a traditional and human point of view, Exodus is the classic story of liberation, in which God is the beneficent liberator of the enslaved and oppressed people. The psychological perspective from the point of view of soul is different. Yahweh was originally a Canaanite nature-rooted Bull and Storm god, along with El and Baal, and like the other male Canaanite nature deities, he had a goddess consort. The story of Exodus from the psychological perspective is the story of Yahweh's self-emancipation from his nature-based essence. Soul was undergoing a revolutionary change, pushing off from its ground in nature and moving toward a nature-transcending, spirit-based existence. The new spirit of Yahweh, symbolized by the Hebrew people, is "oppressed" within the Egyptian world of polytheism, when actually Yahweh had planned his own total immersion in Egypt.

Returning to Genesis for a moment, let's recall one of Abraham's encounters with Yahweh. Abraham had already heard four promises that he would have untold descendants and land, and yet, still nothing happened, and especially no children of his own that would lead to future descendants. He is frustrated and angry, and after yet another promise of land, Abraham demands to know how he can trust Yahweh to keep his word. In response Yahweh cuts a covenant with Abraham, the archaic ritual of cutting animals in half that we witnessed in the last chapter. But, in the middle of this covenant ceremony of ritual slaughter, a strange thing happens:

> As the sun was going down, a deep sleep fell upon Abram, and a deep terrifying darkness descended upon him. Then the LORD said to Abram, "Know this for certain, that your offspring shall be aliens in a land that is not theirs and shall be slaves there, and they shall be oppressed for four hundred years; but I will bring judgment on the nation that they serve, and afterward they shall come out with great possessions." (Gen 15:12–14)

This is clearly a reference to the time in Egypt, and from the Bible's point of view, Yahweh is in charge of all the significant action, events, and decisions. God himself sets the stage and makes sure things happen the way he wants them to happen.

Following the line of Abraham's descendants, Isaac, Jacob, and Joseph, the narrative moves through Joseph directly into Egypt. Throughout that story, Yahweh stays in the background and is almost invisible, but, he is present enough to make

---

9. I explore the contemporary phenomenology of soul in chapter 9.

sure Joseph in Egypt is extraordinarily successful.[10] As the story unfolds, the Hebrew people, that is, Abraham's tribe, end up in Egypt themselves because of famine, and who is in charge of the crops, the rain or the lack of rain? The Bull-Storm god Yahweh. The text is very clear that Yahweh is the direct cause of the seven-year nationwide famine that engulfs Egypt and spreads beyond. To say that these are literary and plot-driven foregone conclusions is to step outside of the narrative and view it externally from the point of view of the logic of humanistic consciousness, modern rational, consciousness. Humanistic consciousness is not wrong, but it is decidedly different from the soul perspective. The theological point of view also sees that God is thoroughly in charge but fails to see that God was undergoing a profound transformation from within. From the point of view of soul, Yahweh was Truth writ large and deeply throughout at least a thousand years of Western civilization. When the Bible was the ground of Truth, it was not a literary work but revelation, the *word of God*. And, thus it shaped the syntax of our Western consciousness.

Pharaoh has a well-known dream of "seven sleek and fat cows" that are devoured by "seven ugly and thin" cows. The dream motif repeats with "seven plump and good ears of grain" swallowed by "seven thin and blighted ears of grain."[11] Brought before Pharaoh and asked to interpret the dream, Joseph replies, "It is not I; God will give Pharaoh a favorable answer." After he hears the dreams Joseph replies:

> Pharaoh's dreams are one and the same; God has revealed to Pharaoh what he is about to do . . . There will come seven years of great plenty throughout all the land of Egypt. After them there will arise seven years of famine, and all the plenty will be forgotten in the land of Egypt; the famine will consume the land . . . And the doubling of Pharaoh's dream means that the thing is fixed by God, and God will shortly bring it about. (Gen 41:25-32)

Pharaoh is greatly impressed by Joseph's interpretation and sees that the spirit and wisdom of God is in him.

> Pharaoh said to his servants, "Can we find anyone else like this—one in whom is the spirit of God [a god]?" So Pharaoh said to Joseph, "Since God [a god] has shown you all this, there is no one so discerning and wise as you. You shall be over my house, and all my people shall order themselves as you command." (Gen 41:38-40)

Pharaoh, in effect, gives Joseph the keys to the kingdom and puts him in charge of preparing the Egyptian nation during the seven years of abundance for the inevitable seven years of famine. An interesting note is that Pharaoh doesn't argue about which god, or whose god, is at work here. The English word *God* is used to translate the Hebrew word *elohim*, which is the plural form of *El*, a basically generic term for "a

---

10. Gen 39:2, 21, 23; 41:37.
11. Gen 41:1-8.

god."[12] Pharaoh recognizes a divine agent at work in Joseph's insight and in return gives Joseph a great deal of power to use his insight and wisdom to protect the kingdom of Egypt. Who is really at work in the text? For the biblical narrative, and for us as soul's interpreter, it is clear that Yahweh is running the show, setting the stage for his own purposes. This becomes crystal clear in Joseph's own understanding of the larger situation. Joseph's family, his father, Jacob, and his brothers, are also suffering the famine in Canaan. Later, after Joseph's brothers have come to Egypt to buy grain, he tells them:

> "Come closer to me." And they came closer. He said, "I am your brother, Joseph, whom you sold into Egypt. And now do not be distressed, or angry with yourselves, because you sold me here; for God sent me before you to preserve life. For the famine has been in the land these two years; and there are five more years in which there will be neither plowing nor harvest. God sent me before you to preserve for you a remnant on earth, and to keep alive for you many survivors. So it was not you who sent me here, but God; he has made me a father to Pharaoh, and lord of all his house and ruler over all the land of Egypt. Hurry and go up to my father and say to him, 'Thus says your son Joseph, God has made me lord of all Egypt; come down to me, do not delay. You shall settle in the land of Goshen, and you shall be near me, you and your children and your children's children, as well as your flocks, your herds, and all that you have.'" (Gen 45:4–10)

Joseph interprets his life circumstances in terms of the purposes of *elohim*, who is also Yahweh. It is as if Yahweh needs to be imprisoned in Egypt in order to escape from Egypt, which is how I read the paradox of this literary determinism describing soul's general condition as archaic soul. Later, during Jacob's journey to Egypt to reunite with his lost son, Yahweh tells him that he, Yahweh, is going to Egypt too:

> When Israel set out on his journey with all that he had and came to Beersheba, he offered sacrifices to the God of his father Isaac. God spoke to Israel in visions of the night, and said, "Jacob, Jacob." And he said, "Here I am." Then he said, "I am God, the God of your father; do not be afraid to go down to Egypt, for I will make of you a great nation there. I myself will go down with you to Egypt, and I will also bring you up again." (Gen 46:1–4a)

Yahweh is in charge here, not human persons. In fact, for my reading, the Hebrew people of this drama, Joseph, Jacob, and his family, represent the movement and

---

12. The NRSV translates *elohim* here simply as "God," while Fox translates as "a god." Natural polytheism is very tolerant and inclusive of gods and goddesses in general. Pharaoh is not concerned with which god is helping Joseph, but clearly a god is helping. But, Fox's translation differentiates in that when Joseph speaks it uses "God" and when Pharaoh speaks it uses "a god," for the same word *elohim*. The NRSV generally blots out the natural distinctions between multiple gods that existed in the polytheistic environment of Joseph and Pharaoh, which again reminds us of the modern mind's habituation to monotheism as the one and only truth.

development of Yahweh. As Yahweh's self-image, the people and their exodus from Egypt dramatize the intense and fierce struggle of soul to escape from natural polytheism. This struggle takes place in terms of a war of the gods and an interior war of a god against himself.

A narrative presents human persons and events occurring in chronological time. The Abrahamic stories, and especially the story of Joseph, are wonderfully and even typically human. Let us keep in mind, however, that this very humanness seduces us to read the stories as primarily human and historical, so that we fail to see soul's movement, the logic of Yahweh's truth, as immersed, even imprisoned, in nature as the Bull-Storm god he once was. Egypt symbolizes Yahweh's polytheistic status, his truth as a nature god. The story of the exodus out of Egypt makes narratively visible what is logically invisible. Of course, the Exodus story is told in hindsight from the point of view of Yahweh already liberated. This is what the Bible is, a work of reflection in the rearview mirror so to speak, a reflection and interpretation, not a record of historical events, but of soul's new status, of Yahweh as the new form of consciousness that soul is striving to become. The Bible tells its story from the point of view of the already liberated Yahweh, a firmly monotheistic point of view, even though certainly not yet a fully achieved monotheism. Remember the status of Yahweh before his liberation, which was the context of that liberation. The Hebrew people were the self-image of Yahweh, and the people and Yahweh share the same status, symbolized by their oppression in Egypt. This is an internal affair: Yahweh for and against himself.

Moses and Yahweh: Two Peas in a Pod

Although Moses and Yahweh appear as two distinct personalities, or entities, they are manifestations of the same soul impulse. They share identical phenomenology: They are both bull-headed, impulsive, fiery killers, and they are singularly focused on one objective: to liberate Yahweh from himself.

Yahweh and Moses are killers, murderers in fact, but of course this is not principally how we remember them. Yet, liberation requires violence against the state of being that is experienced as oppressive, and the book of Exodus has plenty of violence and blood. Murder in this story will be the actual act of liberation, and Moses' first act is indeed murder:

> One day, after Moses had grown up, he went out to his people and saw their forced labor. He saw an Egyptian beating a Hebrew, one of his kinsfolk. He looked this way and that, and seeing no one he killed the Egyptian and hid him in the sand. (Exod 2:11–12)

Tradition remembers Moses as the first prophet, the first priest, the lawgiver, even the first Messiah (king) (not literally, but in spirit), but "murderer" is not on that list, although kings are often warriors, and warriors are out for victory by spilling blood. I contend that this easily overlooked moment in Moses' life reveals the true logic of the monotheistic impulse that both Moses and Yahweh embody. That impulse advances and establishes itself by way of a bloody war and a bloody divorce. Violence and killing are the path, and this path becomes a genocidal one. And, yet, while the narrative sheds much blood and has many people and peoples killed, the real killing from the point of view of soul is deicide, that is, the killing of the gods and goddesses, which itself is the killing of Yahweh's own nature-based bull-storm-god self. Psychologically, this is soul's war against itself, for itself, on the way to a new form of consciousness. In terms of archaic soul, this war is the struggle of a new consciousness (informed by the logic of literacy and writing) to establish itself by pushing off from its original immersion in nature, where it is primarily in an illiterate state of oral traditions. For our reading, this story is soul's dream of itself, the unfolding of its logic as consciousness; it is not primarily about historical peoples fighting each other (which is not to deny the empirical human suffering that follows soul's logical transformations).

In Exodus, Yahweh appears as a new character not seen in Genesis, a warrior with a constitution of fire. He needs a general on earth to carry out his program, and Moses is chosen in the context of a fiery revelation that binds them to each other. After Moses killed the Egyptian overlord, he fled Egypt because he became a marked man. He married, had a son, and worked for his father-in-law as a shepherd in Midian. We can think of him as a rebel leader in exile, although he has not yet been commissioned. That happens next on a mountain, undoubtedly the ritual site of a local deity, where he meets a god of fire:

> Moses was keeping the flock of his father-in-law Jethro, the priest of Midian; he led his flock beyond the wilderness, and came to Horeb, the mountain of God [El]. There the angel of the LORD [Yahweh] appeared to him in a flame of fire out of a bush; he looked, and the bush was blazing, yet it was not consumed. Then Moses said, "I must turn aside and look at this great sight, and see why the bush is not burned up." When the LORD [Yahweh] saw that he turned aside to see, God [El] called to him out of the bush, "Moses, Moses!" And he said, "Here I am." (Exod 3:1–4)

El, the angel (or messenger) of Yahweh, and the fire are one and the same deity, the same god of fire, and an unnatural fire at that, as it does not burn the bush. Fire is the primary character of this Yahweh: He is intense, passionate, fierce, and quick to a consuming anger. Yahweh's anger is almost always "hot" and "kindled," a fiery wrath. He is a commanding, active presence, who, like fire, radiates his claim, his purposes and demands. Moses can resist this god's claim on him, but he cannot escape because fire is also Moses' disposition, and to try to escape the claim of the fiery warrior god would be to deny his own essence ("He went out from Pharaoh in flaming anger").[13] In the end, of course, the fiery liberating purpose of Yahweh and Moses wins out. But,

---

13. Fox, *Five Books*, Exod 11:8; NRSV, "And in hot anger he left Pharaoh."

throughout this story there is massive resistance internal to soul's own constitution, which in the context of our story is natural polytheism refusing to give up its hold. The resistance is more often than not personified as the Egyptians and the Hebrew people, but interestingly enough it is Yahweh who resists himself. His fierce and unbending intent is to free the Hebrew people from Egyptian oppression, but he continually gets in his own way.

Remembering that Yahweh set up the Egyptian situation, we see that Yahweh himself is the real source of resistance. Yahweh's original nature is a Bull-Storm god, one among many deities in the natural polytheistic cosmos. The Exodus story is the struggle of Yahweh to liberate himself from himself. Egypt symbolizes the status of Yahweh as a Bull god, a nature god, as soul immersed in the natural world, which is also evident in Yahweh's natural consort relationship with Asherah. The resistance to Yahweh's divorce occurs at every level, including Moses, the Hebrew people, Pharaoh, and Yahweh himself. With the word *resistance*, I am not saying it is wrong or mistaken. It might be better to say *inertia*, the natural tendency of any condition or system to maintain and preserve itself. Soul operates dialectically, always in conflict with itself. When a new soul-direction emerges, in our case the new form of Yahweh, soul's former version of itself gets characterized in a negative light, expressed in Yahweh's hate of the goddess and also his self-hate in the story of the golden calf and the creation of idolatry.

Immediately after Moses meets the fire god El (the burning bush), Yahweh speaks to Moses:

> Then the LORD [Yahweh] said, "I have observed the misery of my people who are in Egypt; and I have heard their cry on account of their taskmasters. Indeed, I know their sufferings, and I have come down to deliver them from the Egyptians, and to bring them up out of that land to a good and broad land, a land flowing with milk and honey, to the country of the Canaanites, the Hittites, the Amorites, the Perizzites, and the Hivites, and the Jebusites. The cry of the Israelites has now come to me; I have also seen how the Egyptians oppress them. So come, I will send you to Pharaoh to bring my people, the Israelites, out of Egypt." But Moses said to God [El], "Who am I that I should go to Pharaoh, and bring the Israelites out of Egypt?" (Exod 3:7–11)

Here is a synopsis of the program that stalled with Abraham and is reinvigorated with Moses. The original promise to Abraham has been waylaid in Egypt for four hundred years (according to the narrative), but now Yahweh pushes to finish the job. One wrinkle is that the land of "milk and honey" is already inhabited by indigenous peoples and by other nature gods and goddesses; in fact, the Hebrews are themselves from Canaan. Let us also remember that land, people, and gods/goddesses are a unity, an integrated whole, including a cultural way of life, which is true in Egypt as well. The "promised land" is not free and empty territory, but that step of the journey takes place later. Clearly, Yahweh wants a place, a land, and a people, for himself, and so he commissions Moses, but Moses is tentative and hesitant. Moses says this job is way over his head; he can't do it. Over and over, Moses resists his calling, which is symbolic of soul's inherent resistance to this change. First, Moses argues that he and the people need to know God's name; then he argues that the people will not listen to him or believe him; next, he complains that he is not eloquent and is a terrible speaker ("I am slow of speech and slow of tongue"). Each time God provides a reassuring reply, but Moses can only say, "O my Lord, please send someone else." Resistance (inertia in the face of change) runs deep. Finally, the fire breaks through and reaches Moses: "Then the anger of the LORD [Yahweh] was kindled [burned] against Moses, and he said, 'What of your brother Aaron, the Levite? I know that he can speak fluently'" (Exod 4:13–14). Yahweh's fire reaches Moses' fire, and they ignite together. Understood psychologically, this moment is their shared fire burning through its own inertia, nonetheless inertia will accompany this movement every step of the way.

Another instance of Yahweh's self-contradiction appears in a peculiar episode during Moses' journey from Midian back to Egypt. This is one of those strange brief insertions found in the Bible that seem to come out of nowhere. Easily overlooked because it does not make sense and has no connection to the narrative, it relates back to the circumcision rite. After the revelation of the fiery bush and the extended conversation in which Yahweh chooses Moses to undertake the great task of liberation, this happens:

> On the way, at a place where they spent the night, the LORD [Yahweh] met him and tried to kill him. But Zipporah [his wife] took a flint and cut off her son's foreskin, and touched Moses' feet [genitals] with it, and said, "Truly you are a bridegroom of blood to me!" So he [Yahweh] let him alone. It was then she said, "A bridegroom of blood by circumcision." (Exod 4:24–26)

Did Yahweh already forget who Moses is? Yahweh warned Moses not to get too close to the fiery bush, and direct contact with a deity in antiquity could be dangerous, even fatal, for humans. Of course, fire is literally dangerous, quickly flares out of control, and so why would a fiery god be any different? Yahweh is not a "nice" god, but a wild bull, an unpredictable storm, an archaic nature god. There is no rational explanation for this strange textual insertion except as a witness to soul's dialectical self-contradiction, as well as nature's own self-contradiction, vacillating between life-sustaining abundance and life-destroying famine. Yahweh the warrior is a dangerous power, and the sacrifice of circumcision blood protects Moses. Even though Moses and Yahweh are the same fire, it appears that Moses had to be bound to Yahweh even more tightly, at least through the apotropaic (and here, virtual) rite of circumcision. A blood sacrifice appears to satisfy the nature god's own sacrificial impulse, as well as the archaic soul's blood imperative. This reminds me of Yahweh's urge to have Abraham kill Isaac, which would have thwarted Yahweh's own intended ambition. Here, Yahweh's impulse to kill Moses would put an end to his intended self-liberation; in the face of his own grand plan, Yahweh seems also to be his own worst enemy. In these strange self-contradictory texts, soul is fighting with itself. The archaic nature-bound soul exists side by side with a soul straining to transcend its nature-bound status for the sake of a new cultural identity in which soul will infuse word and make texts sacred. Such strange textual anomalies do not need rationalization when we understand that soul is a dialectical self-relation that progresses through self-negation and sublation. This is a cultural dream with its own internal logic and purpose.

Next, however, something even more unusual occurs. Yahweh's tendency to block his own goal continues. Yahweh tells Moses up front—and thus, he is also telling himself—that he himself will prevent Pharaoh from letting the people go:

> And the LORD [Yahweh] said to Moses, "When you go back to Egypt, see that you perform before Pharaoh all the wonders that I have put in your power; but I will harden his heart, so that he will not let the people go." (Exod 4:21)

Wait a minute! Yahweh wants to free his people from Egypt, and yet he himself will prevent it? Indeed. Throughout the entire process of convincing Pharaoh to let the people go, Yahweh hardens Pharaoh's heart over and over to prevent it. The reason the biblical text gives for Yahweh's self-contradictory behavior is that in this way Yahweh will prove what a powerful and mighty warrior he is to the Egyptians, to the world, and of course, to himself:

> Say therefore to the Israelites, "I am the LORD [Yahweh], and I will free you from the burdens of the Egyptians and deliver you from slavery to them. I will redeem you with an outstretched arm and with mighty acts of judgment. I will take you as my people, and I will be your God [El]. You shall know that I am the LORD [Yahweh] your God [El], who has freed you from the burdens of the Egyptians. I will bring you into the land that I swore to give to Abraham, Isaac, and Jacob; I will give it to you for a possession. I am the LORD [Yahweh].'" Moses told this to the Israelites; but they would not listen to Moses, because of their broken spirit and their cruel slavery. (Exod 6:6–9)

The images of "outstretched arm" and "mighty acts of judgment" refer to a warrior's powerful acts of violence, destruction, and conquest. In spite of Yahweh's great boasts, however, more resistance shows itself in the people's demoralized and despairing state. In fact, after Moses' first demand to Pharaoh to free the Hebrew people, the Egyptians merely doubled-down on the Hebrews, intensifying the forced labor and oppressive conditions, leading Moses to complain to Yahweh that nothing has changed and that Yahweh is an ineffectual do-nothing.[14] Yahweh simply doubles down himself, bringing ten plagues, or disasters, upon the Egyptians to convince them to follow Moses' demand for freedom.

The ten disasters follow in succession, each one more horrible than the last. If we took them literally, just three of them would have ended life in the Egyptian kingdom

---

14. Exod 5:1–22.

with the complete destruction of all plant life and all livestock. Yet, after each one, Pharaoh's heart is hardened, and he refuses to let the Hebrew people go. In a few instances, Pharaoh himself authors his own pigheaded callousness, but Yahweh is really the active agent: "But the LORD [Yahweh] hardened the heart of Pharaoh, and he would not listen to them, just as the LORD had spoken to Moses" (Exod 9:12). But Yahweh also wants Pharaoh to know why this liberation project is dragging on:

> Then the LORD said to Moses, "Rise up early in the morning and present yourself before Pharaoh, and say to Him, 'Thus says the LORD, the God of the Hebrews: Let my people go, so that they may worship me. For this time I will send all my plagues upon you yourself, and upon your officials, and upon your people, so that you may know that there is no one like me in all the earth. For by now I could have stretched out my hand and struck you and your people with pestilence, and you would have been cut off from the earth. But this is why I have let you live: to show you my power, and to make my name resound through all the earth.'" (Exod 9:13–16)

Again, the same message:

> Then the LORD [Yahweh] said to Moses, "Go to Pharaoh; for I have hardened his heart and the heart of his officials, in order that I may show these signs of mine among them, and that you may tell your children and grandchildren how I have made fools of the Egyptians and what signs I have done among them—so that you may know that I am the LORD [Yahweh]." (Exod 10:1–2)

Now Yahweh's goal is clear. He will not settle for being one victorious warrior among others. He will be the greatest warrior, the renowned warrior, the most powerful warrior in the known world! This is the legacy and the reputation he wants. And in fact, his mighty liberation work in Egypt will remain his calling card for future generations, especially when they doubt that Yahweh will follow through on his promises. Looking ahead a bit, Yahweh's identity as the Great and All-Powerful Warrior will become a problem and a liability when, as the next chapter will show, history does not cooperate, and Yahweh the warrior must confront failure. For now, however, Yahweh is the most powerful warrior, and the tenth and last disaster Yahweh visits on the Egyptians will prove it.

This has been a cat and mouse game, Yahweh toying with the Egyptians by ruining everything all around them but not yet killing any Egyptians. Now it turns deadly. The story of Passover is probably one of the best-known in the Bible: Yahweh carries out a death curse on the Egyptian people that finally convinces Pharaoh to free the Hebrews. The focus of the Passover rite is on the protection afforded to the Hebrew people and their subsequent liberation from Egypt. Yet the story is also one of widespread ritual slaughter. Although it is not remembered as the Slaughter of the First Born, this is exactly Yahweh's power as warrior, to give life and to bring death. This last disaster will be spectacular:

Yahweh's Violent Rupture: Soul's Revolution

> The LORD [Yahweh] said to Moses, "I will bring one more plague upon Pharaoh and upon Egypt; afterwards he will let you go from here; indeed, when he lets you go, he will drive you away." (Exod 11:1)

Then Yahweh tells Moses what is in store:

> Thus says the LORD: About midnight I will go out through Egypt. Every firstborn in the land of Egypt shall die, from the firstborn of Pharaoh who sits on the throne to the firstborn of the female slave who is behind the handmill, and all the firstborn of the livestock. (Exod 11:4-5)

But, Yahweh is not finished intensifying the internal pressure of the whole situation, still he hardens Pharaoh's heart:

> The LORD [Yahweh] said to Moses, "Pharaoh will not listen to you, in order that my wonders may be multiplied in the land of Egypt." Moses and Aaron performed all these wonders before Pharaoh; but the LORD [Yahweh] hardened Pharaoh's heart, and he did not let the people of Israel go out of his land. (Exod 11:9-10)

Soul's real conflict is internal with itself, and so symbolically, Yahweh's real conflict is with the other nature gods and goddesses. This is explicit in another description of the plague to come:

> It is the passover of the LORD [Yahweh]. For I will pass through the land of Egypt that night, and I will strike down every firstborn in the land of Egypt, both human beings and animals; on all the gods of Egypt I will execute judgments: I am the LORD [Yahweh]. (Exod 12:11b-12)

The "passover" of the Lord is the Lord's slaughter of the innocent, those who happened to be born first. Even though we know today this did not happen historically, that such a thing could not actually happen, it is still a remarkable image of indiscriminate slaughter. Yes, of course, Yahweh discriminates between Egyptians and Hebrews—that is the whole point. But the emphasis on the passing over of the Hebrew people conveniently enables us to turn a blind eye to God carrying out a vast ritual slaughter of innocent human persons:

> At midnight the LORD [Yahweh] struck down all the firstborn in the land of Egypt, from the firstborn of Pharaoh who sat on his throne to the firstborn of the prisoner who was in the dungeon, and all the firstborn of the livestock. Pharaoh arose in the night, he and all his officials and all the Egyptians; and there was a loud cry in Egypt, for there was not a house without someone dead. (Exod 12:29-30)

Our "God" has genocidal tendencies. Even though we are not reading the Bible literally, nor on a human level, if we do not gloss over the imagery of this story, we are struck by a horrifying slaughter of innocents. In the story, thousands are killed for no reason other than that Yahweh had to prove how great and powerful he was. Another point to note here, however, is that Yahweh does not really care for human beings. Human life per se is relevant only if it supports Yahweh's greater aims. Yahweh is out for himself, and his rallying cry is "I am the Lord!" Yahweh will not spare anyone his penchant for slaughter if they do not adhere to this new truth of his: "I am Yahweh!" Nature itself is impersonal, natural phenomena occur with no regard for the effect on people. This would be true of the nature gods of polytheism as they were not dependent on people for their existence and cared little for people as such, though people were completely dependent on nature and the nature gods and goddesses. However, the new Yahweh was a different sort of deity. He was completely dependent on the self-image he had created, the Hebrew people (who later became Israel, who then became the Jews). Yahweh cared about his people only to the extent that they paid attention to him exclusively. For Yahweh, human beings had no value in their own right and continue to exist only at the pleasure of Yahweh.[15] He will have no compunction slaughtering the Hebrew people if they deviate from the truth that he is and insists that he is. Violence seems to be an innate quality of Yahweh, an integral aspect of his vitality. I want to stress that these observations are not judgments of Yahweh. Rather I underscore the phenomenology of Yahweh, which reflects the phenomenology of soul, otherwise overlooked and glossed over. These violent and impersonal characteristics show us the cold distance of soul, in contrast to our modern romantic and comforting images of soul.

Liberation, and resistance to liberation, seem to belong to each other. A new people, a new god, a new idea, do not emerge except against terrific resistance. This is because a people, a god, an idea, can emerge only within an already existing field of peoples, gods, and ideas. The existing truths are the womb of the new, and yet, they will fight against the birth of the new, a labor that is always in danger of failing. The new will push against what already exists in order to establish itself, to bring itself forth; the new will undertake the labor to make itself real. This is true of Yahweh's labor to establish himself and distinguish himself within the crowded field of nature gods and goddesses. Yahweh's ultimate desire is not merely to stand out in the crowd, however, just as his efforts for a bloody and messy divorce are not aimed only to separate. No, he wants to eradicate all the other gods and goddesses, become dominant himself and rule over all. This is not an indictment of Yahweh's power trip, nor a judgment on the evils of patriarchy, but an observation of soul's telos. Soul's telos is to overcome itself and to give birth to a new form of consciousness. It is not really about power per se, especially not as humans view it, but the internal struggle within soul when oral and preliterate culture was ruptured by the emergence of literacy and the written word. As far as the form of consciousness of public mind was concerned, this changed everything. Clearly, literacy has overthrown the preliterate world.

---

15. Innate human dignity is a modern idea, an ideal of humanism, which I explore in chapter 8.

Yahweh's Violent Rupture: Soul's Revolution

The dynamic interplay between liberation and resistance continues throughout the story of Exodus. Even as the Hebrews are escaping Egypt, Yahweh the warrior still has to prove himself:

> I will harden Pharaoh's heart, and he will pursue them [the Hebrews], so that I will gain glory for myself over Pharaoh and all his army; and the Egyptians shall know that I am the LORD [Yahweh]. (Exod 14:4)

Pharaoh and his army pursue the Hebrews, and the Hebrews, now terrified, cry out, "For it would have been better for us to serve the Egyptians [here we can add 'gods'] than to die in the wilderness" (Exod 14:12). Moses may be aligned with this new Yahweh, but the Hebrew people are not. They have been in Egypt for over four hundred years, and the Egyptian gods are their friends, their known world. Yahweh's fight to establish himself is a constant uphill battle. The final battle with Pharaoh occurs with the miraculous parting of the sea and the defeat of Pharaoh and his army. Finally, Pharaoh and the Egyptians are overthrown. Is the resistance to change overthrown? No, now the resistance simply shifts to the Hebrew people, who must wander in the wilderness for years, in profound uncertainty about what is next. Soul's struggle with itself grinds on every step of the way. Archaic soul, nature-polytheism, the very essence of the context of the biblical narrative, will soon suffer an even more violent splitting within itself.

Violent Divorce and Self-Castration

Yahweh needed tremendous energy to divorce Asherah, pull himself out of Egypt, castrate himself as a Bull-Storm god, and leave behind his nature essence. This tremendous and violent impulse is at the heart of the biblical story. The centuries-long process of soul splitting itself off from its identity as a nature-deity in order to become transcendent, imageless, word, and spirit, in the biblical story of this process, required great fierce red-hot energy. As that energy, Yahweh the Bull-Storm god, a great warrior, a fierce and impersonal brute force, was focused on only one thing: *Itself*, declared absolutely with the words, "I am Yahweh!"

"On the third new moon" after their escape from Egypt, Moses and the Hebrew people come to the Sinai and God's mountain. Here the decisive communication occurs, when Yahweh defines himself as a non-nature deity and cuts himself off from his bull nature. Yahweh's fire nature is on full display:

> Now Mount Sinai was wrapped in smoke, because the LORD [Yahweh] had descended upon it in fire; the smoke went up like the smoke of a kiln, while the whole mountain shook violently.
>
> . . .
>
> Now the appearance of the glory of the LORD was like a devouring fire on the top of the mountain in the sight of the people of Israel. (Exod 19:18; 24:17)

God's Autopsy and the Living Truth of Soul

The presence of Yahweh makes the mountain unsafe for everyone except Moses. A clear boundary is established to keep the people at a distance, otherwise they will die.[16] Yahweh is a *terrible* deity in the full sense of the word. The area around Yahweh is like a war zone: If you don't watch out, if you make a mistake, you die. If you do not obey the rules, you die, and Yahweh sets up an extensive set of rules, beginning with what are known as the Ten Commandments. The central focus of these commands is to establish Yahweh as separate from and different from all the other nature gods and goddesses and, also, to divide him from himself. The first four directives consolidate Yahweh's identity over and against his own polytheistic essence:

> I am the LORD your God, who brought you out of the land of Egypt, out of the house of slavery; You shall have no other gods before [or, besides] me.

> You shall not make for yourself an idol, whether in the form of anything that is in heaven above, or that is on the earth beneath, or that is in the water under the earth. You shall not bow down to them or worship them; for I the LORD [Yahweh] your God [El] am a jealous God [El], punishing children for the iniquity [worshiping other gods] of parents, to the third and the fourth generation of those who reject me . . .

> You shall not make wrongful use of the name of the LORD your God, for the LORD will not acquit anyone who misuses his name.

> Remember the sabbath day, and keep it holy [separate]. Six days you shall labor and do all your work. But the seventh day is a sabbath to the LORD your God; you shall not do any work . . . the LORD blessed the sabbath day and consecrated it. (Exod 20:2-11)

The first directive is simply to turn away from the multitude of gods and goddesses everyone is familiar with, those they worship, sacrifice to, and honor. However, the nature gods and goddesses are the source of Life itself, so the prospect of turning away from *them* and focusing only on the *one* presents a problem. As we will soon see, it also means to forget about Yahweh's original bull nature. Yahweh's requirement to turn away from all the other gods and goddesses in the context of cultural natural polytheism was really quite extraordinary! This is indeed a revolutionary moment in soul's development.

The second directive intensifies the radical nature of these new requirements. Polytheistic culture was a symbol-saturated world. Carved wood, cast-metal symbols, and the like, large and small, were all around, alive with the presence of the gods they

---

16. Yahweh tells Moses: "You shall set limits for the people all around, saying, 'Be careful not to go up the mountain or to touch the edge of it. Any who touch the mountain shall be put to death. No hand shall touch them, but they shall be stoned or shot with arrows; whether animal or human being, they shall not live'" (Exod 19:12-13).

represented, but also natural and taken for granted in their ubiquity, common everywhere in public spaces, homes, and temples. For us today, the words *idol* and *idolatry* are thoroughly saturated with powerful negativity because the Bible absolutely excoriates such images and practices. We need to recall that so-called idols were natural images produced by soul and for soul. The nature gods and goddesses had a visceral and sensual presence in these objects, and thoroughly taken for granted, these symbols embodied a transpersonal presence that was the natural logic of soul in antiquity. The emerging Yahweh, however, hated the other gods and goddesses, and he was constantly at war against them. When Yahweh promised to conquer the land of Canaan for the Hebrew people, he really meant the conquest of the other gods and goddesses:

> When my angel goes in front of you, and brings you to the Amorites, the Hittites, the Perizzites, and the Canaanites, the Hivites, and the Jebusites, and I blot them out, you shall not bow down to their gods, or worship them, or follow their practices, but you shall utterly demolish them and break their pillars in pieces. (Exod 23:23-24)

The pillars (symbolic of trees) were symbols of the goddess, often referred to as Asherah, using the name of the goddess associated with the archaic Bull god Yahweh:

> You shall not plant any tree as a sacred pole [Asherah] beside the altar that you make for the LORD your God; nor shall you set up a stone pillar—things that the LORD your God hates. (Deut 16:21-22)

Punishment for wavering from acknowledging only Yahweh, for honoring other gods and goddesses, was death:

> If there is found among you, in one of your towns that the LORD your God is giving you, a man or woman who does what is evil in the sight of the LORD your God, and transgresses his covenant by going to serve other gods and worshipping them—whether the sun or the moon or any of the host of heaven, which I have forbidden—and if it is reported to you and you hear of it, and you make a thorough inquiry, and the charge is proved true that such an abhorrent thing has occurred in Israel, then you shall bring out to your gates that man or that woman who has committed this crime and you shall stone the man or woman to death . . . So you shall purge the evil from your midst. (Deut 17:2-5, 7b)[17]

---

17. See Deut 13:6-18 for another example of the death penalty which extends to the "sacrificial ban" placed on an entire village. If a family member, brother, wife, son, daughter, entices you to worship other gods, "show them no pity or compassion and do not shield them. But you shall surely kill them; your own hand shall be first against them to execute them . . ." If an entire town is led astray to worship other gods, "you shall put the inhabitants of that town to the sword, utterly destroying it and everything in it—even putting its livestock to the sword. All of its spoil you shall gather into its public square; then burn the town and all its spoil with fire, as a whole burnt offering to the LORD your God. It shall remain a perpetual ruin, never to be rebuilt. Do not let anything devoted to destruction stick to your hand, so that the LORD may turn from his fierce anger and show you compassion." Here

Idol and idolatry in their native context were not evil, but natural expressions of nature worship and the divine in nature. This was soul's original most natural expression, its immersion in nature, in all indigenous and early cultures. Later, Christianity, especially during the medieval period in Europe, would extend the hate of soul in nature by equating idol and idolatry with the devil and devil worship. When Christianity first began to infiltrate pre-Christian Europe, it was fairly tolerant of the already existing nature worship practices and the other gods and goddesses. As Christianity became more established, however, it turned more aggressively against so-called pagan practices. Christianity was the continuation of soul's struggle to emancipate itself from its immersion in nature, and at a terrible and tragic cost to human life. Soul was after something for itself, needing to break out of its containment in the natural world.

The third directive—not to make wrongful use of the name of God—meant never to use the name of the god in practices of magic and divination or in making false oaths. To use the name of one's god in an oath was to make a binding statement, and this directive warned against using an oath to cover up personal lying, deception, or fraud ("In the name of Yahweh, this pre-owned Cadillac is in great shape!"). The name of the god is a source of power, and magic rituals and divination were common in polytheistic culture. The new Yahweh is drawing a tight and exclusive circle around himself and his people.

The fourth directive about keeping the sabbath holy is another exclusive claim by Yahweh on time itself. The Hebrew word for *sabbath* simply means rest and refers to the seventh day on which God rested after creating the world in six days. This day of complete rest is a requirement in order to turn one's attention exclusively to Yahweh. It is Yahweh's time. Not optional, it is a claim that this time belongs only and absolutely to Yahweh, and at the same time, it is an absolute claim on the attention and devotion of Yahweh's created self-image, the Hebrew people. On this day, all attention is turned to Yahweh and only to Yahweh. The word *holy* is another Hebrew word that is often misunderstood. The Hebrew word translated as holy is *qadosh*, and it literally means "to be set apart for a special purpose."[18] Today holy has come to mean set apart from the common, or the secular, identifying a sense of the sacred and divine in itself. This modern understanding of *holy* comes about because modern consciousness splits apart the so-called holy and profane, but in antiquity, for archaic soul, such a split consciousness did not exist. Our modern understanding of holy is an abstraction

---

is another example where human life has less value than absolute loyalty to Yahweh. And, "devoted to destruction" meant that everything in the town belonged to Yahweh (no looting allowed) because everything had been contaminated by the cultic ritual practices offered to the other gods. Such complete destruction is itself a kind of human sacrifice (of his "enemies") to the god Yahweh. Here too we see the pervasive logic of archaic soul evidenced in the fear of contamination. Identity in the context of archaic soul was grounded in a *tribal*, that is, group logic, a "we" inclusive of land-people-gods. It is impossible for us today to appreciate the substantial reality of such contamination because our identity is grounded in the ontological certainty of being separate individuals, and notions of group contamination have no reality in our modern consciousness.

18. See https://www.ancient-hebrew.org/definition/holy.htm.

because we have completely lost all contact with the original context of what the word holy would have meant in a polytheistic culture. To keep the sabbath holy meant to keep Yahweh and this particular time separate from the other gods and goddesses and apart from any other cultic ritual practices associated with other deities.

The first four commandments are exclusively devoted to separating the new Yahweh from his original natural bull-god essence, that is, from archaic soul. However, I have gotten a bit ahead of myself here in relation to the narrative sequence of our story. These commandments are delivered a bit later, after Moses has spent a long time on the fiery mountain with the fiery god. Now we will return to Mount Sinai and Yahweh's continuing struggle with his bull nature.

In the scene on Mount Sinai, Yahweh was a terrible fire god, and an overwhelming volcanic storm: "The appearance of the glory of the Lord was like a devouring fire on the top of the mountain in the sight of the people of Israel." Into this "devouring fire" Moses went: "Moses entered the cloud, and went up on the mountain. Moses was on the mountain for forty days and forty nights" (Exod 24:18). During his time on the mountain, the narrative tells us that Moses received many rules and regulations governing social and religious behavior, detailed instructions about how to build cultic ritual objects, such as the special seat for Yahweh (the ark of the covenant), the dwelling tent for Yahweh (the tabernacle), and all its ritual objects and furnishings; how to ordain the priests who will oversee ritual practices and sacrifices and what clothing the priests should wear. All these details, while quite alien and tedious to our modern ears, are social and religious structures to ensure Yahweh is the one and only god of the Hebrew people. In spite of Yahweh's effort to separate himself from his bull nature, some of the details for both the altar and sacrifice reveal Yahweh's original bull essence. Here are Yahweh's instructions for the altar:

> You shall make the altar of acacia wood, five cubits long and five cubits wide; the altar shall be square, and it shall be three cubits high. You shall make horns for it on its four corners; its horns shall be of one piece with it, and you shall overlay it with bronze. (Exod 27:1–2)[19]

The horns were like a bull's, or oxen's, and they were the most powerful and protected part of the altar. Clearly, this is an altar for a Bull god. Part of the ritual for the ordination of the priests (at that time, Aaron and his sons of the tribe of Levi), included the following sacrifice of a bull:

> You shall bring the bull in front of the tent of meeting. Aaron and his sons shall lay their hands on the head of the bull, and you shall slaughter the bull before the LORD [Yahweh], at the entrance of the tent of meeting, and shall take some of the blood of the bull and put it on the horns of the altar with your

---

19. A cubit was an ancient Near Eastern measure based on the length from the elbow to the tip of the longest finger; about one and a half feet.

finger, and all the rest of the blood you shall pour out at the base of the altar. (Exod 29:10–12)

The fat from the bull's entrails, liver, and kidneys are burned on the altar. Two rams are also slaughtered, the blood dashed against the altar, and also applied to the lobe of Aaron's right ear, the thumb of his right hand, and the big toe of his right foot, thus symbolically bathing his entire body in the sacrificial blood. Yahweh details how the rams are to be cut up and washed; then, he says, "Turn the whole ram into smoke on the altar; it is a burnt offering to the LORD; it is a pleasing odor, an offering by fire to the LORD [Yahweh]" (Exod 29:18). Yahweh was essentially a horned god, like other gods of his time and place (Baal and El), and the bull was his most powerful representation. But Yahweh, in our text, also symbolizes soul's conflict with itself, the conflict between the practices and the logic of archaic soul and a newly emergent form of soul, a new Yahweh, who is separating from his animal, nature essence, struggling to free himself from the sensual imagery of his own substance. Soul's self-contradiction is evident as the vestiges of archaic Yahweh persist in the very text (Bible) that is trying to expurgate them.

The Golden Calf and the First Nuclear Fission

Now comes one of the best-known pivotal events in the long process of the new Yahweh turning against himself, and this is a most violent turning. It occurs at the end of Moses' long forty days and nights with Yahweh at the top of mount Sinai—an event known simply as the "golden calf."

> When the people saw that Moses delayed to come down from the mountain, the people gathered around Aaron, and said to him, "Come, make gods for us, who shall go before us; as for this Moses, the man who brought us up out of the land of Egypt, we do not know what has become of him." Aaron said to them, "Take off the gold rings that are on the ears of your wives, your sons, and your daughters, and bring them to me." So all the people took off the gold rings from their ears, and brought them to Aaron. He took the gold from them, formed it in a mold, and cast an image of a calf [bull]; and they said, "These are your gods, O Israel, who brought you up out of the land of Egypt!" (Exod 32:1–4)

If it is a calf, it is a bull calf, but more than likely the word *calf* is belittling and disparaging.[20] No one worshipped calves. The gold would have been forged into a radiant, golden bull, the natural Yahweh in his powerful glory. This is one of those "events" that, no doubt, never happened historically, but it is clear textual evidence of Yahweh's original bull essence with the people eagerly calling the golden bull "your gods, O Israel, who brought you up out of the land of Egypt!" Aaron built an altar before this

---

20. Giegerich, "Nuclear Bomb," 74.

golden image, and the people made sacrifices, ate and drank and partied ("rose up to revel"). Caught up in a playful celebration, even rowdy excess, the people enjoy the golden bull's exuberance and radiant vitality, the joyful exhibition of the power of life, and the living presence of their natural god Yahweh. In this vigorous animal form, their god is not a frightening volcanic eruption, but the presence of nature's irrepressible fertility and bounty. However, the new Yahweh on the mountaintop, the giver of the new sacred written word to Moses, has become aware of the celebration down below and is overcome with a murderous outrage:

> The LORD said to Moses, "Go down at once! Your people, whom you brought up out of the land of Egypt, have acted perversely; they have been quick to turn aside from the way that I commanded them; they have cast for themselves an image of a calf [bull], and have worshiped it and sacrificed to it, and said, 'These are your gods, O Israel, who brought you up out of the land of Egypt!'" The LORD said to Moses, "I have seen this people, how stiff-necked they are. Now let me alone, so that my wrath may burn hot against them and I may consume them; and of you I will make a great nation." (Exod 32:7–10)

Naturally, the narrator, writing a polemic in favor of monotheism, casts the bull worship as a perversity, as something horrible and disgusting, when in fact it was the most natural and innocent thing in their world. But Yahweh sees it as betrayal and treason, deserving of death, now! The new Yahweh's doctrine is zero tolerance—total obedience to this emergent impulse to cut itself off from its own bull nature, or death! No middle ground, no reminders, no rehabilitation. Yahweh would even make of Moses a second Abraham, and begin all over again. From the point of view of soul, the new truth hates the old truth. The narrative is a symbolic depiction of the development of soul, the turning of the new emergent syntax of consciousness against the currently existing one. It is a powerful emotional story told from the point of view of the hyperpersonal and emotionally reactive Yahweh. The impersonal nature of soul is reflected in the fact that Yahweh does not care about the people in any personal way. He cares about them only insofar as they carry out his demands and goals, providing him, so to speak, with a "body" as his people. Soul is indifferent to us human people, contrary to our modern humanistic ideals about innate human dignity and worth. Soul is dedicated to itself and itself alone, and we will continue to see this illustrated in Yahweh's personality. Moses, however, brings a personal argument to dissuade Yahweh from his murderous impulse. Interestingly, his persuasive leverage hinges on appealing to Yahweh's reputation and vanity in relation to the Egyptians:

> But Moses implored the LORD his God, and said, "O LORD, why does your wrath burn hot against your people, whom you brought out of the land of Egypt with great power and with a mighty hand? Why should the Egyptians say, 'It was with evil intent that he brought them out to kill them in the mountains, and to consume them from the face of the earth'? Turn from your fierce

wrath; change your mind and do not bring disaster on your people. Remember Abraham, Isaac, and Israel your servants, how you swore to them by your own self, saying to them, 'I will multiply your descendants like the stars of heaven, and all this land that I have promised I will give to your descendants, and they shall inherit it forever.'" And the LORD changed his mind about the disaster that he planned to bring on his people. (Exod 32:11–14)

Yahweh settled down, and Moses, carrying the commandments of the covenant, written on both sides of two stone tablets by the hand of Yahweh himself, descends from the mountain to where the people are still celebrating and dancing, worshiping the golden bull. But when Moses, who shares Yahweh's temperament, sees the golden bull, he is enraged:

> As soon as he came near the camp and saw the [golden bull] and the dancing, Moses' anger burned hot, and he threw the tablets from his hands and broke them at the foot of the mountain. He took the [bull] that they had made, burned it with fire, ground it to powder, scattered it on the water, and made the Israelites drink it. (Exod 32:19–20)

And that is not all. After Moses upbraided Aaron, shaming him for cooperating in this great sin, giving him a guilty conscience for participating in the most natural of rituals, another rage, a murderous rage, erupts in Moses himself. No matter that he convinced Yahweh to curb his consuming rage for blood, now Moses goes on a rampage:

> When Moses saw that the people were running wild . . . then Moses stood in the gate of the camp, and said, "Who is on the LORD's side? Come to me!" And all the sons of Levi gathered around him. He said to them, "Thus says the LORD, the God of Israel, 'Put your sword on your side, each of you! Go back and forth from gate to gate throughout the camp, and each of you kill your brother, your friend, and your neighbor.'" The sons of Levi did as Moses commanded, and about three thousand of the people fell on that day. Moses said, "Today you have ordained yourselves for the service of the LORD, each one at the cost of a son or a brother, and so have brought a blessing on yourselves this day." (Exod 32:25–29)

Even though I am reading this story as soul's dream of itself, as a symbolic moment in soul's development (it most assuredly never happened historically as described), I still cringe at the astonishing cold brutality and the utter indifference to the bonds of family and friendship. Kill a family member with a sword for the sacrilege of worshiping Yahweh the bull? There is nothing impersonal in such an act (if it were actual). But, as a symbolic story of soul's ruthless movement, the new truth hates the old truth, and is merciless in creating the new truth:

> [Soul] sticks to one content (its prime matter) and works it, works it usually cruelly, in order to push off from its initial natural form and to reach higher,

more distilled forms of the same ... It is destructive, negating, sublating work imposed upon the matter as if from outside the uroboric-okeanic containment, with a view to *change* the form of truth itself, to bring about a fundamentally new level of truth.[21]

The new Yahweh symbolizes soul's new syntax of consciousness, and this Yahweh is the new shape of truth that soul is adopting for itself.

That blow of the sword was a terrific cut through the very heart of Yahweh's own bull nature. He cuts himself off from himself, reflected in the great carnage of human sacrifice. There is no denying this is a human sacrifice for the god, a bloody slaughter for the ritual of ordination (Levi was the tribe of those who served as priests). It brings "blessing," which means Yahweh smiles on and condones the blood-letting in service to him. Here we also see confirmed the clear identity of Yahweh/Moses. The only thing missing is the burning of the fat of the bodies on the altar for a "pleasing odor" to Yahweh. The anger of Yahweh is not yet appeased. He follows up by sending a plague on the people (Exod 32:35), and although he then sends them on their way to the land he has promised them, he states, "But I will not go up among you, or I would consume you on the way, for you are a stiff-necked people" (Exod 33:3). His simmering resentment could break out uncontrolled at any time. This entire scene is another symbolic demonstration of Yahweh as *contra naturam*. The willingness to cut down family members is the narrative symbolic logic of cutting through that natural form of truth that celebrates the bull. To kill the bull worshippers is the symbolic expression of Yahweh the bull castrating his own bull essence, lifting himself out of immersion in the natural world. Nothing is innately wrong with the truth that is the Bull god, but it is now overcome by a new form of truth that shows zero tolerance for the Bull god. This is soul's own interior dialectical self-contradiction, working itself out within this iconic drama central to the development of Western consciousness.

The cry of Moses, "Who is on the Lord's side?" rings out, and continues to ring down through the ages. This text represents a tremendous turning point in the life of soul, paralleling Abraham's watershed moment with Isaac, except in this instance, a human sacrifice is carried out on a large scale, evidence of the immense cut that is now thrust through the very heart of being itself. The violent drama and the enormous energy required to effect this change in soul is what leads Giegerich to refer to this biblical event as the "first nuclear fission." Soul, so to speak, cuts deeply into its own flesh, cuts through its bull nature, cuts off its natural-essence as nature. This was the divorce from Asherah, the bull castrating itself. For the history of consciousness, it was a decisive act that can never be undone. Granted it has taken two thousand and more years to complete the soul-transformation set in motion with this act, but this ancient text reveals soul's wrenching turn against itself, the symbol of a revolutionary rupture.

---

21. Giegerich, "Movement of the Soul," 318.

God's Autopsy and the Living Truth of Soul
The Rupture's Consequences for Consciousness

This change envisions a future, a *historical* future, that breaks free of its prior absolute self-enclosed containment in nature. It symbolizes the creation of *historical* time, a new quality of consciousness able to envision a future goal. Nature-bound time is contained in the concrete cycle of the seasons, the hunt, the rhythms of agriculture, cultic rituals; it cannot abstract a future. The shift in the nature of time reflects the shift in the nature of the god: "This story narrates a fateful event in the history of this God himself. This scene dramatically announces a change within God. God separates himself from an aspect of himself. God's nature splits."[22] Although this chapter focuses on one specific narrative event that encapsulates the act of splitting, the entire Bible enacts the split in God's nature and its consequences. On the one hand, God is a magnificent golden bull, a shining numinous presence, exciting celebration, feasting, and dancing, and on the other hand, God is an imageless mountaintop transcendence of the (abstract) written word, prohibiting any symbolic representations of himself, and ritually killing everyone who playfully and innocently dances with the golden bull. In this light, God the bull ritually commits suicide, slaughtering himself in his bull nature in order to create a new kind of soul truth in a purely spiritual unearthly dimension.

Several significant changes illustrate the radical difference between the phenomenology of the archaic bull Yahweh and the new spirit Yahweh.[23] First, the god moves from a manifest visible image to a completely invisible presence. The real bull was the epiphany of the god. The destruction of the golden bull and its worshippers is the symbolic end of all natural epiphanies. God will now appear as written word, as commandments, laws, and regulations, that is, torah. He rejects his bull form and becomes spirit.

Second, the nature gods were immanent powers of the earth: Yahweh *was* storm, wind, thunder, lightning, rain, fertility, vigorous bull. The new Yahweh is outside of the earth, supernatural, transcendent, and he creates all of nature from nothing, simply by his word. Yahweh abandons his immediate earthly presence in animal and image and becomes a removed, distant, heavenly, more abstract object of faith. This new god represented soul's creation of our linguistic literate world. We no longer live immediately in nature; we relate to nature now from outside, so to speak, through the word, through language. Yahweh inaugurates the meaning-world that language, especially literacy, mediates; it becomes our immediacy, the sea we swim in. The thrust of the sword irrevocably thrusts us, humankind, into a new world of meaning.

Third, this split in god's essence is the division between the mythological gods of nature and the religious monotheistic god of heaven; from down here to up there, from many to one. The mythological gods and goddesses are many, each particular to specific locales, tribes, and cities. The new god is absolutely one and single, a pure mono-theos, transcending specific location (except that for a while he does want

---

22. Giegerich, "Nuclear Bomb," 74.
23. Giegerich, "Nuclear Bomb," 76–77.

his own territory, the "promised land," and his own house, i.e., temple, although the temple was to centralize worship and replace local shrines). Later, both the "promised land" and the temple will be over thrown, and Yahweh exiled with no cultic center. Ultimately, he comes to transcend place and time by becoming a god of the book (Torah). As book, as written language, now the new home of spirit Yahweh, soul abstracts itself from nature, becoming free and mobile, not tied or limited to location or time. Today we take reading and writing so completely for granted that it is difficult to appreciate what a tremendous shift in cultural consciousness this change brought about.

Fourth, in leaving behind his presence in nature, his bodily concrete reality, Yahweh becomes idea, and idealized idea. In a future development, the New Testament, he becomes the idealized idea of *love*. Natural phenomena, the living presence of storm and bull, do not require belief or faith or obedience because their existence as phenomena, and soul's presence as those phenomena, was obvious to everyone, a public truth. But now, soul, as the new Yahweh, pushes off from natural phenomena and becomes a fiercely jealous God who demands absolute obedience and loyalty, with capital punishment the consequence of disobedience. Why? Because if this new god does not have human witnesses, he will cease to exist himself. The dependence between this god and his created self-image is absolute. The new god of spirit, idea, and word will be dependent on endless interpretations and reinterpretations, ever renewed faith and study, and thus the growth of midrash and the Talmud, extracanonical writings like the Apocrypha and the Pseudepigrapha, and legends, all to ensure the new Yahweh is kept alive. Yahweh writes himself into existence.

A fifth characteristic of this revolutionary change in soul is a shift toward a kind of literalism for God. Within archaic soul, or myth-ritual cultures, there are no mere so-called dead objects or scientific weather patterns. Yahweh as golden bull, or living bull, or storm, was the living presence of soul suffused with the image:

> God was the visible sight of the golden luster and the powerful bull shape, the sight of the *image* shining forth from that which we today would call a dead object. And the worshipers of the Golden Calf did not by way of mystification "believe" in the image as if it were anything different from what it actually was: an image, nothing more. For everybody knew of course that it had just been cast from their own jewelry. But anybody could immediately *see* from the bull's radiating imaginal quality that this was God. The essence of God was originally precisely in the radiation and in the numinosity inherent in this metaphoric shine.[24]

Moses' blow of the sword, and Yahweh's own fierce wrath at the worshippers, symbolize soul. In leaving behind its bull form, soul is also discarding its innate meaningful shine and radiance in natural phenomena. Now God becomes a kind of literal absolute metaphysical entity *behind* natural phenomena, and he reinforces his new status by,

---

24. Giegerich, "Nuclear Bomb," 77.

again and again, positing himself as the one true God, who presides *over* all of reality. The new Yahweh abstracts himself from nature and now exists as a decontextualized truth, in this sense a kind of literal (literary) truth that is wholly apart (holy) from its former natural appearance. The notion of archaic soul characterizes societies that are prehistoric, preliterate, and oral in nature, and thus are embedded in local contexts. As long as language is primarily spoken and not yet text-based, it remains bound to concrete places and times. The *written* word escapes the local context of both place and time, and by becoming mobile and decontextualized, moves to another level of abstraction. New Yahweh has written himself into becoming a decontextualized abstract God. We have heard that "the pen is mightier than the sword," but in this case, it was the sword of Moses (who acted for Yahweh) that created the "pen" in the first place. The thrust of the sword into the essence of archaic soul, created the space for a new consciousness, embodied as the written word, to begin to flourish.

The ten commandments (and all the other commandments) are Yahweh's universal abstract self-definition that is no longer tied to any particular locale or time. Soul is free now in a new way at a higher level of abstraction and differentiation, which we can understand in terms of sublation. The archaic Yahweh negated himself and at the same time preserved himself in a new form as a new syntax of consciousness. While this new Yahweh needed a context, it would not be tied to specific local natural phenomena. Rather, Yahweh's new context was a new people, who he himself made into a mobile people, pushing Abraham out of his original natural context, pushing Moses out of Egypt, and creating a new "promised land." Yahweh took possession of this people, made them his self-image, in order to ensure and make real his own existence. I am talking about the work of soul here, and soul is experienced on the human side of its dialectic, or the human side of the psychological difference, as a claim, an imperative. This is experienced not necessarily as a personal claim, but rather as a claim on a whole society, as that living idea that everyone takes as true, as the thing to do or the way to be. Yahweh was that living idea that became the living idea for a people, that shaped how to be, what to do, what to think, primarily through "Yahweh's own writings," the Tanakh (as soul's speech about itself). Legend tells us that Moses received the entire Torah (all five books) from God on Mount Sinai. One of the central characteristics of soul is that it will make itself real in the world. A select people, separate (holy) from other people, came into being for the sake of Yahweh's self-ordered mission. The definition of this people, along with Yahweh's new self-definition, is described in the written word, first the torah (the law) and then the other writings. The *written word* in the form of the Tanakh eventually becomes the sacred location of Yahweh's presence; the *book* becomes the center of new kinds of cultic and ritual practices and new styles of sacrifice (as mind). In this way, soul, as the logical form of consciousness, created a new form of itself, a new form of truth.

Idolatry, the Abstraction of Nature and Liberation

By creating itself as the one true God, soul at the same time made idols and idolatry the evil and abhorrent opposition to the new God. Before the one true God emerged, there were no *idols*, only mythic nature gods and goddesses and their ever-present symbols. The one *true* God and the *false* idols create each other; they come into existence at the same time. For the one true God to be elevated, the entire cosmos of nature gods and goddesses had to be reduced to idols and idolatry, had to become bad, evil, an abomination. The shine that once radiated from the natural manifestations of the gods was taken away when the one true God ascended, and as a result, the bull lost its immanent radiance as divine presence, and became simply animal. In more general terms, the earthly world became god-less. Soul abandoned nature, and the logic of materialism was born. The natural world became mere matter, the stuff of physics, inanimate, and meaningless. The story of Exodus is Yahweh's exodus from nature, leaving it behind for his own transcending "absolute spiritualization," while the living vital soul images (gods and goddesses) that had suffused material reality were made morally abhorrent and destroyed as evil idols. Soul was negating its unconscious containment in the womb of nature for a new form of consciousness that would be free and mobile. The possibility of a new kind of relationship with nature was also created.

Idols and idolatry remained a temptation throughout the narrative of the Tanakh, and the people were always drawn back to the gods and the ritual practices those gods called forth. Of course, "drawn back" is the view in hindsight from the point of view of soul's new position articulated in the Bible. The people were simply doing what soul's presence in nature had always called them to do. It was hard to follow the one true God who was no longer in nature. The one *true* God versus the *false* idols meant that soul had now taken on a singular definition of what was the highest value, of what could be "God" and what could not be "God." The notion of temptation, although the word implies a negative moral judgment, suggests that the shine and presence of soul is still all around, but these other forms of soul are now judged as not of God. The only highest *God* is now defined in a singular way, more of an abstraction demanding faith, and any natural spontaneous manifestations of soul are demeaned and belittled or destroyed. Under the one high God, written ethical guidelines are now what govern behavior and practice. When the gods are present in nature, soul's presence in reality exerts its binding claim, and humankind responds to the implicit ethics embedded in ritual existence. The condition of archaic soul is a world of known ethical norms, an ordered world (although many of those ethical norms would be abhorrent to us, such as human and animal sacrifice, and of course, the closed and clearly defined social roles of tribal existence would be intolerable for modern persons). The ethical requirements of the new God demand something else, demand the use of a new factor, the will, the exercise of will power, to stay committed to the new way of life laid out by the Ten Commandments (symbolic of all the new ethical norms laid out in the Torah) and to stay faithful to the new God. But, how did this new factor, the will, emerge?

As a new soul principle, the will is the new Yahweh himself, in that the new Yahweh willed himself into being by way of the very cut into and the splitting of his being. When Moses and Yahweh first met at the burning bush and Yahweh named himself, "I Am Who I Am," the Yahweh who emerges as a new form of existence is very active. The name can also mean "I Am What I Do" or "I Will Act."[25] Yahweh's essence was action first, thought and reflection later. Just as nuclear fission releases enormous energy, Giegerich suggests that the nuclear fission at the heart of God's being, the splitting off of God from his bull essence, released, or was the creation of, the will, a new energy with direction. Although I am speaking in terms of two here—Yahweh's bull nature and Yahweh's spirit nature—archaic soul was not two parts somehow held together. Archaic soul was a seamless unity, a unified reality, a primordial oneness of the living presence of nature and soul. Only today can we speak of soul and nature separately, as distinct, and only because of what happened in the archaic past as related in Exodus.

One of the central qualities of soul is its compelling and binding nature. When Yahweh-Bull was a unity, the people in its presence were compelled to celebrate, revel, and sacrifice; they were called to ritual behavior as a group. The compelling power of soul was also bound within natural phenomena and was, in this sense, not free. The will was the will of nature, and not a will for itself. I surmise that the unity of Yahweh-Bull, or archaic soul in general, directed the power of what later became the will and kept it contained within ritual and natural phenomena. The original unity of archaic soul holds everything together. The will in a strict sense does not exist. When Yahweh and Moses erupt, and the zeal of Moses' sword cuts through the heart of Yahweh's bull essence, the compelling and binding nature of soul is released from its natural containment and becomes the metaphysical principle, the will. "The age-old story of the Golden Calf is thus, *in the context of the history of our Christian West*, also the myth of the birth of the modern ego, whose innermost essence is the will."[26] Here *ego* does not refer to the individual, but to what has become the mode of being of the modern world. In this sense, the modern ego characterizes the spirit of our age, a product of and a function of the new liberated Yahweh as will: "It is not we who have an ego, the ego or the will has us and our world."[27] The will was not an already existing force that caused Moses' blow of the sword cutting soul in two; it did not exist before this act:

> Rather, by bursting the [original unity of archaic soul] apart, the blow of the sword is the *primary* uprising of the will, the act through which the will releases itself into existence for the "first" time. The will is born out of itself, out of the "sudden" exercise of willing. It is its own origin.[28]

25. Miles, *God*, 99.
26. Giegerich, "Nuclear Bomb," 82.
27. Giegerich, "Nuclear Bomb," 82.
28. Giegerich, "Nuclear Bomb," 82. Where I have inserted "original unity of archaic soul," Giegerich

Yahweh's Violent Rupture: Soul's Revolution

In cutting himself off from his bull nature, the new Yahweh created himself. Nothing else could create the new Yahweh. In his biblical context, he simply bursts onto the scene and creates a world of his own, beginning with the creation of a cosmos and then the creation of his people, all of which is Yahweh's creation of himself. It is almost as if, when the bull was deprived of its soul shine and reduced to a mere piece of gold or biological bull, soul usurped, so to speak, the energetic quality, or essence of bull, and converted it into the will, the will as sublated bull. The form of bull is discarded, negated, but the quality of bull nature is converted into Yahweh's at times bull-headed character. As *will* embodied as Yahweh, soul is now free to leave the bull and his repetitive ritual practices behind and create history, a history that will unfold in terms of a future. Now personified as spirit-transcendent-Yahweh, will is the new form of soul itself:

> It was an act of will that blasted God, earthly reality, and the nature of man, all three, out of the medium of [soul], and thus subjected them to itself—to the will or ego established by this very act of subjugation—as the new medium of existence as a whole.[29]

These reflections on the will (and Yahweh) creating itself in the act of the sword's blow bring to mind Giegerich's reflections, in his essay "Killings," on how soul "killed itself into being." After centuries of ritual sacrificial slaughter, through countless repeated blows of the axe or spear into the heart of self-enclosed and self-contained life, soul created a space for itself to begin to emerge as a new quality of consciousness, exemplified in the story of the Golden Calf. The new Yahweh who emerges in the Exodus story is the new quality of soul released through the long process of archaic ritual sacrificial slaughter. The Yahweh that emerges in the Golden Calf story is a liberated will, now free to create something new for itself. To think of all this in the terms of "Yahweh divorcing Asherah" seems rather tame in the light of the idea of a "nuclear explosion" at the heart of archaic soul, that completely overturned "the foundations of existence." Both metaphors are relevant, but what I want to remember is that the changes in soul I am tracing are violent and cataclysmic revolutions in the nature of consciousness itself. Violence is not a characteristic we normally associate today with soul, but if we stick to our text, the Bible, we cannot help but see the necessary and creative role violence played in soul's self-development, the ongoing story of the living truth of soul.

---

has "imaginal mode of Being." This essay was written in 1985, and Giegerich was not yet using the term "soul" as he does in later writings and as I am throughout this book. The influence of both James Hillman and Martin Heidegger are in evidence as he speaks about the splitting apart of the imaginal nucleus of Being. I believe that my insertion is an adequate translation of his earlier formulation and maintains continuity with the notion of soul as I am using it and as Giegerich uses it himself in later writings.

29. Giegerich, "Nuclear Bomb," 82–83. Here again I have replaced an older formulation of Giegerich's ("the anima, i.e., of the imaginal") with "soul." The idea of "anima" is from Jung and remains confined within the inner world of the individual, while "soul" is a much larger concept pointing to the logical form of consciousness of a historical era.

Chapter 5

Yahweh Defeats Himself to Save Himself

Consciousness Becomes Bookish

> How weighty to me are your thoughts, O God!
> How vast is the sum of them!
> —PS 139:17

Once the soul has entered the stage of thought, there is no way back.[1]

Thought is in itself dynamic and progressive. It has its origin in an act of negation, of "pushing off from" what preceded it, and it exists only as this permanent self-origination or autopoiesis.[2]

THE VIOLENT WARRIOR YAHWEH brought his people out of Egypt to the promised land, and set about establishing themselves on their own land. However, soul undergoes its own development by way of self-negation, and now the great warrior god will undergo a harrowing transformation. The covenant will teeter on the precipice of collapse because its absolutist demands are impossible to maintain, making failure inevitable. Both the people and Yahweh will approach the edge of extinction during Assyrian and Babylonian invasions and exile, and survival will demand a radical change. The form of consciousness that Yahweh the warrior represents will first unravel, then through a

---

1. Giegerich, "Thought," 12.
2. Giegerich, "Thought," 10.

kind of involution, turn toward silent contemplation of word and book. The goddess Asherah will quietly insinuate herself as a quality of Yahweh's new literate nature, and the mind of Yahweh will become more highly valued than his actions in the world. Soul is on its way to a new syntax, a new form of thought itself, another stage in its liberation from nature's embrace. Although the story is about Yahweh, our reading is about the evolution of *meaning*, the struggle of the logical form of consciousness to emancipate itself to a new level of reflection not possible heretofore.

Within the context of the biblical narrative, the defeat and failure of the triumphant warrior god Yahweh was inevitable. Yahweh forced failure upon himself when the agreement (i.e., covenant) he imposed on himself and the Hebrew people laid down impossible standards and unattainable demands. Yahweh wanted to be the one and only deity for Israel, without imagery or symbolic representation, a deity transcending nature and, at the same time, with complete control over nature. Yahweh wanted to defeat and replace all the other gods and goddesses. This was not an intellectual matter by any means. As an analogous thought experiment, imagine declaring, both to humankind and to a nature fertility Bull god: "You must not think about sex, dream about sex, desire sex, talk about sex, and last but not least, you must not have sex! You must turn away from sexuality!" Let's see how long that command against nature is kept! Of course, the covenant was not against sex. But, the command to turn away from the nature gods and goddesses was just as unnatural for the Hebrew people and for Yahweh in his bull form as well. The prohibition was only one-half of the agreement. The contract was not merely denial and negation, but a promise of abundance and greatness, an abundance of descendants, land, nationhood, protection, and flourishing, if (*If*) the first half of the contract (worship me and me alone) was kept. The sticking point is, it was impossible to keep such a covenant, even for Yahweh himself.

From the psychological perspective, soul is undertaking an enormous project, separating itself from nature, and becoming word and spirit. Consciousness is undertaking a cataclysmic transformation, extracting itself from its containment in nature, and raising itself to a new status, in the form of a transcendent monotheistic deity. The Bible is the record of this long struggle internal to soul. It is not just the people who could not maintain the high standards of the covenant, but Yahweh himself could not maintain his own absolutist ideal. As we view this now, we see that it took approximately two thousand years for soul, in the guise of the "one, true, spirit God," to finally achieve the status of thought proper, to become a form of consciousness that has achieved independence from, is no longer embedded within, the natural world.

Yahweh's self-negation was an integral part of the gradual historical process of spiritual-monotheism separating itself from nature-polytheism. This is soul's story of itself, emancipating itself as a form of consciousness named Yahweh from its identification as nature. While the Exodus story showed us a decisive and definitive action whereby soul splits itself apart from nature, the historical books of the Bible, especially 1 and 2 Samuel and 1 and 2 Kings, reveal a long and troubled process whose repeated outcome is more often than not failure. No one, not even Yahweh, can live up to the demands of the covenant: "Worship me and me alone, absent natural and sensual imagery!" An absurd analogy, to try and scale the enormity of this undertaking by soul, would be to expect animals to leave their instincts behind and turn their allegiance to learning human language. The myth-ritual phase of culture, the time of the polytheistic nature deities, was thousands of years older than the Judeo-Christian and modern phases of human culture. The prehistoric and preliterate phase of culture when human existence was barely separated from animal existence lasted about a hundred thousand years.[3]

The pages of the Bible reveal a huge and violent revolution within soul itself, a revolution of consciousness during which the archaic status of consciousness that had its highest expression in human and animal sacrifice is left behind. The part of the story we explore now begins during the years of the Jewish kings, and then records a process of destruction through successive invasions by more powerful empires. Finally, Yahweh's transformation is voiced through a series of prophets.

The Impossible Covenant Defeats Itself

The trouble begins in earnest with Solomon, the biblical son of David and one of the early kings of monarchic Israel. Living during the tenth century BCE, Solomon is a large figure in Israel's history, and even larger still in Jewish and Christian legend. He represents power, wealth, and especially wisdom; he built the first temple to Yahweh.[4] Finally, Yahweh has a concrete place to call his house, a central location that will draw all hearts, minds, and ritual practices to him. He guarantees his presence there forever if, and it is a very big *if*:

> When Solomon had finished building the house of the LORD and the king's house and all that Solomon desired to build, the LORD appeared to him a second time, as he had appeared to him at Gibeon. The LORD said to him, "I have heard your prayer and your plea, which you made before me; I have consecrated this house that you have built, and put my name there forever; my eyes and my heart will be there for all time. As for you, if you will walk before me, as David your father walked with integrity of heart and uprightness, doing according to all that I have commanded you, and keeping my statutes and my ordinances, then I will establish your royal throne over Israel forever, as I

---

3. Harari, *Sapiens*, 41.

4. Interestingly, while Solomon's temple lives large in the imagination and in importance, the tenth century BCE is far away (three thousand years), and there is no archaeological evidence that such a temple existed. Literary evidence from such an early date is also rare. Even the existence of Solomon himself is subject to debate (Fox, *Early Prophets*, 562–66). Still, my concern is not with specific historical facts, but with the general historical trajectory that the Bible represents as the myth of God's origins, and psychologically as soul's speech about itself.

promised your father David, saying, 'There shall not fail you a successor on the throne of Israel.'" (1 Kgs 9:1–5)

The "commands, statutes, and ordinances" of Yahweh are simply that he alone is worshiped, and worshiped in his non-nature essence as imageless spirit, as absolutely transcendent. If the contract is kept, Yahweh promises his presence, and a royal dynasty, forever, an eternal guarantee of his presence. However, *if* Yahweh's commands are not kept, he continues:

> If you turn aside from following me, you or your children, and do not keep my commandments and my statutes that I have set before you, but go and serve other gods and worship them, then I will cut Israel off from the land that I have given them; and the house that I have consecrated for my name I will cast out of my sight; and Israel will become a proverb and a taunt among all peoples. This house will become a heap of ruins; everyone passing by it will be astonished, and will hiss; and they will say, "Why has the LORD done such a thing to this land and to this house?" Then they will say, "Because they have forsaken the LORD their God, who brought their ancestors out of the land of Egypt, and embraced other gods, worshiping them and serving them; therefore the LORD has brought this disaster upon them." (1 Kgs 9:6–9)

If the people forsake Yahweh, the exact opposite is promised: *total* destruction and ruin. If the people do not keep the covenant that promises them life, then it becomes a contract of death. Of course, if this is not just a threat, if Yahweh goes all the way on his promise to destroy Israel and the temple, then he destroys himself. This is how Yahweh begins to paint himself into an inescapable corner. If Yahweh remains true to his word, and if his zero tolerance has no wiggle room whatsoever, then he himself is finished. Without his people, he does not exist. Whether an actual historical person or not, Solomon is the biblical personification of Yahweh's own divided and torn nature. In spite of his great wisdom, Solomon welcomes the polytheistic cosmos into his kingdom, inspired by his love of women:

> King Solomon loved many foreign women along with the daughter of Pharaoh: Moabite, Ammonite, Edomite, Sidonian, and Hittite women, from the nations concerning which the LORD had said to the Israelites, "You shall not enter into marriage with them, neither shall they with you; for they will surely incline your heart to follow their gods"; Solomon clung to these in love. Among his wives were seven hundred princesses and three hundred concubines; and his wives turned away his heart. For when Solomon was old, his wives turned away his heart after other gods; and his heart was not true to the LORD his God, as was the heart of his father David. For Solomon followed Astarte the goddess of the Sidonians, and Milcom the abomination of the Ammonites. So Solomon did what was evil in the sight of the LORD, and did not completely follow the LORD, as his father David had done. Then Solomon

> built a high place for Chemosh the abomination of Moab, and for Molech the abomination of the Ammonites, on the mountain east of Jerusalem. He did the same for all his foreign wives, who offered incense and sacrificed to their gods. (1 Kgs 11:1–8)

One thousand wives could equal one thousand gods and goddesses: Polytheism (the soul-infused natural world) is deeply entrenched. Naturally, the text places the blame for Solomon's turning away from Yahweh on both his advanced age and the influence of his wives. Even at this stage of Israel's collective memory, the text attempts to soften the judgment of Solomon's apostasy. But, my concern is not with men or women and their frailty and failures in matters of faith. Rather, Solomon is the interior conflict of soul itself, striving against its own negation. Yahweh as spirit-tendency is negating his own nature-essence, but then, in the guise of his creature's self-image (Solomon), he falls right back into his nature-essence, his manifestation as one of countless nature deities. It is helpful when reading the Tanakh to remember that the phrase "did what was evil in the sight of the LORD," and the word *abomination*, are code explicitly pointing to the worship of other gods and goddesses and the turn away from Yahweh's spirit-form as the one true god. Yahweh's response is anger and reprisal:

> Then the LORD was angry with Solomon, because his heart had turned away from the LORD, the God of Israel, who had appeared to him twice, and had commanded him concerning this matter, that he should not follow other gods; but he did not observe what the LORD commanded. Therefore, the LORD said to Solomon, "Since this has been your mind and you have not kept my covenant and my statutes that I have commanded you, I will surely tear the kingdom from you and give it to your servant." (1 Kgs 11:9–11)

However, Yahweh postpones tearing the kingdom apart until after Solomon dies, for the sake of the memory of Solomon's father, David. Even this tiny sliver of wiggle room is not enough to prevent what comes next. After Solomon's death, competing power struggles within the government lead to the nation's division into a northern kingdom of Israel and a southern kingdom of Judah, where Jerusalem is located. Over the succeeding years, the kings ruling over these two realms fared no better than Solomon, and most "did what was evil in the sight of the LORD." The divided kingdoms remind us that Yahweh is divided, a deity struggling to separate himself from his original bull nature:

> Then Jeroboam [king of Israel] said to himself, "Now the kingdom may well revert to the house of David [kingdom of Judah to the south]. If this people continues to go up to offer sacrifices in the house of the LORD at Jerusalem, the heart of this people will turn again to their master, King Rehoboam of Judah; they will kill me and return to King Rehoboam of Judah." So the king took counsel, and made two calves [bulls] of gold. He said to the people, "You have gone up to Jerusalem long enough. Here are your gods, O Israel, who

> brought you up out of the land of Egypt." He set one in Bethel, and the other he put in Dan [Bethel and Dan are the southern and northern boundaries of the northern kingdom of Israel]. And this thing became a sin, for the people went to worship before the one at Bethel and before the other as far as Dan. (1 Kgs 12:26–30)

Again, the text makes the motivation for this apostasy a human one, Jeroboam's personal and political self-interest to stay alive and remain king. For the text, the problem hinges on the idea that Yahweh is in the right and the people are in the wrong. The people are frail, weak, stubborn, rebellious, and resistant. The text, of course, cannot see the struggle and conflict within Yahweh himself, Yahweh's self-contradiction between his bull nature and his spirit nature, because from within the logic of spiritual monotheism, the text is erasing, forgetting, Yahweh's bull nature. From the biblical story's point of view, the issue is always a human moral problem, human evil and sin, and note again the derogatory and belittling term "calves," when in fact these had to have been golden bulls, in all their shining, magnificent power. *They* are the gods (plural—there were many local forms of Yahweh, just as there were many Baals) who rescued the people from Egypt. This is more biblical evidence that Yahweh was indeed a Bull god and worshipped as such by Israelites. But, in trying to become a spirit god, Yahweh was divided against himself, showing us soul's internal struggle against its own self-negation.

His consort Asherah also continues to be a problem, as she remains a persistent presence, and Yahweh's animosity does not get rid of her so easily. A local prophet, Ahijah, tells Jeroboam that the continuing presence of Asherah will be their downfall:

> The LORD will strike Israel, as a reed is shaken in the water; he will root up Israel out of this good land that he gave to their ancestors, and scatter them beyond the Euphrates, because they have made their sacred poles [Asherim], provoking the LORD to anger. (1 Kgs 14:15–16)

A note on this verse in the New Revised Standard Version (NRSV) tells us that "sacred poles were symbols of the Canaanite fertility goddess Asherah, who is mentioned about forty times in the Hebrew Scriptures as a temptation to the Israelites." The word *temptation* functions as the moral judgment of the monotheist who is writing the historical overview of the books of Kings. Asherah's presence confirms that Yahweh is recognized in his bull nature, and as a pair, they are the powerful fertility of nature itself. Asherah is a temptation only from the point of view of spirit-Yahweh; but, for Bull-Yahweh, she is his always-present and welcome consort. The "first nuclear fission" incident of the golden bull at the base of Mount Sinai, although narratively dramatic and definitive, was not the end of the struggle by any means. Yahweh's continued war with himself, soul's violent effort to tear itself free of its immersion in nature, is a long-range historical project.

The southern kingdom of Judah also remained thoroughly polytheistic:

> Judah did what was evil in the sight of the Lord; they provoked him to jealousy with their sins that they committed, more than all that their ancestors had done. For they also built for themselves high places, pillars, and sacred poles [Asherim] on every high hill and under every green tree; there were also male temple prostitutes in the land. They committed all the abominations of the nations that the Lord drove out before the people of Israel. (1 Kgs 14:22–24)

For the psychological interpretation, I want to emphasize that the people are the mirror of Yahweh (his self-created self-image), and thus Yahweh is an abomination to himself. This conflict internal to Yahweh continues to build throughout the books of Kings, which chart the course of Yahweh-Israel from the end of the monarchy after Solomon to the end of both kingdoms, Israel and Judah, victims of the expanding empires of Assyria and Babylon. From the point of view of the Bible, the new spirit-Yahweh's point of view, Israel and Judah were conquered by foreign powers because they both continued to do what was evil in the sight of Yahweh. Assyria invaded Israel in 721 BCE, carried everyone away and resettled the population in Assyrian cities, where they eventually simply disappeared, absorbed into Assyrian culture. The northern kingdom of Israel did not survive, could not maintain its identity in exile, as Judah later did in Babylon. As far as Yahweh was concerned, the foreign invasion was a rightly deserved punishment, fully explained in the following:

> This occurred because the people of Israel had sinned against the Lord their God, who had brought them up out of the land of Egypt from under the hand of Pharaoh king of Egypt. They had worshiped other gods and walked in the customs of the nations whom the Lord drove out before the people of Israel [the indigenous peoples cleared out of the "promised land"], and in the customs that the kings of Israel had introduced. The people of Israel secretly [not so secret really] did things that were not right against the Lord their God. They built for themselves high places [altars for ritual sacrifice to other gods/goddesses] at all their towns, from watchtowers to fortified city; they set up for themselves pillars and sacred poles [Asherim] on every high hill and under every green tree; there they made offerings on all the high places, as the nations did whom the Lord carried away before them. They did wicked things, provoking the Lord to anger; they served idols, of which the Lord had said to them, "You shall not do this." Yet the Lord warned Israel and Judah by every prophet and every seer, saying, "Turn from your evil ways and keep my commandments and my statutes, in accordance with all the law that I commanded your ancestors and that I sent to you by my servants the prophets." They would not listen but were stubborn, as their ancestors had been, who did not believe in the Lord their God. They despised his statutes, and his covenant that he made with their ancestors, and the warnings that he gave them. They went after false idols and became false; they followed the nations that were around them, concerning whom the Lord had commanded them

> that they should not do as they did. They rejected all the commandments of the LORD their God and made for themselves cast images of two calves [bulls]; they made a sacred pole [Asherah], worshiped all the host of heaven [solar, planetary deities], and served Baal. They made their sons and their daughters pass through fire [child sacrifice]; they used divination and augury; and they sold themselves to do evil in the sight of the LORD, provoking him to anger. Therefore the LORD was very angry with Israel and removed them out of his sight; none was left but the tribe of Judah alone. (2 Kgs 17:7–18)

This exhaustive list of what was wrong with the Israelite people, wherever they lived, shows clearly that while the text focuses on the moral depravity of the *people*, the real problem was the ubiquity of the nature gods and goddesses ("every high hill and under every green tree"). Yahweh's ancient condemnation of the nature gods and goddesses and the ritual practices associated with them, is the basis of the pervasive moral condemnation Western Christianity levied against every other mythological or religious practice it encountered. The broad judgment of idolatry demeaned every other religious practice as morally inferior, evil, and dangerous; it became identified with the devil or Satan. All indigenous nature-based cultures were seen as heathen devil worshipers. Sadly, and certainly from the human perspective deeply tragic, this is what happened during the more than two thousand years it took soul to extract itself from nature and become literate word and abstract thought, for soul to develop the free life of mind we take for granted today. In fact, the freedom of thought is so thoroughly taken for granted that we really have no idea that it began somewhere else and is a fairly recent historical development. It is hard for us to appreciate the enormity of soul's achievement: that thought itself is an emergent property, and *consciousness* is actually *contra naturam*. The written word, as the newly emergent logic of soul, with its absolute demand to be free, had to negate the archaic form of *meaning* that was embedded, and completely at home, in image, symbol, and natural phenomena.

Judah also suffered extreme punishment. Only 134 years later, in 587 BCE, the Babylonians invaded the southern kingdom of Judah (hence eventually the name *Jews*), and destroyed Jerusalem and Solomon's temple, which had escaped the Assyrian invasion. The Babylonians deported many of the Judean people, especially the educated elites, religious and governmental officials, those skilled in crafts, and soldiers. The land, the temple, the people, Israelite society itself, was overcome and overthrown. This was an actual historical event, the end of Israel and the Jewish people as a sovereign nation, as well as the end of Yahweh's primary identity, the mighty warrior. The Israeli tribes of the northern kingdom had vanished into the Assyrian empire, and the same fate could have befallen Yahweh. He was a minor local deity and could have easily disappeared into the mists of ancient history. Who has ever heard of El, Baal, Chemosh, Moloch, Asherah, among many others lost to time?

From Yahweh's point of view, however, the story in the biblical texts has a different import. The expanding and conquering foreign empires that destroyed Israel and

Judah were, after all, working for Yahweh, punishing his people for their wickedness. Again, what was their wickedness? Ignoring Yahweh's new directive and covenant and following the call of nature, just as they had always done for thousands of years. Their wickedness was to be immersed in archaic soul. So, while Yahweh, the great warrior who had conquered Egypt, thought he was in control of international affairs, managing other nations for his own purposes, he ultimately ended in defeating himself. Yahweh's zero-tolerance for the natural ritual polytheism at the core of his own essence expressed itself with brutal punishment against the people who were disloyal and disobedient in following their natural norm. Yahweh's attempt to power his way through the polytheistic universe, to expunge the nature deities and especially his consort Asherah, to be the one and only true god, had failed. His once-sovereign kingdom was divided, then conquered, demolished, and dissolved into practically nothing. The nature gods and goddesses were still stronger than he was. Matters went too far. The Jews were truly lost and exiled, and now Yahweh was on the edge of losing himself. Yahweh's severe hard line was on the verge of becoming Yahweh's unintentional suicide. In the attempt to preserve himself and his covenant, Yahweh was about to destroy himself. If he destroys his covenant partner, what becomes of him? If he obliterates his people, he obliterates himself. In order not to disappear altogether, he must change.[5]

Yahweh: Soul's Self-Negation and Sublation

Can Yahweh promise to destroy himself and forgive himself, over and over, more or less, at the same time? On the one hand, he will erupt with brutal and unforgiving cruelty, committing genocide, or promising to, in the blink of an eye, while on the other, he is solicitous, tender, forgiving, and gracious. I remind myself that the narrative of Yahweh and the Israelite people is soul's speech about itself. Yahweh and the people are a unity representing the travail of soul and the evolution of cultural-historical consciousness. Biblical Yahweh and Israel are not simply separate entities in a special kind of relationship, as is conventionally understood. As our exemplar of soul, they are Yahweh-Israel, a character in and of itself. Together as one, they represent a stage in soul's development. (I want to be clear that I am interpreting *Israel*, *the Jews*, and *Yahweh* as symbolic literary characters displaying ancient soul's dream of itself. This has nothing to do with Jewish people or the nation of Israel.) Although it often appears that Yahweh is the emotionally unstable one, we have to see both Yahweh and the people as a single unstable character. The people as a whole, as 1 and 2 Kings (and Exodus) amply demonstrate, are just as unstable, just as unpredictable, just as unreliable and untrustworthy, as Yahweh. And while it also appears that Israel suffers the horrible punishments Yahweh inflicts, Yahweh also suffers terribly and is just as vulnerable.

---

5. For these insights, I am indebted to Miles's interpretation in *God*, 187–202.

The psychological perspective lets us see, through the personification of Yahweh-Israel, soul's self-negating struggle with itself. Soul is divided against itself. Soul is both the new literate, spiritual, and monotheistic consciousness *and* the archaic preliterate nature-rooted consciousness from which it is trying to emerge. This is the struggle of the logical structure of consciousness in relation to itself, taking place in and through real people and a real god. As has been said over and over by Jews and Christians, the God of the Judeo-Christian tradition is historical. Therefore, this god is vulnerable to the vagaries of history (in spite of the claim by that same tradition that its god transcends history and is in charge of history). The very real danger is that if Yahweh snuffs out Israel, he snuffs out himself. Why the wild and extreme emotional oscillation?

Soul Is Truth / Truth Is Soul

Truth hates untruth. Truth hates its prior form as it pushes off to create a new truth. Soul's movement is an inside job, in that truth negates itself. The self-negation at the heart of soul is the dynamic that moves soul forward. Yahweh has a troubled relationship with his own truth, which highlights the relationship between *soul* and *truth*. Within the context of psychology as the discipline of interiority, soul and truth are synonyms for the singular and implicit *logical form of consciousness* that gives a culture its identity, its sense of reality, and its orientation to the world. Speaking very broadly again—very broadly, given our modern historical vantage point—in mythological and religious culture, the gods, or God, let's say the Divine, was the source of truth, or was itself truth. All ultimate, and most not-so-ultimate things, were explained in terms of the Divine. God, and/or gods, were the singular source of Meaning and the final explanation of what is. The ontological and epistemological buck stopped with God. In our modern culture, science and its materialistic basis form the bottom-line assumption that is truth. For science, and thus for modern culture in general, the ontological ground of the universe is matter and energy and the natural laws that govern them. For us, no spiritual forces or deities govern the universe.

In god-oriented cultures, there were also problems with God, or the idea of god, but it was not possible to question the existence of God, or gods, because they were the all-encompassing taken-for-granted Truth. The gods framed or formed the very nature of general consciousness, or what I also call public mind. Usually we cannot question the frame we live within because our fundamental consciousness is identical with the frame (remember the analogy of fish not knowing what water is; water is simply their medium of being). Today, in our current late phase of modernity, we recognize problems with science and the idea of science, but when we think about causation, or the nature of life and the nature of the universe, our first thought is not in terms of a god, or God, but rather physics, cosmology, and biology. Yes, plenty is unexplained, but we do not resort to the idea of a god to account for it. We put our trust (faith) in the scientific method and the scientific point of view. Each point of view has its limitations, which begin to emerge more or less in hindsight and when that form of consciousness is beginning to negate itself. My emphasis is on how soul's form has been changing over the centuries, and will continue to do so.

Such a broad overview of soul's historical process allows us to see that truth does change, and when that happens, what was truth before becomes untruth, and the new truth tends to hate what has become untruth. Soul changes itself through the process of self-negation, a series of negations. Thus, Yahweh was a truth in transition, making its former truth (nature-based Bull god) an untruth. Yahweh was a truth turning on itself, hating itself in order to transform (negate and sublate) itself into a new truth (an imageless nature-transcending god). The new truth hates—and with a fierce passion—the former truth it once was, turning it into an abhorrent, abominable untruth (idolatry). As a nature god, Yahweh is nature: impersonal, cruel, unforgiving, violent, and capricious on the one hand, and then generous, bountiful, nurturing, and gracious on the other. Nature is, in this sense, emotional (the flow of natural forces), not rational, not a conscious entity. In a similar way, Yahweh is emotional, not rational. We say that history itself is, in a sense, emotional, not rational, as in history, power rules. Power, as an impersonal force, spreads itself out and absorbs what is around it. Nature is impersonal and has a life of its own. Power is impersonal and has a life of its own. Yahweh is impersonal and clearly has a life of its (his) own, but, at the same time, Yahweh's life reacts to and is completely dependent on Israel. Yahweh's reactivity to Israel is symbolic of his reactivity to his own self-contradictory nature. Yahweh is the emotional personification of soul's process of self-negation, transforming itself into a new syntax of consciousness.

As Storm-Bull god, Yahweh existed not as a text, but as natural phenomena. Yahweh as nature exists without reflection. What we think of as prehistoric cultures were preliterate cultures, organized through oral communication, not writing.[6] Although the new Yahweh, the spirit Yahweh, is first and foremost emotionally reactive and explosive, this Yahweh works his way into existence as a text-based god. He is, so to speak, a literary linguistic creation, soul creating this new form of itself, as a text, as book. On Sinai, although Yahweh is indeed volcanic, his new true manifestation is as text, as word, as ten commandments, and he destroys his golden bull manifestation. The written word, so to speak, cuts itself off from the golden bull. Spirit-Yahweh comes into existence through writing, which represents a new level of consciousness, of thought and reflection, as well as a new level of freedom for consciousness. As bull, Yahweh is bound to the earth; as written word, Yahweh is unbound from time and place. Through its existence as written text, the Yahweh form of consciousness begins to become a rational, thoughtful, and reflective form of consciousness.

---

6. Of course, this is a very broad historical statement. The details of the development of writing are far more complex. My focus remains on the development of forms of consciousness within the Judeo-Christian Western context.

Yahweh Defeats Himself to Save Himself

History Turns Yahweh in on Himself

Historically, the kingdoms of Israel and Judah were crushed and absorbed by the spreading power of the Assyrian and Babylonian empires. Here's what is most remarkable and astonishing. Within the Yahweh-Israel soul-world, Yahweh interpreted this final breaking of the already broken covenant, this final destruction of Yahweh's warrior identity, as evidence that he no longer needed to be the warrior himself. From his new, higher elevation, he could delegate other nations to do his work, mete out his punishment to Israel. Amazingly, Israel interpreted its crushing defeat and destruction as self-criticism of its failure to keep the covenant, as just punishment for its failure. It's an astonishing turn to see the very people who suffered the calamity interpret this great historical tragedy as self-criticism. However, without trying to suggest any hidden determinism, there is a sense that it had to go this way because Israel had no identity without its god Yahweh; Yahweh had to be in charge of Israel's destiny. In this meaning-world, suffused by Yahweh's truth, the notion of secular history, and the random vagaries of power politics and innocent victims, did not exist.

The secular view is possible only today, in the context of our modern atheistic and rational culture; our idea of truth is no longer theistic in any sense. Yahweh and Israel were inseparable, and right goes to might. While foreign nations defeated Israel, it was not through their might, but the greater cosmic might of the high God, Yahweh/El, who was Lord of the universe. In other words, within the logical form of consciousness of antiquity in which gods, or God, was the source of truth, the crushing defeat of Israel and Judah, and the scattering and exile of the Jewish people, was implicitly meaningful as the handiwork of Yahweh. Yahweh engineered complete punishment, gave free rein to his overpowering rage at the wickedness and abominations of the people, and almost destroyed everything that gave the people their identity and thus his identity. Yet, in spite of the destruction, a tiny sliver of hope, a small promise for a future remained. Yahweh did not completely commit suicide this time; he could not simply snuff himself out. To go forward, in order for the sliver of hope to blossom, Yahweh had to become a different kind of deity. He had to resolve his internal contradiction by overcoming himself. The warrior god had to become something that was at first unrecognizable: The warrior had to give up his power, his weapons, and his rage, and become bookish, to become a reader and a student. An inconceivable new truth was taking shape.

At least from our modern and reasonable (domesticated) understanding of deity, we might expect some divine understanding and compassion toward the people's disobedience during this process of change, patience with both the people and himself. Just the opposite is the case. Not the least bit reflective, still very much volcanic and violent storm, Yahweh rages at the people who have betrayed him, erupting in a burning, fiery fury. They disobey him over and over. In the book of Isaiah, we find a stunning record of the crisis that confronts Yahweh at the time when, historically, Assyrians and Babylonians destroyed the nation of Israel. This time, he almost succeeds in punishing the people by destroying them without the possibility of starting over. He almost obliterates his people and thus himself because without his people reflecting Yahweh to himself, he is nothing, he does not exist.

Isaiah: Prophet of Fire

The first words of Yahweh spoken by Isaiah paint the circumstances with which we are already familiar:

> Hear, O heavens, and listen,
> O earth;
> for the LORD has spoken:
> I reared children and brought
> them up,
> but they have rebelled against
> me. (Isa 1:2)

Yahweh addresses both heavens and earth (plural). He has in mind his human creatures (earth), but also the other gods and goddesses (heavens), as well as his own divided self, which is torn between earth (bull) and heaven (written word). The children he reared and brought up are the Hebrew slaves he rescued from Egypt and brought into the promised land, where they established a sovereign kingdom. They rebelled, however, and rebelled continually, against Yahweh's command for absolute fealty. The people's sin and wickedness reflects soul's conflict with itself, soul pushing against its immersion in nature, pushing upward to a new truth as spirit and word. The text depicts this soul-conflict as rebellious Israel, the object of Yahweh's rage:

> The ox knows its owner,
> and the donkey its master's crib;
> but Israel does not know,
> my people do not understand.
>
> Ah, sinful nation,
> people laden with iniquity,
> offspring who do evil,
> children who deal corruptly,
> who have forsaken the LORD,
> who have despised the Holy
> One of Israel,
> who are utterly estranged! (Isa 1:3–4)

Yahweh sarcastically places Israel lower than animals, for even the beasts know their master, understand that their life depends on obedience. With Yahweh, the need for obedience and survival cuts both ways. The irony lies in the words *Holy* and *estranged*.

Holy means separate and apart, and so also isolated and estranged. The holiness (separateness and apartness) of Yahweh means he no longer has divine companions; he is separate and estranged from the natural phenomena that guaranteed his existence. The natural world, the physical world, exists independent of human persons; the nature gods/goddesses were pure nature. The problem for Yahweh is that as he leaves his natural essence behind, he becomes utterly dependent on his human counterparts, the self-image of himself that he created for this very purpose. Yahweh is not only a jealous god, as he often proclaims, but also a dependent god, dependent on his human creatures for his existence.

With some humor, I can say Yahweh suffered from overwhelming separation anxiety, but his anxiety is rooted in his terror of oblivion, no laughing matter. Soul is in a literal life-and-death struggle for the new status of consciousness Yahweh represents. Separation anxiety suggests a human neurotic condition that can be overcome through reflection on the anxiety. Yahweh's anxiety or jealousy cannot be introspected, not only because he is not human, but because Yahweh will die, cease to exist, without his human mirror. The emotions in this story are very human, but this is not at bottom a human struggle, but rather the struggle of soul to liberate itself. The jealousy must be acted out in order for soul to complete its negation of the Bull god so the sublated new consciousness can emerge. Jealousy is never the emotion of one who is secure in their own existence, and thus Yahweh cannot tolerate being ignored:

> Why do you seek further beatings?
> > Why do you continue to rebel?
> The whole head is sick,
> > and the whole heart faint.
> From the sole of the foot even to
> > the head,
> > there is no soundness in it,
> but bruises and sores
> > and bleeding wounds;
> they have not been drained, or
> > bound up,
> > or softened with oil. (Isa 1:5–6)

> If you are willing and obedient,
> > you shall eat the good of the
> > > land;
> but if you refuse and rebel,
> > you shall be devoured by the
> > > sword;
> > for the mouth of the Lord has
> > > spoken. (Isa 1:19–20)

> Therefore says the Sovereign, the
>   Lord of hosts, the Mighty
>   One of Israel:
> Ah, I will pour out my wrath on
>   my enemies,
>   and avenge myself on my foes!
> I will turn my hand against you;
>   I will smelt away your dross as
>   with lye
>   and remove all your alloy. (Isa 1:24–25)

The Jewish people are thoroughly corrupt and sick and, thus, must suffer Yahweh's moral outrage, his punishing wrath. Yahweh's gracious care is completely conditional on obedience; otherwise, complete destruction. And yet, hidden in the phrase "smelt away your dross," is the half-realization that the wickedness is not total, purification is possible; at the heart of the people (and thus, himself) is something worth preserving. In spite of his wholesale emotional condemnation of the people, Yahweh wants to preserve just enough to permit a new beginning. His motive is selfish as his true aim is to preserve his new emergent identity, his newly transcendent free-of-nature identity, which is hardly secure and barely surviving. His need to punish miscalculates, and he finds he does not have the control of international politics that he thought he had. His identity as "Sovereign, the Lord of hosts, the Mighty One of Israel," must adapt and change in the face of the changing political, social, and religious world of Israel. Soul, in this new form of Yahweh, must adapt to historical circumstances and undergo an inner transformation that sublates defeat and failure into something unexpectedly new.

Yahweh Defeats Himself

Brought to his knees, humiliated by failure, and humbled by the necessity of his own suffering, Yahweh is in danger of disappearing altogether, swallowed by the swirling chaos of history. His emotional outbursts, his fiery insistence on obliterating disobedience and rebellion, marched him deep into a box canyon, from which there is no exit. His nature as a warrior god locked itself in a dead end from which there is no escape. He must suffer his contradiction all the way through in order to survive at all, but his survival will have to be in a new, and eventually, unrecognizable form. The warrior god is suffering a fatal crack in the invincible armor he has worn with great success. Or, to turn to his fire identity, the fiery rage, his hot fierce anger, melts the armor he wears, rendering him helpless and disfigured, and yet, this very transformation saves Yahweh from total oblivion, a struggle recorded in Isaiah. The psychological reading of Isaiah is not concerned with whether Isaiah or Yahweh is speaking. The prophet *is* the mouthpiece of Yahweh, so the entire book of Isaiah is Yahweh speaking about himself, just as the psychological truth about the Bible is "soul's speech about itself."

Yahweh Defeats Himself to Save Himself

The various voices in Isaiah "contradict one another freely and frequently," and "these seemingly contradictory messages all come from the same divine source."[7] While it is the same divine source, the one Yahweh of our text, this God, Yahweh, is agitated and in trouble, undergoing immense suffering, a suffering unto death:

> It is when the Lord is speaking to Isaiah that he goes most deeply and recklessly into himself, providing the most searching inventory of his own responses to the agony occasioned in his own life by the agony he has inflicted on his chosen people. To read these responses is to pass through this crisis in the life of God in the company of the God who is suffering it.[8]

In Isaiah, the idea of transformation collides with the idea of total destruction. Transformation requires a death:

> Therefore, as the tongue of fire
> >   devours the stubble,
> > and as dry grass sinks down in
> >   the flame,
> so their root will become rotten,
> >   and their blossom go up like
> >   dust;
> for they have rejected the
> >   instruction of the Lord
> >   of hosts,
> >   and have despised the word of
> >   the Holy One of Israel.
>
> Therefore the anger of the Lord
> >   was kindled against his
> >   people,
> >   and he stretched out his hand
> >   against them and struck
> >   them;
> >   the mountains quaked,
> and their corpses were like refuse
> >   in the streets.
> For all this his anger has not
> >   turned away,
> >   and his hand is stretched
> >   out still. (Isa 5:24–25)

---

7. Miles, *God*, 195.
8. Miles, *God*, 202.

God's Autopsy and the Living Truth of Soul

Let's not pass over this image too quickly: "and their corpses were like refuse in the streets." Imagine this scene. Is it only a metaphor? It tells us something true about God. This was Yahweh! Is it still true about God? That is a mostly irrelevant question as God is not the issue today, but it still reflects the cold impersonal cruelty of soul. Although we are constituted by soul, soul does not really have us in view except as we indirectly serve its purposes. Yahweh reflects the same phenomenology—he is clearly not concerned with the Israelites in any truly personal way, only to the extent that they further his aims. This tone is also typical of Isaiah the man, as he was as hot-headed as Yahweh. He was initiated into the service of Yahweh by a hot coal to his mouth:

> Then one of the seraphs flew to me, holding a live coal that had been taken from the altar with a pair of tongs. The seraph touched my mouth with it and said: "Now that this has touched your lips, your guilt has departed and your sin is blotted out." (Isa 6:6–7)

Like Moses, Isaiah was initiated by fire into the service of the fiery Yahweh; he became a fire prophet and therefore would speak for Yahweh, his speech and Yahweh's speech united in the same fiery purpose. Was fire the strongest image soul had available to purge the nature gods and goddesses, their earth-bound nature, from the substance of Yahweh? After fire consumes, what is left?

Yahweh is, in a sense, speaking out loud to himself, a kind of self-reflection, though not of course self-conscious because Yahweh does not know what he is saying. As fire, he is an impulsive deity who finds out what he has said later when it is written down. As written, Yahweh's speech, his word, will be reflected on over and over as history (soul) writes itself. At this moment, he actually keeps himself ignorant and unconscious when he says:

> Keep listening, but do not
>   comprehend;
> keep looking, but do not
>   understand.
> Make the mind of this people dull,
>   and stop their ears,
>   and shut their eyes,
> so that they may not look with
>   their eyes,
>   and listen with their ears,
> and comprehend with their minds,
>   and turn and be healed. (Isa 6:9b–10)

Here Yahweh confesses that he keeps his mind dull, keeps himself deaf and blind, so that he cannot understand, cannot turn and be reconciled with himself. This state of enforced ignorance (or, unconsciousness) reinforces a complete state of denial that intensifies the tension of the inner conflict. There will be no reconciliation, only a final explosion, a complete negation. The intensification of Yahweh's inner contradiction here is reminiscent of Yahweh hardening Pharaoh's heart over and over, building up to the final violent exodus from Egypt. In the new situation, things are coming to a head, reaching an extreme condition, by which the prevailing form of soul will pulverize and destroy itself for the sake of the new consciousness. Yahweh adheres to his warrior identity, bent on punishing what is abhorrent about himself, his nature embedded bull-god essence and the presence of other gods and goddesses. Earlier Yahweh had declared,

> On that day [of judgment/punishment] people will throw
> > away
> to the moles and to the bats
> their idols of silver and their idols
> > of gold,
> > which they made for themselves
> > to worship,
> to enter the caverns of the rocks
> > and the clefts in the crags,
> from the terror of the LORD,
> > and from the glory of his
> > majesty,
> when he rises to terrify the
> > earth. (Isa 2:20–21)

What is Yahweh's terror, how will he terrify the earth? His answer is in his response to how long he will keep himself ignorant, blind, and deaf:

> Until cities lie waste
> > without inhabitant,
> and houses without people,
> > and the land is utterly desolate;
> until the LORD sends everyone
> > far away,
> > and vast is the emptiness in the
> > midst of the land.
> Even if a tenth part remain in it,
> > it will be burned again,
> like a terebinth or an oak
> > whose stump remains standing
> > when it is felled. (Isa 6:11b–13)

What does the Lord want to destroy with raging fire, burning wrath? The goddess. A footnote in the NRSV states that while the last line of the above quotation is obscure and textually corrupt, it could be reconstructed along the following lines: "like the terebinth [of the goddess] and the oak of Asherah, cast out with the pillar of the high places." As we saw in the previous chapter, Asherah was the original consort of Yahweh, the natural companion of Bull-Yahweh; she was a Canaanite mother goddess associated with lions, serpents, and sacred trees. The pillar and high places are symbols and ritual objects that mark the sacred locations of the nature gods and goddesses. In the ancient Near East, trees were goddesses, and goddesses, trees. The Hebrew people worshipped Asherah as the partner of Yahweh, the original nature fertility god Yahweh. Yahweh's conflict is with himself; he is mixed up and impure within himself. Yahweh yearns to be pure, but he cannot manage it. He rages at his own impurity, his own uncleanness. If the goddess and all she represents is so entwined with the reality of Yahweh, can Yahweh really destroy the goddess without destroying himself? Yahweh treads dangerously close to his own contradiction, inherent in the conflicting impulses of consciousness (nature polytheism vs. spirit monotheism) of the time.

Soon after Yahweh asserted he was deaf, blind, and confounded, the opposite image appears, its negation:

> The people who walked in
>   darkness
>   have seen a great light;
> those who lived in a land of deep
>   darkness—
>   on them light has shined.
> . . .
> For a child has been born for us,
>   a son given to us;
> authority rests upon his shoulders;
>   and he is named
> Wonderful Counselor, Mighty
>   God,
>   Everlasting Father, Prince of
>   Peace. (Isa 9:2, 6)

Yahweh entertains a new image of himself as a child, a counselor, father, and prince of peace, an extreme contrast to the proud, defiant, boastful Lord of power politics, and the fire-breathing punisher. This text is traditionally interpreted in terms of messianic kingship and the promise of Yahweh to establish an eternal kingdom of peace, justice, and righteousness. It was also famously taken up in the Matthew gospel's birth story of the Christ. Within the traditional interpretation, this image refers not to Yahweh but to what Yahweh promises to do. But, as soul's dream of itself, this is Yahweh's speech about himself, telling us he is changing, changing his self-image, his self-understanding. Does he want to become, or is he forced to adopt (although still like a "Mighty God") the new attributes of a child, a father, a counselor, and a god of peace? The great value placed on power and the ability to destroy the opposition is crumbling and dying—the pride of place that power and total domination have held is eroding. Another clue to this reversal of values is found in the well-known passage about the peaceable kingdom:

> The wolf shall live with the lamb,
>   the leopard shall lie down with
>   the kid,
> the calf and the lion and the
>   fatling together,
>   and a little child shall lead them.
> The cow and the bear shall graze,
>   their young shall lie down
>   together;
> and the lion shall eat straw like
>   the ox.
> The nursing child shall play over
>   the hole of the asp,
> and the weaned child shall put
>   its hand on the adder's den.
> They will not hurt or destroy
>   on all my holy mountain;
> for the earth will be full of the
>   knowledge of the LORD
>   as the waters cover the sea. (Isa 11:6–9)

Although this text is in the future tense, it tells us what is happening to Yahweh's warrior identity now. Yahweh's image of wolf and lion, the powerful predators hungry with ambition to be the one and only Lord of creation, is reversing itself. The very idea of divine power is undergoing a sea change, and the Yahweh who was bent on "punish and destroy" is undergoing an alchemical transformation from within. The intimation of another way to be Yahweh is forcing itself upon him. In this text, the natural order of nature, the predator-prey relationship, is negated. The passage accentuates the *contra naturam* principle that threads itself throughout the Bible. The Bible records soul's movement and development as a series of negations, pushing off against its original home in nature. Soul is not negating the natural world as we understand it today. *Soul is negating its understanding of itself as immersed in nature.* The problem is not with nature itself, but with how public mind, the syntax of consciousness, the sea of meaning that is soul, understood itself. This is a transformation of the logical form of consciousness, not a rejection of nature; it did not change the impact of the natural world on human beings, but it does change how human beings will be oriented to nature. Soul as presence *as* nature is leaving nature behind for a new status as transcendent spirit; meaning is relocating itself in the written word, a new style of logos. Soul continues its movement of self-liberation, requiring a revolutionary extraction from a former state.

Yahweh wants to turn his failure, his defeat, into a new beginning, a new world, a new creation. The images of a "new world" or a "new creation" are metaphors for soul's transformation of consciousness. The "new world" is not another physical creation, nor is it primarily a new social order. Rather, it is the changing of the general form of consciousness at large (which will lead to new social orders). From a psychology with soul point of view, the *world* is always the world of consciousness, the culture-wide world of meaning. Our human world is the shared *meaning* that gives us our being and identity. In our biblical text, the general form of consciousness personifies itself as Yahweh, and if the new form of consciousness he represents is to survive, he must suffer the death of the identity that led to this crisis. Yahweh's epic failure is the transforming catalyst. Yahweh himself must die and be born anew, that is, negated and sublated. The new form of consciousness, up until now personified by the heroic triumphant warrior, must undergo a radical metamorphosis.

The Rejected Goddess Insinuates Herself

The goddess has been Yahweh's bane, the constant irritant, the other truth that drives him crazy with rage. He has expended great effort to exterminate Asherah and the other gods and goddesses in order to focus all of the attention of his people on him and him alone. And yet, he has failed to do so. Then what next? What might the historical crisis at the hands of Assyria and Babylon, the dilemma of his failure as a warrior, lead to?

Reading the Old Testament books in their order in the Tanakh reveals a curious omission which, at this point, Miles makes explicit:

> By ceasing to be what for so long he seemed to be, he has *become* mysterious. But because this new awareness is joined to an equally unprecedented tenderness, it leads to the further compelling question of why the Lord has been so complete a stranger to the tender emotions.[9]

The question arises as to Yahweh's relation to love. Today we say "God is love," but that was certainly not the case for Yahweh:

> Until this point in his history, the Lord God has never loved. Love has never been predicated of him either as an action or as a motive. It is not that he has had no emotional life of any sort. He has been wrathful, vengeful, and remorseful. But he has not been loving.[10]

Yahweh has been preoccupied with burning off or cutting out the nature-bound aspects of himself, those dimensions of the myth-ritual status of soul that, in the ancient context, were especially associated with the goddess. However, here I want to highlight

---

9. Miles, *God*, 236.
10. Miles, *God*, 237.

an attribute of the goddess that arises in Yahweh's effort to banish her: her status as *rejected* and *abomination*. Consumed by the war with himself, consumed by wrath, Yahweh has no room for love, or the "tender emotions." On a slash and burn mission of eradication, Yahweh has run into the dead end of this approach and sits in failure and defeat. He cannot exterminate himself. He must come to terms with the *rejected* goddess in some way. Yahweh is faced with an unexpected kind of self-negation. As a result of his fierce and violent efforts to reject the goddess, he himself is now rejected, he himself has failed and knows defeat, he has become an abomination to himself. This is the very transformation soul needs in order to take the next step: the way of the suffering slave. Yahweh's rejection of his bull nature and his consort goddess, of the gods and goddesses in general, is the narrative portrayal of soul's self-negation, soul negating one form of itself for another form of consciousness. Now the triumphant warrior Yahweh has to undergo another negation, negating the power of the warrior for its opposite, the inconceivable form of a suffering slave.

The Suffering Slave

The book of Isaiah is actually two books (if not three), the first of which is composed of Isaiah's own writing, chapters 1–39; an unknown author called Second Isaiah composed chapters 40–66 considerably later. Historical and literary criticism date Isaiah himself during the time when the Assyrian empire absorbed the northern kingdom of Israel, 742 to 701 BCE. Second Isaiah was composed as Babylon falls to Persia around 539 BCE. The historical circumstances, the style of writing, and the expressed concerns are very different for first and second Isaiah, and yet it remains one book, a continuity, the second part a development and amplification of the first. This reflects Yahweh as he suffers a radical discontinuity with himself and yet remains continuous with himself—for the Bible, he is the one deity, Yahweh, the Lord God. This is how sublation works: Soul negates the current form of itself while preserving its essence in a new form; the earlier form is changed and incorporated within a larger or higher status of consciousness. The Bible itself reflects this progressive process of negation and sublation (a kind of digesting and metabolizing a new meaning). As a whole it is one book, while at the same time it is a collection of many books composed gradually over several hundred years. And from the point of view of Christianity, the New Testament negated and sublated the entire Tanakh, and turned it into an "Old Testament." For the psychological viewpoint, the Bible is a single soul-document that portrays a historical development of soul.

Second Isaiah includes four poems known as Servant Songs (42:1–4; 49:1–6; 50:4–11; 52:13—53:12). The fourth and longest one is the well-known Suffering Servant, the essence of which is reflected in the Christian myth of Christ. For the ancient texts and their world, the Hebrew word that is translated as *servant* really means *slave*, and the idea of a slave is closer to the ancient social reality than our modern understanding of servant. The idea of servant softens the meaning and leaves open the possibility that the servant has a choice. The idea of slave is a hard reality; the slave has no choice. In our text, the suffering servant is a suffering slave. This perspective sharpens the exigency of the coming transformation: Yahweh is slave to his own nature. The idea of slave is truer to the soul process at work here: there is no choice. Soul's movement is inexorable. We do not have a choice but neither does soul, subject to itself as slave to master in which the slave-master pair is a dialectical unity. Slave/master is a unity in which each creates the other, and neither exists without the other. They are a differentiated unity, and dialectical in that they contain each other. The slave is the master's own other, and the master is the slave's own other. They constitute a unity and a difference at the same time. This is the structure of soul, as all its internal contradictions are dialectical; soul is ouroboric, its continual self-negations create, destroy, and create itself, again and again. As the world of *meaning* that we are, soul is self-contained, always at work on itself.

The poems are soul documents, and we need not be concerned with the scholarly arguments about who the suffering slave is because in the psychological perspective, the suffering slave is Yahweh, the image of soul's ongoing self-negation and sublation. Simply put, the poem of the suffering slave is soul, as Yahweh, absorbing a quality of the goddess that he created (complete loss of power and rejected status) negating his warrior identity. The suffering slave is an image of the dirty secret of transformation: It must pass all the way through suffering and death before any healing as new consciousness, a more complex and inclusive consciousness, can emerge. So-called healing is not possible without death. The idea of healing tugs at personal concerns, but here we are not on the personal level at all, we are on the level of soul's great work as cultural consciousness, public mind.

The poem asserts the great value of the slave (he is "exalted and lifted up") and how this new value confounds traditional expectations and subverts conventional thinking:

> See, my servant shall prosper;
>   he shall be exalted and lifted up,
>   and shall be very high.
> Just as there were many who were
>   astonished at him
>   —so marred was his
>   appearance, beyond human
>   semblance,
>   and his form beyond that of
>   mortals—
> so he shall startle many nations;
>   kings shall shut their mouths
>   because of him;
>   for that which had not been told
>   them they shall see,

and that which they had not
> heard they shall
> > contemplate. (Isa 52:13–15)

The slave is hard to recognize, so different is he from ordinary expectation. He will force the prevailing thought paradigms (kings) to question what they think they know ("shut their mouths because of him"). The very ground of Yahweh's assumption about himself is called into question and subverted. The established and prevailing self-image of Yahweh is corrupting itself from within:

> He had no form or majesty that
> > we should look at him,
> > nothing in his appearance that
> > we should desire him.
> He was despised and rejected
> > by others;
> > a man of suffering and
> > acquainted with infirmity;
> and as one from whom others
> > hide their faces
> he was despised, and we held
> > him of no account. (Isa 53:2b–3)

The suffering slave image thoroughly negates the expected form of the warrior, of triumphant power. Is this the influence of the "tender emotions," is love at work undermining Yahweh's preoccupation with power and dominance? Yahweh has been in a fierce fight against the goddess, attempting to stamp her out, but now he is himself infected by her. On his knees in failure and defeat, Yahweh does not notice that the despised and rejected goddess, the very goddess associated with infirmity and suffering, finds an entrance and sneaks into Yahweh's very being, but in the guise of an unrecognizable quality:

> Surely he has borne our infirmities
> > and carried our diseases,
> yet we accounted him stricken,
> > struck down by God, and
> > > afflicted.
> But he was wounded for our
> > transgressions,
> > crushed for our iniquities;
> upon him was the punishment that
> > made us whole,
> > and by his bruises we are
> > > healed. (Isa 53:4–5)

God's Autopsy and the Living Truth of Soul

Yahweh is speaking about himself. The suffering slave is a mirror of Yahweh, a self-image of Yahweh. Yahweh strikes down, afflicts himself. Yahweh acknowledges that he is unrecognizable in his state of failure and defeat and, at the same time, accepts this status. The new truth of suffering at his own hands is what makes "whole" and "healed."

Yahweh's admission that he is unrecognizable to himself as one despised and rejected, just as he despised and rejected the goddess, is what makes room for the goddess in his constitution, and in such a form that is not recognized as the goddess. Both Yahweh and the goddess are transformed, their identities changed, unified in a new self-understanding still known as Yahweh. No longer will Yahweh be the Bull-Storm god, with his consort Asherah at his side. That form of Yahweh has pushed itself all the way to its logical end as the warrior who would punish himself into oblivion. Instead of bringing himself to an end and disappearing into the mists of time, Yahweh opts for change by way of love and suffering, a metamorphosis that makes him unrecognizable. Ishtar, Aphrodite, Astarte, and Asherah are names for various goddess soul-forms prevalent in the ancient Near East, and she has insinuated herself inextricably into Yahweh's being:

> He was oppressed, and he was
>   afflicted,
>   yet he did not open his mouth;
> like a lamb that is led to the
>   slaughter,
>   and like a sheep that before its
>   shearers is silent,
>   so he did not open his mouth.
> By a perversion of justice he was
>   taken away.
>   Who could have imagined his
>   future?
> For he was cut off from the land
>   of the living,
>   stricken for the transgression of
>   my people. (Isa 53:7–8)

> Yet it was the will of the Lord to
>   crush him with pain.
> When you make his life an
>   offering for sin,
>   he shall see his offspring, and
>   shall prolong his days;
> through him the will of the Lord
>   shall prosper.
>   Out of his anguish he shall
>   see light,

> he shall find satisfaction through
>> his knowledge. (Isa 53:10–11a)

The silence of the lamb is not meek submission, but rather the silence imposed by the complete lack of adequate categories and concepts to name what is happening to Yahweh. Yahweh has to see that his own insistence on absolute obedience—on destruction of the people as punishment for *dis*obedience—is itself a perversion of justice. But that perversion has led to this image of Yahweh as suffering slave, utterly unexpected and unimaginable. That Yahweh is suffering such a horrible fate cuts him off from his former self-understanding. With the idea of anguish giving birth to light and knowledge, a glimmer of a new consciousness emerges. But the poetic language can only hint at the tremendous transformation taking place at the heart of Yahweh (i.e., soul), a transformation that will take centuries to unfold and understand itself. The change that is underway will be widespread:

> The righteous one, my
>> servant, shall make many
>> righteous,
>> and he shall bear their iniquities.
> Therefore I will allot him a
>> portion with the great,
>> and he shall divide the spoil
>> with the strong;
> because he poured out himself
>> to death,
>> and was numbered with the
>> transgressors;
> yet he bore the sin of many,
>> and made intercession for the
>> transgressors. (Isa 53:11b–12)

The slave is Yahweh himself, a slave to his need to undergo a suffering transformation. Yahweh's changing nature changes the nature of reality (the syntax of consciousness). Everyone who participates in this reality, the shared and corporate reality of Yahweh, therefore, is also changed at that deep level of shared cultural identity. Yahweh is not a discrete entity, even though he appears to be one, a very strong and definitive one at that. He is a personification of soul, and for psychology, he represents the logical (unconscious background) form of consciousness that is undergoing a profound change. Yahweh's story as soul's autobiography is also Western civilization's autobiography. *Yahweh* represents a collective form of consciousness, an implicit and unconscious worldview, and that general worldview is undergoing a deep change. Soul is undergoing a negation at its own hands. The death of Yahweh's warrior form is soul's negation of its own identity as a cultural norm, for the sake of a new more inclusive ground of consciousness that sublates the warrior god who began as a nature-based deity. His transformation subverts the taken-for-granted norms about him as a deity. This form of consciousness is beginning to turn inward.

Culture and language together form a unity that is a kind of womb of meaning within which we live. As soul, this is the water in which we swim, and as the "water" changes, we are also changed, unfortunately, whether we like it or not. Yahweh was the water a particular people swam in, and as the Yahweh-water changed its character, it changed those within its embrace. Therefore, when the text says, "The righteous *one*, my servant, shall make *many* righteous," it refers to this deep change in the nature of reality, the social and cultural reality of the Israelite people that was called Yahweh. That divine entity symbolized the shared and unconscious ground of meaning shaping the general sense of being that everyone was, and individual personalities existed within that larger field. Thus, the poem's references to the healing and making whole of the people through the suffering of the slave, I read as the transformation of Yahweh, which psychologically, is the transformation of the Mind (soul) of the people. It is all of a piece. When soul changes, when the syntax of consciousness changes, we are changed along with it; at that deeper impersonal level, we *are* soul. Soul (the syntax of consciousness) is the basis of our being. The Yahweh stance of consciousness is reorienting itself, and that reorients the world.

We can also speak in terms of Yahweh learning something new about himself. God's self-knowledge develops through his relationship with humankind by trial and error:

> But one way or another, framed as it is by God's words in its opening and closing verses, this haunting poem represents a change in God's mind that is even more important than his crossing, or his near crossing to love.
>
> And the change has come about, just as every previous change has come about, by the unmistakable subversion of his ostensible intentions . . . Perhaps because God has no life other than the one he lives through mankind, because, in other words, there is no purely divine experience from which he might benefit, nearly all his key experiences seem to subvert his intentions. After each of his major actions, he discovers that he has not done quite what he thought he was doing, or has done something he never intended to do.[11]

The transformation of Yahweh is inextricably bound up with a transformation of humankind. In this story of Yahweh, God is not omniscient, but a learning god, groping along with his created self-image, and a new kind of history is the result:

> The inference that one might make looking at the entire course of his history to this point from the outside is that God is only very imperfectly self-conscious and very slightly in control of the consequences of his words and

---

11. Miles, *God*, 250.

> actions. Even inside that history, his own inferences come one at a time, often gropingly after the fact.
>
> . . .
>
> Though drastically unlike mankind in some ways, God is like his creatures in that he too lives his life one stage at a time and, his protestations to the contrary notwithstanding, he is painfully unable to foresee his end in his beginning.[12]

A good description of soul itself. Just as this biblical God is neither omnipotent nor omniscient, so soul—that roiling edge of now recognized as history and culture as which soul self-actualizes—tries this and that, not knowing ahead of time what will catch fire, what will take off and establish itself as soul's next manifestation. Soul gropes along, never able to grasp what the next unintended consequences will be. Whatever they are, soul will both adapt to and push off from what emerges. Only our relatively long view of history, looking back over hundreds and thousands of years, gives us the perspective to discern general trends that were nearly invisible in the moment. Isaiah is a record of Yahweh undergoing change, suffering and adapting to unexpected historical contingencies. Yahweh was the form soul took at that time and place, and the Bible is the record of Yahweh's changing form, embodying a future without knowing what the future would be. Yahweh's scope of operation is refocusing to reflect the gradual transformation of his identity, the changing form of consciousness.

What is happening to Yahweh? From the school of historical contingency, defeated by brute powers beyond his control, Yahweh learns that he must reinterpret himself, reshape his identity away from the bull god and the war god who would conquer and rule over nations. He begins to withdraw into himself and rethink the values that have brought him to this point. The six books, Haggai, Zechariah, Malachi, Psalms, Proverbs, and Job (in that order in the Tanakh), reveal the direction of Yahweh's changing sense of self. Yahweh becomes progressively absent as far as his actual and felt presence is concerned, both with his people and in the Tanakh: By the end of Job, we encounter the "sound of divine silence."[13] Yahweh seems to have shut down his political operations and entered a prolonged period of inward contemplation.

The Divorce Proceedings Falter

The appearance of the Suffering Slave in Isaiah allowed us to consider how the goddess was having an unexpected impact on Yahweh's changing nature. In Malachi, it is possible to discern a new relationship developing between Yahweh and Asherah. Yahweh's goal was to violently separate himself from his fusion with the goddess Asherah. The evidence in the Tanakh for Yahweh's consort is negative, seen clearly in his railing against her. Contemporary archaeology and philology forces us see the early Yahweh/

---

12. Miles, *God*, 251.
13. Miles, *God*, 254.

Asherah union very clearly. In an indirect reference in Malachi, Yahweh speaks as if he were an abandoned wife:

> The LORD was a witness between you and the wife of your youth, to whom you have been faithless, though she is your companion and your wife by covenant. Did not one God make her? Both flesh and spirit are his. And what does the one God desire? Godly offspring. So look to yourselves, and do not let anyone be faithless to the wife of his youth. (Mal 2:14–15)

Here Yahweh's self-understanding introduces a new metaphor as he casts himself in the feminine role of rejected wife. At this stage of Yahweh's development through the pages of the Tanakh, a different kind of question is raised about the relationship between the goddess and the character of Yahweh.

Starting with Exodus through Deuteronomy, continuing with the historical books, Joshua to Kings, and on through the major prophets Isaiah and Jeremiah, Yahweh is at war with other peoples and their gods and goddesses, their carved and cast symbols (idols) in wood, stone, and metal, their ritual practices and places of worship. Yahweh wants to blot them out, wipe them from the face of the earth. Yahweh's hate of the goddess was the energy needed to separate from a fused and natural relationship with her, which was also Yahweh's own natural bull essence. In the ancient polytheistic context, what was odd and unusual was the thrust of Yahweh to separate himself from the goddess. The covenant agreement between Yahweh and his people, which the biblical texts reinforce over and over, was a soul-impulse for the ideal of one true transcendent God. As we have seen, this was far ahead of actual daily practice. The violent imperative that was then Yahweh became the seed of a new consciousness that has realized itself as *consciousness* only in modern times.

Let us remember that Yahweh's violent rejection of his goddess consort was not a marginal theme in the Tanakh. It is a major story line that colored the differentiation of consciousness it was bringing about:

> The exclusion of Asherah must not be seen as, on the Lord's own part, anything less than a violently emotional revulsion. In [Yahweh's] eyes, Israel's worst crime, the crime that finally provokes him to destroy Jerusalem and then to blot out even the remnant of Judah, is King Manasseh's horrifying decision to place a sculpted image of Asherah in the Lord's own temple.[14]

Here is another lengthy text, which records all of the abominable things Manasseh instituted. Let's also remember that these were not anomalous evils, but the prevailing norm of the time:

> Manasseh was twelve years old when he began to reign; he reigned fifty-five years in Jerusalem . . . He did what was evil in the sight of the LORD, following the abominable practices of the nations that the LORD drove out before the

---

14. Miles, *God*, 265.

people of Israel. For he rebuilt the high places that his father Hezekiah had destroyed; he erected altars for Baal, made a sacred pole [Asherah], as King Ahab of Israel had done, worshiped all the host of heaven [solar, planetary deities], and served them. He built altars in the house of the LORD, of which the LORD had said, "In Jerusalem I will put my name." He built altars for all the host of heaven in the two courts of the house of the LORD. He made his son pass through fire; he practiced soothsaying and augury, and dealt with mediums and with wizards. He did much evil in the sight of the LORD, provoking him to anger. The carved image of Asherah that he had made he set in the house of which the LORD said to David and to his son Solomon, "In this house, and in Jerusalem, which I have chosen out of all the tribes of Israel, I will put my name forever; I will not cause the feet of Israel to wander any more out of the land that I gave to their ancestors, if only they will be careful to do according to all that I have commanded them, and according to all the law that my servant Moses commanded them." But they did not listen; Manasseh misled them to do more evil than the nations had done that the LORD destroyed before the people Israel.

The LORD said by his servants the prophets, "Because King Manasseh of Judah has committed these abominations, has done things more wicked than all that the Amorites did, who were before him, and has caused Judah also to sin with his idols; therefore thus says the LORD, the God of Israel, I am bringing upon Jerusalem and Judah such evil that the ears of everyone who hears of it will tingle. I will stretch over Jerusalem the measuring line for Samaria, and the plummet for the house of Ahab; I will wipe Jerusalem as one wipes a dish, wiping it and turning it upside down. I will cast off the remnant of my heritage, and give them into the hand of their enemies; they shall become prey and a spoil to all their enemies, because they have done what is evil in my sight and have provoked me to anger, since the day their ancestors came out of Egypt, even to this day." (2 Kgs 21:1–15)

Yahweh is enraged at the presence of his wife in his house! "Violent emotional revulsion" is correct, as Yahweh wipes Jerusalem as one wipes a dish. Yahweh's revulsion is with himself, his struggle to separate his newly emergent spiritual self from his archaic nature-bound self. For such a transformation of soul's very constitution to be successful, the energy of moral outrage and violent hate were required. The differentiation that soul wanted was not simply an intellectual one; it had to be a moral problem to generate the emotional energy and power necessary to force the separation. In the previous chapter, we saw the metaphor of nuclear fission applied to this gigantic revolution in consciousness. In the context of this amazing rage, it is all the more remarkable that Yahweh likens himself to the image of the abandoned wife, when Asherah herself is the abandoned wife of Yahweh. The image of Asherah as discarded slips in seemingly unnoticed, and Yahweh identifies with her as discarded, in the same way that the Suffering Slave was discarded. The image of Yahweh as powerful warrior, successful up until now, has turned dysfunctional, no longer sustainable or tenable. The warrior form of Yahweh is now discarded as Asherah was discarded. Through a reversal of fortune Yahweh is forced to face what he himself enforced, the status of being rejected and defeated. Though not recognized as such, the goddess slips back in to Yahweh's character.

Yahweh was not always in conflict with himself. When humankind was created as his self-image in that early creation story, he spoke in the plural, "Let *us* make man in *our* image, after *our* likeness," and "they" created a man *and* a woman.[15] These are not abstract masculine and feminine principles, but rather the actual primal life forces of the natural world that must exist together, both in heaven and on earth. The Bible's story of Yahweh, however, moves him away from this natural pairing; biblical Yahweh is most decidedly a single male deity. It is not the feminine, a modern construct, that is being denigrated—a modern judgment with no place in this phenomenology of soul. Rather, spirit-Yahweh claims all truth for himself and denies any truth to the nature-bound goddesses and gods. By claiming "all truth" for himself, he instituted a new dominant status of soul, which worked away on itself for a time in seeming silence. When the Christian movement of soul absorbed the Tanakh into its self-understanding, this vision of soul truly spread its cultural-historical wings.

Historically, we know that Yahweh was entangled with a goddess from the beginning. This was Yahweh's normal and original status as a nature god in the polytheistic universe. As the trajectory of Israelite history and the history of the developing character of Yahweh as portrayed by the Bible unfolds, the goddess is progressively excluded from the character of Yahweh. Still, in spite of this powerful ideological thrust of the Tanakh, in spite of Yahweh's insistence on divorcing Asherah, the goddess enters, unmistakably though not quite recognizable, into Yahweh's character by way of a back door:

> In the aftermath of the Judeans' return from their Babylonian captivity, God will become gradually more androgynous. The analogous femininity implicit in his characterization of himself as abandoned wife—a femininity, obviously of weakness—is not unconnected with the deeper change to come. It is a condition for and prelude to it. For now, however, God is neither female nor androgynous. He may best be described as a chastened and shaken male, even when he compares himself to an ill-supported wife, and the answer to the question *Is there a goddess inside this God?* rather than *No*, is *Not yet*.[16]

Yahweh's status is reduced from that of the proud and grand warrior to that of a "chastened and shaken male," but this image is contained within the metaphor of a weak and vulnerable wife. After the exile and the return to Judah and Jerusalem, things were not at all what Yahweh promised. The three post-exilic prophets

---

15. Miles, *God*, 265.
16. Miles, *God*, 267.

(Haggai, Zechariah, Malachi) convey a very different tone from the prophets writing before and during the exile:

> [There is] a clear suggestion of disappointment and dejection among the Judeans and, in God, an unwonted narrowness of perspective and shrillness of tone. The promises God made through Isaiah and the earlier prophets have clearly not been kept. A semblance of national life has been reconstituted, but to those with clear memories it is no more than a semblance. *The Judeans and their God both find themselves with identities sharply modified by history.*[17]

Not only human beings must adapt to straitened historical circumstances, God too must adapt and change. It is one thing to say that God, or any god, is a cultural construct and that as culture changes, the God too will obviously change. Thinking in terms of "cultural constructs" is a human perspective, the view that human agents create their own gods. This is the reductive perspective from externality, and fails to see the autonomy of the animating principle of culture that psychology calls soul: the logical form, or syntax, of consciousness, the internal truth of any culture. The idea of a "cultural construct" should be reversed: "God" (i.e., the syntax of consciousness) constructs culture rather than the reverse. Yet, it is not a simple reversal, because soul creates culture with and through human agents.

The Judeans and their God must accept severely reduced cultural statuses compared to what they had achieved during their sovereign nationhood. Their history now demanded new identities, new senses of selfhood, that would reflect the new status of truth in Yahweh's separation from nature. In a sense, Yahweh shifts from an extraverted stance toward the world and becomes more introverted in relation to himself. The original effort had been to conquer the outer world. Now in the face of defeat, Yahweh turned to conquering the world of the mind and heart. Yahweh personifies a historical process, transforming himself from a self-evident mythological nature deity to a theological object of faith. He is still a very real ontological truth, but of a very different order. Looking ahead to our modern era, Yahweh literally dissolves and becomes a psychological (logical) notion of truth, although this final dissolution goes through Christianity.

Yahweh's Shame and the End of Prophecy

Yahweh is ashamed of his failure. Is shame one of the tender emotions? Not really. But neither is it fiery rage and dominating anger. Shame is much more than embarrassment; it feels like annihilation of one's self, a psychological and social kind of death. Shame is exactly the emotion that induces one to hide, to go silent, to long for invisibility, and this seems to be what Yahweh is doing when, in Zechariah, he prohibits prophecy:

---

17. Miles, *God*, 267–68, emphasis added.

> On that day[18] says the LORD of hosts, I will cut off the names of the idols from the land, so that they shall be remembered no more; and also I will remove from the land the prophets and the unclean spirit. And if any prophets appear again, their fathers and mothers who bore them will say to them, "You shall not live, for you speak lies in the name of the LORD"; and their fathers and their mothers who bore them shall pierce them through when they prophecy. On that day the prophets will be ashamed, every one, of their visions when they prophesy; they will not put on a hairy mantle in order to deceive, but each of them will say, "I am no prophet, I am a tiller of the soil; for the land has been my possession since my youth." (Zech 13:2–5)

"Prophecy is a mistake the Lord will not make twice," Miles says.[19] A prophecy against prophecy, and if the prophet is ashamed of being a prophet, then God is ashamed of being God, as the two are a unity in the context of soul's speech about itself. The prophet speaks and acts for, and as, God. God is ashamed of himself, induced by his terrible failure as a warrior, his abject suffering as a slave, and the insinuation of the goddess in a new form. As a result, he will go silent and adopt a different focus. The Psalms are another hint at the new direction of the continually self-negating Yahweh, from earth-bound golden bull to liberated mindedness and thought.

Psalms: The Lord Goes Dark

Yahweh now enters a period of protracted silence. Yahweh's purposes and character are so thoroughly changed that Yahweh simply disappears. From here on (in the Tanakh) the Lord does not speak to humankind again. Yahweh, so to speak, goes dark.

This does not mean that the conversation stops, but rather it becomes one-sided. Even though Yahweh is now silent, the people keep the conversation alive. Or, the people, human beings, now keep Yahweh alive, keep Yahweh relevant. Soul is undergoing another transformation. In our psychological context, soul is a unity constituted by Yahweh and humankind. Up until now, Yahweh's initiative has kept the development of Yahweh and his people in motion. Now the initiative shifts to the human side. This supports the central idea that soul is shifting from its embodiment as sensual nature to forms of spirit as mindedness, abstraction, and thought. The written word becomes sacred in itself. The location of soul's motive power begins its subtle shift from God to humankind. The "I Am" is on the move.

Until the Psalms, it is rare that an ordinary person speaks to Yahweh. Rather it has been the towering figures of Jewish history who speak to Yahweh and to whom

---

18. "That day" refers to the eschatological coming great day of God, when Jerusalem will be cleansed of sin, the covenant reestablished, and God will rule over the world. Such "end of history and final judgment" mythologies reflect decisive transformations in the logical form of consciousness, when a prevailing reality is negated and a new reality is emerging.

19. Miles, *God*, 271.

Yahweh speaks, and who carry out Yahweh's great plans for the Israelite nation as a whole. That exclusive conversation now changes. With the Psalms, it is more often the anonymous and ordinary individual who speaks with Yahweh about simple ordinary human concerns and suffering, and in their speaking to Yahweh, they tell us something about him:

> The Psalms often read like interviews with the obscure: anonymous foot soldiers and taxpayers who testify to the character of their leader most convincingly not by what they say about him but by what they say to him.[20]

Previously the speech of Yahweh concerned the guilt or innocence of the whole nation, as guilt or innocence was shared by the corporate body of Israel. Now, in the Psalms, the individuals who speak to Yahweh assume that Yahweh is available and open to hearing their personal problems, their private concerns with guilt or innocence. This corresponds with the change in Yahweh's status, his reduced stature, his coming down to earth, and along with this change in status another shift in emphasis is found in the Psalms. *Knowledge* of Yahweh and attentiveness to the *precious* thoughts of Yahweh come to the fore:

> How weighty to me are your
>   thoughts, O God!
>   How vast is the sum of them!
> I try to count them—they are
>   more than the sand;
>   I come to the end—I am still
>   with you. (Ps 139:17–18)

The Revised Standard Version (RSV) translation reads, "How *precious* to me are thy thoughts, O God!" Both *weighty* and *precious* are the same Hebrew word, and now it is the *thoughts* of God that are more numerous than the sands, rather than the offspring of Abraham. The shift is from Yahweh's *action* in the world to an increased value of Yahweh's *thoughts*, Yahweh's mind. This change signals not just the shrinking of Yahweh's worldly political influence, his loss of status as a warrior, but a shift of soul's orientation from action to thought. Yahweh turns within so to speak, away from international political concerns in favor of his infinite and weighty thoughts. The torah (the law), that "uniquely extended externalization of the mind of God,"[21] increases in value and power as the place where Yahweh's presence is concentrating.

The first psalm sets the theme for the whole collection, putting study of the torah front and center:

---

20. Miles, *God*, 273.
21. Miles, *God*, 277.

> Happy are those
>> who do not follow the advice of
>>> the wicked,
> or take the path that sinners tread,
>> or sit in the seat of scoffers;
> but their delight is in the law [torah] of
>> the Lord,
>> and on his law they meditate
>>> day and night.
> They are like trees
>> planted by streams of water,
> which yield their fruit in its
>>> season,
>> and their leaves do not wither.
> In all that they do, they prosper.
>
> The wicked are not so,
>> but are like chaff that the wind
>>> drives away.
> Therefore the wicked will not
>> stand in the judgment,
>> nor sinners in the congregation
>>> of the righteous;
> for the Lord watches over the
>> way of the righteous,
> but the way of the wicked will
>>> perish. (Ps 1:1–6)

Rather than a prophetic condemnation of a whole nation, this psalm shows a way for an individual to fulfill the covenant and reap its rewards. The Psalms hardly ever mention prophecy or prophets and pass over those extended "thoughts of the Lord" in utter silence. The absence of any concern with prophecy in the Psalms matches Yahweh's declaration in Zechariah that prophecy cannot be trusted, cannot be controlled. The Psalms set a new value on torah itself; torah now embodies God's wisdom and a way of life anyone can follow. Study of torah is a much more manageable project, a project of written words people can live by, and that Yahweh finds acceptable. Although Yahweh never speaks in the Psalms, Yahweh is always assumed to be a beneficent presence, a willing listener. The shift in the tone of address to Yahweh is a change in Yahweh himself:

> What is new in the Psalter, what seems to represent a distinct and pervasive change of emphasis in it, is the shift of attention from national to personal and familial welfare and from aggressive public and political themes to the quiet study of the law.[22]

22. Miles, *God*, 282.

Yahweh Defeats Himself to Save Himself

The law (torah) is becoming a good in itself, something significantly different from what it was when delivered by the volcanic Yahweh at Sinai, a demanding mandate and binding covenant with an entire people and history. Now things are more personal and intimate, and Yahweh's *mind* itself assumes a higher and more precious value. Remembering that the people are God's self-image, the Psalms become the autobiographical musings of Yahweh, Yahweh's own journal writings. Here Yahweh contemplates his own shortcomings and limitations, turning his attention to self-understanding and self-knowledge. If the larger historical circumstances initiated something like Yahweh's mid-life crisis, then he is reexamining the values he began with. In fact, those values, the push for national expansion and international conquest, have failed, and now what is left are the core values, the torah, which must be relearned in an entirely new set of circumstances, outer and inner. If the first push of Yahweh was in a sense horizontal, now it has turned vertical, exploring in depth the pathways of his own mind. In the Psalms, Yahweh is in dialogue with himself, finding a new identity in the torah. Yahweh and torah become identical, the torah functioning as a kind of incarnation of a new Yahweh: from passionate warrior active in the world, to passionate study, contemplation, and thought. As noted above, Yahweh is silent: The people take the initiative by impressing the mind of God on the mind of God:

> And by a paradoxical move, the Jews are taking the law imposed on them and imposing it on him by their very delight in it, by their very celebration of it as his precious thoughts. The idea of morality as an end rather than a means, as a good in itself rather than an instrument to achieve some other good, is an idea even at this point still in the making. A happy family life is, after all, no mean reward. And by, as it were, retrojecting God's projection of himself, his law, back onto him, by personalizing it and inserting their acceptance of it into a personal relationship with him, the Jews who collected the Psalms, dividing them into five books, mirroring the five books of Torah, moved that idea an enormous step toward accomplishment.[23]

The narrative of the Tanakh presents the people and Yahweh as distinct entities, but from soul's point of view, they constitute a unity and a difference that is in conflict and dialogue with itself: They represent a single soul (or truth) that is changing and evolving through time. With the Psalms, soul advances its development as written word and reflective thought. Soul does this by forging a new identity between the *biblical* people and Yahweh, one in which the presence and reality of Yahweh is the *word* of Yahweh, his torah. Soul is accentuating the precious and weighty value of the *written word*. Yes, the written word is here identified with the word of Yahweh, which is the presence of soul and its *claim* as written word as sacred text. Study of torah becomes the greatest practice by which to venerate Yahweh and effectuate the presence of Yahweh. Studying the book is the new credo, soul's powerful impulse to leave its

---

23. Miles, *God*, 285.

immersion in the natural world. In this sense, writing and reading are against nature, *contra naturam*. The written word is the new medium of soul's self-reflection, as the world of *meaning* separates itself from the natural world. Still, the biblical Yahweh remains a complex of contradictory character traits.

The humanistic orientation of Miles's interpretation emphasizes the growing value of morality, which views the torah in terms of human relations, as well as personalizing the Yahweh-humankind relationship as if they are separate entities. The psycho-logical impulse of the torah, however, is to tear Yahweh apart, away from his bull-storm-god self, in favor of a spiritual, transcendent, and imageless deity. Morality is a genuine human concern, certainly an aspect of the development that is unfolding, but soul is not interested in human morality in itself, but rather its own evolution as the syntax of consciousness, the logical form of consciousness, in contrast to its content. Torah is now the focus of soul's logos, a natural extension of the internal logic at the heart of the Sinai explosion, soul continuing to cut itself free from its embeddedness in nature in favor of a new and freer logical status as mindedness. Yahweh's transition into Torah is another of the Bible's many mythological representations of the emergence of the written word, a new level of freedom of mind and consciousness.

Proverbs: The Goddess Abstracted

Even though Yahweh is often referred to in Proverbs, he is—compared to what we have seen so far—quite marginalized, not unlike the frame of a painting—necessary of course, but silent and off to the side.[24] *Wisdom* is a feminine personification who expounds general moral maxims, those qualities that lead to success or failure in life. Wisdom places the burden of responsibility on the human person. If you follow Wisdom's instruction, you will fare well, and if not, you will fail and suffer, but it will be your own fault, not Yahweh's punishment. This is akin to what we popularly think of today as the law of karma.

Proverbs introduces us to "a larger, anonymous, and impersonal tradition of secular wisdom"[25] common throughout the ancient Near East. This body of insight into the human condition is almost an alternative and competitor to "the law" (torah) and sets up a bit of a rival situation with Yahweh. Although Wisdom is *Lady Wisdom*, she is not quite properly a goddess, but as a mysterious personification who has a very intimate relation with Yahweh, she performs a kind of goddess function. She was Yahweh's prized creation, his very first thought:

> The LORD created me at the
>   beginning of his work,
>   the first of his acts of long ago.

---

24. Miles, *God*, 291.
25. Miles, *God*, 290.

Yahweh Defeats Himself to Save Himself

> Ages ago I was set up,
>> at the first, before the beginning
>>> of the earth.
>
> When there were no depths I was
>> brought forth
>
> . . .
>
> Before the mountains had been
>> shaped,
>> before the hills, I was brought
>>> forth—
>
> . . .
>
> When he established the heavens, I
>> was there,
>> when he drew a circle on the
>>> face of the deep,
>
> when he made firm the skies
>> above,
>
> . . .
>
> when he marked out the
>> foundations of the earth,
>> then I was beside him, like a
>>> master worker,
>
> and I was daily his delight,
>> rejoicing before him always,
> rejoicing in his inhabited world
>> and delighting in the
>>> human race. (Prov 8:22–31)

Although the text makes Yahweh the creator of Wisdom, if she is his first thought, then she is a spontaneous creation in her own right. In a sense, she creates herself as the mind of Yahweh, the spontaneous quality of mind and thought itself. Here, the impulse of Yahweh's mind to abandon nature for the liberation of thought is personified as goddess. This brings to mind the first woman, Eve, who personified the thought of disobedience, which brought freedom from the Garden. Wisdom is Yahweh's delight and joy in the process of creation, creation being Yahweh's own thoughts. Yahweh created everything with the spoken word; his *word* is action, his *ideas* substantial. The idea of Wisdom in Proverbs, in the context of the Bible as a whole, is an intuitive personification of the mind of God, a sublated form of the goddess, interiorized as the mind of Yahweh:

> The LORD by wisdom founded the
>> earth;
>> by understanding he established
>>> the heavens;

God's Autopsy and the Living Truth of Soul

> by his knowledge the deeps broke
> open,
> and the clouds drop down the
> dew. (Prov 3:19–20)

Wisdom, understanding, and *knowledge*—modes of thought and mind—operate as the creative function of mind, Yahweh's mind as the fount of existence itself. Here we get a glimpse of consciousness, noetic meaning, as the creator of the world, thought as the origin of our world. Consciousness makes the world an object of reflection, which is actually the world of *meaning* reflecting on itself—this is the effect of text and literacy. Of course, these are God's thoughts, God's mind. Only millennia later do we see the result of the historical sublations of the mind of God in Jung's realization that "human consciousness created objective existence and meaning."[26] This was a *human* insight achieved without God, after God departed as soul became modern consciousness.

Wisdom is the source of right living:

> Happy are those who find
> wisdom,
> and those who get
> understanding,
> for her income is better than
> silver,
> and her revenue better than
> gold.
> She is more precious than jewels,
> and nothing you desire can
> compare with her.
> Long life is in her right hand;
> in her left hand are riches and
> honor.
> Her ways are ways of
> pleasantness,
> and all her paths are peace.
> She is a tree of life to those who
> lay hold of her;
> those who hold her fast are
> called happy. (Prov 3:13–18)

These lines begin and end with the word *happy*, which could easily be the word *blessed*, implying that Yahweh smiles on those who live true to wisdom. Wisdom is identified with a *tree of life*, which connects her directly to ancient Near Eastern goddesses identified with trees, and especially to Asherah, whose symbols were the sacred wooden

---

26. See above p. 51–52 when Jung, on his trip to Africa, realized the cosmic significance of human consciousness, which I interpret as consciousness becoming conscious of itself.

pole and tree.[27] The focus of these maxims is the individual and what right living entails, and much of it involves what we would call common sense. The maxims against greed, pride, deceit, seduction, laziness, and such are universal in appeal and apply to everyone. Within Proverbs we find Yahweh's torah (his law and his way) abstracted in universal moral terms, outlining ethical guidelines for daily life.

Wisdom or Consciousness?

The guiding precept of Wisdom is "fear of the Lord." The overarching truth Wisdom wants to teach, which informs all the practical teachings, is the repeated phrase (with slight variation), "The fear of the Lord is the beginning of knowledge" (Prov 1:7), or "The fear of the Lord is the beginning of wisdom" (Prov 9:10), and similar at 15:33.[28] Is a secular version of this aphorism even possible when the real otherness and unpredictable truth of that terrible deity is gone for us? Miles does offer a possibility: "The first thing a man of understanding must understand is that there is much that he will never understand."[29] However, I wonder if understanding the limit of understanding inspires or incites fear? It seems to me fear, in "fear of the Lord," is not merely metaphoric, not simply transferrable as awe. The modern mind is completely fenced in, protected from any kind of terrible otherness confronting it. Yahweh was an ontological fact, controlling the universe, and humankind was exposed and unprotected. The archaic fear is alien to modern consciousness, because ever since the Enlightenment, the logical form of consciousness that permeates our modern world tells us we are in control (logically), even though empirically, we admit we are not in control of many things. Along with "modern soul" is there some kind of perhaps sublated modern *fear* we could be subject to? I would update this maxim psychologically to "Consciousness begins when soul is sighted." Not my personal self-awareness, which I happily and innocently take for granted, but that consciousness which transgressed into the world and first appeared as the gods gazing at us. As one of the epigraphs of chapter 3 reminds us,

> The terrific quality is due to the fact that the event of consciousness is in fact something outrageous, because it bursts, invades frighteningly, into ordinary natural life.[30]

Consciousness is not our creation, and it is not our superior status (as is our conceit). To be wise today is to grasp the contradiction that while humankind is the vehicle of consciousness, consciousness (i.e., soul) is truly independent of us! To grasp the

---

27. There may also be some wordplay here on the word *asherah*. "The word for 'happy' (*meushar*) shares most of the same basic consonants with the word *asherah*" (Smith, *Memoirs*, 115). The archaic goddess/Yahweh connection lingers in spite of the attempt to eradicate her.

28. "The fear of the Lord is instruction in wisdom."

29. Miles, *God*, 291.

30. Giegerich, "Killings," 227.

history of soul is to be afraid, and this is not a position the modern humanistic ego will accept lightly. We are in a position, as I attempt to show through this book's historical overview, to know consciousness for what it is, not as a secondary attribute of human persons, but the only context of our very world, consciousness aware of itself as consciousness. *Consciousness* is both nothing (no-thing) and everything at the same time. Fear is an appropriate reverberation at the insight that *consciousness* is our home, but this modern consciousness means we are alone in the universe, metaphysically naked, unprotected in a wilderness-of-soul not of our making.

Looking Ahead

While Yahweh remains Yahweh throughout Proverbs, mysterious and finally unfathomable, still he is silent here, and the voice of feminine Wisdom is loud and prominent. She is the speaker and claims her place right alongside of, and equal to, God—the mind of Yahweh, expressing itself as a feminine presence, takes on an intimate and personal relational quality with the new soul-form emerging as a book, as bookish, as sacred writing.

In the next chapter, when we read the book of Job, the wisdom of Yahweh's self-knowledge will take a troubling turn, a decisive turn, as consciousness transgresses to a new status. During a stunning and powerful dialogue, in which both Yahweh and Job stand their ground in relation to each other, Yahweh, at a cost, achieves new insight into himself. A new frailty will emerge in Yahweh's self-understanding, as he becomes more dependent on humankind for sustenance and existence.

We speak of Yahweh's transformation: the historical crisis in the life of God that led to a changed identity, the shift from conquest to study, from the nation to individuals, and an unusual incorporation of the goddess into Yahweh's character. Still Yahweh is a complex, unstable, problem. These changes are only hints of a future that from this point could not be known. Although Yahweh may be changing, his darker and dangerous aspects do not simply disappear. They may recede, but they can also storm back into the foreground at a moment's notice. The question that arises as we turn toward the book of Job is, "Can God [impulsive, violent, fiery] be trusted?"[31]

---

31. Miles, *God*, 302.

Chapter 6

Job: A Crack in the Armor
Consciousness Glimpses Itself

> But it might be phenomenologically more accurate to note that in its first immediate form a new consciousness always approaches us from without, from abroad, as it were. It is truly encountered as the stranger or enemy out there who has never before been *in* us.[1]

> The shadow is not only *experienced* out there, it is also *kept* abroad. Against what is the defense directed? I would say, against the insight that the shadow belongs to *me*.[2]

YAHWEH HAS BEEN THROUGH some remarkable transformations. He began as a Bull-Storm god, one of many ancient Near Eastern Canaanite nature deities, along with his consort Asherah and fellow companion gods, El and Baal, among others. The Exodus story vividly expressed his violent rupture, when he cut himself off from his nature-based essence on the way to becoming an imageless god, a god without a body, transcending nature as spirit and written word. He established himself as a god of literacy with the Ten Words (Ten Commandments) he engraved on stone tablets, writing his new identity into existence:

> I am the LORD [Yahweh] your God [El], who brought you out of the land of Egypt, out of the house of slavery; you shall have no other gods [elohim] before me. You shall not make for yourself an idol [carved image] . . . You shall not bow down to them or worship them; for I the LORD [Yahweh] your God [El] am a jealous God [El], punishing children for the iniquity of parents, to the third and the fourth generation of those who reject me, but showing steadfast love to the thousandth generation of those who love me and keep my

---

1. Giegerich, "First Shadow," 91.
2. Giegerich, "First Shadow," 92.

> commandments. You shall not make wrongful use of the name of the LORD [Yahweh] your God [El], for the LORD [Yahweh] will not acquit anyone who misuses his name. (Exod 20:1–7)

Yahweh divorced Asherah and demanded absolute devotion from his chosen people, the Israelites. Yahweh rejected the truth of the other nature gods and goddesses, turning them into false gods, and rejecting all natural wood, stone, or cast metal images of himself, denouncing them as idols. He rejected and destroyed his own embodiment as nature, as bull.

In his rage at the people's continuing disregard for their mutual contract (covenant), even after they are delivered to the promised land, Yahweh destroyed them, his nation and his house (temple), through invasions by Assyria and Babylon. In this, Yahweh failed as warrior, continuing his transformation into a God of words, thoughts, and texts, abandoning the realm of international politics. However, this new Yahweh remained dependent on the belief, faith, and obedience of his human partners.

In the story of Job discussed in detail in this chapter, we see a decisive transformation. Yahweh's very righteousness—rewarding "those who love me" and punishing "those who reject me"—is challenged by his treatment of Job. Wrapped in his own integrity, a human being stands toe to toe with the Creator and forces Yahweh to acknowledge his own wrongdoings. This marks a further erosion of Yahweh's superiority as the Lord God who dominates human affairs: He is revealed as no longer *only* just.

What Soul Is Saying about Itself

We have been tracing Yahweh's story as an evolution of soul, and his self-transformation over the course of these Bible stories represents an extraordinary shift of the foundation of consciousness. Let's remember that Yahweh, as symbolic of soul's speech about itself, is not an entity separate from humankind. He represents the psychological form of consciousness in antiquity undergoing a revolution within itself.

As a nature god, Yahweh's existence was self-evident in natural phenomena such as lightning, rain, wind, earthquake, and bull; as such, he did not in general require faith, worship, or service *in order to* exist. Soul inhabited nature as the gods (personifications), and the existence of the natural gods was not in question. Humankind participated in the natural powers (*elohim*)[3] and the natural flow of life through ritual practices involving material symbols, human and animal sacrifice, ritual sexual practices, and agricultural offerings. Once Yahweh had pushed off from his natural base, however, he became dependent on obedience to the command: "Hear, O Israel: The LORD [Yahweh] is our God [El], the LORD [Yahweh] alone [is one]. You shall love the

---

3. *El* and *elohim* are archaic words for a high God and plural gods found in Ugaritic texts, and were absorbed into the Tanakh as words for the singular Yahweh. Both Yahweh and El/elohim are used interchangeably in biblical thought as we've seen, along with the gods' manifestations as bull and storm. Nature gods were indeed powers and *elohim* were elemental powers.

Job: A Crack in the Armor

Lord [Yahweh] your God [El] with all your heart, and with all your soul, and with all your might" (Deut 6:4–5). His human subjects needed to bend all their attention to the new spirit God because *this* God could exist *only as* the reciprocal covenant that bound the God and the people together, giving them both their identity. This transformation encountered deep resistance in both Yahweh and the people: Neither wanted to give up the other gods and goddesses. Yet, as a soul-event, as a manifestation of soul's telos, Yahweh's direction was away from locally earth-bound nature and toward the freedom and mobility of spirit and meaning embodied in written, more abstract concepts.

The new form of consciousness that Yahweh represented could not tolerate being ignored, and there was no grey area. It was all or nothing. Yahweh, the self-appointed creator of the universe, the mysterious source of Wisdom and knowledge, the source of all, was nevertheless dependent on his created self-image, humankind (in the biblical narrative, the Hebrew/Israelite people), for his existence. And yet, all of this change left another divine logic unchanged, a logic embedded in the nature of the relationship between god and humankind in antiquity. This is related to the fact that although God is a jealous God, his punishment is not arbitrary: Yahweh would punish those who rejected him and reward those who loved him. A reason and purpose governed Yahweh's violence.

Yahweh's justice was related to a more universal logic, stating that the gods, or God, bestowed blessings or curses in accord with the human person's state of righteousness or wickedness. Good people received health and wealth from God, and bad people received punishment through ill health and poverty and loss. If your life was cursed with bad luck or tragedy, you must have sinned in some way. The corollary was, by definition, the gods are always right, and humankind is always wrong. As he pushed off from nature into a new form, Yahweh was still all powerful, demanding obedience and submission. The logic of consciousness in antiquity, the taken-for-granted truth, was that the gods were the final authority.

Something extraordinary happens to this logic with the story of Job, which undermines and subverts the unconscious and unquestioned logic that God was right and the human person wrong. In order to see the striking nature of this subversion, we must read Job in a new light, a perspective that is possible only today. For over two thousand years, the story of Job has ended with the image of a patient and submissive man who acquiesced to the overwhelming power of God. This image kept the conventional logic of God in place: God is almighty, and his purposes are beyond human comprehension. Therefore, the correct human orientation is to be quiet and accept our lot in life. Questioning God is merely a rhetorical gesture because in the end we can only submit and recognize that God does not need us to add anything to his creation. Especially, God does not need us to add anything to him. The general prevailing logic of antiquity regarding God and humankind was that God does not need to change; humankind needs to change (repent).

This traditional theological, or pious, reading of Job, is no longer tenable, especially for a modern "God-is-dead" consciousness. As long as humankind was living inside "child-of-God" consciousness, viewing God as the superior and wiser being was appropriate, was, in fact, unavoidable as the prevailing logic of consciousness. However, a contemporary reading of Job turns the tables. That reading of Job shows that, in fact, he does not submit; he proves to be morally superior to God, thus undermining the traditional God logic. Job is the image of soul negating itself. Job is the crack in the armor, allowing the unilateral power, value, and rightness that existed only on the God side of the dialectical equation of God/Man to flow to the human side. Job breaks open the idea that God is unfathomable, beyond mankind's ken, and beyond question. God remains superior with regard to power and might, but Job introduces a *moral* superiority rooted in his integrity and consciousness. The Lord, well—his bullying tendency was running out of steam. The soul-logic of the God is changed irreversibly because Job would not budge from the conviction of his integrity. Job refused to release God from the moral question about his terrible suffering: "Why have you done this to me?" To show how tendentious translation and traditionalist theology has led to a misleading reading of Job, I will undertake a close examination of the story, in service to my interpretation of soul's speech about itself. We will see how the I Am, which up to this point is God's sole possession, begins to tilt toward humankind as a result of Job's challenge.

The Biblical Location of the Book of Job

The Jewish Tanakh places Job after the prophets, whereas the Christian Old Testament places Job before the prophets. The significance of this placement is that in the Tanakh, we read Job in a very different literary context, which is a pivotal and major crisis in the life of God. In the Tanakh, Job appears in the context of the failure of Yahweh: the destruction of the kingdoms of Judah and Israel, the destruction of his house (the temple), and the scattering and exile of the Jewish people (his self-image). Yahweh, who boasted that he was the greatest warrior of all time and that he would conquer the whole world, has been humiliated, diminished, and backed into a corner. Yahweh is in the midst of an identity crisis in which his very self must change. This is tantamount to soul learning something from experience and making an adjustment, the way a conquered people must readjust their self-understanding. Soul's adjustment is at a deeper level, as its internal telos reinterprets itself in the light of new circumstances. From the psychological perspective, the confrontation between Job and Yahweh expresses another facet of this adjustment. Historically, this adjustment took place during the sixth and fifth centuries BCE, the time of the Babylonian invasion and exile and the writings of the prophets. From the psycho-logical point of view, the prevailing logical form of consciousness was undergoing a change, and that soul change worked itself out in terms of the mutual identity crisis of Yahweh and the Jewish people. Within the symbolic and literary context of the Bible, Yahweh and the Israelite people are one soul truth, a dialectical unity in that they create and define each other. Together they manifest one idea, the logical constitution of soul at that time. With Job, this idea clashes with itself, adapts, and changes.

Yahweh Makes an Obscene Bet

Clearly no one today takes the Bible at face value, at least not the book of Job, because to do so would require true moral outrage at the character of God. Of course, those who read it from outside the bubble of theological propriety are outraged. The outrage arises because, as Miles puts it, ancient Israel's vision of ultimate reality was the "hyperpersonalized" Yahweh. Yahweh is not an abstract idea or ideal, but an intensely personal, emotional, conflicted, and contradictory presence. To move beyond the deeply ingrained conventional notions of God (that God is only good), we have to allow ourselves to be emotionally affected by the emotionally conflicted Yahweh and the outrageous behavior of this alien and antique god. No matter how much modern thought may abstract the idea of God as Love, or philosophically redefine God in nontheistic terms, those of us raised in the Judeo-Christian West cannot help carry the "hyperpersonalized" Yahweh within us (even if only implicitly and unconsciously). The Bible has been at the heart of what defines Western civilization for well over a thousand years. Even if we are intellectually enlightened, the emotional hyperpersonalized Yahweh is still part of our historical-cultural DNA. And while Job gets all the attention in this story, Yahweh, or God, is the problem. He is at the heart of the drama and, it turns out, he is all too fallible.

First we meet Job, and he is an impressive figure:

> There was once a man in the land of Uz whose name was Job. That man was blameless and upright, one who feared God and turned away from evil. There were born to him seven sons and three daughters. He had seven thousand sheep, three thousand camels, five hundred yoke of oxen, five hundred donkeys, and very many servants; so that this man was the greatest of all the people of the east. (Job 1:1–3)

An interesting fact about the book of Job is that the name Job is not known in Israel, and he is not an Israelite. Neither is it clear where the land of Uz might have been, but it is not associated with Israelite territories. Maybe it was located in what is now southern Jordan and Israel, known then as the kingdom of Edom. The name Job would have been a bit strange to the Israeli ear, with an archaic ring. Similar names are known in even older ancient Near Eastern texts (second millennium BCE).[4] Yet, the story of Job has been completely absorbed into the Jewish psyche, and the god here is Yahweh, even though in Job, the Hebrew words *El* (singular) and *elohim* (plural) are

---

4. *New Interpreter's Bible*, 4:344–45.

used often, and translated as God. And, as noted earlier, the words "the Lord" in the text stand in for the never pronounced Hebrew name of God, *yahweh*. The story of Job has been absorbed into the story of Yahweh, soul's story about itself, and is fully integrated into Yahweh's history and soul's history (the history of consciousness).

Job is portrayed as an enormously wealthy man, the greatest man in the surrounding land, a man of power, influence, and regard. While wealth is not always partnered with an agreeable personality, Job is "blameless and upright," fears God, and turns away from evil. Job is wealthy, powerful, and *good*, and good is really his defining quality. I assume that the strength of Job's self-confidence and moral conviction is equal to his great wealth and power, and that his integrity is rooted in his own core goodness and formidable character. Job actively lives in right relationship with God, and the powerful El, or Yahweh, is the cornerstone of his life. Job knows that the appropriate religious rituals and acts mediate the problem of sin in relation to God and that God is responsive to such rites:

> His sons used to go and hold feasts in one another's houses in turn; and they would send and invite their three sisters to eat and drink with them. And when the feast days had run their course, Job would send and sanctify them, and he would rise early in the morning and offer burnt offerings according to the number of them all; for Job said, "It may be that my children have sinned, and cursed God in their hearts." This is what Job always did. (Job 1:4–5)

Job does not take God for granted. Job trusts God and believes that God will deal justly with him, that God's behavior will be fair in accord with Job's right behavior. Job is a large, impressive public figure, and it turns out God is very much aware of him and takes great pride in Job.

The next scene sets the stage for the rest of the story, and it throws a monkey wrench into our assumptions about how the heavenly realm is administered:

> One day the heavenly beings came to present themselves before the Lord, and Satan also came among them. The Lord said to Satan, "Where have you come from?" Satan answered the Lord, "From going to and fro on the earth, and from walking up and down on it." The Lord said to Satan, "Have you considered my servant Job? There is no one like him on the earth, a blameless and upright man who fears God and turns away from evil." Then Satan answered the Lord, "Does Job fear God for nothing? Have you not put a fence around him and his house and all that he has, on every side? You have blessed the work of his hands, and his possessions have increased in the land. But stretch out your hand now, and touch all that he has, and he will curse you to your face." The Lord said to Satan, "Very well, all that he has is in your power; only do not stretch out your hand against him!" (Job 1:6–12)

Really?! Wouldn't we expect the powerful Yahweh to laugh in Satan's face and tell him to get lost? Instead it seems the Lord's self-doubt leaves him vulnerable to manipulation. And now he has taken a dare and will begin gaming and gambling with a human person? Job trusts the Lord implicitly, and the Lord is obviously proud of his servant Job, whose integrity and goodness are so great that the Lord finds "no one like him on the earth." And, now this, the Lord will betray Job's trust on a dare? And, who is this Satan that draws the Lord into such an obscene bet? The Hebrew behind "Satan" is *ha-satan*, which means "the accuser,"[5] a common noun, not a proper noun. This Hebrew word has no connection to the much later New Testament term Satan that is equated with the devil, but our tradition has inexorably linked them. In "going to and fro on the earth," the accuser seems to function as the eyes and ears of God, as surveillance and informant, to accuse those who do not honor God. In this sense, the satan is God's own judgment and perhaps suspicion of human persons.

In this story, the satan is God's own doubt about Job. The satan raises the question of Job's motivation for "fearing God." Does Job love and honor God only because God has blessed Job with health, wealth, and power? Or, is Job's integrity toward God truly pure, with no expectation of reward? This is the doubt that has crept into God's mind, and now God's mind suffers a conflict in the form of the God-satan wager. A reminder here that for my psychological interpretation, the "mind of God" represents the prevailing logic of consciousness, which was not conflicted about itself. The story of Job, with these personified characters, God, satan, Job, and others, tells the story of a deepening conflict within the currently prevailing logical form of consciousness. The satan's challenge to God is that if God takes away all that Job has, Job will curse God to his face. God has a special pride in his servant Job that obviously reflects back to himself, and so now God's honor is on the line. Who is really being tested here, Job or God? The traditional interpretation of Job is that his faith in God is tested in the face of crisis and calamity. The meaning, or lesson, of the story of Job is framed in terms of *human* suffering and how human beings respond to suffering, tragic events, and great loss. The question of human faith and suffering, of orientation to God in the midst of suffering, is the conventional focus for interpretation. The traditional interpretation is blind to any God-problem. That there might be a core and devastating problem with God is not part of the conventional picture.

The story begins with the assumption that the character of God has a dependable and trustworthy logic. In antiquity, this also meant a dependable and trustworthy logic was inherent to the nature of reality, of life, and the universe. It was assumed that humankind could trust in the basic fairness of God's blessing and God's punishment, but this view is exactly what the Job story challenges. The beginning of the story is not merely the narrative set-up, the circumstances, that lead to Job's suffering, but a shockingly fundamental question about the trustworthiness of God. Whatever the satan is, it opens the crack in God's armor, as God's self-doubt about Job and his relationship with Job leads to a most gratuitous and vicious attack on Job's life. Remember that the human person is Yahweh's created self-image, and now Yahweh's doubt about Job is

---

5. The Jewish Publication Society (JPS) Tanakh translates, "Adversary."

also self-doubt. Psycho-logically, soul is in conflict with itself. The self-assured and self-evident God-logic (the syntax of consciousness) of antiquity is now in question, cracking. God's self-assured pride in Job is showing a fault-line.

After God gave the satan power over everything Job possessed, "the satan went out from the presence of the LORD." In the next seven verses, one servant after another comes to tell Job how the Sabeans stole his oxen and donkeys and slaughtered his servants, how lightning came and burned up all his sheep and servants, how the Chaldeans raided his camels and killed his servants, and finally how a great storm killed all of his children while they were feasting together. Everything gone in one day! Although these terrible losses are presented as the tragic circumstances of ordinary life, the weather and marauding thieves, we know who is behind it all. If narratively satan makes it happen, it is God who allows it; psychologically, God's actions bring this cruelty on Job. Gratuitous violence against a perfectly good human being, a "blameless and upright" man? What are we to make of it? This is only the beginning, but at the start, Job proves the satan wrong and preserves God's honor:

> Then Job arose, tore his robe, shaved his head, and fell on the ground and worshiped. He said, "Naked I came from my mother's womb, and naked shall I return there; the LORD gave, and the LORD has taken away; blessed be the name of the LORD." In all this Job did not sin or charge God with wrong-doing. (Job 1:20–22)

Job knows what everyone, of his time, knows; he lives within the assumed ancient knowledge that God is the final source of all, God gives and takes, God provides blessing and curse, God is the source of life and death, and this most of all, there is a God-logic to life, God's purposes are reasonable and just. Job has not yet observed the crack in God's logic. And, of course, Job has no idea the satan is involved; for Job, God is an undivided unity.

The heavenly scene repeats itself, and again the "sons of God" present themselves with God (which is a reminder we are in a polytheistic cosmos). We hear the same introductory exchange between the satan and God, and then God says to the satan:

> "Have you considered my servant Job? There is no one like him on the earth, a blameless and upright man who fears God and turns away from evil. *He still persists in his integrity*, although you incited me against him, to destroy him for no reason." Then Satan answered the LORD, "Skin for skin! All that people have they will give to save their lives. But stretch out your hand now and touch his bone and his flesh, and he will curse you to your face." The LORD said to Satan, "Very well, he is in your power; only spare his life." (Job 2:3–6, emphasis added)

Now the satan calls God's hand and raises the stakes, and God accepts! Gaming at its best, when the stakes are high and the risk takes you to the edge! Is the adrenaline flowing, excited about this wager, this dare? The self-doubt digs deeper into God, the division within God penetrates the divine self-confidence. God is in trouble because certainly he cannot back out now, but is he concerned, is he feeling at all shaky in his conviction about Job? God's one-sided image of himself—his pride in Job is pride in himself (his honor)—is threatened, and the degree of his dependence on Job is all the greater. What if Job does not live up to God's expectation that Job will never turn his back on God?

The line I want to emphasize and draw attention to, the line that God leads with at this turn, and that carries all of God's pride and hope, is, "He still persists in his integrity." This is the heart and soul of Job: He "persists in his integrity." This is the very thing that will later back God into a corner, confronting God with himself, that is, with his obscene wager. In the story, Job is absolute integrity, and he knows this about himself. It is the key to the rest of the story, but we are not sure that God feels secure in this assertion. At the end of the story, I will ask if Job does indeed persist in his integrity throughout, to the very end, or does Job withdraw his integrity, and even betray his integrity? This is also a key element in the simple literary integrity of the story, and it plays a central role in whether or not Job subverts and undermines the traditional God-logic of antiquity. My psycho-logical reading is not concerned with the problem of human suffering per se, but rather with the transformations of Yahweh and Job. I view them not so much as personalities as exemplars of consciousness, the historical travail of consciousness as it is portrayed in this story, one that is at least two thousand five hundred years old.

The satan does his worst and the suffering of Job intensifies:

> So Satan went out from the presence of the LORD, and inflicted loathsome sores on Job from the sole of his foot to the crown of his head. Job took a potsherd with which to scrape himself, and sat among the ashes. Then his wife said to him, "Do you still persist in your integrity? Curse God, and die." But he said to her, "You speak as any foolish woman would speak. Shall we receive the good at the hand of God, and not receive the bad?" In all this Job did not sin with his lips. (Job 2:7–10)

Now the terms of the wager are complete. Job has been reduced to abject misery, and everything has been taken from him, all his wealth and power, his children, and now his health. Everything external that can be taken away has been stripped, and he is in a sense completely naked. Even his wife withdraws any comfort she might provide and deplores his "integrity" as mere stubbornness, urging him to turn his back on God. This is exactly what Job will not do, however, and this is the key to what follows. His integrity does persist, and he knows God is the origin of all that comes his way. And here is the intriguing dimension of the story: Job will not abandon God (even though God has abandoned him, but, of course, he does not know this, yet), but neither will he abandon himself. He stays adamantly true to both God's truth and his own truth; he will stand his ground and face God directly. So far, "the satan," as God's own riven conscience, places God under duress, creates a strain, a doubt and conflict within God about himself. After this final challenge from the satan, the narrative turns, and the satan disappears for the rest of the story. Eventually, Job will step in to confront God with what Job knows to be God's own actions. Job will be God's mirror, confronting God with God's truth as Job knows it, in contrast to what God thinks is his own truth. But, first, Job will face challenges to his integrity from his so-called friends, the representatives of the prevailing and conventional God-logic.

God in Conflict with Himself

The story now comes down to earth so to speak, and the action shifts from the heavenly casino to the earthly realm where Job suffers, the one chip (of ultimate value) with which the godly gamblers are playing. Coming to visit Job, three friends engage in a series of dialogues about Job's guilt or innocence and the nature of God. How should we view these dialogues? Are they simply the *human* struggle with the idea of God, an intellectual theological argument on the human level, or is the very truth of God at stake in these conversations? In my view, they are really God's dialogue, his internal argument about his true nature, spoken through these human avatars playing roles that voice God's conflicting views about himself. For psychology, God's conflict is soul's autobiographical struggle, consciousness negating itself for a transformation, soul's living truth working on itself.

The three friends journey to Job and are grief-stricken at the sight of him:

> Now when Job's three friends heard of all these troubles that had come upon him, each of them set out from his home—Eliphaz the Temanite, Bildad the Shuhite, and Zophar the Naamathite. They met together to go and console and comfort him. When they saw him from a distance, they did not recognize him, and they raised their voices and wept aloud; they tore their robes and threw dust in the air upon their heads. They sat with him on the ground seven days and seven nights, and no one spoke a word to him, for they saw that his suffering was very great. (Job 2:11–13)

The community of friendship shares the terrible grief, and their simple presence makes Job's awful losses a little easier to bear. Or, does it? Although his friends, at first, offer a more consoling presence than his wife did, after the seven days of silence, while Job does not curse God, he gives voice to the depths of what we would call depression and grief and curses the day he was born:

> Let the day perish in which I was
>   born,
>   and the night that said,
>   "A man-child is conceived."
> Let that day be darkness!
>   May God above not seek it,
>   or light shine on it.

> Let gloom and deep darkness
> claim it.
> Let clouds settle upon it;
> let the blackness of the day
> terrify it.
> That night—let thick darkness
> seize it!
> ...
> Why did I not die at birth,
> come forth from the womb and
> expire?
> Why were there knees to receive
> me,
> or breasts for me to suck? (Job 3:3–6, 11–12)

Job declares he would be at peace and better off dead. He is deeply distressed and troubled:

> Truly the thing that I fear comes
> upon me,
> and what I dread befalls me.
> I am not at ease, nor am I quiet;
> I have no rest; but trouble
> comes. (Job 3:25–26)

One would hope that Job's friends might end their silence with supportive words in Job's favor. But, no, the first words from Eliphaz are meant to remind Job who God really is and that he better take a hard look at himself. At first he commends Job for having been, in the past, the strong one who supported the weak and uplifted the stricken, but now he is the one who is down:

> But now it has come to you, and
> you are impatient;
> it touches you, and you are
> dismayed.
> Is not your fear of God your
> confidence,
> and the integrity of your ways
> your hope?
>
> Think now, who that was
> innocent ever perished?
> Or where were the upright cut
> off?

God's Autopsy and the Living Truth of Soul

> As I have seen, those who plow
> >iniquity
> and sow trouble reap the same.
> By the breath of God they perish,
> >and by the blast of his anger
> >>they are consumed.
> . . .
> Can mortals be righteous before [more than]
> >God?
> >Can human beings be pure
> >>before [more than] their Maker?
> Even in his servants he puts no
> >trust,
> >and his angels he charges with
> >>error;
> how much more those who live in
> >houses of clay,
> >whose foundation is in the dust,
> >who are crushed like a moth. (Job 4:5–9, 17–19)

Eliphaz wants Job to recognize the prevailing view of God as just and good, of human persons as sinful and error-filled, getting what they deserve. Horrible things must happen for a just reason, rooted in the frailty and innate limitation of being human. Eliphaz presses his argument with the idea that suffering is not only punishment but discipline for the sake of improvement:

> How happy is the one whom
> >God reproves;
> >therefore do not despise the
> >>discipline of the Almighty.
> For he wounds, but he binds up;
> >he strikes, but his hands heal.
> He will deliver you from six
> >troubles;
> >in seven no harm shall touch
> >>you.
> . . .
> You shall know that your tent is
> >safe,
> >you shall inspect your fold and
> >>miss nothing.
> You shall know that your
> >descendants will be many,
> >and your offspring like the grass
> >>of the earth.

> ...
> See, we have searched this out; it
>   is true.
> Hear, and know it for yourself.
>   (Job 5:17–19, 24–25, 27)

The implicit form of consciousness prevailing here is that God knows what he is doing, has superior knowledge, and we are disciplined for our own good.

Job challenges this logic of punishment and discipline, claiming the scale of his suffering is so great that such a notion is untenable. The punishment is way over the top and does not fit any "crime" of Job's:

> O that my vexation were
>   weighed,
>   and all my calamity laid in the
>   balances!
> For then it would be heavier than
>   the sand of the sea;
>   therefore my words have been
>   rash.
> For the arrows of the Almighty
>   are in me;
>   my spirit drinks their poison;
>   the terrors of God are arrayed
>   against me. (Job 6:2–4)

This is not "discipline," but cruel and unusual punishment. Rejecting Eliphaz's argument, Job says nothing is left of his relationship with God; again, he would be better off dead. Job has no more resources, no more strength. He asserts that he has "not denied the words of the Holy One"; nothing can be gained by waiting out the so-called "discipline." Job attacks his friends for their superficial words, comparing their arguments to the fleeting streams that fill quickly with melting snow, but run dry and empty as soon as it gets hot. Job is angry and challenges them: "Teach me, and I will be silent; make me understand how I have gone wrong" (6:24). This is an ironic, even sarcastic challenge, because Job knows he has done no wrong, and he turns his complaint directly to God:

> Therefore I will not restrain my
>   mouth;
>   I will speak in the anguish of
>   my spirit;
>   I will complain in the bitterness
>   of my soul.
> ...

> If I sin, what do I do to you, you
>   watcher of humanity?
> Why have you made me your
>   target?
> Why have I become a burden to
>   you? (Job 7:11; 20)

Although Job and his friends start out with the same idea about God—that human beings reap God's justice, or not, depending on their own actions—Job knows something about himself that will not let him merely submit to this notion of God. Job knows he is in the right, and therefore, God must answer his bold question: why?

First, however, Bildad, accuses Job of maligning God, arguing that there must be sin infecting the whole family:

> How long will you say these
>   things,
>   and the words of your mouth
>   be a great wind?
> Does God pervert justice?
>   Or does the Almighty pervert
>   the right?
> If your children sinned against
>   him,
>   he delivered them into the
>   power of their
>   transgression.
> If you will seek God
>   and make supplication to the
>   Almighty,
> if you are pure and upright,
>   surely then he will rouse himself
>   for you
>   and restore to you your rightful
>   place. (Job 8:2–6)

If Job will only admit that he is somehow in the wrong and ask God's forgiveness, surely God will make things right again. Job knows this will not work because this is not the problem. There is, however, another problem: the matter of scale between creator and creature. Though Job wants to contest with God, he is very aware that God has the upper hand, the strength to overpower Job, to ignore him:

> If I summoned him and he
>   answered me,
>   I do not believe that he would
>   listen to my voice.

> For he crushes me with a tempest,
> > and multiplies my wounds
> > > without cause;
> > he will not let me get my breath,
> > > but fills me with bitterness.
> > If it is a contest of strength, he is
> > > the strong one!
> > > > If it is a matter of justice, who
> > > > > can summon him?
> > Though I am innocent, my own
> > > mouth would condemn me;
> > > > though I am blameless, he
> > > > > would prove me perverse. (Job 9:16–20)

For Job, the idea that God is just and even-handed is becoming ridiculous:

> It is all one; therefore I say,
> > he destroys both the blameless
> > > and the wicked.
> When disaster brings sudden
> > death,
> > > he mocks at the calamity of
> > > > the innocent.
> The earth is given into the hand of
> > the wicked;
> > > he covers the eyes of its
> > > > judges—
> if it is not he, who then is it? (Job 9:22–24)

Ultimately, there is no level playing field on which they might meet. Job may be innocent, but he faces insurmountable odds in bringing his case before God:

> For he is not mortal, as I am,
> > that I might answer him,
> > > that we should come to trial
> > > > together.
> > There is no umpire between us,
> > > who might lay his hand on us
> > > > both. (Job 9:32–33)

Job continues to insist on his innocence, raising a challenge to God's own reasons for creation in the first place. What is the point of creating this life, your people, if all you do is turn around and destroy it? Ultimately, the question is "Why? Why do you destroy what you create?"

> I loathe my life;
> I will give free utterance to
> my complaint;
> I will speak in the bitterness of
> my soul.
> I will say to God, Do not
> condemn me;
> let me know why you contend
> against me.
> Does it seem good to you to
> oppress,
> to despise the work of your
> hands
> and favor the schemes of the
> wicked?
> . . .
> Your hands fashioned and made
> me;
> and now you turn and destroy
> me.
> . . .
> Why did you bring me forth
> from the womb? (Job 10:1–3, 8, 18)

Zophar brushes aside Job's complaint. Now he weighs in with his zeal for the traditional view of God, basing his argument on the idea that God is so inscrutable that Job should not even waste words in complaint. In fact, Job is downright ignorant of God's true magnitude and wisdom. Zophar pumps up God's greatness, claiming that, in any comparison to God, we are all sinful by default; we simply need to accept this truth and repent. But first, Zophar can't restrain himself from belittling Job, and then at the last, insulting him:

> Should a multitude of words go
> unanswered,
> and should one full of talk be
> vindicated?
> Should your babble put others to
> silence,
> and when you mock, shall no
> one shame you?
> For you say, "My conduct is
> pure,
> and I am clean in God's sight."

> But oh, that God would speak,
>   and open his lips to you,
> and that he would tell you the
>   secrets of wisdom!
>   For wisdom is many-sided.
> Know then that God exacts of you
>   less than your guilt
>   deserves.
>
> Can you find out the deep things
>   of God?
>   Can you find out the limit of
>   the Almighty?
> It is higher than heaven—what
>   can you do?
>   Deeper than Sheol—what can
>   you know?
> Its measure is longer than the
>   earth,
>   and broader than the sea.
> If he passes through, and
>   imprisons,
>   and assembles for judgment,
>   who can hinder him?
> For he knows those who are
>   worthless;
>   when he sees iniquity, will he
>   not consider it?
> But a stupid person will get
>   understanding,
>   when a wild ass is born
>   human. (Job 11:2–12)

That last verse, "But a stupid person..." is a condescending insult, equivalent to something like, "You'll understand . . . when pigs fly." According to Zophar's view, Job's understanding of God is so limited, like all human understanding, his only choice is to accept that he is in the wrong, and that God is in the right: Only submission to the greatness of God will ease his suffering:

> If you direct your heart rightly,
>   you will stretch out your hands
>   toward him.
> If iniquity is in your hand, put it
>   far away,

> and do not let wickedness reside
> > in your tents.
> Surely then you will lift up your
> > face without blemish;
> > you will be secure, and will not
> > > fear.
> You will forget your misery;
> > you will remember it as waters
> > > that have passed away.
> And your life will be brighter than
> > the noonday;
> > its darkness will be like the
> > > morning.
> And you will have confidence,
> > because there is hope;
> > you will be protected and take
> > > your rest in safety. (Job 11:13–18)

For Zophar, and the traditional view expressed here, God is able to perceive the sinfulness within that Job is unable to perceive himself. Only living in right relation to God will guarantee Job's hope and safety, and so his terrible suffering is clearly a sign that he is out of right relation with God. Only regaining right relation will improve his situation. Quite simply, Job needs to repent, not God. But, Job thinks otherwise.

The arguments of Job's friends express God's anxiousness that Job concede some sinfulness in order to preserve God's honor. If Job really is one hundred percent innocent, then God is in trouble. If Job will acknowledge that God is bigger and wiser than he is, however, and therefore more in the right than Job, then the prevailing God-logic, the prevailing logic of consciousness that God is Just, will be preserved. The ancient prevailing truth, named "God," is at stake.

Job contends he already knows everything his friends expound about God. He is as smart as they are (12:3), and furthermore, their words are only common sense. Even the animals know about God's greatness and his final control over the created order: "But ask the animals, and they will teach you; the birds of the air, and they will tell you" (12:7). However, Job will not rest with common sense. Job condemns his friends' arguments as worthless platitudes:

> As for you, you whitewash with
> > lies;
> > all of you are worthless
> > > physicians.
> If you would only keep silent,
> > that would be your wisdom!
> . . .

> Your maxims are proverbs of
> ashes,
> your defenses are defenses of
> clay. (Job 13:4–5;12)

Job's plan now is to take his case directly to God, to lay it all on the line, no matter the outcome. Job's stance is grounded in his integrity. His truth is congruent with his whole being, and he will conceal nothing as he addresses God:

> But I would speak to the
> Almighty,
> and I desire to argue my case with God.
> . . .
> Let me have silence, and I will
> speak,
> and let come on me what may.
> I will take my flesh in my teeth
> and put my life in my hand.
> See, he will kill me; I have no
> hope,
> but I will defend my ways to
> his face.
> This will be my salvation,
> that the godless shall not [dare to]
> come before him.
> Listen carefully to my words,
> and let my declaration be in
> your ears.
> I have indeed prepared my case;
> I know that I shall be
> vindicated.
> Who is there that will contend
> with me?
> For then I would be silent and
> die.
> Only grant two things to me,
> then I will not hide myself from
> your face:
> withdraw your hand far from me,
> and do not let dread of you
> terrify me.
> Then call, and I will answer;
> or let me speak, and you reply
> to me.

> How many are my iniquities and
> > my sins?
> > Make me know my
> > > transgression and my sin.
> > Why do you hide your face,
> > > and count me as your enemy? (Job 13:3;13–24)

Job is no longer content to argue about God, but now addresses God directly, demanding an answer. Nothing is wrong with him, Job claims, but rather something is wrong with the created order, something wrong with this God who is behaving toward Job in this cruel and unjust way. Job wants God to show up, as in a court of law, and face Job's complaint. Job is certain he will be vindicated and accuses God of hiding from him, avoiding his questions. Job puts God on the spot. If Job has sin on his hands, then he wants God to tell him directly. This will no longer be a theological argument about how God's greatness by itself defines Job's necessary sinfulness. Job will now stand as his undivided wholeness before God and hold God to account. Job, in effect, lays himself bare before the ultimate lie detector, completely confident in his innocence. Anyone with sin on their hands or heart (the godless) would not dare show up before God so openly. Job is utterly clear about how he has experienced God in his suffering, how thoroughly he has been tortured by God. He lays his suffering at God's feet, and maintains his claim that God has absolutely no reason to have done this:

> He has torn me in his wrath, and
> > hated me;
> > he has gnashed his teeth at me;
> > my adversary sharpens his eyes
> > > against me.
> They have gaped at me with their
> > mouths;
> > they have struck me insolently
> > > on the cheek;
> > they mass themselves together
> > > against me.
> God gives me up to the ungodly,
> > and casts me into the hands of
> > > the wicked.
> I was at ease, and he broke me in
> > two;
> > he seized me by the neck and
> > > dashed me to pieces;
> > he set me up as his target;
> > > his archers surround me.

> He slashes open my kidneys, and
>   shows no mercy;
> he pours out my gall on the
>   ground.
> He bursts upon me again and
>   again;
> he rushes at me like a warrior.
> . . .
> My face is red with weeping,
>   and deep darkness is on my
>   eyelids,
> though there is no violence in my
>   hands,
>   and my prayer is pure. (Job 16:9–17)

Job's cry to hold God accountable to himself, holds God accountable to God as well. God cannot escape the moral imperative that Job's integrity presses upon God:

> O earth, do not cover my blood;
>   let my outcry find no resting
>   place.
> Even now, in fact, my witness [God] is
>   in heaven,
> and he that vouches for me is
>   on high.
> My friends scorn me;
>   my eye pours out tears to God,
> that he would maintain the right
>   of a mortal with God,
>   as one does for a neighbor. (Job 16:18–21)

While Job does not know the heavenly circumstances that set his terrible suffering in motion, Job has no doubt that God knows he is innocent. After being thoroughly chastised by his so-called friends, Job turns to God. In spite of everything, he assumes that God is a trustworthy witness, and that God will uphold Job's right to bring his case against God. The words, "do not cover my blood; let my outcry find no resting place," echo the words of God after Cain had murdered Abel: "Listen; your brother's blood is crying out to me from the ground!" (Gen 4:10) With these words, Job accuses God of murder, not punishment for sinfulness. With this charge, Job challenges the very idea that God has about himself (as presented by his friends): that he is just. Will God stand and face the accusation? Job expects God to uphold God's integrity in maintaining the dignity of Job (his mortal creature, whom God fashioned with his own hands) to stand before God and make his case. Job expects God, in this sense, to take a stand against himself; he appeals to God against God. Does Job in these lines have some inkling of a divided state in God that needs to be called out and addressed? Job is accusing God of injustice (while not gainsaying his justice), while everyone else, the prevailing God-logic, is convinced that God is *only* just! And, even more so, that mere mortals have no right to view God as anything less (or more). Now Job, a mere mortal, dares to think outside the prevailing logic of God's nature; he *knows* that God is more than the prevailing view, that God is more complex and difficult, that God is just *and* unjust. Certainly we, as readers, see this truth at the very beginning of Job, when God and the satan get into it. It takes a person of exceptional moral integrity and confidence—especially after they have lost everything, family and friends and community—to stand their ground and force this truth of God into the open, where it is truly visible and known.

Job asserts that his truth will last forever and that he is certain he will win out:

> O that my words were written
>   down!
>   O that they were inscribed in a
>   book!
> O that with an iron pen and with
>   lead
>   they were engraved on a rock
>   forever!
> For I know that my Redeemer
>   lives,
>   and that at the last he will
>   stand upon the earth.
>   (Job 19:23-25)

The "Redeemer" could also be vindicator, but there is no reason to capitalize the term, as it is not a name, but a common noun. There is some interpretive controversy over who the "redeemer" is, but what is clear is that whether God or a family member, Job is secure in himself. Or, as I argue, Job's "vindicator" is his integrity. And yet, when he recognizes the extent of God's injustice he is shocked, and shaken to his core:

> As for me, is my complaint
>   addressed to mortals?
>   Why should I not be impatient?
> Look at me, and be appalled,
>   and lay your hand upon your
>   mouth.
> When I think of it I am dismayed,
>   and shuddering seizes my flesh.
> Why do the wicked live on,
>   reach old age, and grow mighty
>   in power? (Job 21:4-7)

Job: A Crack in the Armor

Job enumerates many more examples of how the wicked are never punished, more evidence that his suffering and the prosperity of the wicked belie the now tired refrain that God is just—Job is disgusted with the notion:

> How then will you comfort me
> > with empty nothings?
> There is nothing left of your
> > answers but falsehood. (Job 21:34)

Finally Job silences his three friends with an oath declaring his innocence:

> As God lives, who has taken
> > away my right,
> and the Almighty, who has
> > made my soul bitter,
> as long as my breath is in me
> > and the spirit of God is in my
> > nostrils,
> my lips will not speak falsehood,
> > and my tongue will not utter
> > deceit.
> Far be it from me, to say that you
> > are right;
> > *until I die I will not put away*
> > > *my integrity from me.*
> I hold fast my righteousness, and
> > will not let it go;
> > my heart does not reproach me
> > > for any of my days. (Job 27:2–6, emphasis added)

Job stakes his oath ("As God lives") on the very God he is accusing of murder and injustice. Job's oath is, in a sense, a counterdare to the satan's—Job dares God to prove him wrong, to answer to Job's integrity. The oath ("far be it for me") irrevocably binds Job and God in the struggle for truth—neither one can evade the oath. He has pushed God into a corner, backed him up against the wall, and something must give. We will want to remember the phrase, "until I die I will not put away my integrity from me," when, at the end of Job, we examine Job's last words to God. For now, although God will indeed speak soon, there is one final paroxysm on the part of the traditional claim that God is just. Another character, who apparently has been there all along, waiting his turn, deferential because of his youth, emerges from the shadows. Elihu, a self-righteous young firebrand who feels compelled to save God's good name, has been holding his tongue, but he is now quite angry that Job seeks to justify himself rather than God.

Elihu Attempts to Shame Job

Elihu[6] appears to be the last attempt to defend the "God is Just" argument in the face of Job's criticism and challenge. But in fact, Elihu represents the next to last attempt (before God finally speaks) in which God tries to justify himself as a just God, to defend himself against Job. For the psychological view, the speeches between Job and his friends and Elihu represent God in conflict with himself: that is, a new God-idea (form of consciousness) is struggling to emerge against the resistance of the prevailing God-idea (the "God is Just" form of consciousness). The late-comer Elihu's speech, perhaps inserted long after the original text was written, is also a desperate attempt to shut down the inevitably eroding impact of Job's integrity on the prevailing view of God.

Elihu has been sitting silently in the background, his traditionalist leanings seething with self-righteousness. He is furious with Job for justifying himself rather than God, and angry with Job's three friends because their talk has been ineffectual (32:2–3). Elihu has six chapters all to himself; he is long-winded and bombastic, barely able to contain himself:

> For I am full of words;
>   the spirit within me constrains
>   me.
> My heart is indeed like wine that
>   has no vent;
>   like new wineskins, it is ready
>   to burst.
> I must speak, so that I may find
>   relief;
> I must open my lips and
>   answer. (Job 32:18–20)

Elihu criticizes Job for arrogance and self-justification. He faults Job for accusing God of injustice, arguing that the important thing Job forgets is God's greatness in all ways over any mortal. Why does Job even bother to contend against God? (33:12–13). Elihu believes he has the final answer, and he wants to put Job in his place and establish his

---

6. The appearance of the Elihu character presents a problem appropriate to historical criticism, but not to my interpretation, so I place this comment here. The historical-critical lens shows us almost all biblical texts are composite productions of more than one writer and editor, sometimes occurring over several hundred years. Despite a few odd literary moments, the book of Job hangs together overall, but the six chapters (32–37) devoted to Elihu alone contain enough anomalies to suggest this material was not from the original author of Job. Although I find the literary history of the biblical texts fascinating, and also illuminating at times of the history of soul, the focus here is on the literary integrity of the text as it has come to us. The text, as it exists today in both the Tanakh and Old Testament versions, has been the form of soul shaping Western civilization for a good fifteen hundred years. The text as given reflects the soulful DNA of Western civilization's psychological inheritance, and this is what I am interpreting. So, it does not matter whether or not the Elihu material was added two or three hundred years after the original Job story; it is there, it belongs to the Job ethos, and thus to this interpretation.

view of God as the final arbiter, but it feels like he is trying to win his argument by the force of his own will, as he invokes his own oath on behalf of God:

> Therefore, hear me, you who
>   have sense,
> far be it from God that he
>   should do wickedness,
> and from the Almighty that he
>   should do wrong.
> For according to their deeds he
>   will repay them,
> and according to their ways he
>   will make it befall them.
> Of a truth, God will not do
>   wickedly,
> and the Almighty will not
>   pervert justice. (Job 34:10–12)

To even think God unjust and promote such an idea is itself a sin:

> Job speaks without knowledge,
>   his words are without insight.
> Would that Job were tried to the
>   limit,
> because his answers are those of
>   the wicked.
> For he adds rebellion to his sin;
>   he claps his hands among us,
> and multiplies his words against
>   God. (Job 34:35–37)

Elihu's last words capture the spirit of his tirade:

> The Almighty—we cannot find
>   him;
> he is great in power and justice,
> and abundant righteousness he
>   will not violate.
> Therefore mortals fear him;
>   he does not regard any who are
>   wise in their own conceit. (Job 37:23–24)

So there we have it. God is great and Job is not, therefore Job must be in the wrong and deserves what he gets. In fact, his affliction is simply a teaching from God to get back in line with God's truth. What really exercises Elihu seems to be Job's arrogance, his presumption to criticize God and think that he is better than God. It is

God's Autopsy and the Living Truth of Soul

not too hard to see that Elihu, not aware of his own arrogance, is perceiving that very trait in Job.

But, and this is an important question: How do we know that Job is not an arrogant self-aggrandizing character, simply defending himself against any deeper self-reflection? Certainly, we would think that the terribly tragic and suffering circumstances of his life would drive him to self-examination, and they do. That is the ground of his integrity. He even runs through a long list of possible wrongdoings, such as lust, dishonesty, mistreatment of others, idolatry, hypocrisy, and so on, calling on God to judge him rightly if he has done any of these things:

> If I have walked with falsehood,
>   and my foot has hurried to
>   deceit—
> let me be weighed in a just
>   balance,
> and let God know my
>   integrity! (Job 31:5–6)

The strongest reason we know that Job is not simply arrogant and egotistically justifying himself at God's expense is the fact that Job has never cursed God, never abandoned God, never dismissed God. Job has been steadfast and courageous in facing God with his truth and asking for an answer. Job remains in relationship with God, and he forsakes neither himself nor his God. As seen earlier, Job makes himself vulnerable and naked before truth, that is, God. This is not the stance of an arrogant person. Elihu represents a desperate attempt on the part of the God-is-just logic to preserve itself against the unshakable ground of Job's integrity.

Now it is God's turn to speak, to respond to Job. And, God does indeed speak. It is reasonable to assume that God has heard Job, heard every word, not only from Job, but from his three friends and Elihu. How will God respond? What can we expect? Will God explain himself? Will God give an accounting of a set of horrific circumstances that do not make sense? Will God reveal the wager with the satan? Will God show some tenderness to Job? If we expect an affirmative answer to any of these questions, we will be disappointed.

The Storm Voice Responds to Job

Throughout the story of Job, he and his friends often use the words *God* and *Almighty*, translating *El* or *elohim* and *Shaddai*, somewhat generic terms for gods and "powers." But at this juncture, the narrator introduces God's response to Job as, "Then the LORD answered Job out of the whirlwind." This is Yahweh, the storm god, whose character is also informed by his bull and warrior qualities. What will this God-character have to say to Job about his suffering?

Job: A Crack in the Armor

> Then the LORD answered Job out
>   of the whirlwind:
> "Who is this that darkens counsel
>   by words without
>   knowledge?
> Gird up your loins like a man,
>   I will question you, and you
>   shall declare to me." (Job 38:1–3)

The appearance of the storm god, in the form of the voice from a whirlwind, is a premonition of how he will answer Job, that is, as a Wild Wind. Rather than understanding and compassion, the storm god responds with bluster, attempting to blow away Job's concerns. The narrator introduces "the LORD" as the speaker, which is somewhat unusual in that Yahweh has always introduced himself when addressing a human person, such as Moses; in that case, Yahweh announced himself as, "I am the God of your father, the God of Abraham . . ." (Exod 3:6).

A storm is speaking (or is it shouting?), so listen for the thunder in Yahweh's confrontation with Job: Those opening lines are a thunderous blast. Dispensing with any protocol niceties, God launches into a harangue, questioning Job's intelligence and challenging his manhood. He has indeed heard every word Job has spoken, and now feels a pressing urge to defend himself against Job's complaint, charge, and demand. Yahweh seems to feel all too acutely the truth of Job's claim, rooted in Job's integrity, which Yahweh himself lauded aloud at the beginning. It appears that God indeed is feeling the sting of shame at his wager with the satan. Yahweh goes on a powerful counterattack, whose only intent, given Job's circumstances, is to overwhelm and intimidate Job, change the subject, and shout him down. Instead of addressing Job's complaints and questions about justice and injustice in relation to Job's clear and unquestionable integrity, Yahweh talks only about power, his power: How great and magnificent his power is, and how small, helpless, and ignorant the mere human creature by comparison. I want to note here that Yahweh is echoing the view of himself that Job's three friends and Elihu promoted because later in this story, Yahweh will contradict himself.

God, interestingly enough, resorts to bullying, as if Job has not already been bullied enough with tragic losses, terrible misery, and sickness unto death, finally reduced to a barely human sack of skin and bones. Now, of course, we the reader see all of Yahweh's cards, he's played them all, the beautiful bright ones and the horrific dark ones. His bombastic tirade, taking four chapters, may be his final attempt to cover up the terrible dark cards of arbitrary injustice. By holding fast to his integrity and innocence, Job will reveal the totality of Yahweh, the gods, the powers, that rule life and the universe. Knowing nothing of Yahweh's wager with the satan, Job is still somewhat naive, innocent in his view of God as primarily just, as he holds fast to his conviction

God's Autopsy and the Living Truth of Soul

that God will vindicate him, will explain the tragic losses, the misery, and the torture that Job suffers.

Now God is in a bind and has to hide his satanic side, which in this instance got the better of him. How can God admit this failure on his part, this weakness, and save face? And, who is he trying to hide this knowledge from? Didn't we hear at the beginning of Genesis that the gods know all about the tree of the knowledge of good and evil? Perhaps that is the problem: They know *about* it, but they do not *know* their own complicity in it, their own personal good *and* evil. More likely, the early nature-based gods and goddesses had not yet risen to the level of a moral problem. Nature is neither good nor evil; it simply *is*, nature is Fate, and nature's consequences do not imply any moral judgment. On the other hand, Yahweh is leaving the natural world behind, abandoning his own nature essence, and thus he becomes subject to a higher level of reflection, which takes place through writing. The book of Job is a writing that enables a higher, more differentiated level of reflection that would be impossible in earlier mostly oral cultures. Because Yahweh insists on a moral code he himself has created, he is himself subject to that code. If Yahweh wants to become a higher more comprehensive level of consciousness, he has to become aware of his totality by way of his created self-image, who is not simply the character Job, but the author of Job, or perhaps more accurately, the literary work, the book of Job itself. It is the literary work (and its several authors) that gives voice to soul's account of itself, a literary witness to soul's travail, subject to interpretation, translation, and more interpretation over centuries. This is soul's way, reinterpreting itself over and over, without end.

Yahweh tries to hide this knowledge from himself. Clearly Yahweh (El, *elohim*) is both a creator god and a destroyer god, but does he know this about himself? If the arguments of Job's three friends and Elihu are taken at face value, then no, he does not. The prevailing knowledge that God has about himself, the prevailing ancient Near Eastern God-logic, is that God rewards the good and punishes the bad. The tension and the conflict in the book of Job is between two images of God, the taken-for-granted "God is Just" God, which, as the status quo, resists the emergence of the subversive and shocking *consciousness* of God as a terrible unpredictable duality of both good *and* evil. The Yahweh who speaks from the whirlwind cannot face this knowledge about himself, at least not yet, and thus he has to continue shouting at Job. Yahweh will crank the power meter all the way up in order to show Job just how insignificant he is and demonstrate that he really has no standing, no right, to question the Lord!

The author of Job is grappling with the intuition that something is terribly wrong with the prevailing worldview, the prevailing God-logic, that God is Just. He was not the only one in the ancient Near East who was questioning the belief that the gods reward the good and punish the wicked: It is obvious that the wicked live long and productive lives, and the good suffer arbitrarily. The story of Job may be the first extended meditation on the problem this notion of God presents by pitting the so-called truth of the gods against an idealized human person. At the beginning, God and Job share an identical integrity, they both live within a shared mutual trust and admiration. Job fears God and turns away from evil, and God is immensely proud of his servant Job. Their mutual mirroring of each other is based in the prevailing belief that God is Just. However, the crack in this mirror occurs not on the human side of the equation, but the God side. God's integrity is compromised by the satan's insinuations and the ensuing wager. God may be beaming with pride in Job—why, we may even detect affection for Job—but as soon as the satan suggests Job might stop reflecting God's glory and integrity back to him, God becomes cold and callous, turning Job's fortunes over to the satan without another thought. How easily God falls apart into seemingly quite separate good and evil dimensions. This is exactly the way the Job author sees things. Reality does not measure up to the tacit, taken-for-granted notion that "God is Just." Yahweh's power speeches are another approach to the argument in favor of God's justice. The human arguments from Job's friends have not swayed Job. Now Yahweh will try his argument, perhaps the only argument he knows, that of "might makes right." Through an overwhelming show of dominance, Yahweh will try to convince Job to forsake his integrity and subjugate himself to reflecting God's glory back to God.

I want to interject here that I am thinking psychologically. Perhaps I want to remind myself that I am thinking psychologically. Though I talk about "God" extensively, "God" no longer exists. I am thinking the idea "God" as a historical representation of a phenomenological and psychological process, a stage in the evolution of consciousness. Soul has left the form of itself that was "God" behind and now functions as psychology, aware of itself as consciousness (psychology as soul's speech about itself). My thinking is a process of soul-making: A psychological interpretation of God and the Bible as historical artifacts of a now bygone form of consciousness is the way that psychology interprets itself, soul interprets itself today and at the same time creates itself, creates its new form. In the mythological and religious ages, divine agents revealed truth and were identified with truth; today, truth is a function of interpretation. As I continue to examine Yahweh's power speech, I want to remember that this form of consciousness was resisting change to its own constitution. Because God represented the foundation of reality (the syntax of consciousness, the water we swim in, public mind), what is at stake between God and Job is nothing less than the nature of reality.

As noted, Yahweh makes no preliminary introduction. He charges at Job, like a bull seeing red, with intimidating words, attempting to put Job on the defensive. First, he accuses Job of not knowing what he is talking about: "Who is this that darkens counsel by words without knowledge?" Then he pulls rank and attempts to put Job in his place by essentially demanding that he get ready for some real questions (as if Job's questions to God are trivial), "Gird up your loins like a man, I will question you, and you shall declare to me." But, what kind of questions? Is Yahweh going to interrogate Job, looking for cracks in his integrity, weaknesses in his self-confidence? Will Yahweh inquire about Job's well-being, show any interest in Job's situation? Not

God's Autopsy and the Living Truth of Soul

in the slightest. All of Yahweh's questions are rhetorical. He launches into a lengthy boast about himself, how he created the earth and the heavens, how only he knows the foundations of creation, the limits of land and sea, how he is the great manager of the known and the unknown:

> Where were you when I laid the
>   foundation of the earth?
>   Tell me, if you have
>   understanding.
> Who determined its
>   measurements—surely you
>   know!
>   Or who stretched the line upon it?
> . . .
> Or who shut in the sea with
>   doors
>   when it burst out from the
>   womb?—
> . . .
> Have you commanded the
>   morning since your days
>   began,
>   and caused the dawn to know
>   its place?
> . . .
> Have you entered into the
>   springs of the sea,
>   or walked in the recesses of the
>   deep?
> Have the gates of death been
>   revealed to you,
>   or have you seen the gates of
>   deep darkness?
> Have you comprehended the
>   expanse of the earth?
>   Declare, if you know all this. (Job 38:4–18)

Yahweh has a way with sarcasm, mocking sarcasm. Hasn't he smashed Job down far enough? Why the condescending rhetorical questions? Perhaps he is trying to undermine Job's self-confidence by emphasizing how little Job knows. Job has never questioned Yahweh's might nor his power and control over creation, yet Yahweh seems to feel the need to thunder these divine truisms. Why the thunder? Why the magnified posturing? Why poke at Job with sarcasm? It is hard to remember that at the beginning of the story, in his heavenly counsel with the other gods, Yahweh showed pride and great respect for Job. If he has heard Job's questions, and if he did take pride in Job's integrity, Yahweh now shows complete and utter disregard for Job's concerns and Job's personhood. It is as if Yahweh himself is trying to forget that little wager with the satan.

Yahweh makes quite a show of his meteorological superiority to poor little Job:

> Have you entered the storehouses
>> of the snow,
>> or have you seen the
>> storehouses of the hail,
> which I have reserved for the time
>> of trouble,
>> for the day of battle and war?
> [remember Yahweh is a Warrior-Storm god]
> What is the way to the place
>> where the light is
>> distributed,
>> or where the east wind is
>> scattered upon the earth?
> Who has cut a channel for the
>> torrents of rain,
>> and a way for the thunderbolt?
> ...
> Has the rain a father,
>> or who has begotten the drops
>> of dew?
> From whose womb did the ice
>> come forth,
>> and who has given birth to the
>> hoarfrost of heaven? (Job 38:22–29)

What on earth is the point of flinging the obvious in Job's face? Of course Yahweh has complete control over the natural world, but that has never been Job's concern nor his complaint. Out of his complete confidence in his innocence, Job has addressed a *moral* question to Yahweh, but Yahweh continues to ignore Job's concern by focusing on his own magnificence and power at Job's expense. Why this overpowering emphasis on what Yahweh can do and Job cannot? What does the weather and the structure of the cosmos have to do with Job's moral charge? Yahweh is obsessed with his power here and completely ignores the question of justice.

Yahweh boasts of his cosmological prowess, with more sarcasm:

> Can you bind the chains of the
>> Pleiades,
>> or loose the cords of Orion?

> Can you lead forth the Mazzaroth [zodiac]
> > in their season,
> > or can you guide the Bear with
> > its children?
> Do you know the ordinances of
> > the heavens?
> Can you establish their rule on
> > the earth? (Job 38:31–33)

Job is certainly getting schooled about his real place in God's view of things. Yahweh expands with more powers over the weather (38:34–38), and then shows off his zoological mastery over a number of wild animals, the lion, mountain goat, deer, wild ass, wild ox, ostrich, and a thrilling description of the courage and strength of the horse in battle (39:19–25), the hawk and eagle, all framed as rhetorical questions, pointing out what Job is incapable of in relation to God. All Yahweh's powers are thrown at Job as challenges that emphasize Job's weakness and ignorance in relation to natural phenomena. They completely miss the point. All the bombast emphasizes Job's small feeble stature (as a mortal) in comparison to Yahweh. Let's remember Job is already utterly miserable at Yahweh's own hand, and the attempt to humiliate Job essentially makes Yahweh look ridiculous. No one looks good kicking a defenseless creature. Still, Yahweh closes his lengthy boast with another direct challenge to Job:

> And the LORD said to Job:
> > "Shall a faultfinder contend
> > with the Almighty?
> Anyone who argues with God
> > must respond." (Job 40:1–2)

Job finally gets his chance to speak with Yahweh directly. Job could reset the terms of the argument, remind Yahweh of his fundamental question about the morality of Yahweh's treatment of him. Job, obviously, has no trouble with words; he is fluent and eloquent and could easily recall his argument and state his claim again, acknowledging at the start that he is speaking as an inferior mortal to his superior deity. Instead, Job gives the Lord as good as he gets, and with far fewer words:

> Then Job answered the LORD:
> "See, I am of small account; what
> > shall I answer you?
> > I lay my hand on my mouth.
> I have spoken once, and I will not
> > answer;
> > twice, but will proceed no
> > further." (Job 40:3–5)

Job: A Crack in the Armor

Job returns sarcasm with sarcasm, with mock deference. On the one hand, traditionalists will see Job's silence here as humility, as forbearance, as submission, as acceptance of Yahweh's greatness and superiority. Job's moral challenge is a mere human misunderstanding and simply has no place on the scale of Yahweh's magnificence.

In the ancient world, "God" was the final epistemological and ontological category, and human knowledge, human being, was simply submitted to that finality. Another word for "God" in this ancient context was Fate. One's fate was indeed simply accepted because Fate was decreed from beyond, and human consciousness did not yet have the status to question or judge Fate. This is why the story of Job is so important, for Job is the one who cracks the armor of Fate, he cracks the impenetrability of that logical form of consciousness. The narrative presupposition about Job's character is that it is thoroughly consistent within itself, that his integrity holds. He does not fall apart the way Yahweh's character has, and thus, his words here do not support a traditionalist interpretation. Job's answer is both sarcastic and ironic: Job is not buying what Yahweh is selling. Job is essentially saying, "Yes, I am smaller than small compared to you. What's new about that?! So what could I possibly say to *you*. But, I know that you have heard my moral charge, otherwise why would you thunder your absurd questions at me. I have nothing more to say. I rest my case!" My paraphrase is a bit wordy,[7] but Job shows a brilliant economy of words, just enough to demonstrate that his silence is not submission.[8] Job's brief response that he will speak no further asserts that silence in the face of such thunder is enough, for it should be clear to Yahweh that he has not moved Job one inch from his moral stand. A more literal translation of these verses, by Miles, reinforces the defiant rather than deferential interpretation:

> Look, I am of no account. What can I tell you?
>   My hand is on my mouth.
> I have already spoken once: I will not harp.
>   Why go on? I have nothing to add.[9]

I want to emphasize and keep in view that Job remains who and what he is. He is not having second thoughts or doubts about his position, about himself. He has staked everything—and I mean everything (remember who he is arguing with)—on his truth, the integrity of his whole being. Early in his conversation with his friends he declared:

> Let me have silence, and I will
>   speak,
>   and let come on me what may.
>   I will take my flesh in my teeth,
>   and put my life in my hand.

---

7. Or, in a terse vernacular, Job looks God in the eye and quietly, simply says, "Bullshit!"
8. Miles, *God*, 318.
9. Miles, *God*, 317.

> See, he will kill me; I have no
>> hope,
> but I will defend my ways to
>> his face. (Job 13:13–15)

Job is not about to bend, to change his mind. Job's status as "a man who fears God and turns away from evil" is unchangeable. His integrity is not a part of him that he can take off or put on; it is who he *is*. His wager is to stake his very life on his innocence, and he dares God to prove him wrong.

Job stands his ground, and this seems to incite the storm god, Yahweh, as he again shouts at Job and charges him with insubordination:

> Then the LORD answered Job out of
>> the whirlwind:
> "Gird up your loins like a man;
>> I will question you, and you
>> declare to me.
> Will you even put me in the
>> wrong?
>> Will you condemn me that you
>> may be justified?
> Have you an arm like God,
>> and can you thunder with a
>> voice like his?" (Job 40:6–9)

Perhaps Yahweh feels himself in a tight spot that is getting tighter. Perhaps Job is seeing through the grandiose posturing, seeing an aspect of Yahweh that Yahweh resists seeing. I also want to highlight again the significance of the fact that neither Job nor Yahweh forsake the other. They remain connected and in relationship; they are, in effect, one consciousness that is struggling with itself. From the psychological point of view, they are not separate entities but one dialectical unity that is working through a self-negation, sublating one form of itself ("God is Just") into another larger consciousness of itself ("God is Just *and* Unjust"). Yahweh continues with one more power tirade emphasizing Job's lack of power (40:10–14), and then seemingly goes off on a tangent with lengthy descriptions of two great animals, Behemoth (hippopotamus) and Leviathan (crocodile). Although they are recognizable as actual animals, Yahweh gives them the dimensions of primordial mythical beasts, elemental powers of nature that only Yahweh can control and manage, more examples of Yahweh's unsurpassable and unchallengeable power.

Throughout Yahweh's speeches, he seems to focus only on his muscles, his physical prowess, his creation of and management of the physical world. Not once does he acknowledge Job's concern for justice, nor does he mention his own concerns for justice, which Yahweh has in fact done in other places. Job's actual condition, his tragic loses and misery, seem to have become a forgotten afterthought. Still, always present in the background is the principle determining the argument. This is no intellectual discussion about the nature of God. This is a life-and-death moral confrontation, the life and death of integrity. The very idea of God, the core assumption about the nature of God, God's very truth, is under attack, and Yahweh must feel increasingly vulnerable in the face of Job's steady, steely conviction that he is indeed innocent and guiltless, and that Yahweh has some answering to do. An obscene wager set the story in motion, and so, Yahweh must know at some level that he has to face his satan, but he seems incapable of doing so alone. This is why Job is so fascinating, and why the confrontation between Job and Yahweh has been such a powerful and lasting force in the evolution of Western consciousness.

As I argued earlier, Job is not caught in arrogance. The argument for Job's uncontaminated innocence and integrity is clear. He has lost everything. He speaks out of his total loss from within the prevailing logical form of consciousness in which God is the source of all, and misfortune is not God's random act of cruelty but God's punishment and discipline. Within this context, Job's supreme self-confidence in his undivided integrity is free of arrogance or what we might call ego.[10] Job is not egocentric, but God-centric. In his position, his stance, and his truth, he stakes his whole being, his totality, on knowing his rightness in the face of God's acts against him. Job knows that God knows he is blameless because he challenges God to point out his iniquity, his wrong-doing. He knows that if God would deign to meet him in court to argue their case, Job would win. Job willingly lays himself open before the ultimate lie detector. God would have to admit that Job is blameless, that God lost control of himself, caught up in his self-doubt and fearing the loss of his honor and position of supreme power. The key to Job's integrity is that he does not abdicate himself, and he does not forsake God. Thus, God must face the music, face his own true nature, which is that he is *both* arbitrarily cruel and arbitrarily good.

The Job/God drama is soul's negation of this particular God-logic, which tips the scales of power from the God side of the equation to the human side. The I Am consciousness that in Exodus belonged only to the God now begins its transit to the human being. Job's rock-solid stand on his moral integrity illuminates a new picture of God, and the human child of God begins to grow up at the expense of the until now all-powerful parent god. Job becomes an I Am in his own right. The story of Job represents a revolution in consciousness at large, soul's logic turned against itself for the sake of a new logic of consciousness. Job's challenge shifts some of the cosmic value of consciousness, first experienced "out there" as the figure of God, into human consciousness now engaged in a moral confrontation with God's injustice. God's

---

10. Here I use this modern term metaphorically to draw attention to Job's total orientation. The "ego," as we understand it today, did not exist in antiquity, although we saw the seed of the "ego as will" appear in the event at Sinai. The modern ego emerges during soul's development through modernity, which I will examine in chapter 8.

God's Autopsy and the Living Truth of Soul

justice can no longer be taken for granted. There is a crack in the armor. The logical status of humankind is raised at the expense of the logical status of Yahweh. This is a change not in content of consciousness but at the level of syntax; the water we swim in is irrevocably transformed. Next comes Job's final response to the Lord and the key verse by which this new interpretation stands or falls.

42:6—Job Is Yahweh's Mirror

Throughout the book of Job, the dialogue and speeches are lengthy and beautiful. The speakers multiply metaphors and images, charges and countercharges, making their points with exquisite poetry. Yet, here at the end, Job makes his stunning final stand with a surprising economy of words. Because these final few words of Job's are the hinge on which everything turns, a close examination of the translation is warranted.[11] The general tone of the conventional translation found in all Bibles is as follows (here NRSV):

> Then Job answered the LORD:
> "I know that you can do all
>   things,
>   and that no purpose of yours
>   can be thwarted.
> 'Who is this that hides counsel
>   without knowledge?'
> Therefore I have uttered what I
>   did not understand,
>   things too wonderful for me,
>   which I did not know.
> 'Hear, and I will speak;
>   I will question you, and you
>   declare to me.'
> I had heard of you by the hearing
>   of the ear,
>   but now my eye sees you;
> Therefore I despise myself,
>   and repent in dust and ashes." (Job 42:1–6)

It would appear from these final lines that Job, against my entire argument to this point, and against Job's own declarations (and remember his oath, "Until I die I will not put away my integrity from me." 27:5b), does indeed cave and buy what Yahweh is selling. That is, he seemingly acknowledges that Yahweh is superior, that he, Job, does not know what he is talking about, and that he will change (repent) his mind and submit to being a mere mortal, as if he is saying: "What on earth got into me? Who was I

---

11. In what follows I am indebted to Miles's (*God*) technical expertise and interpretive brilliance.

to even think that *I* could question *you*?" Now, supposedly chastened, Job appears to plead temporary insanity and confess his guilt. His integrity vanishes before our eyes! The pious position that "God is right and God knows best," is the way tradition has interpreted this text for at least two thousand years. The NRSV even enshrines this point of view in a terse epigraph on that very page. In the upper left or right corner, all NRSV pages include a very brief summary of the content or main point of that page. On the page where we find Job's final reply are the words: "Job is humbled and satisfied." Given Yahweh's speeches, this certainly sounds like his desired outcome, and this remains the prevailing contemporary theological view: The Lord is right, he is more powerful and mysterious than we are, quite beyond our understanding, and thus we should simply crawl back into our cowed little status of obedience and forget about questioning the Lord. Is this satisfying? Modern consciousness (modern soul) is not satisfied.

I will now examine several critical translation details that completely reverse the traditional interpretation and preserve Job's integrity. Of course, simply from the argument of Job's integrity, the traditional interpretation of Job's final statement actually makes Job abdicate and forsake himself, which from a purely literary standpoint, lacks narrative integrity. How is it that a story founded on the *integrity* of Job, vouchsafed by both God and Job, at the end simply makes that very integrity disappear as if it never existed? From simply a literary critical point of view, the traditional ending is senseless. But, the problem is deeper. We will see how the traditional view of God as the superior entity glosses over and twists the meaning of words that actually offer an entirely different and subversive point of view. My claim is that Job remains true to himself to the very end. It is God who has to change, that is, repent.

The first line of Job's response reads, "I know that you can do all things." It sounds as if Job is simply confessing that indeed God is a superior power, and that perhaps he is getting ready to change his position. This, however, is not what is written in the Hebrew text, but rather what would be, in Hebrew, traditionally read out loud. The "I know" is completely dependent on a peculiarity of the Hebrew text, which uses two notations at certain points to tell a public reader whether or not to read out loud what is written, or an alternative.[12] In this case what is written is, "You know that you can do all things." In a public reading, an attitude of reverence would predominate

---

12. "But Job's recalcitrance becomes bolder if we read the text as *written* in the Hebrew and not as conventionally pronounced (and therefore translated) over the centuries. The annotations to the Masoretic or standard Hebrew text of the Tanakh include what are called *ketib* and *qere* indications. The former word means 'written,' the latter means 'read' (the imperative), in Aramaic, which succeeded Hebrew as the spoken language of Jews living in Palestine and became the language of these annotations. For reasons of sense, but also, on occasion, for reasons of reverence, the synagogue reader was instructed by these marginal notations to read another word than the one he found written in the text. In Job 42:2 he was instructed to change the word *yada'ta*, 'you know,' to *yada'tiy*, 'I know.' Change verse 42:2 in the RSV translation by just that much—from 'I know that thou canst do all things' to 'Thou knowest that thou canst do all things'—and its air of confession and submission immediately becomes ambiguous and potentially ironic" (Miles, *God*, 319).

and could not have Job throw Yahweh's boast back in his face, and so the reader is instructed to change "You know," to "I know," keeping Job in his submissive place as a mere mortal. Job's actually words, "*You know* that you can do all things," denotes an immediate change in tone and attitude. Job's assertion is ironic, undercutting Yahweh's authority. As Job pushes Yahweh's boast right back, he follows up with a direct quote of Yahweh's, pushing that too back in Yahweh's face: " 'Who is this that hides counsel without knowledge?' "[13] Job takes Yahweh's accusation of Job's ignorance and gives it back, telling Yahweh, shockingly, that he is the one who is obscuring the truth and obfuscating the real issue. Job is well aware that Yahweh has consistently and brazenly ignored Job's claim. So, Job in his next line, "Therefore I have uttered what I did not understand, things too wonderful for me, which I did not know," is saying, "Well, I guess what I said about you, really amazing wonders, was indeed the truth, and I did not know how right I was at the time." Here Job does indeed turn the tables on Yahweh, actually to an extent belittling Yahweh. When we hear the sarcasm and irony, we know that Job now understands that he was indeed speaking the truth about Yahweh; he has not been cowed by Yahweh's bombast in the least.

Next Job flings another word of Yahweh's back, quoting Yahweh to Yahweh, because now it is Job's turn to declare his truth:

> Hear, and I will speak;
> > I will question you, and you
> > > declare to me.

Yahweh threw these words at Job twice during his power monologue. Once at 38:3, and again at 40:7, when he challenged Job:

> Gird up your loins like a man;
> > I will question you, and
> > > you declare to me.

Such a charge really means, "Buck up and be a man, because I don't think you can handle what I am going to throw at you." The effect is bullying, a belittling and intimidating challenge from a superior and more powerful adversary. Although Job does not tell God in so many words, to "gird up his loins like a God [bull?]," he does demand that Yahweh "listen up!" The words "Hear, and I will speak," is not a direct quote, but they amplify the quotation, "I will question you . . ." The New International Version (NIV) translates "Hear" as "Listen now." The imperative is commanding in "Listen!" as in, "For your own good, Listen Now!" Asserting himself on equal ground, Job confronts Yahweh in return. By using Yahweh's own words, he gives notice he is not

---

13. Given that biblical text is often quite dense, I know I have trouble noticing something like single quotation marks that indicate Job is quoting God back to God, which is why I have intentionally given the double and single marks extra separation in this rendering.

intimidated, and now it is Yahweh's turn to stand down and listen: Job has something to say of equal weight.

> I had heard of you by the hearing
> of the ear,
> but now my eye sees you.

The ambiguity in these words is not so much their general meaning, which is fairly obvious, but rather what they signify. The contrast between the hearing of the ear and the seeing of the eye refers to secondhand, or indirect, knowledge compared to firsthand and immediate knowledge through experience: "I have heard people talk about you, but now I have actually met you." But, what could Job be referring to with "hearing" and "seeing"?

In general, commentators view Job's "hearing" as related to what his three friends, and Elihu, have been telling him about God, and his "seeing" as referring to the experience of the theophany of the voice from the whirlwind. At this obvious surface level, the assumption is that Job's direct experience of God's mighty stormy presence reframes all of his moral justice claims as petty: coming from a limited *human* perspective and actually irrelevant in the face of God's grandeur. Such an interpretation stays on the surface of the text, is too literal, and in the end, is controlled by the theological presuppositions that the God is always superior to human inferiority. All the traditional readings of Job assume an unquestioned theism that permeates the interpretation of Job up to the present, which distorts, obscures, and actually eliminates Job's own truth. The deeper problem here is not Job but God, and the overriding struggle is God with God. Or, within the psychological perspective, soul negating itself for the sake of a new form of consciousness.

What Job has "heard" is the prevailing truth of his time, as well as his own knowing absorbed from the culture and his life experience up to and before God's wager with the satan: that God is indeed Just, and that life is ultimately fair in that divine sense. Job's friends try to make Job the problem, and although he shares with them the same general idea about God, Job knows he is innocent. He knows the problem does not lie with him. Job has not only "heard about" God from his friends, he has absorbed the idea about God that is the taken-for-granted logical form of consciousness of his culture, his age, shared more or less by everyone. In this sense, what Job "heard" about God is what he already knew and assumed about God; this was his starting point. But, now he has moved beyond that starting point. Job stands out as the lonely and solitary challenger of this worldview, a posture that isolates him from his family, his friends, his society, and God. Job is one estranged, alone with his integrity, his truth.

In contrast to what he "heard," what is it that Job "now sees"? In my view, when Job says, "but now my eye sees you," Job means that his direct experience of God, *his* "theophany," includes everything that has happened to him before and after God's wager with the satan, including Yahweh's lengthy bragging about his power, completely ignoring the moral question of justice. Job's tragic losses, his terrible physical misery, his tortured moral consciousness, and the strange bullying speech from the whirlwind—all these accumulate, along with the great blessing he enjoyed before, as his direct and personal experience of God. That is Job's true theophany! After the first round of tragic losses he said,

> Naked I came from my mother's womb, and naked I shall return there; The LORD gave, and the LORD has taken away; blessed be the name of the LORD.
> (Job 1:21)

He affirms that his life experience, no matter how good or how bad, is the Lord's blessing. Then he is inflicted with horrible sickness, and his wife, who at that point has suffered as much as if not more than Job himself (having lost all her children), screams that his stubborn integrity is stupid. "Curse God and die," she says. In return, Job simply affirms, "Shall we receive the good at the hand of God, and not receive the bad?" (2:10b)[14] Job does not doubt that his misfortune, his tragic and horrific circumstances, are in fact the result of God's own hand. They are, therefore, God's presence in his life, and by implication, a theophany. Of course, this is not the traditional notion of theophany, but given Job's special intimacy with God, it does not make sense to privilege only the "voice from the whirlwind" as theophanic. Job's whole life, his being, is saturated with Yahweh/God's presence. And yet, Job does not settle for simple acceptance of Fate. What Job wants to know is, "Why? Why the arbitrary tragic suffering?" This is a brand-new question! What God has done to him makes no sense, and that is why the interpretation of the final lines of Job's response is critical to Job's position. *How* the final line is read is the key to the interpretation that reveals what Job now "sees," that is, what he *knows* in that biblical sense of intimate direct experience.

The traditional translation leaves no doubt about Job's turnabout, that he has indeed changed his mind, seen the error of his arguments, and submits:

> therefore I despise myself,
>   and repent in dust and ashes.

I, on the other hand, argue that the traditional translation sacrifices Job and his truth on the altar of theological piety, a tradition that probably began with the Greek translation of the Hebrew Bible, the Septuagint (third and second centuries BCE). The problem hangs on one word, a word that does not appear in the Hebrew but was supplied by the Greek translators, and that word is *myself*. What the verb *despise* refers to is not immediately apparent in the Hebrew. Miles makes the problem clear:

> In the Hebrew, however, this verse is ambiguous, and in the RSV's resolution of the ambiguity no word has less support from the original than the word *myself*. This last word, supplied in the Greek of the Septuagint and, one way or

---

14. Here again we see the traditional ancient attitude toward Fate: acceptance without complaint or argument.

another, in nearly every translation since then, might be described as the thin air to which is anchored the filament from which hangs the thread by which the traditional interpretation dangles. Against the traditional interpretation, it is likely that though Job is in the grip of profoundly changed and negative feelings about *something* at this point, the something is not himself.[15]

Eliminate the word "myself," and what remains is typical Hebrew poetic parallelism of two verbs and two nouns, as follows:

> therefore I despise and repent,
>   dust and ashes.

Now it is clear something has changed for Job as a result of what he now *sees*, and most likely what he sees in a new light is, God.[16]

The Hebrew word translated as *despise* means rejection and includes a powerful physical revulsion, a visceral horror about something dreadful. The word translated as *repent* is problematic because it can lean toward the typical notion, as in "I am sorry *about*," or it can also point to sorrow and compassion, as in "I am sorry *for*." The meaning depends on context, which will determine how the ambiguous preposition present in the Hebrew, *'al*, is translated. With the ghost object "myself" eliminated, the two verbs, "despise and repent," need an object, which now appears to be "dust and ashes." But, what do "dust and ashes" refer to? This is important because the meaning of the ambiguous preposition, *'al*, is determined by the nature of the noun that follows: If it is a person then it would mean "for," but if something else, then "about."

"Dust and ashes" is a common metaphor in the Hebrew Bible, referring to different things. When Abraham is negotiating with God over the destruction of Sodom, "dust and ashes" refers to mortal human beings, in this case, himself, "I who am but dust and ashes" (Gen 18:27). But, it can also function as a synonym for repentance itself. In that case, the following translation is possible: "I am sorry about dust and ashes," which would mean, "I repent of repentance." If Job is repenting of repentance, what could he be repenting of? What might he fundamentally change his mind about, or completely turn away from? Given that Job has stoutly defended his innocence and rejected the claims of his friends that he repent of some sin, it could mean something like, "I am not buying into the worldview that says I should repent, because I have nothing to repent," or, "I repent of the worldview, I repent of the image of God, that states I should repent." This direction of interpretation does not tell us anything new

---

15. Miles, *God*, 323.

16. In what follows I summarize a complex and lengthy exegetical and linguistic argument developed by Miles in an endnote of his own almost five pages long (*God*, 425–30). He probes the inherent ambiguity of the Hebrew words, and his argument, in my view, is entirely convincing and consistent with his literary analysis. His reading does not place an undue interpretive load on any one word, and he does not twist meanings of words out of their normal bounds in order to fit his point of view. Perhaps, too, the fact that Miles is free of any theological allegiance (Jewish or Christian) enables this fresh and revolutionary reading to emerge.

God's Autopsy and the Living Truth of Soul

and is simply Job repeating his already well-established position: that in his innocence he has nothing to repent. It also does not help us with the "despise" or "revulsion" part of his statement. Miles does not follow "repent of repentance," and prefers "dust and ashes" as a reference to humankind in general. This means that the word for "repent" leans in the direction of "sorry for," and leads Miles to settle on the following as the final words of Job, first somewhat literally, "Now my eyes have seen you; therefore, I feel revulsion and compassion over dust and ashes," or with a more natural phrasing, "Now that my eyes have seen you, I shudder with sorrow for mortal clay."[17]

This reading preserves Job's integrity and does not introduce a radically novel and alien interpretation that would have him forsake his totality, his truth. With the unnecessary object, "myself," removed, we see clearly that Job is the one (the only one) who sees the unalloyed totality of Yahweh, the one who really *sees* the full catastrophe that is Yahweh, in all his beauty *and* horror. Yahweh is not simply just or unjust, but truly *both* and *not always with reason*; clearly in Job's case, there is no justification for Yahweh's arbitrary cruelty. If the pious traditionalist interpretation is allowed to stand (as it has for two millennia), then Job's entire argument, the fundamental moral value on which he has staked his life, is summarily judged worthless and dismissed. In fact, Job's strong challenge to the prevailing idea of God demonstrates that the God-idea has already been crumbling from within.

Job's final response to Yahweh's bluster is again a brilliant economy of words. Miles's translation captures the tone more satisfying to modern consciousness:

> Then Job answered the Lord:
> "You know you can do anything.
>   Nothing can stop you.
> You ask, 'Who is this ignorant muddler?'
> Well, I said more than I knew, wonders quite beyond me.
> 'You listen, and I'll talk.' you say,
>   'I'll question you, and you tell me.'
> Word of you had reached my ears,
>   but now that my eyes have seen you,
> I shudder with sorrow for mortal clay."[18]

The so-called theophany, the voice from the storm, has served only to confirm Job's slowly dawning personal epiphany: Yahweh may bestow blessing, as he did on Job originally, but Yahweh is also a cruel monster, devoid of reason. Job's insight shudders through his whole being; he is revolted by this dark truth, and a spontaneous compassion arises for vulnerable humankind. Job's insight encompasses a complex, penetrating realization that arouses horror and sorrow at now really knowing an inescapable truth. Yahweh is indeed a towering power, but human beings can only hope for justice,

17. Miles, *God*, 428.
18. Miles, *God*, 325.

and just as equally suffer inexplicable misery. A mask or veil that had preserved an assumed reasonable balance of divine power has been torn away. Now, through Job, humankind sees a very different truth. But, an even more surprising thing happens at the same time, as Yahweh is also burdened with this insight about himself. Job's knowledge, as he is God's created self-image, is also Yahweh's self-knowledge.

The Lord of the whirlwind, the storm god, made a last-ditch effort to prop up the conventional, prevailing view of gods, whose great power over all of life makes them always in the right, so that humankind must bow down and submit. The Job story reveals a crisis that was already stirring in the taken-for-granted view of the gods. The prevailing truth of the gods is unraveling, and human consciousness becomes less innocent as it expands. The syntax of consciousness is undergoing a fundamental change, which is soul's internal self-transformation. The biblical symbol for this is the tree of the knowledge of good and evil. We might say that the tree of the knowledge of good and evil had remained in the garden of Eden in a state of unconsciousness, and now, through Job, it becomes more conscious of itself, producing *knowledge* of evil in an unexpected place. The knowledge of good *and* evil is reflected by Job back to Yahweh, and Yahweh now must also bear the disturbing burden of his own complex unpredictable nature. Although the satan character disappeared early from the narrative, this interpretation means that Job has pulled the satan out of the background. It is now integrated consciously, by way of human reflection, into the logical form of consciousness known as Yahweh. I also want to emphasize that this interpretation, Miles's and mine, is a function of modern soul, a reading of the story through the lens of "God is dead." Such a reading has been impossible until now, over two thousand years after the original story was written down. Only because the god of literacy (Yahweh) appeared and texts became sacred, has soul been able to work on itself over the centuries, reading, rereading, and reinterpreting its foundational texts. Soul does not exist, soul cannot work on itself, without the world of meaning preserved and conveyed by the written word in interaction with the living life of mind in the here and now.

The book of Job is a literary monument to a soul-project that had already been underway throughout the culture at large, or public mind. The work that is the book of Job is a soul-work, a soul-document, that reveals, and thus helps make real, soul's internal self-negating transformation of itself and advances consciousness to a new status.

Yahweh Agrees with Job, After All

Immediately following Job's final words to Yahweh, there is an interesting brief *non sequitur* that seems to not make sense. Ever since chapter 3 in the book of Job, the writing style has been poetry, or poetic discourse. All the speeches are in a traditional Hebraic poetic form, and the narrator does not say much except to introduce each speaker. Now, after Job's final words, in which he brings Yahweh's light *and* dark totality to consciousness for both himself and Yahweh, after forty chapters of poetry, the poetic discourse breaks off and the narrator enters with the following words:

> After the LORD had spoken these words to Job, the LORD said to Eliphaz the Temanite ... (Job 42:7)

I will get to what Yahweh said to Eliphaz in a moment, but this introductory phrase gives the impression that the Lord has not heard a word of what Job just said. And instead of poetry, the prose narrative that framed the story in the beginning seems to reassert itself, and the book of Job comes to its conclusion quickly in only eleven more verses. Here's the puzzle: What words of the Lord is the narrator referring to? The words of the storm speech are the only words of Yahweh to Job so far, so could the narrator be referring to some words that are now missing? At this stage of the narrative, it would make more sense if the sentence were phrased, "After Job had spoken these words to the Lord, the Lord said to Eliphaz..."

This disjuncture in the text and the resulting dissonance lead some commentators to conclude that the prose frame represents an independent folk story: Included are the introduction of Job and the wager between Yahweh and the satan leading to his terrible misfortune in the first two chapters and the concluding prose narrative from 42:7–17, where Job's fortunes are restored. This means that the main part of the book, the many discourses between Job, his friends, and Yahweh, could be from another author; when the two were brought together, any inconsistencies were overlooked. Historical criticism suggests this possibility in its analysis, but that does not change the literary, theological, and psychological impact of the story as a whole, and its reception during two thousand plus years of the Judeo-Christian tradition and Western civilization. Further, what Yahweh goes on to say to Eliphaz the Temanite reveals that Yahweh is divided against himself, something we have seen now from the beginning; here it is in Job too. My focus holds the history of the text as one moment within the larger context of what the text suggests as it stands. Just as in a dream, where disparate and illogical contents occur side by side, the contiguity holds the meaning. In this case, Yahweh's next words to Eliphaz are,

> My wrath is kindled against you and against your two friends; for you have not spoken of me what is right, as my servant Job has. Now therefore take seven bulls and seven rams, and go to my servant Job, and offer up for yourselves a burnt offering; and my servant Job shall pray for you, for I will accept his prayer not to deal with you according to your folly; for you have not spoken of me what is right, as my servant Job has done. (Job 42:7–8)

Now, isn't this just like Yahweh, who is handicapped in relation to the *tender* emotions? Yahweh admits to Job that his perception of Yahweh is correct, but he does so by boiling up with rage against his friends and threatening to kill them. Yahweh agrees with Job, but gruffly and indirectly.

Traditional commentators think that Yahweh, in his reference to Job being right, is referring only to Job's final words, and especially verse 6, where Job supposedly says, "I despise myself and repent in dust and ashes." But why would these words make Job right and his friends wrong, if in fact they were encouraging Job to repent, and, so to speak, despise himself? This is true even if Yahweh's words of 42:7 are from the original frame story and do not have the entire collection of poetic dialogues in view, referring instead to the original view of Job as the icon of perfect piety and loyalty to God. What on earth did Job's friends do to warrant the murderous wrath of Yahweh? Such inconsistencies probably point to a now-unknown textual history, but the logic of historical criticism destroys the possibility of a meaning interior to the text as it is. Rather, for the psychological interpretation, the text's disjuncture and dissonance are about Yahweh himself. Yahweh is conflicted and contradicts himself. His entire speech to Job was one of power, self-aggrandizement, and denial that he might be culpable of anything in relation to Job; he stridently denied any moral responsibility. Thus, when the narrator's wording suggests that Yahweh was deaf to Job's final insight into his nature—and then in the next breath has Yahweh himself affirm and agree with Job's insight in the strongest possible terms—we see Yahweh shifting from unconsciousness to consciousness (so to speak) in the blink of an eye. I am reading the text not from the viewpoint of the human persons who composed and edited it (which they did), but from the viewpoint of the living truth of soul. Yahweh's struggle is with himself and his self-image: "Am I a Just god or not?" What the text shows here is that Yahweh shifts from his earlier one-sided ideal self-image to his new inclusive horrifying self-image in one sentence.

My interpretation reveals that Yahweh has in fact heard Job's complaint and that Job's moral judgment of Yahweh has penetrated Yahweh's self-knowledge. Yahweh's agreement that Job is right rather than his friends must include the entirety of the discourses in which Job repeatedly and unrelentingly presented the case for his innocence and challenged Yahweh to explain himself, contra his friends. I conclude that Yahweh listened most attentively. Otherwise, Yahweh's speech from the whirlwind and his now emotional outburst against the friends fall apart and make no sense (that is, the traditional interpretation is now senseless). The inconsistent vacillations of Yahweh are in fact the heart of his unity as the personification of soul's self-negating progression: On the one hand Yahweh negates Job's challenge, and then on the other, Yahweh negates his negation of Job, which is the negation of himself. Yahweh negates himself in favor of Job's insight that Yahweh is indeed the problem and that the satan is a permanent and irredeemable part of Yahweh. Job actually preserves Yahweh's unity, a terrible complex and problematic unity to be sure, which Job's insight has brought to a new level of consciousness. Yahweh's self-negation at the hands of Job is a further step in his undoing. Yahweh is in fact bringing himself to an end, for as a power (*elohim*), the power that was his—or better, that he *was*—is transferring to the human.

God's Autopsy and the Living Truth of Soul

For my psychological interpretation, the structural logic of consciousness itself, which Yahweh and Job represent, is changing.

Miles came to a similar conclusion using the language of winning and losing in this cosmic duel between Job and Yahweh:

> What is primary is whether or not God succeeds in forcing Job's attention away from God and back upon Job himself. If God can force Job somehow to stop blaming God and start blaming himself, God wins. If God cannot do that, God loses. In contemporary political language, the question is whether God can make his opponent the issue. Despite spectacular effort, God, in my judgment, fails in his attempt to do this, and Job becomes as a result the turning point in the life of God, *reading that life as a movement from self-ignorance to self-knowledge.*
>
> If God defeats Job, in short, Job ceases to be a serious event in the life of God, and God can forget about his garrulous upstart. But if Job defeats God, God can never forget Job, and neither can we. The creature having taken this much of a hand in creating his creator, the two are, henceforth, permanently linked.[19]

In the psychological interpretation, the idea of Job "defeating" God has to do with the evolution of the unconscious structure or syntax of consciousness in general. In this story, consciousness is initially presented as the "God is Just" position, the prevailing taken-for-granted cultural position of the time, which Job, his friends, and Yahweh all accepted. That was the unconscious or logical form of consciousness that the deity was, what the deity represented; the god *was* this truth. Then the satan entered and tossed this prevailing, comforting, and reassuring assumption up in the air. The appearance of the satan and the obscene wager was perhaps the first crack in the armor of Yahweh's then current self-image, shared by his human creatures. That state of affairs was still unconscious, still unseen, until it ran up against Job.

As a literary character, Job is obviously an ideal type. He is not a real human being but rather the personification of the thought that all is not right with the "God is Just" assumption. Job represents the negation of the prevailing form of consciousness. Job is the ideal innocent and guiltless subject of Yahweh, Yahweh's pride and joy, and so the wager between Yahweh and the satan cannot go unseen, cannot get past security, so to speak. Job is the inspector who will test Yahweh's actions. Unaware of the wager, Job sees no split between Yahweh and the satan. For Job, all good and all evil come from Yahweh. Thus, Yahweh cannot sneak anything past Job because Job will not, cannot, budge. Job is the philosophical premise, or the thought experiment, testing the "God is Just" notion. Job represents a new consciousness that soul is working toward, and Job's ideal status represents soul up against itself, forcing soul to become more conscious of itself, forcing consciousness to become conscious of its

---

19. Miles, *God*, 429–30, emphasis added.

disturbingly complex and dual nature, forcing it out into the open. Job, Yahweh, and the satan are of a piece, a dialectical unity of soul undergoing an internal transformation, with tremendous ramifications for soul's future. The direction in which soul is moving is reflected in Yahweh's historical development as a cultural phenomenon. *Yahweh* was that logical form of consciousness in which a social group, or civilization, existed, its public mind. By standing firm, Job forces soul, or Yahweh, to negate itself; it must now see itself as a more inclusive and complex unity. The original position of consciousness is negated when it becomes part of a new more comprehensive form of consciousness in the process of sublation. With the help of Job, Yahweh negates and sublates himself into a new larger comprehension of himself.

Not only does Yahweh agree with Job, but he atones to Job by way of a double restitution:

> And the LORD restored the fortunes of Job when he had prayed for his friends;
> and the LORD gave Job twice as much as he had before. (Job 42:10)

In spite of Yahweh's earlier power speech, in which he hardened his own heart against Job and denied Job a hearing, Job's insistent moral question did penetrate the consciousness, the heart, of Yahweh, and he feels some remorse and regret for how he has treated Job.[20] After Job's final words, reflecting Yahweh back to Yahweh as the terrible vision of unpredictable fairness *and* cruelty, giving rise to Job's "shudder with sorrow for mortal clay," Yahweh can no longer hide from himself. The mirror that is Job will not break, and Yahweh must stand there in its light, revealed in the totality of his truth, forever. Of course, the traditional interpretation insists that the story shows a deferential, humble, and repentant Job recanting his challenge to God, and finally at the close, God rewards him with a storied "happy ending." In this view, nothing would have changed, and most probably, if this really were the case, we would have to wonder why the story was remembered and preserved at all. But this view has come to an end. If the book of Job were merely a simple folk tale expressing a pious truism, it would have remained an isolated and forgotten piece of minor popular fiction. However, it became, and has remained, a profoundly troubling drama about fundamental truths. The fact that it was drawn into the canon of Yahweh's self-presentation and development cannot be avoided because it was supremely relevant to that development. Yahweh's double compensation to Job at the end is another indication Yahweh was affected and changed. Yahweh agreed with Job, after all.

For my psychological reading, the story of Job is a critical and central event in soul's autobiography. This psychological interpretation, aided by Miles's careful reading and translation, and founded in Giegerich's notion of psychology as the discipline

---

20. "Does the Lord also regret what he did? If the Lord has nothing to apologize for, and that is certainly his contention when he rebukes Job from the whirlwind, he would also have no reason to give Job 'twice what he had before' (Job 42:10). But as we saw in Second Isaiah, when the Lord promises double compensation, he implies that his own actions have gone too far. The Lord's action here, if not explicit repentance, is unmistakable atonement and implicit repentance" (Miles, *God*, 312).

of interiority (what I also call modern soul), is itself another step in the autopsy of God, tracing Yahweh's serial self-negations to their logical conclusion: Consciousness becoming aware of itself as consciousness.

Consciousness

This book, as God's autopsy and the living truth of soul, traces the historical unfolding logical form of consciousness, the logical form that structures consciousness during different eras. We are doing this by cutting into God's body, the Bible, and with new analytical interpretive tools, discovering new truths. At the beginning of the story of God's life, God created the tree of the knowledge of good and evil and prohibited the human creature from eating its fruit. That prohibition also prevented God from becoming conscious of the "knowledge of good and evil" because humankind is God's self-image; in his human reflection, God's life moves from "*self-ignorance to self-knowledge.*" Within the Creation story, we noticed that God was not fully conscious of his own creation because the serpent (created by God) spoke out and betrayed God's own prohibition, telling Eve, "You will not die; for God knows that when you eat of it your eyes will be opened, and you will be like gods, knowing good and evil" (Gen 3:4–5). Either God was lying (not tenable because God is not a person), or "God" represents one moment in soul's dialectical self-negating process. The serpent was an unconscious doubt in the mind of God that leaked out and negated God's original position (do not eat!) with a new position (eat!). This resulted in a far more complex relationship with his created self-image than Yahweh could have anticipated. Soul progresses through a process of self-negations, and these negations unfold throughout the biblical God's relationship with himself and with his created self-image, humankind. This is how the logical form of consciousness develops. It is soul's inexorable *telos*. But, soul's telos is not part of a formal teleology with a known goal because the future is unknowable. Soul is the roiling edge of now. Soul will continually negate itself into new forms, and find out where it is going by going. Soul creates itself in the moment, and the *future* is only a kind of untethered, abstract, and empty idea. Only in hindsight can soul's direction be provisionally detected, and this psychological interpretation is only one among many.

With Job a new kind of consciousness emerges, a *moral* consciousness. Job's moral stance within his integrity negates and sublates the prevailing power-dominant consciousness of the gods. The new moral consciousness emerges; the unconscious prevailing logical form of consciousness of the time undergoes a shift in the balance of power. Job is a new consciousness of the terrible truth of Yahweh, but not just for himself. As Miles affirms, "But the God who is seen in this vision is new not just for Job but also for God himself":

> The vision with which the Book of Job ends recognizes no principle operating independently of God, to which both divinity and humanity must submit. There is, in other words, no higher, impersonal synthesis beyond personal good and personal evil. The Lord God himself is ultimate in this vision, and therefore evil and good must be found simultaneously and personally in him if they are found anywhere. If Zephaniah rejects, as error, the claim "The Lord will do nothing, good or bad," the counterclaim, the scandalous truth the Book of Job places in evidence, is not "The Lord will do only good"; it is "The Lord will do good, and he will do ill." Within so hyperpersonalized a vision of ultimate reality as ancient Israel had, "the slings and arrows of outrageous fortune," as Hamlet calls them, are slung and shot by Shaddai himself.[21]

The phrase, "Within so hyperpersonalized a vision of ultimate reality as ancient Israel had," is a critically important historical perspective on soul's manifestation. We cannot, as we are wont to do today, abstract God, and thus extract God, out of the good-and-evil problem. A persistent unconscious, unquestioned theism runs through almost all conventional theology and official commentary on the Bible. For my interpretation, and for modernity in general, *God-is-dead* consciousness rules the day; but the prevailing theism that still dominates most notions of God is a whitewashed and domesticated "God is love," a "gracious God of goodness." This is an ahistorical God as it is purported to transcend temporal limits, to exist outside of time, and beyond our human judgments. As the simplistic argument goes, it is not God who changes, but human perception or consciousness of God. This is one way the now obsolete theological and metaphysical categories of omnipotence, omniscience, the absolute, the infinite, and the eternal creep uncritically back into thinking about God. When these now illegitimate, that is, unsublated categories impose themselves, any sense of the truly historical (thus changing) character of Yahweh is lost, along with the historical character of soul. Yahweh *was* the soul-truth of his time and place, the way soul manifested itself, the "hyperpersonalized vision of ultimate reality." If the *historical* truth of soul (and Yahweh) is not recognized, then the revolutionary significance of Job for consciousness is irretrievably lost.

As Job calls out the Lord's cruelty, he is the mirror reflecting the truth of the Lord's cruelty to the Lord himself. Because of Job, the Lord knows something about himself that he did not know before. Not that God was not cruel before, but now he—and we—*know* that cruelty really is part of his essence, and because of this new crack in the nature of things, he cannot be trusted. That humankind is God's self-image is a psychological truth (interpretation) given by the Bible itself. Therefore, knowledge gained by humanity is knowledge gained by God. A new dimension of consciousness of and for the Lord has emerged with Job. The innocence of the Lord and the innocence of Job have shattered. The emotional power of Job's final realization might sound something like this:

---

21. Miles, *God*, 327.

God's Autopsy and the Living Truth of Soul

> I had heard about you secondhand [it is assumed you are fair], but now I have experienced your terrible truth directly [your unreasonable cruelty]. You are a cruel and savage monster, and I am terrified and grieve for humankind.

A new soul-truth emerged and everything changed, but this change was on the logical level of soul. It still had a long way to go to work itself out in empirical cultural consciousness. From the perspective of this psychological interpretation, first soul changes, goes through a negation and sublation, and then gradually works its way into the real as manifest cultural truth.

The book of Job is traditionally a theological text, and in the older traditional sense, a revelatory text, a text from God and inspired by God. My psychological interpretation does not read the text in terms of God, but rather as soul's speech about itself, which self-consciously places God and Job in the historical evolution of consciousness. The conventional theological meaning within which suffering has been contained has also kept God in the right and humankind in the wrong. In this equation, God and the human person are not equals by any means—God is viewed as the great cosmic parent and humankind is the lesser dependent child.

From the psycho-logical point of view, the book of Job is not a meditation on, nor an answer to, the problem of human suffering. It is rather an expression of a fundamental transformation of soul, of a deeper, collective consciousness. A human person stands up to and challenges the collective form of consciousness personified by *Yahweh*. The human creature begins to balance the equation, calling the prevailing idea of God into question. Job represents the logic of human consciousness beginning to outgrow its "child of God" status, moving toward becoming an adult on its own terms (which will take another two thousand years). Again, this is a modern psycho-logical interpretation, and not an interpretation that would have made sense two thousand five hundred years ago in its ancient context. Today we can interpret the narrative of Job as a move of consciousness in which a man stays true to himself and questions the essence of God. Both God and the man are changed as a result.

The value of the book of Job lies in how it articulates a controversy and contradiction that were hidden at the very core of deity and had remained invisible to consciousness. The satan and Yahweh, taken together and understood as Yahweh's doubt about himself and humankind, represent a general doubt soul was having about itself, one that was generating controversial ideas and gathering steam in antiquity. The story of Job raised the question in dramatic fashion, making it visible to thought: What is the real nature of the gods who bring suffering, trauma, and tragedy to the innocent, who have done nothing to deserve it? The traditional reading of Job's retreat to self-loathing is the triumph of conventional piety (then and now) over the undeniable question that was growing, and continues to grow, inexorably louder.

Psycho-logically, with Job's insight, soul sublates an aspect of itself—the power of the gods to dominate consciousness—into the power of humankind to know another truth: that the gods are not consistent, predictable, and above all, not trustworthy. The fact that the randomness of human suffering is now a *known* attribute of the God weakens the Gods' power; it weakens the assumed authority of the prevailing powers (gods). Although the text never says so explicitly, Job in effect is saying to the Lord, "Now I see more clearly than ever that Satan is your partner in crime." The logic here is that Job's consciousness, as God's self-image, is also God's consciousness. I am not talking about Job and God as real entities, but rather as literary manifestations of consciousness gaining a new consciousness of itself; using the mythological language of the Bible, this results in the silencing of God. In the Tanakh, after Job, God never speaks again. It is as if the traditional syntax of consciousness has been silenced, and the silence continues through to the end of the Tanakh, an image, perhaps, of this new troubling thought contemplating itself in the background. God has always been a problem to himself, self-contradictory, self-conflicted, and yet also with a direction, seeking something. Job adds a new dimension of consciousness to the problem of God, which continued to work on itself in antiquity using the language (and meanings) it had at its disposal, the language of gods and God, messiahs and christs, and their continual transformation as soul's historical progressive self-negations (sublations).

In the next chapter, Yahweh will undergo a profound transformation necessitated again by historical forces beyond his control, a negation and sublation, that leaves him unrecognizable. Another empire, Rome, turns its massive military powers against the Jewish people and their God, forcing soul to turn and reinterpret itself in an entirely new direction.

Afterthought

And, then sometimes, it is put ever so succinctly:[22]

Pearls Before Swine © 2017 Stephan Pastis. Reprinted by permission of Andrews McMeel Syndication. All rights reserved.

22. *San Francisco Chronicle*, October 5, 2017, section E, "Datebook," 15.

Chapter 7

Yahweh Kills Himself, Christ Sublates the Flesh

Consciousness Tackles the Impossibility of Incarnation

> He saw the heavens torn apart and the Spirit descending.
> —MARK 1:10

> The curtain of the temple was torn in two, from top to bottom.
> —MARK 15:38

WHEN GOD CHANGES, THE constitution of consciousness itself changes. In antiquity, God and the gods were the ground and the overall context of life and meaning. They were not simply intellectual ideas inside the minds of humankind. They were the shape or form of the Mind of humankind. I am tracing the historical transformations of the *shape* of public mind represented by the Judeo-Christian tradition. When Job faced off with God, it was not just, as in Miles's words, that God lost and Job won, and then they could go on and have another contest and see who won the next round like some sports teams. When God "lost," it was a transformation of the logical form of consciousness. When Job's integrity stood absolute in the face of God's cruelty and revealed that cruelty, the syntax of consciousness that God represented was transformed throughout. It was not simply an aspect of God that was changed or altered; the God-form of consciousness was irrevocably altered through and through. It is interesting to note that Job was a perfectly innocent man who suffered horribly for no apparent reason, which reminds us of the suffering slave in Isaiah, as well as a kind of prefiguration of the Christ, a wholly innocent man who suffers horribly. But Job does prefigure soul's movement toward the Christ drama insofar as the Job drama altered the equation of power between deity and humankind. Job's moral superiority over God tilts, just enough, the power equation in favor of humankind. The *I Am* of Yahweh begins its journey to leave Yahweh and locate itself in the human subject as its *I am*. We will see this tilt take a quantum shift with the idea of the *incarnation* and, over centuries, the incarnation gradually becomes dominant in soul's thought of itself.

The Christian story continues soul's autobiography, soul speaking about itself, soul negating and sublating itself. Just as Yahweh was soul's form of a new emergent mode of consciousness, the transformation of the logical form of consciousness, so also was Jesus Christ. My focus is on the *Christ* as the symbol of a changing logic of consciousness, which involves the negation of Yahweh and the emergence of a completely new truth, *incarnation*. For the Christian view of reality, Jesus Christ was the full incarnation of God, that God was a fully human man, which presented a special problem for the mind of antiquity and, for different reasons, still confounds the modern mind. The Christian view creates a thorny and confusing dilemma for the modern mind because the modern mind has a very different understanding of *history* than the mind of antiquity. It is precisely the point of view of modern soul, as it recognizes the historical differences between forms of consciousness, that enables us to understand what Jesus Christ meant for soul two thousand years ago. I will clarify what is at stake between the ancient and modern mind's thinking about Jesus and how the logic of modernity confuses contemporary thinking in relation to the purported historical claims about Jesus Christ. For my purposes, however, the existence or not of a historical man Jesus is irrelevant. It is the texts themselves viewed as soul-documents that reveal the psychological truth of the changing syntax of consciousness, and the very substantial reality of the *syntax of consciousness* is my concern. I will focus on the incarnation as a once-upon-a-time *living idea* of consciousness, for the *living ide*a is the lifeblood of the living truth of soul. The historical person of Jesus, in our modern sense of historical person, was never an interest of Christianity (until the modern period). Rather, the entire focus of the gospel stories and the christological arguments of the first several centuries of early Christianity was on the meaning and significance of the new category of incarnation, which combined the general *categories* of God and man in a new and unheard of way, profoundly changing both in the process. I approach the figure of Christ, the incarnation, and the christological arguments from the perspective of soul speaking about itself. Christianity was an emergent consciousness during late antiquity and had a particular historical soul-meaning at its time. Although Christianity still exists in various forms today, it has no meaning for soul any longer. Soul has no use for Christianity today as its historical work developing a new syntax of consciousness was achieved long ago. Christianity, as a real soul truth, or a true soul presence, was finished by the time of the emergence of the Enlightenment (mid-1600s), if not before. My continuing autopsy of the *God* phenomenon aims to understand how and why this happened.

The Unusual Christian Position

Christianity's special problem presents itself in terms of a remarkable distinction between Yahweh and Christ. No one thinks that Yahweh was a human person walking around on earth, or that he had a human mother and father and siblings. Christianity, however, claims just that for its Christ. According to Christian doctrine, Jesus Christ was a human person who was born like all human babies and died just like all human adults, although it is true that both his birth and death, as told in the biblical stories, were indeed special non-ordinary events. Christianity also insists that Jesus Christ was God, that he was *the* incarnation of the one true God, so that the person of Jesus Christ was the full presence of God, walking, talking, and relating pretty much like any other human person. However, Jesus, as God, was capable of doing things that the ordinary person would find impossible.

Here are three examples of the Christ's extraordinary abilities that are generally well known:

1. He turned the water in six large stone water jars at a wedding in Cana of Galilee into wine, over 120 gallons, and very good wine at that (John 2:1–10).

2. He brought a dear friend of his, Lazarus, who had been dead and entombed for four days, back to life (John 11:1–44).

3. He walked on the water of the sea of Galilee during a storm and also calmed the storm (John 6:16–21 / Mark 6:47–51).

Such miraculous and supernatural actions on the part of Jesus appear throughout the gospels, and they clearly mark him as a man apart from the ordinary. These actions show Jesus' power over the natural world and ordinary existence, but they are never the gratuitous magic tricks of a human person. Within the narrative, they serve to reveal the glory of God and God's special relation with Jesus Christ, and they especially serve to identify Jesus with Yahweh, for it was Yahweh (i.e., God) who previously had decisive and absolute power over the natural world, as well as life and death. For the psychological perspective, the non-ordinary events, whether performed by a man or a god, do not raise questions about the laws of physics and whether or not such things are possible. Such modern rational questions that critique the theological reading of the Bible are what paved the way for the psychological reading. For my reading, however, the rational conundrums are left behind because reading the Bible as a dream allows us to use completely different categories (consciousness instead of physics). All the non-ordinary events depicted in the gospel stories point to the main non-ordinary event of the incarnation. This is the central idea-event I am concerned with in coming to terms with Christianity as one of the stages of soul's self-transformation. To repeat, I am not reading the biblical text as a historical record of actual past events, but as a soul-document symbolically depicting soul's (i.e., consciousness's) historical development.

The Septuagint

It is well known that developing Christian thought was heavily influenced by Greek philosophy, but it is less well known that Jewish thought had come under the pervasive Hellenizing influence that permeated the greater Mediterranean area. In the late fourth century BCE, Alexander the Great displaced the Persian empire and brought Greek culture and language to the Middle East. The Greek language eventually became the *lingua franca* of an extensive Greek empire. During the second century BCE, the Hebrew scriptures, already translated into Aramaic, were translated into Greek in the city of Alexandria, Egypt, where there was a large Jewish population and everyone spoke Greek. This edition of the Tanakh, as it was more than a translation, became known as the Septuagint.[1] Almost all Jews throughout this Greek empire, themselves thoroughly imbued with Greek culture, came to consider the Septuagint their sacred scripture, the word of God.

This is important for my perspective because Christianity was originally a purely Jewish development, a Jewish idea, a Jewish vision. All the New Testament writers, except perhaps the author of Luke's gospel and Acts, were Jewish, and all the New Testament writings were in Greek. The context of the New Testament writings was the Jewish scriptures, as the New Testament explicitly saw itself as the completion and fulfillment of the unfinished business of the Tanakh. The text of the Tanakh that the New Testament writers had access to was the Septuagint. However, the unfinished business of the Tanakh was Yahweh's unfinished business, really another failure, which was his centuries-long unfulfilled promise to restore Israel's national sovereignty. Christianity was soul's solution to this problem through a radical transformation of Yahweh himself. In this new soul-form of consciousness, Yahweh became a new and unheard of integration as a God-man entity, and this included the interpenetration of Jewish and Greek thought.

At the end of Job and the Tanakh itself, we found that Yahweh went silent and became increasingly remote. In the Septuagint, as well as the New Testament, the Greek word *theós* replaces all references to Yahweh and *kyrios* replaces the word *Lord*. In other words, the hot-tempered, emotional, and intensely personal Yahweh who erupts so powerfully from the pages of the Tanakh is gradually replaced by a Greek conception of a God who is more of an idealized abstract principle, far removed from the human world, a fully transcendent deity.

The Name Christ and Its Internal Contradiction

In the New Testament, the name that becomes prominent is Jesus and Jesus Christ. The word *christ* however is neither Jesus' last name nor a proper noun. Christ is the Greek word for the Hebrew word *messiah*, and quite technically the designation

---

1. Septuagint means "seventy," and is abbreviated as LXX. A legend states it was the work of seventy translators. See also, Miles, *Christ*, 257–58.

should be "Jesus the Christ." It is, of course, usage over centuries that triumphs, not grammatical correctness. "Christ Jesus" is another common form. The real point is that Jesus became the Christ so completely and thoroughly that the words Jesus and Christ became synonymous and interchangeable. What has become in Christian society so familiar and common was, in its original Jewish context, utterly shocking and even outrageous. In the Tanakh, a messiah was a king, literally meaning "the anointed one," and the king was a warrior anointed by God. Moses was the original messiah, as well as king and priest, although he never had these titles explicitly, and Joshua was the warrior who inherited Moses' mantle for the push into the promised land, while David and Solomon were the preeminent anointed kings of Israel. Yahweh himself was messiah in his warrior identity, and all these historical warrior types, Israel's great heroes, glorified the identity associated with messiah. The messiah, either as Yahweh, or as an anointed king, was the rescuer, the savior, of the *nation* of Israel, the one who would restore national autonomy and the truth of the One True God.

It may be difficult for us to keep in mind that the *nation* of Israel was not simply a political idea or identity, but rather the *nation of Israel* and the *truth of the One True God* were identical concepts, identical truths. In their ancient context, one does not exist without the other. The Christian messiah (Jesus Christ), in shocking and really unbelievable contrast, was the exact opposite of the Jewish version because he was a crucified messiah! A helpless, defeated, dead messiah. There was absolutely no room in Yahweh's self-understanding for such an idea, such an identity. The revolutionary reversal of the idea of messiah, however, led to the Christ of Christianity as a king and a conqueror, but not in the expected terms of military and political freedom for Israel, then living under the oppressive conditions of the Roman empire. No, Christianity inaugurated an entirely new quality of consciousness, which was, in its terms, a spiritual kingdom not of this (material) world. The Christian christ/messiah is the complete contradiction, from within, of the Jewish messiah. That is, the Jewish messiah, that is, Yahweh, negates itself as he/it transforms itself into the Christian christ.

The Christian christ symbolized a significant shift in the syntax of consciousness, the logical form of consciousness, that was mythologically expressed as the "salvation of the world." Psychologically, the idea of *world* is a symbol for consciousness, that general consciousness that constitutes our world, the world in which we actually live as beings of language, culture, and meaning. Psychologically, the "salvation of the world" symbolizes the transformation of the syntax of consciousness. Christianity and the Christ represent a revolutionary change of soul's logic because the warrior god Yahweh undergoes a fatal and final transformation.

Yahweh's (Literacy's) Hope for Worldly Dominion

Yahweh had been the living idea that represented the syntax of consciousness embodied by those people who gathered under the name Israel. The messianic impulse embodied by Yahweh was the revolutionary logical form of consciousness that emerged as literacy. As Yahweh, the form of consciousness became literate and historical, soul's impulse for its own emancipation from its not-conscious embeddedness in the natural world. The impulse of literacy (emancipation) expressed itself in an expansive imperative that gathered the whole world to itself, as expressed in the following from Isaiah:

> Assemble yourselves and come
>   together,
>   draw near, you survivors of the
>   nations!
> They have no knowledge—
>   those who carry about their
>   wooden idols,
> and keep on praying to a god
>   that cannot save.
> Declare and present your case;
>   let them take counsel together!
> Who told this long ago?
>   Who declared it of old?
> Was it not I, the Lord?
>   There is no other god besides
>   me,
> a righteous God and a Savior;
>   there is no one besides me.
>
> Turn to me and be saved,
>   all the ends of the earth!
>   For I am God, and there is
>   no other.
> By myself I have sworn,
>   from my mouth has gone forth
>   in righteousness
>   a word that shall not return:
> "To me every knee shall bow,
>   every tongue shall swear." (Isa 45:20–23)

and,

> I will give you as a light to the
>   nations,
>   that my salvation may reach to
>   the end of the earth. (Isa 49:6b)

On the ground as it were, the empirical expression of soul's impulse took the form of the longing of both Yahweh and Israel for independence, a real political-social national identity and the freedom to live and worship God on their own terms. And most especially, *political* freedom also meant freedom from the intrusion of the other goddesses and gods. Yahweh—the core, singular intention of Yahweh—was to be the One and Only God of the Israelites, and, eventually, of the whole world. The assumption was that the intent would be realized as a concrete social-political reality, a real national existence under the rule of the One True God. Of course, this did not happen in terms of its concrete social expectation, but, if we look around today, literacy (as a form of consciousness) indeed has conquered the world.

Christianity, on the other hand, took the impulse of literacy and historicity in a new direction. It both subverted and sublated the Yahweh intent for concrete national sovereignty. Soul negated itself again, as Christ was the sublated Yahweh, the idea of messiah turned upside down and inside out. With what I will broadly call the Christ-event of the first century of the Common Era, the fierce warrior god Yahweh took another decisive step in the process of negating himself again. Yahweh became a completely new kind of messiah in the form of the Christian Christ, and he created this new form by crucifying and killing himself, resurrecting himself, and inaugurating a new world, which was a new logical form of consciousness, known then as the incarnation, "the Word made flesh." And, what could be a more fitting symbolic expression of the literacy impulse than the *Word* becoming *flesh*?

The Christian *Flesh* Abstracted

Throughout the Tanakh, Yahweh creates himself by cutting himself off from his nature-god manifestation, becoming a spirit God who transcended the natural world. Through that manifestation as Yahweh, soul (the syntax of consciousness) went through a revolutionary transformation. As represented by the New Testament, that very same Yahweh who had cut himself off from nature now underwent another revolutionary self-negation (transformation). The Christ was the Divine Logos (Word) become flesh, the incarnation. However, through an unusual inner contradiction, the *flesh* of the Incarnate Christ was, in a sense, evaporated in a higher level of abstract differentiation, symbolized in the New Testament texts by both the resurrection and the ascension. Resurrection and ascension are not about a biological body or a material world. While they have to do with a raising up (Christ was the Risen One), what is raised up is the *conception* of the world itself; a new higher status of consciousness emerges and changes our world, the syntax of consciousness. It took about three to four hundred years from the time the New Testament writings appeared for the idea of the incarnation to *think* itself through and establish itself as the ground of a new fundamental cosmic reality.

The logic of Yahweh-consciousness reordered itself so that the reality of flesh was sublated into the reality of spirit. And spirit is of mind and thought, not the body politic. I read the Christian "crucifixion of the *body*" as the crucifixion of the religious-political hope that Yahweh would defeat imperial Rome in the same way that he had defeated Pharaoh and the Egyptian army, restoring Israel's sovereignty as a nation. That hope was burning in the Jewish heart. It was explicitly voiced by Jesus' followers, when, after the resurrection, they asked, "Lord, is this the time when you will restore the kingdom to Israel?" (Acts 1:6) In the following scene in Acts the risen Christ speaks, and his answer to their question effectively negates the hope for national sovereignty nurtured by centuries of Yahweh's promises. Jesus' answer is ambiguous and evasive, and as he speaks of the spirit, he becomes spirit himself:

> "It is not for you to know the times or periods that the Father has set by his own authority. But you will receive power when the Holy Spirit has come upon you; and you will be my witnesses in Jerusalem, in all Judea and Samaria, and to the ends of the earth." When he had said this, as they were watching, he was lifted up, and a cloud took him out of their sight. (Acts 1:7–9)

The Word that became flesh (Christ) is lifted up, into a cloud and out of sight. These are images of *meaning*, embodied as language, rising to another level of abstraction (literacy/writing). Of course, these are pictorial and narrative symbols intuitively expressed by these texts. Psychology attempts to *think* these images and reveal them as the thoughts they were, giving voice to a new form of consciousness. Psychology cannot take the images at face value, and asks what *meaning* (thought) is saying about itself as a new form of *meaning* (thought).

Throughout the New Testament writings, the Jewish (and thus Yahweh's) longing for a concrete political kingdom is often the foil against which the Christ teaches that his kingdom will not conform to the deeply held hope:

> Once Jesus was asked by the Pharisees [Jewish religious authorities] when the kingdom of God was coming, and he answered, "The kingdom of God is not coming with things that can be observed; nor will they say 'Look, here it is!' or 'There it is!' For, in fact, the kingdom of God is among [or within] you." (Luke 17:20–21)

The Christ event shifted the logic of traditional expectations. The logic of chronological time, of a literal expectation, was negated, and the expectation of a bodily (political, military) solution was dissolved. The *body* of (concrete) hope for national sovereignty was itself irretrievably crucified, pulverized, and destroyed. The resurrection is not really a *bodily* resurrection, not the resuscitation of a corpse, but the emergence (appearance) of a new idea and a new truth. The new idea is as *real* as the body is real, but not as a political corporal reality. The text states Christ, in his bodily form, was lifted up and absorbed by the clouds of heaven, and he disappeared from sight. The *reality* the body symbolizes has been sublated into another logical form of consciousness that is just as real. The *body*, so to speak, has been lifted up into the air, and become air, evaporated into spirit. This reality is not visible to the natural eye but is accessible to the mind's eye, the eye of spirit. The activity the Christ expects of his disciples is their proclamation of the new transformed logic of consciousness, which took the form of the new truth of the *reality* of the crucified-resurrected Christ. Through the Christian phenomenon, Yahweh transformed himself to such an extent, negated himself so thoroughly, that he also disappeared, completely absorbed into the Christ story, as far as soul was concerned.[2] Soul had taken a wholly unexpected turn. The Word (soul's new emancipated form) continues its journey of abstraction (self-liberation).

The Christian truth asserting itself was incarnation: Jesus Christ was one hundred percent God and one hundred percent man, simultaneously united and distinct. The opening lines of the book of John (written around 100 CE) declare the new state of affairs as already accomplished:

> In the beginning was the Word [logos], and the Word was with God, and the Word was God. He was in the beginning with God. All things came into being through him, and without him not one thing came into being. What has come into being in him was life, and the life was the light of all people. The light shines in the darkness, and the darkness did not overcome it. (John 1:1–5)

The text continues, identifying Jesus Christ with the Word; as Word (Greek, *logos*), Jesus *was* God, and like God, uncreated. They were coequal and equally primordial. Yet, while Jesus Christ was of the same substance, same essence, as God, and while they were the same yet distinct, the new idea of the incarnation swallowed Yahweh and thoroughly digested the Yahweh form of consciousness. However, in the Christian story, Christ *is* God. Therefore, Yahweh swallowed himself, thoroughly digested himself, and trans-formed himself into a new form, both beyond and inclusive of his former self. That new form was the Christ as the crucified-resurrected messiah.

The thought "Yahweh swallowed himself" could not have been imagined or pictured in the mythology of its time. It is a thought we can have today, but still, it must be thought (not imagined). This is a ouroboric thought in which an idea (Yahweh) turns in on itself, negates itself, and becomes a new (sublated) thought, which, as embodied in the Tanakh, had already seen glimmers of itself. Perhaps the New Testament narrative was the best way that soul could think this thought in its given time and place, through the intuitive images and stories it had at its disposal, with Yahweh, messiahs, and christs going through a kind of implosion (using the extreme contradiction of the *crucified* messiah).

The entire history of Yahweh, the entire narrative of the Tanakh, was absorbed and reinterpreted in the light of the incarnation. Christ sublated Yahweh, or better,

---

2. Of course, the Yahweh of the Tanakh still existed for the Jews, but soul, in my view, following the historical trajectory of Western consciousness, was leaving the form of Yahweh behind.

Yahweh Kills Himself, Christ Sublates the Flesh

Yahweh sublated himself as the process of soul's self-negation, and the result became Christ. This was an autonomous historical soul process, not the intentional doing of early church fathers, politicians, theologians, or Roman emperors, although all these persons played a role in the cultural movement of the syntax of consciousness. Soul, in the form of cultural ferment, thinks its own thoughts, and those thoughts are what animate the heart of culture as a soul-project. The *idea* of incarnation thought itself into existence, using human persons as the medium of its thinking. *Jesus Christ* represented a new category of consciousness that absorbed the former category that was Yahweh. The very substance of God, the metaphysical truth and foundation of reality, was undergoing a revolutionary change, which created an inherent conflict between the new Christ and the prevailing Yahweh:

> He was in the world, and the world came into being through him; yet the world did not know him. He came to what was his own, and his own people did not accept him. But to all who received him, who believed in his name, he gave power to become children of God, who were born, not of blood or of the will of the flesh or of the will of man, but of God. (John 1:10–13)

The essence of Yahweh was preserved, but his form was changed so radically he no longer recognized, or comprehended, himself. From the point of view of the changing syntax of consciousness, the phrases "the world did not know him" and "his own people did not accept him" symbolize the radical rupture in the syntax of consciousness that was Christianity. In the gospels in general, and especially in the book of John, it is usually the Jewish authorities, but also the Jews in general, who reject the Christ and the new truth that the Christ represents. But for the psychological reading, the "Jews" in those early soul documents symbolize the prevailing Yahweh form of consciousness that could not recognize the new form of consciousness represented by the Christ. I do not take the Jews, the Christ, and Yahweh here as actual people or religious entities, as this is soul's dream of itself I am interpreting. Instead, these religious figures symbolize soul's development as the syntax of consciousness, undergoing negations and transformations on the impersonal cultural level. As representative of the former structure of consciousness, or syntax of consciousness, Yahweh was not able to recognize the new form, the new syntax, and the idea of "the Jews" functioned as the literary personification of the conflict between the old and new logic of consciousness. The shift of logical status is also indicated by the distinction between those born of the flesh (natural and material) and those born of God (abstract and spirit).

The *flesh* and *body* associated with the incarnate Christ, insisted upon by the Christian truth, were neither biological nor material in nature. *Flesh* and *body* were in fact theological concepts performing a theological function, establishing the realness of the location of the idea of incarnation. From my vantage point, the incarnate flesh and body are psychological concepts because they have to do with a new development of soul. They point to the transformation of the nature of reality itself, insofar as our reality is shaped by the logical form of consciousness.

The *living idea* that was Christ, the "Word become flesh," had the power to bestow a new status on human persons, who would be *born* as such from God, and not of blood, flesh, or man. The new *world* (spiritual, not material) was not of this world (flesh), and yet it was through the so-called flesh that the Word was creating its new status as unfleshed. The incarnation contained an inner contradiction, in that although Yahweh was said to have become a human person, incarnate, the kingdom he spoke of now was not a political kingdom but one of spirit. The so-called flesh of the Christ is itself a *flesh* not of this world, and it represents a new reality, a new status of consciousness. In this sense, as the Word became flesh, the flesh became Word, that is, it was sublated into a noetic *substance* having to do with the new status of spirit, mind, and consciousness.[3]

Truth Creates Itself

The performative and right-now process that is soul takes place among real historical people, and the changes of soul are worked out—or we should say, acted out—in the social cultural context. But the changes themselves are not really about people at all, but about soul changing its form. Another way to think of soul is as *implicit* (unconscious) shared public *meaning*. It is the basic structure of *meaning*, or the orientation of *meaning* that changes throughout history. It is not individual and personal consciousness that changes at first; rather the general background form of consciousness, the syntax of consciousness, the basis of truth itself, is undergoing a transformation. It infects and grips many who do not really understand why this is *the truth*:

> And the Word became flesh and lived among us, and we have seen his glory,
> the glory as of a father's only son, full of grace and truth. (John 1:14)

The new truth was self-evident. It had already happened, or was already happening, and the declaration that the "Word became flesh" was simply stating what was already known, that the glory, grace, and truth of the enfleshed Word, the Father's only Son, was already *the truth*. For the people within whom this idea came alive, this new truth was a gripping reality that could not be denied. It was like being infected by an inner knowing. In general, during its earliest stages, no one voluntarily converted to Christianity who was not already pregnant with the idea of the reality of the new Christ, inchoate as it might have been (in the early years, there were many christianities). When culture changes, many people have an incipient sense of an emergent new worldview that remains unarticulated until others find a way to give voice to what is a fundamental new consciousness. Such were the gospel stories about the Christ. The gospels, especially the book of John, would have addressed not the conscious level of

---

3. Thanks to Harry Henderson for this particular turn of insight. Personal communication.

individuals, but the already present, implicit, and unarticulated emergent living idea that was, so to speak, in the air.

The Christ event, or the incarnation, was far more radical than what had happened in the Job story. With Job, Yahweh was shaken and changed, but he was still Yahweh. With Christ, soul's logical life completes a transformation that had begun hundreds of years earlier, and an entirely new logical form of consciousness emerges. The Christ phenomenon was another historical step, in narrative and theological form, of soul's ongoing push away from its embeddedness in nature and myth, becoming word and thought. But, the real problem for soul, for consciousness thinking about itself, was how the incarnation was to be understood. It took hundreds of years for this one idea to think itself to a satisfactory self-understanding.

The notion of the incarnation forced the previously unthinkable, the complete union of God and a man, to generate conflicting fresh and novel ideas, and through that conflict to establish a new sense of ultimate reality. The incarnation would change the ontological ground of the *real*. The incarnation was not simply a new human intellectual idea in the history of ideas sense; it was much more than simply another content of consciousness. The incarnation was soul's transformation of its very constitution, which came about through the unification of what were incompatible categories, God and Man: A new truth creating itself.

The idea of Jesus Christ as the incarnate God was, at its time, brand new, and yet, this new idea was such that it rewrote the entire history of the world from the beginning and posited itself as the origin of the world. The opening lines of John's gospel establish the Christ's own origin myth. It simply and directly asserts the Word's original being, and the Word's unity and identity as God, such that God is fundamentally changed. At the beginning of Genesis Yahweh posited himself as unique and original in his own right, without dependence and non-derivative; he set himself up as the enemy of the nature gods and the enemy of himself as a nature god. So, the new form of consciousness, "Jesus Christ," posits himself as unique and original, and his *enemy* is the Yahweh-consciousness, personified as the *Jews* in various ways.

I want to be clear that the terms *Jews* and *Pharisees*, as they were depicted in the gospels, are for me psychological, or soul, terms that refer to soul's prior logical form as Yahweh, from which soul pushed off. For my psychological reading, the Jews and Pharisees were the symbolic representations of the former logical form of consciousness that simply could not, because of its logical constitution, comprehend the new logical form of Christ. Yahweh was the former syntax. Jesus Christ, as the new syntax, brought Yahweh into the new syntax as a semantic content and narratively acted out that change by making the Jews the enemy of the Christ. The *idea* of the Jews symbolized the old form of consciousness, or the old syntax, which could not grasp the new consciousness, or syntax, that Christ represented. These were the narrative masks soul adopted, so to speak, in order to articulate this stage of its self-negation and self-creation. Tragically, although soul's changes are impersonal, human persons experience them as intensely personal, often with fatal consequences. Soul has no interest in killing people—actually it is not interested in people at all—and yet, people unconsciously act out the changing logic of soul and kill each other over the differences in soul-consciousness. The changing face of truth has, it seems, both unintentional deadly and liberating consequences for human beings. But truth itself does not have human beings in view; it is concerned only with its own logical life, its project of self-creation.

The Impossibility of Incarnation

Two thousand years ago, during late antiquity when the rule of the nature gods and goddesses was fading, the problem the newly emergent Christian truth presented was understanding what exactly the notion of incarnation meant. Over the first several hundred years there were plural christianities with conflicting ideas about that truth. The christological arguments were life-and-death disputes over essential concepts that, as universals, were concrete realities. God was the foundation of truth and reality, and how God was to be thought in the light of the incarnation became a special problem for soul. The christological controversies were arguments soul was having with itself about its new constitution, its new logical form. The primary and fundamental category with which soul thought about itself and expressed itself had been exclusively devoted to gods and God. Now soul had to include another category at this most fundamental level, the category of man, the human person. This, for many, was unacceptable.

Celsus, a second-century Greek philosopher in the tradition of Plato and a critic of Christianity, asserted that the supreme God was utterly transcendent. He argued that God "cannot have created the body, or indeed anything mortal, and only Soul can have come from Him directly; and the idea of His coming down to men must be rejected as involving a change in Him, and a change necessarily for the worse."[4] For the prevailing consciousness of antiquity, along with the influence of Platonism, the idea of God and the idea of Man did not mix and could not cohere into a unity by definition. In antiquity, a god could take human form for a moment in order to impart a teaching or a lesson, or to inspire. As an example, in the book of Joshua, as Joshua was approaching Jericho, "he looked up and saw a man standing before him with a drawn sword in his hand." When Joshua asked him who he was, he answered, "As commander of the army of the Lord I have now come" (Josh 5:13–15). Joshua immediately fell on his face in worship knowing he was Yahweh/God. To further emphasize the identity of this figure with God, he said to Joshua, "Remove the sandals from your feet, for the place where you stand is holy," recalling Yahweh's command to Moses

---

4. Kelly, *Early Christian*, 20.

at the burning bush. The commander of the army of the Lord is the Lord (Yahweh) himself, but this was a temporary apparition.

The incarnate Word, the Christ, was something entirely different, not simply of magnitude, but an entirely new ultimate category that would indeed change the nature of reality. The Christian form of the messiah, Christ, was not a temporary apparition, but the permanent indivisible unity, yet distinctness, of God and Man. This was an entirely new concept, a radically new notion about the nature of God and the nature of humankind, because it stated that both God and humankind had changed in a fundamental way, but what was changing was the logical form of consciousness. With the incarnation, ultimate reality and truth had taken on an unheard of new form, that of a man, while also being wholly God. Soul's thinking this new thought was a painful struggle that took centuries.

Again, the Rift between Ancient and Modern Consciousness

There truly is a radical difference between the consciousness of antiquity and our (taken-for-granted) modern consciousness. I explored this difference in the chapter on Abraham and archaic soul. Here I hope to deepen our appreciation of this difference as it is central to understanding the meaning of incarnation in late antiquity. The consciousness of antiquity was grounded in divinity, God, and the gods as original and final causes and the foundation of what was real. Ideas themselves had a substantial reality that is hard for us to grasp; ideas for us are simply personal thoughts, and quite insubstantial at that. Plato's notion of ideal forms is a good example of the ancient form of consciousness. In his thinking, all material things are but imperfect and shadowy manifestations of an original perfect form that exists in a real realm that is accessible to the mind. The ideal forms are the *universals* that are really real, while we and the world of things are the *particulars*, which are but shadows or mere reflections of the universal original form. The *ideas*, and the gods, were the true *substance* of reality, in Greek known as the *hypostasis*, or, "that which stands under." The substance of reality, which stood under all appearances, was true and real, and all appearances depended on it. Things and people, as the *particulars*, did not have any truth in themselves but drew their truth from the *universals*. Moses (as representative of humankind in general) did not have a personal *I am* but was dependent on the *I Am* of Yahweh, which as Yahweh's name, was Yahweh's true identity (Exod 3:11–14). For our psychological perspective, the realness of the universals in antiquity was how soul manifested, while the particulars were devoid of soul. This book is about how that state of affairs changed through history. Today it is as the particulars that soul manifests, and the universals are just words, subjective opinions, and no longer substantial public truths.

Today consciousness is grounded in human persons and the laws of matter, which as described by science are the original and final causes and the foundation of reality. Truth today is generally identified with concrete material facts, not God, or gods and spirits. It is axiomatic that we are the authors of our own destiny, we are the agents of history. It is no longer a god who determines the course of creation. This unquestioned assumption permeates all conventional humanistic thinking today, making it hard to appreciate what the problem of the incarnation was all about when it emerged. The difference between how antiquity thought and how we think is critical and decisive for understanding the meaning of Jesus Christ and the incarnation as one of soul's ancient manifestations. The christological problem of the incarnation is not soul's problem today. What there is of any contemporary genuine interest in Jesus tends to focus on who he was as a historical man, which is to be expected for an age dominated by scientific historical consciousness.

The questions—that is, the critical questions of our time—are not really theological anymore but historical, or scientific. For most people who take the scientific worldview for granted, Jesus as the divine Son of God, or the Second Person of the Trinity, is a nonissue, an incomprehensible outdated mythology. Modern interest in Jesus looks to the "carpenter from Nazareth" as a sage or wisdom teacher, an ordinary man like us. There is, however, a deeper problem which is that modern consciousness has not truly divested itself of what might be called a christological hangover. For over one thousand years, the presence of the Christ and Christianity saturated Western civilization and defined its consciousness. But, the notion of saturation puts Christ here and Western consciousness there. It is more accurate to say the idea, or the fundamental category, *Christ* names what constituted the syntax of Western consciousness. As personified image, Christ was the implicit orientation of consciousness itself. In contrast, contemporary thinking is preoccupied with Christ as a *content* of thought, as a man, an entity, a God, but no longer the shape of thought itself.

During the Christian era, Christ was both the content of Western thought, and at the same time, the invisible logic, the logical form, of Western thought, throughout the Middle Ages and the Renaissance, which then gave birth to the Enlightenment and modernity. Although as a culture, Western civilization may no longer be officially religious in the traditional sense, the deep effects of Christian thought still linger, often unnoticed, influencing how we think about Jesus Christ and leading only to confusion because we do not understand the historical differences of consciousness. Modern thought about Jesus Christ is utterly confounded because it does not understand the difference between the logic of the ancient consciousness that gave rise to the incarnation and the logic of our modern consciousness. Today, our humanist consciousness, in general, has no idea of what was at stake in the idea of the incarnation and can focus only on a supposed historical man, and can think only about that "historical man" as a content of consciousness.

Modern consciousness is confused about Jesus Christ because of the fundamental rupture between ancient consciousness and modern consciousness. The logic of modern humanistic and historical consciousness is innately incapable of grasping what was important for ancient consciousness. In other words, modern consciousness is incapable of grasping the reality of the gods and of God in their ancient function as the logical form of consciousness, as the substantial nature of reality itself. The modern form of consciousness has reduced the gods and God to contents of consciousness, and they now exist only as semantic items within a larger syntax that is fundamentally scientific and historical. The gods, and God, are now the stuff of history books, not present reality. The emergence of humanism and science is the subject of the next chapter, but humanism and science were themselves the result of the self-negating and sublating project of soul that the Christ represented.

The soul-negations initiated by Yahweh and Christ planted the seed of modern consciousness, which is constituted by the logic of humanism and science. The rupture between modern and ancient consciousness is such that modern consciousness no longer has access to that former form of consciousness. Our circumstance with regard to the changed fundamentals of consciousness is not a little like trying to grasp what existence would have been like before we acquired language. The problem is that once we acquire language, it is impossible to go back behind that acquisition and *know* what it was like before language. Once the fundamental basis of consciousness undergoes a historical change, it is like being born—there is no going back inside the womb that was our former consciousness. As noted in chapter 3, we are on this side of the watershed of history when human sacrifice ended and Yahweh emerged. Another kind of watershed occurred, more modern to be sure, but just as momentous, when Enlightenment historical consciousness became interested in a "historical Jesus" distinct from the divine Christ. So, we can catch a glimpse of that former pre-critical, God-centered consciousness by examining the emergence of the modern quest for the historical man Jesus, the attempt, especially during the eighteenth and nineteenth centuries, to view him as a historical person rather than as the Divine Logos, as God incarnate. The very ability to even conceive of Jesus as an ordinary human person quite apart from his divine status is a purely and striking modern development.

The Quest for the Historical Jesus as the Rupture of God's Time

During the eighteenth and most especially the nineteenth century, a new awareness of history was applied to the Bible. This involved the distinction made between historical events which had to accord with scientific facts and the laws of physics, and the supernatural and miraculous events recorded in the Bible. The notion of *truth* itself began to line up with scientific facts rather than with the sacred revelation provided by scripture, long the source of truth. What had been unified for over a thousand years in the idea of the incarnation (God and man are a unity in the person of Jesus Christ) was broken apart when historical-critical scholarship made the distinction between a Jesus of history and a Christ of faith. It is important to note that the distinction between a historical Jesus and a theological Christ is barely 250 years old, set within the context of the almost two thousand years of Christian civilization. This distinction was itself an indication of the development of soul; modern consciousness, with its growing emphasis on a scientific history grounded in material facts, rather than theology's basis in revelation. During the High Middle Ages, theology was the queen of the sciences (*science* originally meaning *knowledge*) because theology represented the prevailing logical form of consciousness, with all other knowledge gathered under it and subordinate to it. As the queen of the sciences, theology also represented the public status of truth, which was equated with biblical revelation and the theological doctrines based on that revelation. With the rise of historical truth as a new way to view scripture and the nature of reality, theology's days on the public throne of truth were numbered. Of course, there were terrific fights over the rise of historical consciousness, but theology was eventually forced to retreat from its dominance as public truth to the much smaller inner and private subjective world of personal faith. In fact, today the Jesus of history is more likely to be the common designation in the public domain because historical scientific consciousness is public truth, while the Christ of faith has receded to the domain of private belief and what can be considered the cottage industry of theological academia and the church.[5]

Albert Schweitzer illustrated the impact of historical consciousness on theological understanding when he stated, "Before Reimarus, no one had attempted to form a historical conception of the life of Jesus."[6] Schweitzer's book *The Quest of the Historical Jesus: A Critical Study of Its Progress from Reimarus to Wrede* is a brilliant survey of nineteenth-century research on the life of Jesus. During that period—and for the first time—critical historical thinking, which we can equate with the developments of the Enlightenment, began to make inroads on the church's exclusive focus on revelation and supernaturalism.

Hermann Samuel Reimarus (1694–1768) was a professor of oriental languages in Hamburg, Germany. With a mostly historical orientation, he was a proponent of a rational religion known as Deism, a point of view that sought to combine reason and faith by positing a transcendent God who did not intervene in history by way of supernatural, miraculous events. Reimarus would have remained an unknown figure had not Gotthold Ephraim Lessing dared to publish his writings as anonymous fragments in 1778. Reimarus never published anything he wrote, as it would have been a professional death sentence to openly critique the church's dogmatic positions. His intense interest in a historical understanding of both the Old and New Testaments produced four thousand pages critiquing the idea of revelation, the church's beliefs, and the Bible, but he shared his work only with a small circle of friends.

---

5. A good example of this phenomenon was the publication of Reza Aslan's *Zealot: The Life and Times of Jesus of Nazareth* in 2013 by Random House. While the depiction of Jesus as a zealot is not new, this book about the historical person of Jesus was published by a major publishing company, garnered a great deal of attention, and became a best seller. Books focused on Christology and theology are published by small industry-specific religious houses and never make it to the best-seller list.

6. Schweitzer, *Quest*, 13.

Yahweh Kills Himself, Christ Sublates the Flesh

Focusing on a fragment from Reimarus titled "The Aims of Jesus and His Disciples," Schweitzer characterizes Reimarus's writing as downright exciting:

> The language is as a rule crisp and terse, pointed and epigrammatic—the language of a man who is not "engaged in literary composition" but is wholly concerned with the [historical] facts. At times, however, it rises to heights of passionate feeling, and then it is as though the fires of a volcano were painting lurid pictures upon dark clouds. Seldom has there been a hate so eloquent, so lofty a scorn; but then it is seldom that a work has been written in the just consciousness of so absolute a superiority to contemporary opinion. And withal, there is dignity and serious purpose; Reimarus' work is no pamphlet.[7]

The title of this fragment is telling. The assumption that Jesus, as a historical person, had *aims* of his own was actually quite shocking in contrast to the traditional theological assertion that Christ was the obedient divine Son of God, the Messiah who fulfilled on earth God's cosmic plan for the salvation of the world.[8] The notion that Christ might have had a will of his own was unthinkable: Christ was obedient to God's will unto death. Over the one thousand years before Reimarus, Christ was understood as the incarnation of God fulfilling his foreordained role. That was the Christian logic of consciousness that made it impossible to think about Jesus in modern historical terms. The all-prevailing influence of the "logical form of consciousness" determines not so much *what* we see, but *how* we see at all.

The Christian logical form of consciousness was primarily mythical-religious, pre-scientific, and pre-critical, and it was fully defined and self-contained in its own metaphysical world. Christian truth had become a complete cosmos in accord with christological ideas that were taken as revealed in the gospel stories about Jesus and gradually, over centuries, became established as public truths. The metaphysical truths of Christianity became the foundational ground of consciousness itself, the prevailing logic or syntax of consciousness, which could not be questioned until that background form of consciousness began to change. It was not that Christianity forbade a rational historical exploration of the human Jesus, it was that such ideas, such modes of thought, did not exist yet.

Time itself was contained within the metaphysical world God established; it was a function of the logical form of consciousness identified with divinity. Although Christian time was historical and anticipated a future Second Coming of Christ and an eschatological end of time, this was always *God's* time. The experience of time was still completely self-contained within the idea of God, as well as in the annual ritual calendar of the church, every year repeating the sacred holy days (Christmas, Easter, and Pentecost being the most obvious) marking the life of Christ, of the church, and of common Christian culture at large. In about the ninth century, the pope decided

---

7. Schweitzer, *Quest*, 15.
8. Schweitzer, *Quest*, 17.

that time would be divided between BC (before Christ) and AD (Anno Domini, the year of the Lord), thereby transforming the meaning of all time. Today time has no metaphysical significance, and the contemporary secular convention divides time between BCE (before the common era) and CE (common era), but even this secular convention still relies on the historical Christ-moment as an anchor for numbering our historical years.[9] The emergence of scientific historical consciousness broke open the God-enclosed definition of time and created a secular linear sense of progress as humankind became the agent of its own historical destiny. Secular historical time ruptured the enclosed containment of Christian time, shattering the ontological security associated with God's time. Now time is infinite and meaningless.

It took well over a thousand years for Enlightenment thinking, Reason, science, and historical consciousness to emerge and become a force critiquing and competing with the Christian worldview. Soul's irony is that the Enlightenment was the direct result of the incarnation of the Mind of God as the Word. As the Word become flesh, Christ leads directly to Reason becoming a human function. Schweitzer's review of scholars attempting to form a historical conception of Jesus during the nineteenth century shows the gradual, difficult, and painful emergence of historical consciousness challenging the prevailing Christian logic of consciousness. The growing interest in a historical understanding of Jesus is one development of modernity, or what we today take for granted as modern consciousness. Hate was a significant component in that development.

The Painful Struggle of Historical Consciousness

Schweitzer recognized that *hate* was a creative force in the production of the historical work of Reimarus, expressed in his historian's scorn for supernaturalism (the miraculous acts of God) as the foundation of Christianity. Although Lessing published the Reimarus fragments, he did not fully agree with his views. Lessing was himself a fully born product of the Enlightenment, and he recognized the great value of Reimarus's critique, bringing the fragments to public view despite the reservations of Reimarus's family and his own friends. Lessing believed that the concept of revelation would either be destroyed or reformulated, declaring, "The Christian traditions must be explained by the inner truth of Christianity, and no written traditions can give it that inner truth, if it does not itself possess it."[10] Lessing himself took a significant risk in making these new ideas public in the face of a social climate where Enlightenment ideas were novel, challenging, and heretical. The prevailing truth (Christian dogma) and a new truth (Enlightenment rationality) were becoming fully engaged in a struggle for the life and soul of an entire civilization.

---

9. At scale, scientific categories of time, geological, evolutionary, and cosmological, obliterate this distinction, as well as our very short period of human history.

10. Schweitzer, *Quest*, 16.

Yahweh Kills Himself, Christ Sublates the Flesh

The historical development of Enlightenment consciousness was a soul-internal process, soul negating itself from within, for the sake of another form of consciousness. Through a centuries-long process, the Divine Logos, Christ, transformed itself and became the rational word of natural reason, which then turned on itself, by way of critical historical consciousness, and undermined the very foundations of Christian truth. Soul creates a new truth from within a prevailing truth, and when that truth has fulfilled itself, has come to completion, soul turns and undercuts that truth in service to a new truth that is born from the very heart of the prevailing truth (the process of sublation). Soul pushes off from itself in such a way that soul negates itself in a process of creating a new truth from within that negation. Simply put, soul creates itself and destroys itself, in order to create itself again, the innate process of consciousness captured in the image of the ouroboros, the serpent that eats its own tail. This process works itself out through the medium of culture and history, which I want to emphasize is only possible because of books: writing, reading, and more writing and more reading. *Thought, writing, and reading are where soul forms itself.* While I continue to speak of this movement as a kind of natural "process" of soul, from the outside (empirical society) it certainly looks like, and often is, an aggressive and hostile project attacking the old truth in order to establish the new.

Schweitzer recognized that this enormous cultural upheaval required the emotional intensity of hate as a critical force in order for soul to break free of its own prior form of truth. The new truth had to attack the old truth, but the old truth would not go down quietly; it would ruin the lives of those who betrayed it. In his introduction to the historical survey he was about to undertake, Schweitzer acknowledged the important and central place that hate occupied:

> There is no historical task which so reveals a man's true self as the writing of a Life of Jesus. No vital force comes into the figure unless a man breathes into it all the hate or all the love of which he is capable. The stronger the love, or the stronger the hate, the most life-like is the figure which is produced. For hate as well as love can write a Life of Jesus, and the greatest of them are written with hate: that of Reimarus . . . and that of David Friedrich Strauss. It was not so much hate of the Person of Jesus as of the supernatural nimbus with which it was so easy to surround Him, and with which He had in fact been surrounded. They were eager to picture Him as truly and purely human, to strip from Him the robes of splendor with which He had been apparelled, and clothe Him once more with the coarse garments in which He had walked in Galilee.
>
> And their hate sharpened their historical insight. They advanced the study of the subject more than all the others put together. But for the offence which they gave, the science of historical theology would not have stood where it does to-day.[11]

---

11. Schweitzer, *Quest*, 4.

God's Autopsy and the Living Truth of Soul

While Reimarus was well aware of the fate that would befall him if he published his thoughts, the same concern did not stop David Strauss, who, at twenty-seven, published his *Life of Jesus* in 1835, in two volumes of some fourteen hundred pages. Soon after its publication, he lost any opportunities to teach, a terrible loss for him, and thereafter had to subsist (though, not badly) on an inheritance. But he suffered nonetheless, and yet he did not regret staying true to his integrity:

> I might bear a grudge against my book, for it has done me much evil. It has excluded me from public teaching in which I took pleasure and for which I had perhaps some talent . . . it has made my life a lonely one. And yet when I consider what it would have meant if I had refused to utter the word which lay upon my soul, if I had suppressed the doubts which were at work in my mind—then I bless the book which has doubtless done me grievous harm outwardly, but which preserved the inward health of my mind and heart, and, I doubt not, has done the same for many others also.[12]

The hate that impelled Strauss was the fierce intensity of the new truth of critical historical consciousness. Rather than reducing this hate to a personal emotion belonging to Strauss alone, I view it as a soul phenomenon that he could not ignore. No, the hate was the power and insistence of the new truth, soul's new truth, driven to pursue its own logic all the way, cutting into itself and releasing its new form, pushing off from the Christian form of the Divine Logos (the Word become flesh). Reimarus and Strauss were pregnant with a new truth, and for their own sanity, they had to be true to it. In this respect, soul is inhuman and impersonal, and its imperative had a devastating impact on Strauss's professional and personal life. Schweitzer emphasizes, early in his monumental overview of the nineteenth-century quest for the historical Jesus, the human suffering accompanying the emergence of a new logical form of consciousness:

> The world had never seen before, and will never see again, a struggle for truth so full of pain and renunciation as that of which the Lives of Jesus of the last hundred years contain the cryptic record.[13]

Remember the role of hate in Yahweh's push to re-create himself. In his new form as imageless and transcendent, the one and only God, he hated the nature gods and goddesses. He hated himself in his bull manifestation, had to cut himself free of his nature essence, castrating the bull and divorcing his goddess consort Asherah. At least from the point of view of the biblical stories, Yahweh's hate led to many deaths and much suffering, including genocide and deicide, the destruction of local indigenous peoples, the slaughter of his own people at times, and the destruction of the nature gods and goddesses. These intensely emotional dramas and historical struggles reveal soul's self-negating processes, as it created new forms of consciousness out of the previously

---

12. Schweitzer, *Quest*, 5.
13. Schweitzer, *Quest*, 5.

achieved consciousness, with no thought to the consequences for the human persons involved. Soul operates on a historical scale that is not under our control, the flux and flow of ideas that shape civilizations, the conflict and violence of the real and powerful ideas that structure and generate culture. When they emerge as history, we can look back and try to understand what on earth has been happening over the centuries.

By examining the emergence of the historical-critical approach to the figure of Jesus, I want to draw attention to the gulf that exists between our modern scientific historical consciousness and the God-suffused and Christ-centered consciousness of the ancient world and the early centuries of the Christian era, as well as medieval Europe. In those days, God was Truth and Reality *par excellence*, and human persons knew themselves as children of God, subjects of that ultimately authoritative Truth and Reality. In Western society today, it is mostly taken for granted that we are free individuals, democratic in spirit, agents of our own destiny; authoritative truth and reality are grounded in the principles of science, and the bottom line is a material universe governed by the laws of physics. We are no longer children of God dependent on God, but historical agents in our own right. In our modern view, the universe in itself has no purpose unless we create one. During the beginnings of Christianity, the struggle over how to understand the incarnation, how to bring God and a man together without diminishing God, engendered immense conflicts over matters that were truly ultimate, that had life-and-death consequences for the very essence of Truth and Reality.

Tearing Open and Emptying

The two images of *tearing*, "torn open" and "torn in two," the epigraphs at the head of this chapter, frame the story of the incarnate Word (Jesus Christ) as beginning and end in the Gospel of Mark. Both the tearing of the heavens at Jesus' baptism and the tearing of the temple curtain at his crucifixion are symbolic of the emptying of the traditional abode of Yahweh. In the first, the *heavens* represent the traditional and natural home and location of Yahweh and the gods in general. The heavens are up above, associated with clouds, sky, mountains, sun, moon, stars, and planets. The heavens are *up there*, and earth is *down here*. The heavens are far away, beyond our ken, out of reach. The heavens represent the logical status of soul, and of consciousness, in the same way that earlier in Exodus, we saw that the *I Am* belonged to Yahweh, and not Moses, a property of the gods and not of humankind. The heavens are the realm of the *universals*, the true, and the real. What we consider our personal consciousness today, as well as its functions, was during antiquity a gift of the gods, a gift from heaven. The gods bestowed true thought, insight, reason, creativity, and revelation. The status of heaven and the status of Yahweh were the same. All the more startling, then, when heaven is torn apart and empties itself:

God's Autopsy and the Living Truth of Soul

> In those days Jesus came from Nazareth of Galilee and was baptized by John in the Jordan. And just as he was coming up out of the water, he saw the heavens torn apart and the Spirit descending like a dove on him. (Mark 1:9–10)

The heavens torn open and the descent of the Spirit during the baptism of Jesus Christ symbolize an irrevocable change in Yahweh. The birth symbolism is unavoidable, and it represents a change that cannot be reversed. Once the heavens emptied themselves of Yahweh's presence, the heavens were empty once and for all. Looked at psychologically, the spirit *is* Yahweh, not a part of Yahweh or a messenger of Yahweh. Yahweh has left home for good; he has emptied himself of himself. When Abraham left his ancestral home, *home*, understood psychologically, was not a geographical location but a status of consciousness. When soul leaves home, it negates one form of itself, one form of consciousness, on the way to coming home to itself again as another higher, or more inclusive form of consciousness. Yahweh has done this to himself over and over. Now he is not just leaving his animal and nature essence behind, he is leaving his transcendence behind. The development of the Tanakh as a book symbolizes the process of Yahweh becoming *written word*. This is embodied in the growing significance of torah as sacred writing and the increasing value of human study of torah (itself a form of prayer, which is giving one's full attention to Yahweh). When a text becomes *sacred*, we know that soul's claim has changed its location, in this case, from sensual shining bull to abstract written word; the text became the shining revered presence of God.

With the Christ, the Word took another turn and became *flesh*: "And the Word became flesh and lived among us, and we have seen his glory" (John 1:14). In this ancient context, even if historical biological flesh is intended, this is not the mere meaningless biological flesh of modernity. It would have been psychological flesh, that flesh with a new soul-meaning coming into it. The "Word became flesh" is the incarnation, and that was a theological *idea* and not a concrete historical event as a flesh and blood person (as modernity would think it). Of course, for Christianity, the incarnation was (and, is) a historical claim of the first order: God became a real historical man! But in antiquity such a statement had a very different status than it does for us in modernity. When modern consciousness thinks about the incarnation, it automatically thinks in concrete, material, historical terms. For the mind of antiquity, the very substantial *idea* of God and its profound transformation was at stake. For modern consciousness, the incarnation is a content of consciousness, putting an inevitable distance between us and the idea. It can no longer be the *substantial idea of the incarnation thinking itself* into truth by way of the medium of human persons. As far as soul is concerned today, the idea of incarnation is obsolete because it has accomplished its historical purpose, transforming the syntax and status of consciousness. In soul's dream of itself, the incarnation was the symbolic expression of the radical change in the syntax of consciousness two thousand years ago. It was the continuation of soul's move away from the universals, ideal principles, and God, toward the particulars, specifically the human subject. The problem of the incarnation in antiquity was not about how an actual human person and a god united, but how the *idea* of the new relationship between the *universal* and the *particular* was to be resolved. I want to be clear about which syntax of consciousness was doing the thinking back then because it was not modern consciousness, which did not yet exist. The categorical problem the incarnation was working on, thinking through, was specific to that time and place. The orientation of *meaning* in antiquity was very different from today's, and the problem it had to think through with the incarnation was soul's task then.

The dramatic tearing of the temple curtain at the crucifixion is a mirror image of the first tearing but in an earthly location. The curtain of the temple refers to an expensive, rich, and large heavy drapery that concealed the holy of holies, a protected space where the ark of the covenant was kept. The ark *was* the throne of Yahweh on earth among the people.[14] Ritually protected, the curtain veiled the most holy and sacred space in the temple. Only the high priest could enter the holy of holies, and only once a year, on the Day of Atonement (Yom Kippur). While a symbolic event in the gospel story, the tearing of this curtain also reflects the actual destruction of the temple by the Romans in 70 CE. Not only does Yahweh empty himself of his transcendence in the first tearing, but he also loses his literal house again, and this time for good. It is never rebuilt. Yahweh and Judaism were forever changed. Five to seven hundred years earlier, Yahweh had nearly unwittingly destroyed himself when he chose to use the Assyrians and Babylonians to punish the Israelites; his first house (temple) was destroyed and his people dispersed. Now, history converges on Yahweh more harshly with fatal results. He does destroy himself by way of the Romans, but this time he was not using the Romans for his own ends. With regard to the Romans, Yahweh the warrior god was powerless and helpless, and he knew it.[15] The temple was Yahweh's abode on earth, the one and only house of the Lord. The tearing of the curtain during the crucifixion was another indication of the link between Jesus Christ and Yahweh, and the translocation of the heavenly temple-housed Yahweh to the earthly Jesus walking

---

14. The ark was a portable chest or cabinet, which, according to Exodus, was made by Moses following Yahweh's instructions, roughly 4' by 2.5' by 2.5' (Exod 25:10–22). It housed the tablets of the covenant (Ten Commandments) between Yahweh and the people, and it was also the throne of Yahweh. It was the most sacred and powerful object as it *was* the presence of Yahweh in the midst of the people, and as the container of the covenant it was the material manifestation of what bound the people and Yahweh together. When the Israelites were wandering in the desert and when entering the promised land, the ark was carried with them, leading the way. Touching this holy object was forbidden. In one instance, David was bringing the ark to Jerusalem on an ox-driven cart, when the cart lurched and the ark was in danger of falling, so Uzzah reached out his hand and took hold of it to protect it, with unfortunate consequences: "The anger of the LORD was kindled against Uzzah; and God struck him there because he reached out his hand to the ark; and he died there beside the ark of God" (2 Sam 6:7). David, now afraid of the ark, left it in another's care and did not bring it to Jerusalem. The sacred power of the ark, equal to Yahweh's presence, was unpredictable and dangerous.

15. Miles, *Christ*, 112, 150–51, 171–78, 226–27.

among the people every day. No person tore the curtain in two. It was a cosmic event, essentially Yahweh tearing himself open: Yahweh finally and fully emptied himself of himself, of his traditional form (he essentially killed himself, an early prefiguration of the "death of god").

The crucifixion scene is marked by another dramatic emptying. On the cross, before he breathes his last, and before the temple curtain is torn, "Jesus cried out with a loud voice, 'My God, my God, why have you forsaken me?'" (Mark 15:34) Traditional theological explanations reduce this cry of despair to Jesus' human nature separate from his divine nature. The psychological reading allows us to see this cry as God forsaking himself, as another sign of the negation of God by God. God's self-negation is, of course, soul's move against itself as it pours out its status of transcendence for a new status as incarnate. With transcendence truly emptied, what happened to God? The crucifixion cannot be separated from what happened after, as those events were a unity. The incarnate status—and thus implicitly, all of humankind and the natural world, the world of the *particulars*—was then itself raised to a new higher status, through the symbolic events of resurrection and ascension. Crucifixion, resurrection, and ascension constitute the sublation of the *flesh*, that is, the natural world of Yahweh consciousness, into a higher and more inclusive form of consciousness, a new differentiated consciousness that includes Yahweh in a totally new form, the form of the crucified messiah, the crucified king, the crucified warrior.

Before the gospel images of the divine emptying were penned, the idea of God emptying himself appeared in the letter to the Philippians (ca. 62 CE):

> [Christ Jesus], though he was in the form
> of God
> did not regard equality with
> God
> as something to be exploited,
> but *emptied* himself,
> taking the form of a slave,
> being born in human likeness.
> And being found in human form,
> he humbled himself
> and became obedient to the
> point of death—
> even death on a cross. (Phil 2:6–8, emphasis added)

The Greek word for "emptied" is a verb form of *kenosis*, literally meaning "to empty out." The NIV translates that verse as, "but made himself nothing." Here, the self-evident and innate *value* of God (the universal) negates itself and, in the process, begins to take on the form of the human subject (the particular) in a strange, uncanny, and unpredictable reversal. The lines following the *kenosis* text affirm the translocation of the fundamental value of the universal to the particular:

> Therefore God also highly
> > exalted him
> > and gave him the name
> > that is above every name,
> > so that at the name of Jesus
> > every knee should bend,
> > in heaven and on earth and
> > under the earth,
> > and every tongue should confess
> > that Jesus Christ is Lord,
> > to the glory of God the Father. (Phil 2:9–11)

Recall the Isaiah text quoted at the beginning of this chapter, "To me every knee shall bow, every tongue shall swear" (Isa 45:23), and remember it was Christianity, with a fascinating fervor, that spread itself over the globe. In Isaiah Yahweh also cast himself in the image of a suffering slave, a description of a new kind of messiah, an emptying of the traditional and expected warrior Yahweh (Isa 52:13—53:12). The tearing open of Yahweh and the self-emptying of Yahweh form a radical reversal of the logical status of consciousness. When the text says that God gave Christ "the name that is above every name" and goes on to say, "that Jesus Christ is Lord," I read, "Jesus Christ is God," just as the first verse affirms, "he was in the form of God." The narrative of Christ's passion, his betrayal and crucifixion, with its profound depths of emotion, depicts God working through Jesus Christ. The characters of Christ and God depict soul's account of itself. The crucifixion story is God's crucifixion, his suffering transformation, which is the passion of *consciousness* tearing itself out of its transcendent abode for a new dwelling on earth: a revolutionary shift in the syntax of consciousness.

I have said soul does not know where it is going ahead of time. During those early centuries when the Christ-event was making itself felt, many different kinds of gospels were written about Jesus Christ, most of which have not survived.[16] Including the letters of Paul, which also belong to the intuitive groping of soul to understand itself in its newly emerging forms, we should really think in terms of multiple christianities appearing and competing. Fragments of about thirty-five other gospels have been recovered, and the Gospel of Thomas has survived in its entirety.[17] All this early Christian literature points to an upsurge of a new form of soul, or consciousness, that was beginning to emerge and shape itself. Particularly important in this effort by soul to articulate itself, were the emerging christological controversies that sought to understand the

---

16. Carse, *Gospel of the Beloved*, vii.

17. The Gospel of Thomas is completely different from the four official gospels as it consists entirely of disciples posing questions to Jesus and Jesus' answers, and does not include any narrative and nothing of the crucifixion and resurrection, although it is obvious (or should be) that the "Jesus" who is speaking, designated the "Living Jesus," is the personified voice of the new consciousness associated with the Christ-event.

precise nature of the incarnation: How could God and a man (absolutely incommensurate categories) come together in a full unity and yet remain distinct?

Yahweh, who personified the prevailing logical status of soul, was torn open and emptied. The psychological lens views the Christ drama as the negation of soul, soul's self-negation and self-sublation, which was worked out imaginally and mythologically as the suicide of Yahweh. The gospel story presents a sacrifice of a son by a father (remember Abraham and Isaac), and because in this story Son and Father were *one*, were identical, that act amounted to God killing himself, sacrificing himself, as the narrative image of soul's transformation. Reading the Bible as soul's account of itself, it was not a man who was crucified on a cross, but God who crucified himself. And further, it was the substantial *idea* of a particular kind of god that crucified itself.

God Tortures Himself to Death on a Cross

It was not a man who was hung on the cross and died, but a god, and that god was Yahweh. Within the context of soul's historical development, the changing form of *meaning*, Jesus as *historical* man did not exist for consciousness until the eighteenth century. Whether or not there was an actual historic man who conforms more or less with the Jesus of the gospel texts is not the question here. Before Reimarus, it was God, God as Christ the Word, as Christ the Son (the substantial unity of the Father, Son, and Holy Spirit), who went through the humiliating death of crucifixion and the subsequent world-changing process that was called resurrection and incarnation. The strange new idea of the incarnation was born out of the horror of Yahweh's failure vis-à-vis the Romans. Yahweh was tortured and hung on a cross—the Romans preferred form of public torture and execution, used to punish criminals as well as sedition, especially those Jewish rebels who sought to reestablish Israel's national sovereignty. The Jewish people were well acquainted with public execution by crucifixion under the Romans. It was a gruesome and horrible form of slow torturous death reserved for slaves, the lowest classes, criminals, and enemies of the state. The Jewish historian Josephus records that a Jewish revolt in 4 BCE was crushed by the Roman military leader Varus when he crucified two thousand rebels.[18] The Roman response to Jewish uprisings was crushingly cruel.

After the Babylonian conquest and exile in 587 BCE, the Israelite people never experienced national autonomy and sovereignty again (until the modern state of Israel). After the Babylonians came the Persians, then the Greeks, and finally the Romans. My interpretation of Yahweh in the Tanakh sees him change and begin to shed his warrior status and lose interest in political conquests. However, that interpretation is analyzing the logical or syntactical level of consciousness. Empirical society takes much longer to catch up to soul's logical changes. The idea of Yahweh the liberating warrior

---

18. *Wikipedia*, s.v. "Publius Quinctilius Varus," last updated May 4, 2022, https://en.wikipedia.org/wiki/Publius_Quinctilius_Varus.

was very much alive for the Jews in general and specifically took the form of messianic rebellions against the oppressive presence of those larger empires, especially when religious practice and temple worship were infringed or threatened. Yahweh's character may have undergone profound changes, but he had never surrendered his promise to restore Israel to its former glory as a national state.[19] Multiple messianic leaders and rebellious groups emerged over the years, especially under the growing hardships imposed by the Romans during the first century CE. The so-called Zealots, popularly thought to be an underground rebel group, was really a coalition of various groups that came together during the devastating revolt of 66 to 70 CE, when the Romans destroyed the Jerusalem temple. I view these rebel groups as social personifications of the warrior god Yahweh because they were fully informed by Yahweh's promises over the centuries. Of course, terrible social and economic conditions fomented revolt, but the warrior impulse is Yahweh himself, and Yahweh's fundamental concern was not simply to rescue the people, but to establish himself as the one and only true God.

The warrior Yahweh of the Tanakh was passionate and violent, and even as his own internal logic changed, the warrior impulse was intensely alive in those messianic leaders who emerged to lead Jewish insurgents against Rome's oppressive intrusions. The political and military messianic impulse was the outward expression of the warrior Yahweh, because these messianic movements fought for values and principles that defined Yahweh. They believed that only the military overthrow of the foreign oppressor—in essence the political-cultural representation of false gods—could preserve and make the One True God real and sovereign. The other gods and goddesses, and the imperial overlords who represented them, had to be destroyed in order for the Lord God to achieve its sovereign freedom.

Symbolically, when the Jerusalem temple was destroyed in 70 CE, it was also the death of warrior Yahweh, I would even say, the crucifixion of warrior Yahweh. The gospels themselves were all written soon after this horrific event, when the hammer of Rome fell and added to the suspicion that Yahweh had failed.[20] Even though Jerusalem had been leveled and thousands of Jews killed, another revolt erupted about sixty-five years later, 132–136 CE, under the leadership of the messiah Simon Bar Kokhba. This too was crushed, and Rome went so far as to change the name of Jerusalem to Aelia Capitolina and banned Jews from entering the city under pain of death. The new name honored the Roman Emperor Hadrian (Aelia) and the god Jupiter (Greek Zeus)—a temple to Jupiter was built where the Jewish temple had stood. Now the warrior Yahweh, as well as Jewish national identity, was truly obliterated.[21]

---

19. Miles, *Christ*, 80.

20. The dates are approximate and speculative, but it is generally accepted that the gospels appeared in the first decades after the destruction of the temple: Mark, about 70; Matthew and Luke, about 85; John 90, or even as late as 135 CE.

21. Miles, *Christ*, 110, 175.

God's Autopsy and the Living Truth of Soul

The emergence of the Christian story in late antiquity was the emergence of the truly unthinkable. The all-powerful warrior god Yahweh is himself crucified by the Romans in the form of the messiah, the "king of the Jews." The Christian idea completely reverses the meaning of messiah. The Christian messiah is not God's chosen military commander who will lead the people to freedom, although the gospels depict Jesus' disciples as expecting this very thing. The Christian Messiah is God himself. Jesus Christ on the cross was God on the cross, the final end of warrior Yahweh who had passionately promised to win sovereign freedom for his people. The shift from Yahweh to Christ, for the psychological perspective, is the shift to a new logical form of consciousness. Here is the second death of God (counting the death of the Bull god Yahweh as the first), the death of the Yahweh form of God, the Yahweh logic of consciousness which had informed the Jewish people for at least several centuries.

In the gospel narrative, God himself chooses to die this way, a self-sacrifice by the basest and most humiliating public form of death that a human person could then suffer. The crucifixion is presented as a choice that Jesus makes, while at the same time it was foreordained. The fact that foreshadowing dominates the gospel stories, the fact that ninety percent of all the preliminary story-telling is really a prologue to the main event, crucifixion-resurrection, makes it clear that the gospel stories are not about a human person named Jesus who would not have known ahead of time what was going to happen. The gospels, understood as soul's dream of itself and not literal history, have the character of intuitive and naive depictions of a soul-event that had already happened logically. The gospel stories, the Christ stories, read psychologically, are the attempt on the part of soul to articulate a violent wrenching of the syntax of consciousness into a new form. The narrative form of this story, like a dream, was the way soul gave an account of itself. The outer event of the desecration and destruction of Jerusalem reflects the psychological meaning of the gospel stories, in which the death of God on the cross represents a radical transformation of the prevailing logic of consciousness. In the context of the history of consciousness, this death of God was a real event with far-reaching unexpected consequences.

Coupled with Yahweh's choice to die, the *I Am* that was Yahweh's identity relocates and identifies itself with the Christ: "Jesus said to them, 'Very truly, I tell you, before Abraham was, I am'" (John 8:58). The *name* of God, especially in antiquity, is at the same time, the real presence of the God. Up to this point, the consciousness that has been named *I Am* (an autonomous subject) was constituted only by Yahweh. Now the *I Am* takes on the form of the Christ and, as a new logical form of consciousness, assumes an identity as a new God-form. The textual context for this assertion also reveals the pain and dissonance accompanying the dislocation of God's identity. Jesus Christ makes the statement identifying himself with God at the end of a lengthy argument with the "Jews." Immediately after he declares himself the *I am*, "They picked up stones to throw at him, but Jesus hid himself" and escaped. The anger at Jesus when he claims an identity with God really has nothing to do with Jewish people and symbolizes the problem that arises when soul negates one form of itself, sublating itself: Yahweh cannot recognize himself as Christ. The Yahweh form of God cannot recognize himself in his new identity, his new logical status. Not unlike someone who, living in two dimensions, would be unable to "see" the third dimension.

The Christ makes many "I am" statements throughout John's gospel in which he identifies himself with attributes of God. "I am the bread of life. Whoever comes to me will never be hungry" (John 6:35), recalls the event in Exodus when God rained bread from heaven for the Hebrews wandering in the desert (Exod 16:4). All the attributes of God are now incarnate: "I am the light of the world" (John 8:12); "I am the gate" (John 10:9); "I am the good shepherd" (John 10:11); "I am the resurrection and the life" (John 11:25); "I am the way, and the truth, and the life" (John 14:6); "I am the true vine" (John 15:1); and, "The Father and I are one" (John 10:30). As a thoroughly new location of the I Am, the Christ is a kind of transitional figure as the I Am constitution of consciousness (as subject) moves toward humankind. Soul does not make this move for the sake of humankind, but for its own sake, for the sake of its further differentiation as consciousness. Soul is freeing itself from its form as transcendent deity and trending toward the realization of itself as consciousness, when consciousness will become conscious of itself, after it moves through the Enlightenment. At the time of its emergence as the Christ, however, the theological and ontological status of Christ as *both* the Son of God *and* son of man was of absolute importance. Now the critical problem was how to understand the reality of God in the light of the new status of Christ, and this is what would drive the fierceness and urgency of the looming christological arguments.

The Lord God was a warrior (the fierce energy of bull and storm) who engaged in holy war, destruction, execution, murder, vengeance, torture, the sacrificial ban—the Lord God was a warrior god in all its bloody truth. As Christ, on the cross, the Lord God submits himself to himself. The Lord God submits himself to his own violence, to torture and crucify the very idea of warrior and military conquest. Yahweh's ambition for a military, political, and social victory for the One True God to reign supreme was negated. The warrior god submitted to his own inner nature and crucified the idea of crucifixion, if we view crucifixion as symbolic of the method imperial power uses to maintain itself. The first real goal of Yahweh was not to liberate his people from Egypt or Rome, but to liberate himself and become the One and Only True God. Yahweh's enemy, Yahweh's competition, were the nature gods and goddesses, which represented the former form of consciousness he himself was. The intrusion of Rome into Israelite life was the intrusion of a polytheistic cosmos into Yahweh's domain. What really mattered for soul, in the form of warrior Yahweh, was whether or not Yahweh, through the exercise of power, could reestablish himself as sovereign in this material world. In the face of Rome and crucifixion, that hope ended in total and abysmal failure, a complete extinction.[22]

22. The hope and expectation of material and political sovereignty under Yahweh was completely

God's Autopsy and the Living Truth of Soul

On the cross the Warrior God was crucified and extinguished. That negation yielded a resurrection, which in itself was a negation, the negation of *death*. But death here was not biological death, the death of the body, even though the story insists it was a *bodily* resurrection. The death that was overcome symbolized the alienation of humankind from God, the alienation that God brought about in the garden of Eden, an alienation that was itself a new consciousness. More than the willful disobedience of Eve and Adam, God's own unwitting partnership with the serpent led to that necessary advance of consciousness marked by disobedience and death. Now, in the form of Jesus Christ, God's submission to failure and death was the narrative form of soul's self-negation and sublation for another status of consciousness. After the crucifixion, the Yahweh form of consciousness spiritualized itself into a form the narrative states was an ordinary body; but the *resurrected* body passed through walls and doors, and then ascended into heaven. The *idea*, the reality, that was Yahweh collapsed in on itself. Messianism, the impulse into the outer social, political world, turned in on itself, and an entirely new kind of world, a *spiritualized* world, opened up, inaugurated by the Word becoming flesh and the flesh becoming Word.

The notion of the *word* here is all important. As noted earlier, Yahweh was the personification of the emergence of written language, literacy, and the profound revolutionary transformation of consciousness that entailed. The transformation of meaning (soul) into writing changed the world, our world (*world* as our form of consciousness). With Christianity, the evaporation of the flesh into Word and Word coming into a reality all its own also changed the world with a new syntax of consciousness. Christianity and the Christ was the way this new form of consciousness presented itself to the intuitive imagination of humankind, and the form with which it worked on itself thinkingly over centuries. Today it is possible to see the psychological meaning of these symbols that have held humankind in their grip for so long. Soul's journey is consciousness on the way to becoming conscious of itself.

The resurrected *body* of the Christ was a new idea (the Word made flesh) that emerged and represented the completion of the sublation process (dissolving Yahweh). The process of *crucifixion-resurrection* must be seen as a unity expressing the negation of Yahweh and the transformation of Word and flesh into another logical status. The new idea, incarnation, soul's new form, would bedevil the conventional categories soul had at hand (*God* and *man*) for hundreds of years, as it sought to think itself into a comprehensible truth. This thought process would have to completely rethink the idea of God and the idea of mankind so they could coexist as a new concept. The new concept became an entirely new basis of mind at large, a new logic and

---

extinguished, on the logical level of soul. Of course, on the empirical social level, the Tanakh and the Jewish people continued to exist, and developed in a new direction themselves. But, Yahweh, as a soul-force, became the Christ, creating the Christian cosmos, where the dynamism of soul continued to work on itself.

status of the syntax of consciousness. It was a new reality, a new world of meaning, and would shape and create a new civilization.

It is simply irresponsible to take Christianity's insistence on the *bodily* nature of the incarnation literally, literally that is, from the perspective of our modern, scientific, and materialistic logical form of consciousness. The *idea* of the incarnation in its ancient context was soul's attempt to make the new spiritual nature of the Word/logos *real*, substantial, in its new form, as the crucified(-resurrected) Yahweh Warrior god. The emergence of the new *concept* incarnation took place in the context of a thought world whose logical form of consciousness was constituted by the self-evident truth and reality of the universals, the reality of the gods and goddesses, at the same time that it asserted the irreality and sinful status of the body, the flesh, the realm of the particulars (more on this status below). The incarnation changes the logical status of the flesh and the body, the material world, alongside the status of the ideal world of the universals. Today we live in a very different thought world, which is that we exist as a logical form of consciousness that takes the particulars, the material world, materialism, as the *real*; for us, words and ideas are not real and substantial as they once were. When modern consciousness thinks about the incarnation, it cannot help but think in terms of our literal physical bodies (the "dead" body of physics and biology), but that was not the case when Christianity emerged and the arguments over the nature of the incarnation raged. What was really at stake was the logical concept of body, the nature of the *idea* "body" as a real in its own right.

The Christological Controversies as Soul's Speech about Itself

Even though the New Testament has thoroughly Jewish roots and sees itself as the fulfillment of Yahweh's longing, as we've seen, the theological atmosphere of the Mediterranean at the time was heavily influenced by Greek philosophy. Both Platonism and Stoicism contributed to an extreme transcendent monotheism deeply resistant to being tampered with, diminished, or tainted in any way. The supreme high God was absolutely singular and remote, and this God's relationship to the created order had to be through some variation of a descending hierarchy of lesser deities. So, when the Gospel of John, which was itself authoritative as God's revealed truth, stated, "In the beginning was the Word [logos], and the Word was with God, and the Word was God. He was in the beginning with God" (John 1:1–2), and goes on to identify the Word with Jesus Christ, who was a human person, just what was the status of Christ in relation to God? How could Christ be equal to God without diminishing God? How could Christ be united with such an extremely transcendent God without losing his true and full humanity? What exactly was the status of Jesus Christ as God's Word? This was a thought problem of the first order, and its solution was, in my opinion, what led directly to the Enlightenment and the development of Reason as a human function. During the first few hundred years of the Christian era, from about 90 to 450

CE, many brilliant minds tackled the problem of Christ's exact relationship with God, causing a great deal of confusion and intense conflict. It was the most creative period of Christian thinking, laying the groundwork for all future thought.[23] The christological controversies were soul's new playground.

The incarnation had a deep global purpose, the salvation of humankind from sin and death. According to the Christian worldview, sin and death came into the world by way of Adam and Eve's original disobedience in the garden of Eden when they ate the fruit forbidden by God. The original sin of Adam permeated all of humankind and acted as a permanent wedge, a deep disconnect, between humanity and God. The Christian solution to this problem was to have God negate himself in such a way that manhood (Jesus) and Godhead became coequal within one being, the incarnate Jesus Christ. Only the precise balance of sameness and simultaneous distinction uniting God and Jesus could bring about the full and complete re-union between God and humankind. Soul was creating a new logic of consciousness on the field of conflicting ideas, and only getting it right would prove satisfactory. If that delicate balance of the union of God and Christ did not prove satisfactory, the redemption of the realm of humankind, equivalent to the realm of matter and the world at large, would fail. Of course, "redemption," understood psychologically, represented the transformation of the syntax of consciousness.

Prior to the incarnation idea, God was defined as the uncreated, self-subsisting, indivisible, and impassable, wholly transcendent One: an absolute monotheism. Nothing could infringe on the essence and oneness of God. Claiming that Jesus Christ was also God threatened the inviolate integrity of God. Thus, for some christological thinkers, Jesus was viewed as only a man inspired by God, or Jesus was accorded a kind of semi-divine status, over and above all other created creatures, but was himself still an entity created at some point by God, and thus was subordinate to God. But, wait, if Christ is subordinate to God, actually less than God, then how can the redemption of the realm of humankind come about? It would remain a partial redemption, and the ontological status of humankind would remain inferior. And, consciousness would remain suspended in a kind of "beyond" state, in heaven. The form of consciousness known as "God transcendent," a divine subject, seemed to want a further differentiation through becoming a human subject (of course, this is hindsight talking when I say, "seemed to want").

This was the problem Arius (256–336; a priest in Alexandria, known to orthodoxy as an arch-heretic) presented during the early fourth century. He believed that

> since it is unique, transcendent and indivisible, the being or essence of the Godhead cannot be shared or communicated. For God to impart His substance to some other being, however exalted, would imply that He is divisible and subject to change, which is *inconceivable*. Moreover, if any other being

---

23. Kelly, *Early Christian*, 3.

were to participate in the divine nature in any valid sense, there would result a duality of divine beings, whereas the Godhead is by *definition unique*.[24]

Any new addition to the idea of the Godhead was absolutely unthinkable for the ancient form of consciousness. For Arius, the truth of absolute monotheism could not be touched. That was the existing point of view about God, the given syntax of consciousness: God was absolutely One and untouchable. Christianity, however, introduced an alien element into this elemental idea, and Arius represented one form of the resistance to the alien idea that a human person could be fully equal to God without diminishing God or multiplying Gods. Arius's viewpoint was pervasive and influential enough to threaten the unity of the church throughout the Roman empire, which is why the Roman emperor Constantine convened a council at Nicaea in 325 CE, where he required the assembled bishops to come up with a commonly agreed doctrine. In this case, the presence of the emperor encouraged everyone to achieve a solution. The Nicene Creed was the result:

> We believe in one God, the Father almighty, maker of all things, visible and invisible;
>
> And in one Lord Jesus Christ, the Son of God, begotten from the Father, only-begotten, that is, from the substance of the Father, God from God, light from light, true God from true God, begotten not made, of one substance with the Father, through Whom all things came into being, things in heaven and things on earth, Who because of us men and because of our salvation came down and became incarnate, becoming man, suffered and rose again on the third day, ascended to the heavens, and will come to judge the living and the dead;
>
> And in the Holy Spirit.
>
> But as for those who say, There was when He was not, and, Before being born He was not, and that He came into existence out of nothing, or who assert that the Son of God is from a different hypostasis or substance, or is created, or is subject to alternation or change—these the Catholic Church anathematizes.[25]

This statement affirmed that Jesus Christ and God were of the same substance. It also strongly asserted that Jesus Christ was coeternal with God, that he was not created or made by God. Any point of view contrary to this was condemned and denounced. Slowly the reality (i.e., *idea*) of human being and the reality (i.e., *idea*) of God were merging, when previous to the thought-problem of the incarnation, they were separated absolutely. The creed does not make any mention of what I earlier referred to as the tearing open and the self-emptying of God. In the creedal statements the notion that God was ever lessened in any way is never broached. The problem

---

24. Kelly, *Early Christian*, 227, emphasis added.
25. Kelly, *Early Christian*, 232.

posed by the incarnation was to articulate just how a man and God could be joined without detracting from either. The idea of the incarnation stimulated tremendous creative activity as thought grappled with the nature of ultimate reality. From the psychological perspective, the theological conflicts were where soul (i.e., consciousness) was coming to terms with its new logic, its new syntax. At the same time, another problem that was implicit in the Nicene Creed, yet to be thought through, was how there could be both one (the Incarnate) and yet two (God and man) that were both identical in their sameness and yet distinct and whole in their own right. This problem had to do with how Jesus as divine Word and Jesus as human person could be both the same and not the same, at the same time. The Council of Nicaea came up with an official public document, a statement of truth (creed) everyone present signed, but the conflict and ferment around these ideas did not decrease.

While the Arian tendency lessened Jesus' identity with God and so diminished Jesus' divine status, an opposing tendency lessened Jesus' humanity. Apollinarius's (ca. 310–ca. 390; bishop of Laodicea, Syria) attempt to bring the two together ended up substituting the divine Word for Jesus' human mind. Apollinarius wanted to affirm only one fundamental nature in the person of Christ, in contrast to those who wanted to affirm two natures, but in the process, he affirmed the flesh, the human body, of Jesus and then animated it with the spirit of the Word rather than the spirit of Jesus' own human will. Because he united Jesus' flesh with the divine essence, others objected that this view was docetic (Greek: to seem), which implied that Christ only *seemed*, or appeared, to be human. Here again, the full redemption of the realm of humankind fails if Christ is not fully human and only *seems* to be human, but the failure is in the opposite direction from Arius, in that God, or the divine Word, fails to become fully and completely human:

> It was man's rational soul, with its power of choice, which was the seat of sin; and if the Word did not unite such a soul with Himself, the salvation of mankind could not have been achieved. In a famous phrase of Gregory Nazianzen, "What has not been assumed cannot be restored; it is what is united with God that is saved."[26]

How to think the essence of the incarnate Jesus Christ presented a most terrible and ongoing problem for soul. Any formulation remained inherently unstable. Was he of one nature or one person, or was he of two natures, or two persons? If he is of one nature, how do you avoid losing either the divine or the human element in that oneness, and the tendency was almost always to lose some aspect of the human element. If he is of two natures, how exactly are the divine and human element connected, how do they function together, or do they function separately depending on the circumstances? The problem for these thinkers was the depiction of Jesus Christ in the gospels themselves, which were sacrosanct, the received authoritative revelation of

---

26. Kelly, *Early Christian*, 296–97.

God. The gospel depiction of Jesus Christ was the self-revelation of God, and so all the details in the gospels and all of Jesus Christ's actions had to be taken seriously. In some instances, Jesus is ignorant, weak, and subject to change and growth, these qualities taken as the expression of his human nature. At other times, he is clearly omniscient and omnipotent, qualities taken as the expression of his divine nature.

The gospels represent an intuitive, naive narrative expression of this new stage in the development of soul, or consciousness, taking the form of the coming together of God and man. But, after the gospels tell their story, the truth they implicitly contain becomes a problem for soul to think through explicitly, especially because it contradicted the prevailing theology of God's transcendent, undivided oneness. The idea of the incarnation was thinking itself, and stumbling along as it did so. As soul tried to work through the coming together of God and man, it had to work with these two already existing categories. All the solutions had something unsatisfactory about them, no matter how much each position insisted in its own way on keeping both categories (God and man) united and distinct at the same time. But, the real point here is that throughout all the christological struggles, soul, or consciousness, was working on itself over the centuries. Through this process in which soul was thinking its own thoughts, the real transformation of consciousness came about because the solution that soul needed could only come about as thought itself. If we hold too tightly to the concrete and empirical, or positivistic, categories of God and man, then thought will always fail to unite them because it falls prey to the naive imagination where God and man exist as concrete categories. Through the process of thinking, soul achieved the sublation of both the *idea* of God and of man into a new thought that was negative in the sense that it does not have concrete existence, but is pure thought. The *real* idea of God, as a *substantial* universal, was undergoing a transformation. The living *concept* of God and the living *concept* of man, as actual truths and realities for ancient public mind, had to negate each other to create a new thought that was neither but both at the same time. Soul had to create a new fundamental category. The living concepts that constituted public mind at the beginning of the Christian era were undergoing a self-negation in order to self-create a new form of shared public mind. The early christological formulations and their jostling for position were the dynamic thought process that was soul forging a new way to think about itself. A new living concept (the incarnation) that would transform the nature of reality was thinking itself into existence.

The position of Gregory Nazianzus (329–89; Archbishop of Constantinople), in opposition to Apollinarius, asserted two natures (here summarized by Kelly):

> Thus there are "two natures concurring in unity" in the God-man, and he is "twofold," "not two, but one from two"; and of course there are not "two Sons." His two natures are distinguishable in thought, and can be referred to as "the one" and "the other," but there are not two Persons; rather, "they both form a unity by their commingling, God having become man and man God." So far

from conceiving of this union as a moral one, or as a union of "grace" like that between God and His prophets and saints, Gregory states that the two natures "have been substantially conjoined and knit together."[27]

Nazianzus argues for "two natures" but tries to be clear this is a "twofoldness" in contrast to "two." He insists there are not "two Sons" and there are not "two Persons," and that this distinction occurs on the level of thought: that is, as a differentiation of qualities, not two different quantities. The logical shift that is working itself out is in the direction of a highly-sophisticated differentiation of consciousness that continues to develop because of the ongoing conflicts. The problem for Nazianzus's way of thinking is that it came up short in accounting for the natural limitations of Christ's human mind. His propensity for words like *mingling* and *fusion* led to the divine Word overtaking the functions of Jesus' human mind. Although he was thinking the incarnation on a higher level, weaknesses still appeared in the overall argument that naturally prompted corrections from other thinkers.

The very fact that the same words were used in the attempt to articulate contrasting positions in subtly different ways led to ongoing confusion, misunderstanding, and conflict. The primary Greek words at play in the ongoing arguments were, *Ousia* (essence, being, substance), *hypostasis* (highest principle, being, concrete individual existent), *prosopon* (person, individual) and *physis* (nature). All were brought to bear to define the true essence of the God-man. The unavoidable shadings of emphasis brought by different thinkers, intensifying and deepening the thinking process, was the very way soul thought itself into a new form of consciousness. The inability to get it right meant that thought had to continue to work on itself. The nature of the divine Word, the syntax of consciousness, is what was undergoing a transformation. As Kelly highlights, "The fundamental point which should be remembered is that for these writers the *ousia* of Godhead *was not an abstract essence but a concrete reality.*"[28] However, as concrete reality, this "substance" was not a visible thing but an invisible reality, a concrete soul truth. Naturally, the modern mind finds it hard to grasp this reality because the logic of our consciousness does not allow for concepts and ideas to have a concrete reality, and certainly not any existence independent of the *human* mind.

Is there anything today, by way of analogy, that might give us a sense of an invisible concrete reality? My mind goes to the realm of physics: perhaps electromagnetic fields, electricity itself, atomic and sub-atomic particles. All of these are basically invisible, but we believe they are concrete realities. This might help us understand that our modern logical form of consciousness, grounded in materiality and cause and effect, automatically, tacitly, lends these invisible *things* their *substance* and reality. In the same way, in antiquity the logical form of consciousness was constituted by the reality and substance of the universals, principles, and absolutes that informed thinking.

---

27. Kelly, *Early Christian*, 297.
28. Kelly, *Early Christian*, 268, emphasis added.

The christological controversies were working not with free-floating abstract mental concepts, but with the ground of reality, the fundamental stuff of the universe, the truth and reality of God, God's Word (the logos), and the way God related to the world and to humankind. These were living ideas, ultimate substantial truths, the stuff of reality itself, not intellectual abstractions in our modern sense, today sneered at as ivory tower pursuits, unconnected to reality.

Two Greek words that were at the heart of these debates reveal a subtle and seemingly trivial difference that was in fact decisive and profound: *homoousios* (*homo*; same + *ousia*; substance) and *homoiousios* (*homoi*; like or similar + *ousia*; substance). The struggle was to decide whether or not the Son—that is, Jesus Christ—was of the *same* or a *similar* substance as the Father, or God. As seen above, the Nicene Creed came down decisively on the side of *same* substance. Opponents tended to exaggerate each other's positions, and the opponents of the *homoousios* (same substance) feared that the real humanity of Jesus Christ would be lost if he was of the *same* substance of the divine, while the opponents of the *homoiousios* feared that if Jesus Christ was only of a *similar* substance, then there would be two gods with a trend toward polytheism. In that historic moment, the fights over these differences were intense and bitter, resulting in charges of blasphemy, as well as bans and exile when one camp had power over the other. In hindsight, I would say that the eventual reconciliation on the side of Father and Son being of the *same* substance was the direction soul needed to go. The new truth of incarnation needed to forge an entirely new category of reality in the heat of conflict and necessity. It could not settle for the already existing categories simply remaining side by side—the negation of the prevailing categories (Man and God) had to go all the way. *God* had to die on the cross, fully forsaken and fully dead, in order for the unheard-of *resurrection and ascension of the body* to occur. Thought itself (soul) insisted on thinking into reality a new concept, a new category, of reality—incarnation.

The ancient *concept* of matter considered *matter* as inherently evil in itself,[29] and matter, inclusive of the material-created order, included the flesh of the human body, as well as the general human condition, already alienated through its sinful status as matter. This was the logical status of matter (the natural world), the flesh, the body, in antiquity. Also, *evil*, in that ancient context, was a metaphysical problem and concern, and not a matter of human behavior. Today our humanistic mindset (form of consciousness) associates evil with human ethical matters and no longer thinks of evil in metaphysical terms. When God died (for modernity), Satan and the devil (the personifications of metaphysical evil) also died, that is, became irrelevant (metaphors).

The ancient alienated state of affairs, containing an inherent longing for redemption, had to find a way to be joined with God again. For the Neoplatonists, even though

---

29. According to Plotinus (205–70 CE), a Neoplatonist and one of the greatest thinkers of the ancient world, "Matter in itself, that is, unilluminated by form [eternal idea], is darkness or non-being, and as such is evil" (Kelly, *Early Christian*, 16).

matter was evil, the natural world was created from the One and thus contained a given longing to reunite with that higher truth. Within that metaphysical context, the human soul's desire was to make the ascent to higher insight and knowledge, but it first had to free itself from the body and the seduction of sense perception—the body was a problem, not an asset. This Neoplatonic orientation to ultimate reality is a reminder that God had succeeded in becoming totally transcendent, leaving the world behind, which dovetailed nicely with Yahweh's own trajectory. My psychological reading of Yahweh's journey to transcendence revealed how the sinful (separate from god) state of the world had been created by Yahweh's own self-divorce and self-castration, separating himself from his earlier fusion with nature as a Bull god. If the God(s) (personified soul) had left nature behind, and nature became mere nature, or only nature, no longer soul-infused with a god or goddess presence, the transformation of the evil status of the world would require the God to unite again with the created order, but on a higher logical order of thought. Soul could not simply return to permeating the natural order as it had done earlier, as that had been an immersive and undifferentiated state. The prehistoric, preliterate, and myth-ritual form of consciousness was decisively over.[30] And, so, if a new union was to be achieved, it had to be on a higher level of differentiation of the mode of consciousness itself. As incarnate Son of God, as incarnate Word, the Christ was an intensification in the realm of *thought* of a new union of God and the created order that had divided itself under both the idea of Adam's original sin and Yahweh's own abandonment of the created order, that is, his negation of himself as a nature god.[31]

The attempt to redeem the world under God's rule by way of a sovereign nation of Israel had failed and was now lost—that would have been an outward attempt at redemption in prevailing worldly terms; an external fix, so to speak. And, that form of worldly redemption would have remained on the semantic level (political and social), rather than achieving a true syntactical change, a change of the form of consciousness. The project of the so-called salvation of humankind now had to proceed on another level of thought itself, which is what the idea of the incarnation necessitated. But, even though the historical furnace of thought produced public statements of truth

---

30. It is interesting to note a parallel development in Greek thought in a legend reported by Plutarch during the early first century CE. It "tells of a voice requesting a passenger on a merchant ship to report, when the ship reached Palodes, that the Great Pan was dead. When the ship was becalmed off Palodes, the man complied with the request, and a great wailing was heard from the shore" (Lindow, *Swedish Legends*, 100). Pan was a pure nature god, archaic soul personified, in his part human and part animal representation—the human only partially emerged from the natural world. Bull-Yahweh represented a similar condition of consciousness. Christians of the time claimed that Christ's birth killed all (pan) the nature "demons" (and they were right, insofar as the Christ's birth symbolized the new emergent logical form of consciousness moving further away from the natural world).

31. Giegerich presents another approach to our theme through linking the death of Pan (and his relationship with Echo) with the ascension of Christ: "What the death of Great Pan implicitly heralded, but what it had as yet been incapable of expressing, or capable of expressing only in a negative way, became thus explicit in the Christian idea of Christ's Ascension" ("God Must Not Die!," 236).

(creeds) that gave shape to the new consciousness, it also led to deep and persistent divisions leading to different cultural outcomes, such as the division between the Western (Rome) and Eastern (Constantinople) churches, which was in part brought to a head by the christological settlement achieved at Chalcedon in 451. The difference that contributed to such a decisive split in Christian civilization was based on whether Jesus Christ had two natures (dyophysite), the West, or one nature (monophysite), the East. The Chalcedon settlement included the following statement:

> In agreement, therefore, with the holy fathers, we all unanimously teach that we should confess that our Lord Jesus Christ is one and the same Son, the same perfect in Godhead and the same perfect in manhood, truly God and truly man, the same of a rational soul and body, consubstantial with the Father in Godhead, and the same consubstantial with us in manhood, like us in all things except sin; begotten from the Father before the ages as regards His Godhead, and in the last days, the same, because of us and because of our salvation begotten from the Virgin Mary, the *Theotokos* [God-bearing or Mother of God], as regards His manhood; one and the same Christ, Son, Lord, only-begotten, made known in two natures without confusion, without change, without division, without separation, the difference of the natures being by no means removed because of the union, but the property of each nature being preserved and coalescing in one *prosopon* and one *hypostasis*—not parted or divided into two *prosopa*, but one and the same Son, only-begotten, divine Word, the Lord Jesus Christ, as the prophets of old and Jesus Christ Himself have taught us about Him and the creed of our fathers has handed down.[32]

This declaration affirmed that it was not only the flesh, or body, of Jesus that was united with the divine Word, but his mind, his rational soul, as well. It also strongly affirmed that the two natures, manhood and Godhead, were distinct and at the same time united in one *prosopon* and *hypostasis*, which meant *one singular objectively existing reality or substance*. The *unity* and *difference* of the God-man were affirmed to exist simultaneously as a singularity.

But, what about the phrase, "like us in all things except sin"? The idea of sin in its traditional theological context simply means *separation*, separation, that is, from God. On a superficial level, sin is most often thought of as bad behavior, transgressing a moral principle. What makes that a sin is the action separates the person from God. We might call this semantic sin, ordinary ethical human behavior. On the other hand, the "original sin" in the Christian context was the disobedience of Eve and Adam, as this is what separated them (and humankind) from God. We might call this syntactic sin, or logical sin. It is the category (concept) of sin as it exists within a particular form of consciousness that is at stake. "Adam and Eve" are a mythological/theological idea, never human persons who did a bad thing. The Christian affirmation was

---

32. Kelly, *Early Christian*, 339–40.

that Jesus Christ was never separate from God: recall the beginning of John's gospel ("In the beginning was the Word [logos], and the Word was with God, and the Word was God"), and the Nicene Creed affirmation that Christ was *begotten* not *made*. The fact that Christ is without sin means all of humankind is absolved of its sin, that is, absolved of its *logical* separation from God. How does one man save all men? "Christ" is not a man per se, but rather a manifestation of the logical form of consciousness that constitutes our human being and constitutes being in general. In the language of Christian theology, all of creation is now new, because the syntax of consciousness is now new. In terms of our biblical texts that symbolize this cosmic transformation of consciousness, the Tanakh becomes the "Old Testament"—the meaning the Tanakh constituted is incorporated (sublated) into the new shape of meaning that became the "New Testament." However, this was hardly a perfect balance, and as this idea played out through history, because the human person is declared to be of the same *substance* as the God, eventually the status of God does indeed reduce and the status of humankind increase.

The inclusion of the two natures left many unsatisfied and contributed to more unrest and conflict, as well as more councils. The underlying conflict between the two natures position (dyophysite) and the one nature position (monophysite) was one of the major contributing factors to the Great Schism of 1054 when the Western and Eastern churches officially went their separate ways, severing all ties (actually excommunicating each other). Speaking generally, in the West, under Roman Catholicism, which embraced the two natures, the humanity of Jesus has been more prominent, while in the East, in the Eastern Orthodox church, the embrace of the one nature led to an emphasis on the divinity of Christ. Thus, Western culture has tended to be more worldly and practical, while the Eastern orientation has been more otherworldly and mystical. Of course, many other practical, political, cultural, and geographical factors contributed to the schism, but how the incarnation was understood was a major factor conditioning the underlying logic of consciousness that permeated and shaped culture. The "Word made flesh" did just that, as *Word* and *man*, as *ideas* that were living realities interpenetrated each other, as they thought their way into a new category with its own ontological status. God and man were now an indissoluble union, and there was no retreating from this new idea, no escaping it, no avoiding it. The Christian basis of mind (*Word*) became a new world (*flesh*), affecting everyone whether Christian or not. But the incarnation was not a stable idea; it never did settle into a final secure form. In its Christian guise, soul continued to think itself through many conflicting variations, and some would become ortho-dox (right opinion), but that orthodoxy, as history shows, would take different forms with different culture-shaping outcomes. The next massive historical change in the syntax of consciousness will come with the Enlightenment, preceded and prepared for by the Reformation when Christianity's inherent instability led to another decisive split.

Soul Thinks Itself from Incarnation to Enlightenment

I argue that the right balance in the conception of the incarnation leads to the Enlightenment. I say this because the emergence of Reason as a human function (not a divine gift) is the direct result of the divine Word (logos), understood in antiquity as the source of the rational soul in humankind, incarnating itself and thus necessitating itself to think itself into a new form of consciousness. The idea of the incarnation continued to think itself through centuries of European culture, until the Enlightenment, when the incarnate Word is realized as human thought itself, rather than God's mode of thought in man. Through the soul process of self-negation and sublation, the divine Word became natural reason. I believe this probably would not have happened if the two dimensions of being constituting the incarnation, God and Man, had not been held in an absolute and yet unresolvable tension.

In antiquity, the given concepts of *God* and *man* were already established as metaphysical truths, and thus their definitions were immutable and ultimate. Although the incarnation did become a new category of soul, in the end, it could never reconcile itself with its own definition because the logic of the two constituting components (God and man) would maintain their incommensurate tension. In spite of the enormous thought that went into the notion of the incarnation in its Christian form, it remained on the level of image, of picture (the story of a God and a man)—it did not move to the level of thought proper, in spite of the tomes written about that image, that is, the Christ. For that to happen, the incarnation would have to dissolve itself through another self-negation and sublation on the way to another higher level of thought. In a sense, the incarnation was the result of an unholy alliance between fundamentally incompatible categories, though this would be the very dynamism driving it forward. The fundamental contradiction of the logic of the given concepts themselves, the concepts of God and man at the heart of the incarnation, drove soul to negate itself again in what became known as the Enlightenment.

The syntax of the consciousness that constituted God (i.e., the universals) had to empty itself so that the value of humankind (i.e., the particulars) could increase in value, significance, and freedom. In the mythological language of the time, the particulars, humankind and matter, were enslaved to sin, subject to death and fate (they lacked true value in themselves). They had no innate autonomy, value, and subjectivity; the true subject, value, and autonomy belonged to God alone. Humankind was not yet in possession of a self that was its ownmost self, free and no longer simply subject to an external destiny (symbolized by death, fate, and God's time). The truth of being a free subject belonged to God exclusively until the incarnation brought about the translocation of the free subject, and soul as a subject could continue to develop itself by way of the idea of *Christ* (historically, a revolutionary new subject). This became the human function of Reason. The Logos, divine, remote, and transcendent, needed (wanted?) to impregnate matter in the form of the human person, as the thinking subject: "from divine substance to human subject."³³ The mythological image of the Annunciation, when the angel Gabriel announced to the virgin Mary that she would conceive a son by way of the Holy Spirit, is the intuitive anticipation of this historical development, that resulted in the Enlightenment. Of course, within the contexts of the current monotheistic religions themselves, the definition of God as supreme, absolute, and eternally transcendent did not and does not change, but it does become a semantic content within a new syntax of consciousness. Today soul is not invested in the formal theological definition of God. When the definitions of the God-man were truly living ideas, however, soul was working on itself, thinking itself as living thought into a new reality. Once the most fertile christological period was over, say during the sixth century, Christianity continued to work on itself throughout the Scholastic period. As Western Christian thought developed itself over hundreds of years, soul was fermenting its new meaning in the background as the *I am*, and the possibility of a truly autonomous human subject insinuated itself as a cultural truth, first emerging tentatively during the Renaissance in the idea of humanism, and then with a vengeance during the Enlightenment.

---

33. "The soul had shed its previous logical form of substance and otherness and taken on the form of subject" (Giegerich, *What Is Soul?*, 273). See esp. section 3.4, "The Soul's Home-Coming: From Substance to Subject," 272–80.

Chapter 8

Reason: The Sublation of Christ (Death of God)

Consciousness—from Substance to Subject

The "end of meaning" [= death of God] is a logical, syntactical transformation and comes about through the *integration* (and thus also sublation) of the whole former status of consciousness into the structure of consciousness itself.[1]

The enormity of real meaning may become a little more plausible to us when we keep in mind that the *real* (existing) meaning of *our modern existence* is the journey, pursued systematically and with great fervor, into meaninglessness, or the systematic, step-by-step work upon the abrasion of meaning as such down to nothing.[2]

SOUL, IN THE FORM of the "I Am" subject, has sublated itself through successive forms:

Yahweh:	"I Am Who I Am"
Christ:	"I am the way, the truth and the life"
Descartes:	"I think therefore I am"

These historical moments, personified by these figures, show us the historical process whereby soul has left the universals and invested itself in the particulars, as well as leaving the sensual picture world of myth and religion and become abstract thought proper. As the shared public mind of meaning that invisibly orients us to the world, soul has undergone a deep transformation in which the reality of divine substance and the universals has changed itself into the subjectivity of humankind, the human function of reason, and the ultimate value of the material world of particulars (today the

---

1. Giegerich, "Ego-Psychological Fallacy," 359.
2. Giegerich, "Sacrifice of Isaac," 181.

public expects physics—rightly or wrongly—to answer ultimate questions, not theology). In this chapter, I explore how soul left behind the world of religion and became the world of modernity and science, how soul became the truth that we believe is universal. The Bible has, so to speak, done its work, and I now examine the new form of consciousness, humanism, and how it manifested through the lives and thought of specific pre-Enlightenment and Enlightenment figures, who were enlisted in soul's service to develop *reason* as a human function.

Autonomous Soul

Something truly monumental and extraordinary happened as the ages of mythology and religion gradually faded and what is called the modern age developed. The age of science and humanism did indeed supersede the age of myth and religion. Just as the attitude of the new spirit god Yahweh was one of superiority to the nature gods and goddesses, and the attitude of Christ as the incarnation of the Logos was one of superiority to Yahweh (and also all the nature gods and goddesses who became equated with the devil), so the attitude of science and humanism was (is) also one of superiority toward all forms of mythology and religion, dismissing that entire form of consciousness as unscientific superstition. As I have noted, soul negates its former status in its process of self-transformation, and it does not do so politely. Soul exhibits a fierce and violent intolerance toward its former state. This is primarily because the process, as it occurs on the large historical cultural scale, is blind and unconscious. Human persons are not the authors of this work; what changes is the unconscious, impersonal basis of mind itself, the actual syntax of consciousness, the invisible context of thought. Obviously, human persons enact the work of the background cultural-mind, or soul, but we are not its creators. We did not create Mind any more than we created Life. We find ourselves *minded* just as we find ourselves *alive*. We act out soul's unfolding ideas, meanings, and projects far more than we direct them. This is because we *are* the passions of the unfolding mind; that is, we exist first of all as unconsciously identified with the deep basis of mind. Like the image of the *water* that we swim in without knowing what we swim in, *the prevailing matrix of consciousness is our being* (we live *as* the virtual world of meanings). In its immediacy during the historical moment, public mind, or soul, does not have the capacity or distance to reflect on itself. The passage of time, historical distance, makes it possible to see the prior basis of mind with some perspective. As with both Yahweh and Christ, these deep changes of the logical form of consciousness take hundreds of years and have life-and-death consequences for the human persons and populations caught up in these historic shifts of soul.

Reason: The Sublation of Christ (Death of God)

Soul: Substance to Subject

As the late Middle Ages waned and Christianity exhausted itself, a period interestingly named the Enlightenment emerged, a Western European development of consciousness conventionally dated from about 1685 to 1815, known also as the Age of Reason (it is probably self-evident that this new age named itself). The main ideas that emerged during this period—reason, individualism, and skepticism—were the logical development of about one thousand years of Christian history. The well-established Christian syntax of consciousness, the ground of society and its institutions, fought the implications of the rise of Reason, even employing state-sponsored heresy spies in the process. Nevertheless, the movement of Reason underway was not of people but of soul, and Reason did indeed become the new basis of mind, the new logical form of consciousness. It is striking to note that soul as Reason did not personify itself as a god or deity the way it had with the polytheistic nature gods, the god Yahweh, and the god Christ, but rather soul became a *function* of the mind of humankind in general. Functioning as Reason, soul did indeed kill off the form of itself manifesting as deities once and for all. Reason came to be essentially a-theistic, and as a *human* function, it took a stand against the gods and God. Soul in the form of Reason became the basis of what we today take for granted as science and humanism, and for science and humanism, God is not the basis of mind, our own natural reason is. Of course, scientists and humanists can believe in a god, but this god is a content of personal consciousness, as "God" is no longer the taken-for-granted general basis of consciousness. Today, people can believe whatever they want and pursue all kinds of hobbies, but spinning wheels and steam locomotives, for example, are no longer at the center of our society's economic systems, even though some are passionately devoted to maintaining them. When Christianity was the basic form of consciousness, people generally did not choose whether or not to be a Christian because it was already the given form of culture and society one simply inherited. Today anyone can put on or take off a belief system, a spiritual orientation, or a religion like the latest fashionable pair of jeans.[3] Modernity means there is no soul in religion anymore. Science, in a general sense, is what soul became during the Enlightenment. The large cultural sense of soul can be thought of in terms of the overall *shape* of consciousness that we, in a sense, inhabit. God is no longer that shape. God has in fact been downgraded to being only one idea, one moment among many, within a new shape of consciousness called Enlightenment and Reason. The overall *shape* of consciousness determines how we think about the contents of consciousness, the things of our inner and outer world. This is the distinction between syntax and semantics. Soul *is* what we *are* as our being and existence, and soul in this view is not an unchanging eternal truth, but a historical, changing, and self-developing truth. As soul changes, our fundamental conception of what it means to be human changes.

3. This does not mean individuals cannot have profound and meaningful religious and spiritual experiences and convictions. A religious orientation and belief can still be genuine and authentic for individuals, but it is no longer the water we, as a culture, swim in.

God's Autopsy and the Living Truth of Soul

The Gods Were Real Indeed, But . . .

The broad historical overview I propose, from Yahweh to psychology, from prehistoric oral cultures all the way to today, posits the living truth of soul at the heart of this autopsy of God. The psychological analysis of the logical form of consciousness that animates historical and cultural activity uncovers the surprising factor discovered in the skeleton of God's corpse: Soul is that autonomous *factor*. It enables an entirely new perspective on formerly perceived mythological and theological entities and metaphysical (ontological) substance or presence. Enlightenment consciousness came to the mistaken conclusion that the gods and goddesses, all mythology, had never been real and were merely the result of primitive thought processes and superstition. Psychology recognizes that the gods and goddesses were indeed very real, but they were the form of the mind itself, public mind, the form of consciousness, which now has changed and become something entirely different. In its cultural form of Enlightenment, soul sublated its earlier personified deity-forms into Reason as a function of the human mind. The "I Am" of God became the "I am" of Christ, which then became the "I am" of the ordinary person, and as this change took place, soul's manifestation as deity truly disappeared. God, as a substantial autonomous subject (I Am) in its own right, essentially dissolved as an entity of otherness and reemerged as a subject (I am) in the human person. As humankind (in Western Europe) awakened to its new autonomy with Reason, it looked around and discovered that it was now alone in the cosmos for the first time. The divine parents had "died," and humankind, the former "child of God," was now an adult without God. It is as if, under the gaze of this autopsy, we see how the body of God simply evaporated into nothing, thin air, becoming the process of thought itself, consciousness at large. It is my contention that the new "nothing" (no-thing) of consciousness is just as *real* as God once was.

The notion of the *autonomy* of soul should not be surprising in the context of a phenomenological view of soul's historical manifestations. Historically, the gods and goddesses in general, and Yahweh and Christ in particular, were autonomous, authoritative, and superior real entities *vis-à-vis* human persons. They were objective truths independent of human will and direction. In fact, human will and direction were always subject to the will and direction of the gods. The notion that human persons are the agents of their own fate, the creators of their own world, and that the human mind is free and independent, as well as the origin of culture, is a very recent development. Our feeling of human superiority and agency really emerged during the last three hundred years (the eighteenth through the twentieth centuries), while the early emergence of our modern frame of mind can be found in the sixteenth and even the fifteenth century. However, the first impulse for what is called the Enlightenment actually finds its origin in the ancient and decisive act of Yahweh cutting himself off from his bull nature. The seeds of the modern form of mind and its freedom that we take for granted today were the deities Yahweh and Christ.

Reason: The Sublation of Christ (Death of God)

When he cut himself off from his own nature as Bull and Storm god, Yahweh was the early herald of that still far off modern development known as the Enlightenment. No one at the time could have predicted the outcome, but looking back we can see its *telos*. Yahweh became a fierce and passionate critic of the nature gods and goddesses, which is how truth split itself off from its ground, its reality in sensual earthy nature, and became a transcendent independent deity, the one true god in contrast to the "false" (nature) gods, the idols of idolatry (the natural worship of symbols). Soul's project as Yahweh was to erode the image nature of truth and to become image-less and abstract (literate). Although tending toward a more noetic form, soul remained thoroughly identified with the personification Yahweh, the hyperpersonalized Yahweh. Soul continued its movement as the Christ sublated Yahweh and became the incarnate Word, another hyperpersonalized form, but this time in the form of a "historical human person," which then transcended itself through self-torture, suicide, and resurrection/ascension. The Word became *flesh* and established a new status of consciousness as a spiritual kingdom that paradoxically transcended the world of the flesh. In uniting with the flesh, the Word raised the logical status of the flesh (the natural order) out of its sinful, shadowy state to a new higher-valued status. Through the incarnation, both God and Man sublated each other into a new category that had not existed before, but that category remained unstable. Soul continued to think this new thought by way of Christology over centuries. Soul's process of self-negation continued, carried out by hundreds of thinkers over the years, as essentially the Logos (divine Word) attacked itself again, negating its form as a deity, and became a free and critical function of the human mind as well as a newly autonomous human subject. *Soul was shifting itself from its location outside humankind as a God, to a location within humankind as a function, the function of Reason.*

From Biblical Text to Historical Thinker

The primary text for my reading of soul's living truth and God's autopsy up until now has been the Bible, in both its Jewish and Christian forms. The texts of the New Testament date to the first and second centuries of the Common Era, and so it seems that soul, in a biblical sense, stopped appearing as a sacred text, understood as the direct revelation of a god, about two thousand years ago. Of course, Christianity, in its own self-understanding, *knew* it was the *final* revelation of truth. And this points to a significant aspect of soul's phenomenology, that when it achieves its new status it is totalizing. This is because the old soul status has been completely negated, and the new soul status *is* all the water we swim in; there are no other perspectives in view until soul begins negating itself again, as we explore now. The texts in which soul continued to write its truth next were the writings, thoughts, and lives of seminal thinkers, and the logic of soul, soul's telos, established by my interpretation of the biblical texts, is visible in the cultural development and thought of Western civilization. A close reading of the Medieval period, the one thousand years from the fifth to the fifteenth centuries (which I am not undertaking), would also show the gradual movement of consciousness as the primary and authoritative value shifted from the universals to the particulars, from God to humankind.[4]

In this chapter, I touch on a handful of iconic thinkers who exemplify the momentous shift in the syntax of consciousness that soul was undertaking at the end of the medieval period and into the Enlightenment. The ideas that show the progression of soul are not merely intellectual ideas that we would ordinarily think of as contents of consciousness (history of ideas). These are living ideas that seize hold of certain people, who then must work and live them out. They are ideas that disturb and change the lives of those who must think them, as we saw with Reimarus and Strauss and the quest for the historical Jesus. Before I introduce specific historical figures, I want to explore the psychological structure of *integrity*, as I believe it shows us the dialectical movement of soul in relation to these individuals. I have spoken of soul as cold, distant, and impersonal and not under human control, but the impact of soul is indeed very personal. For me, the idea of *integrity* is where we can recognize soul "incarnating" in human individuals. Soul lays a burden on them, an ineluctable creative task, and integrity leads that person to take up the burden and see it through.

Integrity as Soul's Presence

I have been focused on soul as the impersonal form or syntax of consciousness that defines the character of a cultural and historical era. Soul is that general "water" we all swim in without being explicitly aware of it, while it orients our awareness to the world. And from this perspective, people, as the ones who think and create, are the medium that soul works with as it generates new ideas in the context of already established ideas. But, soul is not a potter shaping, like clay, human thought—that is a traditional metaphysical or theological image. Soul *is* the living dynamic interplay of the conflict of ideas throughout culture, and humankind is the medium in which this living process occurs. Although it is never just one person who generates the new idea out of his personal consciousness, soul seems to take hold of iconic individuals throughout history who become remembered historically as symbolic of cultural sea changes in the nature of consciousness. The quality these people exhibit is integrity, in that they embody in their thought and life a new truth, and they stake their lives on that truth no matter the consequences. We saw this quality of integrity in the story of Job.

Integrity is the name I give to soul manifesting in individuals, noted especially when they find they must take a stand because they are gripped by a truth they cannot deny. Further, this truth puts them at odds with the prevailing version of soul that has

---

4. Interpreting the medieval period would include, of course among many others, Meister Eckhart (1260–328). Here is one telling aphorism that indicates the direction of soul's thinking: "Between God and me there is no 'between.'"

already long established itself. Soul creates a truth that becomes the prevailing cultural truth and then negates itself in the process of forming a new truth. Job's fully embodied and wholly heartfelt integrity enabled him, forced him, to take a stand against not just the prevailing view of God, but against God himself. This alienated him from those who held the prevailing established ideas about God (his friends, his wife, his social world), and from the very truth of the God with whom he was in conflict. Job was a man alone who stood for his truth. He could not forsake himself, nor could he forsake his God, and this dual conviction constituted his integrity. Integrity has this twofold structure and internal tension that results in unavoidable suffering, a suffering brought on by truth.

Integrity is the dialectical process of being both gripped and gripping in turn. Job knew that he was guiltless before God, and this knowledge gripped him, but Job also had to take hold of his guiltlessness with his whole being and take his stand in the face of this very God and all the social pressures that urged him to stand down. He had to take hold of the internal imperative of what he knew to be true, stake his life on it, and let it become his ground. When a truth grips an individual and the individual in turn takes hold of that truth, soul begins to crystallize a new truth in a social/cultural context. Many are gripped by soul but do not then truly take hold of what has gripped them; they do not wrestle with it. People have powerful moving experiences, receive a glimpse of a new truth, but if it does not become a problem that must be interpreted in relation to the wider cultural world, it goes nowhere; it remains merely a personal experience and does not enter the public arena. People often have moral conflicts about matters in their lives or in society, but they find myriad ways to avoid truly grappling with them. What grips a person is not something to be merely copied, imitated, or acted out, but to be interpreted and shaped.

Another illustration of the dialectical nature of integrity, as described by Giegerich, is Jung's relationship with the concept of *soul*, in which both "being gripped" and "grasping" play a role:

> Jung had been reached and touched, indeed "gripped," by the Notion of the soul. And because he had been touched and gripped by it, he had a grasp, a *Begriff*, a Notion, of it and he could grasp it. Both oppositional aspects (active and passive) belong together. The *living* Notion that we are concerned with here is the dialectical unity of "being gripped" and of "grasping," of *begriffen sein* and *begreifen*.[5]

The notion of soul for Jung was not merely an intellectual idea that he came up with or generated out of his own thinking. It was a *living* idea that touched Jung with a life of its own. It became his ground and standpoint, "the center and the circumference of his vision and reflection."[6] It put him at odds with the conventional Enlightenment ratio-

---

5. Giegerich, *Soul's Logical Life*, 41.
6. Giegerich, *Soul's Logical Life*, 42.

nalism and materialism that was the dominant cultural paradigm within which Jung was educated and worked. The psychology that Jung developed was one of the new visions that emerged during late modernity at the beginning of the twentieth century, which began to undermine the very foundations of modernity. Jung was one of several major transitional figures who represented the beginning of the end of Enlightenment consciousness, and I will explore his significance in the next chapter. Here I am interested in the structure of integrity as a soul phenomenon and how it manifests as the individual. Not every stance of integrity is necessarily a cultural soul phenomenon, and it is important to distinguish between personal soul and cultural soul (the *opus parvum* and the *opus magnum*).[7] The mutual relationship of "being gripped" and "grasping" is what constituted Jung's relationship with soul, and it oriented not just how he thought, but how he lived. In this regard, Jung's integrity involved him in a "great work" that had a broad impact on culture. But, even in personal moments of integrity the same structure is at work, when a truth takes hold of us and we commit to taking a stand on that truth, come what may.

My first thinker, Francesco Petrarch, does not exemplify integrity as much as he represents the movement of soul from divine substance to human subject in the form of the emergence of humanism during the Renaissance, preparing the way for the Enlightenment.

Francesco Petrarch

Francesco Petrarch (1304–1374), the founder of humanism, was another exemplar of soul's movement toward becoming a human subject. He represents the development of a new faculty of the human mind itself that was being recognized as "human possibility." He championed and affirmed the development of the human mind: "Petrarch argued . . . that God had given humans their vast intellectual and creative potential to be used to their fullest."[8] Although a devout Catholic, he saw no conflict between faith and the development of *human* possibilities. Petrarch initiated the Renaissance's intellectual preoccupation with Greek and Roman classical literature and history, finding it far superior to anything of his contemporary period. Petrarch was a bridge between the classical world of antiquity and the opening of the modern world beginning with the Renaissance and continuing to the Enlightenment. He worked to bring together the value of human intellectual, aesthetic, and moral development through the contemplation of the ancient writers in concert with the prevailing Christian view of divine revelation and a cosmos ordered and governed by God. Petrarch was a deeply sensitive man who preferred the work of the mind in solitude. Because of the fame of his intellectual work, especially his poetry, and his orientation to the world promoting *human* development, he stands as another historical icon of soul's shifting valence as

---

7. Giegerich, *What Is Soul?*, 73.
8. *Wikipedia*, s.v. "Petrarch," last updated April 26, 2022, https://en.wikipedia.org/wiki/Petrarch.

a result of the incarnation when full divine and ontological status had been given to humankind by way of the soul's project called "Jesus Christ." The soul value of the "I Am" was shifting from God to humankind, from the universals to the particulars, and Petrarch was an early emissary of this process, helping to prepare the consciousness that enabled Martin Luther to take his stand.

Martin Luther

At the moment of taking a stand, a person may have purely personal motives in mind, with no intention to shake the foundations of consciousness. Hindsight reveals the cultural significance of that action so that certain historical figures become household names down through the centuries as their name comes to mark a turn in cultural consciousness that they themselves were not seeking to initiate.

This was certainly true of Martin Luther (1483–1546), who stands out as a significant figure on the threshold of the Enlightenment, which he preceded by over a 150 years. Luther's famous ninety-five theses, posted in 1517, were originally simply a call for an academic discussion among colleagues of the church's practice of selling indulgences (buying forgiveness of sin with money) along with other doctrinal matters. The hoped-for discussion never took place, and the theses took on a life of their own, published and disseminated throughout Europe. The Roman Catholic church, at the time the only church in Europe and the most powerful political institution as well, brought these matters to a head with a heresy trial in 1521. Luther was asked to withdraw several of his statements in order to avoid being branded a heretic, but he responded with his well-known declaration:

> I cannot and will not recant anything, for to go against *conscience* is neither right nor safe. Here I stand, I can do no other, so help me God. Amen.[9]

It took several years for Luther to realize that integrity was at stake in these matters. What he originally intended as an academic discussion had become a contest over truth itself, and it was the church's truth in conflict with his own. To state it simply, the church based its authority on the New Testament revelation that Christ as God incarnate was the first and final truth and reality, as well as the church's history of tradition and practices. During the early centuries of the church's development, there was no ontological distinction between God's revelation, the church's doctrine and traditions, and the church as institution: It was all created and sanctioned by God, the ultimate universal principle. The Middle Ages was ruled by the logical form of consciousness constituted by Christ as God Incarnate, as absolute truth. The ontological unity of God, church, and political authority manifested as day-to-day reality, the societal expression of the prevailing syntax of cultural consciousness. In that syntax

---

9. *Wikipedia*, s.v. "Martin Luther," last updated April 13, 2022, https://en.wikipedia.org/wiki/Martin_Luther (emphasis added).

of consciousness, the "I Am," as the universal principle, was identified with God, with Christ, and the church.

In that social-religious context, it is quite astonishing really that Luther took his stand on *himself*. In that historical moment, Luther represented the shifting of ontological value to an individual, as he stood on and refused to forsake his integrity; he was gripped by a new value of soul. This created a crisis for the prevailing mode of truth, and the prevailing logical form of consciousness, and so the church had to take steps to protect its truth. Luther is an example of soul negating itself (or God as the ultimate metaphysical value) and increasing the value of humankind (the universal principle is losing value, and the particular is gaining value). Luther based his authority, his claim to truth, on the Bible, but—and this is the crucial difference and the shift—*his own* reading of the Bible. The *authority* of the primary source of God's revelation, the Bible, and most especially the New Testament, which was ontologically identified with the church's reading (doctrine, tradition, institutional, and papal authority) was claimed now by an individual. Luther, as *himself*, as an individual, claimed *his* reading of the Bible was the ultimate source of truth, placing him in a fundamental conflict with the church, which claimed its reading of the same Bible was the ultimate source of truth. This was a profound change in the logical status of truth, in the context of what had been a veritable ontological womb of Christian truth for almost one thousand years.

Once Luther had been condemned as a heretic and excommunicated, he could have been put to death. Standing up to God and challenging the prevailing truth had dire consequences. Still, the fact that the ninety-five theses spread throughout European society indicates that soul's self-negation and change was underway. A new idea (truth) was in the air but remained inchoate until articulated by Luther. If "Luther" had appeared too early, he would have disappeared in the historical record, which is what happened to some extent to a forerunner a hundred years earlier, Jan Hus (1369–1415). Hus was burned at the stake for taking his own principled stand on the role and practices of the church, the nature of the Eucharist, and other theological topics. A well-regarded and popular theologian and priest in the kingdom of Bohemia (now Czech Republic), Hus was an early reformer, and his teachings, after his death, led to the Hussite wars rebelling against the Roman Catholic rulers. These rebellions failed, and the area was returned forcibly to Roman Catholicism.[10] Such convulsive historical events reveal soul's agitation as it developed new ideas that would rupture the closed syntactical world of European Roman Catholic consciousness. These historical events helped pave the way for Luther, resulting from the shifting basis of mind, the transformation of the syntax, or structure, of soul (i.e., consciousness at large).

The ontological unity of the Christian basis of mind was beginning to fall apart, and the high value that imbued consciousness as the identity of the "I Am" of God, was shifting from God and Christ to the mind of humankind. The human mind was

---

10. *Wikipedia*, s.v. "Jan Hus," last updated May 2, 2022, https://en.wikipedia.org/wiki/Jan_Hus#Apology_of_the_Catholic_Church.

gaining freedom, becoming a subject, its own "I am," in its own right. This shift is the direct result of the incarnation. In a sense the incarnation was beginning to work against itself. By individualizing and humanizing itself as Luther's truth, it took a stand against its societal and institutional ontologized form of truth (represented by the church).[11]

My next example of integrity is Francis Bacon who took a stand in conflict with the dominance of the universals in the world of academic thought prevailing in the universities.

Francis Bacon

Standing on the threshold of the Enlightenment at the turn of the seventeenth century is Francis Bacon (1561–1626), a major figure in the history of Western thought, who became seriously misunderstood. Bacon was important to soul's movement because his introduction of the inductive process of reasoning was another indication of the shifting balance of power between the universals and the particulars, between God and humankind. Up until his time, the tradition of deriving knowledge was based on deduction from generalizations, universal principles, metaphysical assumptions, and divine revelation. The universal principles of philosophy, and God's divine revelation, the Bible, were *the* source of truth, and thus knowledge had to be derived from these higher principles and truths. This basic assumption had guided thought through antiquity and into the Elizabethan era (1558–1603) of Bacon's time. In that framework, knowing began in heaven, descending from on high by way of abstract argument. Bacon's process of induction reverses this direction of thinking, and insists that scientific reasoning should begin with the careful observation of natural phenomenon. From the thorough gathering of data, on the ground, as it were, generalizations and principles are built from the bottom up, grounded in the empirical observation of nature.

In Bacon's time, the Bible was the source for understanding the natural world as divinely created and ordered, and the Bible's "chronology" determined that the universe was about six thousand years old. The natural world was taken for granted as a given and basically ignored as a source of knowledge itself. Nor was it possible to consider that humankind could improve upon the natural world. In fact, the general cultural tone in Elizabethan England was one of decay, that the fallen and sinful state of humankind permeated nature itself, and everything was in decline:

> Man's fall from the perfect Garden was believed to have infected nature itself. The microcosm, man, had destroyed the macrocosm, nature. The human drama of the Fall and the Redemption was being played out upon the brief stage of a few trifling millennia. Eternity, the timeless eternity of the spiritual

---

11. For an in-depth analysis showing how soul forged the modern "I" by way of Martin Luther's terrible religious anguish see, Giegerich, *Historical Emergence*, 35–134.

> world, was near at hand. By contrast, the long story of geological change and evolution was unknown. The smell of an autumnal decay pervaded the entire Elizabethan world. Over all that age . . . there was a subdued feeling in men's hearts that the sands in the hourglass were well-nigh run. It was autumn, late autumn, and God was weary of the play.[12]

When an intuitive sense of the "End of the World" permeates a culture, we can be sure that the underlying logical form of consciousness, soul, is undergoing a profound change of self-negation as a new form of soul begins to emerge. Something is coming to an end, but it is not the physical world that we think of as "out there," but rather that form of consciousness that is the unconscious and assumed human cultural world. The human world of the prevailing order of meaning (soul) was dying, and a new order of meaning was emerging. It was as if soul, in its medieval Christian form, had exhausted itself—that particular form of consciousness had done its work, and a new status of consciousness had begun to unfold. The historical iconic figures I am touching on were the ones marked by soul's creative ferment to develop the new idea, and they often suffered as a result, as they were ahead of their time and misunderstood. Through Bacon's integrity, soul entered culture as an idea that expressed a new soul-truth, which gripped him and could not be denied. Integrity demands the individual give voice to that soul-truth and suffer the social consequences of rejection and dismissal, or worse.

At Bacon's time, Aristotle, alongside the Bible, was the other infallible authority in the fields of education and learning. Argument was focused on metaphysical controversies and abstract conceptions, the realm of the universals, while nature was largely ignored. The Greeks and Romans, known through their classic literature, were viewed as great and glorious cultures that far exceeded the possibilities of Bacon's time and preoccupied prevailing thought. Truth was to be sought in the paramount value of the universals and in the much more highly valued cultures of the past. When Bacon went to Cambridge at the early age of twelve he sensed something was not right with the prevailing educational foundations:

> "Men of sharp wits," Bacon was later to describe his tutors, "shut up in the cells of a few authors, chiefly Aristotle, their Dictator." A strong admiration for the lost classic literature could not conceal the fact that at Cambridge learning was largely pretense, that all was of the past. Men endlessly wove and rewove a spider web of ideas derived from Greek and Roman sources.[13]

Trapped in a past and a logical form of consciousness constituted by the universals, a form that was losing much of its sheen, European culture (soul's workshop) was slowly developing a new style of consciousness, and Bacon was one of its early spokespersons.

Although Christianity had its own version of the eternally fixed and stable character of nature as God's created order, Greek thought, too, had its version of the

---

12. Eiseley, *Man Who Saw*, 58.
13. Eiseley, *Man Who Saw*, 24.

eternal fixity of nature, governed not by observation but by the universality of general principles, the universals. Aristotle was a keen observer of nature and spent two years on the island of Lesbos staring into the lagoons.[14] He was fascinated by sea life and particularly puzzled by those creatures that defied conventional categories, and seemed to be neither plant nor animal, such as sponges. It was clear to him nature existed on a scale, or continuum, and that individuals went through transformations and cycles of life, including birth, growth, decay, and death, but he could not consider the notion of evolution because his consciousness was governed by the general form of consciousness of antiquity: the predominance of universal truths, which in the case of nature meant the eternal unchanging form of species:

> Flesh might bloom and decay, but the shape of the human body, the cicada body, the fish body—all those shapes and functions remained unchanging. Aristotle's nature was steady-state and beautifully, eternally continuous.
>
> Although he had broken with Plato's conception of ideal forms, nonetheless he believed that knowledge could be based only on what was fixed and not in flux. Only the fixity of individual forms through the eternity of species makes Aristotelian nature and thus knowledge possible.
>
> When the ancients argued about creation, their narratives were not inflected by stories of a man and a woman in a garden or a god moving across the face of the waters; their arguments turned on different questions, about whether the universe had been shaped by gods or atoms colliding chaotically or was the outcome of a design deep within all animal and plant forms.[15]

Thinking, from ancient times through the Middle Ages, whether Israelite, Christian, or Greek, always began with theoretical general principles, universal truths, and moved down from there. That form of consciousness was still functionally absolute during Francis Bacon's life, and this was what he was up against in trying to promote the thinking process of induction. Bacon challenged the prevailing orthodoxy that species were eternally unchanging:

> The transmutation of species is, in the vulgar philosophy, pronounced impossible, and certainly it is a thing of difficulty, and requireth deep search into nature; but seeing there appear some manifest instances of it, the opinion of impossibility is to be rejected, and the means thereof to be found out.[16]

Today, the idea of the "transmutation of species" has become commonplace. But given the prevailing logic of consciousness of Bacon's time, it was a radical, even revolutionary idea because it shattered the very logic of consciousness within which the idea of "impossibility" was embedded. The conviction that species change was impossible was not merely a wrong or misguided idea that could be corrected by science.

14. Stott, *Darwin's Ghosts*, 20–40.
15. Stott, *Darwin's Ghosts*, 39–40.
16. Eiseley, *Man Who Saw*, 80.

More profoundly, the very conviction that species change was impossible was rooted in the foundational logic of a consciousness that *knew* that general principles and universal ideas were absolute truths! Soul itself undermined the absolute nature of that truth because soul attacked itself from within itself. Bacon does not represent a merely intellectual controversy. Bacon was one of the spokespersons for a transformation of the logic of consciousness on the same level as Yahweh's challenge to the polytheistic gods and goddesses, and the Christ's transformation of Yahweh. These shifts in the foundation and syntax of consciousness are major earthquakes that change everything on the surface.

The cultural public mind that Bacon was challenging was not yet truly living in the present, and the consciousness that would observe and question nature without starting from universal principles had not yet emerged. Bacon symbolizes soul's turn to the natural world as an internal revolution of consciousness:

> Bacon saw more clearly than any of the other Renaissance writers that the development of the experimental method itself, the means by which "all things else might be discovered" was of far more significance than any single act of invention.
>
> It was Bacon's whole purpose, set against the Scholastic thinking of medieval times, "to overcome," as he remarks in another of his works, the *Novum Organum*, "not an adversary in argument, but nature in action." *Truth, to the medieval schoolmen of the theologically oriented universities, rested upon the belief that reality lay in the world of ideas largely independent of our sense perceptions.* In this domain the use of a clever and sophisticated logic for argument, rather than observation of the phenomena of nature was the road to wisdom.
>
> Francis Bacon . . . presented an "engine," for the attainment of truth; namely, induction. We must refrain, Bacon contended, from deducing general laws or principles for which we have no real evidence in nature. Instead, because of our human tendency to leap to unwarranted conclusions, we must dismiss much of what we think we know and begin anew patiently to collect facts from nature, never straying far from reality until it is possible through surety of observation to deduce from our observations more general laws.[17]

The frame of mind that Bacon introduced has been attacked as the origin of humankind's alienation from nature because it established the general principles of the scientific method, which objectified nature, and led directly to the industrial revolution. This, of course, did happen. Nature, instead of being God's creation, became raw material for industrial production.

However, such a critique fails to see the larger soul context of this development. Although humankind lived within nature, it was an unconscious fusion offering no possibility of a conscious relationship with nature. In general, humankind's attention was absorbed by truth and reality identified with the universal ideas, and,

17. Eiseley, *Man Who Saw*, 53–54, emphasis added.

metaphorically, we "looked up" in order to know truth. Bacon represented the shift away from this upward looking to a looking around down here and now. As the value of the universals declined and the value of the particulars increased, soul (public mind) actually began to become conscious of nature as something separate from itself; soul (public mind) began to notice the natural world and to see it in a new light. Even more, this was a step in the process of humankind becoming aware of itself because now humankind becomes the location for soul's subjective sense of self. Humankind begins to become an *I am*, feeling and knowing itself as an agent in its own right, whereas in antiquity the universals, the gods, were the ultimate agents. Along with proposing the new principle of reasoning, Bacon realized that this way of approaching the natural world gave humankind the means to improve upon nature and culture through the process of discovery by way of inductive reasoning. Mind gained a new independence, valuing engagement with the natural world through curiosity and practicality, as well as feeling new powers for social and cultural self-improvement. Here again, the trend of soul toward freedom and independence is at work.

René Descartes

René Descartes (1596–1650), like Bacon, found his thinking at odds with the received truths. He cut all ties with the traditions of the past, and went his own way. The very fact that Descartes could declare independence from the philosophical tradition and base his findings on his own experience and thinking was significant. It shows again that the power of the universals to bind thinking to its general principles was already seriously weakened; Descartes was making his way in the context of an already increasing cultural relativism. Martin Luther's ninety-five theses, challenging the absolute authority of the church, symbolized the growing decline of the logic of revelatory theological truth. A popular writer, Michel de Montaigne (1533–1592), published a series of *Essays* at the end of the sixteenth century that challenged the traditional and absolute standards of religion and morality. Montaigne believed that everything was in a constant state of flux, and so he was pushed to an extreme skepticism: "Since nothing can ever be grasped with certainty in the turbulence of the world, he [Montaigne] is led to a full-blooded Pyrrhonism summed up in his famous slogan: 'Que sais-je?'" (What do I know?)[18] His views were quite popular, also indicating that he was expressing something of a new Zeitgeist, a new logic of consciousness. The increase in *human* authority, questioning and challenging divine and traditional authority, was, in effect, throwing the long-established eternal truths up in the air. The "ground" that culturally had been taken for granted up to that point—the logical form of consciousness of antiquity, of the universals, of God—was dissolving. The crumbling of the foundations

---

18. Guignon, *Heidegger*, 22.

was unnerving and disorienting. Descartes found that he needed to create a new approach to knowledge in the face of the encroaching relativism:

> What is needed in order to overcome the ravages of relativism is a method that will lead us to certain and indubitable truths. Descartes resolves "to rid myself of the opinions which I had formerly accepted, and commence to build anew from the foundation."[19]

As he cut himself off from the traditional source of knowledge in the handed down theoretical universal principles, Descartes also found he could not trust his sense perception of the world. He realized things were not always what they seemed, and therefore the only trustworthy source of knowing that was available to him had to be grounded in his own thinking. Even though he could doubt everything, he could not doubt that it was he that doubted. The fact that he was a thinking being proved to him that he existed and that he could rely on his thoughts as the indubitable foundation that he sought. This insight is what gave rise to the famous declaration *cogito ergo sum* (I think, therefore I am):

> The crucial decision made by Descartes is to determine the ground of understanding as lying in the *self*-certainty of the knowing subject. With this shift in the conception of the source of true understanding, the anthropocentrism and subjectivism of the modern age begins.[20]

Now the "I am," which had been identified with the divine "I Am" of Yahweh and Christ, becomes the individual human subject who thinks. The translocation of the Divine "I Am" has tremendous consequences for the nature of the relationship between the human subject and the world. The Divine "I Am" was soul's constitution of the world itself, that is, the human world, the world of meaning, of consciousness at large. As God's world, the human connection with the world was guaranteed, axiomatic, a given. Now the new "I am" as human subject is so thoroughly buried in the human subject that the world is lost. Humankind, because of the revolution of the syntax of consciousness that Descartes symbolizes, becomes ontologically split off from its world. This turn of events is what gave us the infamous Cartesian mind-body dualism. A fundamental separation—really, an ontological division—opens up between the knowing subject and what can be known, most especially knowledge of the material world.

It was not just thinking that gave Descartes the certainty he was looking for, it was skeptical thinking, skepticism about the traditional way of knowing the world. Previously, "knowing the world" was, in a sense, given automatically to God's created beings because we and the world were God's created world. Knowledge was given by way of divine reason, and God was the basis of shared, public truth. *God*, the name of

---

19. Guignon, *Heidegger*, 23.
20. Guignon, *Heidegger*, 23.

that historical logical form of consciousness, constituted the syntax of public mind. There was no doubt about the world at all, just as there was no doubt about God—God's truth was given and absolute. But in Descartes's world, the Absolute was fading, dissolving, weakening, no longer self-evident and trustworthy, as humankind flexed its muscle as the inheritor of the "I Am," its own possession: "The *res cogitans* discovered by Descartes's methodological doubt comes to replace God as the essential substance that determines the Being of beings."[21] The "Being" of beings refers to that self-evident ontological value I associate with soul and the logical form of consciousness. Descartes's new thought symbolizes the way in which this fundament is transforming itself, shifting its location, changing its mode of being.

The Loss and Gain of "I Think, Therefore I Am"

The Cartesian shift is both a loss and an achievement on the part of soul. It shows us "a picture of the inner self as completely self-defining, with no essential bonds to anything else in the cosmos."[22] But, the cost of this freedom of mind, of soul's newfound freedom, is that soul, as human rationality, is cut off from itself by way of skepticism, locked up, so to speak, in the human mind. Soul has created a divide, a separation, within itself, between subject and object. During antiquity, the greater subject, God, vouchsafed the world. Now, having lost the safety and security of the greater subject and now a subject himself, Descartes is confronted with a new freedom, but also a new relationship with the object, the world out there. The world becomes an "out there," external for the first time, as the human subject becomes self-contained. Mind and its relation to matter becomes a problem for the first time. The big question, the central epistemological question that would dominate European philosophy for three hundred years, now becomes, how can the rational mind, which is immaterial, know the material world? The mind and the natural world had become incommensurate categories—an uncrossable gap had opened between them. As a consequence, the material world had now become just that, mere *matter*. The core ontological value that safeguarded the natural world as God's creation had in fact withdrawn from the world as soul re-created itself as a rational human mind. Left behind was a purely materialistic world, nature as matter no longer imbued with soul, nature now devoid of any innate meaning. Let's remember this movement of soul began with Yahweh (not Bacon) cutting himself off from his bull nature—the soul sheen radiating from the golden bull irretrievable dulled, and the resulting annihilation of the archaic form of consciousness (nature gods and goddesses).

This momentous logical and ontological shift is the fulfillment of soul's drive for materialism and humanism, which become the modern Western world's onto-logical and psycho-logical foundation. The growth of modern human-centered consciousness

21. Guignon, *Heidegger*, 17.
22. Guignon, *Heidegger*, 18.

means that what was once soul's highest value and dignity, the universal status of theological and philosophical ideas, has now been reduced and dismissed as prejudice, superstition, ungrounded assumption, and speculation. Scientific logic uses the word *myth* to denote the worldviews dominated by gods and goddesses from *outside*. The new humanistic logic of consciousness is, as it were, no longer *inside* that form of consciousness, and the word myth means untrue, false, subjective fantasy, and ignorance. This modern divide is very much in line with Yahweh's distinction between idols (false gods) and the one true God (old truth vs. new truth). Descartes's method distanced us from the world of traditional beliefs, and his systematic doubt and skepticism freed us from custom and tradition, setting up the human subject as a self-contained neutral and objective observer of the world. This was a gain for humankind, but a loss for Being:

> When the *subject* is interpreted as the ground of all beings, Being comes to be understood as something merely at man's disposal. Nature and the world are regarded as something on hand for fulfilling our utilitarian ends. In this process, Being loses its gravity and weightiness.[23]

This is philosophical language for the simple phrase, "God is dead." It means God is no longer an autonomous presence confronting humankind, but rather an idea in the mind of man that mankind can manipulate for its own needs. The notion of God is now at our disposal, kept handy as a benign comforter, our security blanket—gone is the God, fear of whom is the beginning of wisdom, the God who was an objective terror. Nature is no longer guaranteed as God's created order but is now simply the stuff of physics, chemistry, and biology, a de-souled matter, available for our use.

Of course, this state of affairs, our alienation from nature and the infamous subject-object dualism of Western consciousness, has long been under attack. What the critique of the Cartesian legacy fails to realize is that this state of affairs is the work of soul, not of humankind. No one set out to kill God and de-soul nature. It happened. It started with Yahweh himself. From the psychological and soul perspective, it has, in fact, been God who has killed himself, in stages. Soul is a happening in which we participate. The psychological and phenomenological description of soul's historical development is not a judgment that something has gone wrong, or that humankind has gone off the rails. Like an autopsy, my analysis cuts into the subject in order to discover the agent of death, a fact-finding process without moral judgments. The soul perspective interprets a new autonomous factor in history and culture that humankind does not control. Viewing the Cartesian legacy psychologically, as soul's speech about itself, is a new perspective on historical development. Sublation is at work, soul's inherent tendency to negate itself and continue its own self-generation. This interpretation is neither theological nor humanistic/historical, but soul-consciousness historical. In light of soul as its syntax, consciousness is a new category with which to understand the history of consciousness itself. If anything, the soul perspective is

---

23. Guignon, *Heidegger*, 19, emphasis added.

itself an implicit critique of humanism's conceit about humankind's self-importance and supposed control of history. We are not, after all, the agents of history that we have thought ourselves to be. We are the instruments of the syntax of consciousness (again, remembering the "water we swim in") which is an independent factor in its own right. To reverse the analogy, I would say humankind is the medium within which soul swims and does its work.

The Idea of *God* Hangs On

Descartes himself realized there was a fundamental problem in how knowledge of the external world was to be achieved and secured as reliable. I do not here need to follow Descartes's arguments in detail to understand his predicament in starting out from extreme doubt and skepticism. Soul had unwittingly backed itself into a blind alley, and in the context of Descartes's thinking, could not imagine a way out of this predicament. Certainly, this prepared the ground for the new status of soul as a human subject, but how could Descartes be sure that a demon, an evil God, was not distorting his thinking and perceptions. Here we see an early expression of modernist anxiety at the loss of God. But, the idea of "God" was still enough of a factor in the lingering syntax of consciousness that Descartes could appeal to God to back up his doubt. The possibility of an evil God troubled him enough that he posited God as a God who could not be a deceiver God. Descartes had one foot in the new syntax and the other foot in the old syntax. How this actually worked for Descartes need not concern us here, but this move on his part to invoke a non-deceiver God indicates that as soon as the human mind has to posit a particular definition of God in order to secure the mind, then we know that God is no longer what he was. God is no longer a *self-evident* autonomous truth over and against the human person, but is now imported by the rational mind to prop up its rationality. When a "proof of God" must be mounted then it is clear that metaphysical doubt and skepticism have won the day. Only a *form of consciousness* that is the result of the dissolution of God (Enlightenment reason) would feel any need to "prove" God's existence, providing further evidence for my thesis that as the syntax of consciousness moved into its Enlightenment mode, it was undergoing a profound and irreversible transformation.

Positing God Contradicts Itself

When God was truth, that is, the prevailing logical form of consciousness, no thought of proof even entered the picture, because *God* was the form of the mind itself. To return to the analogy of the windshield for the logical form of consciousness, when mind *is* the windshield, it is basically impossible to see the windshield until something goes wrong with it. The question of whether or not the windshield exists just cannot arise because the windshield is the given ground of existence itself. Or, following the metaphor of the water we swim in, when the mind *is* the water, it is next to impossible to see or know the water, let alone question the existence of the water. If consciousness *is* the water, how can consciousness *know* that it is the water? It cannot because it is identical with it. Only the historical distance we enjoy today enables consciousness to take the turn and look back on itself and see former forms of itself as if from outside. A psychology with soul is just that perspective of consciousness that now recognizes this self-reflexive structure of consciousness. The loss of God as the fundamental basis of consciousness, while not recognized consciously (yet) by early Enlightenment thinkers, was felt, or intuited, as a loss of something important that needed to be retained, maintained, and secured. Thus, the *conscious* mind, sensing this loss but not understanding it, attempted to rescue God, in the face of the fact that when God was God, when God was self-evident truth, God needed no rescuing.

Only a mind that has lost God as its syntax can feel any nostalgia, insecurity, or anxiety about the missing God that was and then, in a kind of regressive reflex, attempt to base God on another kind of logic that actually has nothing to do with God. Either God is or he isn't, *sui generis*. God cannot be based on any other foundation, and certainly not a rational proof. Once God *as foundation*, as syntax, of consciousness, is gone, there is no going back, in the same way that when childhood or adolescence or young adulthood are passed, lived through, there is no going back—as forms of consciousness, those stages of life are gone forever. This is the nature of reality for us, our psychological truth. Today, belief in God can only be an ego-project, the ego exerting efforts to sustain its belief in God because the notion of God no longer has any truth in it. Or, it is a sincere personal belief, genuinely held by an individual, but in this form, it is a content of personal consciousness, because it is no longer the syntax of societal consciousness. From the psychological perspective, God was a former status of consciousness (and thus, a real truth in its time) that soul has lived through and left behind. Today we are beginning to realize that consciousness itself *is* our foundation, and consciousness is not a thing (it is no thing), nor is it an absolute; consciousness is the "foundation" that is not a foundation. And, just as God could not be based on any other foundation, so consciousness today cannot be based on any other foundation except itself. Consciousness, insofar as it has come home to itself in our post-Enlightenment world, must be understood as being its own foundation. Soul, the syntax of consciousness, or public mind, is a historical process and a happening, mercurial, only the moment itself (although that "moment" can be a historical era). Soul is never static, it is performative. Soul is inherently unstable because its fundamental dynamic is self-negation.

The Bible and the Enlightenment

Most Enlightenment thinkers did not have anything against God per se. Just about all of them took God for granted and believed that their new methods of thought, of scientific experimentation, would reveal God's mysteries and were in service to God. They were not out to do away with God. What people in general think, however, is not necessarily what soul is up to. Even those innovative thinkers who introduce world-changing and civilization-altering ideas will themselves continue to hold on to remnants of the old order without realizing what they are doing, as Descartes showed us above. Albert Einstein is a modern example. When confronted with the unpredictable chaos (the predominance of probability and randomness) of quantum mechanics, he famously asserted, "God does not play at dice with the universe." This does not mean that Einstein believed in God (he was an atheist) but rather, that he could not tolerate the idea that the beautiful and precise laws of nature (physics) might be founded on uncontrollable probability and randomness. While not a theist, Einstein's insistence on predictability in nature is a remnant of the secure and stable logical form of consciousness constituted first by God and then, for him, by Reason (the dogma of the nineteenth century was scientific determinism).

The idea of *God* is a historical cultural artifact, and just because the underlying logical form of consciousness that personified itself as God was dissolving does not mean that the existing cultural artifacts (institutions, practices, beliefs) associated with God will just disappear. The idea of God will indeed hang around, as is all too clear today, even after five hundred years of Enlightenment science and secular society. The empirical and material aspects of civilization, and especially humankind itself, change much more slowly than soul does—soul is always out ahead of us. How the Bible came to be read as a result of Enlightenment thinking is a good example of soul's power to negate itself. The inductive method of Bacon's careful observation of facts and Descartes's pervasive doubt and skepticism were applied to the Bible itself. If the universal truth of God was fading, then the Bible as the "word of God," as God's direct revelation, comes into question. The Bible loses its luster as a sacrosanct inviolable text and becomes a fallible literary work written by human persons. The Bible can be questioned rather than only revered.

As seen in the previous chapter, it was not until the late eighteenth century that the Bible began to be critically evaluated from the point of view of reason. Luther is an example of how the God-centered logical form of consciousness read the Bible uncritically. Although he took a stand against the authority of the institutional church and some of its doctrinal claims, he held the New Testament as irrefutable in every detail. Luther's view of the Gospels is presented clearly by Schweitzer:

> Luther had not so much as felt that he cared to gain a clear idea of the order of the recorded events. Speaking of the chronology of the cleansing of the Temple, which in John falls at the beginning, in the Synoptists near the close, of Jesus' public life, he remarks: "The Gospels follow no order in recording the acts and miracles of Jesus, and the matter is not, after all, of much importance.

If a difficulty arises in regard to the Holy Scripture and we cannot solve it, we must just let it alone."[24]

The discrepancy in the gospels over when the cleansing of the Temple occurred during the life of Jesus simply did not arouse Luther's curiosity, nor did it generate a logical contradiction in his mind to which he must pay attention. Luther's mind was contained within a form of consciousness in which such questions did not have any weight. Within the context of Christian civilization and the Christian logical form of consciousness, the living idea of Christ *is* the windshield, *is* the water. In that context, the gospels are soul's direct expression of itself, God's direct and immediate self-revelation. The text was not a literary human document, it was the word of God, and it was completely wrapped in a God-centered and a Christ-centered form of consciousness, which had not yet developed into a historical, critical, scientific consciousness. The modern questions of historical criticism and literary criticism were simply not an issue because the text *was* the speech of God, or soul's speech about itself, but in the guise of Christ. Psychology with soul views the *Christ* phenomenologically, not as a person or an entity, nor as a God, but as the name for a wide and deep matrix of consciousness that *was* the syntax for an entire cultural and historical epoch.

The chronological contradiction of the stories about the cleansing of the Temple in the gospels—obvious to rational consciousness—was simply not a matter of concern for Luther. Luther's lack of concern generalizes to the insight that rational and logical contradictions, those gospel events and scenes that are contrary to natural law and create obvious (to us) historical and literary dissonance in the texts of the New Testament, were simply not the concern of the form of consciousness that gave rise to the New Testament. The New Testament, like the Bible as a whole, is more like a dream than history, more like a poem than a record of events. That soul developed itself to think critically and historically about the Bible was a major break with its own way of thinking, for the Bible was one of the ways that soul thought itself into existence. And, in this sense, when soul begins to think critically about the Bible, it is beginning to think critically about itself. That Christ, as the personified incarnate Logos (the Word), would become Reason by way of sublation, and then turn on itself and read itself critically, read itself in a new light, really does not seem all that surprising in hindsight. And, yet, this was a radical and world-shaking shift on the part of soul.

The Christ Critiques Itself

The Christ phenomenon (*Christ* in the psychological sense as the syntax of consciousness) was originally a critic in its own right. Christ created a new order, Christ was a new status of consciousness, that critiqued the natural or worldly order of biology, family, and politics, placing all of it within the category of *sin*. Psychologically

24. Schweitzer, *Quest*, 13.

understood, the idea of *sin* at that time would stand for the prevailing form of consciousness that the new *Christ* form of consciousness was pushing off against, similar to how Yahweh had created the idea of *idols* to push off from in order to create himself. Christ and the kingdom of God were in this world, but not of this world. The Christian critique of material wealth and power, setting itself up as a spiritual world apart ruled by the value of love,[25] was the creation of a new critical consciousness. That this consciousness would turn against itself is simply soul being true to itself and its dialectic: soul creates itself, negates itself, and through sublation becomes a new form, or syntax, of consciousness. The Logos subverted itself as Logos by changing its logical form because it took the incarnation seriously. It was utterly essential for soul that the ontological status of humankind became equal to that of God, so that eventually the "I am" of Christ, as the light, the truth, and the way, eventually became the light, the truth, and the way of Reason, not as divine Reason, but as the natural light of reason innate to each human person. Through the process of sublation, Reason, as a function of humankind, receives the transfer of the ontological value of God, as the ontological value of God diminishes. The Enlightenment was symbolic of a fundamental change in the location and nature of the fundamental syntax of consciousness. Along with Bacon and Descartes, another early harbinger of the new critical differentiation was Benedict Spinoza, who also suffered the consequences of being true to his integrity. Spinoza's inner and outer life were both representative of the historical change of consciousness he symbolized, and so I include more of his biography in the following.

Benedict Spinoza

Spinoza (1632–1677)[26] was born Jewish and took his Christian first name later. His grandfather had fled from Portugal to France to avoid the Inquisition and even professed Catholicism to escape persecution. Spinoza's father took refuge in the more tolerant Netherlands, where he became a prosperous merchant. Spinoza was educated by the best Jewish teachers and worked in his father's import business. He soon became more interested in scholarship and gave himself to philosophy full time. When he was twenty-four the first break occurred, and I would call it the first differentiation: Spinoza was excommunicated from his own Jewish community because he lacked respect for the Jewish religious authorities. Rather than simply accept the received teachings, he began to think for himself. Spinoza took to associating with Christian free thinkers, and at that time, he gave up his Hebrew name Baruch, for the Latin

---

25. The concept of *love* taught by the Christ was not a personal emotion or feeling as we think of it today. It was an objective differentiation in which one's personal sense of self was subordinated to, and contained within, a larger "spiritual" truth: "If you love me, you will keep my commandments. And I will ask the Father, and he will give you another Advocate, to be with you forever. This is the Spirit of truth, whom the world cannot receive, because it neither sees him nor knows him" (John 14:15–17).

26. Dawes, *Historical Jesus Quest*, 1–26. Dawes's chapter on Spinoza is titled "The Divorce between History and Faith."

Benedict (blessed). When he was thirty-eight, he published *Theological and Political Discussion* anonymously in an attempt to protect himself (but his authorship became widely known anyway). Spinoza had committed himself to freedom of conscience and freedom of thought.

Spinoza believed the individual had the freedom to interpret the Bible according to historical reason, independent of faith, theological dogma, and the parochialism of the quarreling and bitter feuding of religious parties. He was one of the earliest thinkers to begin the divorce between history and faith, to push apart reason and theology. Spinoza was suffering the shift of the weight of truth from its exclusive identity with the universals to include and value the particular, which in this case, was his own thinking, which saw truth in history and reason. During the previous centuries, during the building of the great cathedrals and still in his day, both Jewish and Christian scholars took for granted the divinely guaranteed accuracy of the Bible. The biblical view of the world was universally held to be true, and to question the fundamental assumptions supporting it was dangerous.

In his reading of the Bible, Spinoza began to see things differently, and he made the critical distinction between meaning and truth. Faith provided the *meaning* of the text, while history was the source of its *truth*. He found it impossible to continue to twist and distort the historical truth in order to make it match the meaning given by faith. This basic distinction between what God means and what history records marked a new stage in the history of both the Jewish and Christian interpretation of the Bible. Such a division would have been unthinkable to rabbinic, patristic, and medieval interpreters, or even those of the Reformation. This differentiation between theological meaning and historical truth would lead, in another century or two, to that modern distinction between the Christ of faith and the Jesus of history.

Spinoza took the inductive orientation that Bacon had introduced to the study of nature and applied it to the Bible, taking as authoritative the method of collecting data on the ground, in contrast to expecting revelation from heaven:

> I hold that the method of interpreting Scripture is no different form the method of interpreting Nature, and is in fact in complete accord with it. For the method of interpreting Nature consists essentially in composing a detailed study of Nature from which, as being the source of our assured data, we can deduce the definitions of the things of Nature. Now in exactly the same way the task of Scriptural interpretation requires us to make a straightforward study of Scripture, and from this, as the source of our fixed data and principles, to deduce by logical inference the meaning of the authors of Scripture. In this way—that is, by allowing no other principles or data for the interpretation of Scripture and study of its contents except those that can be gathered only from Scripture itself and from a historical study of Scripture.[27]

---

27. Dawes, *Historical Jesus Quest*, 6.

For Spinoza, just as knowledge of nature came from the observation of nature and not higher universal principles or ideals, so scripture was to be the sole source of knowledge about scripture, through the careful study of texts and the application of the natural light of reason.

Through Spinoza's thinking, the shifting value of consciousness led to undermining the authority of the biblical picture of the world through the application of the natural light of reason to scripture. Spinoza continued a trend begun by Martin Luther, in which the individual becomes the authority in interpreting scripture. Spinoza declared, "For since the supreme authority for the interpretation of Scripture is vested in each individual, the rule that governs interpretation must be nothing other than the natural light that is common to all, and not any supernatural right, nor any external authority."[28] Though Spinoza found a new dimension of freedom in relation to the Bible and his religious tradition, being true to his integrity cost him his Jewish community and his name. He died at forty-four after a long illness.

Spinoza made explicit what was implicit in Martin Luther's stand: The *individual* is now the "supreme authority for the interpretation of Scripture." Just as Bacon and Descartes argued for the necessity and the right to break with philosophical tradition and think for themselves, Spinoza stands for the absolute right of the individual to think freely and independently in relation to the Bible and religious ideas. Whereas the traditional form of thought, the form of consciousness of antiquity and the Middle Ages, fused biblical truth and historical truth into one soul-truth, a new differentiation of consciousness emerged with the thinkers of the Enlightenment. The power and authority of religious leaders and religious institutions were also fused with that form of consciousness identifying God as absolute truth, which is why Martin Luther's stand a hundred years earlier was so monumental. Spinoza takes his stand on the distinction between historical truth and biblical meaning, insisting that historical truth must not be tortured to fit the biblical or religious meaning of the text. The logic of truth is shifting its location from universal to particular. Secular, or rational, historical consciousness begins to assert itself in the face of the prevailing theological consciousness. It will take another two hundred years, however, for the full effect of historical consciousness to penetrate and transform biblical interpretation.

Ernst Troeltsch: History Subverts Revelation

From the point of view of soul, the Logos (Christ as divine Word) now turned against itself, in the same way that Yahweh had turned against himself. By way of the thinkers of the Enlightenment, soul in the form of Christ as divine Logos was sublating itself into human reason-logos. I might even personify this process and say, as the Logos, now the new light of natural reason, read about itself in traditional texts—that is, as

---

28. Dawes, *Historical Jesus Quest*, 26.

critical reason read the Bible, especially the gospels—it began to notice discontinuities, inconsistencies, contradictions, and differences in the gospel revelation of Jesus Christ. The Logos (critical reason) became bothered, even distressed, by these rational problems presented by the texts in a way that Luther had not. The absolute theological truth of Christ the divine Savior of the World was fading, and the gospels were seen in the light of history, informed by critical reflection and empirically observed (historical) facts. Historically, from soul's point of view, the taken-for-granted truth of Christian theological doctrine had done its work, over approximately one thousand years, of changing the mode of consciousness. The Divine Logos had now become critical of itself through the eyes of human natural logos. What I might call religious realism, that status of consciousness in which the Bible, in all its details, was truth itself, was, in effect, changing itself from within and becoming historical/humanistic realism. The power, value, authority, and reality of the universals was transferring itself to the particulars. The very nature of *truth* was changing as it shifted its location from divine revelation to natural, empirical facts, and these natural facts gained more weight and significance within the newly emergent form of historical consciousness.

The divorce between faith and reason, or between theological authority and historical authority, in the interpretation of the Bible was well underway during the nineteenth century. Ernst Troeltsch (1865–1923),[29] although not specifically a biblical scholar, was well aware of what was at stake in the growing dominance of historical consciousness and its conflict with the prevailing theological orientation. Born in Augsburg, Germany, he was one among many who continued to further the development of historical consciousness begun by Spinoza two hundred years earlier. Although by the late nineteenth century the historical sense of reality was more securely established, the dogmatic absolutism of Christian theology continued to assert itself, refusing to see that its theological methods had been thoroughly undermined and dissolved. Troeltsch was one of the founders of what became known as the "history of religions school." This perspective viewed Christianity as one religion among many, a product of the historical and cultural context of its time. The "historical sense" of reality was still working its way into the general consciousness, where it confronted the still prevalent dogmatic assertion that *Christianity was the supreme and absolutely unique and final revelation of God.* Because of the absolute nature of this direct revelation from God, Christianity was thought to stand apart from all other historical phenomena and transcend historical contingencies. Within such a dogmatic position, Christianity and its God were ahistorical. The growing "historical sense" was breaking open such an absolutizing and closed theological world of Christian consciousness, or in psychological terms, the syntax of *historical* consciousness was taking over the value and weight that had informed the *Christian* syntax of consciousness.

Troeltsch was arguing against those theologians whose method took the authoritative concept of revelation for granted, basing their dogmatic claims on that

---

29. Dawes, *Historical Jesus Quest*, 27–53.

fundamental principle. He noted that the dogmatic method established its *facts* beyond ordinary history. The revealed facts presented in the Bible—for example, Jesus Christ's purported self-proclaimed messianic self-consciousness—were then protected and "safeguarded by a miraculous transmission and sealed by an inward testimony in the heart."[30] The dogmatic method attempted to establish a separate epistemological territory immune to the "historical sense" and fenced off from the effects of historical criticism. For the dogmatic theologians, Troeltsch saw, everything depended on the external manifestation of supernaturalism, and the miraculous was the authoritative foundation for that metaphysical principle. Those theologians created two "histories" and asserted the separation of the history of salvation and ordinary history, remaining astonishingly insensitive to the consequences flowing from the historical method. Using a biblical metaphor,[31] Troeltsch intuitively recognized the process of sublation in how the "historical sense" transformed everything from within:

> I am referring to *the historical method as such* [Troeltsch's emphasis], to the problem of "Christianity and history," which is to be understood not as the defense of Christianity against particular results of historical criticism but rather as the effect of modern historical methodology on the interpretation of Christianity itself. Once applied to the scientific study of the Bible and church history, *the historical method acts as leaven*, transforming everything and ultimately exploding the very form of earlier theological methods.[32]

Leaven, in its ancient Jewish context, was associated with corruption, decay, and evil.[33] While our ordinary associations with leaven and baking bread are positive, from the flour's point of view, leaven is a subversive element, working invisibly from within, negating and transforming the structure of the flour itself. Once flour is leavened, there is no unleavening—the change is pervasive and permanent. Troeltsch definitely intuits the profound effect historical consciousness has already had on theological consciousness. The theologians employing what he called their dogmatic method were really engaged in a rearguard action, helpless against the new Enlightenment consciousness and the historical sense that had already come to characterize

---

30. Dawes, *Historical Jesus Quest*, 40.

31. "To what shall I compare the kingdom of God? It is like leaven which a woman took and hid in three measures of flour, till it was all leavened" (Luke 13:20–21).

32. Dawes, *Historical Jesus Quest*, 30–31, emphasis added.

33. The Jewish remembrance of Passover, the origin myth of Yahweh (for Israel), must be celebrated with *unleavened* bread, and all leaven must be removed from the house. The New Testament associates leaven with the hypocrisy of the Pharisees (Luke 12:1). Paul states: "Therefore, let us celebrate the festival, not with the old yeast, the yeast of malice and evil, but with the unleavened bread of sincerity and truth" (1 Cor 5:8). Contemporary scholarship sees a subversive element in the fact that a woman engaged in an ordinary daily task is associated with the kingdom of God, in contrast to Yahweh-consciousness, which would be associated with masculine warrior triumph. See Herzog, *Parables as Subversive*. (The amount of flour in the parable is ridiculous, and no doubt an exaggeration, as "three measures" translates to about one bushel, or 144 cups.)

the understanding of reality. Soul works on itself by way of infection, corruption, and contamination, subverting established meaning with new meaning. This is not simply two different semantic meanings existing side by side. A previous syntax of meaning is destroyed and at the same time incorporated into a new syntax. Although theology still exists today as one semantic meaning among others, its power as the syntax of all meanings has been destroyed by historical consciousness.

According to Troeltsch, the principles that inform historical consciousness are contained in three basic ideas. These principles also show us how profoundly consciousness has shifted from the idea that Christianity was the product of immediate and direct divine revelation. The first involves criticism and probability. Every historical document, including scripture, must not be taken at face value but must be critically evaluated. The historical sense is based on the knowledge that all such documents can present only a probable and changeable picture of the past. The second idea is analogy. In general, the past is like the present, and people behave more or less the same, and the same kinds of distortion we recognize in the present have occurred in the past. The third is correlation, which tells us that all historical phenomena occur and develop in the context of the total stream of history and culture. There is nothing so unique that it transcends its context. In contrast to these historical principles, the dogmatic theological method wants "absoluteness as an immediate derivation from God" and conceives of the absolute as a "faith that absolute values have been supernaturally revealed at one point in history."[34]

Troeltsch recognized that the Bible had become one historical text among others and could not be a sequestered truth set apart. The metaphor of leaven shows just how thoroughly the new understanding of humankind's basic historical nature had pervaded and changed consciousness. In the light of historical consciousness, the Bible was no longer the revered and authoritative revelation of God's purpose, but simply another historical text that itself must submit to rational questions about the reliability of what it purports to tell us. Within the traditional theological mode of consciousness, humankind was submitted to the Bible's authority as revealed truth. The act of submission turns when, in the light of historical consciousness and human reason, the Bible was submitted to the scrutiny of Descartes's "I am" and its critical questions, which seek to discover truth from scratch rather than simply accept it as given from the past or from on high. This really did change everything, a monumental revolutionary transformation of consciousness.

From Public to Private: Theology Retreats

The dogmatic method's attempt to cordon off Christian revelation into its own history reveals the profound change that had already happened to the logical ground of religion. The world of Christianity had been the taken-for-granted truth of the public

---

34. Dawes, *Historical Jesus Quest*, 49.

domain, and in this sense, it was not a "religion" separate from the prevailing culture: it was the culture. But now, under threat from the encroaching truth of historical consciousness and the Enlightenment, Christianity was no longer safe in the public square and had to retreat to the private and subjective sphere of individual faith, which was thought to be protected from scientific criticism. Religion was transformed from a public truth to a private one, becoming completely subjective. The terms by which religion was understood had changed without anyone realizing the nature of the change. The change was fairly silent and momentous. During antiquity and the medieval period, religion was in fact a public truth, the unquestioned and accepted basis of reality. Now it was reduced to something personal and private, a matter of the heart. Religion shifted its location from the outer world of the public commons to the private inner world of the individual. It became a content of consciousness and therefore a person could choose to accept or reject it. Religion had lost its position as the syntax of consciousness, when it was the larger general cultural form of consciousness, which is a given and not a choice. We live as the syntax of the consciousness of our time and place whether we like it or not; we do not choose it, we are born into it.

In one sense (though not to be taken literally), religion made a strategic or tactical retreat in the face of the hegemony of reason and science, which was becoming the prevailing public truth everyone accepted and took for granted. To survive in some form, religion had to leave the epistemological field that empiricism and positivism had conquered, retreating to the subjective world of feeling and personal belief where the factual empiricism of science was helpless to advance. Science could show there was no God or heaven up in the skies, and it could convince us resurrection from the dead was just not possible, not true, but it could not "disprove" anyone's subjective and personal beliefs and feelings, the individual's faith. So, religion subjectivized itself in order to escape the implications of reason and science. This very move demonstrates that God had already succumbed to the implications, the leaven, of reason and science, and that *God* as the basis of mind, as the logical form of consciousness, had indeed *died*. The death of God, however, was not what Troeltsch had in mind.

Troeltsch was not against Christianity or God; he was against the "theological dogmatic method" that split history into two histories and denied the leavening effect of the "historical sense." Instead of a supernatural and supreme revelation happening once, he saw "reason" at work through history in general when he said, "it is indispensable to believe in reason as operative in history and as progressively revealing itself." He believed that Christianity was the "highest ethical and religious force," that "Christianity was the supreme religious force of history," and he held "the conception of history as a disclosure of the divine reason."[35] What interests me is that Troeltsch's insight—"the historical method acts as leaven, transforming everything and ultimately exploding the very form of earlier theological methods"—does not penetrate the notion of God itself. Troeltsch's argument is limited to contrasting the historical method

---

35. Dawes, *Historical Jesus Quest*, 46, 47.

and the dogmatic method, and while he sees history in general as the place where God progressively reveals himself, God himself does not seem changed by the historical process. Rather, it seems that Troeltsch reserved an ahistorical transcendent status for God. Troeltsch's own thinking did indeed play a role in the leavening action of the historical sense, but his thinking did not penetrate all the way through the theological point of view. He stopped at the problem of *method* and did not penetrate the logos of theos (God) itself. He is another example of how each thinker contributes limited insights that promote the leavening, sublating, historical process. Soul develops itself by fits and starts, trial and error, through many expressions of itself throughout history and culture. The explicit recognition of a change in the status of God comes with Nietzsche (they were contemporaries), whom I take up next.

Friedrich Nietzsche

The achievement of the Enlightenment included a move in the social-political sphere from the form of consciousness organized according to monarchical principles to a consciousness organized according to democratic principles. Democratic values affirm the dignity of each individual, the right to one's own thoughts, and a vote in determining the leaders of government and the welfare of the commonwealth. The value and authority once contained in the universal, which manifested in the special figures of God, king, or priest, has sublated itself into the particular, the individual human person. Within Christianity itself, this shift is reflected in the emergence of Protestantism ("the priesthood of all believers") out of Catholicism (where one pope rules). Within the modern form of consciousness, the dignity of the human person is taken for granted as a self-evident truth. The modern form of consciousness is often called secular humanism or scientific materialism. The basis of truth, and the ground of reality, is now the human being and no longer God. The logical consequence of the Enlightenment is that *God is dead*, which comes to explicit expression at the end of the nineteenth century through Friedrich Nietzsche (1844–1900).

Nietzsche's *The Gay Science* was first published in 1882. As Walter Kaufmann, Nietzsche's preeminent translator, makes clear, the word *gay* has nothing to do with homosexuality, and *science* does not mean the natural sciences. Rather, what Nietzsche wanted to convey was that the serious pursuit of knowledge (*Wissenschaft*) can be lighthearted and perhaps *sunny*, in contrast to what was for Nietzsche a typical German heaviness and stodginess. *Gay* for Nietzsche connotes poetry, dancing, and laughter and is meant to be anti-German, anti-academic.[36] And yet in this "lighthearted" book one of his best-known, deadly serious statements appears: "God is dead." He introduces this idea with the story of a *madman* who announces the news. Is the news tragic, is it a lament, is it a triumphant proclamation, or is it simply news? I will let you decide. In order to feel the quality of Nietzsche's short parable, I reproduce it here in

---

36. Nietzsche, *Gay Science*, 4–7. (Another title translation is *The Joyful Wisdom*.)

its entirety. I read it psychologically, as soul's speech about itself, a statement heralding a change in the syntax of consciousness that had already occurred. The madman declares, quite passionately, that we ourselves have killed God, but as soul's speech about itself, soul has killed soul. Nietzsche presents a clear-eyed picture of both what has happened and the tremendous implications resulting from the sublation of the Divine Logos into the logos of reason:[37]

> *The madman.*—Have you not heard of that madman who lit a lantern in the bright morning hours, ran to the marketplace, and cried incessantly: "I seek God! I seek God!"—As many of those who did not believe in God were standing around just then, he provoked much laughter. "Has he get lost? asked one. Did he lose his way like a child? asked another. Or is he hiding? Is he afraid of us? Has he gone on a voyage? Or emigrated?"—Thus they yelled and laughed.
>
> The madman jumped into their midst and pierced them with his eyes. "Whither is God?" he cried; "I will tell you. *We have killed him*—you and I. All of us are his murderers. But how did we do this? How could we drink up the sea? Who gave us the sponge to wipe away the entire horizon? What were we doing when we unchained this earth from its sun? Whither is it moving now? Whither are we moving? Away from all suns? Are we not plunging continually? Backward, sideward, forward, in all directions? Is there still any up or down? Are we not straying as through an infinite nothing? Do we not feel the breath of empty space? Has it not become colder? Is not night continually closing in on us? Do we not need to light lanterns in the morning? Do we hear nothing as yet of the noise of the gravediggers who are burying God? Do we smell nothing as yet of the divine decomposition? Gods, too, decompose. God is dead. God remains dead. And we have killed him.
>
> "How shall we comfort ourselves, the murderers of all murderers? What was holiest and mightiest of all that the world has yet owned has bled to death under our knives: who will wipe this blood off us? What water is there for us to clean ourselves? What festivals of atonement, what sacred games shall we have to invent? Is not the greatness of this deed too great for us? Must we ourselves not become gods simply to appear worthy of it? There has never been a greater deed; and whoever is born after us—for the sake of this deed he will belong to a higher history than all history hitherto."
>
> Here the madman fell silent and looked again at his listeners; and they, too, were silent and stared at him in astonishment. At last he threw his lantern on the ground, and it broke into pieces and went out. "I have come too early," he said then; "my time is not yet. This tremendous event is still on its way, still wandering; it has not yet reached the ears of men. Lightning and thunder require time; the light of the stars requires time; deeds, though done, still require time to be seen and heard. This deed is still more distant from them than the most distant stars—*and yet they have done it themselves.*"

---

37. Nietzsche, *Gay Science*, 181 (§125).

God's Autopsy and the Living Truth of Soul

> It has been related further that on the same day the madman forced his way into several churches and there struck up his *requiem aeternam deo*. Led out and called to account, he is said always to have replied nothing but: "What after all are these churches now if they are not the tombs and sepulchers of God?"

Honestly, I still get goose bumps when I read this. What an extraordinary statement of soul's modern project abrading meaning down to nothing! The cosmos which once had God at its center is now directionless and rudderless, fundamentally empty of meaning and purpose. The very cosmos that was God, the God-centered and God-infused cosmos, has faded away—or, as Nietzsche dramatizes, killed by the knives of Reason we wield—we are God's murderers. Can we own up to a crime of such horrific proportions? Probably not, because "this deed is still more distant from them than the most distant stars—and yet they have done it themselves." And yet, is it really a crime? No, it is not a crime, and it is not of our doing, but there is a responsibility we bear if we are to come to terms with this profound revolution in consciousness. Nietzsche brings home the historic magnitude of this change in the world order, which psychologically, is that monumental transformation of the logical form of consciousness that had been in the works ever since Yahweh cut himself off from his essence as a nature god. The modern *death of God*, which we think is a purely modern phenomenon, is the logical result of the death of gods (Yahweh) and the suicide of God (Christ).

However, to speak of the death of God is still to think in terms of God, to still cling to the logic of the consciousness of a former time. This is one of the madman's significant points: "This tremendous event is still on its way, still wandering—it has not yet reached the ears of man." The death of God was a logical event, a soul event, that had already happened, and yet, while it has become the general consciousness of modernity, it is not yet consciously understood as an already accomplished truth. The idea of death is psychologically a symbol of change and transformation. The death of God is the *death* of a form of consciousness that consciousness itself generated. Soul negates itself in order to fulfill itself in another form. The death of God is the phrase the God form of consciousness uses to name its own demise, but it is only the *death of God* from that point of view. From the psychological viewpoint, it is the negation and sublation of one form of soul's logical life into another. It is the self-negating and self-transcending process of consciousness, the historical movement of public mind. Today the *God* category is obsolete, and new categories are needed in its place.

The matter is no longer about God at all, but rather, an evolution of consciousness. However, as I am at pains to show, not the consciousness of individuals, but consciousness as such, the consciousness now aware of itself as consciousness—the logical form of consciousness. The fundamental category that God has been can be released. The category of *consciousness* has sublated the entire God tradition and become a new category. The end of God as the source of public truth is a movement on the part of soul, a movement of liberation and emancipation of consciousness from its former syntax. The change presents humankind with a new dimension of freedom.

Yet, Nietzsche's story makes very clear that the *death of God* truly is a terrible loss, a terrific emotional shock, and humankind does not know how to deal with it. This is a real human problem.

What Does Soul Want?

The form of soul as a god has dissolved itself into the form of reason and become a human subject. Though now free in a new way, the human subject is also truly alone, metaphysically alone, in a cosmos devoid of any external moral compass or external teleology. No divine purpose, no salvation plan, surrounds us, containing us any longer. For a while, the modern period saw its own "salvation plan" in the hands of Reason and science, the idea that, now enlightened, we can save ourselves. The optimism of the nineteenth century was crushed by two world wars and the advent of the nuclear age, along with the growing anxious sense of general meaninglessness. The hope of "salvation," nevertheless, still crops up in relation to technology's promise to save us.

These different kinds of salvation plans, divine or human, are soul-constructs developed and refined over centuries. If we can discern anything, it seems soul has some kind of intent and direction, but my view of soul as history itself eliminates any final goal as soul is by definition open ended, creating itself in the moment, and, to cap it off, does not have the welfare of the human species in view. The whole enterprise, culture and universe, appears to be a trial and error process, creating itself as it goes, building on itself in unpredictable ways: "Let's see what happens if this is done." Soul, as the inexhaustible production of meanings, is infinite, cannot reach an end, for the same reason that while language as a linguistic object may be finite (the alphabet is not infinite), the world of meaning remains qualitatively infinite. Only if civilization burns itself out will soul come to an end at this place called earth, but that would certainly not be a planned end, not a goal. This leaves humankind in an awkward position. We have been, it would seem, born out of the womb of mythology and religion, and now, parentless, we are on our own. The supreme self-confidence of reason has faded, and radical freedom entails radical anxiety. It is not for nothing that our modern time has been called the Age of Anxiety.

The general tendency has been to focus on what has been lost, and to blame ourselves, as Nietzsche did, feeling guilty that we have killed the gods and nature. There is a pervasive feeling that humankind has made a massive mistake. But, is it really a human mistake, or simply a massive change that we did not orchestrate and do not understand? To indulge in guilt is to view history from a human-centric and personalistic point of view, and it prevents us from grappling with a larger perspective that might help us understand what is happening, even if it does not put control in our hands. In fact, rather than guilt, grief would be a more appropriate response to the loss. Grief would mean acceptance of the loss, and then allowing that loss to teach us, teach consciousness, about this new environment, new world, that is consciousness itself. Loss requires an adaptation to the truth of that loss. Guilt is a kind of denial that the loss has actually occurred. Our responsibility is to face the historical circumstance, whatever it is. The Enlightenment was the age of human agency, the time of science and humanism, the time of human flowering and optimism. With Nietzsche and the turn of the twentieth century, that flower has withered and the optimism has turned to a darker pessimism. Though infused with despair and hopelessness at the emptied universe, pessimism is also colored by another turn of soul toward an astounding view of the universe, of life, and of the place of consciousness—soul now sees itself as *consciousness*! Our age of meaninglessness actually has a historical meaning.

A Very Brief Review

Yahweh was the internal critique of the logic of the fusion of nature-gods-goddesses, pushed off through his exodus to become a free transcendent god of spirit and writing. Christ was the internal critique of the logic of Yahweh and greatly expanded the freedom of the Word through an incarnation with humankind. Reason was the internal critique of the logic of Christ and developed itself further as human subject. Looking ahead, psychology with soul itself will be the implicit internal critique of the logic of science and humanism, soul seeing itself as pure form or syntax, becoming conscious of itself as consciousness. Is soul pushing for another kind of exodus, from what, toward what?

The notion of each stage of soul critiquing the former stage does not mean that the former logic was wrong, although that is certainly the explicit position of the new logic. The critique happens because the next form of consciousness has achieved a more expansive and inclusive perspective on the former syntax of consciousness, and so includes it in a wider frame of reference. The new syntax has expanded and thus turns the old syntax into a content; or the old syntax becomes a content in the context of the new syntax. But the new has to push off, push against, the old. Each new status of soul is a new freedom, a new truth that sees itself as liberated from its prior form of truth. Freedom, and not necessarily human freedom, seems to be an inherent quality of soul's self-development.

In the next chapter, I explore how modernity and reason reached their own end through a turn against themselves, another self-negation on the part of soul, and how our current stage of soul's project is producing a consciousness that is now aware of itself as consciousness, resulting in the dissolution of all foundations. Philosophy and physics have become aware of this new state of affairs, but psychology with soul, psychology as the discipline of interiority, psychology concerned with truth, gives this new status of consciousness its rightful place in the history of Western Judeo-Christian culture.

Chapter 9

Soul's Thought of Itself Today Is *Consciousness*

Ouroboric Consciousness

The soul is no longer "out there." Subjectively this may be experienced as alienation. The psychological difference that formerly existed *between* man and the soul / the natural world / transcendence, now imparts itself on man himself. It is now an internal difference. Man can now gain a distance to himself. He exists now *as* a difference, a duality, a tension: the difference between his more egoic, pragmatic orientation, on the one hand, and his potential of a soulful mode of experiencing and reacting. The soul, having lost its transcendent and substance quality, is now a mode or style in man.[1]

GOD'S AUTOPSY HAS REVEALED striking transformations of the structure of meaning, the syntax of consciousness. By cutting into the dead body of God (the body of religious texts), we found Reason had digested and incorporated that body (through negation and sublation) into its own mode of thought. Soul—in the form of modernity, the most recent historical form of consciousness—left the dead body behind as a snake would shed its skin and took up a new life, as the incarnate Word dissolved into Reason and human subject. Soul, however, is never finished with itself. Our most precious possession, our modern sense of self as subject, as I, is suffering through its own self-negation. Something untoward is happening, and we are dissolving before our own eyes.

This chapter focuses on pivotal events at the beginning of the twentieth century, and although that is now about one hundred years ago, we are for all intents and purposes in soul's present tense, and a strange present tense it is. I will explore how Reason undermined itself, turned itself inside out. Here at the end of the book, we reach our beginning, which is those contemporary soul conditions that give rise to

1. Giegerich, *What Is Soul?*, 279.

psychology with soul—the serpent of consciousness bites its own tail. Although psychology with soul has become explicit only in the last fifty years,[2] it is the perspective that allows this reading of soul's approximately five-thousand-year history. The logical form of consciousness, the water we swim in, finds its origin in preliterate consciousness and has shape-shifted itself through several forms of consciousness since then, long before the *idea* of *consciousness* could be thought. With the first chapter, I planted my interpretive stake in the idea of *modern soul*. I showed how I would approach the history of Western consciousness, not with another hermeneutic but with a completely new category, a hermeneutic that includes all hermeneutics heretofore, the category of *soul*. Now I will show how our current circumstances have come about by way of consciousness coming home to itself, becoming conscious of itself as consciousness, and why this has turned our world upside down.

I will examine how soul escaped (another exodus) the self-enclosed subjectivity of modernity's *cogito*, or what we might call humanism's ego. Our flights into outer space escaped the earth's gravity, and we now look back on ourselves from a distance, seeing our little blue planet in the unimaginable new context of a vast dark abyss. In the same way, consciousness has gotten outside of itself and sees itself in a completely new light for the first time: Consciousness itself is no longer tethered to an Absolute. The personal thinking ego is no longer the ground of certainty. The *I*—what we know and depend on as the modern subject—is also a historical construct resulting from soul's self-transformation. The soul created the ego, and now it is undermining the ego, actually sublating the ego into a larger context of self-reflecting consciousness. The ground we have trusted to remain solid and fixed is now fluid and moving. The death of God is also, dialectically, the death of the ego (that is, the Cartesian *cogito*).

Now come home to itself, consciousness is a radical openness of fecund wilderness, escaping domestication and colonization. The accomplished logic of soul's previous forms—Yahweh, Christ, and Reason, established as the Absolute—were totalizing foundations encompassing all of reality, and thus were, in their effects, exclusive, totalitarian, imperialistic, and colonial. In world-shaking contrast, the logic of the serpent of consciousness is dialectical, excludes nothing, and recognizes self-negation as its essence. The new consciousness will not tolerate an ego that exists simply to defend itself. Rather, it requires a grounded and open *I* that takes its stand in truth, but a truth that always negates itself for the ineluctable next truth. We are now in the realm of dialectical consciousness: "Forget being either or, be both and more and moving."[3]

The Cartesian-Enlightenment form of consciousness has run its course; it has negated itself and given birth to a new logical form of consciousness resulting in remarkable and shattering upheavals throughout contemporary global culture. Even so,

---

2. I base this time frame on Giegerich's earliest essays of the late 1960s and early '70s.

3. This line is taken from the activist poem "Co-sensing with Radical Tenderness" by the collective Gesturing Toward Decolonial Futures (GTDF). Their work seeks to name and disidentify from modernity's norms of thinking and being, and explores decolonial ways of being with ourselves, each other, and the world. See https://decolonialfutures.net/rt-recording/.

it is still too early for clarity about what is happening to us. Our world is so thoroughly saturated and enveloped by the compelling presence of media and technology that it is difficult to still claim we are in charge. The world is running away from us. The current monumental changes enveloping us are the result of soul, in the form of Reason, turning on itself. In its current self-negation and creation, soul is sabotaging and corrupting the lofty ideals of humanism that many of us still take for granted: human dignity, personal freedom, and agency. These foundational values are dissolving as the syntax of consciousness explores new ways to be in constant motion, always fluid, erase all boundaries, and obliterate context, certainties, and the notion of truth itself.

Reason Betrays Itself

Here I will review the accomplishments of the Enlightenment form of consciousness in order to bring home the revolutionary changes currently roiling our world. Through the triumph of mathematics to describe and predict natural phenomena, the success of the scientific method, and the ideology of scientific materialism and determinism, Reason became identified with absolute certainty and truth, especially during the eighteenth and nineteenth centuries. Reason, in its Enlightenment status as absolute certainty, replaced God as the locus of truth. However, none of the thinkers of the Enlightenment wanted to remove God—in fact, they believed they were uncovering God's handiwork. Nevertheless, while God as a conscious idea remained firmly in the minds of the people and cultural institutions, *God* as the logical form of consciousness was undergoing soul's own self-negation and sublation, culminating in the death of God. Just as Yahweh betrayed himself by becoming Christ, and Christ betrayed himself by becoming Reason—keeping in mind that these names are the personifications of the syntax of consciousness—it follows that Reason will betray itself through soul's ongoing process of self-creation, self-negation, and sublation into a new logical form of consciousness. To be clear, this does not eliminate the functional value of reason and critical thinking; instead, it negates the status of *absolute* that Reason had attained as modernity's syntax of consciousness. The methodology of science is obviously effective; the questions it asks get worthwhile results; and skepticism is a valuable critical function. As the foundational logic of a worldview, however, Reason's self-understanding is undergoing a profound change. After it achieves the status of public mind and public truth, each stage of consciousness becomes critical of its achieved form and pushes off from that form of itself. The new truth converts the old truth into an untruth. Consciousness, as soul (truth), will always eventually become critical of itself.

Descartes, the icon of the Enlightenment, represents soul's achievement of a new ontological ground, which manifested itself as the human subject: the conscious, skeptical, and rational thinking subject. The conscious thinking subject became the certain foundation, the ground of truth that once belonged to the gods, or God. Reason became the arbiter of truth, functioning as it did through the scientific method and especially mathematics. Soul and truth are synonyms, and as soul changes, so does the nature of truth. During the Enlightenment, truth became identified with mathematical certainty, which gives us an abstract and impersonal description of the functioning of nature, in contrast to antiquity when gods, goddesses, and God were at the heart of nature's functioning. Mathematical certainty provided new levels of precision in relation to causes and effects, and at this stage of its development during the Enlightenment, it was not subject to ambiguity, nor mystical or occult influences.

Isaac Newton (1642–1726) solidified the interpretation of nature in terms of mathematical relationships, grounding knowledge in precise empirical data rather than metaphysical or theological principles. In his mathematical calculations and his experimental measurements of time and weight, Newton was able to make calculations at a level of exactitude never seen before, or even thought possible. Newton, along with the other foundational thinkers I have included, was himself pre-Newtonian. For him and others of this period, nature was intensely alive with the mystery of God's active presence, while his legacy became a mathematically defined nature devoid of spirit. Newton was also one of the great alchemists of the early Enlightenment period, but he kept these researches completely private, and his alchemical manuscripts were not discovered until after his death.[4] Newton is representative of any great mind that is both ahead of its time and simultaneously thoroughly embedded in its time. This reflects the general dynamic of soul, always in conflict with itself, always out ahead of itself and thoroughly entrenched in itself at any given time. Soul manifests as the cauldron of culture, its internal and ongoing conflict of meanings.

Humankind was exhilarated by the newfound discoveries of nature's secrets, the possibilities of science, and the promise of understanding and controlling nature itself, as well as a vision of endless self-improvement of both society and human capacity through the powers of conscious rationality and scientific method. Here I emphasize *conscious* because Enlightenment consciousness was identified with the ability to consciously use reason and the promise and hope of scientific determinism. The seventeenth and eighteenth centuries enjoyed a terrific optimism, which Reason itself would betray. However, as the nineteenth century came to a close, this rock-solid ground of soul and truth began to crumble in the face of several new emerging ideas.[5] One of the most prominent was the psychological notion of *the unconscious* as an unavoidable dimension of the human person. The unconscious is anything but conscious or rational. With the idea of the unconscious, soul negated its Enlightenment certainty and its newfound rational ground. The idea of the *unconscious* became a living and culture-changing idea—it was an idea whose time had come. The two best-known psychological figures promoting the unconscious were Sigmund Freud (1856–1939) and Carl Jung (1875–1961).

4. Gleick, *Isaac Newton*, 106.
5. Also of note is that the first half of the twentieth century was marked by two horrific world wars, (1914–1918) and (1939–1945), which I interpret as symbolic of the vast and deep cataclysmic upheaval soul was undergoing, turning Enlightenment achievement and optimism on its head, subverting the foundation of Reason, and inaugurating a new cultural pessimism, insecurity, and anxiety.

During the Enlightenment, scientific curiosity was applied to every nook and cranny of nature, including the human person. First the body was probed and examined, and then the mind. But as the mind was first observed, it was not immediately noticed that this was the beginning of mind observing mind, the mind observing itself. This also led to growing awareness of the peculiar relationship between mind and culture: there is no mind without culture, and there is no culture without mind. I find myself thinking in terms of a mind-culture field, as they are, in effect, one and the same thing, or better, they are both constituted by one and the same field. Of course, this *field* is not a positivity, not a material thing, not even an invisible electromagnetic field, not a field that can be defined by physics or mathematics. A mind-culture field is a linguistic field of shared meanings and significance. The cultural field, or soul, is a field of active and dynamic ideas which is entirely *negative* in the sense that thought has no measurable mass (in contrast to the positivity of the physical world). In this regard, soul itself is a negativity, while its manifestations are positivities, remembering that soul has no existence apart from its manifestations.

With regard to public mind as a shared field of meaning, my personal so-called mind is not really *my* private possession. Even though the hard-won fight of the Enlightenment for the right and freedom to think our own thoughts was a positive achievement, that very achievement was a public achievement by public mind. Every individual mind is first of all constituted by public mind. In this larger soul sense, the social-cultural mind in all of its activity is reflecting on and working on itself. The Enlightenment freed the subject from one form of public mind, from what had become the stifling and oppressive nature of the religion and tradition of a culture-wide church-centered dogmatism, but the newfound liberation of Reason and free thinking was itself a new form of public mind. It was soul's liberation of itself for a new freedom of thought, another soul exodus. It was not that religion in itself was wrong or mistaken (although its institutional expression had become widely problematic), but that soul transformed itself from *divine substance* to *human subject* on the level of logical form or syntax. Religion, as soul expression, shifted from being the water we swam in to being one of the fish swimming in the new water of Reason. Religion became a sublated content within the new logic of scientific consciousness.

In what follows I will explore how *the unconscious* and two other ideas that emerged at the beginning of the twentieth century undermined the status of Reason as an *absolute*, dissolving the reigning background form of consciousness. These ideas negate (and sublate) the Enlightenment's established foundations:

1. Psychology: Through the discovery of the unconscious, we learn that we are not who we think we are.

2. Physics: The uncertainty principle reveals our knowledge of matter as fundamentally limited and unstable.

3. Philosophy: The metaphysical category of Being (formerly itself an Absolute) is seen as contingent, historical, and identical with time itself.

Reason, as the Enlightenment-achieved ground of our being, gave us what we thought to be the *certain* knowledge that reality and we ourselves were fundamentally stable and consistent. The new ideas that emerged during the twentieth century suggested another fundamental truth that is unstable and inconsistent. From a world of stable nouns, we have moved into a world of process verbs. However, this is not just a matter of exchanging fixity for process. Now soul understands itself as a dialectical unity of noun-verb. This is not simply a matter of either/or (stability or instability), but both/and (stability-instability as a dialectical unity). Such is the relationship of soul (interiority) and world (manifestation): One does not exist without the other. This new understanding of the unity of soul and world is the result of a further sublation of the logic of incarnation. It is also what enables us to understand *psychology*, not as one of the sciences but as sublated religion *and* science.[6]

The Idea of *the Unconscious* Undermines Reason

Freud understood the unconscious as each individual's storehouse of repressed instinctual desires (sexuality, greed, aggression), which were always in conflict with societal reality and ego ideals. Although this view of human nature certainly undermined the naive Enlightenment belief that we were in complete charge of reality, the logic of Freud's thinking still viewed the unconscious in the Cartesian terms of subject here and object there. Freud's mind naturally assumed the worldview of the sciences, not the worlds of philosophy, theology, or hermeneutics: Freud, as a medical scientist, believed he was discovering objective data, not interpreting subjective phenomena. For him, the unconscious was made up of primarily biological drives that the individual, as a social being, had to master. Freud went further and began to unearth the secrets of the unconscious by offering a way to interpret dreams, and he developed the "talking cure" of psychoanalysis. As a result, the idea of *the unconscious* took off, capturing the public's imagination and stimulating other great thinkers. At the opening of the twentieth century, soul was turning in a whole new direction (Freud's *The Interpretation of Dreams* was published in 1899), undermining Reason's foundation of certainty. While Freud's idea of the unconscious held the seed of a new soul syntax—and we should really understand it as soul's new idea about itself—the syntax of Freud's own thinking was thoroughly determined by Reason, by the Enlightenment form of consciousness. It would require another thinker, as it always does, for soul to continue thinking the thought *the unconscious* in a deeper way and thus to develop its implications for a change in the very foundation of consciousness.

---

6. Giegerich, *Soul's Logical Life*, 66–67; and above p. 25–26; 37–38.

Psyche (Consciousness) Is Both Subject and Object

Jung recognized that psychology, in investigating the psyche (by which he meant human soul and human mind), had an inescapably circular nature. When we talk about the psyche, he realized, the psyche is talking about itself. When we investigate the psyche, the psyche is investigating itself. The psyche is not an object out there that we can look at dispassionately or objectively, as separate from us, because *we are the psyche (subject) observing the psyche (object)*. For Jung, the only way to deal with what would be a vicious circle in traditional philosophy was to be aware of it and openly admit this is the case: "Never forget that in psychology the *means* by which you judge and observe the psyche is the *psyche* itself . . . In psychology, the observer is the observed. The psyche is not only the *object* but also the *subject* of our science."[7] This insight arises when the human-centered, individualized, and private self-understanding of mind (the Cartesian subject) steps back from itself and sees itself in a much larger encompassing framework, a cultural scope of mind or soul. Jung's insight frees soul (psyche) from its Cartesian confinement in the so-called self-contained individual mind and reveals its ouroboric, self-reflexive, dialectical structure. Mind and culture are inextricably bound together as soul, the one soul—as mind-culture, soul as a unity. Even as biological life shows an inexhaustible variety within one Life, so with soul. Soul (as culture) shows an inexhaustible variety, and it is one soul. In the same way, language shows infinite variety, and language itself is one unified phenomenon. Just as we know that Life was not created by humankind, we need to realize Mind, or consciousness, was not created by humankind either. Consciousness at large, the form of consciousness, is a phenomenon in its own right and cannot be reduced to humankind as its substrate; consciousness is self-generating.

Jung's insight into the circular nature of soul dissolves the Cartesian logic that divides the encapsulated and isolated person (mind/subject) from the external world of otherness (matter/object). The ontological division between mind and matter established by Cartesian epistemology and Enlightenment ontology was an achievement of soul's project of ongoing self-emancipation and liberation. The mind/matter divide (science) and the democratic freedom of the human subject, although logically isolated from the world, was primary for a few hundred years, until Jung's realization of the circular essence of the psyche (soul) simply dissolves the gap between mind and matter. Mind and matter are no longer ontological separate categories because the logical form of consciousness (culture itself as shared mind) has become the unified circular truth that defines our existence. As Jung notes:

> If I shift my concept of reality on to the plane of the psyche—where alone it is valid—this puts an end to the conflict between mind and matter, spirit and nature, as contradictory explanatory principles. Each becomes a mere

---

7. Jung, *Tavistock Lectures*, ¶ 277.

designation for the particular source of the psychic contents that crowd into my field of consciousness.[8]

Mind and matter, once separate fundamental categories, are now brought together in an entirely new logic of a subject-object unity. We used to think that the physical world was ontologically external and separate from us, but now we know that *all knowledge* of the world, of ourselves, is cultural knowledge, constituted by shared consciousness, meaning, mind. All knowledge is soul knowledge—that is, mediated as consciousness—and soul (the world of meaning) is the only way we know the world. For us, there is no world without soul, which is the same as saying, there is no knowledge of the world without consciousness. All knowledge is mediated through language, which mediates meaning. We do not know anything of ourselves, our world, our universe, that is not languaged. With this awareness of soul, there can no longer be a clear demarcation between world, soul, and humankind.[9] Our only access to the physical world of stuff is by way of our *world of meaning* (soul). It certainly appears, or so science tells us, that the physical universe existed long before soul and language emerged. But is it possible to really know this with some kind of knowing that is not already embedded in all of our narratives of knowing and meaning? All that we identify as "evidence" does not exist apart from the already existing narrative soul tells about itself. Given the lack of an Archimedean[10] point, we have to accept that all knowledge is first of all, for us, soul knowledge. There is no such thing as abstract data, brute facts, without a context. All data already exist as part of a larger soul narrative that is always changing. We are creatures of soul and language, we are creatures of consciousness, and Jung's insight is the awakening of *consciousness* to itself as *consciousness*, as a phenomenon quite independent of us.

As Jung also noted, we cannot get outside of ourselves to see ourselves from another vantage point: "There is no Archimedean point from which to judge, since the psyche is indistinguishable from its manifestations. The psyche is the object of psychology, and—fatally enough—also its subject. There is no getting away from this fact."[11] This means that all forms of knowledge are now known to be within this circle, and the circle is *fatal* only to soul's former syntax or logical form. In fact, it is literally fatal, in that just as the logic of Reason killed the logic of God, so the logic of the circular nature of soul/consciousness kills the ontologically split (subject/object) logic of Reason. And, while the *logic* of Reason has been dissolved, the *function* of reason

---

8. Jung, *Basic Postulates*, ¶ 681.

9. I will explore this problematic idea again below in a discussion of physics and the undermining of the Cartesian world view.

10. Archimedes, one of the great mathematicians and engineers of antiquity (third century BCE), claimed he could move the earth if he had a solid place to stand on and a long enough lever. The idea of an "Archimedean point" is attributed to Descartes, who hoped to find that one certain and indubitable point on which to found his philosophy. It came to refer to the possibility of standing outside of oneself and see things with a kind of "God's-eye" objectivity, which was the ideal hope of science.

11. Jung, "Psychology and Religion," ¶ 87.

has been preserved in the nature of consciousness itself. We are now beset with a new unsettling problem as we realize consciousness is truly aware of itself as consciousness and as circular. Reason was unconscious of itself and thus naive in its approach to the object, to nature. Reason becomes conscious of itself as consciousness when it applies its critical rigor to itself as a phenomenological method, free of the illusion of the so-called separate object out there. Within the circle of consciousness, there is no longer any "out there" because we realize the object is now a function of consciousness or soul. Subject and object are bound together within the web of meanings and significance that is our world, that constitutes our existence (the world of [written] language). Soul as subject sees itself in the *object* and recognizes the inextricable entanglement that constitutes its knowledge of itself and of the world.

The Dialectical Unity of I and Other

This insight fundamentally changes our relationship with the *other* and also has social implications. The other (whether a thing, a person, or group—especially that person or group we love or hate) is not an isolated difference out there but is itself constituted by consciousness. For soul and for us, the other is always soul's and our own other. Consciousness creates the other's otherness, which is first experienced at a personal level as foreign, threatening, and dangerous. If we understand that consciousness constructs otherness as it constructs us, that it is consciousness's—and my—own other, then a new relationship with that otherness becomes possible. What appears as different or other is, in fact, according to the circle of consciousness, simply another hitherto unknown dimension of myself. However, this change of consciousness requires a dissolution of the original position (subject vs. object) that constructed the other in the first place. For the ego position, or the ideological position, this is a death. Our first instinct is to avoid the death of a personal truth: It *is* our identity, and so we demonize and dehumanize the other to protect our limited truth and thus fail to see the other in ourselves. To do that, to see ourselves through the eyes of the other and realize we are also other to them, means our truth would have to adjust and modify itself, to die a little or a lot. To see things this way shows more clearly the great value of consciousness and the freedom from ideological possession that is now possible. It is difficult to realize such consciousness, yet this work is soul work on the cultural and personal levels.

The self-consciousness that recognizes we are constituted by consciousness (language, meaning, culture, history) dissolves the hard and fast Cartesian dualistic categories of mind and matter and dethrones the materialistic logic of the scientific worldview. The scientific method remains a valuable way to ask questions and find answers, but now we understand that every question is already an interpretation containing its own answer, and every interpretation is already colored by interest, concern, desire, and curiosity within a cultural context. Science still works, but its foundation is no longer fixed and eternal—it is a method, not a dogma.

There is no longer a certain and fixed foundation external to us based on a God or Reason. There is only the ongoing construction of temporary foundations as consciousness continually creates itself: The ship builds itself as it sails. The end of logical certainty (which is on a different level from pragmatic or practical certainty) does not, of course, occur only within psychology. Science (the inner logic of science) itself becomes uncertain and has to enfold uncertainty into its own self-understanding.

The Uncertainty Principle in Quantum Mechanics

Albert Einstein (1879–1955) fundamentally changed our understanding of the physical universe when at the turn of the twentieth century, he developed his theories of relativity (his first and most famous papers were published in 1905). His best-known equation, $E = mc^2$ (energy equals mass times the speed of light squared), established the equivalence of mass and energy, heretofore completely separate categories, another manifestation of the new thought forms that were thinking a unified universe, and, by analogy, a unified view of reality. Einstein's equation is a thought that soul had about itself, in the same way that Jung's insight into the circular and unified nature of consciousness, the unity of subject-object, was also a thought soul was thinking about itself. This is basically the same thought manifesting itself in different areas of knowledge, psychology and physics, expressing the new thought of unity soul was developing, in contrast to Cartesian dualism.

Newton conceived of space and time as separate absolutes that could not affect each other. Newton worked out how the motions of bodies in space were the result of external forces, and he developed the methods to mathematically calculate and measure motions and forces very precisely. Einstein believed that Newtonian mechanics by themselves were not sufficient to be reconciled with the laws of electromagnetic fields, described by James Maxwell in 1864.[12] This led Einstein to his special theory of relativity, which brought together the discrete notions of space and time into the unified idea of *spacetime*.[13] The word *relativity* suggests that the idea of *certainty* is breaking down, but this was not the case. Einstein's relativity was orderly and predictable. Yet, Einstein's new way to think about space, time, gravity, and light helped pave the way to quantum mechanics, which led to the uncertainty principle in 1927.

---

12. Maxwell is probably the greatest scientist we have never heard of. Considered by other physicists to be the third most influential physicist of the modern age, behind only Newton and Einstein, he showed that electricity, magnetism, and light were different manifestations of the same phenomenon. His equations for electromagnetism are another manifestation of soul's developing self-understanding of its own unity through the discovery of the unified ground of seemingly disparate phenomena.

13. *Wikipedia*, s.v. "Albert Einsten," last updated May 31, 2022, https://en.wikipedia.org/wiki/Albert_Einstein#Theory_of_relativity_and_E_=_mc2.

The radical shift in the logic of consciousness that the uncertainty principle represents is apparent when viewed in the context of the absolute mathematical precision of Newton's universe. That precision had led to an absolute faith in mathematical determinism expressed by Pierre Simon de Laplace (1749–1827), a brilliant mathematician and astronomer, known as the "French Newton," who refined and updated many of Newton's mechanical calculations. The following statement by Laplace, considered the first articulation of *scientific determinism*, shows how soul, as Reason, had sublated (incorporated) primary characteristics that would traditionally be associated with God:

> We may regard the present state of the universe as the effect of its past and the cause of its future. An intellect which at a certain moment would know all forces that set nature in motion, and all positions of all items of which nature is composed, if this intellect were also vast enough to submit these data to analysis, it would embrace in a single formula the movements of the greatest bodies of the universe and those of the tiniest atom; for such an intellect nothing would be uncertain and the future just like the past would be present before its eyes.[14]

Such was the faith in the certainty of mathematical formulae, that once all the data was in for every item of nature, of every force and position, a single equation would reveal the past and future of the universe, for all time: *Nothing would be uncertain.* This was the achievement of soul as Reason, an absolute faith in itself to uncover every aspect of nature. During Reason's exhilarating triumph through the eighteenth and nineteenth centuries, humankind's optimism for self-improvement without a supernatural interventionist God was at its height. Soul, as Reason, was certain of itself, and self-doubt was nowhere on the horizon. Today we smile at such an extravagant claim, but our smile simply acknowledges that the foundation of consciousness (its syntax) has changed again.

The uncertainty principle came into consciousness as Werner Heisenberg worked on the mathematical foundations of quantum mechanics.[15] Quantum mechanics has to do with the physical properties of what we still call matter and energy at the smallest conceivable scale, although at this scale the terms are particles and waves, although *particle* on the quantum level has no relation to our commonsense notion of particle. Quantum mechanics focuses on how energy functions at this level, the behavior of light and electromagnetic fields. On our human scale, things in general have a continuous flow about them: Light is not broken up into bits, it does not blink or flicker. At the quantum level, however, light is in fact made up of quanta, discrete packets of energy that can be measured. The packet of light energy is called a photon, and the packet of energy we find in the elements of matter (gold, iron, carbon, etc.)

---

14. Gleick, *Isaac Newton*, 183–84; *Wikipedia*, s.v. "Pierre-Simon Laplace," last updated April 8, 2022, https://en.wikipedia.org/wiki/Pierre-Simon_Laplace.

15. *Wikipedia*, s.v. "Uncertainty principle," last updated April 4, 2022, https://en.wikipedia.org/wiki/Uncertainty_principle.

is the electron. What Heisenberg discovered is that even if the position of an electron is known precisely, it is impossible to know its velocity (speed plus direction), and vice versa. When its velocity is known, its position cannot be known except as a *probability* within a certain range. Unfortunately for "Newtonian certainty" and Laplace, this introduced a limit on our ability to know what a given quantum system will do.

Unpredictability is now a fundamental trait of the universe. Certainly, on our everyday level of functioning, the unpredictability at the heart of matter does not affect us, as our chairs, stairs, cars, and coffee cups do their job with enough stability to get on with things. At the quantum level, the problem of uncertainty is real and has to be taken into account when making calculations. Stephen Hawking, taking the principle further by including the nature of black holes, concludes that the unfolding of the universe, the future, is fundamentally unpredictable. Our understanding of the nature of reality itself has been changed, he says in a 1999 lecture titled "Does God Play Dice":

> Although quantum mechanics has been around for nearly 70 years, it is still not generally understood or appreciated, even by those that use it to do calculations. Yet it should concern us all, because it is a completely different picture of the physical universe, and of reality itself. In quantum mechanics, particles don't have well defined positions and speeds.
>
> It is just a pious hope that the universe is deterministic, in the way that Laplace thought. I feel these scientists have not learnt the lesson of history. The universe does not behave according to our pre-conceived ideas. It continues to surprise us.

We can think of the "pious hope that the universe is deterministic" as a nostalgic longing for a "God" of some kind, some basis of certainty. But why? Why does the hope for a deterministic universe persist? For me, the "lesson of history" is that *historical time* is the very nature of things, and that history (soul as process, as happening) is fundamentally unpredictable. Hawking continues his line of thought and brings it home:

> To sum up, what I have been talking about is whether the universe evolves in an arbitrary way, or whether it is deterministic. The classical view, put forward by Laplace, was that the future motion of particles was completely determined, if one knew their positions and speeds at one time. This view had to be modified, when Heisenberg put forward his Uncertainty Principle, which said that one could not know both the position, and the speed, accurately. However, it was still possible to predict one combination of position and speed. But even this limited predictability disappeared, when the effects of black holes were taken into account. The loss of particles and information down black holes meant that the particles that came out were random. One could calculate probabilities, but one could not make any definite predictions. Thus, the

> future of the universe is not completely determined by the laws of science, and its present state, as Laplace thought. God still has a few tricks up his sleeve.[16]

This talk was Hawking's reply to Einstein's hope that "God does not play at dice with the universe," and he doubled down on the persistence of uncertainty with his own well-known quip, "Not only does God definitely play dice, but He sometimes confuses us by throwing them where they can't be seen."

When Hawking uses the word *God* in this lecture, he is simply following Einstein's use of the same figure of speech. Both Hawking and Einstein were atheists, so we might assume that when they use the word God, it functions as a popular metaphor to refer to a kind of essence of the universe. However, Hawking is affirming that the so-called "material" universe will continue to elude our grasp. It is said that about 95 percent of the universe is made up of dark matter and dark energy, and the visible matter of the universe is only about 5 percent.[17] Therefore, a vast majority of unknown "stuff" is necessary to account for observable anomalies at the present time. We do not know where we (the universe) came from, we do not know why we are here, and we do not know where we are going. There is no fixed foundation in this particular story of the universe. By analogy we can think of the 5 percent of the visible (known) universe as the horizon of consciousness. The fluid, fragile, and vulnerable condition of consciousness—not a thing in itself, a no-thing, or "nothing" (a negativity)—is what we are and the only home we have. We exist *as* consciousness, a linguistic world of meanings, itself always in process, in motion. We exist *as* no-thing in the midst of no-thing. Philosophy, too, came to this conclusion by way of Martin Heidegger's (1889–1976) analysis of Being.

Being (as Metaphysical Foundation) Reconsidered

Early in the twentieth century, philosophy also came to the realization that the pursuit of the final articulation of *the* Foundation was an illusion. For philosophy, this was equivalent to the death of God. The pursuit of such a Foundation had been at the heart of the Western philosophical tradition. The thinkers of antiquity conceived of the Foundation as already *given*, whether as God or Being, as the *a priori*, already known ground of truth. All thought flowed from this already established Foundation. With the Enlightenment and Descartes, the Foundation moved to the human person, and the subject's own thinking process became the indubitable ground of certainty. This Enlightenment shift of the Foundation, however, created another problem, in that it created the ontological gap between the subject and the object, between the thinker and the world. Yes, Descartes's "I think therefore I am" (*cogito ergo sum*), guaranteed

---

16. See https://www.hawking.org.uk/in-words/lectures/does-god-play-dice. This talk is accessible and fun to read, showing flashes of Hawking's characteristic earthy humor. You can even listen to "his voice" as a speech synthesizer recording.

17. See https://science.nasa.gov/astrophysics/focus-areas/what-is-dark-energy.

the thinker's existence (for that cultural context), but this achievement generated the other problem of how does the thinker *know* the world, how does the thinker come to be in contact with the world and know that what is known is true? This quandary set up an epistemological problem that troubled philosophy for three centuries because soul had split itself off from, or differentiated itself from, the material world, and "God" was no longer the guarantor of knowledge. Although the *cogito* established a new foundation, it also set up the new problem of how the world could be known, which remained an inherent instability generating continued thought. The incarnation had established a new foundational category, but its reconciliation of God and Man was also inherently unstable and incomplete, continuing to generate thought. For the Enlightenment, the new status of consciousness remained an unconscious presupposition; that is, it was the new truth, for the time being, even though it was incomplete. The *cogito* was soul's true advance during the Enlightenment, but also, because it was the *syntax* of consciousness, its inherent instability or incompleteness remained out of sight and unquestioned until the twentieth century.

Descartes established the unquestioned presupposition, the inherent instability of the *cogito*, when he posited the subject, the human person, as an isolated, neutral, objective observer who also transcended any cultural context. Such a move amounted to the withdrawal and isolation of Being (I would add, soul) within the human subject and turned the outer world into a "scientific object." But not only the world, we ourselves became "scientific objects" cut off from Being (the former truth of soul as a divine presence had been neutered):

> The Enlightenment ideal of freedom from prejudice and authority, together with the quest of an absolutely generalized objectivity through decontextualization, leads the scientific mode of existence to deny its essential situatedness in the world into which it is thrown. Heidegger regards the withdrawal into the Cartesian *ego cogito* as a necessary concomitant of scientific objectification. In modern technological "framing," he says,
>
> > man has risen into the "I"-hood of the *ego cogito*. With this stance, all entities become objects. Entities, as objective, are absorbed into the immanence of subjectivity. The horizon no longer illuminates from out of itself.[18]

This, of course, was exactly what soul as Reason wanted, freedom to think its own thoughts, free of the prevailing authoritarian theological dogma that had come to dominate soul's thinking. And for this, naturally, soul needs a "thinker," which is the human role in soul's movement. Freedom from the oppressive authoritarian context also led to the loss of all context, and the atomized individual became the new Foundation, the new ground of authority. This was not just a social or political rejection of the church's authoritarianism, but the negation of the logical form of consciousness that made religion and God's reality possible in the first place. This was soul's

---

18. Guignon, *Heidegger*, 191.

self-negation of its religious nature and form for the sake of becoming a free-thinking subject. When Heidegger states in the above quotation that "the horizon no longer illuminates from out of itself," he means that the world beyond the human subject no longer contains any inherent truth. All truth has been absorbed by the subject, and things have been reduced to mere (dead) objects. The earth as God's created order, and thus inherently meaningful and truthful, has been erased (seen clearly expressed in Nietzsche's parable). With this fundamental change of modernity, the ground of general consciousness, public mind, gained a new freedom, and at the same time, anxiety and alienation (the *human* experience of this change) became the hallmarks of late modernity. Within this context, Heidegger realized that the epistemological preoccupation of philosophy was misguided: The human person as an isolated subject, and an objective neutral observer did not exist.

In *Being and Time*, Heidegger interprets the human condition as always already thrown (born) into a cultural context of meanings and significance; we always already have a purposeful engagement with everyday things and people. *Being*, in Heidegger's thinking, is neither something mystical nor transcendent, and yet, this most familiar of all concepts is also the most obscure. Being at its most obvious is simply the verb *to be*. We all know what the phrases, "The sky *is* blue," "We *are* here," or "I *am* well," mean without thinking about the meaning of Being. We already have an implicit understanding of Being in that we know how *to be* in the world without thinking about it. We do not require an explicit theoretical articulation of the nature of Being in order to be a human being. We already know how to be human beings automatically, and we learn unselfconsciously, automatically, within our environment and within ourselves how to exist, how to survive, how to be what we are. Being already knows how to be. Being, in its most general sense, is our taken-for-granted essence, and this simply means that a baby knows how to be a baby without being taught how to be a baby, and so on. We might say that Being is the specifically *human* instinct for how to be. In thinking about this *essence* philosophically, Heidegger also wants to know if there is something absolute and eternal about it. Is there a Foundation, a final meaning of Being, somewhere within or beneath all the infinite cultural and personal variety? The quest for a final truth is what initially motivated Heidegger:

> Heidegger's goal, at least during the period when *Being and Time* was composed, is in fact to find *trans*historical and *trans*cultural structures that underlie any possible interpretations. Seen in this way, the existential analytic is aimed at finding a firm foundation for ontology, and this goal strikes us as rather similar to that of Cartesian foundationalism.[19]

Ontology refers to the philosophical project of fully thinking out the meaning of Being, which is the attempt to articulate the ultimate nature of reality. The word *psychology*, composed of the Greek words *psyche* and *logos*, means making soul's speech

---

19. Guignon, *Heidegger*, 63.

about itself explicit, or making soul's truth explicit. Similarly, ontology, also composed of two Greek words, *ōn* (being, essence) plus *logos*, means making Being's speech about itself explicit, or making the meaning of Being explicit. In its aim to make the ultimate principles of Being explicit, ontology is philosophy's analogue to theology, the attempt to articulate explicitly the nature of God as the ultimate principle. From the point of view of my history of consciousness (soul), both philosophy and theology realize the same thing at more or less the same time—the notion of a transcendent Absolute is dead. By the end of the nineteenth century, God was dead. Through what was really the failure of *Being and Time*, the attempt to realize a full conceptualization of Being that could be the final transcendental Foundation, is also dead. These cultural ideas reveal soul's account of itself and the death of the Absolute, while a real end coincides with the birth of something else. At the same time, the absolute isolation of modernity's Cartesian subject has come to its end, and its self-negation gives birth to a new kind of differentiated unity.

The Reunification of Being and World

Heidegger uses the German word for existence, *Dasein*, to refer to humankind in general. *Dasein* is Da-sein, and can be translated literally as the "there-of-Being," which conveys the principle that Being is always embedded in a *there* that is humankind and culture. As the "there-of-Being," Da-sein is the term that designates the existential analysis of *Being's existence as a world*, which is our world. Thus, Heidegger thinks of Being, not as a transcendent metaphysical other, but always constituted as "Being-in-the-world," and that *world* is the social, cultural web of implicit *meanings* and *purposes*.

This way of thinking the structure and context of existence (human beings) means that we are always embedded in specific historical and cultural worlds that we first of all take for granted. As children, we absorb our social context like a sponge and never think about it consciously, as we are shaped by the unspoken assumptions, values, rules, and behaviors that then inform our relations to others and ourselves. Only later, as adults, do we begin to make our interpreting, theorizing, and philosophizing explicit, and even then, our thinking is always influenced ahead of time by the ideas that define the cultural world we inhabit. Of course, new and creative interpretations emerge, but they must always push against the already existing ideas that have shaped us. The structure of Dasein as Being-in-the-world also means that Being does not exist, cannot exist, without its *there*. Being itself exists only as a *there*, or a here and now. Today, Being must be conceived as completely contingent with existence. Heidegger will discover that the traditional metaphysical idea of Being as transcendent and ahistorical is now inconceivable. Such a conception of Being can no longer be thought because the syntax of consciousness has changed. Being can be thought only as *in-a-world*. This view of Being parallels the view that soul exists only as its cultural manifestations. Here we see the sublated logic of the incarnation: the Word (God) is inextricably united with the flesh: God-in-flesh, Being-in-world.

With the obvious truth of the phenomenological structure of Dasein as always already embedded in meaningful contexts, there can be no such thing as a neutral, isolated, contextless human being. And it would be better to say that Dasein is not a thing embedded *in* meaning, but that Dasein—that is, humankind—is made of meaning, exists *as* meaning, and can exist only as meaning. Dasein in this sense is the *there-of-meaning*. We are not passive observers receiving impressions from the world, but rather active participants always already engaged meaningfully and purposefully with our world. With this realization of the basic nature of Dasein, the idea of a human person without a given context of meaning becomes meaningless and incoherent. This is obvious to us today, but this obviousness is because the logic of consciousness has already changed, and our context today is that soul has already dissolved the notion of an isolated Foundational subject.[20] Heidegger's analysis of existence demonstrates not only that we are contextualized in meaning, but that *everything* is contextualized in meaning. There are no such things as so-called raw facts, raw data, or bare material things, as everything we encounter is mediated by language and meaning ahead of time. Everything that exists for us is already embedded in some kind of narrative or story of meaning that already encompasses all of our history and culture. The linguistic world of meaning is one world and its history.[21]

Foundations Crumble

The notion of the Cartesian subject had served its purpose during the Enlightenment when it rejected its original context of received traditional ideas, the given meanings in which it had been embedded, especially the Christian syntax of consciousness. The Cartesian subject became its own foundation, its own syntax. Now, during late modernity, soul has been outgrowing this idea of itself as Foundation. The traditional notion of Foundation as something fixed is crumbling. Heidegger is another example, along with the ideas of the unconscious and the uncertainty principle, of soul discovering this about itself and carrying out the self-negation of itself as Foundation. Soul as Foundation, in the form of a primordial universal fixed truth, is leaving itself behind and emerging as the no-thing of a happening: Being and we, as soul, *are* an open-ended process of meaning always creating, destroying, and re-creating itself.

---

20. The rise of ecological awareness of the complete interrelatedness of the total natural environment is also evidence for the logical dissolution of the idea of the isolated subject and object. For recent challenging thought on this topic, see *Dark Ecology*, by Timothy Morton.

21. So Jorge Luis Borges, *Collected Fictions*: "Even in the language of humans there is no proposition that does not imply the entire universe; to say 'the jaguar' is to say all the jaguars that engendered it, the deer and turtles it has devoured, the grass that fed the deer, the earth that was mother to the grass, the sky that gave light to the earth" (252). "There is not a simple page, a simple word, on earth—for all pages, all words, predicate the universe, whose most notorious attribute is its complexity" (345).

God's Autopsy and the Living Truth of Soul

Heidegger's analysis of Dasein (existence), as constituted by the structure of Being-in-the-world, is another instance in which the infamous Cartesian subject-object dichotomy dissolves. Subject and object now constitute together a differentiated unity, as it is now quite impossible to imagine a subject disconnected from its world (its "meaningful" objects). Being-in-the-world means that all objects are already embedded in a *world* of meanings. Heidegger never uses the term *consciousness* because for him it was too tightly bound to the Cartesian discrete subject, or ego. For me, *consciousness*, as representative of soul, is a comprehensive term that points to the world of meanings that unites subject and object in their mutual meaningful relations, and without which they have no existence (for us) whatsoever. Just as the Newtonian discrete categories of space and time were dissolved by Einstein's spacetime continuum, so the Cartesian view of subject and object as discrete things is dissolved by Heidegger's idea of Being-in-the-world (as well as Jung's insight into the structure of psyche and Giegerich's view of soul), leading me to think in terms of a *subjectobject* continuum, or better, dialectic. As Heidegger tells us, "Dasein *is* its world existingly."[22] Dasein's world is a world of given linguistic and cultural meaning that continually destroys and recreates itself.[23] We are essentially creatures of meaning, which is the world of consciousness we inhabit, or that we *are*. In being a world, and living a world, we do not have consciousness, we *are consciousness*.

Heidegger's ambitious hope in *Being and Time* was to articulate a fundamental ontology that was ahistorical, to bring to complete theoretical expression a final truth that would withstand the vagaries of culture and history. A "fundamental ontology" would be the fully thought out articulation of the essence of reality, which would stand as a final statement of the truth. Failure of such an enterprise was inevitable when Heidegger realized that Being *is* time. Truth is fundamentally historical, and Being *is* always time and culture, ever changing, and always, as to the future, open and unpredictable. For Heidegger, Dasein's fundamental historicity means Dasein is not a metaphysical object, but a *happening*:

> "Historicity" refers to the temporal axis of Dasein's Being when it is regarded not as an object but as the *happening* of a life as a whole. Heidegger defines "historicity" as "the temporalization structure of temporality" through which Dasein "*is stretched along and stretches itself along*" between birth and death. As "temporalizing as such," historicity captures the dynamic structure of Dasein's way of taking up the possibilities into which it is "delivered over" by projecting itself onto its ownmost possibility of Being-a-whole.[24]

We are much more than individual persons who happen to live within history, with history viewed as a stream of time somewhat independent of us. We *are* the history

---

22. Heidegger, *Being and Time*, 416.
23. In later writing Heidegger says, "Language is the house of Being" ("Letter," 63).
24. Guignon, *Heidegger*, 214.

of our time living itself out over the total time between birth and death. If we think of being and time as a continuum, then we can imagine ourselves as stretched out from our beginning (birth) to the end, as we also stretch ourselves into those possibilities presented to us along the way. Our existence is stretched as time and also stretches itself into its truth. If we are going to realize the truth that is ours, and ours alone, then we must also meet that which stretches us and also stretch ourselves toward that truth. It is no longer possible to think of Being as a transcendent metaphysical fixed truth or universal principle. Being is time, Being is historical, *beingtime* is soul's new logic today.

The circular and historical nature of Being appears with the insight that it is Dasein (us) who asks the question of the meaning of Being. Dasein is always already (as the there-of-Being) thinking from within a cultural context, and the cultural context shapes our thoughts. Thus, when we think about the nature of reality, we are that reality, already constituted by a cultural context, thinking about itself. All cultural contexts are historical in that they change and develop. Dasein, as that being that raises the question of the meaning of Being, is thereby Being asking the question about itself. I would paraphrase Heidegger's succinct aphorism, "Dasein *is* its world existingly," as, humankind manifests soul's thoughts thinking themselves.

We, as Dasein, already have an implicit understanding of Being in that we automatically, or unconsciously, know how to be. This does not always go well by any means, but it does mean that our being knows how to cope, to adapt, to survive, and to thrive in a variety of life circumstances. The making explicit of Dasein's pre-ontological (unconscious) understanding of Being is a process of interpretation that makes the unconscious understanding conscious (or, ontological, explicit). For example, we survived our childhood because we already knew how to be, and our pre-ontological understanding of how to be has enabled us to adapt, cope, learn, achieve, and become what we are today. Perhaps, later in adulthood through a process like psychotherapy, we become conscious and make explicit what we have already known pre-ontologically. Our so-called neuroses or dysfunctional adaptations were the way the know-how of Being, as our being, became itself within the confines of our family and society.

Through psychotherapy, as one example, we become conscious of our unconscious adaptations, which is a process of interpreting what has already been understood, and thus we gain a bit of freedom of choice in relation to our behavior and thoughts. The movement from implicit *understanding* of Being to explicit *interpretation* Heidegger calls the *hermeneutic circle*: "Any interpretation which is to contribute understanding must already have understood what is to be interpreted."[25] This circular structure is the way Being discloses itself, by way of the unconscious understanding of Being that Dasein already is. We, as Dasein, manifest the *understanding* of being that we already are by way of lived life. This is another way to see the circular structure and process of soul, moving from implicit to explicit.

---

25. Heidegger, *Being and Time*, 194.

This is not a vicious circle any more than the gift of divine reason would have been thought circular in antiquity. Only the modern rational (and logically solipsistic) ego can consider such a circle a trap. The Cartesian ego cannot imagine anything beyond itself because it is constituted as, and totally self-contained as, its rational "I-hood." The syntax of its consciousness remains identified with itself as "I," and thus for this form of consciousness, there is no God, no unconscious, no soul, only itself (and let us remember, this was its achievement). Heidegger's analysis of Dasein and Being as fundamentally circular and historical breaks open the self-enclosed ego to a mode of Being beyond itself, but within which it is included. In dissolving the subject-object dichotomy the hermeneutic circle affirms that we are always meaningfully involved with the world in pre-ontological undisclosed ways. When I speak of soul-work as that process of allowing soul to think its own thoughts, this is the psychological way of entering the hermeneutic circle consciously to interpret its implicit understanding of its Being-in-the-world. For example, we already know what a dream means, no matter how bizarre, because it is our own thought; it is just not a thought from the ego, and the ego will not understand it. It is not a thought from day-consciousness, but a thought from night (or soul) consciousness. What we need is to find the means to allow it to tell us what it means, which for starters, could simply be the assertion that the dream does mean something and is not random nonsense. Psychology as the discipline of interiority begins with the discipline of first focusing on the dream images themselves, while allowing the everyday commonsense ego to recede. Then the dream images can begin to tell us about themselves, and their inherent intelligibility can begin to reveal itself. It is as if the dream is held within a hidden syntax that does not match our ego commonsense syntax. Letting the dream's hidden syntax reveal itself is the process of letting its implicit meaning become explicit.

No Foundation: Soul Happens as Now

The essence of Dasein (people), the essence of culture, and the essence of Being itself is historical, which means essence never stands still and never escapes its time-bound nature. If this is our essence and the essence of Being, then we must give up the quest for a final and fixed Foundation. Instead of deep, atemporal, and fixed structures of Being, Heidegger comes to understand Being and Dasein as a *happening*:

> "The basic position and attitude of our questioning is in itself historical; it stands and maintains itself in happening, inquiring out of happening for the sake of this happening." Fundamental ontology is part of the world-historical happening of Western thought and, therefore, cannot be conceived of as the attempt to find ahistorical, transcendental structures that lie outside of that happening.[26]

---

26. Guignon, *Heidegger*, 234.

This reminds me of the uncertainty principle, in that we cannot pin down location and velocity simultaneously. If we want a solid Foundation (something pinned down), then we lose sight of historical process (an analogue for velocity), and if we focus on historical process, then we have to let go of any Foundation. The only Foundation possible is the *foundation* of the ever-moving and changing historical now, as well as a conception of truth as fluid, itself historical, changing. Soul has succeeded in dissolving the very notion of Foundation, and the soul-world, the truth, we inhabit now is Foundationless. Truth itself has become a happening.

Review of the Foundation's Self-Sublations

Throughout this book, I have been tracing the syntax of consciousness through its varied historical manifestations, as it transformed itself from nature gods to Yahweh, from Yahweh to Christ, from Christ to Reason, and from Reason to psychology. Psychology here is focused on soul, representing the status of consciousness as conscious of itself as consciousness. Each stage of consciousness was a Foundation unto itself, establishing itself as Foundation, and experienced implicitly and self-evidently as Foundation. At each stage, the established Foundation negated and sublated itself, because its interiority, its meaning, is a dynamic form of cultural consciousness, which is always restless and in conflict with itself. The dominant cultural ideas and thoughts are how the syntax of consciousness manifests itself in any given age. The following overview, which follows the same narrative arc as the overview of the *I Am* seen in chapter two, highlights how the logical form of consciousness has always defined itself as a Foundation. This will lead to an interesting question about the status of consciousness today and its relation to what is generally thought of as the "physical world" by way of the insights of modern physics.

Yahweh as Foundation

The first manifestation (for my purposes) of the syntax of consciousness presenting itself as the Foundation of everything occurs in the opening lines of Genesis in the Tanakh, through the voice of the omniscient narrator:

> In the beginning when God created the heavens and the earth, the earth was a formless void and darkness covered the face of the deep, while a wind from God swept over the face of the waters. Then God said, "Let there be light"; and there was light.

The ancient text asserts that God, at the beginning, created the "heavens and the earth" and everything that is in heaven and earth. As the creator of all that is—and yet uncreated himself—God is the primordial Foundation. Psychologically, the idea of *God* was the personified form of the syntax of consciousness that created itself as a new form of consciousness within the context of the polytheistic cosmos of the ancient Near East. As God, God posited himself as the Foundation and functioned, as the syntax of consciousness, as the Foundation. Humankind does not create this foundation; the foundation creates itself. It is the logic of a society's shared or collective consciousness as a people. Someone did not think this up and then persuade others that it was true because the *syntax* of consciousness is not a *content* of consciousness—it is the ground of consciousness itself, or as I have also said, the shape of consciousness. God as Foundation emerged as truth of its own accord through the dynamic cultural ferment of ideas that think their own thoughts by way of human culture, which is its medium. This level of consciousness, the logical form of consciousness or soul, at first presents itself as intuitive revelation or vision. As such, it is self-evident and lays a claim, even a kind of possession, on human persons. It is first experienced as if it were a god, and thus also as if external to humankind. Yahweh was experienced as the self-evident Foundation of all life and the Truth directing the action.

Christ as Foundation

The God who was the Foundation that gave rise to the Tanakh sublated itself as a new Foundation in the form of the Christ that gave rise to the New Testament. The opening lines of the Gospel of John state this clearly:

> In the beginning was the Word, and the Word was with God, and the Word was God. He was in the beginning with God. All things came into being through him, and without him not one thing came into being.

The *Word* is *Christ*, and he too is in the beginning, just as God was. Christ as Foundation is posited as equal to the original Foundation God, but he is different; he incorporates and adds a new dimension to the original Foundation God. The opening lines of John state something else was present at the beginning that was also God, but it was not yet explicit, or I would say, conscious. The Word, as it emerged in Christianity, was a further differentiation of the original Foundation. Now it was the Word that was the Foundation of "all things," and "not one thing came into being" without the Word. Christianity was a significant stage in the evolution of consciousness, and the name Christ, as the incarnate Word, became the Foundation, absorbing the earlier foundation and bringing it into a new status of consciousness. *Christ* was the name of the logical form of consciousness that established itself as Foundation.

Reason as Foundation

The Foundation that was Christ also negated itself through sublation in the development of Enlightenment Reason. Here I revisit Simon de Laplace's statement in reference to the positing of Reason as the Foundation of absolute certainty:

> We may regard the present state of the universe as the effect of its past and the cause of its future. An intellect which at a certain moment would know all forces that set nature in motion, and all positions of all items of which nature is composed, if this intellect were also vast enough to submit these data to analysis, it would embrace in a single formula the movements of the greatest bodies of the universe and those of the tiniest atom; *for such an intellect nothing would be uncertain and the future just like the past would be present before its eyes.*[27]

Reason, as the name of a new form of consciousness, has sublated the quality of God as the Foundation of the universe into its own self-understanding. Here again, the form of consciousness posits itself as Foundation. It is easy to critique Laplace's statement as naive, but that critique is from the human-centered point of view, through the human ego. Laplace's statement simply represents soul's achievement of a new syntax of consciousness, a cultural-historical process that worked its own way into a new status of general consciousness, new *water* so to speak, that we swim in. We do not control how the *water* changes, but we do adapt to the new qualities and circumstances of consciousness, because at our deepest level, this is what we *are*. In fact, we become that new form of consciousness without really knowing that it happened. Through these major historical and cultural epochs, consciousness—that is, the logic of consciousness, in each of its historical manifestations as *God*, as *Christ*, and as *Reason*—posits itself as, and is, the self-evident Foundation of the world. And, of course, I mean the Foundation of the only world we know, which is the linguistic (literate) world of *meaning*.

Consciousness as "Foundation"

From within the age of Reason, a new age is emerging, which I call the age of Psychology. Our age is fundamentally psychological because in many different ways and at many different levels, it is preoccupied with the circular nature of consciousness that is aware of itself as consciousness. Until now, consciousness has been the invisible means by which the world is apprehended and experienced, and consciousness has been oriented outward toward objects and ideas, both material and metaphysical. Consciousness has been thoroughly conditioned by its orientation to a physical world within which it exists, and it has been naturally preoccupied with that three-dimensional world. Consciousness has also taken, in a naturally naive way, the so-called spiritual or metaphysical world as an objective external reality. This natural orientation of consciousness is what is changing, has changed, in a radical and profound way. Thomas Kuhn's insight into the nature of scientific paradigms can be generalized and paraphrased as, "when you're in the paradigm, you can't see the paradigm," which is true for the prevailing logical form of consciousness of each historical epoch.

---

27. Gleick, *Isaac Newton*, 183–84; see also Wikipedia, s.v. "Pierre-Simon Laplace," emphasis added.

However, consciousness, as a phenomenon in its own right, may be the most invisible "paradigm" of them all (as far as we know today), and this lens or eye that allows us to see anything at all is finally becoming somewhat visible to itself. We have been naturally preoccupied with *what* we see without having any idea about *how* we see. Psychological consciousness gives a glimpse into how we see, now that consciousness is becoming *aware of itself* as such. This "awareness of itself" is the new "foundation," but it is not a "foundation" in any sense we have ever known; it is the anti-foundation because it dissolves all prior forms of Foundation into *nothing*, that is, *consciousness*. Our challenge today is to learn to think consciousness, to learn what thinking, thinking itself, means.

Having become psychological, seeing itself as soul's logos, consciousness does not have itself as one more content along with all the other contents of consciousness. Consciousness can now see that the objects it interacts with are reflections of itself; consciousness is the medium by which we know anything at all. All knowledge and experience is reflected as consciousness (in the modes of language, history, memory, culture, meaning, and story). Consciousness, in seeing itself seeing itself, is fundamentally circular and self-reflexive, and these structural characteristics define soul as well because consciousness at this level, and soul, are synonyms. This *consciousness* is first of all not personal, not individual-centered. It is a human species-wide factor constituted by language and culture as the medium of meaning that exists first, and which makes personal and individual consciousness possible at all. This ouroboric consciousness, this "foundation," gives no pretext to fixity or finality—it is happening, movement, performative, a river.

Consciousness as Torrent

From the beginning, culture has always been the medium of soul's self-reflection, and the first medium that enabled soul's historical self-reflection in earnest was writing, books. As noted so far, the Bible played a central role in Western soul's self-development, as it was read and interpreted over and over, spawning millions of books, all conflicting with and building on each other. But we have not had the conceptual categories until today to recognize this historical process as the movement of consciousness. Today the circular and self-reflexive nature of consciousness is understood theoretically through philosophy and psychology, but it is also reflected in popular culture where, of course, it is simply acted out without any conscious understanding. Now electronic media are pushing this process faster and faster. Radio would be the first electronic medium that began to accelerate this process as a mass medium as which soul talked to itself. With television soul achieved another status in now watching itself almost instantaneously, recording and reporting on itself live. Television has become absolutely ubiquitous, and it is almost impossible to find a public space that television has not infiltrated. Although television has become completely filtered, edited, and produced, it is always focused on Now, the live present moment, and it pushes this moment to us with increasing intensity and heightened emotionality. No one planned out how television would operate. It simply developed as a mode of soul operating on itself. Television is a loop so entirely focused on the immediacy of Now that it ends up flattening out consciousness; the torrent of televised images leaves no room for thought and reflection. In this way, soul keeps itself on the surface of things and cancels out depth.[28] In the world of television, silence is nonexistent. Any moment of stillness in which deeper reflection could occur has been eliminated. No stopping. Constant rushing movement. Continual emotional spikes hooking our attention, but remembering nothing. This torrent is not limited to television as it has come to infect culture at large. Why has this torrent become soul's cultural norm?

What happened next is that television gave birth, metaphorically speaking, to billions of small replicas of itself as smart phones. Every smart phone is also a camera, connected via the Internet to the World Wide Web. Selfies (photographing oneself using a smart phone) are an expression of the fascination soul has with itself as conscious of itself, reflecting itself. The video platform YouTube (and more recently, Zoom and TikTok) have become enormously popular almost instantaneously because they too are a medium by which soul reflects itself to itself. Why are our screens, colorful, bright, animated, even "alive," so fascinating and mesmerizing? We may complain that we are addicted to our smart phones, preoccupied with content truly empty of any substance, that we have become a culture of distracted watchers. This may indeed be true, but again, this is the human-centered perspective. Our natural tendency is to focus on how all of this affects *us*, positively or negatively, but what's happening is not really about us.

Psychologically, the burgeoning technology and media-saturated culture is soul's speech about itself, soul operating on itself, another manifestation of soul's thoughts thinking themselves. Contemporary culture is soul, a new syntax of consciousness, propagating itself without knowing where it is going nor why it is going at all. But, while it is going, and at increasing speed, one thing we do know is that the ground of consciousness, the form of consciousness, has changed in a revolutionary way, and consciousness appears to be liberating itself from all its traditional moorings and notions of truth. It is almost as if soul in its extreme preoccupation with itself through the medium of digital technology is trying to become conscious of something. Or is popular culture simply the implicit acting out of something that has indeed already happened, that consciousness has come home to itself because it is now aware of itself as such?

The very negation soul is undergoing today is thoroughly undermining the traditional grounds of truth, while creating a new truth that appears abhorrent to us. Consciousness is liberating itself from the self-evident values of humanism. While we publicly affirm platitudes of human dignity and the rights of the individual, the global

---

28. Giegerich, "Function of Television," 290–91.

forces demanding profit devour the environment and human persons. Is consciousness undertaking a new exodus? At the very least we have seen that consciousness wants to liberate itself, and perhaps it will continue in such a direction in spite of what happens to humankind.

Soul, as the logical *form* of consciousness, has found that it was the Foundation of our being, and of itself, all along. Consciousness is its own foundation, the consciousness that is the world of *meaning* (public mind) that we not only inhabit, but that we *are*. And, furthermore, it could very well be that humankind itself is a kind of temporary by-product, even a transitory stepping-stone, of soul's self-transformations. The religious stages of consciousness have clearly been stepping stones of the self-negating and self-developing process of consciousness. Is the human species itself a stepping-stone for the impersonal project of consciousness? We hear the joke that AI (artificial intelligence) will overtake the human species, and if it is kind will keep us as pets, if it does not eliminate us. Such thoughts point to the transformation of the logical form of consciousness, and have the flavor of apocalyptic end of the world fantasies. Ever since the publication of *Frankenstein* two hundred years ago, our anxieties about technology have continued to grow.[29] Science fiction in general is not really about the future but about what is happening now.

Consciousness and Physics

What does it mean to say that consciousness of consciousness is our new foundation? In the sense that consciousness is our human-world—as such it is inescapable—it is our foundation, but, as we see, a much less stable one than it seemed to be until now. We can gain another line of insight into how consciousness sees itself by way of the field of modern physics. Now, to be sure, traditional physics as a science is incompatible with psychology (with soul) as the discipline of interiority, to the extent that they each represent completely different orientations to reality. Physics operates from the external point of view, and its objects are thoroughly outside of itself; it is focused on nature as an object "out there" and making measurements of quantities. Psychology with soul is devoted to interiority, which is the awareness of the structure of consciousness itself, realizing there are no so-called objects outside of itself. Nothing (for us) exists outside of the world of meaning that makes us what and who we are. Within psychology, self and other, or object, are always a dialectical unity constituted by consciousness itself. Psychology with soul is concerned with interpreting meanings (not measuring quantities).

Although classical physics has had a very different ontological orientation in contrast to psychology with soul, modern physics has itself become infected and infiltrated by the awareness that consciousness plays a role in what the physicist observes

---

29. Shelley, *Frankenstein*, 1818.

and "discovers." In fact, some physicists are beginning to wonder if consciousness itself is not implicated as a constitutive factor in the existence of the physical universe.

When Carl Sagan (1934–1996) stated that "Man is the matter of the universe contemplating itself,"[30] he established a circular relationship constituted by both the *universe* and *consciousness*. We know that exploding stars are the furnaces in which all the atomic elements that make up life are created. We do not believe a God created us full blown and already endowed with consciousness. We do believe in the evolutionary interpretation in which life evolved from simple to complex forms, and the physical stuff of the universe also developed from simple elements to the more complex. This cosmic story is a narrative of meaning created by the historical development of consciousness (public mind), leaning heavily on the meaning conveyed by the word *evolution*. This scientific view of the cosmos and life is itself a shared public linguistic construction that has developed over time. This does not mean no cosmos exists outside of language. Rather, it means that we know this cosmos only by way of language, or better, by way of the meaning that language mediates for us and the history of this meaning. We (i.e., soul) can only think these thoughts because language is itself soul's medium for thinking about itself.

Sagan's statement that humankind is the medium by which the universe (matter) contemplates itself is a circular logic, and within that circularity we can question the *a priori* assumption that it all started with not-conscious matter. The logic of our modern consciousness is oriented to believe that inanimate matter (hydrogen, etc.) is the source—or what came first—and then from this primal stuff first animate life evolved, and now culture and consciousness have emerged. We can consider a different arrangement in which *consciousness*—again, not personal ego-consciousness—is essential to the means by which matter has manifested. However, to make this reorientation we have to overcome the logic or syntax of our modern Enlightenment consciousness, which is founded in scientific materialism. For our modern form of consciousness, matter is ontologically superior to spirit—matter/energy is *real* while mind and ideas (consciousness) are merely personal and subjective, and not real in any concrete sense. Therefore, it is next to impossible to imagine, to think, that anything other than inanimate matter or inanimate natural forces could be the ground of the Beginning. To think otherwise is to drift back into religious, spiritual, or who knows what kind of crazy ideas. It is very hard to imagine or think a nonmaterial origin of the material universe without reverting to earlier mythos- and theos-centered forms of consciousness.

---

30. While I have long been moved by this statement attributed to Carl Sagan, I have been unable to find its exact source, other than its ubiquitous presence on popular quote websites (where sources are never cited). This general idea is not new to scientists and astronomers, but Sagan made it popular. Two similar statements by Sagan are: "The cosmos is within us. We are made of star-stuff. We are a way for the universe to know itself" (Sagan et al., "Shores of the Cosmic Ocean"); and, "We are the local embodiment of a Cosmos grown to self-awareness. We have begun to contemplate our origins: star-stuff pondering the stars" (Sagan, *Cosmos*, 364).

In spite of this very barrier within our thinking, and because soul is negating its Cartesian logic, this is exactly the territory we enter with the realization that consciousness is conscious of itself. New ways to think are introduced when we realize the stuff of the universe is contemplating itself as consciousness. It is not a matter of some kind of "higher" consciousness having created the world, which again, is a personalistic or anthropological model, but rather of giving the impersonal nature of consciousness the consideration it needs for us to understand how it functions independently of us. This is confusing because our natural tendency is to think that *consciousness* is individual or personal consciousness, rather than an impersonal factor, as impersonal as matter and energy. One very simple way to see how impersonal consciousness functions independently of our personal consciousness is to consider the process of measuring something. The units of measurement (inches, pounds, gallons, volts) are themselves a function of an impersonal intelligible meaningful world that is founded in the structure of consciousness. A ruler, a scale, or a voltmeter does not care whether the measurer is hungry, sad, or stupid. If used correctly, it will make a correct measurement that is intelligible within the general, shared, impersonal field of consciousness. In other words, the world of public mind, public meaning, is not dependent on the personal state (consciousness) of the individual person. The world of public mind functions independently of us.

I am not interested in rehabilitating the idea of "God," but I am also not interested in settling for the scientific and humanistic logic of our still-prevailing Enlightenment form of consciousness. The logic of *consciousness of consciousness* pushes us beyond those historical stages of consciousness to consider other interpretations. Whether or not Sagan's statement means that matter itself (hydrogen, etc.) has become self-conscious or is simply another way of saying that consciousness has become conscious of itself, it leads us to the thought of physicist John Wheeler (1911–2008). In the last years of his life philosophical interests dominated his thinking and he was preoccupied with the role consciousness played in the existence of the physical universe.[31] Does consciousness, in the function of our observations of physical phenomenon, help to bring the universe into existence? This prompts the question about what kind of relationship exists between the physical universe and consciousness. Is consciousness discontinuous with the physical universe, having little to do as a logical function (a function of mind, culture) with the existence of the physical universe? We should know that our personal (ego) consciousness and the physical universe exist independently of each other. We also believe that the universe created itself long before human consciousness came into existence. Life itself, the life of nature, plants, and animals, obviously functions quite well without consciousness, that is, the consciousness that we equate with culture, language, history, and so on. Is there another way to understand consciousness, however, such that consciousness may have something to do with how the universe created itself, and continues to create itself?

---

31. Folger, "Does the Universe Exist," 44.

Wheeler was a physicist who worked closely with Albert Einstein and Niels Bohr in developing nuclear fission among other scientific advancements, and he was the one to coin the term *black hole*. Although his name is not well known, he was one of the last titans of modern physics, and he made significant contributions to quantum mechanics and cosmology. Late in life, in his nineties, he was preoccupied with the relationship between consciousness and the universe. Wheeler's mind was drawn to philosophical questions: "We are no longer satisfied with insights only into particles, or fields of force, or geometry, or even space and time. Today we demand of physics some understanding of existence itself."[32] This is an extraordinary statement, given that in former ages an "understanding of existence" was the exclusive purview of theology and philosophy. Here a physicist makes an existential demand on physics itself: that *physics* should provide some answer to the question of the *meaning of life*.

Wheeler is not alone in his concern. I believe the "we" he refers to is the general public's fascination with modern physics and cosmology as well as its hunger for deep answers to the ultimate questions. When the general public hunger for meaning looks to "science" for answers to ultimate questions, it reflects the fundamental logic of modern consciousness, which is informed by Enlightenment Reason and science, grounded in a materialistic view of reality. This is the result of the shift of ultimate value, the *logic* or *syntax* of consciousness, from the universals (God and spirit) to the particulars (matter and humankind). We no longer look for truth in divine revelation, but in the knowledge of science and empirically grounded theories developed by the human intellect. The logic of Science, which rejected all metaphysical and theological questions and answers, now feels the need for answers larger than its own traditional self-understanding. And yet, as Wheeler's thinking will show, the closed materialistic world of traditional physics is cracking open. There is a new awareness of the role consciousness plays in observing and measuring, specifically in relation to quantum functioning, nature at its most elemental level.

Observations in science are the operation of consciousness as an impersonal function interacting with reality. (What is *reality*?) An insight is emerging that sees observation and measurement as ways in which consciousness interacts with itself. (Reality is not just out there as the observed, but reality must now include the *observation as part of the reality it observes*.) Wheeler's statements about the role of observation suggest just such a self-reflexive and circular nature of consciousness in relationship with the universe:

> According to the rules of quantum mechanics, our *observations* influence the universe at the most fundamental levels.[33]
>
> . . .

---

32. John Wheeler obituary, *New York Times*, April 14, 2008, https://www.nytimes.com/2008/04/14/science/14wheeler.html.

33. Folger, "Does the Universe Exist," 44, emphasis added.

> Our *observations* ... might actually contribute to the creation of physical reality. To Wheeler we are not simply bystanders on a cosmic stage; we are shapers and creators living in a participatory universe.[34]
>
> ...
>
> The universe is built like an enormous feedback loop, a loop in which we contribute to the ongoing creation of not just the present and the future but the past as well.[35]

The role of observation is a function of consciousness that is independent of ego or personal consciousness. *Observation* is not, first of all, simply a human person looking at an event or interaction. Rather, *observation* is consciousness itself functioning as *concepts* of measurement, which themselves are a function of language and culture at large. The *concepts* of units of mass, length, speed, time, and so on are themselves thoughts already embedded in linguistic systems of meaning and historical narratives of observations over hundreds, even thousands of years. These define and interact with whatever is being measured and observed. Consciousness itself, not a human person, is observing and then theorizing.

Theory making weaves observations into a larger intelligible framework, which is dependent on previous observations and frameworks, and so creates a new story out of older and prevailing stories. Consciousness is a story-creating function or process, and consciousness always also has the structure of narrative, which we call theory, culture, identity, or explanation, and so on. The logical form, or syntax, of consciousness is the *a priori* orientation of consciousness (the water we swim in), the given story that we all share and accept that orients all our thoughts and observations. This level of consciousness is itself dynamic, creative, and self-transforming. When observations yield results or data that do not fit the already existing story, a new story begins to construct itself to account for the new information. Not just the story, but the syntax that has contained that story is also disrupted, needing to be rebuilt to accommodate the new data. The idea or story of evolution emerged to account for observations that did not fit into the established biblical, theological story. Although by the mid-nineteenth century, the story of a God-created order had already been profoundly undermined, the story of evolution pushed it further to the margins in favor of a story of a self-creating biological process. This also contributed to a changing conception of time, which was already underway because of earlier discoveries about the vast spans of time involved in geological processes.[36] This changing story from God-centered to natural processes-centered happened at the deepest level of consciousness and the very nature of reality for us. More recently, observations at

---

34. Folger, "Does the Universe Exist," 46, emphasis added.

35. Folger, "Does the Universe Exist," 46.

36. Note the historical convergence of the concepts of evolution, geological time, and the historical conception of time, during the eighteenth and nineteenth centuries, all a result of the emergence of Enlightenment consciousness—a completely new narrative of the meaning of time.

the quantum level in physics have challenged the interpretations of classical physics and are themselves part of the emerging transformation of consciousness at its most fundamental, reality-changing level.

Before I go further with Wheeler's insights, I want to introduce a bit of etymology for the word *consciousness*, which will have a bearing on his thoughts about the role of observation and consciousness in creating the universe. The words *conscience* and *consciousness* are intimately related, and they share a common origin. The word *conscience* is composed of the two words *con* and *science*, which originally meant "to know together," a kind of shared knowing with others. The word *science* is from the Latin *scire*, "to know," which probably originally meant "to separate one thing from another, to distinguish." This meaning is related to *scindere*, "to cut, divide, rend, tear asunder, split," from the Proto-Indo-European root *skei-*, "to cut, split." This is the root for words like consciousness, science, and schism.[37] Consciousness has something to do with cutting, dividing, and splitting.

An informal etymological connection I find interesting is based on noticing that in the English language the word *scissors* shares the same three letters, *sci*, as science and consciousness. However, the word *scissors* (which is directly related to cutting) is based on a different Proto-Indo-European root, *kae-id-*, "to strike," which forms words like decision and decide, as well as suicide and homicide. The Latin word for cut is *caedere*, "to cut," "to strike down, fell, slay."[38] These etymological connections are suggestive in that they bring together the notions of cutting, dividing, and killing in the concept of *consciousness*. It appears that consciousness creates reality—that is, our reality—through a process of cutting and killing. Out of the churning possibilities of latent thoughts, implicit and not conscious, consciousness cuts out specific ones and makes them real, while simultaneously killing the possibilities not chosen. This tells us something about the phenomenon of consciousness itself, which operates independently of our personal waking consciousness.

The phenomena of quantum mechanics are very strange in contrast to our everyday understanding of the functioning of physical objects. This strangeness is illustrated, in part, by the uncertainty principle. The uncertainty principle, as we saw above, states that it is impossible, even in theory, to know both the velocity and the position of a subatomic particle. Knowing one destroys the ability to measure the other. As a result, *until they are observed*, subatomic particles and events exist in a sort of cloud of possibility that Wheeler sometimes referred to as "a smoky dragon."[39] The "smoky dragon" is also known as a "quantum potential," a condition in which subatomic particles exist in many possible states at once, traveling in every possible direction, not quite real and solid until they *interact* with something. Our observation and measurement of quantum states is the interaction that creates an actuality out

---

37. See https://www.etymonline.com/word/*skei-?ref=etymonline_crossreference.
38. See https://www.etymonline.com/word/*kae-id-?ref=etymonline_crossreference.
39. Wheeler obituary, *New York Times*, April 14, 2008.

of what was mere potentiality.[40] From within a fundamentally indeterminate state, consciousness determines what will be real:

> Wheeler conjectures we are part of a universe that is a work in progress; we are tiny patches of the universe looking at itself—and building itself. It is not only the future that is still undetermined but the past as well. And by peering back into time, even all the way back to the Big Bang, our *present observations* select one out of many possible quantum histories for the universe.[41]

In the quantum world, a quantum system exists as all of its possible outcomes simultaneously. It exists as a kind of fuzzy, or hazy, indeterminate state of possibilities, Wheeler's "smoky dragon." We might think of it as an unthought thought, a potential, gestating thought. Observation, or consciousness, cuts into the hazy possibilities and makes one clear, explicit, and real, and, in the process, slays the "smoky dragon" (all other possibilities). As observation and interpretation, consciousness, through its work of cutting and killing, effectuates the real.

Although Wheeler does not use the word consciousness directly in the following statement, he goes so far as to say that the basis of the physical world is some kind of "consciousness":

> *It from bit.* Otherwise put, every *it*—every particle, every field of force, even the space-time continuum itself—derives its function, its meaning, its very existence entirely—even if in some contexts indirectly—from the apparatus-elicited answers to yes-or-no questions, binary choices, bits. It from bit symbolizes the idea that every item of the physical world has at bottom—a very deep bottom, in most instances—an immaterial source and explanation; that which we call reality arises in the last analysis from the posing of yes-no questions and the registering of equipment-evoked responses; in short, that all things physical are information-theoretic in origin and that this is a *participatory universe.*[42]

What we think of as the *physical* universe may not be "physical" in the traditional Cartesian and Newtonian way. We certainly have to realize that what are called "particles" at the quantum level have nothing to do with our human-scale grasp of a particle. It might make more sense to think of them along the lines of an implicit concept that has not yet become explicit. In physics, particles were originally thought to be the more or less basic stable building blocks of matter. Now they are seen as only temporary instantiations of an underlying quantum field, the indeterminate "smoky dragon" becoming determinate. We ourselves are functions of consciousness, *and* we are physical beings coterminous with the universe. Both the nature of the so-called physical and

---

40. Folger, "Does the Universe Exist," 47.

41. Folger, "Does the Universe Exist," 47, emphasis added.

42. *Wikipedia*, s.v. "John Archibald Wheeler," last updated November 29, 2021, https://en.wikipedia.org/wiki/John_Archibald_Wheeler.

the nature of consciousness have to be thought again in new terms. Wheeler's idea that what "we call reality arises in the last analysis from the posing of yes-no questions," and that "all things physical are information-theoretic in origin," leads him to the thought of "a participatory universe." The yes-or-no questions or binary choices are consciousness in action, killing and cutting the real into existence, or making what is implicit in the field explicit as an existing particle/concept. These ideas challenge and subvert the entire ground of modernist, scientific, Cartesian ontology. Our traditional scientific understanding of the universe and our place in it is inadequate to the nature of *consciousness* today and its interactive nature.

Of course, physical reality is a hard, unforgiving presence, but the logic governing the consciousness with which we understand reality in general is undergoing a profound change. The traditional categories of mind and matter have been separated by a hard, ontological division within the Cartesian framework. This division, the infamous subject-object dualism, is at the heart of the modern logical form of consciousness that has been our legacy, and it continues to unwittingly influence our thinking. These categories, just like time and space, have undergone a profound transformation, and now they have been sublated into a new understanding of their basis and their relationship. What we need to understand is that the basis of consciousness itself has already changed. Consciousness is no longer divided from itself at the level of its logical form, its syntax. Through the process of becoming conscious of itself, the hard division between subject and object, mind and matter, has been dissolved within the ouroboric, self-reflexive structure of *consciousness*, which is reality itself. The very idea of our "participatory universe" is itself an ouroboric, linguistic construction of meaning that entangles us with a new way to understand so-called matter, and its relationship with mind. Physics itself is edging toward a psychological consciousness that is dissolving the hard-edged concepts associated with Newtonian and modernist thought. The formerly discrete categories of subject and object now mirror each other in a new dialectical consciousness.

The Sublation of Cartesian Categories

Soul in general is implicit thought (not yet conscious thought), which is indeterminate and inexhaustible. Soul is also absolutely negative, that is, it is the process of thought itself as an objective, or impersonal, cultural wide phenomenon. As the dynamic process of thought, soul has no mass whatsoever; it is thoughts thinking themselves, and then these thoughts generate the emergence of real cultural products. Although negative in that it is not an existing thing, soul is a real generative force; ideas, thoughts, are real generative forces. Once the real cultural products have been produced, soul is often ready to move on. The opening of the book of Genesis provides just such a suggestive image of soul speaking itself into existence:

> In the beginning when God created the heavens and the earth, the earth was a formless void and darkness covered the face of the deep, while a wind from God swept over the face of the waters. Then *God said* . . . (emphasis added)

As the narrative presents it, soul is at first formless and void, and then a thought thinks itself, speaks itself, and becomes a concrete reality. The idea of *God* personified the thought that created a scripture and a people and the social organization of that people, as well as cultural and historical ambitions, hopes, and desires. The idea of the *Christ* was the thought that created a scripture, a movement, a civilization, and the dynamic expanding energy of that civilization. Yahweh and Christ are examples of soul-thoughts, fundamental modes of consciousness, that gradually coalesced out of soul's indeterminate infinity and became determinate realities. *Consciousness*, as its etymology suggests, cuts into a wide range of possibilities and makes one specific idea real. The phenomenology of soul overlaps with that of quantum mechanics, to the extent that *particles* are explicit thoughts that have emerged out of the implicit infinity of a quantum potential or smoky dragon. Werner Heisenberg pointed in this direction when he said:

> I think that modern physics has definitely decided in favor of Plato. In fact the smallest units of matter are not physical objects in the ordinary sense; they are forms, ideas which can be expressed unambiguously only in mathematical language.[43]

The basis of reality for Plato was the idea, the ideal form, which had its own substantial reality as a universal, while everyday empirical reality, flesh and materiality, was merely a poor copy, an inferior shadow, the world of particulars. As we have seen, this was the form of consciousness of antiquity, when the ideas and the gods were the highest reality and truth, and the world of matter and human bodily existence was poor and sinful, even evil. Heisenberg is certainly not taking us back to that worldview, but he is helping us see that our thinking about the nature of *matter* has to change. What we unthinkingly consider to be solid, fixed material stuff is not a fixed thing in itself but a function of the logic or syntax of consciousness.

Matter is first of all the *idea* matter, the *concept* matter. The *concept* "matter" mediates our relationship with matter. Of course, none of us interact with *matter* because the idea "matter" is a pure abstraction—we interact with the everyday physical things all around us—but the meaning of the concept "matter" informs our implicit understanding of stuff. The *concept* (*meaning*) of matter is the basis of our relationship with the physical world. On the deep level that Heisenberg and Wheeler are thinking, *mathematical language*, in its ability to sidestep the limits of metaphor, analogy, and the language of ordinary consciousness, is capable of describing the complexities and craziness of the quantum world. Mathematics is a language in itself, operating on a

---

43. Heisenberg, *Natural Law*, 34.

higher level of abstraction that escapes the material world-boundedness of our natural commonly shared ego-consciousness. Ordinary and everyday consciousness has been shaped by our sense experience of the three-dimensional world and the ordinary passage of time over thousands of years.

"Commonsense" consciousness is just that, the common experience of our senses. The quantum world left common sense behind, and so a new language was needed to describe it, and that language is mathematics. In contrast with the Platonic worldview of antiquity, the higher abstraction required to articulate the quantum world does not do so at the expense of the value and reality of the human-scale world. Now we can think in terms of two worlds of *matter*—let's say the Newtonian-scale and the quantum-scale—which exist together as a unity and difference, both worlds (or forms) of matter preserved in a higher, more inclusive conception of reality.[44] This brings me to the sublation of the two concepts *matter* and *mind*, as both concepts are now intertwined in a way that would have been inconceivable for Cartesian consciousness:

> In the Copenhagen interpretation of quantum theory we can indeed proceed without mentioning ourselves as individuals, but we cannot disregard the fact that natural science is formed by men. Natural science does not simply describe and explain nature; it is part of the interplay between nature and ourselves; it describes nature as exposed to our nature of questioning. This was a possibility of which Descartes could not have thought, but it makes a sharp separation between the world and the I impossible.
>
> If one follows the great difficulty which even eminent scientists like Einstein had in understanding and accepting the Copenhagen interpretation . . . one can trace the roots . . . to the Cartesian partition. It will take a long time for it [this partition] to be replaced by a really different attitude toward the problem of reality.[45]

The Enlightenment assumption that natural science can describe nature in an almost supernatural objective and neutral way is no longer tenable. Science and the natural world are the product of an interaction between the natural world and ourselves, and so the idea of consciousness is working its way into science's own self-understanding. The "sharp separation between the world and the I," between subject and object, between mind and matter, simply does not exist for us today. What we *know* of nature is a function of *consciousness* and not simply a description of a supposed absolute otherness of a physical world ("nature as exposed to our nature of questioning").

We and nature are entangled in a new consciousness of that entanglement. Heisenberg is wise to note that while we may have an intellectual appreciation of this new relationship between mind and matter, it will take a long time for this new

---

44. This "two worlds of matter" parallels the phenomenologically similar two dimensions of the human person, ego and soul, known as the "psychological difference." And, here again is another example of sublated incarnation, that is, incarnation thought in completely new categories.

45. Heisenberg, *Physics and Philosophy*, 75.

consciousness to work its way into the explicit syntax of our consciousness and to be recognized as the logical form of the ground of our functioning consciousness. Of course, I would contend, from the point of view of soul, this has already happened. The shift in the basis of consciousness has already occurred, and we are simply working to catch up, to make it explicit. The fact that the syntax of our general consciousness has already changed is what makes it possible for Heisenberg (and others) to have the insight about the changed relationship between mind and matter. Thinkers make the implicit idea an explicit one, and as it becomes a topic of conversation and debate, it spreads itself throughout culture. An idea catches on because the logic of the underlying ground of consciousness has already changed, and we are already that changed consciousness without necessarily being aware of it.

The dissolution of any traditional sense of Foundation also means there is no such thing as a Cartesian *objective reality*, by which I mean an observer-independent reality. Science has been based on the *theoretical ideal* of an objective reality. (On the human scale of everyday reality, there is obviously an objective reality we have to pay attention to, or else.) The entire foundation of Science rests on the belief that a fundamental objective reality exists independently of our observations and that different observers will, ultimately, always be able to reconcile any differences. Science, by way of its methodology through repeated measurements, has the goal of establishing an objective, universally agreed-upon reality. The belief in an objective reality independent of the observer is founded in the logic of the Enlightenment. A recent quantum level experiment has demonstrated just the opposite.

Physicists working on the quantum realm have suspected for some time that at this level, the notion of an objective reality simply does not hold. A new quantum experiment, confirming a prevailing thought experiment, has demonstrated that an objective reality does not exist. At the quantum level of polarized photons, *two independent observers* can measure the *same photon* and find irreconcilable outcomes really do coexist. What the researchers found is that one observer can measure the photon's polarization and record the result, while another observer can observe the same photon in a superposition, which means that a measurement has not taken place. This experiment does not hinge on different points of view or different interpretations—it demonstrates unambiguously that two different realities coexist. The problem for physics is that a measured photon and its superposition cannot coexist, as these are contradictory states of reality itself. A measured photon is a single specific determination of the photon's multiple possible states, which exist simultaneously in a superposition. Once the photon is measured, the superposition collapses or is gone. But not in this experiment. The measured photon and all its superposition possibilities exist simultaneously to two different independent observers. "It turns out that both realities can coexist even though they produce irreconcilable outcomes."[46] This state

---

46. "A quantum experiment suggests there's no such thing as objective reality: Physicists have long suspected that quantum mechanics allows two observers to experience different, conflicting realities.

of affairs has moved the interesting and puzzling thought experiment to the status of a reality that contradicts itself, "forcing physicists to reconsider the nature of reality."

Lest there be misunderstanding here, I want to be clear that citing this experiment is not in any way meant to be a scientific "proof" for the interpretation of soul and consciousness presented here. That would be an attempt from externality, materiality, to ground an interpretation of meaning in something other than itself. That is like science trying, or claiming, to prove the existence of God: they are incommensurate categories. Historically, psychology with soul is already sublated religion and sublated science. The logic (logos) of both religion and science are incorporated in the more inclusive logic (logos) of psychology. With its traditional stance of externality, with the observer outside what it observes, science cannot enter the circle of consciousness and soul, which has now realized that all knowledge is constituted by consciousness. What this experiment does show, for my purposes, is that from within the field of physics, the assumed nature of reality created by the fundamental logic of the scientific endeavor is opened to further questions.

At the beginning of this chapter, I said that reason had undermined itself by way of the psychology of the unconscious, the question of being, and the problems of quantum mechanics. Through the results of this experiment, the categorical logic of Reason continues to undermine itself *theoretically*, raising questions at fundamental levels that crack open persisting basic assumptions, what Heisenberg above called the "Cartesian partition." For me, the experiment is interesting because it supports the idea that consciousness and matter at a fundamental level are a kind of fluid and self-contradictory simultaneity, and that they exist in some kind of poorly understood dialectical relationship. So, what does it mean that the classic Cartesian ontological split between consciousness and matter has truly dissolved? We have always known that culture, history, and human life are temporal, passing, and ephemeral, and we have found some solace in various ideas that some kind of eternal Foundation exists beyond us. Now this notion of Foundation in all its varied religious, philosophical, and scientific forms has truly dissolved, and we find ourselves alone with ourselves, living *as* our world of fluid meaning. There is no Foundation beyond our world of meaning (i.e., soul), and now we see that our world, which is our foundation, is fluidity itself.

The traditional Cartesian categories of mind and matter existed ontologically as completely separate realities. Mind and matter were incompatible modes of Being, and as this division was the very logic of modern consciousness, mind and matter were locked away in what were mutually both alienated and liberated states of being. Mind was cut free in a new way to explore, and matter (de-animated and empty of spirit) was free in a new way to be probed and utilized. The freedom of exploration has led to the now-emerging crazy logic of consciousness, the new logic in which

---

Now they've performed the first experiment that proves it," *MIT Technology Review*, March 12, 2019, https://www.technologyreview.com/s/613092/a-quantum-experiment-suggests-theres-no-such-thing-as-objective-reality/. Thanks to Harry Henderson for bringing this article to my attention.

the undialectical categories of the subjective inner (mind) and the objective outer (matter) are incorporated, sublated, into the logic or syntax of a dialectical subject-object. Dialectical means subject and object are now thought as a differentiated unity instead of a divided duality. As a differentiated unity, mind and matter do not exist independent of each other; they constitute each other's existence. *Mind* and *matter* are concepts, functions of consciousness, and they have been sublated within a larger frame of reference, a new syntax that now defines them as one ($E = mc^2$). This is the result of consciousness having become conscious of itself as consciousness. The self-aware circular nature of consciousness reconciles the traditional opposition of the universal and the particular that has characterized both antiquity and modernity, creating a new indivisible unity. The logic of the incarnation, the God-Man differentiated unity, has been sublated again in the new logic of consciousness that brings mind and matter together in a differentiated dialectical unity. This does not mean that this new view of consciousness is Christian—The Christian form has been left behind, but the phenomenology of soul shows a historical continuity. The logical form of Christianity destroyed itself and at the same time gave birth to a new syntax, Cartesian ontology, which in turn is destroying itself and giving birth to another syntax. The thread is consciousness itself.

The Cartesian *concept* of *matter* is dissolved by the psychological concept of *consciousness*. Just as the Cartesian consciousness sublated the substance and substantiality of the universals into the substance and substantiality of the subject and the particulars, the substantiality of the particulars is now undergoing sublation as consciousness. By probing into the infinite depths of so-called *matter* and finding quantum potentials, quantum uncertainties, and smoky dragons, consciousness finds itself and gazes into its own gazing. What is emerging is a new logic of the unity and difference of the universals and the particulars, which constitutes a higher status of consciousness. There is a historical progression—in antiquity, the universals were more real and true than the particulars; in modernity, the particulars were more real and true than the universals; now a new logic of consciousness is emerging in which the universals and the particulars are united in a necessary and equal dialectic. A new basic truth is creating itself.

Mind and matter do not have an independent existence apart from each other; neither exists without the other. Like $E = mc^2$, mind and matter reflect different aspects of a unified reality. Let us recall that Yahweh and the Jewish people existed as reflections of each other, and that neither could exist without the other. Just so, this new unification of mind and matter is the logic of the incarnation coming home to itself. The incarnation, personified as Jesus Christ, sought to unify and yet differentiate the category of God with that of man: It insisted on their equality and their difference. Today both God and Christ have dissolved as metaphysical entities, as existing forms of consciousness, but the logic of the unity and difference of the universal and the particular has been preserved in a new status of consciousness that is reshaping our late modern world.

Obviously, what we might call Newtonian matter still exists as solidly as ever, and the mathematical description of matter works with marvelous accuracy. It is the logic of the *concept* of matter that is undergoing a change; the notion of matter as a fundamental category of reality is changing. Just as the Newtonian concepts of space and time once existed as discrete, objective, categories, and are now wrapped together as an Einsteinian dynamic spacetime continuum, so the Cartesian ontological categories or concepts of matter and mind no longer exist, as they have become a sublated moment in the new status of consciousness. This means that Newtonian matter, the everyday human scale of the physical world, works very well for us on the semantic level, as a content of our consciousness (our chairs will not dissolve from under us), but the Cartesian and Newtonian *view* of matter is no longer the logic of our consciousness. Just as we have learned to think in terms of a spacetime continuum, we can also learn to think in terms of a *mindmatter* continuum. Perhaps the idea of matter will dissolve even further, in favor of something like *the information*,[47] integrated into the notion of consciousness itself as a new category, which is soul.

The contemporary status of consciousness as conscious of itself is our foundation today. Consciousness has sublated the logic of the Cartesian concepts of mind and matter into its own self-understanding. Not only does consciousness today see itself in the historical foundational texts of civilization, it also sees itself involved in the physical world of matter. The dimension of consciousness we understand as soul, the water we swim in, has created itself through its own historical foundational categories, such as God and Reason. The ideas of mind and matter are now also brought into the fold of consciousness as ways in which soul creates itself. The Foundation, which has always been invisible because it is the water we swim in, has become conscious of itself enough so that we get a glimpse of its operations.

The question of whether or not there is a relationship between consciousness and the physical universe is the wrong question, just as the question about the existence of God is the wrong question. These questions assume the old logical form of consciousness, one that has outgrown itself. The foundational categories have changed in such a way that neither God nor mind nor matter exist in the way that former logical forms of consciousness conceived them. What appears to be true today is that what we call the universe has thought itself into existence, and *consciousness* is that foundational thought.

In the light of these late modern ideas—the unconscious, the uncertainty principle, and the historicity of Being—what was once thought to be solid and stable has dissolved into air.[48] These are not merely new contents of consciousness, new intel-

---

47. "In the long run, history is the story of information becoming aware of itself." Gleick, *Information*, 12.

48. In a different context, Karl Marx had a similar insight one hundred seventy years ago: "All that

lectual ideas. These new thoughts express the new syntax, the logic, of that general consciousness that is the ground of our being, and this has dissolved and evaporated, has become "air." The categorical and fundamental *idea* of a Foundation, or an Absolute, has been sublated as a new category, which is *consciousness*, and this is what defines our existence today. We are constituted by a logical form of consciousness that now sees itself free of any god, foundation, or personification. This consciousness has become aware of itself as consciousness and understands itself as an ongoing process of soul-making, soul negating itself, and creating itself out of that negation. Of course, this view of soul is itself historical and transient, and it will itself dissolve into a new idea when the current concept of soul has fulfilled its purpose. For the time being, it appears that soul's thought of itself today is *consciousness*. This single thought manifests in contemporary culture in many different ways that are both inspiring and also deeply unsettling. Already the electronic communication revolution, especially the Internet and the World Wide Web, has abolished all national boundaries. The international refugee crisis and the rise of authoritarian right-wing political movements in reactive response reflect the general undermining of the sense of foundation and identity and the fearful reaction to this new fluidity. The attempt by nation-states to harden their borders and identities is already too late. Although we have not created our cultural situation, we are responsible for how we choose to respond to it:

> The conception of man as an event or happening caught up in the flow of a shared historical project lights up the transitoriness of human endeavors while emphasizing our deep responsibility to the unfolding historical current in which we are implicated.[49]

What is our "deep responsibility to the unfolding historical current in which we are implicated"? One step on the personal level is to open ourselves to the truth of our historical situation. Truth in its original foundational sense has become impossible. What is the nature of truth today? We are at least responsible to become conscious of the historical situation confronting us, to pay attention to what is happening at large, of what soul is doing today as culture. It is not that there is no truth, but that truth is not what we thought it was or would be. Each age is the manifestation of its own historical soul-truth. As soul changes through its historical development, so truth changes. If the notion of an external and absolute truth has indeed dissolved, what then becomes my responsibility to truth? "Authentic truth here seems to be a matter not of what one knows, but instead of how one lives."[50] This raises some questions worth contemplating: If the truth of our time already exists as the general imperative of contemporary culture at large, what specific claim, if any, does it make on me? Am

---

is solid melts into air, all that is holy is profaned, and man is at last compelled to face with sober senses, his real conditions of life, and his relations with his kind." Marx, *Communist Manifesto*, 44.

49. Guignon, *Heidegger*, 246.
50. Guignon, *Heidegger*, 248.

I aware of a purpose that gnaws at me that wants my attention? What is the question that addresses my life, to which I can only give *my* answer?

The Psychological Difference

The new unity and difference of the universal and particular, the equality and unity of mind and matter, and the ouroboric self-aware nature of consciousness represent the new logical form of consciousness at large. This shape of consciousness, our public mind, our new syntax, is today the home of humankind, but we do not yet know that this is our new truth. This emergent logic of consciousness both negates and preserves the former logic of the incarnation. In the incarnation, God (the universal) and man (the particular) were united and different, but the truth of that logic remained in the shape of a God, a metaphysical truth. Today, after passing through the refiner's fire of the Enlightenment, the unity and difference of the universal and particular have a shape which is neither God nor human person, but *consciousness* itself. This is not a Christian development because Christianity, as a former syntax of consciousness, is obsolete—it is no more, and its categories have been sublated. We are not now little "christs" as it were, we are simply human beings, and it is consciousness itself that has undergone a transformation. What we see is the phenomenological development of soul itself. However, it is also true that we are, in ourselves, implicitly constituted by this new shape of consciousness, yet we are generally unaware of it. The *difference* that was formerly experienced by us as an external soul is now a complex quality of consciousness available to us. The syntax of consciousness that we are today is the cumulative result of all the previous stages, but sublated. We now are the *adults* in our known cosmos. And, I would add, we have a duty to be professional adults, a sobering responsibility.

What I refer to as the *difference* has changed over time. In the ancient past soul presented itself as an Absolute, personified as gods, goddesses, or God, and as that Absolute, soul was experienced as absolutely different and externally other from us. In the more recent past, and still very much alive in our modern form of consciousness, Reason presented itself as an Absolute. Functioning as Reason, soul put nature and the material world into a category that was externally and absolutely different and other from us. Soul in our time is changing yet again. Soul is conscious of itself now as an ongoing process constructing meanings that are embodied as language, and with this self-consciousness, soul's difference is now immanent, internal, self-reflexive. Soul's self-awareness is also our self-awareness, and we have the ability to reflect on ourselves in a new way. As human beings, we experience this difference as the immanent dialectical difference of ego and soul, which itself is not an existing thing, but two different styles of consciousness. We exist automatically as ego consciousness, as personal I-ness that is oriented to practical life tasks and social adaptation, but to achieve the orientation of soul-consciousness takes work. Paradoxically, while soul-work is not an ego work, the ego can choose to orient itself toward soul-work, and in the process, ego is sublated, recedes. The goal is not to achieve a soul-consciousness permanently, like some kind of mystical enlightenment. No, soul is made from scratch each time. It is not unlike playing a musical instrument. One never achieves playing well permanently. Practice, practice, practice, is how playing well is accomplished, and still it fluctuates.

Historically we have never been a difference in relation to ourselves. Human persons were primarily defined and identified in terms of inflexible social roles, and despite clear social differences (semantic), the primary difference was in relation to the gods, and to God (syntax). That difference, on the level of soul, was externalized. During the Enlightenment, the difference was in terms of our relation to nature as the object of science and Reason, the subject-object difference. The identity of the person was singular, or one-dimensional, we were the conscious, rational mind, as there was no notion of any unconscious dimension. For late modernity, the difference appeared in a new form as the personal and subjective idea of "the unconscious," but this was still thought as a kind of personal internal location in humanistic terms. Freud thought it housed the raw instincts that threatened the ego's adaptation and had to be sublimated. Jung developed a nostalgic and romantic "Shangri La" where all the archetypes gathered, in an attempt to rehabilitate a kind of Mount Olympus for a supposed modern understanding of the "gods/goddesses." Ultimately, in Jung's framing, the idea of the unconscious was a neo-religious mystification, actually a regression. However, both Freud and Jung were critically important thinkers for soul's movement away from the Enlightenment form of consciousness, and yet the idea of "the unconscious" as some kind of place or container is not adequate for a truly modern soul. *Consciousness* is, finally, not a thing, nor is it any place. The idea of "the unconscious" is too personal, too humanistic, when there is no such place or thing. There is unconsciousness, yes, but no "the unconscious."

From the point of view of psychology, which is focused on the syntax of consciousness, the idea of the unconscious and the historical difference with the gods is dissolved and reframed as the psychological difference. The idea of difference has interiorized itself in relation to the human subject, and the human subject is constituted by the *psychological difference*. We are an immanent dialectical difference, both ego and soul, both *who* and *what* we are. That is, we are constituted by both a personal identity and an impersonal identity, a personal sense and a soul sense, and both are good and necessary. To recall a sentence from the epigraph at the head of this chapter, "The soul, having lost its transcendent and substance quality, is now a mode or style in man." The difference between us and soul that has historically been external is now internal to consciousness itself, which we experience as if it were our consciousness. However, Giegerich's notion of a "soulful mode of experiencing and reacting" is a potential, not a given. Even though we are constituted by soul, which is the syntax of the newly emerging cultural consciousness, to know the "soulful mode" consciously requires a certain discipline—psychology (with soul) is a discipline of interiority—which is the skill of allowing soul to speak for itself in contrast to our personal (ego) thoughts and opinions. Psychology is the discipline of allowing the ego to recede temporarily in favor of another mode of knowing.

Soul has taken the unusual step of recognizing itself as *consciousness*, or better, as the structure or form of consciousness, as the sea of shared *meanings* in which we swim. Soul now sees—or consciousness now sees—that it is constituted by cultural production, linguistic production, interpretive acts, meaning structured as narrative. Consciousness now recognizes the way in which it has been and is the invisible syntax that is the ground of meaning. Soul is a process of live happenings now. It is the roiling edge of now: alive, dynamic, experimental, restless, adventurous, and a true wilderness in the sense that humankind cannot fence it in, no matter how many legislative safeguards we try to put in place. Soul is by definition infinite and free, *not* subject to our values, neither theological nor humanistic. Soul is not Christian, it is not of any specific religious persuasion, not humanistic. Soul is like evolution or the laws of nature. We can observe these phenomena, understand these phenomena, but we do not control them; they are autonomous in their own right. It is easier for us to appreciate the impersonal quality of nature and natural forces, and much harder to grasp that "our" cultural productions are also impersonal. Soul is of a different order, and while we now have enough historical distance to observe the historical soul, we cannot control where it is going. Soul and its future are inherently unpredictable.

The *psychological difference* is the structure of consciousness that we now are, as well as the conceptual tool with which we can think in a new way about our relationship with ourselves and our world. We have the capacity to reflect on thoughts, feelings, emotions, sensations, dreams, reactions, compulsions, cravings, fantasies, loves, and hates, to not take everything we experience at face value. The psychological difference enables us to see that what we experience as our thoughts, feelings, emotions, and so on, are not ours alone but contain a soul-meaning, both ours and not ours, wanting to become explicit. In other words, while our immediate experience is intensely personal, something else is at work that is not personal. The *difference* is a potential in how we can experience ourselves in relation to ourselves. An internal distance is now available that gives us a little more time and space within ourselves in relation to the world that makes us who we are, both the historical and cultural world of our being and the experience of our personal mind and all it brings. Although the idea that consciousness-at-large is aware of itself as consciousness is a new status of consciousness and the syntax of contemporary culture, for us to cultivate a soul-sensitive consciousness as individuals is still a work and a discipline. As a new structure of our own being and sense of self, soul-consciousness is available to us as never before. Along with the freedom and depth that it offers, it also brings complexity and inner conflict. Consciousness is a burden and a responsibility. Honest consciousness, consciousness of truth, includes depression and anxiety as also soul truths.

Consciousness, especially as self-awareness, was in earlier times deified, seen as a quality imparted by God or as the direct speech of the god itself. In fact, until the late nineteenth century, the human mind was still seen as a faculty created and organized by God and ultimately unknowable by us. The *mind* was a mystery beyond our ken. Today we know that self-awareness is a human function and capacity, which is another indication that the consciousness that once was external to us as a God has transformed itself, sublated itself, and become a human function and capacity.

Now the *difference* is a psychological difference, the difference that defines and constitutes our existence, our own immanent dialectical difference. We ourselves can change our focus as ego and choose to focus on a deeper truth, the thought that thinks itself at the heart of phenomena. This is a process of learning to trust the soul's logos, or the soul's logical life, to trust the autonomous thinking process that is different from our personal thoughts, especially the thoughts of our preferred human values and needs. One way this is experienced is when the ego slips out of sight as we become immersed in a project, a process, a work, or play, when we forget about time, eating, and our surroundings. This is when the ego is sublated within the creative process of soul thinking its own thoughts. The ego slips into the background as soul work becomes the foreground, and we are both aware and not aware that this is happening. This is one way on the personal level when soul as happening happens to us.

"Subjectively This May Be Experienced as Alienation"

On the level of personal human experience, the fact that soul is no longer "out there" is most often experienced as loneliness, anxiety, depression, loss, and alienation. It is why our modern age has been called the Age of Anxiety, why anxiety and depression are widespread mental health phenomena, and why suicide is at an all-time high, especially among the young. Without fully realizing it, we exist not just *over* an abyss, but *within* an abyss of cold, infinite meaninglessness. The planet Earth, in the context of the Milky Way galaxy—or the Milky Way galaxy in the context of the two trillion galaxies in the observable universe[51]—is less than a minuscule dot, less than a grain of sand, less than an ant we step on without knowing. We are a blip in the cosmological scale of the universe. When we step back and survey the vast scale of what we believe we know of our universe (and include what we know we do not know), we are as nothing. This universe of science, of the big bang, has no meaning, no purpose, and we certainly have little effect on it at that scale, even if meaning no longer resides "out there" and now does reside with us. Our connection with personal meaning should not be confused with what soul is doing, however. We are no longer contained within a cocoon of Meaning (as myth, religion, metaphysics) as we once were. We have been born out of the former womb of Meaning (capital *M* meaning as an implicit containing

---

51. *Wikipedia*, s.v. "Observable universe," last modified May 5, 2022, https://en.wikipedia.org/wiki/Observable_universe.

cosmic narrative) and now exist on our own, creators of personal meaning, if there is to be any meaning at all.[52]

This change in our metaphysical circumstances is experienced as a profound loss, but one that remains inchoate and little understood. We look around for human explanations for the widespread insecurity, but the deeper reason is the metaphysical death of God. The freedom of the Enlightenment was tethered to a sense of human community, communal responsibility for ourselves. The freedom let loose today is wild and untethered to any value except freedom itself. However, this freedom is undermined by depression, anxiety, and despair, which freedom attempts to repair with more freedom (technological cures). On the other hand, the psychological perspective lets us see the historical movement of consciousness, and thus the historical meaning of our culture of meaninglessness. It will take a dialectical consciousness to hold both the untethered wild freedom and despairing depression in a unity that includes both and does not act out either. As adults (psychological adults), we can know our condition consciously and choose how to respond. We can hold the prevailing conditions of soul consciously and not take them personally. To suffer them, yes, but not succumb. Traditionally, in the face of suffering, humankind has called on God as its rock of strength, security, deliverance, and refuge: "The Lord is my rock" (Ps 18:2).[53] Today, due to the sublation of soul's syntax (the death of God), we are that rock; it is the syntax of our consciousness made conscious, and we are responsible to be a rock unto ourselves. The *rock* is no longer "out there" somewhere. Our modern consciousness, modern soul, is already the cumulative result of the sublation of the former stages. The sublation of the historical Foundations means that the living concept (reality) of Foundation has been negated *and* preserved. If there is a *rock* for us today, it is *consciousness* itself. Even though we, as mere human beings, may have zero sense of any *rockness* in ourselves in relation to our very real and terrible suffering, simply knowing that the sublated *rock* is a constituent of consciousness can give some support to our being in the world.

The situation we find ourselves in as a human species is not unlike the emergence of the *I* in the development of late childhood. As children, we are at first identified with the family, the *We* of family, mother and father, siblings, relatives. Our *soul*, so to speak, is contained externally in the *We* of the family, the generality, the larger field of being that is the family, tribe, or group. Sometime during late childhood, on the cusp of adolescence, one's own internal sense of *I* begins to coalesce and make itself felt. We find ourselves unexpectedly feeling separate from the family, from the *We*, and find ourselves alone, disoriented, and anxious with the newfound and strange sense of independent *I*. Our sense of identity begins within the containing web of the family and, in our individualistically oriented Western culture, develops into a personal sense of separate individuality. The new experience of separateness can be painful and

---

52. Giegerich, "End of Meaning," 199–203; 230–38.
53. The image of rock referring to God is used about twenty-four times in the Psalms.

disturbing—it takes some getting used to; we must grow into it. At the same time, we feel a new quality of freedom, independence, and agency. At this stage of childhood, some pre-adolescent "adolescent" acting out may appear, behavior that causes trouble and disruption. Shifting to the species level, perhaps today we are barely at the logical level of adolescence, floundering as we are, caught between old modes of consciousness and new forms of consciousness, which are in many ways incompatible. The cusp we are on is dangerous for the human species. We do not know what it is for soul.

I want to emphasize again why the designation *soul* is so important in understanding the tremendous historical changes visible through this overview of the history of consciousness. The changes are not simply intellectual ideas that are in conflict with other intellectual ideas, not simply an academic debate occurring high above ordinary life in a history of ideas stratosphere. Soul has to do with our most intimate and taken-for-granted sense of shared and collective identity as humankind. Soul is the logical form of consciousness, the syntax of consciousness, the water that we swim in—it is the fundamental and invisible (unconscious) orienting consciousness that is at stake in this whole discussion. Soul in general (as an implicit meaning of being) is given to us unthinkingly by culture as what is most real and important. When soul shifts, our deepest and most unconscious values are under attack, threatened, as when a tectonic plate moves, jolting us out of our slumber.

As our assumed orienting consciousness changes, disturbing changes in our normative deep values follow. Sexual orientation, gender identity, and reproduction are tied into what for many are absolute, even divinely ordained aspects of identity and human nature. Today marriage between same-sex couples is growing in acceptance, and a host of gender identities have stepped into the place where traditional cultural definitions allowed only the binary male or female. Reproduction is now possible in the laboratory completely independent of biological sexual relations between a man and a woman. As these changes appear in the social realm, symptomatic of the changing syntax of consciousness (soul), there is tremendous resistance because they threaten theological moral absolutes with which many are ideologically identified. Another example is the area of artificial intelligence (AI), which is gradually infiltrating all aspects of contemporary society; perhaps the most visible example is the promise of self-driving vehicles. Artificial intelligence software is taking over significant areas of human decision-making, and many areas of work are changing because of the growing use of robotics. Human decision-making is getting displaced behind the scenes, infiltrating society in unseen ways. This contributes to a generalized societal anxiety that lacks a clear target, which leads to the targeting of human scapegoats that have nothing to do with the deeper changes soul is undergoing.

Soul is negating itself and moving in a new direction, and this current shift is more threatening to our sense of self as human beings than all the others. The movement of soul during the Enlightenment and modernity seemed to raise humankind to a new status of importance. The current movement of soul seems to be reversing that status, and humankind could be on the verge of becoming somewhat irrelevant historically. From the beginning, soul seems to be about *exodus*, extracting and liberating itself from one form after another. What happens if—or is it even possible that—soul could liberate itself from humankind? The word *consciousness* itself may not capture what is at work in the background of our lives. Just as our bodies are dependent on air, water, and food to survive, so is the human mind dependent on meanings (which is what consciousness is) to be what it is. Soul has been the *meaning* on which we depend to be human. Today global warming dangerously imperils the supply of air, water, and food. Are the *meanings* we depend on to be human also imperiled in ways that are still only dimly intuited? In fact, the humanistic meaning of the concept *human* (of what it has meant to be human) is already obsolete. The global scale of corporations, financial markets, technology, automation, bureaucracy has become so autonomous and impersonal that the human individual is now nothing more than a monetized product (an *it* more than a *who*). All the internet-based services that are "free" simply mean that we the users are the product producing value for the algorithms invisibly operating in the background. This is still another example of the profound shift in syntax that has already happened and remains mostly unseen, only beginning to be recognized by academic researchers.[54]

Our Virtual World of *Meaning*, Squared

Several millennia ago, language emerged, first spoken and then written, a new virtual world within which *Homo sapiens* came to be what we consider as *human*. The human world is the world of language, and language is the "house of Being," to which I will add, language is where and how soul dwells. *Language* is not a collection of alphabets, words, and dictionaries, but the world of shared meanings that language expresses. The black marks on the white page which we call letters and words actually fade away behind the meanings they convey. The letters and words are the apparatus we use to speak and listen, read and write, but the physicality of the words and letters fade into the background, sublated by the meaning they express, and the meaning dominates the foreground. Language is the medium in which meaning (soul) operates (and, of course, *language* is not only words written and spoken, but any system that conveys meaning: dance, visual arts, music, mathematics, software code). Our immediate and primary dwelling as human beings is the virtual world of meanings, and we come to the physical world secondarily and indirectly. We do not inhabit the physical world immediately the way plants and animals do. We are languaged and linguistic beings, and our access to any world whatsoever is through the meaning that language bears; we exist as beings of *meaning* first. When I touch a tree, I do not touch some mere object but the *meaning* the word *tree* evokes. My contact is with the *meaning* of *tree*

---

54. See Zuboff, *Age of Surveillance Capitalism*, and Wark, *Capital Is Dead*.

and all the narratives that give this tree, or trees in general, their cultural meaning. Of course, a real physical tree is present, but my contact with it is as something linguistically and culturally meaningful. No tree is there, for us, apart from its meaning.

It should not be too strange to say, in the light of our world of meaning becoming conscious of itself, that language as the medium of meanings ate the world some time ago. As the medium of meaning, language ate the world and digested us along with it, and now we live within this meaning-world as creatures of meaning (soul). Consciousness, as meaning, is the invisible world we live within, and we are not aware that our reality is already and always mediated and reflected as language/meaning, which is completely invisible to us. We have already long lived, and continue to live, within a virtual world of mind and meanings, which has only recently begun to be a little bit visible to us. The general larger shared world of languaged meanings is that invisible context we all inhabit. Consciousness is not merely personal awareness, nor is it some kind of mystical or mysterious pure empty knowing. Consciousness has no existence without the logos of language and meaning that is the web or matrix we share as human beings; we are already embedded in it and take it for granted. Although, it is more accurate to recognize that rather than being "something" we are embedded *in*, it is what we *are*. Notice how easily my language slips into spatial images (embedded *in*; we inhabit; web, matrix), when the logos of consciousness is simply a way of being, it *is* our being; we *are* consciousness. It is a struggle to articulate the new meaning of soul, because the old or established conventional meaning continues to overlap with the new meaning. Especially for those of us who straddle generational change, the echoes of conventional meanings continue to reverberate within us even as we are called to new meanings. But something untoward is happening to language and meaning itself.

Today, we are confronted with an emerging language that most of us know little about. Software is the language of the digital world, another virtual world, and on the surface, it is a set of commands authored by human persons. Although we write the commands, as these commands become more complex, a certain unpredictable autonomy can become a function of the software itself. Of course, we do not want this unpredictable autonomy to creep into the spreadsheets and databases that run our financial institutions, or the software that flies our airplanes, but in the world of writing, both news stories and fiction, software is becoming intelligibly creative. In fact, one such program became so good that the creators were shocked and fearful enough over the possibilities of its misuse that they withheld it from the public domain.[55] And, as we look around at the world at large, is there any nook or cranny where we will not find software or the influence of software? It would appear that, indeed, "software is eating the world."[56]

---

55. Alex Hern, "New AI Fake Text Generator May Be Too Dangerous to Release, Say Creators," *Guardian*, February 14, 2019, https://www.theguardian.com/technology/2019/feb/14/elon-musk-backed-ai-writes-convincing-news-fiction.

56. Andreessen, "Why Software Is Eating the World."

The phrase "software is eating the world" first appeared in relation to emerging economic possibilities related to software's ability to organize data in ways not possible without the software code. One well-known example is the case of Airbnb, which helps individuals all over the world rent their private homes to others; this is possible only because of the worldwide software network that now exists. However, beyond the profit motive, what could "software is eating the world" mean as a motto for what soul is doing now? Like a dream or myth, we can treat the phrase "software is eating the world" as soul's speech about itself. What is its interiority or truth about the movement of the syntax of consciousness? Not only is software eating the world, but it is doing so in a voracious manner. There is probably no significant area of life that has not already been infiltrated by software and is now dependent on the constant silent humming of the code. More and more human decision-making is getting turned over to software in the form of AI. Is the form of intelligence embedded in software any more *artificial* than the *intelligence* soul's evolution has created, which we consider to be "our" intelligence? Isn't software simply another form of intelligence into which worldwide culture is pouring enormous resources, such that the pervasive influence of software is creating itself, and we are simply the tools it is using in order to do so? The image of "eating the world" is telling because it points to a process of incorporation, digestion, and transformation that is independent of our will. Software is simply the visible manifestation of a new meaning, a form of soul that is creating itself. Software could be an exploratory movement in which soul is experimenting with another exodus. Soul is itself a virtual world unto itself, and although we certainly participate in its creation, its feverish creative exploration seems to be out of our hands.

The ancient gods were an autonomous intelligence to which humankind was subservient, but which we have come to recognize was the external extension of our own intelligence. We have seen that the point of the "gods," from the perspective of soul, the syntax of consciousness, was not the content of that hierarchical relationship, but the form of consciousness that it represented. From the point of view of a psychology with soul, we need to detach ourselves from the idea that *intelligence* is *our* intelligence, recognizing that intelligence is a function of soul, of consciousness, of the dynamic culture-wide play of meanings. What we ordinarily think of as human intelligence is a kind of autonomous function that has gone beyond animal intelligence to create linguistic culture. History built itself on top of biology. The written word pushed off from the oral word. Yahweh and Christ, gods of the written word, dominated and overcame the polytheistic nature gods/goddesses of preliterate culture. We have seen in the examination of Yahweh what a violent effort it was to secure literacy (symbolic of a new form of consciousness). Today another violent upheaval seems to be overturning everything we have held sacred and valuable. Soul as public mind is creating another kind of intelligence that is again pushing off toward another level, toward something else. The syntax of consciousness has transformed itself over the course of three thousand years. What is consciousness, the general basis of consciousness itself, in this new digital form (not the contents of the digital world), doing to itself now?

To view the idea "software is eating the world" as a soul phenomenon is to realize it is not about content, not about how it is impacting us, not about our smartphones mesmerizing and distracting us, not about internet addiction. It is about how the "medium is the massage" (Marshall McLuhan),[57] how all of this is another soul-internal transformation of the syntax of consciousness, the shape of consciousness changing itself, all while we remain none the wiser. While we identify the *virtual* world with technology, the virtual world that defines our existence (language and meaning) may be simply squaring itself, pushing off into another exodus.

Is the extraterrestrial intelligence we are so interested in finding "out there" actually creating itself right here? Just as so-called human intelligence, in its species-wide form as soul, is fundamentally alien to the animal form of intelligence, or even the preliterate status of humankind, perhaps what is creating itself now is a new form of soul that will be equally alien to what we consider *human intelligence*. On the general soul level, we are not as important as we think we are, and yet, in relation to each other on the personal human level, all we have is each other.

Psychology as the Discipline of Interiority

Conventional psychology, within the context of humanism and science, approaches its object (the mind, the person, the subjective world, the soul) from an external point of view. The scientific mind observes and investigates its object from outside. This is normally what we assume without giving it much thought, when we think of psychology. During the nineteenth century, the idea of the soul fell out of use, and the idea of the *mind* took over, and this is when psychology became a clinical science (and interestingly enough, during the twentieth century, psychology became one of the largest scientific professions).[58] This was a natural extension of the Enlightenment and Cartesian consciousness bringing its focus to the mind itself. Another inversion has taken place during the twentieth century, and now psychology, or at least "psychology with soul," knows it is its own object and subject. Psychology is studying itself as psychology, or psyche's logos; consciousness is conscious of its status as consciousness. The *object* of psychology is its own idea of itself:

> Now that the very notion of its object, "the soul," has dissolved from "existing entity" to method or style, psychology has to be defined differently: as the *discipline of interiority*.[59]

---

57. The popular aphorism still attributed to McLuhan is "the medium is the message," but the original title of the book published in 1967 is *The Medium Is the Massage: An Inventory of Effects*.
58. Reed, *From Soul to Mind*, ix–xvi.
59. Giegerich, *Neurosis*, 13.

Soul's Thought of Itself Today Is Consciousness

The concept of *interiority* as a psychological discipline means that soul, now as method or style, is an orientation we can adopt, in fact, it is an orientation we must learn to adopt if we are to live up to where soul is today. We have noticed how abstract everything is today. The mind is not the biological wiring of the brain, but the world of meanings. Matter itself is constituted by quantum processes, a completely abstract realm (mathematics). And, clearly the process of thinking the meaning of Being is abstract thought, thought thinking about itself. And, of course, reflecting this surface-and-depth dialectic, software code is always operating unseen in the background of all our interactions with technology. And yet, by "abstract" I do not mean "in the clouds," but rather, that we can no longer take the surface appearance of things for granted, at face value—we have to look deeper into what appears for its soul-meaning. Soul, as consciousness, is the process of thinking in one form or another—on the personal level, emotions, intuitions, sensations, physical symptoms, addictions, etc., are all fundamentally thoughts, even if buried thoughts. Interiority is the method of turning our attention toward the living concept or thought that is buried in phenomenon, the meaning that animates it. The interiority of a phenomenon is its truth, and its truth is the logic of consciousness the phenomenon manifests. This book is an attempt to read the *interiority* of the Judeo-Christian Western tradition, and the twin notions of "God's autopsy" and "the living truth of soul" point to a specific psychological interpretation of interiority as the history of consciousness.

Just as Yahweh and Christ have faded as the locus of truth, so now humanism and science are fading as the locus of truth. Humanism's innate belief in its own superiority and freedom is in decline. Humanism is also a phase in soul's movement just as myth and religion were. Mind, or soul, has not reached its pinnacle by any means, and the nature of soul as basically infinite, or inexhaustible, precludes that any pinnacle exists to be reached. The basis of mind, or soul, is experimental and restless. It is not satisfied with any of its achievements, and it is not content to remain identified with any of its forms. Soul did not remain identified with the many gods and goddesses, and it did not remain identified with Yahweh and Christ. Soul now appears to be slipping away from its identification with human beings. Perhaps soul is in the process of leaving us behind, which from our personal point of view, is indeed terrifying. The objects of our collective anxiety, the global climate crisis, robotics and automation, artificial intelligence, the overwhelming presence of technology, the impersonal scale of society, are perhaps symptoms of a deeper change we are only dimly aware of. Another cataclysmic transformation of soul is underway, and whether we like it or not, it will initiate us into its new form.

In this regard, one response is to open ourselves to what soul is doing and allow it to teach us what it is. Like a dream, something is going on that is not of our making, and yet, it has some meaning that is not at first obvious. A new syntax is at work that is hard to discern. Simply asking the question of the meaning of this historical moment from the perspective of psychological interiority would open us to a knowing that is first of all broader and deeper than our personal ego fears and preferences. Facing the awareness of just how inhuman consciousness is, seeing soul's historical trajectory, brings everything into a new light never possible before.

One of our new tasks is to face the truth (interiority) embedded in the meaninglessness of existence. As we have seen, the fact that capital-*M* Meaning is not handed to us anymore is soul's own doing. And, eventually, all life on this planet will disappear, either in the short term when global warming could very well overtake us, or in the far long term (billions of years) when the sun expands and swallows the inner solar system. Human life, humankind, has no guarantee of its significance or meaning. Above all else, we ourselves are wholly responsible for how we will live. What do we do when we learn we have a terminal illness, that our life is truly finite? Death is always an unreal abstraction until it confronts us up close, gets in our face. Then we are shaken and we make choices that reveal our values. This is our case now in the context of the death of God, the end of Meaning, and the fact that consciousness is now aware of itself as consciousness. The death of Meaning apparently is the birth of a new meaning, but this new meaning is not going to save us from the gaze of meaninglessness.

The form of consciousness as such is moving on, self-generating, and it may have pulled the rug out from under us already. From the point of view of soul, the hard truth is we are insignificant. However, our personal point of view contradicts our insignificance; from my (our) point of view, I am (we are) of ultimate significance. We are significant (as ego, as personal I) to ourselves; we are our own significance. While the universe, the sun, the planet, the environment, and soul do not deem us significant, the new truth of the end of Meaning is an initiation into psychological adulthood, to be responsible for our own meaning. Our challenge today is to be conscious of our dialectical condition, to be aware that we are both meaningless and meaningful, both insignificant and significant. We must learn to live as constituted by the unity and difference of ego and soul (not either/or, but both and more and moving).

The Challenge and Promise of Dialectical Consciousness

We exist as the deep process of the syntax of consciousness, and there is no escape. One may be able to leave society empirically, go off-grid and live in the woods, but one's consciousness will forever be informed by the prevailing logic. One can even choose to live like a seventeenth-century farmer, but one's mind will forever be twenty-first century. So, while we did not in the first place choose to be born and live here and now, we do have a choice *about how* we will live here and now. We have some choice about living either mindlessly or consciously in the midst of our circumstances.

My book has been introducing dialectical consciousness throughout by way of a theoretical interpretation of Western history. Here at its end, I want to suggest a way this new consciousness can inform our daily personal living. I will briefly draw the outlines of the difference between Cartesian consciousness and dialectical consciousness

Soul's Thought of Itself Today Is Consciousness

in terms of the difference between *either/or* and *both/and*. While dialectical consciousness is happening to us without our being aware of it, we can cultivate a conscious appreciation of dialectical consciousness, allowing it to seep in and gradually transform our way of seeing, thinking, and being. Doing so can help us adapt on a personal level to the topsy-turvy, fluid, and moving world that is overtaking us. Changing our deep-seated Cartesian consciousness is not done easily or quickly, and it is not done by the ego making changes, like moving the inner furniture around. The process is more like learning a new language: practice and immersion—never-ending practice.

The phrases *either/or* and *both/and* refer to different structures of relatedness, and I find it helpful to think them in terms of *me-or-you* in comparison with *me-and-you*. The *you* part of these equations represents more than another person; it is any *other* we are in relation with, such as animals, insects, the biosphere, houses, cars, chairs, civilization, family, friends and enemies, your own thoughts and dreams, your body, yourself. No matter what the *other you* is, we can have either an *or* relationship or an *and* relationship with it, and they are qualitatively different. It should be clear that *me-or-you* sets up an exclusive relatedness structure, while *me-and-you* is an inclusive relatedness structure: each represents a very different logical form of consciousness.

Me-or-you is based in the Cartesian syntax of consciousness in which subject and object are ontologically split apart and the subject (me) assumes the dominant position. When we are *me-or-you*, the *me* must survive at *you's* expense, compete against *you*, dominate *you*, and exclude *you*. There is no soul connection between the *me* and the *you*; there is no relatedness at all except by mutual exclusion. The *or-you* has indeed become devalued to be used by the *me* for its own purposes. The *or-you* is logically excluded by the very structure of either/or Cartesian consciousness; rational logic will not tolerate contradictions. The *me* contradicts the *you*, and the *you* contradicts the *me*; they cannot simultaneously occupy the same ontological status, the same validity, the same truth. The Cartesian syntax of consciousness is our starting point, still the prevailing logic of our embedded consciousness. We cannot extract or exorcise it, but we can make it conscious and see how it works. Either/or is not dialectical.

Me-and-you, in the context of dialectical consciousness, is a relational structure constituted as an identity in which *me* and *you* are known to be of one and the same soul. I am you and you are me. The two are constructed by the circle of consciousness within the realization they are not separate entities, but differentiated by most likely unknown aspects of each other. The *me* does not exclude the *you* as foreign and alien but includes the foreign and alien as the *me's* own foreign and alien strangeness. I recognize that I am strange and alien to myself and that the *you* that I perceive as alien and strange is my own other, since we are both enclosed and sublated, within the serpent of consciousness. *Me-and-you* is logically, structurally, different from the merely semantic "me and you." Me and you, without the hyphens, are simply two separate semantic contents, side by side. *Me-and-you* constitutes a singular logical structure that is recursive and open to the infinity, the wilderness, of soul.

God's Autopsy and the Living Truth of Soul

A negation of exclusion characterizes the *me-**or**-you* relation, in which the *me* negates the substance of the *you*, deletes its existence, erases its substantial validity; this is an undialectical negation. Within the *me-**and**-you* relation, a process of logical self-negation works to disidentify both the *me* and the *you* from itself internally. When I know that I am also constituted by the otherness of the *you*, I can no longer remain unconsciously (ideologically) identified with myself; I become aware of the difference I am within myself. As a dialectical consciousness (like the view of the planet from outer space), I view myself with both a detached and related consciousness; I view myself with suspicion, curiosity, and love. Taking the *other you* as a self in its own right, one that is dialectically also *me* within the circle of consciousness, relativizes and deepens my identity. With the status of dialectical consciousness, my sense of self is torn open to the ongoing and unavoidable infinity and self-negations of soul. In another context—discussing the contradictions inherent in the formulations of medieval alchemy, such as the Philosopher's Stone, which is the stone that is not a stone, and *aqua permanens*—Giegerich says: "This is a contradiction that within the framework of Formal Logic appears as a sign of madness. For this reason you need the Dionysian frenzy of dialectical logic to do justice to it."[60]

The challenge of dialectical consciousness is that it kills the Cartesian ego, it subverts our common sense of self, decentering it. Of course, the ego resists this death with all its might, but it is happening anyway. The promise comes by unwavering and committed contemplation of the new structure *me-**and**-you*, allowing dialectical consciousness to seep into our bones and mind—we will become fluid, flexible, and sturdy, able to surf the new truth and its self-negations. Acknowledge the either/or we still are. Become both/and more and moving.

---

60. Giegerich, *Soul's Logical Life*, 148.

Afterword

White Supremacy Is Christian Supremacy

Yahweh-Christ and the Hidden Logic of Genocide, Misogyny, and Racism

> After Buddha was dead, his shadow was still shown for centuries in a cave—a tremendous, gruesome shadow. God is dead; but given the way of men, there may still be caves for thousands of years, in which his shadow will be shown.—And we—we still have to vanquish his shadow, too.[1]

HERE I WANT TO suggest one possible interpretation of God's "tremendous, gruesome shadow" that casts itself over society like a curse. We are far from finished with the work of the autopsy of God and God's legacy. God may be dead, but God's original deicidal impulse still permeates the deep background of our collective being (just as we still detect the cosmic background radiation of the big bang), translating itself on the human level into genocide, misogyny, and racism, subtly influencing our orientation to the world and each other. I trace the roots of these horrors we visit on each other back to the earliest emergence of the logical forms of consciousness I have called Yahweh and Christ.

Soul, as an autonomous and impersonal self-generating process, does not care about how humankind acts out its logic socially. In general, humankind is not conscious of the logical form of consciousness as it exists at any particular historical time. So, for example, we look back on the era of human and animal sacrifice in horror. How could people possibly have thought that a god would want human sacrifice?! And, yet, there it was. How about the Spanish Inquisition, when people were tortured

---

1. Nietzsche, *Gay Science*, 167 (§108).

in order to save their souls? There again, a logic of consciousness prevailed in which the soul was more real and more valuable than biological life.[2] For that syntax of consciousness, that form of truth, biological life was transitory and ephemeral, and the soul was eternal. Within that logic when the universals had ultimate value, it was better to torture the body to preserve the soul, and of course, in that case, it had to be a "Christian" soul.

Soul is the way meaning, public mind, creates itself, but it does not control how humankind will act in relation to that meaning. Consider the imperial and colonial impulse of Christianity to convert everyone to Christianity. Throughout most of its history, Christianity viewed anything not Christian as of the devil. All indigenous nature-worshipping peoples, polytheistic peoples, were heathen, less than human, and subject to either conversion or destruction. Another example was the existence of slavery as a state-regulated legal enterprise for over two hundred years during the settling and founding of the United States, a supposedly Christian and Enlightenment nation. Certainly, it is an astonishing contradiction that slavery flourished in Christian America (and Christian Europe) at the same time the Enlightenment was displacing Christianity. The hidden logic of Christianity, and the Judeo-Christian impulse, enabled Christian people of a Christian culture to view people from Africa, and the indigenous peoples of the Americas, as less than human, as savages, as animals (because they did not have a Christian soul). Soul was up to something as it transformed itself as the syntax of Western culture, but how human persons enacted what soul was up to was not what soul had in mind at all. As I have said, soul is as impersonal as the weather, and how human persons enact soul's imperative is just not in its purview. In a way, soul does not see human beings, any more than evolution sees individual creatures, and the force we call Life comes and goes throughout the life and death of billions of creatures. We do not imagine that Life cares for any specific individual creature. Soul, the force of living ideas that animate culture, is just as impersonal.

The Hidden Logic of Genocide

Yahweh (and Christ) hated the goddess and those who worshipped the "false" gods and goddesses of the nature-embedded myth-ritual cultures—hated and destroyed the natural symbols that were "false idols." In chapters 4 and 5, this hate was most visible in the Tanakh, but Christianity extended that hate as it spread throughout pre-Christian Europe. Yahweh was the one and only true God. I stated that soul needed the energy of hate to free itself from its embeddedness in nature on its way to becoming imageless transcendent spirit. Through its exodus, Yahweh was leaving bondage to the ground (local natural environment and tribe) and moving into the freedom of

---

2. Although the Spanish Inquisition spanned the late medieval period into the modern period, the working idea of soul was that of antiquity, soul as a real metaphysical substance, of ultimate value.

the air (the unboundedness in principle of the written word). This move on the part of soul, of the syntax of consciousness, appeared as culturally personified in "Yahweh."

For psychology, Yahweh was not the name of some kind of divine entity as we conventionally think of him. "Yahweh" was the name of a form of consciousness that was changing itself from sensual image and natural phenomena to the abstract word of written language. Yahweh was the god of the origin of writing in our Western cultural context, and he represented the movement from preliterate culture to literate culture. This move transformed the logical constitution of *meaning* itself, which was the self-negation and self-development of the syntax of consciousness. This, of course, at least as depicted in the biblical narrative, had terrible and tragic consequences for those who continued to worship Yahweh as a golden bull, as well as those polytheistic cultures which inhabited the "promised land," as they were slaughtered to make room for Yahweh. Writing killed oral culture. My contention is that Yahweh personified the emergence of a new form of consciousness identified with writing, over and against orality. This was acted out culturally in the form of a single transcendent God going to war against the nature-embedded gods and goddesses. It was a struggle in which spirit and word overcame the limits of nature-bound images and the innate limits of consciousness constituted by preliterate orality.

During the movement of Christianity throughout Western Europe and the Americas, even into modernity, indigenous cultures were destroyed and indigenous peoples were enslaved and slaughtered. The first hidden logic of the Judeo-Christian impulse was Yahweh's genocidal tendency, which was not merely a literary metaphor but a drive acted out by people on other people. Again, soul itself did not intend the killing of people, but because soul is the bedrock of who and what we think we *are*, without our knowing that this is who and what we think we *are*, we act out soul's imperative in terrible and unconscious ways. On the level of soul, genocide can be seen as the hidden logic of deicide—Yahweh destroyed all the many other gods and goddesses, which were identified with the natural world, as well as himself in his bull form.

Both Jews and Christians are known as "people of the book." In Judaism and Christianity, the written word of scripture is sacred: the actual Word of God. For Christianity especially, Christ was the *Word* made flesh, and the New Testament as book was sacrosanct. Viewed as the changing syntax of meaning, the advent of writing was genocidal in effect toward preliterate, oral cultures, because it was the end (killing off) of one logical form of consciousness for a radically and qualitatively different form. Oral, preliterate cultures are bound to specific locales, to natural phenomenon, to local gods and goddesses. The spoken word can go only so far. In general, social organization was limited to small and local tribal groups. The written word represented an explosion of consciousness beyond such local limitations, freeing it to travel far and wide and build larger social organizations. The written word is abstract in the original sense of "draw off, or away." The word *abstract* points to ideas and thoughts that do not have concrete, physical existence and are not bound to concrete physical places. Abstract ideas are meanings free of the limitations of orality and geography. The historical development of the abstract idea was symbolized by Yahweh's exodus out of Egypt. Soul's exodus from nature by way of Yahweh and Christ was the move from preliterate to literate consciousness. Soul needed an enormous explosion of energy to break free of its immersion in nature, and that explosive energy took the form of the father-son pair, Yahweh-Christ. One of the consequences of that revolution is that human beings acted out soul's transformations with dire and tragic results for other human beings.

Contemporary liberal Jews and Christians relate to the Judeo-Christian tradition, and the supposed "God" of Judaism and Christianity, as promoting an ethic of social justice. This orientation, however, is a semantic ego project (a product of humanism) that completely misses the hidden logic of genocide. The logic of consciousness that originated with Yahweh and Christ leads directly to the logic of misogyny and racism. Of course, soul's project of literacy is long over, and the victor in the war between non-literacy and literacy is obvious. The hidden impulses of genocide in the latter-day expressions of misogyny and racism are like a long-lasting hangover thoroughly embedded in our deepest and most unconscious sense of self. European white supremacy and its white American heirs are the unconscious logical result of European *Christian* supremacy.

Christian Supremacy Is Racist

James Cone's important book *The Cross and the Lynching Tree* draws a theological and phenomenological line from the crucifixion of Jesus to the lynching tree on which thousands of blacks were murdered. This connection had never been made by either white or black theologians and preachers (although many black artists and writers saw it clearly). For Cone, the connection holds the hope of healing:

> The lynching tree is a metaphor for white America's crucifixion of black people. It is the window that best reveals the religious meaning of the cross in our land . . . If America has the courage to confront the great sin and ongoing legacy of *white supremacy* with repentance and reparation there is hope "beyond tragedy."[3]

The words *white supremacy* define the prevailing problem, the "great sin" in the systemic orientation that infects America at large. Cone wrote the book because "it was my responsibility to address the great contradiction white supremacy poses for Christianity in America."[4] The idea of white supremacy poses its own problem, raising the question of where white supremacy originated. In my view, what is called white supremacy is not simply a demographic and sociological problem that arises when

---

3. Cone, *Cross*, 166, emphasis added.
4. Cone, *Cross*, xvii.

one majority ethnic group in power claims superiority to a different-looking minority. For Caucasians of European descent, superiority starts in the logic of the Judeo-Christian tradition. For more than one thousand years (approximately 500–1600), European Christianity identified itself as the *ultimate, supreme*, and *final revelation* of God, and this self-understanding was the defining logic of European civilization. This was not just about people assuming power, but rather, the logical constitution of the consciousness of European civilization was *identified* with ultimate Truth. (Not to mention the fact, which I will not develop here, that the rational consciousness developed during the Enlightenment also saw itself as inherently superior. As far as *superiority* goes, Christianity and the Enlightenment became a deadly combination in early modern Europe.) Anything not of Christianity, whether nature-worshipping indigenous cultures or any other religion, including Islam and Judaism, was of the devil and inherently evil, necessitating conversion or destruction. Why not choose tolerance and coexistence? Primarily because it is not a matter of conscious choice. The imperative of the water we swim in does its work collectively and unconsciously. And, even though during the early centuries of its move into Europe, Christianity was tolerant of the existing nature-based religions, it gradually became less and less so. Wherever the Absolute appears (and by Absolute, I mean the logical form of consciousness), which in this case informed Christian civilization, the Absolute is, by definition totalitarian, imperialistic, and colonial (zero tolerance of other truths).

White supremacy is Christian supremacy, plain and simple. The term white supremacy has become somewhat of a liberal axiom, which we can hope will deepen the consciousness of the majority white culture about its invisible, assumed, and unconscious racism. At the same time, the term white supremacy cloaks and hides the deeper logic of genocide that resides at the heart of the Judeo-Christian tradition, its roots growing from the seeds called Yahweh and Christ. White supremacy is not first of all a social problem, as its roots are primordially associated with soul's ancient move into writing; the ancient transformation of consciousness that has taken two thousand years and more to work itself throughout society. Today, white supremacy is a deadly and tragic remnant, a left-over secondary effect of the now obsolete Judeo-Christian religion(s). It is unconsciously acted out in human society, informed by the lingering hidden logic of the form of consciousness established by the written word, and remains genocidal, misogynistic, and racist. God's "gruesome shadow" continues to fall over us and our future.

Of course, today it is silly to say that "literacy" in general is genocidal, misogynistic, and racist, and that is not what I am trying to say. (Although let's not forget that literate people do indeed look down on illiterate people, and illiterate people are generally ashamed of being illiterate.) My focus here is on the *genocidal* (*deicidal*) *logic* of Yahweh and Christ in their original ancient contexts, which has led to the human acting out of genocide, misogyny, and racism. In the context of white Christian supremacy, women and people of color are *unconsciously* identified with the old false "goddesses and gods," the false idols, and they suffer the tragic consequences. The original genocidal impulse of Yahweh and Christ and its rampage throughout world history remains unexamined as it pertains to soul's development of itself. This is not a critique of Judaism or Christianity as religions, but an attempt to see deeper into the *logic of soul's movement*, so as to see the logical remnants of deicide and genocide and to acknowledge they are real for everyone, white and non-white.

Although the emergence of literacy was genocidal for preliterate oral culture, literacy also frees consciousness to reflect on itself at a higher level. The written word in books allows soul to reflect on itself over decades and centuries (history), which would be impossible in oral culture. By way of critical theory, literacy has enabled us to see things that would remain invisible otherwise. Writing, like any form of consciousness, is dialectical in that it both reveals and conceals; it kills one idea in order to bring another idea to life. This is why we need a dialectical consciousness in order to come to terms with soul's logical (dialectical) life.

Patriarchy and Misogyny

Misogyny means the hatred of women, and it normally refers to the hateful attitudes of individual male persons toward women; it is considered an isolated interpersonal expression. The roots of misogyny, however, go much deeper than the merely personal. Misogyny in our Judeo-Christian tradition is often traced to the apostle Paul and his injunctions for women to be submissive to men (Eph 5:22) and silent in church (1 Cor 14:34). Long before Paul, however, as we saw in chapters 4 and 5, the logic of misogyny began with God himself, in the form of Yahweh. Yahweh's hatred of the goddess, especially his consort Asherah, was explicit:

> You shall not plant any tree as a sacred pole [Asherah] beside the altar that you make for the LORD your God; nor shall you set up a stone pillar—things that the LORD your God hates. (Deut 16:21–22)

and:

> The LORD will strike Israel, as a reed is shaken in the water; he will root up Israel out of this good land that he gave to their ancestors, and scatter them beyond the Euphrates, because they have made their sacred poles [Asherim], provoking the LORD to anger. (1 Kgs 14:15–16)

The sacred poles referred to in these verses were the actual presence of the Canaanite fertility goddess Asherah, consort of the Bull god Yahweh. In my psychological interpretation, Yahweh was the name of a new logical form of consciousness (spirit, word, and literacy) that soul used to personify itself in its push against immersion in the preliterate natural world; soul was negating itself for a new syntax of consciousness. I locate the roots of misogyny within this drama of Yahweh's hatred of the goddess which has been acted out by men (and systemically institutionalized) against women (which was not soul's intent).

This is the hidden logic at the heart of the feminist term *patriarchy*. Through decades of incisive feminist criticism, patriarchy has been used to identify many social sins, systemic misogyny chief among them from the point of view of feminism.[5] Contemporary analysis shows misogyny is not simply an individual's emotional hatred of women, but rather the systematic orientation of an entire society and its institutions to keep women in a subservient role.[6] The word patriarchy, however, can also cloak and cover its roots in the logical form of consciousness named Yahweh and Christ. That Yahweh and Christ represent the origins of patriarchy in the negative sense has been said before, but I would also suggest that the emergence of writing as a new logical form of consciousness, a new kind of public mind, carried the hidden logic of genocide and misogyny. Misogyny, like genocide and racism, is the social and human acting out of the deeper logic of soul's self-transformations. We need to become conscious of misogyny as a deep-seated, invisible, and unconscious, institutionalized ideology that infects all of us, most especially men, but also women. No one is exempt as it is a social disorder of God's lingering shadow.

Consciousness Is Responsibility

Soul will do what it will do whether we like it or not. However, genocide, misogyny, and racism are not soul's intent; we are not helpless and must take responsibility for our behavior. While soul may not care about how we as human beings act out the movement of the form of consciousness throughout history, when we as persons become conscious of what we are doing, we are wholly responsible for how we behave toward each other. As we have seen, soul has been emancipating itself, increasing its freedom. The reflective process of writing that soul has used in its self-liberating project goes hand in hand with consciousness and freedom. The freedom of consciousness today can no longer be in terms of *me-or-you* but must embrace the entangled freedom of *me-and-you*. Our human freedom has to become a kind of dialectical freedom because with consciousness we are burdened with responsibility. The popular misconception of freedom as an unburdened state relies on the simplistic fantasy in which we define freedom as cut off from social cares (vacation). But, real freedom must be social and entangled in our conflicts and responsibility to each other.

The freedom inherent in consciousness is the potential to become conscious of ourselves, and to even differentiate ourselves from ourselves, to be conscious of our consciousness. Because of the historical movement of consciousness, we are now the adults in the room (cosmos). We bear the responsibility to enhance freedom in human relations. The social problems of genocide, misogyny, and racism exist precisely

5. Solnit, *Mother of All Questions*.
6. Manne, *Down Girl*.

because they function unconsciously at a deep level and inform the invisible systems of society. To make these social ills conscious is to suffer their reality and to realize we are all sick with this collective problem. We can choose to acknowledge and dismantle the social structures and the personal beliefs that perpetuate genocide, misogyny, and racism. The freedom to be conscious is a duty laid on us by soul itself; our choice is to accept it or reject it.

Of course, this reflection on a possible hidden misogyny and racism within the historical origins of the Judeo-Christian syntax of consciousness has little to say about the reality of genocide, misogyny, and racism within non-Christian cultures. Genocide, misogyny, and racism seem to be persistent problems of humankind. Within Christianity, however, they can be tracked to a special problem at the heart of white Christian culture that was nurtured by one thousand years of Christianity. Soul has been focused on its own historical self-negations in the development of new logical forms of consciousness, while European Christian culture has imprinted on white human persons both an unconscious inherent supremacy and an open wound of hate and fear of false gods/goddesses. The supremacy condition, with its accompanying hate, is still acted out against those perceived as alien and threatening to its truth. The psychological perspective offers hope because it enables us to see the "false gods and goddesses" (which white society unconsciously identifies with people of color and women) as belonging to ourselves. When we are conscious of the perceived alien other as a who, who is deeply entangled with our own sense of self, we will not act out soul's logical transformations against others, either other human beings or nonhuman beings. Consciousness gives us choice in how to live and coexist.

Recommendations for Further Reading

I RECOMMEND THE FOLLOWING works by Wolfgang Giegerich as entry points for first-time readers interested in this new psychological perspective. All of his books first published by Spring Journal Books (now out of business) are now available through Routledge.

- "The End of Meaning and the Birth of Man: An Essay about the State Reached in the History of Consciousness and an Analysis of C. G. Jung's Psychology Project."

    Available as a download from, http://www.jungpage.org/pdfdocuments/End-ofMeaning.pdf, and a chapter in, *The Soul Always Thinks*, CEP IV, 189–283.

    This is a compelling essay on the historical status of consciousness today, and a penetrating critique of Jung's understanding of the unconscious.

- "Introduction: The Object of Psychology." *Technology and the Soul*, CEP II, 1–22.

    An excellent overview of Giegerich's reorientation of psychological thinking.

- *What Is Soul?* New Orleans: Spring Journal, 2012. Now Routledge, 2019.

    One of the more accessible book-length treatments of what Giegerich means by *soul*.

- Giegerich, Wolfgang. *Dialectics & Analytical Psychology: The El Capitan Canyon Seminar*. With David Miller and Greg Mogenson. New Orleans: Spring Journal, 2005. Now Routledge, 2020.

I particularly recommend "'Conflict/Resolution,' 'Opposites / Creative Union' versus Dialectics, and the Climb Up the Slippery Mountain," and "The Historicity of Myth." The interpretation of the folk tale "The Princess on the Glass Mountain" is a clear introduction to the idea of *dialectics* in psychology with soul, and "The Historicity of Myth" shows myth is not a source of universal abstract truths, but a time-bound form of soul(mind) that is now obsolete.

- Sandoval, Jennifer M., and John C. Knapp, eds. *Psychology as the Discipline of Interiority: "The Psychological Difference" in the work of Wolfgang Giegerich*. New York: Routledge, 2017.

    This collection of essays by international scholars amplifies the idea of the "psychological difference" from a variety of perspectives.

- https://www.ispdi.org/

    The website for the International Society for Psychology as the Discipline of Interiority. The definitive resource for all things related to psychology with soul.

Although introducing psychology with soul by way of a novel reading of the biblical record is the primary aim of my book, I would be remiss not to highly recommend Jack Miles's two books that have played a significant role in the development of my own thought: *God: A Biography* and *Christ: A Crisis in the Life of God*. It is extremely rare to find eloquent writing and profound scholarship united with a non-confessional and non-tendentious interpretation of the Bible and the figures of God and Christ. Clearly Miles has great respect for and knowledge of the Judeo-Christian tradition, and he does not have an axe to grind either for or against it. He deftly allows the central characters to reveal themselves through their own pages.

Bibliography

Andreessen, Marc. "Why Software Is Eating the World." *Wall Street Journal*, August 20, 2011. https://www.wsj.com/articles/SB10001424053111903480904576512250915629460.

Black, Jeremy, ed. *The World History Atlas*. London: Dorling Kindersley, 2005.

Borges, Jorge Luis. *Collected Fictions*. Translated by Andrew Hurley. New York: Penguin, 1998.

Carse, James. *The Gospel of the Beloved Disciple*. HarperSanFrancisco, 1997.

Childs, Hal. "From God to Psychology: A Sketch of the Soul's Self-Transformation through Myth and History." In *Psychological Hermeneutics for Biblical Themes and Texts: A Festschrift in Honor of Wayne G. Rollins*, edited by J. Harold Ellens, 97–117. New York: T. & T. Clark, 2012.

———. *The Myth of the Historical Jesus and the Evolution of Consciousness*. Atlanta: SBL, 2000.

The Compact Edition of the Oxford English Dictionary. Oxford: Oxford University Press, 1971.

Cone, James H. *The Cross and the Lynching Tree*. Maryknoll: Orbis, 2011.

Dawes, Gregory W., ed. *The Historical Jesus Quest: A Foundational Anthology*. Leiden: Deo, 1999.

Dever, William. G. *Did God Have a Wife?* Grand Rapids: Eerdmans, 2005.

Eiseley, Loren. *The Man Who Saw Through Time*. New York: Scribner, 1973.

Folger, Tim. "Does the Universe Exist if We're Not Looking?" *Discover*, June 2002, 44–48.

Fox, Everett. *The Early Prophets*. A new translation with introductions, commentary, and notes. New York: Shocken Books, 2014.

———. *The Five Books of Moses*. A new translation with introductions, commentary, and notes. New York: Shocken Books, 1995.

Giegerich, Wolfgang. "Blood Brotherhood, Blood Revenge, and *Devotio*: Glimpses of the Archaic Psyche." In *Soul-Violence*, Collected English Papers (CEP) III, 267–315. New Orleans: Spring Journal, 2008. Now Routledge, vol. 3, 2020.

———. "C. G. Jung's Idea of a 'Metamorphosis of the Gods' and the History of the Soul." In *The Soul Always Thinks*, CEP IV, 531–62. New Orleans: Spring Journal, 2010. Now Routledge, vol. 4, 2020.

———. "The Ego-Psychological Fallacy: A Note on 'the Birth of the Meaning Out of a Symbol.'" In *The Soul Always Thinks*, CEP IV, 351–61. New Orleans: Spring Journal, 2010. Now Routledge, vol. 4, 2020.

———. "The End of Meaning and the Birth of Man." In *The Soul Always Thinks*, CEP IV, 189–283. New Orleans: Spring Journal, 2010. Now Routledge, vol. 4, 2020.

———. "First Shadow, then Anima, or The Advent of the Guest: Shadow Integration and the Rise of Psychology." In *Soul-Violence*, CEP III, 77–109. New Orleans: Spring Journal, 2008. Now Routledge, vol. 3, 2020.

———. "The Function of Television and the Soul's Predicament." In *Technology and the Soul: From the Nuclear Bomb to the World Wide Web*, CEP II, 281–308. New Orleans: Spring Journal, 2007. Now Routledge, vol. 2, 2020.

———. "God Must Not Die! C. G. Jung's Thesis of the One-Sidedness of Christianity." In *"Dreaming the Myth Onwards": C. G. Jung on Christianity and On Hegel*, CEP 6, 165–242. New Orleans: Spring Journal, 2013. Now Routledge, vol. 6, 2020.

———. *The Historical Emergence of the I: Essays About One Chapter in the History of the Soul*. London, Canada: Dusk Owl Books, 2020.

———. "Killings." In *Soul-Violence*, CEP III, 189–265. New Orleans: Spring Journal, 2008. Now Routledge, vol. 3, 2020.

———. "The Movement of the Soul." In *The Soul Always Thinks*, CEP IV, 307–23. New Orleans: Spring Journal, 2010. Now Routledge, vol. 4, 2020.

———. *Neurosis: The Logic of a Metaphysical Illness*. New Orleans: Spring Journal, 2013. Now Routledge, 2019.

———. "The Nuclear Bomb and the Fate of God: On the First Nuclear Fission." In *Technology and the Soul: From the Nuclear Bomb to the World Wide Web*, CEP II, 69–99. New Orleans: Spring Journal, 2007. Now Routledge, vol. 2, 2020.

———. "The Sacrifice of Isaac and the Watershed of History: Preparatory and Methodological Remarks Concerning the Topic of Ritual Killings." In *Soul-Violence*, CEP III, 171–87. New Orleans: Spring Journal, 2008. Now Routledge, vol. 3, 2020.

———. *The Soul's Logical Life: Towards a Rigorous Notion of Psychology*. 5th rev. ed. Frankfurt am Main: Peter Lang, 2020.

———. "'Thought': Some Signposts." Introduction to *The Soul Always Thinks*, CEP IV, 1–21. New Orleans: Spring Journal, 2010. Now Routledge, vol. 4, 2020.

———. *What Is Soul?* New Orleans: Spring Journal, 2012. Now Routledge, 2019.

Gleick, James. *The Information: A History, a Theory, a Flood*. New York: Pantheon, 2011.

———. *Isaac Newton*. New York: Pantheon, 2003.

Guignon, Charles B. *Heidegger and the Problem of Knowledge*. Indianapolis: Hackett, 1983.

Harari, Yuval Noah. *Sapiens: A Brief History of Humankind*. London: Vintage, 2011.

Heidegger, Martin. *Being and Time*. Translated by John Macquarrie and Edward Robinson. New York: Harper & Row, 1962.

———. "Letter on Humanism." In *Basic Writings*, edited by David Farrell Krell, 189–242. New York: Harper & Row, 1977.

———. *On the Way to Language*. Translated by Peter D. Hertz. New York: Harper & Row, 1971.

Herzog, William R., II. *Parables as Subversive Speech: Jesus as Pedagogue of the Oppressed*. Louisville: Westminster John Knox, 1994.

Jung, C. G. *The Archetypes and the Collective Unconscious*. 2nd ed. Edited by H. Read et al. Translated by R. F. C. Hull. Collected Works of C. G. Jung (CW) 9.1. Princeton: Princeton University Press, 1968.

———. "Basic Postulates of Analytical Psychology." In *The Structure and Dynamics of the Psyche*, 338–57. 2nd ed. CW 8. 1960.

———. *Civilization in Transition*. 2nd ed. CW 10. 1970.

———. *Memories, Dreams, Reflections*. New York: Pantheon, 1961.

———. *Mysterium Coniunctionis*. 2nd ed. CW 14. 1970.

———. *Psychological Types*. CW 6. 1971.

———. "Psychology and Religion." In *Psychology and Religion: West and East*, 3–111. 2nd ed. CW 11. 1969.

———. "The Tavistock Lectures." In *The Symbolic Life: Miscellaneous Writings*, 5–182. CW 18. 1976.

Heisenberg, Werner. *Natural Law and the Structure of Matter*. London: Rebel, 1981.

———. *Physics and Philosophy: The Revolution in Modern Science*. London: Allen & Unwin, 1959.

Kelly, J. N. D. *Early Christian Doctrines*. Rev. ed. New York: HarperOne, 1978.

Kirsch, Thomas B. *The Jungians: A Comparative and Historical Perspective*. London: Routledge, 2000.

Kuhn, Thomas. *The Structure of Scientific Revolutions*. Chicago: University of Chicago Press, 1962.

Levenson, Jon D. *Inheriting Abraham: The Legacy of the Patriarch in Judaism, Christianity, and Islam*. Princeton: Princeton University Press, 2012.

Lightman, Alan. Introduction to *Flatland: A Romance of Many Dimensions*, by Edwin A. Abbott, 1884. New York: Penguin, 1998.

Lindow, John. *Swedish Legends and Folktales*. Berkeley: University of California Press, 1978.

Manne, Kate. *Down Girl: The Logic of Misogyny*. New York: Oxford University Press, 2018.

Marx, Karl, and Frederick Engels. *The Communist Manifesto*, 1848. In *A Road Map to History's Most Important Political Document*, edited by Phil Gasper. Chicago: Haymarket, 2005.

Metzger, Bruce M., and Michael D. Coogan, eds. *The Oxford Companion to the Bible*. New York: Oxford University Press, 1993.

Miles, Jack. *Christ: A Crisis in the Life of God*. New York: Knopf, 2001.

———. *God: A Biography*. New York: Knopf, 1995.

Morton, Timothy. *Dark Ecology: For a Logic of Future Coexistence*. New York: Columbia University Press, 2018.

Munz, Peter. *The Shapes of Time: A New Look at the Philosophy of History*. Middletown, CT: Wesleyan University Press, 1977.

The New Interpreter's Bible: A Commentary in Twelve Volumes. Nashville: Abingdon, 1994.

Nietzsche, Friedrich. *The Gay Science*. Translated by Walter Kaufmann, based on the second edition of *Die fröhliche Wissenschaft*, 1887. New York: Vintage, 1974.

Norris, Eleanor L. *Reflections of a Passerby: Jesus, Jung, and the Power of Choice*. Asheville, NC: Chiron, 2022.

Reed, Edward S. *From Soul to Mind: The Emergence of Psychology, from Erasmus Darwin to William James*. New Haven, CT: Yale University Press, 1997.

Sagan, Carl. *Cosmos*. New York: Ballantine, 2013.

Sagan, Carl, et al. "The Shores of the Cosmic Ocean." Episode 1 of *Cosmos: A Personal Voyage*, a television miniseries. Public Broadcasting Service, 1980.

Schweitzer, Albert. *The Quest of the Historical Jesus: A Critical Study of Its Progress from Reimarus to Wrede*. Translated by W. Montgomery from the 1st German ed., *Von Reimarus zu Wrede*, 1906. Introduction by James Robinson, 1968. New York: Macmillan, 1961.

Bibliography

Schweizer, Bernard. *Hating God: The Untold Story of Misotheism.* New York: Oxford University Press, 2011.

Shelley, Mary. *Frankenstein; or, The Modern Prometheus.* London: Lackington, Hughes, Harding, Mavor & Jones, 1818.

Smith, Mark S. *The Early History of God: Yahweh and the Other Deities in Ancient Israel.* San Francisco: Harper & Row, 1990.

———. *The Memoirs of God: History, Memory, and the Experience of the Divine in Ancient Israel.* Minneapolis: Fortress, 2004.

Solnit, Rebecca. *The Mother of All Questions.* Chicago: Haymarket, 2017.

Stevenson, W. Taylor. *History as Myth: The Import for Contemporary Theology.* New York: Seabury, 1969.

Stock, Brian. *Listening for the Text: On the Uses of the Past.* Baltimore: Johns Hopkins University Press, 1990.

Stott, Rebecca. *Darwin's Ghosts: The Secret History of Evolution.* New York: Spiegel & Grau, 2012.

Veyne, Paul. *Writing History: Essay on Epistemology.* Middletown, CT: Wesleyan University Press, 1984.

Wark, McKenzie. *Capital Is Dead: Is This Something Worse?* London: Verso, 2019.

White, Hayden. *The Content of the Form: Narrative Discourse and Historical Representation.* Baltimore: Johns Hopkins University, 1987.

Zuboff, Shoshana. *The Age of Surveillance Capitalism: The Fight for a Human Future at the New Frontier of Power.* London: Profile, 2019.

Author Index

Andreessen, Marc, 370n56
Aslan, Reza, 262n5

Black, Jeremy, 105n14
Borges, Jorge Luis, 339n21

Carse, James, 271n16
Childs, Hal, 9n6, 9n7, 25n6
Cone, James H., 380, 380nn3–4

Dawes, Gregory W., 311n26, 312n27, 313n28, 314n29, 315n30, 315n32, 316n34, 317n35
Dever, William G., 124n3

Eiseley, Loren, 300nn12–13, 301n16, 302n17

Folger, Tim, 350n31, 351n33, 352nn34–35, 354nn40–41
Fox, Everett, 86n86, 98n10, 110n23, 110n26, 114n29, 124n5, 130n12, 132n13, 156n4

Giegerich, Wolfgang, 1nn1–3, 16nn1–2, 29, 30, 30nn7–8, 31, 38n10, 49n14, 56nn1–3, 57nn4–6, 62n7, 87nn1–2, 112n27, 113n28, 120n33, 121n24, 122nn35–36, 123nn1–2, 144n20, 147n21, 148nn22–23, 149n24, 152nn26–28, 153, 153n28, 153n29, 154nn1–2, 193n30, 195nn1–2, 284n31, 288n33, 289nn1–2, 295, 295nn5–6, 296n7, 323n1, 324n2, 328n6, 340, 347n28, 364, 367n52, 372n59, 376n60, 385
Gleick, James, 326n4, 333n14, 345n27, 361n47

Guignon, Charles B., 303n18, 304nn19–20, 305nn21–22, 306n23, 336n18, 337n19, 340n24, 342n26, 362nn49–50

Harari, Yuval Noah, 69n10, 110n24, 154nn1–2, 156n3
Heidegger, Martin, 12, 23, 23n5, 69, 69n11, 74, 74n12, 153n28, 335, 336–42, 340nn22–23, 341n25
Heisenberg, Werner, 356n43, 356n45
Henderson, Harry, 256n3, 359n46
Hern, Alex, 370n53
Herzog, William R., 315n32

Jung, Carl, 7n5, 8, 31, 49, 50–52, 54, 54n17, 56, 57, 57n4, 58, 59, 60, 65, 88, 88n4, 95, 192n26, 295–96, 326, 329–30, 329n7, 330n8, 330n11, 332, 364

Kaufmann, Walter, 318
Kelly, J. N. D., 258n4, 278n23, 278nn24–25, 280n26, 282nn27–28, 283n29, 285n32
Kirsch, Thomas B., 7n5
Knapp, John C., 386
Kuhn, Thomas, 345

Levenson, Jon D., 87n3, 119n31, 120n32
Lindow, John, 284n30

Manne, Kate, 380n6
Marx, Karl, 361n48
McLuhan, Marshall, 372, 372n57
Metzger, Bruce M., 106n16, 124n3

391

Author Index

Miles, Jack, 13n8, 35n9, 42n11, 64–65, 67n8, 85n13, 152n25, 162n5, 169nn7–8, 174nn9–10, 180n11, 181nn12–13, 182n14, 184nn15–16, 185n17, 186, 186n19, 187nn20–21, 188n22, 189n23, 190nn24–25, 193, 193n29, 194n31, 199, 227, 227nn8–9, 230n11, 231n12, 234, 235nn15–16, 236, 236nn17–18, 240, 240n19, 241n20, 242, 243n21, 269n15, 273n19, 273n21, 386
Miller, David, 385
Mogenson, Greg, 385
Morton, Timothy, 339n20
Munz, Peter, 9n6

Nietzsche, Friedrich, 2, 12, 19, 21, 47, 318–22, 318n36, 319n37, 321, 337, 377n1
Norris, Eleanor I., 7n5

Reed, Edward S., 372n58

Sagan, Carl, 349, 349n30
Sandoval, Jennifer M., 386
Schweitzer, Albert, 262, 262n6, 263, 263nn7–8, 264, 264n10, 265, 265n11, 266, 266nn12–13, 310n24
Shelley, Mary, 348n29
Smith, Mark S., 88n3, 91n5, 108nn18–20, 124n3, 193n27
Solnit, Rebecca, 380n5
Stevenson, W. Taylor, 9n6
Stock, Brian, 9n6
Stott, Rebecca, 301nn14–15

Wark, McKenzie, 369n54
White, Hayden, 9n6

Zuboff, Shoshana, 369n54

Name Index

Aaron, 134, 137, 143, 144, 146
Abram/Abraham, 11, 61, 87–88, 90–100, 100n11, 101–3, 105–6, 108–11, 113–19, 121, 125, 128–29, 133–34, 145, 147, 150, 221, 235, 259, 268, 272, 274
Adam, 84, 85, 101, 276, 278, 285
King Ahab, 183
Ahijah, 159
Akhenaten, 127n8
Alexander the Great, 249
Aphrodite, 178
Apollinarius, 280, 281
Archimedes, 330n10
Aristotle, 301
Arius, 278–79
Asherah, 13, 91, 123, 124–25, 133, 139, 141, 147, 153, 155, 159, 161, 162, 171–72, 178, 181–82, 183–84, 192, 195, 196, 382
Aslan, Reza, 262n5
Astarte, 91, 157, 178
Aten, 127n8

Baal, 13, 91, 105, 106, 107, 108, 128, 144, 161, 195
Bacon, Francis, 12, 299–303, 309, 311, 312, 313
Bar Kokhba, Simon, 273
Bildad, 204, 208
Bohr, Niels, 351
Buddha, 377

Celsus, 258
Chemosh, 13, 158, 161
Christ. *See* Jesus Christ
Cone, James, 380–81, 380nn3–4
Constantine, 279

Daniel, 68
David, 156, 157, 158, 183, 250, 269n14
Descartes, René, 12, 31, 47, 49, 289, 303–7, 309, 311, 313, 325, 330n10, 335–36, 357

Echo, 284n31
Einstein, Albert, 309, 332, 332n12, 332n13, 335, 340, 351
El, 13, 91, 105, 106, 107, 108, 108n18, 128, 144, 161, 195
Elihu, 218–20, 218n6, 222, 233
Eliphaz, 204, 205, 206, 238
Emperor Hadrian (Aelia), 273
Enlil (god), 105
Esau, 120
Eve, 84, 85, 101, 191, 242, 276, 278, 285

Freud, Sigmund, 49, 50, 326, 328, 364

Gaal, 98n9
Gabriel, 288
Goethe, Johann Wolfgang von, 60
Gregory Nazianzus. *See* Nazianzen, Gregory

Haggai, 185
Hamlet, 243
Haran, 93
Hawking, Stephen, 334–35, 335n16
Hegel, 29
Heidegger, Martin, 12, 23, 23n5, 69, 69n11, 74, 74n12, 153n28, 335, 336–42, 340nn22–23, 341n25
Heisenberg, Werner, 333–34, 356, 356n43, 356n45, 357, 357n45, 358
King Hezekiah, 183

Name Index

Hillman, James, 153n28
Hugo, Victor, 8
Hus, Jan, 298, 298n10

Isaac, 87, 117, 118, 119–20, 121, 128, 134, 147, 272
Isaiah, 166–68, 170, 175
Ishtar, 178
Israel. *See* Jacob (Israel)

Jacob, 98n9, 120, 128, 130
Jacob (Israel), 146
Jeroboam, 158, 159
Jesus Christ, 2, 5, 7, 7n5, 8, 11, 31, 43–48, 43n12, 45n13, 74, 172, 175, 246–50, 252–57, 259, 260–72, 262n5, 274–86, 284n30, 284n31, 289, 290, 292, 294, 297, 310–11, 311n25, 313–15, 324, 343, 344, 345, 356, 360, 371, 373, 380–83, 386
Jethro, 132
Job, 11, 194, 196, 198, 199–245, 247
John (the Baptist), 268
Joseph (son of Jacob), 68, 128–31, 130n12
Josephus, 272
Joshua, 98, 98n9, 258
Jung, Carl G., 7n5, 8, 31, 49, 50–52, 54, 54n17, 56–60, 65, 88, 88n4, 95, 192n26, 295–96, 326, 329–30, 329n7, 330n8, 330n11, 332, 364
Jupiter, 273

Kuhn, Thomas, 345

Laplace, Pierre Simon de, 333, 333n14, 334, 335, 344–45, 345n27
Lazarus, 248
Lessing, Gotthold Ephraim, 262, 264
Lévy-Bruhl, 95
Lot, 93
Luther, Martin, 12, 297–99, 297n9, 303, 309–10, 313

Malachi, 185
King Manasseh, 182–83
Marduk, 32
Marx, Karl, 361n48
Virgin Mary, 285, 288
Maxwell, James, 332, 332n12
McLuhan, Marshall, 372, 372n57
Meister Eckhart, 294n4
Milcom (god), 157
Molech, 158
Moloch, 13, 161
Montaigne, Michel de, 303

Moses, 11, 39–41, 42, 61, 100, 100n11, 123, 125, 131–37, 140n16, 143, 145–47, 149, 150, 152, 170, 221, 250, 259, 267, 269n14
Mulcahy, Gary, 97n8

Nanna, 93, 105
Nazianzen, Gregory, 280, 281, 282
Newton, Isaac, 326, 332, 332n12, 333
Nietzsche, Friedrich, 12, 19, 21, 29, 47, 318–22, 318n36, 319n37, 321, 337, 377n1
Noah, 101

Pan, 284n30, 284n31
Pastis, Stephan, 245
Paul, 271, 315n32, 382
Petrarch, Francesco, 296–97, 296n8
Plato, 258, 259, 301, 356
Plotinus, 283n29
Plutarch, 284n30

Rebekah, 120
Rehoboam, 158
Reimarus, Hermann Samuel, 262, 263, 264, 265, 266, 272

Sagan, Carl, 349, 349n30, 350
Sarah, 115, 116
Sarai, 93, 106, 109
Satan, 200, 201, 202, 203, 245, 283
the satan, 202, 203, 244
Shem, 101
Sin (god), 105
Solomon, 156, 156n4, 157, 158, 183, 250
Spinoza, Benedict, 311–13, 311n26
Strauss, David Friedrich, 265, 266

Terah, 93
Thompson, Klay, 25
Tiamat, 32
Troeltsch, Ernst, 313–16, 317–18

Uzzah, 269n14

Varus, Publius Quinctilius, 272, 272n18

Wheeler, John Archibald, 350–51, 351n32, 353, 353n39, 354–55, 354n42, 356
Wink, Walter, 7n5

Zechariah, 185
Zephaniah, 243
Zeus, 273
Zipporah, 134
Zophar, 204, 210, 212

394

Ancient Document Index

OLD TESTAMENT

Genesis

	13, 39, 75, 81, 85, 110, 128, 132, 257, 343, 355–56
1:1–2	31
1:3	38
1:3–5	34
1:3–10	76
1:26	108
1:26–27	66
1:26–30	77
2:7–9	78
2:15–17	80
2:24	124n5
3:1–5	81
3:4–5	242
3:14–19	86n14
3:21	86
4:10	215
5:1–32	101n12
11:10–26	101n12
11:31	93
12:1	92
12:2–3	102
12:4	98
12:5b–7	98
12:7	98n10
12–50	87
13:16	109
15	113
15:2–5	109
15:7–12	114n29
15:12–14	128
15:17–18	114n29
16:1	109
16:2	109
17:1–6	110
17:1n	110n23
17:5	110n26
17:5n NRSV	110n25
17:9–13	111
17:12	115
17:15–19a	116
18:22–33	100n11
18:27	235
19:24–25	100n11
22:1–19	118–19
35:4	98n9
39:2	129n10
39:21	129n10
39:23	129n10
41:1–8	129n11
41:16	68n9
41:25–32	129
41:37	129n10
41:38–40	129
45:4–10	130
46:1–4a	130
49:24	108

Exodus

	22n4, 31, 39, 132, 151, 155, 182, 195, 267, 269n14
2:11–12	131
3:1–2	40

Ancient Document Index

Exodus (cont.)

3:1–4	132
3:6	221
3:7–11	133
3:9–11	41
3:11–14	259
3:13–15	41
4:13–14	134
4:21	135
4:24–26	134
5:1–22	135n14
6:6–9	135
9:12	136
9:13–16	136
10:1–2	136
11:1	137
11:4–5	137
11:8 NRSV	132n13
11:9–10	137
12:11b–12	137
12:29–30	137
14:4	139
14:12	139
16:4	275
19:12–13	140n16
19:18	139
20:1–7	196
20:2–11	140
23:23–24	141
24:17	139
24:18	143
25:10–22	269n14
27:1–2	143
29:10–12	143–44
29:18	144
32:1–4	144
32:4	108n17
32:7–10	145
32:7–14	100n11
32:11–14	145–46
32:19–20	146
32:19–29	100n11
32:25–29	146
32:35	147
33:3	147

Leviticus

17:11	114
17:14	114

Numbers

24:8	108

Deuteronomy

	182
6:4–5	196–97
11:30	98n9
13:6–18	141n17
16:21–22	141, 382
17:2–5	141
17:7b	141

Joshua

	182, 258
5:13–15	258
24:25–26	98n9
24:26–27	98

Judges

9:37	98n9

1 Samuel

	155

2 Samuel

	155
6:7	269n14

1 Kings

	155
9:1–5	156–57
9:6–9	157
11:1–8	157–58
11:9–11	158
12:26–30	158–59
14:15–16	159, 382
14:22–24	160

2 Kings

	155
17:7–18	160–61
21:1–15	182–83

Job

	14, 181, 194, 198–99, 237, 243, 244, 249
1:1–3	199
1:4–5	200
1:6–12	200
1:20–22	202
1:21	234
2:3–6	202
2:7–10	203

2:10b	234
2:11–13	204
3:3–6	204–5
3:11–12	204–5
3:25–26	205
4:5–9	205–6
4:17–19	205–6
5:17–19	206–7
5:24–25	206–7
5:27	206–7
6:2–4	207
6:24	207
7:11	207–8
7:20	207–8
8:2–6	208
9:16–20	208–9
9:23–24	209
9:32–33	209
10:1–3	210
10:8	210
10:18	210
11:2–13	210–11
11:13–18	211–12
12:3	212
12:7	212
13:3	213–14
13:4—5:12	212–13
13:13–15	227–28
13:13–24	213–14
16:9–17	214–15
16:18–21	215
19:23–25	216
21:4–7	216
21:34	217
27:2–6	217
27:5b	230
31:5–6	220
32:2–3	218
32:18–20	218
32–37	218n6
34:10–13	219
34:35–37	219
37:23–24	219
38:1–3	221
38:3	232
38:3–38	226
38:4–18	224
38:22–29	225
38:31–33	225–26
39:19–25	226
40:1–2	226
40:3–5	226
40:6–9	228
40:7	232
40:10–14	228
42:1–6	230
42:2	231n12
42:6	230
42:7	238
42:7–8	238
42:7–17	238
42:10	241, 241n20

Psalms

	14, 181, 186–90
1:1–6	188
18	106
132:2	108
139:17	154
139:17–18	187

Proverbs

	14, 181, 190–94
3:13–18	192
3:19–20	191–92
8:22–31	190–91
9:10	193
15:33	193

Isaiah

	182
1:2	166
1:3–4	166
1:5–6	167
1:19–20	167
1:24–25	168
1–39	175
2:20–21	171
5:24–25	169
6:6–7	170
6:9b–10	170
6:11b–13	171
9:2	172
9:6	172
11:6–9	172
40–66	175
42:1–4	175
45:20–23	251
45:23	271
49:1–6	175
49:6b	251
50:4–11	175
52:13–15	176–77
52:13—53:12	175, 271
53:2b–3	177
53:4–5	177

Isaiah (cont.)

53:7–8	178
53:10–11a	178–79
53:11b–12	179

Jeremiah

	182

Daniel

1:27–28	68n9
4:18	68n9

Zephaniah

	243

Haggai

	181, 185

Zechariah

	181, 185, 188
13:2–5	186

Malachi

	181, 182, 185
2:14–15	182

APOCRYPHA (NEW TESTAMENT)

Gospel of Thomas	271, 271n17

NEW TESTAMENT

Matthew

	273n20

Mark

	273n20
1:9–10	268
1:10	246
6:47–51	248
15:34	270
15:38	246

Luke

	249, 273n20
12:1	315n33
13:20–21	315n31
17:20–21	253

John

	31, 44, 255, 273n20, 277
1:1–2	277
1:1–5	44, 254
1:10–13	255
1:14	45, 256, 268
2:1–10	248
6:16–21	248
6:35	44, 275
8:12	44, 275
8:58	44, 274
10:9	275
10:11	275
10:30	275
11:1–44	248
11:25	275
14:6	44, 275
14:15–17	311n25
15:1	44, 275

Acts

	249
1:6	253
1:7–9	253

Romans

8:10	45n13

1 Corinthians

5:8	315n33
14:34	382

Ephesians

5:22	382

Philippians

2:6–8	270
2:9–11	271

EARLY CHRISTIAN WRITINGS

Apollinarius	280, 281
Arius	278
Celsus	258
Chalcedon settlement	285
Nazianzen, Gregory	280, 281–82
Nicene Creed	279, 280, 283, 286
Plotinus	283n29

www.ingramcontent.com/pod-product-compliance
Lightning Source LLC
Chambersburg PA
CBHW080406300426
44113CB00015B/2410